Computer Aided Analysis and Design of Machine Elements

Computer Aided Analysis and Design of Machine Elements

(REVISED SECOND EDITION)

Rao V Dukkipati
PhD, PE
Fellow of ASME and CSME
Ex-Professor and Chairman
Department of Mechanical Engineering
Ex-Director, Graduate Programme
Fairfield University
Fairfield, Connecticut
USA

M Ananda Rao
Department of Mechanical Engineering
Andhra University, Visakhapatnam
Andhra Pradesh

Rama Bhat
Department of Mechanical Engineering
Concordia University, Montreal
Canada

Publishing Globally

NEW AGE INTERNATIONAL (P) LIMITED, PUBLISHERS
New Delhi • Bangalore • Chennai • Cochin • Guwahati
Hyderabad • Kolkata • Lucknow • Mumbai
Visit us at www.newagepublishers.com

Published by New Age International (P) Ltd., Publishers
First Edition: 2000
Second Edition: 2006
Reprint: 2015

BRANCHES

- **Bangalore** 37/10, 8th Cross (Near Hanuman Temple), Azad Nagar, Chamarajpet Bangalore-560 018 Tel.: (080) 26756823, Telefax: 26756820 **E-mail: bangalore@newagepublishers.com**
- **Chennai** 26, Damodaran Street, T. Nagar, Chennai-600 017 Tel.: (044) 24353401, Telefax: 24351463 **E-mail: chennai@newagepublishers.com**
- **Cochin** CC-39/1016, Carrier Station Road, Ernakulam South, Cochin-682 016 Tel.: (0484) 2377303, Telefax: 4051303 **E-mail: cochin@newagepublishers.com**
- **Guwahati** Hemsen Complex, Mohd. Shah Road, Paltan Bazar, Near Starline Hotel, Guwahati-781 008 Tel.: (0361) 2513881, Telefax: 2543669 **E-mail: guwahati@newagepublishers.com**
- **Hyderabad** 105, 1st Floor, Madhiray Kaveri Tower, 3-2-19, Azam Jahi Road Near Kumar Theater Nimboliadda, Kachiguda, Hyderabad-500 027 Tel.: (040) 24652456, Telefax: 24652457 **E-mail: hyderabad@newagepublishers.com**
- **Kolkata** RDB Chambers (Formerly Lotus Cinema) 106A, 1st Floor, S.N. Banerjee Road, Kolkata-700 014 Tel.: (033) 22273773, Telefax: 22275247 **E-mail: kolkata@newagepublishers.com**
- **Lucknow** 16-A, Jopling Road, Lucknow-226 001 Tel.: (0522) 2209578 4045297, Telefax: 2204098, **E-mail:lucknow@newagepublishers.com**
- **Mumbai** 142C, Victor House, Ground Floor, N.M. Joshi Marg, Lower Parel Mumbai-400 013 • Tel.: (022) 24927869, Telefax: 24915415 **E-mail: mumbai@newagepublishers.com**
- **New Delhi** 22, Golden House, Daryaganj, New Delhi-110 002 Tel.: (011) 23262368, 23262370, Telefax: 43551305 **E-mail: sales@newagepublishers.com**

ISBN: 978-81-224-1256-7

₹ 599.00

C-14-10-8005

Printed in India at Glorious Printers, Delhi.

PUBLISHING GLOBALLY
NEW AGE INTERNATIONAL (P) LIMITED, PUBLISHERS
7/30 A, Daryaganj, New Delhi-110002
Visit us at **www.newagepublishers.com**

PREFACE

The purpose of the book is to present the useful and general methods for the analysis and design of basic machine elements. The methods discussed are oriented towards the use of a digital computer. The advent of the computer has, of course, had a dramatic impact on design work and techniques such as finite element methods have come to be regarded as natural tools by the stress analysis.

This is to serve as a textbook for engineering students at the senior undergraduate or beginning graduate level course. Students are expected to have studied or their preparation in mathematics should include the elements of determinant and matrix theory, the calculus, and a first course in ordinary differential equations. The book is also quite useful for practicing engineers and designers. All of the essential tools of computer aided design pertinent to the methods described are developed in each chapter. Their structure is made clear through indenting, and a rich use of comments makes the algorithm being implemented quite self-evident. In addition to a good number of illustrative worked examples, the book contains an unusual number of problems for solution by the student. Because of worldwide acceptance of the metric system, this book uses SI units in text material, tables, and problems. However, the U.S. customary units have been retained without interfering with the text material.

AUTHORS

CONTENTS

CHAPTER 1

Computer Aided Aspects of Mechanical Design

1.1 INTRODUCTION

Engineering activity involves building and realizing contrivances, machines or structures to harness the environmental resources and energy for human needs. Design is an integral part of this activity. After the final design is complete, the ultimate realization and use of these engineering products would involve production, marketing, commissioning etc. This book focuses on the design activity in general, and the design of machine elements in particular.

The design activity is the major part of the final realization of any engineering product. This involves the following:

(i) Identification of the need for a specific engineering product.
(ii) Identification of the environmental conditions in which the product has to operate.
(iii) Conceptual design of the product, which draws on the past experience of the designer, aesthetics of the final product, limitations in terms of space, time and cost of production etc.
(iv) Detailed design, involving mathematical modelling and analysis of the component to be designed, to verify whether the design can withstand the environmental conditions under which it has to function. This includes optimization to minimize the production costs, the weight or any other specified objective criterion. Optimization will involve redimensioning and reanalysis under some relevant constraint conditions until the objective criterion is satisfied.
(v) Finally, transmission of the design information in the form of detailed drawings, and material and production specifications to the production shop.

Some of the component activities in the design process need human expertise, whereas some of them are repetitive. Once the methodology is clearly spelt and described, human expertise is not essential. The analysis and optimization activity is one which can be very efficiently implemented in a computer. Once an expert identifies the need for the product, conceptualizes the design, formulates the mathematical model and specifies the method of analysis and optimization criterion, the actual analysis and optimization can be done quickly and efficiently in a computer.

With the ever-widening capabilities of the present day computers, their use can be extended to the initial design phase of conceptualization including aesthetics, visualizing the design with animated graphics during the optimization phase and to the final design phase of preparation of drawings and specifications for transmitting the design information for production.

Elaborating a little bit on these extended uses of computers in the design activity, we can note the increasing use of expert systems in various fields. Expert systems draw upon the experience and expertise of human experts which are stored in their knowledge base. In this way, even a novice designer can benefit from the vast expertise of the entire design community available literally at the designer's fingertips punching keys on the keyboards of expert systems. More about the expert systems will be discussed later in Section 1.4.

The final design information can be directly transmitted to the machines in the production shop. Numerically controlled machine tools and robots involved in specific machining or assembling process can be directly supplied with the design information and instructions from the computers.

The above discussion gives a brief idea of the extent to which computers can be usefully employed in the design exercise. The design exercise, when aided by the capabilities of the computer, is aptly described as computer aided design. It is worth noting that reference to the computer is not the important thing here. A computer is a tool just as calculators, slide rules, logarithmic tables or abacus which were used at various times as aids in performing calculations needed during design. There may be a time in the future when computers as we know today may be replaced by super intelligent machines and the present day computers may find places in science history museums. But the rudiments of the design exercise itself will remain essentially unchanged except that the tools used in the design process will be different. It is in this light that we should see the name computer aided design.

1.2 MECHANICAL DESIGN

Mechanical design can be defined as the selection of materials and geometry which would satisfy specified functional requirements while remaining within the confines of inherently unavoidable limitations. For most of the practical design problems there exists an infinite number of possible design solutions, any one of which might be designated an adequate design. By defining more clear cut and explicit objectives, it is possible to narrow down the vast range of possible solutions.

Associated with any mechanical element are certain inherent undesirable effects and limitations. The environmental conditions in which the element must function may induce undesirable stresses, deflections, vibrations and in addition there may be limitations in terms of space, weight and cost. Also, associated with any mechanical element are certain desirable effects such as power transmission capability, speed capability and usable length of life.

Depending on the design problem at hand, we can explicitly define our design objectives so as to minimize the most significant undesirable effects. This process results in a mechanical design which is the best possible one, among all the numerous possible designs and this is called as the optimum design.

1.3 FORMULATION OF A SPECIFIC DESIGN PROBLEM

Suppose it is required to install a see-saw in a children's park located in a residential area. The design process starts with this identification of the need for the see-saw. A sketch of the sea-saw is shown in Fig. 1.1. Let us identify the conditions under which the see-saw must function.

(a) The average weight of children who would be using it. It is also possible that there may be a child at one end and it may be an adult on the other end. It is also possible that when children are playing on other rides in the park, two adults may use the see-saw. Therefore, it is better to design the see-saw for the worst possible

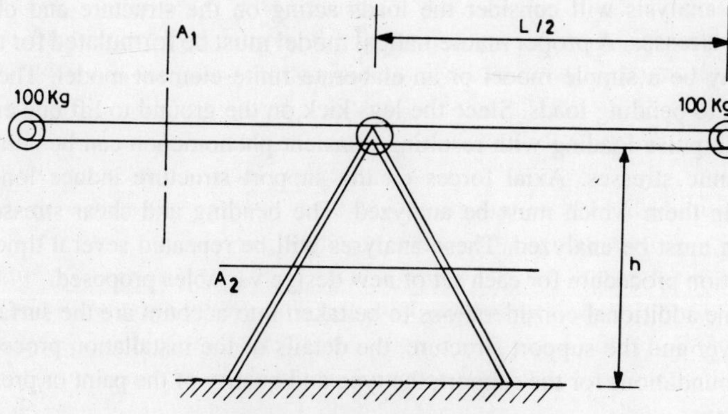

Fig. 1.1 Design of a see-saw

situation of two adults with above average weight.

(b) In addition to the weight, there will be effective forces due to the motion of the riders and the lever itself. The lever, the hinge and the support structure must be able to withstand the dynamic loads to which they are subjected. The stresses on these parts should be within the fatigue limit.

(c) The weather conditions in parks throughout the year must be considered. If it is in a cold country such as Canada, there will be snow in winter. Will it be left in snow or will it be dismantled and stored during winter? Does it rain too much? If the lever is made of wood, it may rot due to too much rain or moisture. If it is made of iron it may rust and will have to be painted regularly.

The above are some typical environmental considerations. Next, a conceptual design must be evolved. Some points to be considered at this stage are:

(a) When very small children are using it, the maximum height to which it goes should be such that an adult must be able to hold the child there for safety. This height may be taken as 1 m, say, and hence the hinge at the center must be at a height of 0.5 m.

(b) Much of the fun in the see-saw is when one side goes up, the child there can look down at the other end and "feel" the height. Similarly, the child at the lower end sees that the other child has gone very high. Hence the angle of elevation must be quite large. This is not possible if the lever is very long. Let us take the total lever length $L = 3$ m resulting in an angle of elevation of approximately 20°.

At this stage, the material, cross sectional shapes for the lever and the support structure, the type of seats and handle etc. may either be decided based on the weather conditions, availability and cost or they may be considered as design variables in the design analysis and optimization process. The cost may be considered as the objective function which must be minimized.

If the material and cross-sectional shapes are chosen, then the allowable stresses are known. Design optimization will obtain the actual cross-sectional dimensions, so as to minimize the cost of the total structure keeping the stresses within safe limits. If the material and the cross sectional shapes also must be obtained through design optimization, then the procedure is more involved. We must decide as to whether the cost of the effort involved in this complicated optimization procedure will be balanced by the savings in cost of the final structure

The analysis will consider the loads acting on the structure and obtain the resulting stresses. A proper mathematical model must be formulated for the analysis. It may be a simple model or an elaborate finite element model. The lever is subjected to bending loads. Since the legs kick on the ground to lift one end of the see-saw, a pulse loading with resulting transient phenomenon can be anlaysed for the dynamic stresses. Axial forces on the support structure induce longitudinal stresses in them which must be analyzed. The bending and shear stresses in the hinge pin must be analyzed. These analyses will be repeated several times during optimization procedure for each set of new design variables proposed.

Some additional considerations to be taken into account are the surface finish of the lever and the support structure, the details of the installation procedure, the type of foundations for the support, the type and quality of the paint or preservative coatings etc.

1.4 COMPUTER AIDED ASPECTS OF DESIGN

Computers can be used efficiently in several aspects of the design process. The capabilities of the computer in terms of storing vast amounts of information, the astonishing speed with which it can retrieve the required information buried in its knowledge base, and also the speed with which it can perform routine and repetitive computations with accuracy for the required analysis and optimization of the design, the graphics capabilities which enable visual representation of the design at every stage in the design, convenience with which design information can be transmitted to the production shop in the form of computer drafted drawings or directly to CNC machines, industrial robots etc, make it a very useful tool for the designer. Some of these computer aided aspects in design will be discussed briefly in this chapter. The analysis and optimization aspects will be dealt with in greater detail in the latter chapters.

1.4.1 Expert System

Expert systems are computers with their knowledge base filled with knowledge gathered from human experts and with capabilities to process this stored knowledge to solve difficult problems in the same way an expert would. This is a new computing technology which has emerged from research in Artificial Intelligence (AI) and can be applied to a variety of technical and nontechnical domains. The knowledge base in expert systems is structured and encoded in such a way that the system can readily explain the rationale in arriving at the answer. It is also possible to operate them in a tutorial mode, allowing a novice to learn how an expert proceeds in solving a problem. Expert systems have been developed in medicine for diagnostic purposes, in computer manufacturing and sales, mineral exploration, telephone systems, power plants, aircraft, insurance risk evaluations and so on. We will limit ourselves to the use of expert systems in design.

The term 'expert system' refers to a computer program which is essentially a collection of heuristic rules (rules of thumb) and detailed domain facts that have been collected from practicing experts over a period of time and have proven useful in solving special problems in the technical area. Expert system may be characterized by their accuracy, speed and cost-effectiveness of information gathering techniques. Some additional properties, many of which are taken for granted in human experts, are:

(a) Ability to explain and justify answers, either using relevant theory or citing relevant heuristic rules or citing past case histories;
(b) Similarities in reasoning procedures to those used by human experts;
(c) Ability to deal with problem situations involving incomplete or uncertain information;
(d) Ability to summarize and point out factors, in the order of their importance, which are responsible in leading to an answer;
(e) Ability to communicate in easily understandable natural language.
(f) Ability to add new pieces of knowledge from each problem solving exercise, which can be readily used in solving problems later.

The steps to be taken to build an expert system involve building up the knowledge base from the simplest elements to the most complex, such as building up the concepts first, then rules, then models and strategies. To start with, test cases are considered to build up initial set of rules and to establish the overall model organization. Once this is complete, more and more details can be put in, primarily with the acquisition of rules. After the building phase is complete, field evaluations are carried out to gain confidence in the system to deal with different problem situations.

A design engineer does not necessarily have to start with the difficult languages used in building expert systems. There are commercially available skeletal programs in natural languages which are known as shells. Expert system shells are computer programs whose knowledge base has been removed, leaving only a shell that can perform the functions of inference mechanism, user interface capabilities and knowledge storage medium. However, the full capabilities of an expert system can be exploited in design only by building custom-built and dedicated expert systems for specific design areas. The most important potential impact of an expert system on the design process are:

(a) Rapid checking of preliminary design concepts, comparing several design alternatives.
(b) Strategies for iterating the design process.
(c) Integration of the various stages of design, manufacture, aesthetics, marketing, use of a product, by having knowledge bases that can be readily distributed for wide access.

Design process starts with synthesis, which is assembling or gathering concepts around which the design is developed. In this phase of design, the emphasis is on exploring a set of alternative preliminary designs, from which the designer chooses one, for more detailed configuration and evaluation. Selection for the layout of the design, selection of materials etc. can be made at this stage.

Expert systems can also be built to analyze and optimize the designs and integrate this activity with the initial conceptual design. However, computer aided design tools are difficult to integrate to embrace all aspects of the design due to their diverse subject manner, diverse algorithms and data structures, and their applications to different stages of the design process such as synthesis, manufacturing and maintenance. Further, often they are programmed by different people in different languages using different operating systems and hardware.

1.4.2 Computer Aided Analysis

Machine elements are required to operate in environmental conditions where they may be subjected to forces, extreme thermal conditions, unfavorable weather conditions and so on. The element must be designed to withstand the harmful effects of the environment and to operate satisfactorily. Hence, the designer must formulate a mathematical model for the element, represent the behavior or the response of the element using differential equations, and analyze for the response when subjected to the environmental conditions. The stresses developed in the element due to the external forces under other unfavorable conditions must be obtained and compared with the maximum stresses that the element can withstand safely.

The mathematical model for the element as well as mathematical models for the external forces must be formulated by the designer. There are several methods available to solve the resulting differential equations describing behavior of the element or the system, of which the element is a part. The past experience in solving similar equations using all the available techniques may be stored in an expert system, which can suggest the best analysis method for the design problem. Alternatively, the designer can make a choice of the analytical method from past experience in solving similar problems. Finite difference methods, transfer matrix methods, finite element methods are some typical methods that can be used for the mathematical representation of the system and direct numerical integration or modal analysis techniques are some possible analysis techniques to obtain the system response when subjected to environmental excitations. More detailed account of some of these techniques will be given in the next chapter.

When the element being designed is quite complex or when the element behavior can be understood only by analyzing the complete system, of which the element is a part, then calculations done manually will be unmanageable and prone to errors. Computers can be very efficiently used for the routine and repititive computations involved in all these analysis methods.

1.4.3 Computer Aided Optimization

It has been mentioned earlier that there are several solutions possible for a design problem. The number of variables in a design problem are enormous. The material properties, overall shape and geometry, detailed dimensions of individual elements in a system, manufacturing methods and the corresponding costs are all parameters that can be chosen so as to optimize a required objective in a design problem. The objective may be to minimize the overall cost of the final product, minimize the weight of the product as in aerospace applications or maximize the strength or maximize the aesthetic appeal.

Some of the design parameters may be changed without any restrictions imposed on them, however, there may be some constraints applied on some parameters. The material may be available only in a particular shape and size, the production shop may have limitations on the maximum and minimum sizes of parts that can be machined, the deflection at a specific point in a part may not exceed certain value due to the space limitations, stresses cannot exceed the safe limits and so on. Hence the optimum design must ensure that all these constraints are satisfied while trying to meet the required objective.

An initial design can be formulated based approximatively on past experience or using heuristic rules which have been put in an expert system. Subsequently this initial design must be analyzed to see whether it can satisfy all constraint requirements. If it satisfies, the next step is to see whether it can be improved by optimizing the objective function. If the initial design does not satisfy all the constraints, the immediate task is to vary the parameters in a logical fashion so as to satisfy the constraint requirements. In either case, the newly proposed design must be reanalysed. In the course of an optimization exercise, several reanalyses may have to be performed.

The large number of analyses necessary in design optimization and proposing new design parameters at every stage by using some meaningful criteria based on the previous analysis is a task which is tedious and better left to the computer. Hence, optimization part of the design process is ideally suited to be carried out in a computer.

1.4.4 Computer Aided Interactive Graphics

Designers conceive their ideas first in the mind, proceed to make some sketches for visual representation, modify the sketches with several alternative shapes and sizes and finally decide on a few choices that are to their satisfaction and also meet the design specifications. Traditionally, the chosen designs will be drawn by a draughtsman using rules, compass, protractors, pens of varying sizes and other devices. Because the task is time consuming and laborious, only drawings of the final design or one alternative design may be drawn in this way. However, with the present day capabilities of the computer along with cathode ray tube display devices it is possible to see the display of the final design in a very short time. If what the designer sees on the display terminal is not satisfactory, changes can be made right then and there to the designers satisfaction.

During optimization, the changing shape of the design can be continously monitored on the display terminal. The final version of the design or many intermediate versions can be plotted readily by using a plotter.

The cathode ray tube screen is like a gridwork and the intercepts of the horizontal and vertical lines, called dots, grids, nodes or pixels are usable points. It is up to the user to effectively utilize these pixels on the screen to be lighted to draw diagrams, graphs, and characters. The displayed image of a curve is composed of the usable points on the screen as shown in Fig. 1.2. The resolution of the graphics unit dictates the appearance of the curve.

The advantage of the computer aided graphics and its display cannot be overemphasized. By proper programming, it is possible to rotate, translate, scale down to reduce the size or scale up to magnify the size, obtain different views of the design, perspective projections of three-dimensional objects, focus on the specific region of the display by windowing etc. Parts lists and bills of materials also can be prepared. Drawings can be checked for tolerancing and dimensioning etc. using the computers quite efficiently.

The workstation replaces the draughtsman's drawing boards and the essential element of any computer aided design (CAD) workstation is the graphic display terminal where all work activities are focussed. A typical workstation would consist of a graphic terminal, either a storage tube type or raster graphics type. To address the computer by menu commands there would be a digitizing tablet on which the menus are mounted, with a joystick for control of the screen cursor. A small screen,

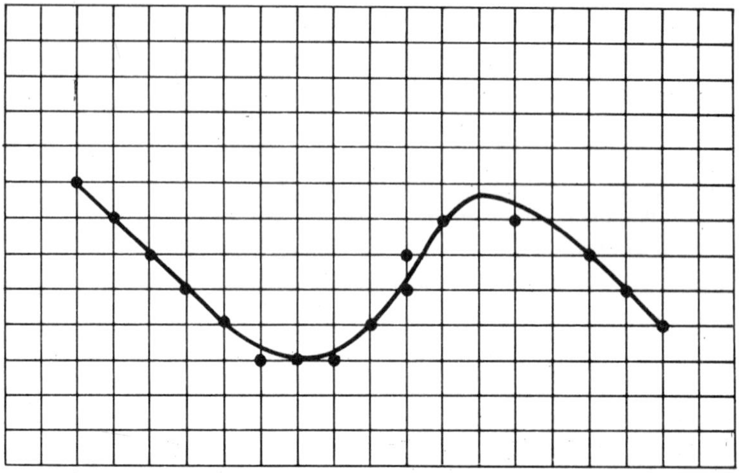

Fig. 1.2 Display of a curve on CRT terminal

non-graphics terminal, would be provided complete with a keyboard, for the display in text form of all user commands together with any prompts, comments or reports generated by the computer.

A plotting machine produces the output copy of the finished design and there are three divisions of plotters, such as:

(i) Line drawing plotters with either pen, ink-jet or electrostatic version.

(ii) Color or shaded fill-in plotters using ink-jet or electrostatic version.

(iii) Photo image plotting machines which plot in photo sensitive materials to produce a direct negative master.

1.4.5 Computer Aided Manufacturing Integrated with Computer Aided Design (CAD/CAM Systems)

The computer aided manufacturing content in a CAD/CAM system include NC machining, production control, process engineering with respect to machining operations.

Numerical controlled machines are capable of doing almost all of the general purpose machining processes such as drilling, turning, milling, punching and nibbling and so on. At the present time NC machines are operated by creating machining programs which are input to the machines form of punched tapes. Direct numerical control form of a CAD system computer would be highly desirable, however, currently this capability is not exploited by many systems. But this technology is not far from realization. At the present time, several companies have elementary examples of DNC (direct numerical control) in that they have eliminated the need for punched tapes and interface the machine with a computer.

1.4.6 Integration of Design Systems

The life cycle of an engineering product can be described by a collection of projects, where each project involves a coherent set of attributes, such as the design, manufacturing, or assembling of an artifact. Traditional CAD systems address some narrow aspect of the design task, and fail to provide any sort of integrated support for product development. Moreover, these traditional tools are typically isolated from each other and often employ incompatible representations of the design, process, requiring manual data transmission between tools. One simple example is the incompatibility between the natural language currently used in an expert system for a preliminary design and the FORTRAN language used in computer software which performs analysis and optimization of the design.

Expert systems are being developed presently which can coordinate the various projects involved in the life cycle of a product to eliminate problems due to lack of communication and compatibility between different areas of concern, such as design and manufacturing. Such a system will ensure that, in achieving the goals of one project, goals of another are not made unreachable.

The program modules of such a system can be classified into three main types:

(i) Design Agent, which manipulates one or more design representations to develop and extend a design in response to a group of specifications. In this module, design decisions can be made automatically, through the use of stored domain knowledge and algorithms, or interactively, by a human designer.

(ii) Design Critic, evaluates a developing design with respect to certain criteria. This module can perform analysis, optimization and can interpret the result and communicate to a design agent.

(iii) Design Translator, maps one design representation into another. The two representations do not have to be informationally equivalent, but the translator module should not disturb any of the design decisions that have been made. For example, a program to generate finite element meshes would use information not present in the design to determine the spacing of grid lines, but the geometric structure of the part being modelled would not be altered. Translators help in communication between agents and design critics.

1.5 CLOSURE

The example of the design of a see-saw discussed earlier, gives an idea about the design procedure. A major portion of this procedure can be carried out in computer. If past experience in designing see-saws for various environmental conditions, soil conditions etc. are stored in the knowledge base of an expert system, then the conceptual design can be carried out using this expert system. Finite element analysis and optimization can be carried out in a computer. Interactive graphics can be used to see the designed structures at various stages during optimization. The design drawings, material specifications and installation procedures can be prepared in the computer itself and passed on to those responsible for fabrication, installation etc. The latter may be machines, robots or people. This exercise may be termed as a computer aided design procedure.

A brief description of the computer aided aspects of design are given in this chapter. Some of computer aided tasks are already in use at the present time, whereas some of them are still in the development stage. The chapter gives the reader a perspective of the enormous possibilities of using computers in the design process. The integration of various computer aided tasks for the complete design is highly desirable in view of the perfection that can be achieved throughout the design phase of a product.

In Chapter 2, a review of different failure criteria will be given, which is quite essential for any design. Chapter 3 will discuss various optimization techniques used in optimizing a design. Chapter 4 will describe the static analaysis procedures for design of structures and components not involving any dynamic loading, while Chapters 5 and 6 will discuss numerical analysis procedures involving transient and dynamic loadings. Chapter 7 will discuss the finite element analysis methods. Chapter 8 will deal with the design of a special class of structures which are cyclically symmetric. Finally Chapter 9 will provide some case studies of specific design exercises.

REFERENCES

1. Dimarogonas, A.D., (1988), *Computer-Aided Machine Design,* Prentice-Hall, New York.
2. Fellows, J.W., (1983), *All About CAD/CAM,* Sigma Technical Press, Cheshire, U.K.
3. Mischke, C.R., (1968), *An Introduction to Computer-Aided Design,* Prentice-Hall, Inc., Englewood Cliffs, N.J.
4. Pao, Y.C., (1984), *Elements of Computer Aided Design and Manufacturing,* John Wiley and Sons, New York.
5. Ryan, D.L., (1981), *Computer-Aided Kinetics for Machine Design,* Marcel Dekker, Inc., New York.
6. Rychener, M.D., (1988), *Expert Systems for Engineering Design,* Academic Press, London.

CHAPTER 2

THEORIES OF FAILURE

2.1 STRENGTH OF MACHINE ELEMENTS

A machine element will function satisfactorily if its strength is sufficiently greater than the stress to which it is subjected during its use. To understand how to design so that the parts do not fail in service, it is necessary to know why they fail.

Machine elements are subjected to various types of loading conditions in service. They may be subjected to tensile or compressive loading, bending loads, torsional loadings and so on. To study the strength of these components it is necessary to carry out controlled experiments on representative specimens by loading them as they would be in service. The specimens must have the same heat treatment, surface finish etc. so as to be representative of the machine elements being designed.

Collection of such extensive data through costly experiments is essential since failure of the machine part may result in loss of production and may endanger human life. Further if the number of such parts being produced are quite large, then the cost of such tests will be very low when it is distributed over every part.

When a specimen is subjected to a tensile loading, it undergoes deformation. If the load is P and the cross sectional area of the specimen is A, then the tensile stress σ is given by

$$\sigma = \frac{P}{A} \tag{2.1}$$

If the original length of the specimen is L and the elongated length when subjected to loading is L', then the deformation is $\Delta L = L' - L$ and the strain, ε is given by

$$\varepsilon = \frac{\Delta L}{L} \tag{2.2}$$

When the load is removed, if the material regains its original shape completely, without any trace of deformation left in it, then the material is said to be elastic and the deformation is elastic deformation. If the material does not completely regain its shape when the load is removed, then the deformation left in the material is called the plastic deformation.

A standard tensile test uses specimens machined to stated dimensions. The original cross sectional area and length are recorded before the test. Specimen is slowly loaded in tension while the load and the corresponding deformations are observed. From the data obtained a stress-strain diagram as shown in Fig. 2.1 may be drawn.

In Fig. 2.1 (a) the proportional limit is the point at which the stress-strain diagram first begins to deviate from a straight line. If the load is removed at the elastic limit point, the specimen will not have any permanent set. Between the proportional limit and elastic limit, the stress-strain relation is not linear, however the material is

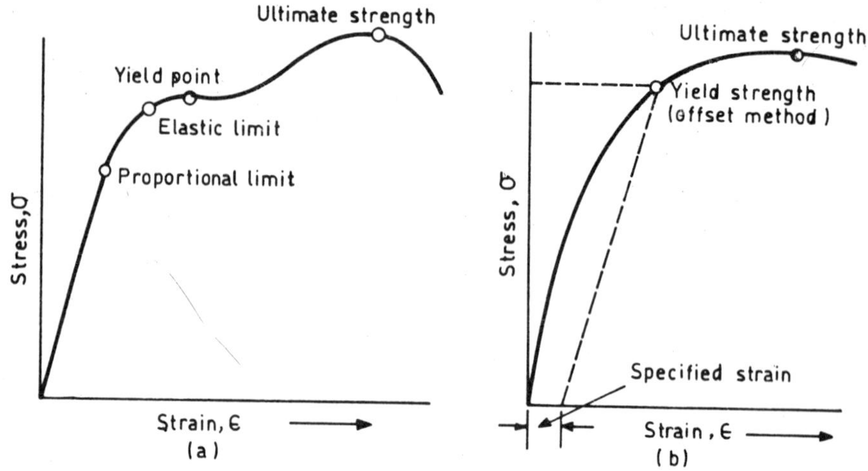

Fig. 2.1 Stress-strain data from tensile test

still elastic. At the yield point the strain begins to increase very rapidly without a corresponding increase in stress. Yield point is not very well defined for some materials. Hence, yield strength is often defined by an offset method as shown in Fig. 2.1 (b). Here yield strength is defined as the stress, when completely removed will cause a specified permanent set in the material, usually 0.2 or 0.5 percent of the original gauge length. The ultimate strength or the tensile strength is the maximum stress reached on the stress-strain diagram. Some materials show a downward trend after the ultimate strength. Some others such as cast iron, fracture when the stress-strain diagram is still on the rising trend. A material having less than 5 percent elongation at fracture is said to be brittle while the one that can elongate more than 5 percent before rupture is said to be ductile.

Compressive strength of materials is much more difficult to obtain experimentally. There are added complications such as the specimen may buckle during loading, the stresses may not be distributed evenly over the cross sectional area, the ductile material may bulge after yielding. For many materials the compressive strengths are approximately same as tensile strengths. When they are substantially different, however, as in the case of brittle materials such as cast iron, the tensile and compressive strengths must be stated separately.

Torsional strengths are determined by subjecting round bars to moment loading and observing the torque and the corresponding angular deflections. A torque-twist diagram, as shown in Fig. 2.2, can be plotted. Similar to the stress-strain diagram in Fig. 2.1, it is possible to see corresponding proportional limit point, yield point and ultimate torsional strengths in Fig. 2.2.

2.2 STRESS

External loads cause stresses in the elements. In a simple tensile test specimen, the load is acting in one direction and the corresponding tensile stress can be easily obtained from Eq. (2.1). However, when the load is applied along all three mutually perpendicular directions on a solid, determination of the stresses is more complex.

Consider a general three-dimensional stress element, showing three normal stresses denoted by σ_x, σ_y, and σ_z along x, y, and z directions respectively, as shown in Fig. 2.3. There are also six shear stresses denoted by τ_{xy}, τ_{yx}, τ_{yz}, τ_{zy}, τ_{xz} and τ_{zx}, as shown in the same figure. Assuming that the element is in static equilibrium, we obtain

$$\tau_{xy} = \tau_{yx},\ \tau_{yz} = \tau_{zy},\ \tau_{xz} = \tau_{zx} \tag{2.3}$$

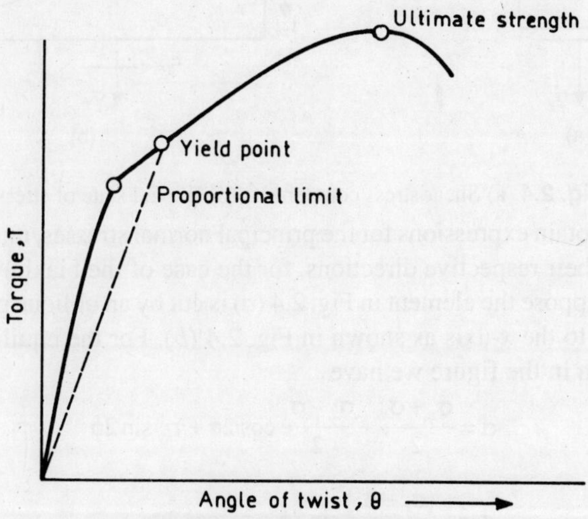

Fig. 2.2 Torque-twist diagram

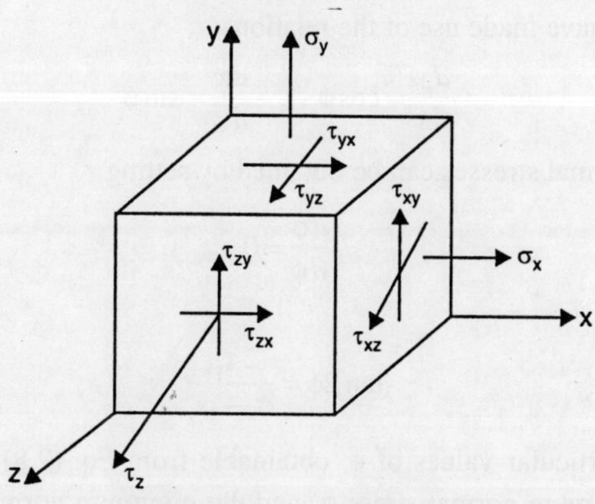

Fig. 2.3 Triaxial state of stress.

As shown in Fig. 2.3, outwardly directed normal stresses are considered as tensile and positive. Positive shear stresses are directed in the positive direction of a reference axis. The first subscript of a shear stress component is the coordinate normal to the element face. The shear stress component is parallel to the axis of the second subscript. The negative faces of the element will have shear stresses acting in the opposite direction which are also considered as positive.

A state of biaxial stress or plane stress, which is the more usual case, is shown is Fig. 2.4. In this case, only the normal stresses will be treated as positive or negative. The senses of the shear stress components will be specified by the clockwise or counterclockwise directions. In Fig. 2.4 τ_{yx} is clockwise and τ_{xy} is counterclockwise.

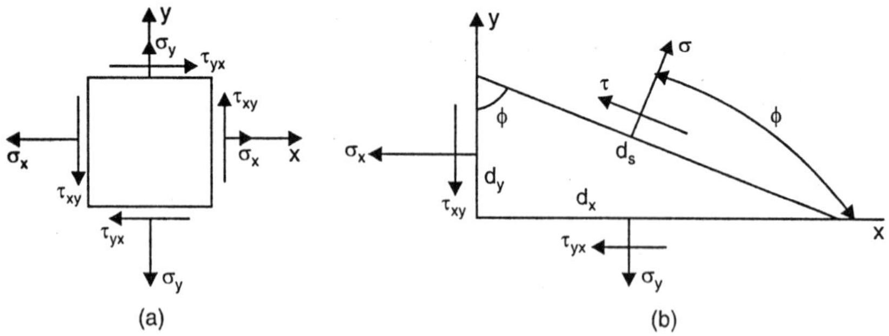

Fig. 2.4 (a) Shear stress components (b) Biaxial state of stress.

Let us obtain expressions for the principal normal stresses, maximum shear stresses and their respective directions, for the case of the biaxial stress shown in Fig. 2.4. Suppose the element in Fig. 2.4 (*a*) is cut by an oblique plane inclined at an angle ϕ to the x-axis as shown in Fig. 2.4 (*b*). For the equilibrium of the portion shown in the figure we have

$$\sigma = \frac{\sigma_x + \sigma_y}{2} + \frac{\sigma_x - \sigma_y}{2} \cos 2\phi + \tau_{xy} \sin 2\phi \tag{2.4}$$

$$\tau = -\frac{(\sigma_x - \sigma_y)}{2} \sin 2\phi + \tau_{xy} \cos 2\phi \tag{2.5}$$

In the above we have made use of the relations

$$\frac{dy}{ds} = \cos\phi \quad , \quad \frac{dx}{ds} = \sin\phi \tag{2.6}$$

The principal normal stresses can be obtained by setting

$$\frac{d\sigma}{d\phi} = 0 \tag{2.7}$$

which yields,

$$\tan 2\phi = \frac{2\,\tau_{xy}}{\sigma_x - \sigma_y} \tag{2.8}$$

The two particular values of ϕ, obtainable from Eq. (2.8) provide the directions of the maximum normal stress σ_1 and the minimum normal stress σ_2. Directions of the principal normal stresses σ_1 and σ_2 are known as principal directions. Substituting Eq. (2.8) into (2.4) we obtain the principle normal stresses as

$$\sigma_1, \sigma_2 = \frac{\sigma_x + \sigma_y}{2} \pm \sqrt{\left(\sigma_x - \frac{\sigma_y}{2}\right)^2 + \tau_{xy}^2} \tag{2.9}$$

The maximum shear stresses are obtained by setting

$$\frac{\partial \tau}{\partial \phi} = 0 \tag{2.10}$$

which yields

$$\tan 2\phi = -\frac{(\sigma_x - \sigma_y)}{2\,\tau_{xy}} \tag{2.11}$$

Substituting Eq. (2.11) into (2.5), the maximum shear stresses are obtained as

$$\tau_{max} = \pm\sqrt{\left(\frac{\sigma_x - \sigma_y}{2}\right)^2 + \tau_{xy}^2} \tag{2.12}$$

By substituting equation (2.8) into (2.5) it is possible to verify that the shear stresses associated with the two principal directions are zero.

Mohr's circle provides a visual representation of the stress state at a point, and helps in keeping track of the directions of the various components associated with plane stress. This is done by showing the normal stresses along the abcissa and the shear stresses along the ordinates as shown in Fig. 2.5. Setting OA = σ_x and OC = σ_y along the abcissa and drawing AB = τ_{xy}, and CD = τ_{yx} along the ordinate direction, we obtain the line DEB as the diameter of the Mohr's circle. It can be noted that E is the midpoint of CA.

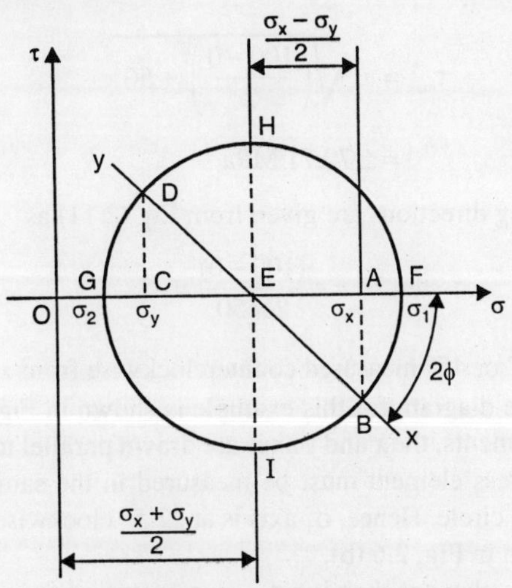

Fig. 2.5 Mohr's circle diagram

Point B in Fig. 2.6 (*a*) represents the stress coordinate σ_x, τ_{xy} on the *x*-faces, and point D represents the stress coordinates σ_y, τ_{xy} on the *y*-faces. Line EB corresponds to *x*-axis and ED to *y*-axis. Angle from EB to ED, measured counterclockwise is 180° which is twice the angle between *x*- and *y*-axes. The abcissa in the Mohr's circle corresponds to principal normal stresses and the ordinate to the shear stresses.

The maximum principal normal stress, σ_1 occurs at F and the maximum principal stress σ_2 at G. The maximum shear stresses, one clockwsie and counterclockwise, occur at H and I, respectively. It should be noted that tensile normal stresses are plotted to the right of the origin O and compressive stresses are plotted to the left of O in the Mohr's circle.

Example 2.1

For the biaxial stress element shown in Fig. 2.4, σ_x = 100 MPa , σ_y = 0 and τ_{xy} = 50 MPa clockwise. **Find the principal stresses and directions and show them on the** stresss element. Draw another stress element to show τ_{max} along with the corresponding normal stresses.

Solution

The principal normal stresses are obtained from Eq. (2.9) as

$$\sigma_1, \sigma_2 = \frac{100+0}{2} \pm \sqrt{\left(\frac{100-0}{2}\right)^2 + 50^2}$$

$$= 120.71, -20.71 \text{ MPa}$$

The corresponding directions are obtained from Eq. (2.8) as

$$\tan 2\phi = \frac{2 \times 50}{(100)} = 1$$

Hence, $2\phi = 45°$, measured clockwise from x-axis. Using Eq. (2.12) the maximum shear stresses are

$$\tau_{max} = \pm\sqrt{\left(\frac{100-0}{2}\right)^2 + 50^2}$$

$$= \pm 70.71 \text{ MPa}$$

The corresponding directions are given from Eq. (2.11) as

$$\tan 2\phi = -\frac{(100-0)}{2 \times 50} = -1$$

Hence $2\phi = -45°$ or 45° measured counterclockwise from x axis.

The Mohr's circle diagram for this example is shown in Fig. 2.6 (a). To draw the principal stress elements, the *x* and *y* axes are drawn parallel to the original axes. The angle ϕ on the stress element must be measured in the same direction as the angle 2ϕ in the Mohr's circle. Hence, σ_1 axis is at 22.5° clockwise from x-axis. The stress element is shown in Fig. 2.6 (b).

To draw the stress element showing τ_{max}, we must find the corresponding normal stresses. These are obtained from Mohr's circle as 50 MPa. Point H is 45° counterclockwise from B on Mohr's circle. Hence, in Fig. 2.6 (c) a stress element oriented at 22.5° counterclockwise from x-axis indicates the normal stress. Corresponding stresses are marked in Fig. 2.6 (c).

2.3 FAILURE UNDER STATIC LOADING

When the external loading is static in nature the following three theories of failure may be considered in the design.

The Maximum Normal Stress Theory

The maximum normal stress theory states that failure occurs whenever the largest principal stress equals the yield strength of the material. If the principal stresses are such that $\sigma_1 > \sigma_2 > \sigma_3$, then failure by yielding occurs whenever $\sigma_1 = S_y$ and failure by fracture occurs whenever $\sigma_1 = S_u$. Here S_y and S_u refer to yield strength and ultimate strength of the material, respectively.

Predictions using this theory do not agree with experiments and may even give results on the unsafe side. For example, in the case of pure torsion, the corresponding principal stress is obtained as $\tau = \sigma_1$, and consequently failure would occur

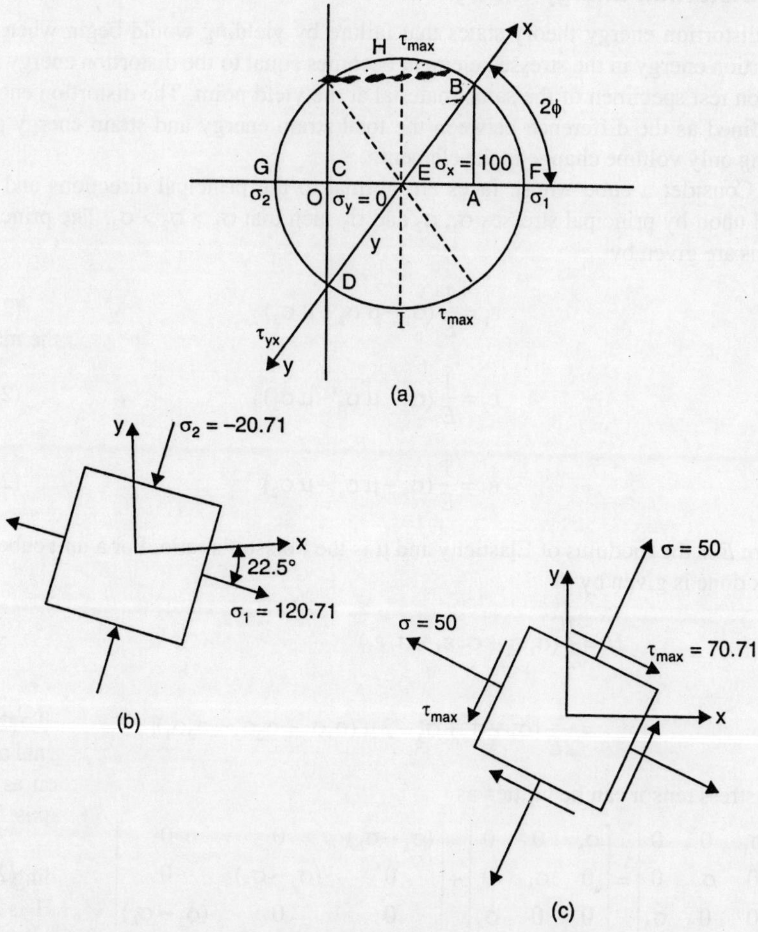

Fig. 2.6 Mohr's circle and stress elements corresponding to Example 2.1

when the shear stress reaches the yield strength or ultimate strength. This prediction does not agree with the experimental observations. However, results from maximum normal stress theory can be used for comparison purposes.

The Maximum-Shear Stress Theory

The maximum shear stress theory states that yielding begins when the maximum shear stress in the element reaches a value equal to the maximum shear stress in a tension test specimen which has reached its yield point. From Eq. (2.12) or from a Mohr's circle diagram with $\sigma_y = 0$ and $\tau_{xy} = \tau_{yx} = 0$, it can be seen that yielding begins when $\tau_{max} = S_y/2$.

Note that this theory predicts that the yield strength in shear is half the yield strength in tension. This theory is easy to use and is always on a conservative side of the test results. It is used only to predict yielding and hence applies to ductile materials only.

The Distortion-Energy Theory

The distortion energy theory states that failure by yielding would begin when the distortion energy in the stressed element becomes equal to the distortion energy in a tension test specimen of the same material at the yield point. The distortion energy is defined as the difference between the total strain energy and strain energy producing only volume change in the element.

Consider a cube whose faces are normal to the principal directions and are acted upon by principal stresses σ_1, σ_2 and σ_3 such that $\sigma_1 > \sigma_2 > \sigma_3$. The principal strains are given by

$$\varepsilon_1 = \frac{1}{E}(\sigma_1 - \mu\,\sigma_2 - \mu\,\sigma_3) \tag{2.13}$$

$$\varepsilon_2 = \frac{1}{E}(\sigma_2 - \mu\,\sigma_3 - \mu\,\sigma_1) \tag{2.14}$$

$$\varepsilon_3 = \frac{1}{E}(\sigma_3 - \mu\,\sigma_1 - \mu\,\sigma_2) \tag{2.15}$$

where E is the modulus of Elasticity and μ is the Poisson's ratio. For a unit cube the work done is given by

$$U = \frac{1}{2}(\sigma_1\,\varepsilon_1 + \sigma_2\,\varepsilon_2 + \sigma_3\,\varepsilon_3)$$

$$= \frac{1}{2E}[\sigma_1^2 + \sigma_2^2 + \sigma_3^2 - 2\,\mu\,(\sigma_1\sigma_2 + \sigma_2\sigma_3 + \sigma_3\sigma_1)] \tag{2.16}$$

The stress tensor can be written as

$$\begin{vmatrix} \sigma_1 & 0 & 0 \\ 0 & \sigma_2 & 0 \\ 0 & 0 & \sigma_3 \end{vmatrix} = \begin{vmatrix} \sigma_h & 0 & 0 \\ 0 & \sigma_h & 0 \\ 0 & 0 & \sigma_h \end{vmatrix} + \begin{vmatrix} (\sigma_1 - \sigma_h) & 0 & 0 \\ 0 & (\sigma_2 - \sigma_h) & 0 \\ 0 & 0 & (\sigma_3 - \sigma_h) \end{vmatrix} \tag{2.17}$$

where the first tensor on the right hand side is the hydrostatic stress tensor responsible for volume change in the material and the second stress tensor causes only angular distortion. The hydrostatic stress σ_h is an average stress given by

$$\sigma_h = \frac{\sigma_1 + \sigma_2 + \sigma_3}{3} \tag{2.18}$$

Following Eq. (2.16) the strain energy producing volume change is given by

$$U_v = \frac{3\,\sigma_h^2}{2\,E}(1 - 2\mu)$$

$$= \frac{(1-2\mu)}{6\,E}\left[\frac{(\sigma_1 - \sigma_2)^2 + (\sigma_2 - \sigma_3)^2 + (\sigma_3 - \sigma_1)^2}{2}\right] \tag{2.19}$$

The distortion energy is obtained as

$$U_d = U - U_v = \frac{(1+\mu)}{3E}\left[\frac{(\sigma_1 - \sigma_2)^2 + (\sigma_2 - \sigma_3)^2 + (\sigma_3 - \sigma_1)^2}{2}\right] \tag{2.20}$$

Note that the distortion energy is zero if $\sigma_1 = \sigma_2 = \sigma_3$.

The distortion energy of a tension test specimen at the yield point is obtained by substituting $\sigma_1 = S_y$ and $\sigma_2 = \sigma_3 = 0$ in Eqs. (2.20) as

$$U_d = \frac{(1+\mu)}{3E} S_y^2 \tag{2.21}$$

Hence, the criterion for failure by yielding is given by equating the distortion energy in Eqs. (2.20) and (2.21) as

$$S_y^2 = \frac{1}{2} [(\sigma_1 - \sigma_2)^2 + (\sigma_2 - \sigma_3)^2 + (\sigma_3 - \sigma_1)^2] \tag{2.22}$$

For the case of biaxial stress, we have $\sigma_3 = 0$ and the yield criterion is given by

$$S_y^2 = \sigma_1^2 - \sigma_1\sigma_2 + \sigma_2^2. \tag{2.23}$$

For the case of pure torsion, we have, $\sigma_2 = -\sigma_1$ and $\tau = \sigma_1$ and consequently the yield criterion is

$$S_{sy} = 0.577\, S_y \tag{2.24}$$

where S_{sy} is the yield strength in shear.

For analysis and design purposes, it is convenient to define a von Mises stress from Eq. (2.23) as

$$\sigma' = (\sigma_1^2 - \sigma_1\sigma_2 + \sigma_2^2)^{1/2} \tag{2.25}$$

Hence the distortion energy theory states that failure by yielding is predicted when

$$\sigma' = S_y \tag{2.26}$$

Example 2.2

The stress state on a machine element is $\sigma_x = 40$ MPa, $\sigma_y = -16$ MPa and $\tau_{xy} = 24$ MPa. If the yield strength of the material is 100 MPa, determine the factor of safety by the (i) maximum normal stress theory, (ii) maximum shear stress theory and (iii) the distortion energy theory.

Solution

This is a biaxial stress situation. Using Eq. (2.9), the principal normal stresses are

$$\sigma_1 = 48.8 \text{ MPa}, \sigma_2 = -24.8 \text{ MPa}, \quad \sigma_3 = 0$$

From Eq. (2.12)

$$\tau_{max} = 36.8 \text{ MPa}$$

(i) From maximum normal stress theory, factor of safety

$$n = \frac{S_y}{\sigma_1} = 2.05$$

(ii) From maximum shear stress theory, factor of safety

$$n = \frac{S_y}{2\,\tau_{max}} = 1.36$$

(iii) From distortion energy theory, factor of safety

$$n = \frac{S_y}{\sigma'}$$

where, $\sigma' = 65$ MPa (from Eq. (2.25))
Hence $n = 1.54$

2.4 FAILURE UNDER DYNAMIC LOADING: FATIGUE

Machine members often fail under the action of repeated or fluctuating stresses, caused by dynamic loading, even though the actual maximum stresses are below the ultimate strength and even below the yield strength. This type of failure is called a fatigue failure. A fatigue failure begins with a small crack in the element at the point of discontinuity such as a change in cross section, a keyway or a hole. Once a crack has developed, the stress concentration effect becomes greater and the crack progresses more rapidly. As the stressed area decreases in size, the stress increases in the remaining area, which fails suddenly. Hence, a fatigue failure is characteized by two distinct areas. The first of these is due to the progressive development of the crack, while the second is due to the sudden fracture.

To determine the fatigue strength of materials under the action of dynamic loads, specimens are subjected to fluctuating forces of specified magnitudes while the cycles or number of stress reversals are counted until destruction of the specimen by fatigue failure. Because of the statistical nature of fatigue, a large number of tests are necessary to establish the fatigue strength of a material.

A rotating beam specimen of the test material is subjected to a bending load at the center in these tests. Initially, the specimens are subjected to stress levels which are somewhat lower than the ultimate strength. The number of revolutions which are equal to the number of stress reversals, are recorded. In the subsequent tests the stress levels are gradually reduced and the corresponding number of stress reversals for failure are recorded. The results are plotted with stress levels on the ordinate and the corresponding number of stress reversals to failure on the abcissa, which is normally reffered to as a *S–N* diagram. A typical *S–N* diagram is shown in Fig. 2.7 for a steel material. In the case of ferrous metals and alloys, the plot becomes horizontal for a specific stress level, when plotted in a log-log scale as in Fig. 2.7.

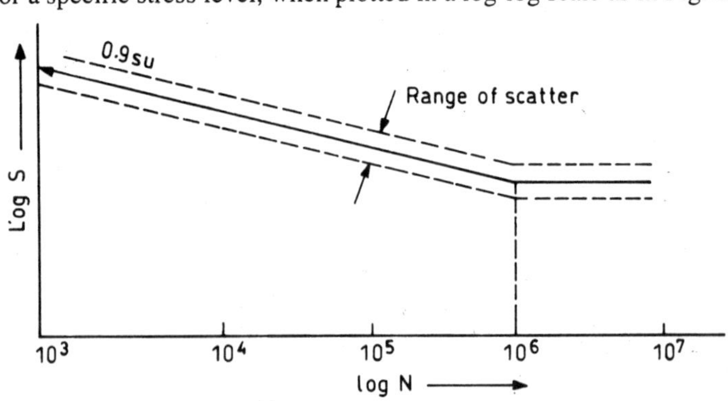

Fig. 2.7 *S–N* diagram for ferrous metals and alloys

The fatigue strength, S_f is shown on the ordinate of the S–N diagram. The fatigue strength corresponding to the horizontal line is called the endurance limit, S_e, or the fatigue limit. If the stress levels are below the endurance limit for the material, it can be safely assumed that the material will not fail by fatigue when subjected to fluctuating type of dynamic loading. For non-ferrous metals and alloys, the S–N diagram does not have a horizontal portion when plotted in a log-log scale, and hence they do not have a clearly defined endurance limit.

2.4.1 Strength for Finite Life

If the machine element is designed so that the stresses in operation never exceed the endurance limit, then it will have infinite life. If the parts are not subjected to continuous cyclic loading and if it is known that they may be subjected to only finite number of stress reversals in their life, they can be designed for finite life. The fatigue strength corresponding to the expected finite stress reversals, N, can be obtained from the S–N diagram. As a rough guide, any part which is expected to have less than 1000 stress reversals in its life can be designed from static design considerations only.

Since there is a scatter in the fatigue test results, the S–N diagram does not have a well defined line for a given material. If we consider the lower values of stress levels in this scattered range, it is found reasonable to assume that a line on the log S–log N plot joining S_e at 10^6 cycles and 0.9 S_u at 10^3 cycles may be used to define the mean fatigue strength S_f corresponding to life N. With this assumption, an equation can be obtained from the S–N line as

$$\log S_f = -m \log N + b \tag{2.27}$$

Using the above values, we have

$$\log (0.9\, S_u) = -m \log (10^3) + b \tag{2.28}$$

$$\log (S_e) = -m \log (10^6) + b \tag{2.29}$$

Solving for m and b we obtain

$$m = \frac{1}{3} \log (0.9\, S_u/S_e) \tag{2.30}$$

$$b = \log [(0.9\, S_u)^2/S_e] \tag{2.31}$$

Example 2.3

The endurance limit of a steel material is 100 MPa and its ultimate tensile strength is 375 MPa. Find the fatigue strength corresponding to the life of 60×10^4 cycles.

Solution

From Eqs. (2.30) and (2.31) we get

$$m = \frac{1}{3} \log (0.9 \times 375/100) = 0.1761$$

$$b = \log [(0.9 \times 375)^2/100] = 3.0565$$

Using Eq. (2.27) we have

$$\log S_f = -0.1761 \log (60 \times 10^4) + 3.0565$$

$$= 2.0390$$

Hence $\quad S_f = 109.3875$ MPa

2.4.2 Cumulative Fatigue Damage

Suppose a machine part is subjected to a cyclic stress of σ_1 for n_1 cycles, σ_2 for n_2 cycles etc. If the life of the part is N_1 cycles at σ_1, N_2 cycles at σ_2 etc. then it is reasonable to assume that the life of the part is reduced by n_1/N_1 by the application of σ_1, n_2/N_2 by the application of σ_2 etc. Application of the stresses σ_1, σ_2 etc. inflict a corresponding damage in the part. When the accumulated damage reaches a certain value, the material will fail by fatigue. This is the basis of the Palmgren-Miner cycle-ratio summation theory, also called as Miner's rule or Miner's hypothesis. Mathematically, the accumulated damage is expressed as

$$\frac{n_1}{N_1} + \frac{n_2}{N_2} + \frac{n_3}{N_3} + \ldots.. = C \tag{2.32}$$

where n_i are the number of cycles of stress σ_i applied to the element and N_i is the corresponding fatigue life at σ_i. The constant C is determined experimentally to be in the range of $0.7 \le C \le 2.2$ for failure. It is convenient to use the value of unity and many designers assume that the failure occurs when the cumulative damage is unity, given by

$$\Sigma \frac{n_i}{N_i} = 1 \tag{2.33}$$

2.4.3 Endurance Modifying Factors

So far we discussed the endurance limit of an ideal rotating beam specimen. Even for this case the tests show scattered results. An actual machine element may be operating under much different conditions than the test specimen. The factors that will affect the endurence limit of materials are:

(a) surface finish
(b) size effects
(c) temperature effects
(d) stress concentration effects
(e) residual stresses
(f) corrosive operating atmosphere
(g) coating or platings on the part.

2.4.4 Fatigue Strength Under Fluctuating Stresses

Quite frequently machine parts may be subjected to stress situation other than complete reversals. A fluctuating stress may vary between a maximum and a minimum without passing through zero. Figure 2.8 shows a fluctuating stress, which has a mean value σ_m, an amplitude σ_a and a related maximum and minimum values. If $\sigma_m = 0$, it corresponds to a purely alternating stress with complete stress reversals.

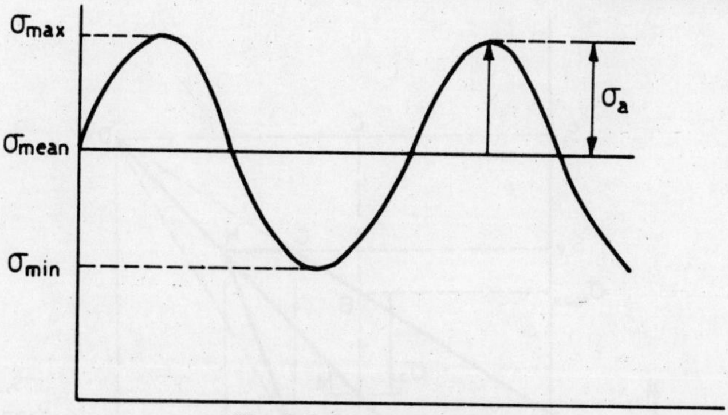

Fig. 2.8 Fluctuating stress

Fatigue strength of materials when subjected to fluctuating type of stress can be obtained from a modified Goodman diagram. This is the simplified representation of data from fatigue test on specimens subjected to fluctuating stresses. Figure 2.9 shows the modified Goodman diagram with all the stress components. The yield strength, S_y and the ultimate strength, S_u are marked on both the abcissa and the ordinate. The endurance limit, S_e is marked on the ordinate both above and below the origin. The mean stress line is 45° line cutting the ultimate strength line at point D. The lines DE and DF are shown from D to cut the ordinate at S_e and $-S_e$, and these lines represent the maximum and minimum stresses respectively.

Mean stress is marked on the abcissa for convenience and carried up to the mean stress line. Tensile mean stress is marked on the right side and the compressive mean stress on the left side. For a given mean stress σ_m, marked on the abcissa, the corresponding point on the 45° mean stress line is M. The intercept MB between the mean stress line and the maximum stress line ED provides the endurance limit when the mean stress is σ_m. Hence, line ED is the endurance limit also.

It should be mentioned here that when the mean stress is tension, most of the experimentally determined failure points fall above line ED. On the compression side, however, the failure points are not affected by the mean stress. Hence when the mean stress is compression, failure is defined by the two lines which are drawn parallel to the mean stress line. When the mean stress is tension, failure is defined by the maximum stress line until it cuts the yield strength line at G. To indicate failure by yielding, the maximum stress line is modified to go from G to H as shown in Fig. 2.9.

For design purposes, the modified Goodman line can be represented as shown in Fig. 2.10. The line from S_y on the ordinate to S_{yc} defines failure by compressive yielding; line from S_y to S_{yt} defines failure by tensile yielding. The failure line on the compressive side is the horizontal line drawn from S_e to the left until it cuts line joining S_y to S_{yc}. On the tensile side lines EG and GH denote the modified Goodman line, indicating failure by fatigue or yielding. The points E, G, D, H, M and B corresponds to those shown in Fig. 2.9.

For finite life design under fluctuating stresses, a S–N diagram may be drawn approximately using the modified Goodman diagram. A line similar to Eq. (2.27) can be constructed assuming that at the mean stress of σ_m, the material can endure 10^6 cycles of stress, σ_a = MB and 10^3 cycles of stress, $\sigma = 0.9\, S_u - \sigma_m$.

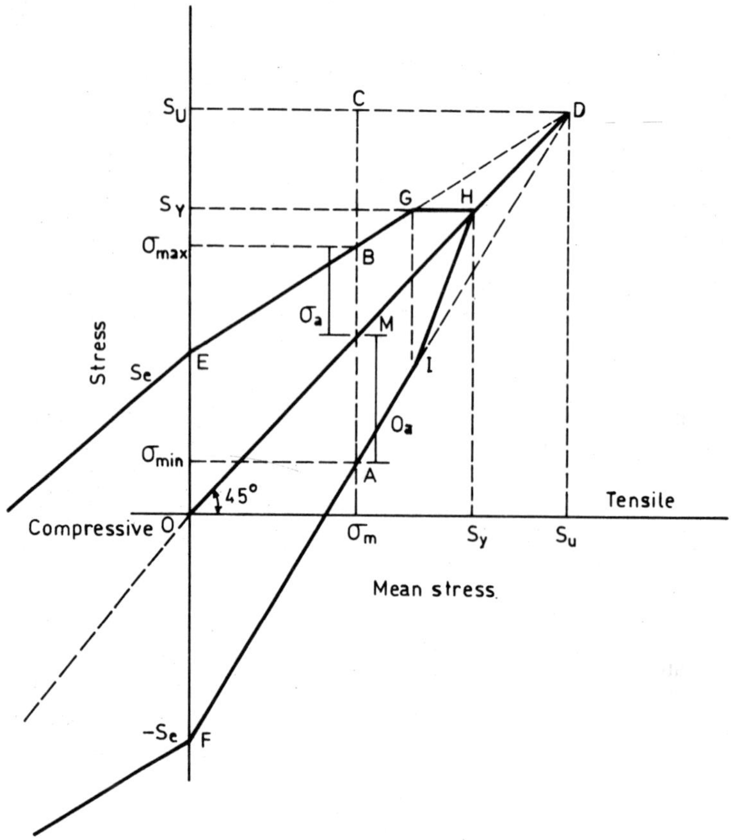

Fig. 2.9 Modified Goodman diagram

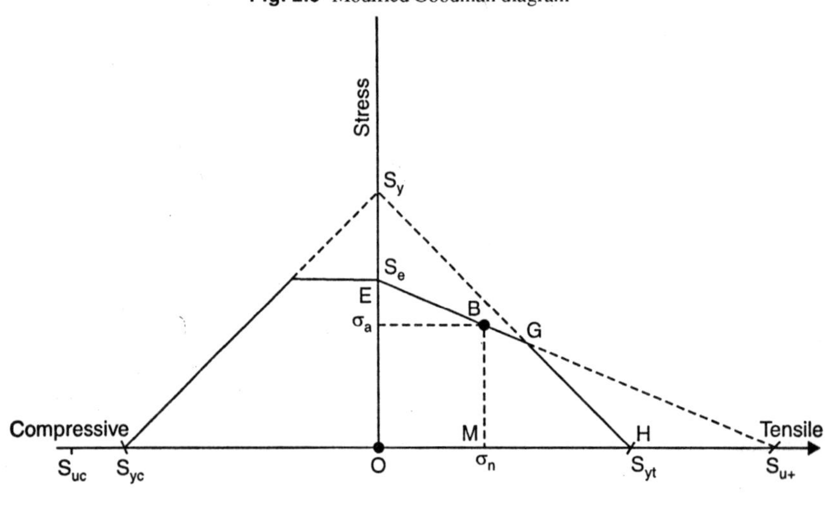

Fig. 2.10 Fatigue diagram for fluctuating stresses

Example 2.4

A machine element is subjected to a fluctuating tensile load varying from 0 to 112 KN. If the element is to be made from the steel having $S_y = 588$ MPa, $S_u = 700$ MPa and $S_e = 116.2$ MPa, determine a suitable diameter for an infinite life and a factor of safety of at least 2.0.

Solution

Let the diameter of the element be *d*. The stress range is

$$\sigma_r = \frac{112}{\pi d^2/4} = \frac{142.8}{d^2} \text{ Kpa}$$

The mean stress is

$$\sigma_m = \frac{112 - 0}{2 \times (\pi d^2/4)} = \frac{71.4}{d^2} \text{ Kpa}$$

The amplitude of the fluctuation is

$$\sigma_a = \frac{\sigma_r}{2} = \frac{71.4}{d^2} \text{ Kpa}$$

Hence we have the ratio of the amplitude of fluctuation to the mean stress as

$$\frac{\sigma_a}{\sigma_m} = 1$$

A fatigue diagram showing the Goodman line is drawn in Fig. 2.11. The intersecting of the modified Goodman line with a line of slope $\sigma_a/\sigma_m = 1.0$ from origin defines two values of strength. S_a is the strength corresponding to stress σ_a, and S_m is a strength corresponding to stress σ_m. For a factor of safety of 2.0, we have

$$\sigma_a \le S_a/2.0$$

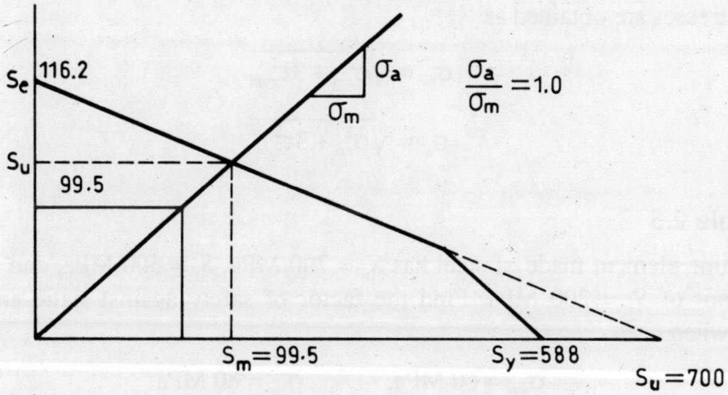

Fig. 2.11 Fatigue diagram for Example 2.4

Consequently, we have

$$\frac{71.4 \times 10^3}{d^2} \le \frac{99.5 \times 10^6}{2}$$

which gives

$$d = 0.038 \text{ m}$$
$$= 3.8 \text{ cm}$$

2.4.5 Fatigue Failure due to Combined Stresses

When a rotating shaft is subjected simultaneously to a constant torque and a stationary bending load, it is experiencing a combined stress situation. At the shaft surface, the torsional stress is $\tau = Tc/J$, where J is the polar moment of inertia of the shaft cross section, T is the applied torque and c is the shaft radius. The bending moment M will induce a normal stress at the shaft surface which is $\sigma = \pm\, Mc/I$, where I is the moment of inertia of the shaft cross section about the neutral axis in bending. This normal stress varies from tension to compression, back to tension and so on as the shaft rotates. If the stresses on the surface of the shaft are analyzed using a Mohr's circle diagram, it will be seen that the principal stresses do not maintain the same orientation, relative to the mark on the surface, as the shaft rotates. The normal stresses σ_x and σ_y as well as the shear stress τ_{xy}, in the general two dimensional stress-state, may have both mean and alternating components.

A method using the distortion energy theory applied to fatigue may be formulated to solve the problem involving combined stresses. Construct two stress elements, one for the mean stresses and the one for the alternating stresses. Draw two Mohr's circle diagrams, one for each element, and the principal mean stresses can be obtained from the other. We can then define a mean and an alternating von Mises stresses as

$$\sigma_{m'} = \sqrt{\sigma_{1m}^2 - \sigma_{1m}\,\sigma_{2m} + \sigma_{2m}^2} \tag{2.34}$$

$$\sigma_{a'} = \sqrt{\sigma_{1a}^2 - \sigma_{1a}\,\sigma_{2a} + \sigma_{2a}^2} \tag{2.35}$$

These two stress components may then be applied to a fatigue diagram using the modified Goodman criterion as shown in Fig. 2.9 as before.

When a single normal stress σ_x is accompained by a shear stress τ_{xy}, the Von Mises stresses are obtained as

$$\sigma_{m'} = \sqrt{\sigma_{xm}^2 + 3\tau_{xym}^2} \tag{2.36}$$

$$\sigma_{a'} = \sqrt{\sigma_{xa}^2 + 3\tau_{xya}^2} \tag{2.37}$$

Example 2.5

A machine element made of steel has $S_u = 700$ MPa, $S_y = 500$ MPa, and an endurance limit of $S_e = 200$ MPa. Find the factor of safety against static and fatigue failure when

$$\sigma_{xm} = 60 \text{ MPa}, \qquad \sigma_{xa} = 80 \text{ MPa}$$

$$\tau_{xym} = 70 \text{ MPa}, \qquad \tau_{xya} = 35 \text{ MPa}$$

Solution

The maximum normal stress is

$$\sigma_{x\,\max} = \sigma_{xm} + \sigma_{xa} = 60 + 80 = 140 \text{ MPa}$$

The maximum shear stress is

$$\tau_{xy\,\max} = \tau_{xym} + \tau_{xya} = 70 + 35 = 105 \text{ MPa}$$

From Eq. (2.36) we obtain the maximum von Mises stress as

$$\sigma_{max'} = \sqrt{140^2 + 3 \times 105^2}$$
$$= 229 \text{ MPa}$$

Hence the factor of safety against static failure is given by

$$n(\text{static}) = \frac{S_y}{\sigma_{max}} = \frac{500}{229} = 2.18$$

From Eqs. (2.36) and (2.37) we get

$$\sigma_{m'} = \sqrt{60^2 + 3 \times 70^2} = 135 \text{ MPa}$$

$$\sigma_{a'} = \sqrt{80^2 + 3 \times 35^2} = 100 \text{ MPa}$$

Drawing these stresses on a modified Goodman diagram as shown in Fig. 2.12, we obtain $S_a = 161.5$ MPa. Hence

$$n(\text{fatigue}) = \frac{S_a}{\sigma_a} = \frac{161.5}{100} = 1.615$$

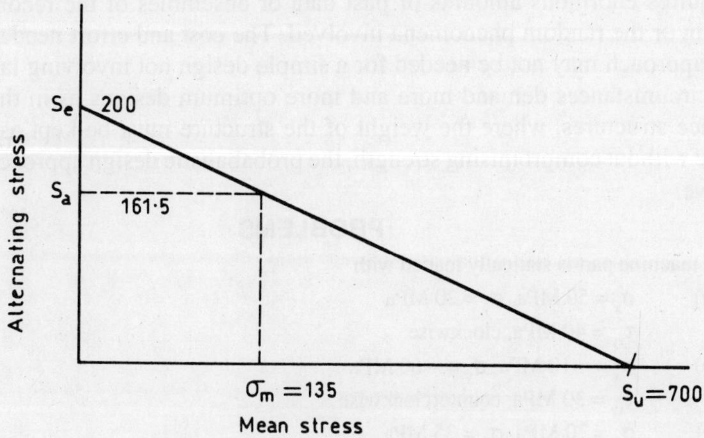

Fig. 2.12 Fatigue diagram for Example 2.5

2.5 FACTOR OF SAFETY

It is practically impossible to evaluate accurately all the different factors, that are involved in the design problem. It may be difficult to determine the various forces to which the element is subjected in operation. The factor may be random in nature also. The accuracy to which a part can be machined in the machine shop will vary from element to element and hence the geometrical dimensions may be slightly different from those specified in the design. The material properties used in the design are average values from past experiments on carefully chosen specimens, whereas the actual material chosen to make the part may have slightly different properties.

To ensure against such uncertainties and unknown conditions, engineering designers used a factor of safety in their design. The working stress to be used in the design is obtained by dividing the yield or ultimate strength by the factor of safety, which must be obviously greater than unity.

Use of a large factor of safety to eliminate all possibilities of failure from worst possible combination of circumstances may not be economical in engineering design. The designer should attempt to reduce the probability of failure to a suitable level which obviously depends on particular situation and application. A failure that involves only a little inconvenience or a minor loss in terms of time and cost might be allowed more frequently than one involving large losses or one involving loss of human life. Provision should be made in design for easy and rapid replacement of parts that are subject to frequent failure. If the product operates under conditions of frequent service inspection, smaller factor of safety can be used.

Since factor of safety is used as a hedge against uncertainties in design, it is, in fact, a factor of ignorance. The uncertainties involved in the design can also be handled using the ideas of probabalistic concepts related to random processes. By this approach the forces acting on the element can be described using statistical analysis considerations in terms of their distributions, mean values, mean square values etc. Uncertainties in the manufacture and in material properties can be included in such a probabalistic analysis. In this method, factor of safety will be replaced by appropriate probabilities attached to each of the uncertainties. However, this requires enormous amounts of past data or ensembles of the records of the uncertain or the random phenomena involved. The cost and effort needed for this design approach may not be needed for a simple design not involving large risks. When circumstances demand more and more optimum designs as in the case of aerospace structures, where the weight of the structure must be kept as small as possible without compromising strength, the probabalistic design approach is more attractive.

PROBLEMS

2.1 A machine part is statically loaded with

(*a*) $\sigma_x = 50$ MPa, $\sigma_y = 20$ MPa
$\tau_{xy} = 40$ MPa, clockwise

(*b*) $\sigma_x = -10$ MPa, $\sigma_y = -60$ MPa
$\tau_{xy} = 30$ MPa, counterclockwise

(*c*) $\sigma_1 = 70$ MPa, $\sigma_2 = 35$ MPa

If the yield strength $S_y = 150$ MPa, find the factor of safety for each of the three static failure theories.

2.2 A state of plane stress consists of a tensile stress $\sigma_a = 10$ *ksi* exerted on vertical surfaces and of unknown shearing stresses. Determine (*a*) the magnitude of the shearing stress τ_0 for which the largest normal stress is 12 *ksi*, and (*b*) the corresponding maximum shearing stress.

2.3 A machine part is designed for a factor of safety of 3, using the distortion energy theory. If the yield strength of the material is $S_y = 350$ MPa and $\sigma_x = 90$ MPa, $\tau_{xy} = 0$, find the value of σ_y.

2.4 A shaft is loaded by a torque of 4000 Nm. The material has a yield strength of $S_y = 340$ MPa. Factor of safety is 2. Find the diameter of the shaft using (*i*) maximum sheare theory (*ii*) distortion energy theory.

2.5 A steel plate 0.5 × 0.25 m, has only normal stresses on all the four edges. After the loads are applied, the dimensions become 0.50015 × 0.24995 m. If the material has $S_y = 450$ MPa and $S_u = 600$ MPa, find the factor of safety by the maximum shear theory.

2.6 A 5 cm diameter nonrotating shaft has a steady bending moment of 1000 Nm. Find the permissible steady torque that can be superposed on the bending moment if the factor of safety is to be 2 by the distortion energy theory. For the material, $S_y = 400$ MPa and $S_u = 550$ MPa.

2.7 The state of plane stress occurs at a critical point of a steel machine component. Given that $\sigma_x = 90$ Mpa, $\sigma_y = -50$ Mpa, $\tau_{xy} = 25$ Mpa and the yield strength is 250 Mpa for the grade of steel used. Determine the factor of safety with respect to yield, using (*a*) the maximum shearing-stress criterion, and (*b*) the maximum distortion-energy condition.

2.8 A shaft of steel with material properties given by $S_u = 600$ MPa, $S_y = 490$ MPa and $S_e = 220$ MPa is subjected to alternating stresses of amplitude $\sigma_1 = 250$ MPa for 1000 cycles, $\sigma_2 = 300$ MPa for 1000 cycles, $\sigma_3 = 350$ MPa for 1000 cycles and $\sigma_4 = 200$ MPa for 2000 cycles. Find the total damage experienced by the shaft.

2.9 A shaft of steel with material properties given by $S_n = 600$ MPa, $S_y = 490$ MPa and $S_e = 220$ MPa is subjected to alternating stresses of amplitude $\sigma_1 = 250$ MPa for 1000 cycles, $\sigma_2 = 300$ MPa for 1000 cycles, $\sigma_3 = 350$ MPa for 1000 cycles and $\sigma_4 = 200$ MPa for 2000 cycles. Find the total damage experienced by the shaft.

2.10 A mechanical part is made of steel with $S_u = 600$ MPa, $S_y = 480$ MPa, and $S_e = 200$ MPa. Determine the factor of safety if it is subjected to a fluctuating stress varying between 40 and 100 MPa.

2.11 A machine component is made of steel with $S_u = 800$ Mpa, $S_y = 600$ Mpa, and an endurance limit of $S_e = 300$ Mpa. Determine the factor of safety against static and fatigue failure when $\sigma_{xm} = 50$ Mpa, $\sigma_{xa} = 90$ Mpa, $\tau_{sym} = 80$ Mpa, and $\tau_{xya} = 40$ Mpa.

REFERENCES

1. Davidson, J.W., Felton L.P. and Hart G.C., Reliability based optimization for dynamic loads *Journal of Structural Division,* ASCE, vol. 103, October 1977.
2. Johnson, R.C. (1980), *Optimum Design of Mechanical Elements,* John Wiley and Sons, Inc. New York.
3. Moses, F., (1973), Design for Reliability—Concept and Applications in R.H. Gallagher and O.C. Zienkiewicz (Ed.), Optimum Structural Design, Theory and Applications, Chapter 13, John Wiley & Sons, New York.
4. Phelan, R.M., (1957), *Fundamentals of Mechanical Design,* McGraw-Hill Book Company, New York.
5. Shigley, J.E., (1977), *Mechanical Engineering Design,* Third Edition, McGraw-Hill Book Company, New York.
6. Spotts, M.F., (1961), *Design of Machine Elements,* Third Edition, Prentice-Hall, Inc., Englewood Cliffs. N.J.

CHAPTER 3

OPTIMIZATION OF THE DESIGN

3.1 INTRODUCTION

Design decisions are quite often made by means, based on the past experience of the designer, in an attempt to produce optimal design. It should be possible, however, to rationalize a significant amount of this decision making process by basing it on analytical techniques.

For a given specification, there may be several possible design configurations or options. The choice of a particular design option can be done either by the past experience of the designer or by an analytical technique, where numbers are attached to each possible option which can be optimized. These numbers can be assigned for various aspects of a design option such as the aesthetic value, simplicity in the production process, availability of required materials and so on.

Once the design option is chosen, the detailed design can be carried out by specifying the design variables such as the diameter of a shaft, length and cross sectional dimensions of a load carrying member, viscosity of a lubricant. An optimization or objective function is set up defining the total value in terms of the design variables given as

$$U(x_1, x_2, \ldots\ldots, x_n) = \text{maximum (or minimum)} \tag{3.1}$$

In certain design situations, the design variables, x_i, may not be completely free to be varied and may be subject to constraints, which may be an equality type or inequality type given by

$$\psi_i\ (x_1, x_2, \ldots\ldots\ldots, x_n) = 0 \qquad i = 1, m \tag{3.2}$$

$$\phi_j\ (x_1, x_2, \ldots\ldots\ldots, x_n) \geq 0 \qquad j = 1, p \tag{3.3}$$

Numerical procedures from the mathematics of operations research can be used to adjust the design variables so that the constraints are satisfied.

In general, the expression for the objective function and the constraints in terms of the design variables are nonlinear in nature. We will discuss some techniques of obtaining the optimum value for the objective function. The methods discussed below are not exhaustive and books on optimization must be referred to for an in depth study. An attempt is made in this chapter to give a glimpse of the optimization procedure.

3.2 UNCONSTRAINED MINIMIZATION OF FUNCTIONS

Consider an unconstrained design problem, represented by

$$U\ (x_1, x_2, \ldots\ldots\ldots, x_n) = \text{minimum} \tag{3.4}$$

The conditions for an extremum given by

$$\frac{dU}{dx_i} = 0 \qquad i = 1, 2, \ldots\ldots n \tag{3.5}$$

These are n number of simultaneous nonlinear algebraic equations which must be solved. The Newton's method of finding the roots of equations can be employed here, however, obtaining a good initial approximation is a tedious task. Further, out of the n possible solutions, a particular solution yielding a minimum must be found. The sign of the second derivative must be found to ensure that the roots correspond to minima and not maxima or saddle points.

3.3 MINIMIZATION WITH CONSTRAINTS USING LAGRANGE MULTIPLIERS

Considering only equality contraints, to start with and assuming that they cannot be used to eliminate some of the variables, the design problem can be given as

$$U(x_1, x_2, \ldots\ldots, x_n) = \text{minimum} \tag{3.6}$$

$$\psi_j(x_1, x_2, \ldots\ldots, x_n) = 0 \quad j = 1, 2, \ldots\ldots, m \tag{3.7}$$

The condition for the optima are given as

$$\frac{\partial U}{\partial x_i} + \sum_{j=1}^{m} \lambda_j \frac{\partial \psi_j}{\partial x_i} = 0 \quad i = 1, 2, \ldots\ldots, n \tag{3.8}$$

where λ_j are m number of Lagrange multipliers. Equation (3.8) may be expressed in an alternative form as

$$\frac{\partial}{\partial x_i}\left(U + \sum_{i=1}^{m} \lambda_i \psi_j\right) = 0 \quad i = 1, 2, \ldots\ldots, n \tag{3.9}$$

There are n equations in either (3.8) or (3.9) and along with the constraint equations, there are $(n + m)$ equations in the n design variables and m Lagrange multipliers which must be solved simultaneously.

The inequality contraints can be handled by converting them into equality constraints by the use of slack variables. Let the inequality constraint be given by

$$\phi_k(x_1, x_2 \ldots\ldots x_n) \geq 0 \tag{3.10}$$

which can be expressed as an equality constraint in the form

$$\phi_k - a_k^2 = 0 \tag{3.11}$$

where a_k is a slack variable introduced which must be adjusted for the solution so that Eq. (3.11) is satisfied. The slack variables are squared to prevent it from dropping out when the derivative is taken and to maintain the slack positive even if a_k goes negative. The set of simultaneous equations to be solved now have the form

$$\frac{\partial}{\partial x_i}\left[U + \sum_{j=1}^{m} \lambda_j \psi_j - \sum_{k=1}^{p} \lambda_k (\phi_k - a_k^2)\right] = 0 \qquad i = 1, 2m \ldots n \tag{3.12}$$

$$\frac{\partial}{\partial a_l}\left[U + \sum_{j=1}^{m} \lambda_j \psi_j - \sum_{k=1}^{p} \lambda_k (\phi_k - a_k^2)\right] = 0 \qquad l = 1, 2, \ldots p \tag{3.13}$$

$$\psi_j = 0 \qquad j = 1, 2, \ldots\ldots m \tag{3.14}$$

$$\phi_k - a_k^2 = 0 \qquad k = 1, 2, \ldots\ldots p \tag{3.15}$$

The negative sign in the third term of Eq. (3.12) is to make λ_k positive. It may be noted that Eq. (3.13) reduces to

$$\lambda_k \, a_k = 0 \quad k = 1, 2, \ldots . p \tag{3.16}$$

requiring that either λ_k or a_k be zero for all k.

3.4 NUMERICAL OPTIMIZATION

In the sections 3.1 and 3.2, analytical methods of finding the minimum of a function with or without constraint was discussed. Vast majority of design optimization problems are quite difficult to solve using the above analytical techniques. Numerical techniques using computers must be employed to solve many engineering opimization problems. In the following several such numerical methods will be developed.

3.4.1 Optimization Involving Single Variables

Even though problem involving optimization of a function with just one variable occurs rarely in practice, the technique discussed here will have application in several strategies used for nonlinear programming involving optimization of function of several variables that will be discussed later.

Let the function to be minimized be $U(x)$. Initially, the minimum is bracketed in a small interval by using incremental search technique. The function is evaluated at x_0, $x_0 + h$, $x_0 + 2h$ ... etc, where h is incremental step. If $U_{j-1} < U_j < U_{j+1}$ where $U_j = U(x_0 + jh)$, then the minimum is bracketed between $x_0 + (j - 1)\,h$ and $x_0 + (j + 1)\,h$. In doing this search, if $U_1 < U_0$, search is continued with $x = x_0 + 2h$, $x_0 + 3h$, etc. in the same direction. Otherwise, search must be done in the opposite direction with $x = x_0 - h$, $x_0 - 2h$, etc.

Once the region of the minimum is bracketed, the bounds of this region can be squeezed and narrowed down to pin point the minimum more accurately. This can be done in an iterative fashion by making two interior evaluations in the interval containing the minimum. This is shown in the Fig. 3.1 which represents a plot of $U(x)$ versus x in the interval. After i number of interations the lower and upper bounds of the interval are designated as l_i and u_i. Let a_i and b_i be the points within the interval symmetrically located so that

$$a_i - l_i = u_i - b_i \tag{3.17}$$

The three possible situations are distinguished by evaluating $U(a_i)$ and $U(b_i)$ and are shown by curves 1, 2 and 3 in fig. 3.1.

Case 1.	$U(a_i)$	$<$	$U(b_i)$:	minimum is in the region	$l_i < x < b_i$
Case 2.	$U(a_i)$	$>$	$U(b_i)$:	minimum is in the region	$a_i < x < u_i$
Case 3.	$U(a_i)$	$=$	$U(b_i)$:	minimum is in the region	$a_i < x < b_i$

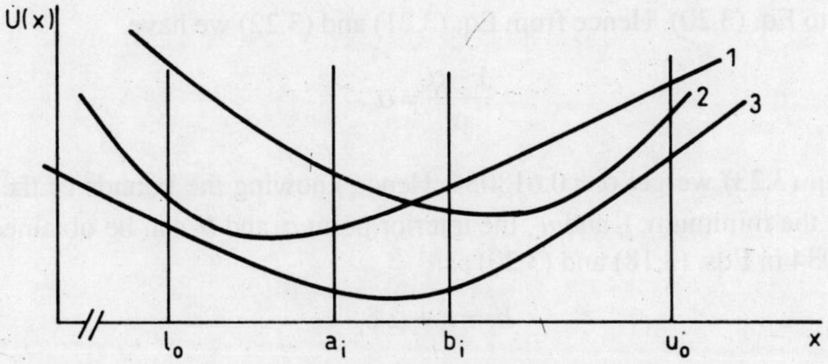

Fig. 3.1 Plot of function over the established interval

The procedure to choose the interior points a_i and b_i is explained with the aid of Fig. 3.2. Designating

$$u_i - l_i = \delta_i$$

$$b_i - l_i = u_i - a_i = \delta_{i+1}$$

$$a_i - l_i = u_i - b_i = \delta_{i+2} \tag{3.18}$$

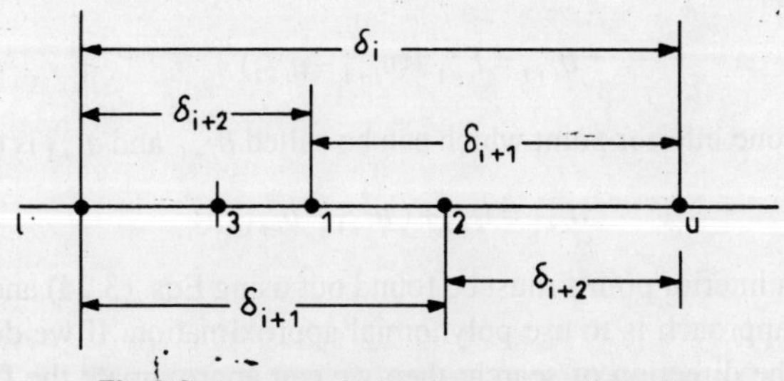

Fig. 3.2 A strategy for locating new interior points

and noting that a_i and b_i are located symmetrically, we have

$$\delta_{i+1} + \delta_{i+2} = \delta_i \tag{3.19}$$

Denoting
$$\frac{\delta_{i+1}}{\delta_i} = \alpha \tag{3.20}$$

and eliminating δ_i between Eqs. (3.19) and (3.20) we obtain

$$\frac{\delta_{i+2}}{\delta_{i+1}} = \frac{1-\alpha}{\alpha} \tag{3.21}$$

If the Case 1 holds good then the minimum is between l_i and b_i and the point a_i is located in this region, whereas if Case 2 is true then the minimlum is between a_i and u_i and b_i will be a point in the interior of this region. In either case, if we want to use one such interior point which is already available, say, a_i for case 1 and b_i for case 2, then we must have the relation

$$\frac{\delta_{i+2}}{\delta_{i+1}} = \alpha \tag{3.22}$$

according to Eq. (3.20). Hence from Eq. (3.21) and (3.22) we have

$$\frac{1-\alpha}{\alpha}=\alpha \tag{3.23}$$

Solving Eq. (3.23) we get $\alpha = 0.618034$. Hence knowing the bounds of the region containing the minimum, l_i and u_i, the interior point a_i and b_i can be obtained using $\alpha = 0.618034$ in Eqs. (3.18) and (3.20) as

$$b_1 = l_1 + \alpha\,\delta_1 \tag{3.24}$$

The other interior point is symmetrical and from Eq. (3.17) or (3.18) it is obtained as

$$a_i = l_i + (u_i - b_i) \tag{3.25}$$

Now, function evaluations are made at a_i and b_i to obtain $U(a_i)$ and $U(b_i)$. After determining which case is satisfied, we can identify the region of the minimum on either between l_i and b_i for case 1 or between a_i and u_i for case 2 or between a_i and b_i for case 3. We can redesignate the new bounds as l_{i+1} and u_{i+1}. For case 1, a_1 is one interior point which can be redesignated as a_{i+1} and b_{i+1} is obtained by symmetrically placing it as

$$b_{i+1} = l_{i+1} + (u_{i+1} - a_{i+1}) \tag{3.26}$$

For case 2, b_i is one interior point which can be called b_{i+1} and a_{i+1} is obtained as

$$a_{i+1} = l_{i+1} + (u_{i+1} - b_{i+1}) \tag{3.27}$$

For Case 3, both interior points must be found out using Eqs. (3.24) and (3.25).

A second approach is to use polynomial approximation. If we define x as the coordinate for the direction of search, then we can approximate the function to be minimized by

$$U(x) = \sum_{i=0}^{n} a_i\, x^i$$

In order to evaluate the a_i s it is necessary to evaluate $U(x)$ at $n+1$ successive values of x. Substituting corresponding known values in Eq. (3.28), we get n linear algebraic equations which can be solved for the $a_i s$. The minimum is then given by solving

$$U(x) = \sum_{i=0}^{n} a_i x^i \tag{3.28}$$

which is

$$\sum_{i=1}^{n} a_i\, i\, x^{i-1} = 0 \tag{3.29}$$

Explicit solutions are easily obtained for n equal to 2 or 3, and these are the common polynomials used. If the minimum is not bracketed, it is desirable to test for a true minimum using the sign of the derivative of Eq. (3.29) at the apparent minimum.

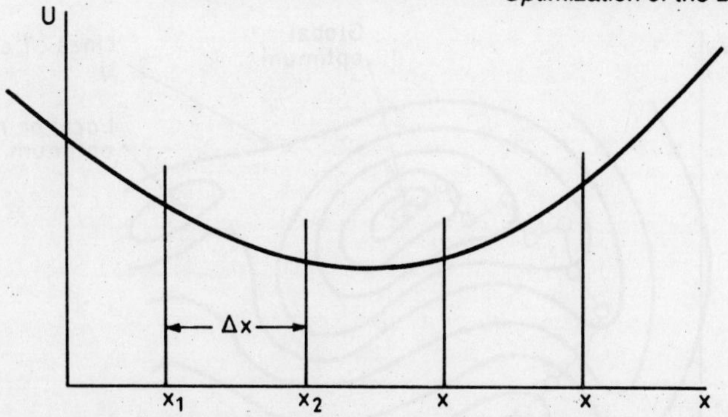

Fig. 3.3 Points used for polynomial approximation of a minimum along a line

If the polynomial has a degree higher than a cubic, Eq. (3.29) could be solved by the Newton-Raphson method.

There are many strategies for generating the n+1 values of x required for the polynomial approximation. The simplest is to take equally spaced points inside the region containing the minimum. Alternatively, if the previously described iterative method is used upto the ith iteration, then the points l_i, a_i, b_i, and u_i can be used to obtain the cubic. Defining these points as x_1, x_2, x_3, and x_4 for simplicity, the Lagrangian polynomial of degree 3 (cubic) is given by

$$P_3(x) = \sum_{i=1}^{4} L_i(x)\, U(x_i) \tag{3.30}$$

where,

$$L_i(x) = \prod_{\substack{j=1 \\ i \neq j}}^{4} \frac{(x - x_i)}{(x_i - x_j)} \tag{3.31}$$

where the π symbol indicates that the product of the quantities following the symbol must be taken. For example,

$$L_1(x) = \frac{(x - x_2)(x - x_3)(x - x_4)}{(x_1 - x_2)(x_1 - x_3)(x_1 - x_4)} \tag{3.32}$$

By putting

$$\frac{dP_3}{dx} = 0 \tag{3.33}$$

and solving we can obtain the estimated x_{min} where the function $U(x)$ has the minimum.

3.5 GRADIENT METHODS

Gradient methods are not as efficient as some of the most recent methods to be discussed later, however, it forms a conceptual basis for many of them. The optimization follows the direction of the gradient in this method.

Consider the optimization function, in two dimensions, representing a terrain as shown in Fig. 3.4. The local direction of steepest descent is given by the negative of the gradient vector components, $-\partial U/\partial x_1$, $-\partial U/\partial x_2$. The gradient vector direction would be normal to the local contour line.

For numerical execution, the partial derivatives are obtained as

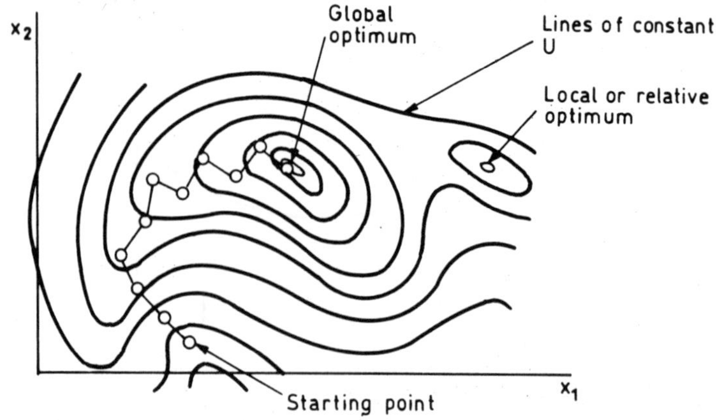

Fig. 3.4 The concept of the gradient method

$$\frac{\partial U}{\partial x_i} = \frac{\Delta U_i}{\Delta x_i} \tag{3.34}$$

where, $$\Delta U_i = U\,(x_i + \Delta x_i) - U\,(x_i) \tag{3.35}$$

and Δx_i is as small as possible without causing round-off errors.

Once the direction of the steepest gradient is found as shown in Fig. 3.5, the search is continued in that direction choosing a step $\delta\bar{r}$ given by

$$\delta\bar{r} = \delta x_i + i\ \delta x_2 \tag{3.36}$$

as shown. The step components have arbitrary absolute values, illustrated in Fig. 3.5. Their relative values are given by

$$\frac{\delta x_1}{\delta x_2} = \frac{\partial U/\partial x_1}{\partial U/\partial x_2} \tag{3.37}$$

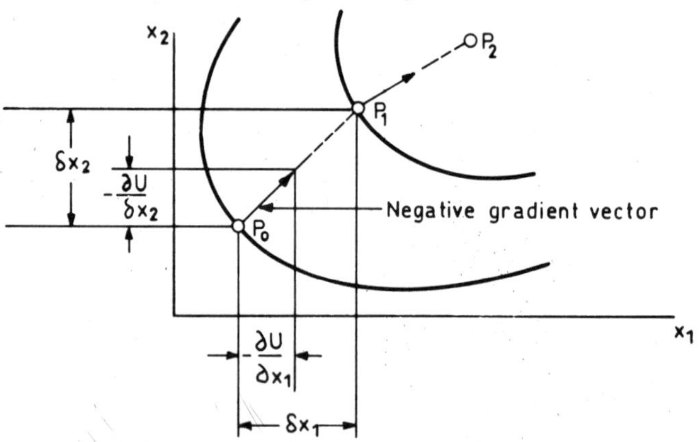

Fig. 3.5 Direction of step in gradient method

A parameter λ can be conveniently used to establish the absolute value of the step size, as

$$\delta x_i = -\lambda \frac{\partial U}{\partial x_i} \tag{3.38}$$

This same expression can be used in the n-dimensional case, for which we assume that the same strategy is applicable. Use of short step sizes makes the process very slow and large step sizes cause zig-zagging because the steps overshoot the range in the gradient vector direction.

An improved version of the gradient strategy is to continue along the gradient direction until a minimum is found along the direction line, using one of the methods of single variable minimization described in Sec. 3.3. The parameter λ is now the variable adjusted. This is illustrated in Fig. 3.6. The search has the tendency to zig-zag badly, particularly when the contours are elliptical in shape, or the function U is near quadratic. This is the reason for the poor success of the method.

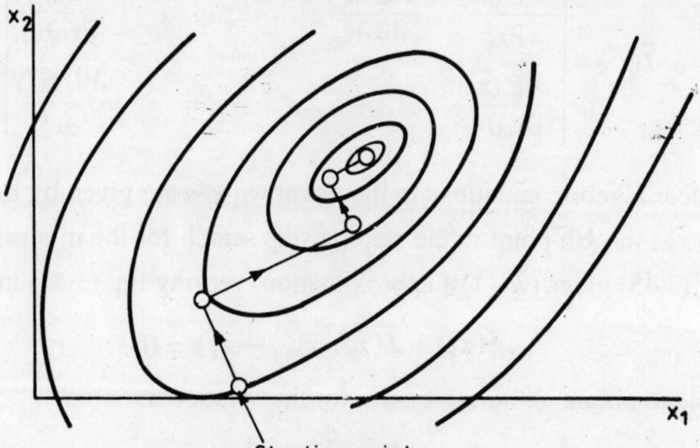

Fig. 3.6 Gradient method using line searches

The stopping criterion for the search could be when the partial derivatives become negligibly small or when successive changes in U become negligible. When an apparent optimum is reached, it is desirable to reduce the step size in the line search to ensure that the search is not stalled in the 'valley'. This is one of the several modes by which searches stall.

3.6 NEWTON'S METHOD

Newton's method is a gradient method and can be conveniently used to optimize functions with several parameters. Let the function to be optimized be $U(\bar{x})$, where $\bar{x}$ is the vector of parametrs $x_1, x_2, \ldots\ldots, x_n$. The function $U(\bar{x})$ can be expanded in the Taylor's series about a point $\bar{x}^*$ as

$$U(\bar{x}) = U(\bar{x}^*) + \sum_{i=1}^{n} \frac{\partial U(x^*)}{\partial X_i}(x_i - x_i^*) \tag{3.39}$$

Newton's method uses only two terms in the series. Expressing in concise form, the above series can be written as

$$U(\bar{x}) = U(\bar{x}^*) + g^{-T}(\bar{x}^*)(\bar{x} - \bar{x}^*) \tag{3.40}$$

where $\bar{g}(\bar{x}^*)$ is the vector of first derivatives given by

$$\bar{g}(\bar{x}^*) = \left[\frac{\partial U(\bar{x}^*)}{\partial x_1}, \frac{\partial U(\bar{x}^*)}{\partial x_2}, \ldots\ldots \right]^T \tag{3.41}$$

The minimum of $U(\bar{x})$ is obtained by setting

$$\frac{\partial U}{\partial x_i} = 0 \tag{3.42}$$

in Eq. (3.40) which yields the set of equations

$$\bar{g}(\bar{x}^*) + \bar{J}(\bar{x}^*)(\bar{x} - \bar{x}^*) = 0 \tag{3.43}$$

where $\bar{J}(\bar{x}^*)$ is the Jacobian matrix of second derivatives given by

$$\bar{J}(\bar{x}^*) = \begin{vmatrix} \dfrac{\partial^2 U(\bar{x}^*)}{\partial x_1^2} & \dfrac{\partial^2 U(\bar{x}^*)}{\partial x_1 \partial x_2} & \cdots\cdots\cdots & \dfrac{\partial^2 U(\bar{x}^*)}{\partial x_1 \partial x_n} \\ \dfrac{\partial^2 U(\bar{x}^*)}{\partial x_n \partial x_1} & \cdots\cdots\cdots\cdots\cdots & & \dfrac{\partial^2 U(\bar{x}^*)}{\partial x_n^2} \end{vmatrix} \tag{3.44}$$

A set of linear algebric equations in the unknown x_i's are given by Eq. (3.43). If $\bar{x}^*$ is taken as $\bar{x}_k$, the kth point in the step by step search for the minimum, then solution of Eq. (3.43) gives ($\underline{k}$ +1)st approximation. Writing Eq. (3.43) in the form

$$\bar{g}(\bar{x}_k) + \bar{J}(\bar{x}_k)(\bar{x}_{k+1} - \bar{x}_k) = 0 \tag{3.45}$$

it is possible to obtain an iterative form for the solution as

$$\bar{x}_{k+1} = \bar{x}_k - [\bar{J}(\bar{x}_k)]^{-1}\bar{g}(\bar{x}_k) \tag{3.46}$$

It is not actually necessary to obtain the inverse of the matrix $\bar{J}[\bar{x}_k]$ to solve for the new approximation $\bar{x}_k$. It is possible to write Eq. (3.45) in the form

$$\bar{J}(\bar{x}_k)\bar{\delta}_k = -\bar{g}(\bar{x}_k) \tag{3.47}$$

Where $$\bar{\delta}_k = \bar{x}_{k+1} - \bar{x}_k,$$

and then solve Eq. (3.47) for $\bar{\delta}_k$ using Gaussin elimination.

The major disadvantage of the Newton's method is the need for determining second-order partial derivatives, which makes it quite impractical for most engineering applications.

3.7 METHODS BASED ON THE CONCEPT OF QUADRATIC CONVERGENCE

3.7.1 Conjugate Directions for a Quadratic Function

The gradient method is expressed as

$$\bar{x}_{k+1} = \bar{x}_k - \lambda_k \bar{g}(\bar{x}_k) \tag{3.48}$$

or in the form

$$\bar{\delta}_k = -\lambda_k \bar{g}(\bar{x}_k) \tag{3.49}$$

which is similar in form to Eq. (3.38)

During each iteration λ_k is selected to minimize $U(\overline{x}_{k+1})$ in the gradient direction. As illustrated in Fig. 3.6, a gradient search tends to zig-zag quite badly, particularly for quadratic functions. If it is possible to establish the best direction to take for a quadratic function, it would likely also be better for most other non-linear functions. This is called quadratic convergence and the approach is rather surprisingly successful. Eq. (3.48) has the general form, in this case, given by

$$\overline{x}_{k+1} = \overline{x}_k + \lambda_k \overline{c}\,(\overline{x}_k) \tag{3.50}$$

where $\overline{C}(\overline{x}_k)$ defines the conjugate direction vector at each step. The general quadratic form is

$$U(\overline{x}) = \frac{1}{2}\overline{x}^T \overline{A}\,\overline{x} + \overline{B}^T \overline{x} + d \tag{3.51}$$

where $\overline{A}$ is a matrix and $\overline{B}$ is a vector.

It is required to determine a means of establishing conjugate directions for an optimization function of this form, and show that they give convergence to the minimum. For this we require $\overline{A}$ to be a positive-definite matrix, which means it must be such that all quadratic terms of Eq. (3.51) are positive. This is equivalent to requiring Eq. (3.51) to be convex so that it has a minimum. $\overline{A}$ will also be symmetric since

$$\frac{\partial^2 U}{\partial x_i\, \partial x_j} = A_{ij} = \frac{\partial^2 U}{\partial x_j\, \partial x_i} = A_{ji} \tag{3.52}$$

and consequently $\overline{A}^{-1}$ is also symmetric. For convenience, let

$$\overline{g}\,(\overline{x}_k) = \overline{g}_k\,;\ \overline{g}(\overline{x}) = \overline{g}\,;\ \overline{C}(\overline{x}_k) = \overline{C}_k$$

Note that the gradient vector of the quadratic (3.51) is

$$\overline{g} = \overline{A}\,\overline{x} + \overline{B} \tag{3.53}$$

Equation (3.50) is iterated for successive steps from i to $(n-1)$, to obtain

$$\overline{x}_n = \overline{x}_i + \sum_{k=i}^{n-1} \lambda_k \overline{C}_k \tag{3.54}$$

Premultiplying both sides by $\overline{A}$ and adding $\overline{B}$, we get

$$\overline{A}\,\overline{x}_n + \overline{B} = \overline{A}\,\overline{x}_i + B + \sum_{k=i}^{n-1} \lambda_k \overline{A}\,\overline{C}_k \tag{3.55}$$

Using Eq. (3.53) this becomes

$$\overline{g}_n = \overline{g}_i + \sum_{k=i}^{n-1} \lambda_k \overline{A}\,\overline{C}_k \tag{3.56}$$

Finally premultiplying by $\overline{C}_{i-1}^T$,

$$\overline{C}_{i-1}^T\, \overline{g}_n = \overline{C}_{i-1}^T \overline{g}_1 + \sum_{k=1}^{n-1} \lambda_k \overline{C}_{i-1}^T \overline{A}\,\overline{C}_k \tag{3.57}$$

It can be demonstrated intuitively that $\overline{C}_{i-1}^T \overline{g}_i$ is zero by the following reasoning. In the $i-1$ step, $\overline{C}_{i-1}$ is followed to a minimum for U, which takes us to $\overline{x}_i$. The search vector must be tangent to a contour line through $\overline{x}_i$ and therefore the gradient $\overline{g}_i$ is normal to $\overline{C}_{i-1}$. Consequently,

$$\overline{C}_{i-1}^T \overline{g}_i = 0 \tag{3.58}$$

This can be demonstrated more rigorously as follows. Consider λ_{i-1} as a variable that is being adjusted to minimize U and bring the search to $\overline{x}_i$. Consequently,

$$\frac{dU}{d\lambda_{j-1}} = \frac{\partial U}{\partial x_1}\frac{dx_1}{d\lambda_{i-1}} + \frac{\partial U}{\partial x_2}\frac{dx_2}{d\lambda_{i-1}} + \ldots + \frac{\partial u}{\partial x_n}\frac{dx_n}{d\lambda_{i-1}} \tag{3.59}$$

Referring to Fig. 3.7, the search vector $\overline{C}_{i-1}$ at the origin has components $C_{1,i-1}, \ldots,$ $C_{n,i-1}$, and the search moves along vector $\lambda_{i-1}\overline{C}_{i-1}$ from x_{i-1} to x_1. In general, then, for any value of $\lambda_{i-1'}$,

$$\overline{x} = \overline{x}_{i-1} + \lambda_{i-1}\overline{C}_{i-1} \tag{3.60}$$

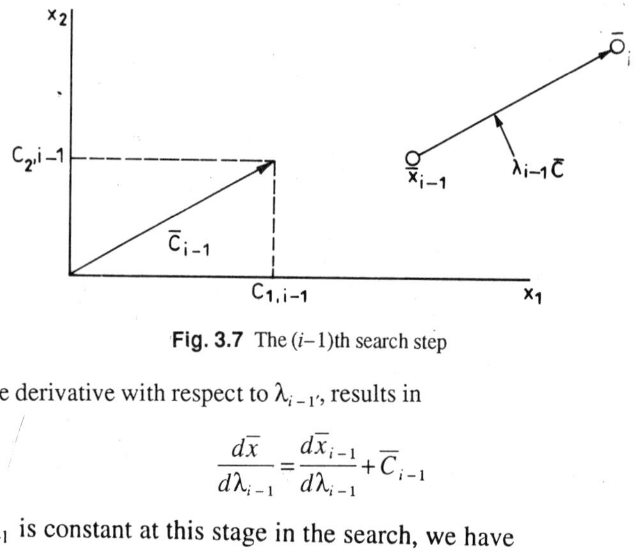

Fig. 3.7 The $(i-1)$th search step

Taking the derivative with respect to $\lambda_{i-1'}$, results in

$$\frac{d\overline{x}}{d\lambda_{i-1}} = \frac{d\overline{x}_{i-1}}{d\lambda_{i-1}} + \overline{C}_{i-1} \tag{3.61}$$

Since $\overline{x}_{i-1}$ is constant at this stage in the search, we have

$$\overline{C}_{i-1} = \frac{d\overline{x}}{d\lambda_{i-1}} \tag{3.62}$$

Thus Eq. (3.59) can be written for any value of $\lambda_{i-1'}$, as

$$\frac{dU}{d\lambda_{i-1}} = \overline{C}_{i-1}^T \overline{g} \tag{3.63}$$

Now at $\overline{x}_1$, $dU/d\lambda_{i-1}$ must be zero for a minimum U. Thus, we have

$$\overline{C}_{i-1}^T \, \overline{g} = 0 \tag{3.64}$$

Consequently, Eq. (3.57) reduces to

$$\overline{C}_{i-1}^T \, \overline{g}_n = \sum_{k=i}^{n-1} \lambda_k \, \overline{C}_{i-1}^T \, \overline{A} \, \overline{C}_k \tag{3.65}$$

The conjugate vectors are defined as those satisfying

$$\overline{C}_i^T \, \overline{A} \, \overline{C}_j = 0 \tag{3.66}$$

for $i \neq j$. Since $\overline{A}$ must be a positive-definite matrix as defined above, the summation term of Eq. (3.65) is zero so that

$$\overline{C}_{i-1}^T \, \overline{g}_n = 0 \tag{3.67}$$

The theory of n-dimensional vectors states that if we construct a set of n-vectors all orthogonal or conjugate to each other, then any other vector can be written as a linear combination of these vectors. Therefore, no other vector can be orthogonal to all of the orignal n vectors other than the zero vector. Since Eq. (3.67) is an expression of orthogonality of the nth gradient vector with all n conjugate vectors, then $\overline{g}_n$ must be zero, which is the condition for the minimum of the quadratic. Thus the minimum of the quadratic can be found in the n steps if the search directions are conjugate.

The conjugate directions in two dimensions are shown in Fig. 3.8. The first search direction is the gradient vector, which is chosen arbitrarily. The second direction is conjugate to the first one. Several methods have been proposed for generating the first search direction and these methods are applied to nonquadratic functions also. It should be noted that Newton's method would go to the minimum in one step if the function to be minimized is quadratic.

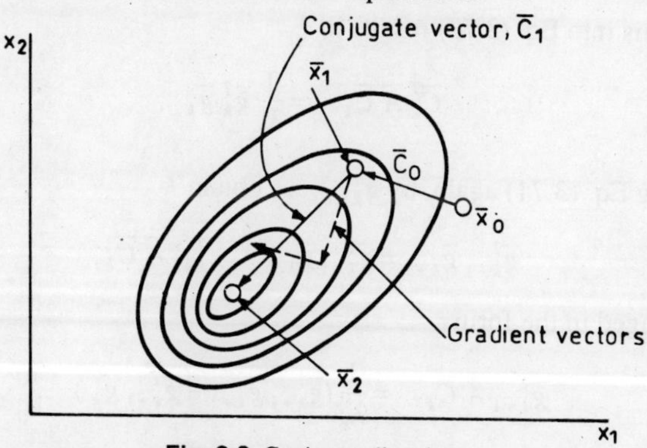

Fig. 3.8 Conjugate directions

3.7.2 Fletcher-Reeves Method

This method [Fletcher & Reeves 1964] is based on the assumption that conjugate directions can be generated by the following expression,

$$\overline{C}_{k+1} = -\overline{g}_{k+1} + \beta_k \, \overline{C}_k \tag{3.68}$$

where β_k must be determined using the fact that $\overline{C}_{k+1}$ is conjugate to $\overline{C}_k$. Eq. (3.68) is premultiplied by $\overline{C}_k^T \overline{A}$, to give

$$\overline{C}_k^T \overline{A}\, \overline{C}_{k+1} = -\overline{C}_k^T \overline{A} \overline{g}_{k+1} + \beta_k \overline{C}_k^T \overline{A}\, \overline{C}_k \tag{3.69}$$

By conjugacy the left-hand side is zero giving

$$\beta_k = \frac{\overline{C}_k^T \overline{A}\, \overline{g}_{k+1}}{\overline{C}_k^T \overline{A}\, \overline{C}_k} \tag{3.70}$$

In order to apply the method to nonquadratic functions we must eliminate $\overline{A}$ from Eq. (3.70). If we examine Eqs. (3.24) to (3.26) , it is clear that we could use the same approach to develop the following special case:

$$\overline{g}_{k+1} = \overline{g}_k + \lambda_k \overline{A}\, \overline{C}_k \tag{3.71}$$

Premultiplying both sides by $\overline{C}_k^T$ gives

$$\overline{C}_k^T \overline{g}_{k+1} = \overline{C}_k^T \overline{g}_k + \lambda_k \overline{C}_k^T \overline{A}\, \overline{C}_k \tag{3.72}$$

The left-hand side is zero by Eq. (3.58) , giving

$$\overline{C}_k^T \overline{A}\, \overline{C}_k = -\frac{1}{\lambda_k} \overline{C}_k^T \overline{g}_k \tag{3.73}$$

Returning to Eq. (3.68) , we premultiply it by $\overline{g}_{k+1}^T$

$$\overline{g}_{k+1}^T \overline{C}_{k+1} = -\overline{g}_{k+1} \overline{g}_{k+1} \beta_k \overline{g}_{k+1}^T \overline{C}_k \tag{3.74}$$

By Eq. (3.58), again the last term is zero, and hence

$$\overline{g}_k^T \overline{C}_k = \overline{C}_k^T \overline{g}_k = -\overline{g}_k^T \overline{g}_k \tag{3.75}$$

Substituting this into Eq. (3.73) results in

$$\overline{C}_k^T \overline{A}\, \overline{C}_k \quad = \frac{1}{\lambda_k} \overline{g}_k^T \overline{g}_k \tag{3.76}$$

Premultiplying Eq. (3.71) again, by $\overline{g}_{k+1}^T$, we obtain

$$\overline{g}_{k+1}^T \overline{g}_{k+1} = \overline{g}_{k+1}^T \overline{g}_k + \lambda_k \overline{g}_{k+1}^T \overline{A}\, \overline{C}_k \tag{3.77}$$

This is rearranged in the form

$$\overline{g}_{k+1}^T \overline{A}\, \overline{C}_k \quad = \frac{1}{\lambda_k} (\overline{g}_{k+1}^T \overline{g}_{k+1} - \overline{g}_{k+1}^T \overline{g}_k) \tag{3.78}$$

Because $\overline{A}$ is a symmetric matrix, we can reorder the left hand side as

$$\overline{C}_k^T \overline{A}\, \overline{g}_{k+1} = \frac{1}{\lambda_k} (\overline{g}_{k+1}^T \overline{g}_{k+1} - \overline{g}_{k+1}^T \overline{g}_k) \tag{3.79}$$

Premultiplying Eq. (3.71) once again, this time by $\overline{C}_{k+1}^T$, we get

$$\overline{C}_{k-1}^T \overline{g}_{k+1} = \overline{C}_{k-1}^T \overline{g}_k \lambda_k \overline{C}_{k-1}^T \overline{A}\, \overline{C}_k \tag{3.80}$$

Due to Eq. (3.58), the first term of Eq. (3.80) on the right hand side is zero, and the second term is zero due to the conjugate requirement. Thus

$$\overline{C}^T_{k-1}\,\overline{g}_{k-1} = 0 \tag{3.81}$$

Eq. (3.68) is used to get

$$\overline{C}_{k-1} = \frac{1}{\beta_{k-1}} \quad (\overline{C}_k + \overline{g}_k) \tag{3.82}$$

which we premultiply by $\overline{g}^T_{k+1}$ and obtain

$$\overline{g}^T_{k-1}\,\overline{C}_{k-1} = \frac{1}{\beta_{k-1}} \quad (\overline{g}^T_{k-1}\,\overline{C}_k + \overline{g}^T_{k-1}\,\overline{g}_k) \tag{3.83}$$

The left-hand side is zero because of Eq. (3.81), and the first term of the right-hand side is zero due to Eq. (3.68). Thus

$$\overline{g}^T_{k-1}\,\overline{g}_k = 0 \tag{3.84}$$

We have thus verified the orthogonality of successive gradient vectors in the use of conjugate search directions.

Returing to Eq. (3.79), we get from Eq. (3.84)

$$\overline{C}^T_k\,\overline{A}\,\overline{g}_{k+1} = \frac{1}{\lambda_k}\,\overline{g}^T_{k+1}\,\overline{g}_{k+1} \tag{3.85}$$

Finally returning to Eq. (3.70) , our original expression for β_k , we use Eqs. (3.76) and (3.85) to get

$$\beta_k = \frac{\overline{g}^T_{k+1}\,\overline{g}_{k+1}}{\overline{g}^T_k}\,\overline{g}_k \tag{3.86}$$

So now we can use Eq. (3.64) to get the final expression for generating each successive search direction.

$$\overline{C}_{k+1} = -\,\overline{g}_{k+1} + \frac{\overline{g}^T_{k+1}\,\overline{g}_{k+1}}{\overline{g}^T_k\,\overline{g}_k}\,\overline{C}_k \tag{3.87}$$

This is applied to the general algorithm expression (3.50) . The search direction used is

$$\overline{C}_0 = -\,\overline{g}_0 \tag{3.88}$$

This method is said to have trouble due to round off errors and a restart with $\overline{C}_k = -\,\overline{g}_k$ after every $n + 1$ iterations is recommended.

3.8 DIRECT SEARCH METHODS–HOOKS AND JEEVES

Hooks and Jeeves method makes local exploratory searches to determine the nature of the function and how to proceed in some accelerated fashion. This method avoids the use of derivatives and not only reduces the time of formulation, programming and computation but also makes the strategy less sensitive to irregular or discontinous functions.

Hooks and Jeeves method can get stuck on constraints because of the fixed orientation of its search coordinates as illustrated in Fig. 3.9 for a two dimensional case. If the contour lines and the inequality constraints line happen to have a certian orientation, and the search approaches from a certain direction, the search becomes stalled as shown in the figure. A new starting point may lead to the right solution and hence a local random search may be added to the strategy when the process gets stuck at a constraint.

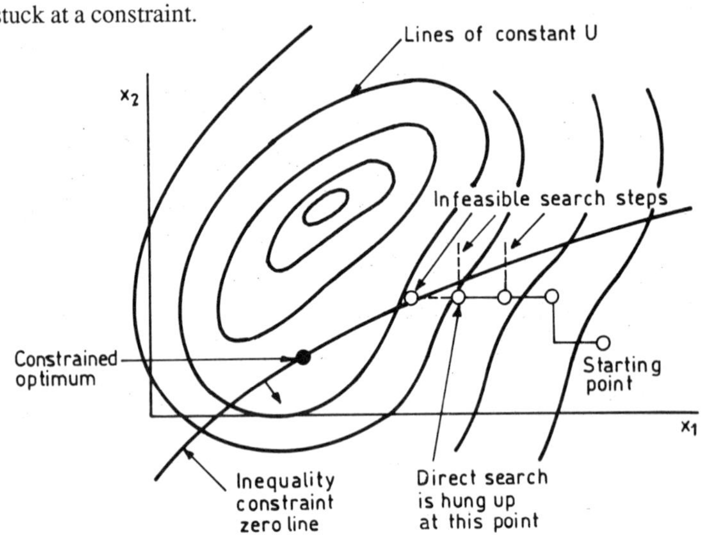

Fig. 3.9 Illustration of how a Hooke and Jeeves direct search can become stalled at constraint lines

3.9 METHOD OF SUCCESSIVE LINEAR APPROXIMATION

It is possible to represent the nonlinear function by linear expressions, which are meaningful if they are restricted to a small local region about some given point. These expressions can be solved by linear programming. Another linearization is then done about the new position and the process is continued.

Let the optimization problem be defined by

$$U = U\ (x_1, x_2, \ldots . x_n) = \text{minimum}$$

$$\psi_j\ (x_1, x_2, \ldots, x_n) = 0 \quad j = 1, m \tag{3.89}$$

$$\phi_s\ (x_1, x_2, \ldots\ldots, x_n) \geq 0 \quad s = 1, p$$

It is convenient to use vector notation, and designate the kth position of the search as $\bar{x}_k$. The linearization is achieved by using a Taylor's series expansion about $\bar{x}_k$, in which all terms above linear are dropped.

$$U = U\ (x_k) + \sum_{i=1}^{n} (x_i - x_i^k)\frac{\partial U(\bar{x}^k)}{\partial x_i} = \text{minimum} \tag{3.90}$$

$$\psi_j\ (x^k) + \sum_{i=1}^{n} (x_i - x_i^k)\frac{\partial \psi_j\ (\bar{x}^k)}{\partial x_i} = 0 \quad j = 1, m \tag{3.91}$$

$$\phi_s(\bar{x}^k) + \sum_{i=1}^{n} (x_i - x_i^k) \frac{\partial \phi_s(\bar{x}^k)}{\partial x_i} \geq 0 \tag{3.92}$$

Using the following notation for convenience

$$c_i = \frac{\partial U(\bar{x}^k)}{\partial x_i} \qquad U = U(\bar{x}^k)$$

$$\psi_j^k = \psi_j(\bar{x}^k) \qquad U_{ji} = \frac{\partial \psi_j(\bar{x}^k)}{\partial x_i}$$

$$\phi_s^k = \phi_s(\bar{x}^k) \qquad V_{si} = \frac{\partial \phi_s(\bar{x}^k)}{\partial x_i}$$

$$\delta x_i^k = x_i - x_i^k$$

Using this notation in Eqs. (3.90), (3.92) gives

$$U - U^k = \sum_{i=1}^{n} c_i \, \delta x_i^k = \text{minimum} \tag{3.93}$$

$$\sum_{i=1}^{n} u_{ji} \, \delta x_j^k = -\psi_j^k \quad j = 1, m \tag{3.94}$$

$$\sum_{i=1}^{n} v_{si} \, \delta x_i^k \geq -\phi_s^k \quad s = 1, p \tag{3.95}$$

Adding to these expressions the relation defining the limits on the δx_i's, designated m_i, we have

$$\delta x_i^k \leq m_i \qquad \delta x_i^k \geq -m_i \tag{3.96}$$

The values of m_i are based on judgement in order to adequately limit the linear approximation. This results in a linear programming form in terms of δx_i's.

The updating of the x_i's, given by

$$x_i^{k+1} = x_i^k + \delta x_i^k \tag{3.97}$$

is repeated until the δx_i's become negligibly small.

The method has convergence problems, but performance can be improved by adjusting the variables after each iterations so that the equality constraints are satisfied. This can be done by using Newton's method for solving simultaneous nonlinear equations.

An initial feasible solution is required in this method.

3.10 CLOSURE

Some strategies for optimizing a function subject to constraints have been discussed. The methods given in this chapter give only a glimpse of the optimization procedure and techniques used to achieve the optimum. There are several other methods not covered in this chapter which are given in greater detail in the references given at the end of the chapter.

Example 3.1 (Polynomial Approximations)

Given the following information, fit a polynomial by quadratic approximation and find the value of X at which $F(X)$ is minimum.

X	F(X)
1	12
2	7
5	20

Solution

The polynomial passing through three points will be of the form

$$F(X) = a_0 + a_1X + a_2X^2$$

Substituting from the table,

$$F(1) = a_0 + a_1 + a_2 = 12$$

$$F(2) = a_0 + 2a_1 + 4a_2 = 7$$

$$F(5) = a_0 + 5a_1 + 25a_2 = 20$$

Solving we get

$$a_0 = 21.67$$

$$a_1 = -12.00$$

$$a_2 = 2.33$$

Hence

$$F(X) = 21.67 - 12.0X + 2.33X^2$$

When $F(X)$ is minimum, we have

$$\frac{dF}{dX} = -12 + 4.66X = 0$$

Hence, when $F(X)$ is minimum

$$X = 2.5751$$

To verify whether $F(X)$ is indeed minimum at $X = 2.5751$, we obtain the second derivative of $F(X)$ with respect to X, which is

$$\frac{d^2F}{dX^2} = 4.66$$

Since this value is positive $F(X)$ is minimum at $X = 2.5751$

Example 3.2 (Powell's Method)

Find the minimum of the function $F(X) = 4X_1^2 + 3X_2^2 - 5X_1X_2 - 8X_1$ starting from (0, 0).

Solution

The starting point is given as

$$X^{(0)} = \begin{Bmatrix} 0 \\ 0 \end{Bmatrix}.$$

By selecting the matrix

$$C = \begin{bmatrix} 1 & 0 \\ 0 & 1 \end{bmatrix},$$

the initial search directions $S^{(1)}$ and $S^{(2)}$ become

$$S^{(1)} = \begin{Bmatrix} 1 \\ 0 \end{Bmatrix}; \quad S^{(2)} = \begin{Bmatrix} 0 \\ 1 \end{Bmatrix}$$

Now we minimize $F(X)$ along $S^{(1)}$ from $X^{(0)}$

Then,
$$X^{(1)} = X^{(0)} + \alpha_1 S^{(1)}$$

$$= \begin{Bmatrix} 0 \\ 0 \end{Bmatrix} + \alpha_1 \begin{Bmatrix} 1 \\ 0 \end{Bmatrix} = \begin{Bmatrix} \alpha_1 \\ 0 \end{Bmatrix}$$

Substituting this value of $X^{(1)}$ in the given function, we get

$$F(X^{(1)}) = 4\alpha_1^2 - 8\alpha_1$$

To find the minimum step length α_1^*,

$$\frac{dF(X^{(1)})}{d\alpha_1} = 8\alpha_1 - 8 = 0$$

which gives
$$\alpha_1^* = 1$$

$\therefore$
$$X^{(1)} = \begin{Bmatrix} 1 \\ 0 \end{Bmatrix}$$

Next we minimize $F(X)$ along $S^{(2)}$ from $X^{(1)}$.

i.e.,
$$X^{(2)} = X^{(1)} + \alpha_2 S^{(2)}$$

Then
$$X^{(2)} = \begin{Bmatrix} 1 \\ 0 \end{Bmatrix} + \alpha_2 \begin{Bmatrix} 0 \\ 1 \end{Bmatrix} = \begin{Bmatrix} 1 \\ \alpha_2 \end{Bmatrix}$$

Substituting this value of $X^{(2)}$ in the given function, we get

$$F(X^{(2)}) = 3\alpha_2^2 - 5\alpha_2 - 4$$

To find the minimum step length α_2^*,

$$\frac{dF(X^{(2)})}{d\alpha_2} = 6\alpha_1 - 5 = 0$$

which gives $$\alpha_2^* = 0.83$$

therefore $$X^{(2)} = \begin{Bmatrix} 1 \\ 0.83 \end{Bmatrix}$$

Update the matrix C as follows:

$$C = \begin{bmatrix} 1 & 0 \\ 0 & 0.83 \end{bmatrix}$$

Hence $$S^{(3)} = \begin{bmatrix} 1+0 \\ 0+0.83 \end{bmatrix} = \begin{bmatrix} 1 \\ 0.83 \end{bmatrix}$$

Manimize $F(X)$ along $S^{(3)}$ from $X^{(2)}$

Then, $$X^{(3)} = \begin{Bmatrix} 1 \\ 0.83 \end{Bmatrix} + \alpha_3 \begin{Bmatrix} 1 \\ 0.83 \end{Bmatrix} = \begin{Bmatrix} 1+\alpha_3 \\ 0.83(1+\alpha_3) \end{Bmatrix}$$

Substituting this value of $X^{(3)}$ in the given function, we get

$$F(X^{(3)}) = 1.95(1+\alpha_3)^3 - 8(1+\alpha_3)$$

To find the minimum step length α_3^*,

$$\frac{dF(X^{(3)})}{d\alpha_3} = 3.9(1+\alpha_3) - 8 = 0$$

which gives $$\alpha_3^* = 1.1$$

$\therefore$ $$X^{(3)} = \begin{Bmatrix} 2.1 \\ 1.7 \end{Bmatrix} \text{ and } F(X^{(3)}) = -8.3400$$

Again, update the matrix C as follows:

$$C = \begin{bmatrix} 0 & 1.1 \\ 0.83 & 0.87 \end{bmatrix} \text{ from which we get } S^{(4)} = \begin{bmatrix} 0+1.1 \\ 0.83+0.87 \end{bmatrix} = \begin{bmatrix} 1.1 \\ 1.7 \end{bmatrix}$$

Now minimize $F(X)$ along $S^{(4)}$ from $X^{(3)}$

Then, $$X^{(4)} = \begin{Bmatrix} 2.1 \\ 1.7 \end{Bmatrix} + \alpha_4 \begin{Bmatrix} 1.1 \\ 1.7 \end{Bmatrix} = \begin{Bmatrix} 2.1+1.1\alpha_4 \\ 1.7(1+\alpha_4) \end{Bmatrix}$$

Substituting this value of $X^{(4)}$ in the given function, we get

$$F(X^{(4)}) = 4(2.1+1.1\alpha_4)^2 + 8.7(1+\alpha_4)^2 - 8.5(1.1\alpha_4^2 + 3.2\alpha_4 + 2.1) - 8(2.1+1.1\alpha_4)$$

To find the minimum step length α_4^*, find $\dfrac{dF(X^{(4)})}{d\alpha_4} = 0$ and solve for α_4. Then we get

$$\alpha_4^* = 0.0143$$

Hence, $$X^{(4)} = \begin{Bmatrix} 2.1 \\ 1.72 \end{Bmatrix} \text{ and } F(X^{(4)}) = -8.3448$$

Now we can see that $|F(X^{(4)}) - F(X^{(3)})| = 0.0048$. If we need more accurate result, we need to minimize $F(X)$ along $S^{(5)}$ from $X^{(4)}$ where $S^{(5)}$ is calculated as follows:

Update the matrix C as follows:

$$C = \begin{bmatrix} 1.1 & 0.016 \\ 0.87 & 0.02 \end{bmatrix} \text{from which we get } S^{(5)} = \begin{bmatrix} 1.1 + 0.016 \\ 0.87 + 0.02 \end{bmatrix} = \begin{bmatrix} 1.12 \\ 0.89 \end{bmatrix}$$

Now minimize $F(X)$ along $S^{(5)}$ from $X^{(4)}$

Then, $$X^{(5)} = \begin{Bmatrix} 2.1 \\ 1.72 \end{Bmatrix} + \alpha_5 \begin{Bmatrix} 1.12 \\ 0.89 \end{Bmatrix} = \begin{Bmatrix} 2.1 + 1.1\alpha_5 \\ 1.72 + 0.89\alpha_5 \end{Bmatrix}$$

Substituting this value of $X^{(5)}$ in the given function, we get

$$F(X) = 4(2.1 + 1.12\alpha_5)^2 + 3(1.72 + 0.89\alpha_5)^2 - 5(\alpha_5^2 + 3.8\alpha_4 + 3.6) - 8(2.1 + 1.12\alpha_5)$$

To find the minimum step length α_5^*, find $\dfrac{dF(X^{(5)})}{d\alpha_5} = 0$ and solve for α_5.

$$\alpha_5^* = 0.0085$$

Hence, $$X^{(5)} = \begin{Bmatrix} 2.11 \\ 1.73 \end{Bmatrix} \text{ and } F(X^{(5)}) = -8.3444$$

Since $|F(X^{(5)}) - F(X^{(4)})| = 0.004$, the iteration process can be stopped here and the optimum value of X is given by

$$X^* = \begin{Bmatrix} 2.11 \\ 1.73 \end{Bmatrix}$$

Example 3.3 (Lagrange Multiplier Method)

Design a tablet containing 1 ml of medicine. It is desired to have maximum possible surface area for fast solubility. From manufacturing point of view no dimension should be less than 2 mm. For two possible shapes of the tablet, formulate the task as an optimization problem. What will be the basis for final design selection?

Solution

Let A = area in square centimetres

h = height in cm

d = diameter in cm and

v = volume in cubic centimetres

Design 1

Let the shape be that of a cylinder. Then we can formulate the constrained optimization problem as follows:

Maximize the surface area, $A = \pi d\,(h + d/2)$

subject to $V = \pi d^2 h/4 = 1$ (since 1 ml = 1 cubic cm)

The side constraints on the design variables are

$$d \geq 0.2$$
$$h \geq 0.2$$

The Lagrange function L can be written as

$$L = \pi d\left(h + \frac{d}{2}\right) + \lambda_1[\pi d^2 h - 4]$$

where λ_1 is the Lagrange multiplier. Further,

$$\frac{\partial L}{\partial d} = \pi h + \pi d + 2\pi dh\lambda_1 = 0$$

Solving this equation for λ_1,

$$\lambda_1 = \frac{-(h+d)}{2dh} \qquad (1)$$

Similarly, we have

$$\frac{\partial L}{\partial h} = \pi d + \lambda_1 \pi d^2 = 0$$

Solving this equation for λ_1,

$$\lambda_1 = -\frac{1}{d} \qquad (2)$$

Similarly, $\dfrac{\partial L}{\partial \lambda_1} = \pi d^2 h - 4 = 0$

Solving this equation for h,

$$h = \frac{4}{\pi d^2} \qquad (3)$$

From equations (1) and (2), we get

$$h = d$$

Substituting this in equation (1), we get

$$h^3 = 4/\pi$$

which gives $h^* = d^* = 1.084$ cm

Design 2

Let the shape of the tablet be a sphere. Then the constrained optimization problem can be stated as follows:

Maximize $A = \pi d^2$

subject to $V = \dfrac{4}{3}\pi\left(\dfrac{d}{2}\right)^3 = 1$

The side constraint on the design variable is

$$d \geq 0.2$$

Now the Lagrange function L can be written as

$$L = \pi d^2 + \lambda \left[\frac{\pi}{6} d^3 - 1 \right] = 0$$

$$\frac{\partial L}{\partial \lambda} = \frac{\pi}{6} d^3 - 1 = 0$$

Solving this equation gives

$$d^* = 1.241 \text{ cm}$$

Design 3

Let the tablet has the shape of a cylinder with hemispherical ends. The constrained optimization problem can be stated as follows:

Maximize $\quad A = \pi d\,(l - d) + \pi d^2$

subject to $\quad V = \dfrac{\pi d^3}{6} + \dfrac{\pi d^2 l}{4} - \dfrac{\pi d^3}{4} = 1$

where l is the total length from end to end.
The side constraints on the design variables are

$$d \geq 0.2$$

$$l \geq 0.2$$

Now the Lagrange function L can be written as

$$L = \pi d\,(l - d) + \pi d^2 + \lambda \left[\frac{\pi d^3}{6} + \frac{\pi d^2 l}{4} - \frac{\pi d^3}{4} - 1 \right]$$

Calculating $\dfrac{\partial L}{\partial d} = 0$ and simplifying, we get

$$l - \lambda\,[0.25 d^2 - 0.5 d l] = 0$$

Solving this equation, we get

$$\lambda = \frac{l}{0.25 d^2 - 0.5 d l} \tag{4}$$

$$\frac{\partial L}{\partial l} = \pi d + \lambda \frac{\pi d^2}{4} = 0$$

Solving this equation gives

$$\lambda = -4/d \tag{5}$$

From equations (4) and (5), we get

$$l = d \tag{6}$$

That means the design turns out to be a hollow sphere. Now there is no need to proceed further, since we got the optimum design (as per the design 2) as

$$d^* = 1.241 \text{ cm}$$

Now let us compare the two optimum designs:

DESIGN	SURFACE AREA (CC)
Cylinder $h = 1.084$ cm; $d = 1.084$ cm	5.537
Sphere $d = 1.241$ cm	4.838

The basis for the best design should be maximum area for fast solubility. The cylindrical shape tablet has more surface area than spherical shape tablet and hence cylindrical shape is preferred.

Example 3.4 (Interior Penalty Function Method)

Find the minimum of the function $F(X) = (X_1 - 1)^3 + (X_2 - 5)^2$

Subject to $\quad -X_1 + 1 \le 0$

$\quad -X_2 + 5 \le 0$

Solution

To find the minimum of a constrained function by penalty function approach, no initial starting point is required, since the method of calculus will be used to minimize the function. The pseudo-objective function ϕ (X, r) is given by:

$$\phi(X,r) = (X_1 - 1)^3 + (X_2 - 5)^2 - r\left[\frac{1}{-X_1 + 1} + \frac{1}{-X_2 + 5}\right]$$

To find the minimum of the pseudo-objective function,

$$\frac{\partial\phi}{\partial X_1} = 3(X_1 - 1)^2 - r\left[\frac{1}{(-X_1 + 1)^2}\right] = 0$$

Simplifying and solving this equation, we get

$$3(X_1 - 1)^2(-X_1 + 1)^2 - r = 0$$

$$3(X_1 - 1)^4 - r = 0$$

$$(X_1 - 1)^4 = r/3$$

$$X_1 = 1 + \left(\frac{r}{3}\right)^{\frac{1}{4}} \tag{1}$$

Similarly, at the minimum of the pseudo-objective function,

$$\frac{\partial\phi}{\partial X_2} = 2(X_2 - 5) - r\left[\frac{1}{(-X_2 + 5)^2}\right] = 0$$

Simplifying and solving this equation, we get

$$2(X_2 - 5)^3 - r = 0$$

$$(X_2 - 5)^3 = r/2$$

$$X_2 = 5 + \left(\frac{r}{2}\right)^{1/3} \quad (2)$$

Rewriting the equations (1) and (2), we get the optimum values as

$$X_1^* = 1 + \left(\frac{r}{3}\right)^{1/4}$$

$$X_2^* = 5 + \left(\frac{r}{2}\right)^{1/3}$$

Substituting these optimum values in the pseudo-objective function gives

$$\phi_{\min}(r) = \left(\frac{r}{3}\right)^{1/2} + \left(\frac{r}{2}\right)^{2/3} + r\left[\frac{\left(\frac{r}{2}\right)^{1/3} + \left(\frac{r}{3}\right)^{1/4}}{\left(\frac{r}{3}\right)^{1/4}\left(\frac{r}{2}\right)^{1/3}}\right]$$

To find the minimum of the original objective function, we have to decrement the value of r. i.e.,

$$F_{\min}(X) = \lim_{r \to 0} \phi_{\min}(r)$$

$$X_1^* = \lim_{r \to 0} X_1^*(r)$$

$$X_2^* = \lim_{r \to 0} X_2^*(r)$$

In interior penalty function method, we have to start initially with a high value of r (say 10^6) and decrement it till we get the optimum solution. The results of this iterative procedure are shown in the following table.

r	X_1^*	X_2^*	$\phi_{\min}(r)$	$F_{\min}(X)$
1000000.0	25.02811	80.97316	61430.98	19644.56
10000.0	8.598357	21.62111	2261.097	714.9528
100.0	3.402811	8.636304	88.32125	27.09534
1.0	1.759836	5.795537	3.781561	1.071570
1.0*E*−2	1.240281	5.174045	0.186458	0.044164
1.0*E*−4	1.075984	5.038077	0.011108	0.018885
1.0*E*−6	1.024028	5.008330	0.000804	0.000083
1.0*E*−8	1.007598	5.001822	0.000068	0.000003
1.0*E*−9	1.004273	5.000853	0.000020	0.000000

It is clear from the above table that when $r = 1.0E{-}9$, the function is minimum and the optimum values are

$$X_1^* = 1.004273$$

$$X_2^* = 5.000853$$

$$F_{\min}(X^*) = 0$$

Example 3.5 (Newton's Method)

Find the minimum of the function $F(X) = 4X_1^2 + 3X_2^2 - 5X_1X_2 - 8X_1$ starting from (0,0).

Solution

The starting point is given as

$$X_{(0)} = \begin{Bmatrix} 0 \\ 0 \end{Bmatrix}.$$

Newton's method is the second order method, meaning that second derivative (Hessian matrix) of the given function is required in each iteration. The gradient and Hessian matrix of $F(X)$ are

$$\nabla F(X) = \begin{Bmatrix} 8X_1 - 5X_2 - 8 \\ 6X_2 - 5X_1 \end{Bmatrix} \quad \text{and} \quad H(X) = \begin{bmatrix} 8 & -5 \\ -5 & 6 \end{bmatrix}$$

$$\nabla F(X^{(0)}) = \begin{Bmatrix} -8 \\ 0 \end{Bmatrix} \quad \text{and} \quad H^{-1}(X) = \begin{bmatrix} 0.2609 & 0.2174 \\ 0.2174 & 0.3478 \end{bmatrix}$$

Now $$X^{(1)} = X^{(0)} - H^{-1}(X^{(0)})\nabla F(X^{(0)})$$

$$= \begin{Bmatrix} 0 \\ 0 \end{Bmatrix} - \begin{bmatrix} 0.2609 & 0.2174 \\ 0.2174 & 0.3478 \end{bmatrix} \begin{Bmatrix} -8 \\ 0 \end{Bmatrix} = \begin{Bmatrix} 2.0870 \\ 1.7391 \end{Bmatrix}$$

Now substituting this value in $\nabla F(X)$ we get

$$\nabla F(X^{(1)}) = \begin{Bmatrix} 0.0005 \\ -0.0004 \end{Bmatrix}$$

$$X^{(2)} = \begin{Bmatrix} 2.0870 \\ 1.7391 \end{Bmatrix} - \begin{bmatrix} 0.2609 & 0.2174 \\ 0.2174 & 0.3478 \end{bmatrix} \begin{Bmatrix} 0.0005 \\ -0.0004 \end{Bmatrix} = \begin{Bmatrix} 2.0870 \\ 1.7391 \end{Bmatrix}$$

Now substituing this value in $\nabla F(X)$ we get

$$\nabla F(X^{(2)}) = \begin{Bmatrix} 0.0005 \\ -0.0004 \end{Bmatrix}$$

Since $\nabla F(X^{(2)}) \approx 0, X^{(2)}$ is the optimum.

$$\therefore \qquad X^* = \begin{Bmatrix} 2.0870 \\ 1.7391 \end{Bmatrix}$$

Example 3.6 (Fletcher–Reeves Method)

Find the minimum of the function $F(X) = 4X_1^2 + 3X_2^2 - 5X_1X_2 - 8X_1$ starting from (0, 0).

Solution

The starting point is given as $X^{(0)} = \begin{Bmatrix} 0 \\ 0 \end{Bmatrix}$.

Fletcher–Reeves method is a first order method, meaning that first derivative (gradient) of the given function is required in each iteration. The gradient of $F(X)$ is

$$\nabla F(X) = \begin{Bmatrix} 8X_1 - 5X_2 - 8 \\ 6X_2 - 5X_1 \end{Bmatrix}$$

$$\nabla F(X^{(0)}) = \begin{Bmatrix} -8 \\ 0 \end{Bmatrix}$$

Now the initial search direction will be

$$S^{(1)} = -\nabla F(X^{(0)}) = \begin{Bmatrix} 8 \\ 0 \end{Bmatrix}$$

Now we begin the search in $S^{(1)}$ direction from $X^{(0)}$. Then

$$X^{(1)} = \begin{Bmatrix} 0 \\ 0 \end{Bmatrix} + \alpha_1 \begin{Bmatrix} 8 \\ 0 \end{Bmatrix} = \begin{Bmatrix} 8\alpha_1 \\ 0 \end{Bmatrix}$$

Substituting this value of $X^{(1)}$ in the given function, we get

$$F(X^{(1)}) = 256\alpha_1^2 - 64\alpha_1$$

To find the minimum step length α_1^*,

$$\frac{dF(X^{(1)})}{d\alpha_1} = 512\alpha_1 - 64 = 0$$

which gives $$\alpha_1^* = 0.125$$

Hence $$X^{(1)} = \begin{Bmatrix} 1 \\ 0 \end{Bmatrix}$$

Now update the gradient as follows:

$$\nabla F(X^{(1)}) = \begin{Bmatrix} 0 \\ -5 \end{Bmatrix}$$

The new search direction from $X^{(1)}$ will be calculated as follows:

$$S^{(2)} \equiv \nabla F(X^{(1)}) + \frac{|\nabla F(X^{(1)})|^2}{|\nabla F(X^{(0)})|^2} S^{(1)}$$

Here $$|\nabla F(X^{(1)})|^2 = 25; \; |\nabla F(X^{(0)})|^2 = 64 \text{ and hence}$$

$$S^{(2)} = -\begin{Bmatrix} 0 \\ -5 \end{Bmatrix} + \left(\frac{25}{64}\right) \begin{Bmatrix} 8 \\ 0 \end{Bmatrix} = \begin{Bmatrix} 3.125 \\ 5 \end{Bmatrix}$$

Then,

$$X^{(2)} = \begin{Bmatrix} 1 \\ 0 \end{Bmatrix} + \alpha_2 \begin{Bmatrix} 3.125 \\ 5 \end{Bmatrix} = \begin{Bmatrix} 1 + 3.125\alpha_2 \\ 5\alpha_2 \end{Bmatrix}$$

Substituting this value of $X^{(2)}$ in the given function, we get

$$F(X^{(2)}) = 4(1. + 3.125\alpha_2)^2 + 75\alpha_2^2 - 25\alpha_2(1 + 3.125\alpha_2) - 8(1 + 3.125\alpha_2)$$

To find the minimum step length α_2^*, find $\dfrac{dF(X^{(2)})}{d\alpha_2}$ and equating it to zero, we get

$$\alpha_2^* = 0.3478$$

Hence, $$X^{(2)} = \begin{Bmatrix} 2.08696 \\ 1.7391 \end{Bmatrix}$$

Now $$\nabla F(X^{(2)}) = \begin{Bmatrix} 0.00018 \\ -0.0000174 \end{Bmatrix} \approx \begin{Bmatrix} 0 \\ 0 \end{Bmatrix}$$

Since $\nabla F(X^{(2)}) = 0, X^{(2)}$ is the optimum point and is denoted by

$$X^* = \begin{Bmatrix} 2.08696 \\ 1.7391 \end{Bmatrix}$$

Example 3.7 (Hooke and Jeeves Method)

Find the minimum of the function $F(X) = 4X_1^2 + 3X_2^2 - 5X_1X_2 - 8X_1$ starting from (0, 0).

Solution

The starting point is given as $$X^{(0)} = \begin{Bmatrix} 0 \\ 0 \end{Bmatrix}.$$

Let the initial step lengths, $$\Delta X_1 = 0.5$$

$$\Delta X_2 = 0.5$$

The value of the given function at $X^{(0)}$ is

$$F(X^{(0)}) = 0$$

Now $$Y_{00} = X^{(0)} = \begin{Bmatrix} 0 \\ 0 \end{Bmatrix}$$

To find the new temporary base point,

$$F = F(y_{00}) = 0$$

$$F^{(1)} = F(y_{00} + \Delta X_1 u_1) = F(0.5, 0) = -3$$

$$F^{(2)} = F(y_{00} - \Delta X_1 u_1) = F(-0.5, 0) = 5$$

Since $F^{(1)} < F$,

$$Y_{01} = \begin{Bmatrix} 0.5 \\ 0 \end{Bmatrix}$$

$$F = F(Y_{01}) = -3$$

$$F^{(1)} = F(Y_{01} + \Delta X_2 u_2) = F(0.5, 0.5) = -3.5$$

$$F^{(2)} = F(0.5, -0.5) = -1$$

Since $F^{(1)} < F$,

$$Y_{02} = \begin{Bmatrix} 0.5 \\ 0.5 \end{Bmatrix}$$

Since Y_{02} is different from $X^{(0)}$, the new base point is taken as

$$X^{(1)} = \begin{Bmatrix} 0.5 \\ 0.5 \end{Bmatrix}$$

Now the pattern direction is calculated as

$$S = X^{(1)} - X^{(0)}$$

$$= \begin{Bmatrix} 0.5 \\ 0.5 \end{Bmatrix} - \begin{Bmatrix} 0 \\ 0 \end{Bmatrix}$$

$$= \begin{Bmatrix} 0.5 \\ 0.5 \end{Bmatrix}$$

$$Y_{10} = X^{(1)} + \alpha S$$

$$= \begin{Bmatrix} 0.5 + 0.5\alpha \\ 0.5 + 0.5\alpha \end{Bmatrix}$$

Substituting this in the given function and simplifying, we get

$$F(Y_{10}) = 2(0.5 + 0.5\alpha)^2 - 8(0.5 + 0.5\alpha)$$

To find the minimum step length,

$$\frac{dF(Y_{10})}{d\alpha} = 4(0.5 + 0.5\alpha) - 4 = 0$$

which gives $\quad \alpha^* = 3$

Hence $\quad Y_{10} = \begin{Bmatrix} 2 \\ 2 \end{Bmatrix}$

Now $\quad F = F(Y_{10}) = -8$

$$F^{(1)} = F(Y_{10} + \Delta X_1 u_1) = F(2.5, 2) = -8$$

$$F^{(2)} = F(Y_{10} - \Delta X_1 u_1) = F(1.5, 2) = -6$$

Since $F(Y_{10}) = F^{(1)}$, reduce the step length to 0.2

Then, $\quad X^{(2)} = \begin{Bmatrix} 0.5 \\ 0.5 \end{Bmatrix}$

$$Y_{(20)} = X^{(2)} = \begin{Bmatrix} 0.5 \\ 0.5 \end{Bmatrix}$$

$$F = F(Y_{20}) = -3.5$$

$$F^{(1)} = F(Y_{20} + \Delta X_i u_i) = F(0.7, 0.5) = -4.64$$
$$F^{(2)} = F(Y_{20} - \Delta X_1 u_1) = F(0.\ 3, 0.5) = -3.64$$

Since $F^{(1)} < F$,

then, $$Y_{(21)} = \begin{Bmatrix} 0.7 \\ 0.5 \end{Bmatrix}$$

$$F = F\ (Y_{21}) = -4.\ 64$$
$$F^{(1)} = F(Y_{21} + \Delta X_2 u_2) = F(0.7, 0.7) = -4.62$$
$$F^{(2)} = F(Y_{21} - \Delta X_2\ u_2) = F(0.7, 0.3) = -4.42$$

Since $F < \min\ (F^{(1)}, F^{(2)})$,

then, $$Y_{22} = Y_{21} = \begin{Bmatrix} 0.7 \\ 0.5 \end{Bmatrix}$$

Since $F(Y_{22}) = -4.64 < F(X^{(2)}) = -3.5$, take the new base point as

$$X^{(3)} = \begin{Bmatrix} 0.7 \\ 0.5 \end{Bmatrix}$$

Now the new pattern direction is

$$S = X^{(3)} - X^{(2)} = \begin{Bmatrix} 0.7 \\ 0.5 \end{Bmatrix} - \begin{Bmatrix} 0.5 \\ 0.5 \end{Bmatrix} = \begin{Bmatrix} 0.2 \\ 0 \end{Bmatrix}$$

$$Y_{30} = X^{(3)} + \alpha S = \begin{Bmatrix} 0.7 \\ 0.5 \end{Bmatrix} + \alpha = \begin{Bmatrix} 0.2 \\ 0 \end{Bmatrix} = \begin{Bmatrix} 0.7 + 0.2\alpha \\ 0.5 \end{Bmatrix}$$

Substituting this in the given function and simplifying, we get

$$F(Y_{30}) = 4(0.\ 7 + 0.2\alpha)^2 + 0.75 - 10.5(0.7 + 0.2\alpha)$$

To find the minimum step length,

$$\frac{dF(Y_{30})}{d\alpha} = 8(0.7 + 0.2\alpha)\ (0.2) - 2.1 = 0$$

which gives $\alpha = 3.1$

Hence $$Y_{30} = \begin{Bmatrix} 1.3125 \\ 0.5 \end{Bmatrix}$$

$$F = F(Y_{30}) = -6.14$$
$$F^{(1)} = F(Y_{30} + \Delta X_1 u_1)$$
$$= F(1.5125, 0.5) = -5.98$$
$$F^{(2)} = F(Y_{30} - \Delta X_1 u_1) = F(1.1125, 0.5) = -5.981$$

Since $F < \min\ (F^{(1)}, F^{(2)})$

$$Y_{31} = \begin{Bmatrix} 1.3125 \\ 0.5 \end{Bmatrix}$$

$$F = F(Y_{31}) = -6.14$$
$$F^{(1)} = F(Y_{31} + \Delta X_2 u_2) = F(1.3125, 0.7) = -6.733$$

Since $F^{(1)} < F$, $Y_{32} = \begin{Bmatrix} 1.3125 \\ 0.7 \end{Bmatrix}$

Now the new direction is

$$S = X^{(4)} - X^{(3)} = \begin{Bmatrix} 1.3125 \\ 0.7 \end{Bmatrix} - \begin{Bmatrix} 0.7 \\ 0.5 \end{Bmatrix} = \begin{Bmatrix} 0.6125 \\ 0.2 \end{Bmatrix}$$

$$Y_{40} = X^{(4)} + \alpha S = \begin{Bmatrix} 1.3125 + 0.6125\alpha \\ 0.7 + 0.2\alpha \end{Bmatrix}$$

Substituting this in the given function and simplifying, we get

$$F(Y_{40}) = 4(1.3125 + 0.6125\alpha)^2 + 3(0.7 + 0.2\alpha)^2 - 5(1.3125 + 0.6125\,\alpha)\,(0.7 + 0.2\alpha) - 8(1.3125 + 0.6125\alpha)$$

To find the minimum step length, find $\dfrac{dF(Y_{40})}{d\alpha} = 0$ and solving, we get

$$\alpha^* = 0.536$$

Hence $$Y_{40} = \begin{Bmatrix} 1.64 \\ 0.81 \end{Bmatrix}$$

Similarly repeating the procedure we get the optimum solution as

$$X^* = \begin{Bmatrix} 2.08696 \\ 1.7391 \end{Bmatrix}.$$

PROBLEMS

3.1 Fit a polynomial by quadratic approximation and determine the values of X at which $F(X)$ is minimum.

X	$F(X)$
1	8
2	5
3	17

3.2 Fit a polynomial by quadratic approximation and determine the values of X at which $F(X)$ is minimum.

X	$F(X)$
1	−7
2	3
3	14

3.3 Find the maximum of the function $F(X) = X_1^2 + 2X_2^2 + 3X_1X_2 - 5X_1$ starting from (0, 0) using Powell's method.

3.4 Find the maximum of the function $F(X) = X_1^2 - 3X_2^2 + 8X_1X_2 - 7X_2$ starting from (0, 0) using Powell's method.

3.5 A total of 360 linear feet of tubes must be installed in a heat exchanger in order to provide the necessary heat-transfer surface area. The total cost of the installation includes:

Cost of the tubes = \$900

Cost of the shell = $30\,D^{2.5}\,L$

Cost of the floor space occupied by the heat-exchanger = $25\,DL$

The spacing of the tubes is such that 25 tubes will fit in a cross-sectional area of 1 ft^2 inside the shell. Determine the diameter D and the length L of the heat exchanger to minimize the purchase cost using Lagrange multiplier method.

3.6 Determine the value of insulation thickness for a furnace wall, which will minimize the cost. Given

Wall temperature = 600°F

Outside air temperature = 70°F
Air film coefficient = 5 Btu/(h)(ft²)(°F)
Thermal conductivity of insulation = 0.04 Btu/(h)(ft)(°F)
Insulation cost per inch of thickness = \$0.80 per ft²
Value of heat saved = \$0.70 per million Btu
Fixed charges = 25 percent per year
Hours of operation = 9000 h/year
Surface area of furnace wall = 125 ft².

3.7 Find the minimum of the function $F(X) = (X_1 + 2)^3 + (X_2 - 6)^2$ subject to $-X_1 + 2 \leq 0$ and $-X_2 + 7 \leq 0$ using interior penalty function method.

3.8 Find the minimum of the function $F(X) = (X_1 - 3)^3 + (X_2 - 7)^2$ subject to $-X_1 + 7 \leq 0$ and $-X_2 + 3 \leq 0$ using interior penalty function method.

3.9 Solve the Problem 3.3 using Newton's method.

3.10 Solve the Problem 3.4 using Newton's method.

3.11 Solve the Problem 3.3 using Fletcher-Reeves method.

3.12 Solve the Problem 3.4 using Fletcher-Reeves method.

3.13 Solve the Problem 3.3 using Hooke and Jeeves method.

3.14 Solve the Problem 3.4 using Hooke and Jeeves method.

REFERENCES

1. Broyden, C.G. (1972), Quasi-Newton Methods, in '*Numerical Methods for Unconstrained Optimization*', W, Murray, (Ed.) Academic Press, New York.
2. Fox R.L. (1971), *Optimization Methods for Engineering Design*, Addison-Wesley, Reading, Mass.
3. Garvin W.W. (1960), *Introduction to Linear Programming,* McGraw-Hill, New York.
4. Gottfried, B.S., and J. Weisman (1973), *Introduction to Optimization Theory,* Prentice-Hall, Englewood Cliffs, N.J.
5. Hadley, G. (1962), *Linear Programming*, Addison Wesley, Reading, Mass.
6. Himmelblau. D.M. (1972), *Applied Nonlinear Programming,* McGraw-Hill, New York.
7. Murray, W., ed. (1972), *Numerical Methods for Unconstrained Optimization,* Academic Press, New York.
8. Powell, M.J.D. (1964), An Efficient Method for Finding the Minimum of a Function of Several Variables without Calculating Derivatives, *Computer J.*, Vol. 7 No. 4. pp. 303-307.
9. Powell, M.J.D. (1969), A Method for Nonlinear Constraints in Minimization Problems, in '*Optimization*', R Fletcher, (Ed.), Academic Press,. New York, Chapter 19.
10. Powell, M.J.D. (1970), A New Algorithm for Unconstrained Optimization, in '*Nonlinear Programming*', J.B. Rosen, O.L. Mangasarian, and K. Ritter, (Ed.), Academic Press, New York, pp. 31-65.
11. Powell, M.J.D. (1974), Uncconstrained Minimization and Extensions for Constraints, in '*Mathematical Programming in Theory and Practice*', P.L. Hammer and G. Zoutendizk, (Ed.), North-Holland, Amsterdam, pp. 31.
12. Powell M.J.D. (1974a), Introduction to Constrained Optimization, in '*Numerical Methods for Constrained Optimization*', P.E. Gill and W. Murray, (Ed.), Academic Press, New York.
13. Powell, M.J.D. (1977), Restart Procedures for the Conjugate Gradient Method, *Math. Prg.*, Vol. 12, pp. 241-254.
14. Sargent R.W.H. (1973), Minimization without Constraints, in '*Optimization and Design*', M. Avriel, M.J. Rijckaert, and D.J. Wilde, (Ed.), Prentice-Hall, Englewood Cliffs, N.J.
15. Schmit, L.A. Jr., (Ed.) (1974), Structural Optimization Symposium, Amer, Soc, Mech. Eng.
16. Siddali, J.N. (1982), *Optimal Engineering Design,* Marcel Dekker, Inc., New York.
17. Spunt, L. (1971), *Optimal Structural Design*, Prentice-Hall, Englewood Cliffs. N.J.

CHAPTER 4

STATIC ANALYSIS

4.1 INTRODUCTION

In many design problems the components have to be designed to withstand static loads only. If the forces acting on the machine component are known, the design is quite simple. However, in complex structures, although loads acting at discrete points on the structure may be well defined, the load on the specific component to be designed is difficult to evaluate. In such cases, the load on a specific component can be obtained by solving a system of equations describing the equilibrium of the complete structure given by:

$$[A]\{x\} = \{b\} \tag{4.1}$$

where $[A]$ is the stiffness matrix of size $(n \times n)$

$\{x\}$ is the displacement vector of size $(n \times 1)$ and

$\{b\}$ is the force vector of size $(n \times 1)$.

Here $[A]$ and $\{b\}$ are known, and $\{x\}$ is to be determined. Eq. (4.1) is a simultaneous linear equations and there are two different analytical approaches to solve them. One is direct solution technique and the other is an iterative solution technique (indirect). Both the approaches have their advantages and certain disadvantages, however, the direct solution technique is most effective. The indirect solution technique (iterative) is more useful to solve a set of ill-conditioned equations.

Matrix methods are commonly used in engineering, mathematics and applied science. Here we discuss briefly the fundamental definitions and concepts of matrix algebra that are necessary to understand the solution techniques discussed later. Special emphasis is given to those aspects of matrix algebra that are useful in Finite Element Analysis (FEA). Finite element analysis in static problems determines the displacements when the applied loads are known. It is possible to successfully solve many engineering problems, using the concepts of matrix methods.

4.2 DETERMINANT AND MATRICES

4.2.1 Determinant

A determinant of second order and its numerical evaluation are defined by the following notation and operation

$$D = \begin{vmatrix} a & b \\ c & d \end{vmatrix} = ad - bc$$

A determinant of nth order has n rows and n columns, and in order to identify the position of its elements, the following notation is adopted

$$\begin{vmatrix} a_{11} & a_{12} & a_{13} & \dots & a_{1n} \\ a_{21} & a_{22} & a_{23} & \dots & . \\ . & & & & \\ . & & & & \\ . & & & & \\ a_{n1} & a_{n2} & a_{n3} & \dots & a_{nn} \end{vmatrix}$$

Minors

A minor M_{ij} of element a_{ij} is a determinant formed by deleting the i th row and the jth column from the original determinant.

Cofactor

The cofactor C_{ij} of element a_{ij} is defined by the equation

$$C_{ij} = (-1)^{i+j} M_{ij}$$

Example 4.1

Given the third order determinant

$$\begin{vmatrix} 2 & 1 & 5 \\ 4 & 2 & 1 \\ 2 & 0 & 3 \end{vmatrix}$$

the minor of term $a_{21} = 4$ is

$$M_{21} \text{ of} \begin{vmatrix} 2 & 1 & 5 \\ 4 & 2 & 1 \\ 2 & 0 & 3 \end{vmatrix} = \begin{vmatrix} 1 & 5 \\ 0 & 3 \end{vmatrix} = 3$$

and its cofactor is

$$C_{21} = (-1)^{2+1} 3 = -3$$

Expansion of a Determinant

The order of a determinant can be reduced by one by expanding any row or column in terms of its cofactors.

Example 4.2

The determinant of the previous example is expanded in terms of the second column as

$$D = \begin{vmatrix} 2 & 1 & 5 \\ 4 & 2 & 1 \\ 2 & 0 & 3 \end{vmatrix}_{3\times3} = 1(-1)^{1+2}\begin{vmatrix} 4 & 1 \\ 2 & 3 \end{vmatrix} + 2(-1)^{2+2}\begin{vmatrix} 2 & 5 \\ 2 & 3 \end{vmatrix} + 0(-1)^{3+2}\begin{vmatrix} 2 & 5 \\ 4 & 1 \end{vmatrix}$$

$$= \begin{vmatrix} 0 & 9 \\ 2 & 3 \end{vmatrix}_{2\times2} = -18$$

Properties of determinants

The following are some properties of determinants.

(1) Interchange of any two columns or rows changes the sign of the determinant.
(2) If two rows or two columns are identical, the determinant is zero.
(3) Any row or column may be multiplied by a constant and added to another row or column without changing the value of the determinant.

4.2.2 Matrices

Real matrix

A real matrix consist of $m\ n$ numbers arranged in m rows and in n columns and all of its elements are real quantities. For example

$$\begin{bmatrix} a_{11} & a_{12} & a_{13} & a_{14} \\ a_{21} & a_{22} & a_{23} & a_{24} \\ a_{31} & a_{32} & a_{33} & a_{34} \end{bmatrix} \text{ is a } 3 \times 4 \text{ matrix}$$

Complex matrix

All the elements of a matrix may be complex. A complex matrix has the form

$$\begin{bmatrix} a_{11}+ib_{11} & a_{12}+ib_{12} & a_{13}+ib_{13} \\ a_{21}+ib_{21} & a_{22}+ib_{22} & a_{23}+ib_{23} \\ a_{31}+ib_{31} & a_{32}+ib_{32} & a_{33}+ib_{33} \end{bmatrix}$$

where the a's and b's are real numbers. If the b's are all zero the matrix is real.

Square matrix

A square matrix is one in which the number of rows is equal to the number of columns. It is referred to as an $n \times n$ matrix or a matrix of order n. The sum of the diagonal elements of a square matrix is called the *trace*.

$$\text{Trace } [A] = \sum_{i=1}^{n} a_{ii}$$

Symmetric matrix

If the elements of any $n \times n$ matrix are symmetrical about the principal diagonal, i.e. If $a_{ij} = a_{ji}$, the matrix is said to be symmetric. A symmetric matrix $[A]$ is given below:

$$\begin{bmatrix} 15 & 5 & 8 \\ 5 & 25 & 7 \\ 8 & 7 & 35 \end{bmatrix}$$

Let $[A]$ be a square matrix. The transpose of the matrix $[A]$ can be written as $[A]^T$ and is obtained by interchanging the rows and columns in $[A]$. A square matrix for which $[A] = [A]^T$ is a symmetric matrix. Note that a symmetric matrix is a square matrix but a square matrix need not be symmetric.

Column and row matrices (vectors)

A column matrix is a matrix with m rows and one column i.e., $m \times 1$. Similarly, a row matrix is a matrix with one row and n columns i.e., $1 \times n$. Column and row matrices are often referred to as vectors.

Diagonal matrix

A diagonal matrix is a square matrix which has zero elements everywhere except on the main diagonal. A diagonal matrix $[A]$ requires that $a_{ij} = 0$ if $i \neq j$ and has the form

$$[A] = \begin{bmatrix} a_{11} & 0 & 0 & \dots & 0 \\ 0 & a_{22} & 0 & \dots & 0 \\ 0 & 0 & a_{33} & \dots & 0 \\ \cdot & & & & \\ \cdot & & & & \\ 0 & 0 & 0 & \dots & a_{nn} \end{bmatrix}$$

Unit or identity matrix

A diagonal matrix which has unit valued elements on the diagonal is a unit or identity matrix. The unit matrix is commonly represented by $[I]$ and is shown as

$$[I] = \begin{bmatrix} 1 & 0 & 0 \\ 0 & 1 & 0 \\ 0 & 0 & 1 \end{bmatrix}$$

Singular matrix

If the determinant of a matrix is zero, the matrix is said to be singular.

Row matrix

A row matrix has $m = 1$

$$\{B\} = [b_1 \; b_2 \; b_3]$$

Column matrix

A column matrix has $n = 1$.

$$\{C\} = \begin{Bmatrix} c_1 \\ c_2 \\ c_3 \end{Bmatrix}$$

Null or Zero matrix

A null matrix is a matrix whose elements are all equal to zero. The common notation for the null matrix is [0].

Anti-or skew-symmetric matrix

A matrix $[A]$ in which $a_{ij} = -a_{ji}$ and $a_{ii} = 0$ is by definition an anti-symmetric or skew-symmetric matrix.

Banded matrix

Matrices relating to engineering problems have a banded nature. In banded matrices non-zero elements have a definite band around the principal diagonal. For a symmetric matrix [A] we can state this condition as $a_{ij} = 0$ for $j > i + m_A$ where $2m_A + 1$ is the bandwidth of [A]. The following matrix is a symmetric banded matrix of order 5. The half bandwidth m_A is 2.

$$[A] = \begin{bmatrix} 3 & 2 & 1 & 0 & 0 \\ 2 & 3 & 4 & 1 & 0 \\ 1 & 4 & 5 & 6 & 1 \\ 0 & 1 & 6 & 7 & 4 \\ 0 & 0 & 1 & 4 & 3 \end{bmatrix}$$

If half bandwidth of a matrix is zero, the banded matrix reduces to a diagonal matrix.

Tridiagonal matrix

A banded matrix which has only one non-zero element on either side of the principal diagonal is said to be tridiagonal. It has a half bandwidth of one.

Transpose

When a matrix [A] has its rows and columns interchanged the resulting matrix is the transpose of [A], denoted as $[A]^T$. For example

$$[A] = \begin{bmatrix} a_{11} & a_{12} & a_{13} \\ a_{21} & a_{22} & a_{23} \end{bmatrix} \qquad [A^T] = \begin{bmatrix} a_{11} & a_{12} \\ a_{21} & a_{22} \\ a_{31} & a_{32} \end{bmatrix}$$

The transpose of a column matrix is a row matrix

$$\{X\} = \begin{Bmatrix} x_1 \\ x_2 \\ x_3 \end{Bmatrix} \qquad \{X\}^T = [x_1 x_2 x_3]$$

Minor

A minor M_{ij} of a matrix [A] is formed by deleting the ith row and the jth column from the determinant of the original matrix.

Let
$$[A] = \begin{bmatrix} a_{11} & a_{12} & a_{13} \\ a_{21} & a_{22} & a_{23} \\ a_{31} & a_{32} & a_{33} \end{bmatrix}$$

$$[M_{12}] = \begin{vmatrix} a_{11} & a_{12} & a_{13} \\ a_{21} & a_{22} & a_{23} \\ a_{31} & a_{32} & a_{33} \end{vmatrix} = \begin{vmatrix} a_{21} & a_{23} \\ a_{31} & a_{33} \end{vmatrix}$$

Cofactor

The cofactor C_{ij} is equal to the corresponding signed minor $(-1)^{i+j} M_{ij}$. From the previous example

$$C_{12} = (-1)^{1+2} M_{12} = -M_{12}$$

Rank of matrix

If a matrix [A], of order $m \times n$, is such that every square submatrix of order greater than r has zero determinant while at least one square submatrix of order r has determinant non-zero, then the matrix $[A]$ is said to be of rank r. The notation $r[A]$ denotes the rank of $[A]$.

Square submatrices formed should not be of any order higher than the smaller of m and n i.e., $r \leq \min(m, n)$ of $[A]$. A systematic procedure to determine rank of a matrix would be to evaluate the determinants of the highest possible order submatrices; then the next highest order and so on. The procedure is continued until a non-zero determinant is found. The rank is of the order of the corresponding submatrix. The procedure is demonstrated in the following example.

Example 4.3

Determine the rank of the given matrix.

$$[A] = \begin{bmatrix} 1 & 1 & 1 & 0 \\ 1 & 2 & 3 & 1 \\ 2 & 3 & 4 & 1 \end{bmatrix}$$

Solution

Since $[A]$ is of the order of 3×4, the maximum possible rank should be 3. This is true when at least one square submatrix of order 3 has non-zero determinant. Otherwise the rank will be at most 2 and it must be investigated for square matrices of order 2.

There can be four square submatrices of order 3 in the given matrix, and these are as follows:

Submatrix	*Its determinant*
$\begin{bmatrix} 1 & 1 & 0 \\ 2 & 3 & 1 \\ 3 & 4 & 1 \end{bmatrix}$	0
$\begin{bmatrix} 1 & 1 & 0 \\ 1 & 3 & 1 \\ 2 & 4 & 1 \end{bmatrix}$	0
$\begin{bmatrix} 1 & 1 & 0 \\ 1 & 2 & 1 \\ 2 & 3 & 1 \end{bmatrix}$	0
$\begin{bmatrix} 1 & 1 & 1 \\ 1 & 2 & 3 \\ 2 & 3 & 4 \end{bmatrix}$	0

Hence it is required to investigate submatrices of order 2.

$\begin{bmatrix} 1 & 1 \\ 1 & 2 \end{bmatrix}$	1

Hence a non-zero determinant is arrived at, and so we can conclude that $r[A] = 2$.

Augmented matrix

A system of linear equations in matrix notation takes the form $Ax = b$, where A is of order $m \times n$, x is of order $n \times 1$ and b is of order $m \times 1$. The augmented matrix $[A_b]$ can be obtained by adjoining column b to matrix A. In terms of partitioned matrices we have $[A_b] = [A : b]$.

As an example let us consider a set of linear equations

$$x + y + z = 6$$
$$x + y - z = 0$$
$$x - y + z = 2$$

Then we have,

$$[A] = \begin{bmatrix} 1 & 1 & 1 \\ 1 & 1 & -1 \\ 1 & -1 & 1 \end{bmatrix}; \{b\} = \begin{Bmatrix} 6 \\ 0 \\ 2 \end{Bmatrix}$$

and
$$[A_b] = \begin{bmatrix} 1 & 1 & 1 & 6 \\ 1 & 1 & -1 & 0 \\ 1 & -1 & 1 & 2 \end{bmatrix}$$

4.3 THE INVERSE OF A MATRIX

In structural analysis, a structure having n degrees of freedom involves solution of n linearly independent equations. In matrix form they may be written as $[A]\{X\} = \{b\}$ where $[A]$ is a non singular square matrix of order $(n \times n)$ and $\{x\}$ and $\{b\}$ are column matrices of order $(n \times l)$. The matrix $[A]$ is said to be singular if the determinant of the matrix is zero.

For a given matrix $[A]$, it is possible to find another matrix $[B]$ of the same order such that

$$[A]\,[B] = [I] \tag{4.2}$$

If such a matrix $[B]$ exists, it is called the inverse of $[A]$ and is denoted by $[A]^{-1}$. A matrix that possesses an inverse is said to be non-singular. Let

$$[A]\,\{x\} = \{b\} \tag{4.3}$$

Premultiplying both sides by $[A]^{-1}$ we have

$$[A]^{-1}\,[A]\,\{x\} = [A]^{-1}\,\{b\} \tag{4.4}$$

since $[A]^{-1}\,[A] = [A]\,[A]^{-1} = [I]$ we get

$$[I]\,\{x\} = [A]^{-1}\,\{b\}$$

or
$$\{x\} = [A]^{-1}\,\{b\} \tag{4.5}$$

Having computed $[A]^{-1}$ it is easy to compute the values of the vector $\{x\}$ by matrix multiplications.

Inverse of a Matrix by Partitioning

The time taken to invert a matrix by a computing machine is roughly proportional to n^3 where n is the size of the matrix. The inversion of a higher order matrix is more conveniently done by the method of partitioning, by dividing the matrices into small size submatrices. This is shown by dotted lines for the matrix given below.

$$[A] = \begin{bmatrix} a_{11} & a_{12} & . & a_{13} & a_{14} \\ a_{21} & a_{22} & . & a_{23} & a_{24} \\ - & - & . & - & - \\ a_{31} & a_{32} & . & a_{33} & a_{34} \\ a_{41} & a_{42} & . & a_{43} & a_{44} \end{bmatrix} = \begin{bmatrix} [B] & \cdots & [C] \\ \cdots & \cdots & \cdots \\ [D] & \cdots & [E] \end{bmatrix} \quad (4.6)$$

In order to obtain the inverse of $[A]$, it is required that the submatrices $[B]$ and $[E]$ are both non singular.

Let $$[A]^{-1} = \begin{bmatrix} [W] & \cdots & [X] \\ \cdots & \cdots & \cdots \\ [Y] & \cdots & [Z] \end{bmatrix} \text{ in the partition form}$$

using Eq. (4.6) in the relation $[A]\,[A]^{-1} - I$ we obtain

$$\begin{bmatrix} [B] & [C] \\ [D] & [E] \end{bmatrix} \begin{bmatrix} [W] & [X] \\ [Y] & [Z] \end{bmatrix} = \begin{bmatrix} [I] & 0 \\ 0 & [I] \end{bmatrix}$$

By matrix multiplications we have

$$\begin{aligned} [B]\,[W] + [C]\,[Y] &= [I] \\ [B]\,[X] + [C]\,[Z] &= O \\ [D]\,[W] + [E]\,[Y] &= O \\ [D]\,[X] + [E]\,[Z] &= [I] \end{aligned} \quad (4.7)$$

Computing the unknown $[W]$, $[X]$, $[Y]$ and $[Z]$ in terms of the known quantities $[B]$,$[C]$, $[D]$ and $[E]$, we obtain

$$\begin{aligned} [Z] &= ([E] - [D]\cdot[B]^{-1}\cdot[C]^{-1} \\ [Y] &= -([E] - [D]\cdot[B]^{-1}\cdot[C]^{-1}\cdot[D]\cdot[B]^{-1} = -[Z]\cdot[D]\cdot[B]^{-1} \\ [X] &= -[B]^{-1}\cdot[C]\cdot([E] - [D]\cdot[B]^{-1}[C])^{-1} = -[B]^{-1}[C]\cdot[Z] \\ [W] &= [B]^{-1} + [B]^{-1}\cdot[C]\,([E] - [D]\cdot[B]^{-1}[C]^{-1}\cdot[D]\,[B]^{-1} \\ &= [B]^{-1} - [X]\cdot[D]\cdot[B]^{-1} \end{aligned} \quad (4.8)$$

The entire inversion is reduced into two matrices of smaller size ie., $[B]^{-1}$ and $([E] - [D]\cdot[B]^{-1}\,[C])^{-1}$. These computations are more rapid than inversion of higher order matrices and hence result in considerable time saving. For a considerably large size matrix the process can be started with the top left-hand corner of the matrix and adding a row and a column at a time until the inverse $[A]^{-1}$ is obtained. This process is known as the *Escalator Method.*

Example 4.4

Solve the set of linear equations given below by matrix inversion using the method of partitioning.

$$10x_1 + 7x_2 + 8x_3 + 7x_4 = 32$$

$$7x_1 + 5x_2 + 6x_3 + 5x_4 = 23$$

$$8x_1 + 6x_2 + 10x_3 + 9x_4 = 33$$

$$7x_1 + 5x_2 + 9x_3 + 10x_4 = 31$$

Solution

The set of linear equations can be written in the matrix form as

$$\begin{bmatrix} 10 & 7 & 8 & 7 \\ 7 & 5 & 6 & 5 \\ 8 & 6 & 10 & 9 \\ 7 & 5 & 9 & 10 \end{bmatrix} \begin{Bmatrix} x_1 \\ x_2 \\ x_3 \\ x_4 \end{Bmatrix} = \begin{Bmatrix} 32 \\ 23 \\ 33 \\ 31 \end{Bmatrix}$$

where

$$[A] = \begin{bmatrix} 10 & 7 & 8 & 7 \\ 7 & 5 & 6 & 5 \\ 8 & 6 & 10 & 9 \\ 7 & 5 & 9 & 10 \end{bmatrix}; \ \{x\} = \begin{Bmatrix} x_1 \\ x_2 \\ x_3 \\ x_4 \end{Bmatrix}; \ \{b\} = \begin{Bmatrix} 32 \\ 23 \\ 33 \\ 31 \end{Bmatrix}$$

The unknown vector $\{x\}$ can be obtained from $\{x\} = [A]^{-1}\{b\}$.

To obtain the inverse of matrix $[A]$, the method of partitioning is used. At every stage, the corresponding $[B]$, $[C]$, $[D]$, $[E]$ submatrices are as given in Eq. (4.6).

First operation

Take the first (2×2) submatrix.

$$\begin{bmatrix} 10 & 7 \\ 7 & 5 \end{bmatrix} [B]^{-1} = 1/10$$

$$[B]^{-1} \cdot [C] = 1/10 \times 7 = 7/10$$

$$[D] \cdot [B]^{-1} = 7/10$$

$$[D] \cdot [B]^{-1} \cdot [C] = 7 \times 1/10 \times 7 = 49/10 \ [Z] = (5 - 49/10)^{-1} = 10$$

$$[Y] = -10.7/10 = -7$$

$$[X] = -7/10.10 = -7$$

$$[W] = (1/10 + 7.7/10) = 5$$

2nd operation

$$\begin{bmatrix} 10 & 7 & . & 8 \\ 7 & 5 & . & 6 \\ - & - & - & - \\ 8 & 6 & . & 10 \end{bmatrix}$$

$$[B]^{-1} = \begin{bmatrix} 5 & -7 \\ -7 & 10 \end{bmatrix}$$

$$[B]^{-1}[C] = \begin{bmatrix} 5 & -7 \\ -7 & 10 \end{bmatrix} \begin{Bmatrix} 8 \\ 6 \end{Bmatrix} = \begin{Bmatrix} -2 \\ 4 \end{Bmatrix} \quad [Z] = (10-8)^{-1} = 1/2$$

$$[D]\,[B]^{-1} = \{8 \quad 6\} \begin{bmatrix} 5 & 7 \\ -7 & 10 \end{bmatrix} = \{-2, 4\} \; [Y]$$

$$= -1/2\{-2, 4\} = \{1 - 2\}$$

$$[D]\,[B]^{-1}[C] = \{-2, 4\} \begin{Bmatrix} 8 \\ 6 \end{Bmatrix} = 8 \quad [X] = -\begin{Bmatrix} -2 \\ 4 \end{Bmatrix} \frac{1}{2} = \begin{Bmatrix} 1 \\ -2 \end{Bmatrix}$$

$$[X]\,[D]\,[B]^{-1} = \begin{Bmatrix} 1 \\ -2 \end{Bmatrix} \{-2 \quad 4\} = \begin{bmatrix} -2 & 4 \\ 4 & -8 \end{bmatrix} \quad [W] = \begin{bmatrix} 7 & -11 \\ -11 & 18 \end{bmatrix}$$

From above

$$[B]^{-1} = \begin{bmatrix} 7 & -11 & 1 \\ -11 & 18 & -2 \\ 1 & -2 & 1/2 \end{bmatrix}$$

3rd operation

$$\begin{bmatrix} 10 & 7 & 8 & 7 \\ 7 & 5 & 6 & 5 \\ 8 & 6 & 10 & 9 \\ 7 & 5 & 9 & 10 \end{bmatrix}$$

$$[B]^{-1}[C] = \begin{bmatrix} 7 & -11 & 1 \\ -11 & 18 & -2 \\ 1 & -2 & 1/2 \end{bmatrix} \begin{Bmatrix} 7 \\ 5 \\ 9 \end{Bmatrix} = \begin{Bmatrix} 3 \\ -5 \\ 3/2 \end{Bmatrix}$$

$$[D]\,[B]^{-1} = \{7\;5\;9\} \begin{bmatrix} 7 & -11 & 1 \\ -11 & 18 & -2 \\ 1 & -2 & 1/2 \end{bmatrix}$$

$$= \{3 \; -5 \quad 3/2\}$$

$$[D]\,[B]^{-1}[C] = \{3 \; -5 \quad 3/2\} \begin{Bmatrix} 7 \\ 5 \\ 9 \end{Bmatrix} = 19/2$$

$$[Z] = (10 - 19/2)^{-1} = 2$$

$$[Y] = -2\,\{3\ -5\ 3/2\} = \{-6 \quad 10 \quad -3\}$$

$$[X] = (-2)\begin{Bmatrix} 3 \\ -5 \\ 3/2 \end{Bmatrix} = \begin{Bmatrix} -6 \\ 10 \\ 3/2 \end{Bmatrix}$$

$$X[D]\,[B]^{-1} = \begin{Bmatrix} -6 \\ 10 \\ -3 \end{Bmatrix} \{3 \quad -5 \quad 3/2\} = \begin{bmatrix} -18 & 30 & -9 \\ 30 & -50 & 15 \\ -9 & 15 & -9/2 \end{bmatrix}$$

Hence

$$[W] = \begin{bmatrix} 25 & -41 & 10 \\ -41 & 68 & -17 \\ 10 & -17 & 5 \end{bmatrix}$$

$$[A]^{-1} = \begin{bmatrix} 25 & -41 & 10 & -6 \\ -41 & 68 & -17 & 10 \\ 10 & -17 & 5 & -3 \\ -6 & 10 & -3 & 2 \end{bmatrix}$$

The solution of the system of equations is

$$\{x\} = [A]^{-1}\{b\}$$

$$= \begin{bmatrix} 25 & -41 & 10 & -6 \\ -41 & 68 & -17 & 10 \\ 10 & -17 & 5 & -3 \\ -6 & 10 & -3 & 2 \end{bmatrix} \begin{Bmatrix} 32 \\ 23 \\ 33 \\ 31 \end{Bmatrix} = \begin{Bmatrix} 1 \\ 1 \\ 1 \\ 1 \end{Bmatrix}$$

4.4 GAUSSIAN ELIMINATION

One of the most effective direct solution techniques for solving a set of linear algebraic equations is the method of Gaussian elimination. The method is an extension of the procedure of eliminating one unknown between a pair of simultaneous equations. Let us consider a set of linear algebraic equations.

$$a_{11}x_1 + a_{12}x_2 + \dots + a_{1n}x_n = b_1$$

$$a_{21}x_1 + a_{22}x_2 + \dots + a_{2n}x_n = b_2$$

$$\dots \qquad \dots$$

$$a_{n1}x_1 + a_{n2}x_2 + \dots + a_{nn}x_n = b_n \tag{4.9}$$

The first step is to eliminate the terms with coefficients a_{i1} where $i = 2, 3, \dots n$. In this the coefficient a_{11} is the pivot. It is assumed that $a_{11} = 0$. If a_{11} is zero or even very small, then an interchange of this row with another one can be done so that the new row 1 will have non zero a_{11}. The above set of equations (4.9) are transformed to

$$a_{11}x_1 + a_{12}x_2 + \ldots + a_{1n}x_n = b_1$$

$$a_{22}^{(1)}x_2 + \ldots + a_{1n}^{(1)}x_n = b_2^{(1)}$$

$$\ldots \quad \ldots \quad \ldots$$

$$a_{n2}^{(1)}x_2 + \ldots + a_{nn}^{(1)}x_n = b_n^{(1)} \tag{4.10}$$

where
$$a_{ij}^{(1)} = a_{ij}\frac{a_{i1}}{a_{11}}a_{ij}\,;\, b_i^{(1)} = b_i - \frac{a_{i1}}{a_{11}}b_1$$

$$i = 2, 3, \ldots, n$$

$$j = 2, 3, \ldots, n$$

The next step eliminates the terms with coefficients $a_{i2}^{(1)}$ where $i = 3, 4, ..., n$. Again, it is assumed that $a_{22}^{(1)} \neq 0$. The equations (4, 10) are then transformed to

$$a_{11}x_1 + a_{12}x_2 + a_{13}x_3 + \ldots + a_{1n}x_n = b_1$$

$$a_{22}^{(1)}x_2 + a_{23}^{(1)}x_3 + \ldots a_{2n}^{(1)}x_n = b_1^{(1)}$$

$$a_{33}^{(1)}x_3 + \ldots + a_{3n}^{(2)}x_n = b_3^{(2)}$$

$$\ldots. \quad \ldots. \quad \ldots.$$

$$a_{n3}^{(2)}x_3 + \ldots + a_{nn}^{(2)}x_n = b_n^{(2)} \tag{4.11}$$

where
$$a_{ij}^{(2)} = a_{ij}^{(2)} - \frac{a_{i2}^{(1)}}{a_{22}^{(1)}}a_{2j}^{(1)}\,;\, b_i^{(2)} = b_i^{(2)} - \frac{a_{i2}^{(1)}}{a_{22}^{(1)}}b_2^{(1)}$$

$$i = 3, 4, \ldots, n$$

$$j = 3, 4, \ldots, n$$

After $(n - 1)$ steps, the set of linear algebraic equations are transformed to

$$a_{11}x_1 + a_{12}x_2 + a_{13}x_3 + \ldots + a_{1n}x_n = b_1$$

$$a_{22}^{(1)}x_2 + a_{23}^{(1)}x_3 + \ldots + a_{2n}^{(1)}x_n = b_1^{(1)}$$

$$a_{33}^{(1)}x_3 + \ldots + a_{3n}^{(2)}x_n = b_3^{(2)}$$

$$\ldots. \quad \ldots. \quad \ldots.$$

$$\ldots. \quad \ldots + a_{nn}^{(n-1)}x_n = b_n^{(n-1)} \tag{4.12}$$

which in the matrix form can be written as $[A]\{x\} = \{b\}$. The matrix $[A]$ has all its elements below the main diagonal as zero and is said to have an upper triangular form. The last equation in the set of equations (4. 12) involves only one unknown x_n and leads to the solution of

$$x_n = \frac{b_n^{(n-1)}}{a_{nn}^{(n-1)}}$$

Knowing x_n , the (n – 1)th equation in (4. 12) will lead to the solution of x_{n-1}. Continuing this way, x_{n-3}, x_{n-2}, . . ., x_1 can all be obtained in that order. The process of obtaining x_n, x_{n-1}, from an upper triangular matrix is called *back substitution.*

Example 4.5

Use the method of Gaussian elimination to solve the following system of linear equations.

$$x_1 + x_2 + x_3 - x_4 = 2$$

$$4x_1 + 4x_2 + x_3 + x_4 = 11$$

$$x_1 - x_2 - x_3 + 2x_4 = 0$$

$$2x_1 + x_2 + 2x_3 - 2x_4 = 2 \quad \text{(a)}$$

Solution

In the first step, eliminate x_1 terms from second, third and fourth equations of the set of equations (a) to obtain:

$$x_1 + x_2 + x_3 - x_4 = 2$$

$$-3x_3 + 5x_4 = 3$$

$$-2x_2 - 2x_3 + 3x_4 = -2$$

$$-x_2 = -2 \quad \text{(b)}$$

Interchange columns in Eq. (b) putting the variables in the order x_1, x_4, x_3 and x_2 as

$$x_1 - x_4 + x_3 + x_2 = 2$$

$$-5x_4 - 3x_3 = 3$$

$$3x_4 - 2x_3 - 2x_2 = -2$$

$$-x_2 = -2 \quad \text{(c)}$$

In the secod step, eliminate x_4 term in third equation of the set of equations 4.3 (c)

$$x_1 - x_4 + x_3 + x_2 = 2$$

$$5x_4 - 3x_3 = 3$$

$$-1/5x_3 - 2x_2 = -19/5$$

$$-x_2 = -2$$

Now, by the process of back substitution

$$x_2 = 2, x_3 = -1, x_4 = 0, x_1 = 1$$

Example 4.6

Solve the following set of simultaneous linear equations using Gaussian elimination method.

$$2x_1 + x_2 - 3x_3 = 11$$

$$4x_1 - 2x_2 + 3x_3 = 8$$

$$-2x_1 + 2x_2 - x_3 = -6$$

Solution

The augmented matrix is

$$\begin{bmatrix} 2 & 1 & -3 & 11 \\ 4 & -2 & 3 & 8 \\ -2 & 2 & -1 & -6 \end{bmatrix}$$

Step 1

$$\begin{matrix} \text{Row } 2 - 2 \times \text{Row} \\ \text{Row } 3 + \text{Row } 1 \end{matrix} \begin{bmatrix} 2 & 1 & -3 & 11 \\ 0 & -4 & 9 & -14 \\ 0 & 3 & -4 & 5 \end{bmatrix}$$

Working on the resulting matrix of step 1

Step 2

$$\text{Row } 3 + \frac{3}{4}\text{Row } 2 \quad \begin{bmatrix} 2 & 1 & -3 & 11 \\ 0 & -4 & 9 & -14 \\ 0 & 0 & \frac{11}{4} & -\frac{11}{2} \end{bmatrix}$$

By back substitution,

$$x_3 = -2, x_2 = -1, x_1 = 3$$

Example 4.7

Using the Gaussian elimination method, solve the system of equations $[A]\ \{x\} = \{b\}$ where

$$[A] = \begin{bmatrix} 1 & 1 & 1 & 1 \\ 2 & -1 & 3 & 0 \\ 0 & 2 & 0 & 3 \\ -1 & 0 & 2 & 1 \end{bmatrix} \text{ and } \{b\} = \begin{Bmatrix} 3 \\ 3 \\ 1 \\ 0 \end{Bmatrix}$$

Solution

The augmented matrix is

$$[A_b] = \begin{bmatrix} 1 & 1 & 1 & 1 & 3 \\ 2 & -1 & 3 & 0 & 3 \\ 0 & 2 & 0 & 3 & 1 \\ 0 & 2 & 0 & 3 & 1 \\ -1 & 0 & 2 & 1 & 0 \end{bmatrix}$$

Step 1 yields the augmented matrix

$$\begin{matrix} \\ \text{Row } 2-2\times\text{Row } 1 \\ \text{Row } 4+\text{Row } 1 \\ \\ \\ \end{matrix} \begin{bmatrix} 1 & 1 & 1 & 1 & 3 \\ 0 & -3 & 1 & -2 & -3 \\ 0 & 2 & 0 & 3 & 1 \\ 0 & 2 & 0 & 3 & 1 \\ 0 & 1 & 3 & 2 & 3 \end{bmatrix}$$

Similarly, steps 2 and 3 yield, respectively, the following augmented matrices.

$$\begin{bmatrix} 1 & 1 & 1 & 1 & 3 \\ 0 & -3 & 1 & -2 & -3 \\ 0 & 0 & \frac{2}{3} & \frac{5}{3} & -1 \\ 0 & 0 & \frac{10}{3} & \frac{4}{3} & 2 \end{bmatrix} \begin{bmatrix} 1 & 1 & 1 & 1 & 3 \\ 0 & -3 & 1 & -2 & -3 \\ 0 & 0 & \frac{2}{3} & \frac{5}{3} & -1 \\ 0 & 0 & 0 & -7 & 7 \end{bmatrix}$$

By back substitution the upper triangular matrix

$$x_4 = -1, x_3 = 1, x_2 = 2, x_1 = 1$$

4.5 GAUSS-JORDAN METHOD

Let us consider a system of linear algebraic equations in the matrix form

$$[A]\ \{x\} = \{b\} \tag{4.13}$$

where, for simplification, $[A]$ is of order 3×3. The augmented matrix is

$$\begin{bmatrix} a_{11} & a_{12} & a_{13} & b_1 \\ a_{21} & a_{22} & a_{23} & b_2 \\ a_{31} & a_{32} & a_{33} & b_3 \end{bmatrix} \tag{4.14}$$

The solution of equation (4.13) is

$$[I]\ \{x\} = [A]^{-1}\ \{b\} = \{\alpha\} \tag{4.15}$$

where $[I]$ is the identity matrix. The augmented matrix is

$$\begin{bmatrix} 1 & 0 & 0 & \alpha_1 \\ 0 & 1 & 0 & \alpha_2 \\ 0 & 0 & 1 & \alpha_3 \end{bmatrix} \tag{4.16}$$

In the Gauss-Jordan method the augmented matrix (4.14) is converted to the augmented matrix (4.16) by a series of operations similar to the Gaussian elimination mathod. In the Gaussian elimination method an upper triangular matrix is deriv d while in the Gauss-Jordan method an identity matrix is derived.

Example 4.8

Solve the following set of equations by Guass-Jordan method.

$$2x_1 + x_2 - 3x_3 = 11$$

$$4x_1 - 2x_2 + 3x_3 = 8$$

$$-2x_1 + 2x_2 - x_3 = -6$$

Solution

The augmented matrix for equation (a) is

$$\begin{bmatrix} 2 & 1 & -3 & 11 \\ 4 & -2 & 3 & 8 \\ -2 & 2 & -1 & -6 \end{bmatrix}$$

Step 1

Divide Row 1 by 2

$$\begin{bmatrix} 1 & \frac{1}{2} & -\frac{3}{2} & \frac{11}{2} \\ 4 & -2 & 3 & 8 \\ -2 & 2 & -1 & -6 \end{bmatrix}$$

Step 2

$$\begin{matrix} \text{Row } 2 - 4 \times \text{Row } 1 \\ \text{Row } 3 - 2 \times \text{Row } 1 \end{matrix} \begin{bmatrix} 1 & \frac{1}{2} & -\frac{3}{2} & \frac{11}{2} \\ 0 & -4 & 9 & -14 \\ 0 & 3 & -4 & 5 \end{bmatrix}$$

Step 3

$$\text{Divide Row 2 by } -4 \begin{bmatrix} 1 & \frac{1}{2} & -\frac{3}{2} & \frac{11}{2} \\ 0 & 1 & -\frac{9}{4} & \frac{7}{2} \\ 0 & 3 & -4 & 5 \end{bmatrix}$$

Step 4

$$\begin{matrix} \text{Row } 1 - 1/2 \times \text{Row } 2 \\ \text{Row } 3 - 3 \times \text{Row } 2 \end{matrix} \begin{bmatrix} 1 & 0 & -\frac{3}{8} & \frac{15}{4} \\ 0 & 1 & -\frac{9}{4} & \frac{7}{2} \\ 0 & 3 & \frac{11}{4} & -\frac{11}{2} \end{bmatrix}$$

Step 5

$$\text{Divide Row 3 by } 11/4 \begin{bmatrix} 1 & 0 & -\frac{3}{8} & \frac{15}{4} \\ 0 & 1 & -\frac{9}{4} & \frac{7}{2} \\ 0 & 0 & 1 & -2 \end{bmatrix}$$

Step 6

$$\begin{matrix}\text{Row } 1 + 3/8 \times \text{Row } 3 \\ \text{Row } 2 + 9/4 \times \text{Row } 3\end{matrix} \quad \begin{bmatrix} 1 & 0 & 0 & 3 \\ 0 & 1 & 0 & -1 \\ 0 & 0 & 1 & -2 \end{bmatrix}$$

Hence the solution is $x_1 = 3,\ x_2 = -1,\ x_3 = -2$.

4.6 CHOLESKY'S FACTORISATION METHOD

Let $[A]$ be a square matrix of order n and let $\Delta_p = \det A_p$ where $[A_p]$ is a square matrix of size p formed by the first p rows and columns of $[A]$. Then if $\Delta_p \neq 0$ $(p = 1, 2, \ldots n)$, $[A]$ can be expressed uniquely in the form $[A] = [L]\,[U]$ where $[L]$ is a unit lower triangular matrix of order n and $[U]$ is an upper triangular matrix of order n.

Here we make use of the above property assuming that the matrix $[A]$ of the given set of equations $[A]\,\{x\} = \{b\}$ satisfies these conditions. The set of equations. can be written in the form

$$[L]\,[U]\,\{x\} = \{b\} \tag{4.17}$$

$$[U]\,\{x\} = \{y\} \tag{4.18}$$

Now it is easy to solve the two equations (4.17) and (4.18) by forward and back substitution respectively. Factorisation of $[A]$ into $[L]$ and $[U]$ can be explained by writing

$$[L] = \begin{bmatrix} 1 & 0 & 0 & \cdots & 0 \\ l_{21} & 1 & 0 & \cdots & 0 \\ l_{31} & l_{32} & 1 & \cdots & 0 \\ \cdots & \cdots & \cdots & \cdots & \cdots \\ l_{n1} & l_{n2} & \cdots & l_{n,n-1} & 1 \end{bmatrix};\ [U] = \begin{bmatrix} u_{11} & u_{12} & \cdots & \cdots & u_{1n} \\ 0 & u_{22} & \cdots & \cdots & u_{2n} \\ 0 & 0 & u_{33} & \cdots & u_{3n} \\ \cdots & \cdots & \cdots & \cdots & \cdots \\ 0 & 0 & 0 & \cdots & u_{nn} \end{bmatrix} \tag{4.19}$$

If $[A]$ and $[L]\,[U]$ are then equated element by element, a system of equations can be obtained which yield l'_{ij} s and u'_{ij} s explicitly in terms of a'_{ij} s.

$[A]$ can also be written in the form

$$[A] = [L]\,[D]\,[U] \tag{4.20}$$

where $[L]$ is a unit lower triangular, $[D]$ is a diagonal matrix and $[U]$ is a unit upper triangular matrix. It is possible to write the $[U]$ matrix as $[D]\,[U]$.

$$[U] = \begin{bmatrix} u_{11} & u_{12} & \cdots & \cdots & u_{1n} \\ 0 & u_{22} & \cdots & \cdots & u_{2n} \\ 0 & 0 & u_{33} & \cdots & u_{3n} \\ \cdots & \cdots & \cdots & \cdots & \cdots \\ 0 & 0 & 0 & \cdots & u_{nn} \end{bmatrix} = \begin{bmatrix} u_{11} & 0 & \cdots & \cdots & 0 \\ 0 & u_{22} & \cdots & \cdots & 0 \\ 0 & 0 & u_{33} & \cdots & 0 \\ \cdots & \cdots & \cdots & \cdots & \cdots \\ 0 & 0 & 0 & \cdots & u_{nn} \end{bmatrix} \cdot \begin{bmatrix} 1 & \dfrac{u_{12}}{u_{11}} & \dfrac{u_{13}}{u_{11}} & \cdots & \dfrac{u_{1n}}{u_{11}} \\ 0 & 1 & \dfrac{u_{23}}{u_{22}} & \cdots & \dfrac{u_{2n}}{u_{22}} \\ \cdots & \cdots & \cdots & \cdots & \cdots \\ 0 & 0 & 0 & \cdots & 1 \end{bmatrix} \tag{4.21}$$

If $[A]$ is a symmetric matrix, it is possible to decompose it into the form $[A] = [L]\,[L]^{-1}$ where $[L]$ is a lower triangular matrix and it is also possible to decompose into the form $[A] = [L]\,[D]\,[L]^{-1}$ where $[L]$ is unit lower triangular matrix and [D] is a diagonal matrix. In addition, the Cholesky factorisation is only suitable for the solution of positive definite matrices, for which all diagonal elements d_{ii} are positive, otherwise complex arithmetic is to be adopted.

Example 4.9

Solve the system of equations using Cholesky's factorisations.

$$x_1 + x_2 + x_3 - x_4 = 2$$

$$x_1 - x_2 - x_3 + 2x_4 = 0$$

$$4x_1 + 4x_2 + x_3 + x_4 = 11$$

$$2x_1 + x_2 + 2x_3 - 2x_4 = 2$$

Solution

The set of equations can be written in the matrix form $[A]\{x\} = \{b\}$

$$\begin{bmatrix} 1 & 1 & 1 & -1 \\ 1 & -1 & -1 & 2 \\ 4 & 4 & 1 & 1 \\ 2 & 1 & 2 & -2 \end{bmatrix} \begin{Bmatrix} x_1 \\ x_2 \\ x_3 \\ x_4 \end{Bmatrix} = \begin{Bmatrix} 2 \\ 0 \\ 11 \\ 2 \end{Bmatrix}$$

Let us decompose $[A]$ in the form

$$[A] = [L]\,[U]$$

where

$$[L] = \begin{bmatrix} 1 & 0 & 0 & 0 \\ l_{21} & 1 & 0 & 0 \\ l_{31} & l_{32} & 1 & 0 \\ l_{41} & l_{42} & l_{43} & 1 \end{bmatrix} \text{ and } [U] = \begin{bmatrix} u_{11} & u_{12} & u_{13} & u_{14} \\ 0 & u_{22} & u_{23} & u_{24} \\ 0 & 0 & u_{33} & u_{34} \\ 0 & 0 & 0 & u_{44} \end{bmatrix}$$

The product of $[L]\,[U]$ gives

$$[L]\,[U] = \begin{bmatrix} u_{11} & u_{12} & u_{13} & u_{14} \\ l_{21}u_{11} & l_{21}u_{12} + u_{22} & l_{21}u_{13} + u_{23} & l_{21}u_{14} + u_{24} \\ l_{31}u_{11} & l_{31}u_{12} + l_{32}u_{22} & l_{31}u_{13} + l_{32}u_{23} + u_{33} & l_{31}u_{14} + l_{32}u_{24} + u_{34} \\ l_{41}u_{11} & l_{41}u_{12} + l_{42}u_{22} & l_{41}u_{13} + l_{42}u_{23} + l_{43}u_{33} & l_{41}u_{14} + l_{42}u_{24} + l_{43}u_{34} + u_{44} \end{bmatrix}$$

Equating the elements of this matrix to the $[A]$ matrix yields the following equations

$$u_{11} = 1 \qquad l_{21}\,u_{11} = 1 \qquad l_{31}\,u_{11} = 4$$

$$u_{12} = 1 \qquad l_{21}\,u_{12} + u_{22} = -1 \qquad l_{31}\,u_{12} + l_{32}\,u_{22} = 4$$

$$u_{13} = 1 \qquad l_{21}\,u_{13} + u_{23} = -1 \qquad l_{31}\,u_{13} + l_{32}\,u_{23} + u_{33} = 1$$

$$u_{14} = -1 \qquad l_{21}\,u_{14} + u_{24} = 2 \qquad l_{31}\,u_{14} + l_{32}\,u_{24} + u_{34} = 1$$

$$l_{41}\,u_{11} = 2$$

$$l_{41}\,u_{12} + l_{42}\,u_{22} = 1$$

$$l_{41} u_{13} + l_{42} u_{23} + l_{23} u_{33} = 2$$

$$l_{41} u_{14} + l_{42} u_{24} + l_{43} u_{34} + u_{44} = -2$$

By solving these sixteen equations we get

$$[L] = \begin{bmatrix} 1 & 0 & 0 & 0 \\ 1 & 1 & 0 & 0 \\ 4 & 0 & 1 & 0 \\ 2 & \frac{1}{2} & -\frac{1}{3} & 1 \end{bmatrix} \text{ and } [U] = \begin{bmatrix} 1 & 1 & 1 & -1 \\ 0 & -2 & -2 & 3 \\ 0 & 0 & -3 & 5 \\ 0 & 0 & 0 & \frac{1}{6} \end{bmatrix}$$

To solve $[A]\{x\} = \{b\}$ we have to solve the two systems

$$[L]\{Y\} = \{b\}$$

$$[U]\{x\} = \{Y\}$$

i.e.,

$$\begin{bmatrix} 1 & 0 & 0 & 0 \\ 1 & 1 & 0 & 0 \\ 4 & 0 & 1 & 0 \\ 2 & \frac{1}{2} & \frac{1}{3} & 1 \end{bmatrix} \begin{Bmatrix} y_1 \\ y_2 \\ y_3 \\ y_4 \end{Bmatrix} = \begin{Bmatrix} 2 \\ 0 \\ 11 \\ 2 \end{Bmatrix}$$

which gives by forward substitution

$$y_1 = 2, y_2 = -2, y_3 = 3, y_4 = 0$$

and hence $[U]\{x\} = \{y\}$ becomes

$$\begin{bmatrix} 1 & 1 & 1 & -1 \\ 0 & -2 & -2 & 3 \\ 0 & 0 & -3 & 5 \\ 0 & 0 & 0 & \frac{1}{6} \end{bmatrix} \begin{Bmatrix} x_1 \\ x_2 \\ x_3 \\ x_4 \end{Bmatrix} = \begin{Bmatrix} 2 \\ -2 \\ 3 \\ 0 \end{Bmatrix}$$

Then by back substitution we obtain

$$x_4 = 0, x_3 = -1, x_2 = 2, x_1 = 1$$

4.7 POTTERS' METHOD

The main feature of this method is its ability to handle simultaneous equations whose stiffness matrix is unsymmetric. The approach of this method is to split the problem into a number of small submatrices. Consider the system of simultaneous equations

$$[A]\{x\} = \{b\} \tag{4.22}$$

where $[A]$ may be sparse with variable bandwidth.

The matrix $[A]$ is split into a number of small submatrices. The matrices $\{x\}$ and $\{b\}$ are also split into the same number of rows as in $[A]$. The modified form of the system of equations is

$$\begin{bmatrix} B_1 & A_1 & \dots & & & \\ C_2 & B_2 & A_2 & \dots & & \\ C_3 & B_3 & A_3 & \dots & & \\ \dots & \dots & \dots & \dots & \dots & \dots \\ & & & & C_n & B_n \end{bmatrix} \begin{Bmatrix} z_1 \\ z_2 \\ z_3 \\ \dots \\ z_n \end{Bmatrix} = \begin{Bmatrix} g_1 \\ g_2 \\ g_3 \\ \dots \\ g_n \end{Bmatrix} \quad (4.23)$$

Small vectors of $\{x\}$ are denoted as z_1, z_2 ..., similarly small vectors of $\{b\}$ are denoted as $g_1, g_2, ..., g_n$.

Considering the first and secod equations of (4.23)

$$[B_1]\{z_1\} + [A_1]\{z_2\} = \{g_1\}$$

$$[C_2]\{z_1\} + [B_2]\{z_2\} + [A_2]\{z_3\} = \{g_2\}$$

Premultiplying the second equation by $[C_2]^{-1}$, we have

$$\{z_1\} + [C_2]^{-1}[B_2]\{z_2\} + [C_2]^{-1}[A_2]\{z_3\} = [C_2]^{-1}\{g_2\}$$

Premultiplying by $[B_1]$

$$[B_1]\{z_1\} + [B_1][C_2]^{-1}[B_2]\{z_2\} + [B_1][C_2]^{-1}[A_2]\{z_3\} = [B_1][C_2]^{-1}\{g_2\}$$

subtracting from the first equation it gives

$$[A_1]\{z_2\} - [B_1][C_2]^{-1}[A_2]\{z_3\} - [B_1][C_2]^{-1}[B_2]\{z_2\}$$

$$= \{g_1\} - [B_1][C_2]^{-1}\{g_2\}$$

$$([A_1] - [B_1][C_2]^{-1}[B_2])\{z_2\} = (\{g_1\} - [B_1][C_2]^{-1}\{g_2\}) + [B_1][C_2]^{-1}[A_2]\{z_3\}$$

This is written as

$$\{z_2\} = [P_2]\{z_3\} + \{q_2\} \quad (4.24)$$

where $$[P_2] = ([A_1] - [B_1][C_2]^{-1}[B_2])^{-1}([B_1][C_2]^{-1}[A_2]) \quad (4.25)$$

and $$\{q_2\} = ([A_1] - [B_1][C_2]^{-1}[B_2])^{-1}(\{g_1\} - [B_1][C_2]^{-1}\{g_2\})$$

From the third equation of (4.23)

$$[A_3]\{z_4\} + [B_3]\{z_3\} + [C_3]\{z_2\} = \{g_3\}$$

Substituting the value of $\{z_2\}$ from (4.24), we get

$$[A_3]\{z_4\} + [B_3]\{z_3\} + [C_3]([P_2]\{z_3\} + \{q_2\}) = \{g_3\}$$

rearranging

$$([B_3] + [C_3][P_2])z_3\} = (\{g_3\} - [C_3]\{q\}) - [A_3]\{z_4\}$$

Premultiplying both sides by $([B_3] + [C_3][P_2])^{-1}$

we get

$$\{z_3\} = -([B_3] + [C_3][P_2])^{-1}[A_3]\{z_4\} + ([B_3] + [C_3][P_2]^{-1})(\{g_3\} - [C_3]\{q_2\})$$

This can be written as

$$\{z_3\} = [P_3]\{z_4\} + \{q_3\} \tag{4.26}$$

where $$[P_3] = -([B_3] + [C_3][P_2])^{-1}[A_3]$$

and $$\{q_3\} = ([B_3] + [C_3][P_2])^{-1}(\{g_3\} - [C_3]\{q_2\}) \tag{4.27}$$

Similarly we can write

$$[P_i] = -([B_i] + [C_i][P_{i-1}])^{-1}[A_i]$$

$$\{q_i\} = ([B_i] + [C_i][P_{i-1}])^{-1}(\{g_i\} - [C_i]\{q_{i-1}\}, \quad (\text{for } i = 3, 4, \ldots m) \tag{4.28}$$

therefore

$$\{z_i\} = [P_i]\{Z_{i+1}\} + \{q_i\} \ (\text{for } i = 3, 4, \ldots m-1) \tag{4.29}$$

Since $[A_m] = 0$, and $[P_m] = 0$ hence $\{q_m\} = \{z_m\}$

The main feature of this method is its capability of handling simultaneous equations whose coefficient matrix is unsymmetric. The intervals need not be of unifrom width. This is very useful to solve the problems of variable bandwidth.

Another advantage of this method is that this can be used as an out-of-core solution by generating $[A_i]$, $[B_i]$ and $[C_i]$ and computing $[P_i]$ and $\{q_i\}$.

In the case of finite element modelling, it is required to assemble the element stiffness matrices such that it should assemble only the portions $[A_i]$, $[B_i]$ and $[C_i]$ of the Global Stiffness matrix. In other words the block matrices must correspond to the corresponding particular partition of the whole structure. It is sufficient to compute the $[A_i]$, $[B_i]$ and $[C_i]$ each time instead of the overall stiffness matrix.

Example 4.10

Solve the following system of linear equations by using Potters' scheme.

$$\begin{bmatrix} 1 & 1 & 1 & -1 \\ 1 & -1 & -1 & 2 \\ 4 & 4 & 1 & 1 \\ 2 & 1 & 2 & -2 \end{bmatrix} \begin{Bmatrix} x_1 \\ x_2 \\ x_3 \\ x_4 \end{Bmatrix} = \begin{Bmatrix} 2 \\ 0 \\ 11 \\ 2 \end{Bmatrix}$$

Solution

Here the coefficient matrix is unsymmetric. Dividing into block matrices, we have

$$[B_1] = \begin{bmatrix} 1 & 1 \\ 1 & -1 \end{bmatrix}, [A_1] = \begin{bmatrix} 1 & -1 \\ -1 & 2 \end{bmatrix}$$

$$[C_2] = \begin{bmatrix} 4 & 4 \\ 2 & 1 \end{bmatrix}, [B_2] = \begin{bmatrix} 1 & 1 \\ 2 & -2 \end{bmatrix}$$

$$\{Z_1\} = \begin{Bmatrix} x_1 \\ x_2 \end{Bmatrix}, \{z_2\} = \begin{Bmatrix} x_3 \\ x_4 \end{Bmatrix}, \{g_1\} = \begin{Bmatrix} 2 \\ 0 \end{Bmatrix}, \{g_2\} = \begin{Bmatrix} 11 \\ 2 \end{Bmatrix}$$

$$[B_1]^{-1} = -\frac{1}{2}\begin{bmatrix} -1 & -1 \\ -1 & 1 \end{bmatrix} = \begin{bmatrix} \frac{1}{2} & \frac{1}{2} \\ \frac{1}{2} & -\frac{1}{2} \end{bmatrix}$$

$$[P_1] = -[B_1]^{-1}[A_1] = -\begin{bmatrix} \frac{1}{2} & \frac{1}{2} \\ \frac{1}{2} & -\frac{1}{2} \end{bmatrix}\begin{bmatrix} 1 & -1 \\ -1 & 2 \end{bmatrix} = \begin{bmatrix} 0 & -\frac{1}{2} \\ -1 & \frac{3}{2} \end{bmatrix}$$

$$\{q_1\} = [B_1]^{-1}\{g_1\} = \begin{bmatrix} \frac{1}{2} & \frac{1}{2} \\ \frac{1}{2} & -\frac{1}{2} \end{bmatrix}\begin{Bmatrix} 2 \\ 0 \end{Bmatrix} = \begin{Bmatrix} 1 \\ 1 \end{Bmatrix}$$

$$\{q_2\} = ([B_2] + [C_2]\,[P_1])^{-1}(\{g_2\} - [C_2]q_1\})$$

$$= \left(\begin{bmatrix} 1 & 1 \\ 2 & -2 \end{bmatrix} + \begin{bmatrix} 4 & 4 \\ 2 & 1 \end{bmatrix}\begin{bmatrix} 0 & -\frac{1}{2} \\ -1 & \frac{3}{2} \end{bmatrix}\right)^{-1}\left(\begin{Bmatrix} 11 \\ 2 \end{Bmatrix} - \begin{bmatrix} 4 & 4 \\ 2 & 1 \end{bmatrix}\begin{Bmatrix} 1 \\ 11 \end{Bmatrix}\right)$$

$$= \begin{bmatrix} -3 & 5 \\ 1 & -\frac{3}{2} \end{bmatrix}^{-1}\begin{Bmatrix} 3 \\ -1 \end{Bmatrix}$$

$$\{q_2\} = \begin{bmatrix} 3 & 10 \\ 2 & 6 \end{bmatrix}\begin{Bmatrix} 3 \\ -1 \end{Bmatrix} = \begin{Bmatrix} -1 \\ 0 \end{Bmatrix} = \{z_2\}$$

$$\{z_1\} = [P_1]\,\{z_2\} + \{q_1\} = \begin{bmatrix} 0 & -\frac{1}{2} \\ -1 & \frac{3}{2} \end{bmatrix}\begin{Bmatrix} -1 \\ 0 \end{Bmatrix} + \begin{Bmatrix} 1 \\ 1 \end{Bmatrix} = \begin{Bmatrix} 1 \\ 2 \end{Bmatrix}$$

Hence the solution is: $x_1 = 1$, $x_2 = 2$, $x_3 = -1$ and $x_4 = 0$.

Example 4.11

Use Potters' method to solve the set of simultaneous equations given by

$$5x_1 - 4x_2 + x_3 = 1$$

$$-4x_1 + 6x_2 - 4x_3 + x_4 = 2$$

$$x_1 - 4x_2 + 6x_3 - 4x_4 + x_5 = 3$$

$$x_2 - 4x_3 + 6x_4 - 4x_5 = 2$$

$$x_3 - 4x_4 + 5x_5 = 1$$

Solution

The given set of equations can be written in the matrix form.

$$\begin{bmatrix} 5 & -4 & 1 & 0 & 0 \\ -4 & 6 & -4 & 1 & 0 \\ 1 & -4 & 6 & -4 & 1 \\ 0 & 1 & -4 & 6 & -4 \\ 0 & 0 & 1 & -4 & 5 \end{bmatrix} \begin{Bmatrix} x_1 \\ x_2 \\ x_3 \\ x_4 \\ x_5 \end{Bmatrix} = \begin{Bmatrix} 1.0 \\ 2.0 \\ 3.0 \\ 2.0 \\ 1.0 \end{Bmatrix}$$

Here the coefficient matrix is a symmetric one.
Forming into groups.

$$[B_1] = \begin{bmatrix} 5 & -4 \\ -4 & 6 \end{bmatrix}, [A_1] = \begin{bmatrix} 1 & 0 \\ -4 & 1 \end{bmatrix}, \{z_1\} = \begin{Bmatrix} x_1 \\ x_2 \end{Bmatrix}, \{g_1\} = \begin{Bmatrix} 1.0 \\ 2.0 \end{Bmatrix}$$

$$[C_2] = \begin{bmatrix} 1 & -4 \\ 0 & 1 \end{bmatrix}, [B_2] = \begin{bmatrix} 6 & -4 \\ -4 & 6 \end{bmatrix}, [A_2] = \begin{bmatrix} 1 \\ -4 \end{bmatrix}, \{z_2\} = \begin{Bmatrix} x_3 \\ x_4 \end{Bmatrix},$$

$$\{g_2\} = \begin{Bmatrix} 3 \\ 2 \end{Bmatrix}$$

$$[C_3] = [1 - 4]\,, [B_3] = [5]\,, [A_3] = 0\,, \{z_3\} = \{x_5\}\,, \{g_3\} = \{1\}$$

$$[B_1]^{-1} = \frac{1}{14}\begin{bmatrix} 6 & 4 \\ 4 & 5 \end{bmatrix}$$

$$[P_1] = -[B_1]^{-1}[A_1] = -\frac{1}{14}\begin{bmatrix} 6 & 4 \\ 4 & 5 \end{bmatrix}\begin{bmatrix} 1 & 0 \\ -4 & 1 \end{bmatrix} = -\frac{1}{14}\begin{bmatrix} -10 & 4 \\ -16 & 5 \end{bmatrix}$$

$$\{q_1\} = [B_1]^{-1}\{g_1\} = \frac{1}{14}\begin{bmatrix} 6 & 4 \\ 4 & 5 \end{bmatrix}\begin{Bmatrix} 1 \\ 2 \end{Bmatrix} = \frac{1}{14}\begin{bmatrix} 14 \\ 14 \end{bmatrix} = \begin{Bmatrix} 1 \\ 1 \end{Bmatrix}$$

$$\{q_2\} = ([B_2] + [C_2]\,[P_1])^{-1}\,(\{g_2\} - [C_2]\,\{q_1\})$$

$$= \left(\begin{bmatrix} 6 & -4 \\ -4 & 6 \end{bmatrix} + \begin{bmatrix} 1 & -4 \\ 0 & 1 \end{bmatrix}\begin{bmatrix} \frac{10}{14} & -\frac{4}{14} \\ \frac{16}{14} & -\frac{5}{14} \end{bmatrix}\right)^{-1}\left(\begin{Bmatrix} 3 \\ 2 \end{Bmatrix} - \begin{bmatrix} 1 & -4 \\ 0 & 1 \end{bmatrix}\begin{Bmatrix} 1 \\ 1 \end{Bmatrix}\right)$$

$$= \left(\begin{bmatrix} 6 & -4 \\ -4 & 6 \end{bmatrix} + \begin{bmatrix} -\frac{27}{7} & \frac{8}{7} \\ \frac{8}{7} & -\frac{5}{14} \end{bmatrix}\right)^{-1}\left(\begin{Bmatrix} 3 \\ 2 \end{Bmatrix} - \begin{Bmatrix} -3 \\ 1 \end{Bmatrix}\right)$$

$$= \begin{bmatrix} \frac{15}{7} & -\frac{20}{7} \\ -\frac{20}{7} & \frac{79}{14} \end{bmatrix}^{-1}\begin{Bmatrix} 6 \\ 1 \end{Bmatrix} = \frac{1}{55}\begin{Bmatrix} 514 \\ 270 \end{Bmatrix}$$

$$[P_2] = -\frac{1}{55}\begin{bmatrix} -81 \\ -80 \end{bmatrix} = \frac{1}{55}\begin{Bmatrix} 81 \\ 80 \end{Bmatrix}$$

$$\{q_3\} = ([B_3] + [C_2]\,[P_2])^{-1}\,(\{g_3 - [C_3]\,\{q_2\})$$

$$= \left([15] + \frac{1}{55}[-239]\right)^{-1}\left((1) + \frac{566}{55}\right)$$

$$= \left(\frac{36}{55}\right)^{-1}\left(\frac{621}{55}\right) = \frac{621}{36} = 17.25$$

$$\{z_3\} = \{q_3\} = 17.25 = \{x_5\}$$

$$\{z_2\} = [P_2]\,\{z_3\} + \{q_2\}$$

$$= \frac{1}{55}\begin{Bmatrix} 81 \\ 80 \end{Bmatrix}(17.250 + \frac{1}{55}\begin{Bmatrix} 514 \\ 270 \end{Bmatrix} = \begin{Bmatrix} 34.75 \\ 30.00 \end{Bmatrix} = \begin{Bmatrix} x_3 \\ x_4 \end{Bmatrix}$$

$$\{z_1\} = [P_1]\,\{z_2\} + q_1$$

$$= \frac{1}{14}\begin{bmatrix} 10 & -4 \\ 16 & -5 \end{bmatrix}\begin{Bmatrix} 34.75 \\ 30.00 \end{Bmatrix} + \begin{Bmatrix} 1 \\ 1 \end{Bmatrix} = \begin{Bmatrix} 17.25 \\ 30.00 \end{Bmatrix} = \begin{Bmatrix} x_1 \\ x_2 \end{Bmatrix}$$

Therefore $x_1 = 17.25, x_2 = 30.00, x_3 = 34.75, x_4 = 30.00$ and $x_5 = 17.25$.

4.8 JACOBI'S METHOD

This is an iterative technique solving with an assumed solution vector and successive refinement by iteration. The system of equations for consideration is

$$\begin{array}{ccccccccccc}
a_{11}x_1 & + & a_{12}x_2 & + & a_{13}x_3 & & \ldots\ldots\ldots\ldots & + & a_{1n}x_n & = & b_1 \\
a_{21}x_1 & + & a_{22}x_2 & & a_{23}x_3 & & \ldots\ldots\ldots\ldots & + & a_{2n}x_n & = & b_2 \\
\ldots & & \ldots & & \ldots & & \ldots & & \ldots & & \ldots \\
\ldots & & \ldots & & \ldots & & \ldots & & \ldots & & \ldots \\
a_{i1}x_1 & + & a_{i2}x_2 & + & a_{i3}x_3 & + & \ldots\ldots\ldots\ldots & + & a_{in}x_n & = & b_i \\
\ldots & & \ldots & & \ldots & & \ldots & & \ldots & & \\
a_{n1}x_1 & + & a_{n2}x_2 & + & a_{n3}x_3 & + & \ldots\ldots\ldots\ldots & + & a_{nn}x_n & = & b_n
\end{array} \tag{4.30}$$

Rewriting the above equations

$$x_1 = (b_1 - a_{12}x_2 - a_{13}x_3 - \ldots\ldots\ldots\ldots - a_{1n}x_n)/a_{11}$$

$$x_2 = (b_2 - a_{21}x_1 - a_{23}x_3 - \ldots\ldots\ldots\ldots - a_{2n}x_n)/a_{22}$$

$$\ldots \quad \ldots \quad \ldots \quad \ldots \quad \ldots \quad \ldots \quad \ldots$$

$$\ldots \quad \ldots \quad \ldots \quad \ldots \quad \ldots \quad \ldots$$

$$x_i = (b_i - a_{i1}x_1 - a_{i2}x_2 ... a_{ii-1}n_{i-1} - a_{ii+1}x_{i+1} ... a_{in}x_n)/a_{ii}$$

$$\dots \quad \dots \quad \dots \quad \dots \quad \dots \quad \dots\dots\dots$$

$$x_n = (b_n - a_{n1}x_1 - a_{n2}x_2 ... a_{nn-1}x_{n-1})/a_{nn} \tag{4.31}$$

This procedure is valid only if all the diagonal elements are non zero. The equations are to be rearranged suitably to avoid the non zero elements in the main diagonal.

Substituting the values of x_i^r' at any stage in the iterative process on the right hand side of equations (4.31) gives the values to the next stage, i.e. x_i^{r+1} . In other words, the scheme is given by the system of equations (4.32) with a superscript r on the right side and a superscript $r + 1$ on the left hand side.
Rewriting the equations.

$$x_1^{r+1} = (b_1 - a_{12}x_2^r - a_{13}x_3^r - \dots - a_{1n}x_n^r)/a_{11}$$

$$x_2^{r+1} = (b_2 - a_{21}x_1^r - a_{23}x_3^r - \dots - a_{2n}x_n^r)/a_{22}$$

$$\dots \quad \dots \quad \dots \quad \dots \quad \dots \quad \dots \quad \dots$$

$$x_i^{r+1} = (b_i - a_{i1}x_i^r - a_{i2}x_2^r \dots - a_{ii-1}n_{i-1}^r - a_{ii+1}n_{i+1}^r \dots a_{in}x_n^r)/a_{ii}$$

$$\dots \quad \dots \quad \dots \quad \dots \quad \dots \quad \dots \quad \dots \quad \dots \quad \dots \quad \dots$$

$$x_n^{r+1} = (b_n - a_{n1}x_1^r - a_{n2}x_2^r - \dots \dots a_{n,n-1}x_{n-1}^r)/a_{nn} \tag{4.32}$$

The sequence x^0, x^1, x^2, ... generated by the equations of (4.32) gives a sequence which converges to the solutions vector x which satisfies the set of equations given in Eq. (4.30), i.e. $[A]\{x\} = \{b\}$.
Eq. (4.32) in the matrix form is as follows

$$x^{r+1} = \{V\} + [B]\{x\}^r \tag{4.33}$$

where

$$\{V\} = \begin{Bmatrix} \dfrac{b_1}{a_{11}} \\ \dfrac{b_2}{a_{22}} \\ \dots \\ \dfrac{b_i}{a_{ii}} \\ \dots \\ \dfrac{b_n}{a_{nn}} \end{Bmatrix}$$

and

$$[B] = \begin{bmatrix} 0 & a_{12}/a_{11} & a_{13}/a_{11} & \cdots & \cdots & \cdots & a_{1n}/a_{11} \\ a_{21}/a_{22} & 0 & a_{23}/a_{22} & \cdots & \cdots & \cdots & a_{2n}/a_{22} \\ \cdots\cdots & \cdots\cdots & \cdots\cdots & \cdots & \cdots & \cdots & \cdots\cdots \\ a_{i1}/a_{ii} & a_{i2}/a_{ii} & \cdots & 0 & a_{ii+1}/a_{ii} & \cdots & a_{ii}/a_{nn} \\ \cdots\cdots & \cdots\cdots & \cdots\cdots & \cdots & \cdots\cdots & \cdots & \cdots\cdots \\ a_{n1}/a_{nn} & \cdots & \cdots & \cdots & a_{n,n-1}/a_{nn} & & 0 \end{bmatrix}$$

The system of equations given in Eq. (4.30) can be written in the form

$$\{x\} = \{v\} + [B]\{x\} \tag{4.34}$$

Now we can construct expressions for $x^{(1)} \ldots x^{(2)} \ldots.$ in terms of $x^{(0)}$

$$\{x\}^1 = \{v\} + [B]x^0$$

$$\{x\}^2 = \{v\} + [B]x^1$$

$$= \{v\} + [B]\left(\{v\} + [B]x^{(0)}\right)$$

$$= \{v\} + [B]\{v\} + [B]^2x^0$$

$$\{x\}^3 = \{v\} + [B]\{x\}^{(2)}$$

$$= \{v\} + [B]\left(\{v\} + [B]\{v\} + [B]^2x^{(0)}\right)$$

$$= \{v\} + [B]\{v\} + [B]^2\{v\} + [B]^3x^0$$

Generalizing

$$x^{(r)} = \{v\} + [B]\{v\} + [B]^2\{v\} + \ldots [B]^{r-1}\{v\} + [B]^r x^{(0)}$$

Finally

$$x^{(r)} = ([I] + [B] + [B]^2 + [B]^3 \ldots [B]^{r-1})\{v\} + [B]^{(r)}x^{(0)} \tag{4.35}$$

Here we notice that ($[I] + [B] + [B]^2 + [B]^3 \ldots [B]^{r-1}$) is a matrix geometric progression. It is possible to obtain the sum of r terms of the above expressions.
Let us denote

$$s_r = [I] + [B] + [B]^2 + [B]^3 \ldots [B]^{r-1}$$

$$= ([I] - [B]^r)([I] - [B])^{-1}$$

provided ($[I] - [B]$) is non-singular. Here we see that as $r \to \infty$ the limit of the sum exists if $[B]^r \to 0$, in this case $s_r \to s = ([I] - [B])^{-1}$.
Hence in Eq. (4.35) x^r will converge to the vector $\{x\}$ provided $[B]^r \to 0$ as $r \to \infty$. Then the vector $\{x\}$ can be written as

$$\{x\} = ([I] - [B])^{-1}\{v\}$$

This means that $([I] - [B])\{x\} = \{v\}$ and hence $\{x\} = [B]\{x\} + \{v\}$. This is just the equation (4.34).

Example 4.12

Use the Jacobi iterative scheme to obtain the solutions of the system of equations correct to three decimal places.

$$x + 2y + z = 0$$

$$3x + y - z = 0$$

$$x - y + 4z = 3$$

Solution

Rearrange the equations in such a way that all the diagonal terms are dominant.

$$3x + y - z = 0$$

$$x + 2y + z = 0$$

$$x - y + 4z = 3$$

Computing for x, y and z we get

$$x = (z - y)/3$$

$$y = (-x - z)/2$$

$$z = (3 + y - x)/4$$

Iterative equations can be written as

$$x^{(r+1)} = (z^{(r)} - y^{(r)})/3$$

$$y^{(r+1)} = (-x^{(r)} - z^{(r)})/2$$

$$z^{(r+1)} = (3 - x^{(r)} + y^{(r)})/4$$

Initial vector is not specified in the problem. Hence we choose

$$x^{(0)} = y^{(0)} = z^{(0)} = 1$$

Then the first iteration gives

$$x^{(1)} = (z^{(0)} - y^{(0)})/3 = (1 - 1)/3 = 0$$

$$y^{(1)} = (-x^{(0)} - z^{(0)})/2 = (-1 - 1)/2 = -1.0$$

$$z^{(1)} = (3 - x^{(0)} + y^{(0)})/4 = (3 - 1 + 1)/4 = 0.750$$

similarly second iteration yields

$$x^{(2)} = (z^{(1)} - y^{(1)})/3 = (0.75 + 1.0)/3 = 0.5833$$

$$y^{(2)} = (-x^{(1)} - z^{(1)})/2 = (-0 - 0.75)/2 = -0.3750$$

$$z^{(2)} = (3 - x^{(1)} + y^{(1)})/4 = (3 - 0 - 1)/4 = 0.500$$

Subsequent iterations result in the following

$x^{(3)} = 0.29167$	$y^{(3)} = -0.47917$	$z^{(3)} = 0.51042$
$x^{(4)} = 0.32986$	$y^{(4)} = -0.40104$	$z^{(4)} = 0.57862$
$x^{(5)} = 0.32595$	$y^{(5)} = -0.45334$	$z^{(5)} = 0.56728$
$x^{(6)} = 0.34021$	$y^{(6)} = -0.44662$	$z^{(6)} = 0.55329$
$x^{(7)} = 0.3333$	$y^{(7)} = -0.44675$	$z^{(7)} = 0.55498$
$x^{(8)} = 0.33391$	$y^{(8)} = -0.44414$	$z^{(8)} = 0.55498$
$x^{(9)} = 0.33304$	$y^{(9)} = -0.44445$	$z^{(9)} = 0.5555$

so to three decimal places the approximate solution

$$x = 0.333 \qquad y = -0.444 \qquad z = 0.555$$

4.9 GAUSS-SEIDEL METHOD

Gauss-Seidel method is also an iterative solution procedure which is an improved version of Jocobi's method. The vector x^{r+1} is an improvement on vector x^r, in an iterative scheme. Jacobi's method calculates x_1^{r+1} in the first equation which can be used in place of x_1^r in the second and subsequent equations. Similarly, x_2^{r+1} is calculated in the second equation and so could be used in place of x_2^r in the third and subsequent equations. In general, x_i^{r+1} could replace x_i^r in the $(i+1)^{\text{th}}$ and subsequent equations. This improvement over Jacobi's method gives Gauss-Seidel iterative scheme.

$$x_1^{(r+1)} = (b_1 - a_{12}x_2^r - a_{13}x_3^r - \ldots - a_{1n}x_n^r)/a_{11}$$

$$x_2^{(r+1)} = (b_2 - a_{21}x_1^{(r+1)} - a_{23}x_3^{(r)} - \ldots - a_{2n}x_n^{(r)})/a_{22}$$

$$x_3^{(r+1)} = (b_3 - a_{31}x_1^{(r+1)} - a_{32}x_2^{(r+1)} - a_{34}x_4^{(r)} - \ldots - a_{3n}x_n^{(r)})/a_{33}$$

$$\ldots \quad \ldots \quad \ldots \quad \ldots \quad \ldots \quad \ldots$$

$$\ldots \quad \ldots \quad \ldots \quad \ldots \quad \ldots \quad \ldots$$

$$x_i^{(r+1)} = (b_i - a_{i1}x_1^{(r+1)} - \ldots - a_{i,i-1}x_{i-1}^{(r+1)} - a_{i,i+1}x_{i+1}^{(r)} - \ldots - a_{in}x_n^{(r)})/a_{ii}$$

$$\ldots \quad \ldots \quad \ldots \quad \ldots \quad \ldots \quad \ldots$$

$$x_n^{(r+1)} = (b_n - a_{n1}x_1^{(r+1)} - a_{n2}x_2^{(r+1)} - \ldots \quad \ldots - a_{n,n-1}x_{n-1}^{(r+1)})/a_{nn} \tag{4.36}$$

Matrix form of the above system of equations can be written as

$$\{x\}^{(r+1)} = \{v\} + [B_L]\{x\}^{(r+1)} + [B_U]\{x\}^{(r)} \tag{4.37}$$

where

$$\{V\} = \begin{Bmatrix} \dfrac{b_1}{a_{11}} \\ \dfrac{b_2}{a_{22}} \\ \ldots. \\ \ldots. \\ \ldots. \\ \dfrac{b_n}{a_{nn}} \end{Bmatrix}$$

$$[B_L] = \begin{bmatrix} 0 & 0 & 0 & \cdots & 0 \\ \frac{a_{21}}{a_{22}} & 0 & 0 & \cdots & 0 \\ \frac{a_{31}}{a_{33}} & \frac{a_{32}}{a_{33}} & 0 & \cdots & 0 \\ \frac{a_{41}}{a_{44}} & \frac{a_{42}}{a_{44}} & \frac{a_{43}}{a_{44}} & \cdots & 0 \\ \cdots & \cdots & \cdots & \cdots & \cdots \\ \cdots & \cdots & \cdots & \cdots & \cdots \\ \frac{a_{n1}}{a_{nn}} & \frac{a_{n2}}{a_{nn}} & \cdots & \frac{a_{n,n-1}}{a_{nn}} & 0 \end{bmatrix}$$

$$[B_U] = \left\{ \begin{matrix} 0 & \frac{a_{12}}{a_{11}} & \frac{a_{13}}{a_{11}} & \cdots & \cdots & \frac{a_{1n}}{a_{11}} \\ 0 & 0 & \frac{a_{23}}{a_{22}} & \cdots & \cdots & \frac{a_{2n}}{a_{22}} \\ 0 & 0 & 0 & \frac{a_{34}}{a_{33}} & \cdots & \frac{a_{3n}}{a_{33}} \\ \cdots & \cdots & \cdots & \cdots & \cdots & \cdots \\ \cdots & \cdots & \cdots & \cdots & \cdots & \cdots \\ 0 & 0 & \cdots & \cdots & 0 & \frac{a_{n-1,n}}{a_{n-1,n-1}} \\ 0 & 0 & \cdots & 0 & \cdots & 0 \end{matrix} \right\}$$

Vector $\{v\}$ is the same as in Jacobi's method; $[B_L]$ and $[B_U]$ are the lower and upper triangular matrices respectively of Jocobi's matrix $[B]$, i.e.

$$[B] = [B_L] + [B_U]$$

Rearranging the equation

$$\{x\}^{(r+1)} - [B_L]\,\{x\}^{(r+1)} = \{v\} + [B_U]\,\{x\}^r \tag{4.38}$$

This can be rewritten as

$$\{x\}^{(r+1)} = ([I] - [B_L])^{-1}\,\{v\} + ([I] - [B_L])^{-1}\,[B_U]\,\{x\}^{(r)} \tag{4.39}$$

The convergence of the solution given by equation (4.39) is assured if $\{([I] - [B_L])^{-1}\,[B_u]\}^r \to 0$. The convergence rate of this method is about twice that of Jacobi's. However, it should be cautioned here that there are situations in which Jacobi's method converges but the Gauss-Seidel does not. But for both the methods the convergence criteria is the same as given in Jacobi's method.

Example 4.13

Using the Gauss-Seidel method solve the system of equations correct to three decimal places.

$$x + 2y + z = 0$$

$$3x + y - z = 0$$

$$x - y + 4z = 3$$

Solution

Rearranging the equations to give dominant diagonal elements, we have

$$3x + y - z = 0$$

$$x + 2y + z = 0$$

$$x - y + 4z = 3$$

This can be rewritten as

$$x = (z - y)/3$$

$$y = -(x + z)/2$$

$$z = (3 - x + y)/4$$

Writing in the torm of Gauss-Seidel iterative scheme,

$$x^{(r+1)} = (z^{(r)} - y^{(r)})/3$$

$$y^{(r+1)} = -(x^{(r+1)} + z^{(r)})/2$$

$$z^{(r+1)} = (3 - x^{(r+1)} + y^{(r+1)})/4$$

We start with the initial values

$$x^{(0)} = y^{(0)} = z^{(0)} = 1$$

Then the iterative scheme gives

$$x^{(1)} = (z^{(0)} - Y^{(0)})/3 = (1 - 1)/3 = 0$$

$$y^{(1)} = (-x^{(1)} - z^{(0)})/2 = (0 - 1)/2 = -0.5$$

$$z^{(1)} = (3 - x^{(1)} + y^{(1)})/4 = (3 - 0 - 0.5)/4 = 0.625$$

Second iteration gives

$$x^{(2)} = (z^{(1)} - y^{(1)})/3 = (0.625 + 0.5)/3 = 0.375$$

$$y^{(2)} = (-x^{(2)} - z^{(1)})/2 = (-0.375 - 0.625)/2 = -0.50$$

$$z^{(2)} = (3 - x^{(2)} + y^{(2)})/4 = (3 - 0.375 - 0.5)/4 = 0.53125$$

Subsequent iterations result in

$x^{(3)} = 0.34375$ $\quad$ $y^{(3)} = -0.4375$ $\quad$ $z^{(3)} = 0.55469$

$x^{(4)} = 0.33075$ $\quad$ $y^{(4)} = -0.44271$ $\quad$ $z^{(4)} = 0.55664$

$x^{(5)} = 0.33312$ $\quad$ $y^{(5)} = -0.44488$ $\quad$ $z^{(5)} = 0.5555$

$x^{(6)} = 0.33346$ $\quad$ $y^{(6)} = -0.44448$ $\quad$ $z^{(6)} = 0.55552$

Hence the approximate solution is as follows

$$x = 0.333 \qquad y = -0.444 \qquad z = 0.555$$

Comparing these results with those of Example 4.12 it can be seen that the rate of convergence is faster in Gauss-Seidel method.

4.10 THE GIVENS FACTORISATION

The Givens method transforms the matrix $[A]$ into upper triangular form by using the rotation matrices. Matrix $[A]$ is premultiplied by a rotation matrix to obtain

$$[P]^T [A] = [S] \tag{4.40}$$

where

$$[P]^T = [P_{n,n-1}]^T \ldots ([P_{n,2}]^T [P_{n-1,2}]^T \ldots [P_{3,2}]^T) \ldots$$

$$\ldots ([P_{n,1}]^T [P_{n-1,1}]^T \ldots [P_{2,1}]^T) \tag{4.41}$$

is the rotation matrix and $[S]$ is an upper triangular matrix. Then the solution to the system of equations $[A]\,\{x\} = \{b\}$ is obtained using the factorisations of $[A]$ by the equation

$$[A] = [P]\,[S] \tag{4.42}$$

This is because $P^{-1} = P^T$. It is also required to reduce the vector $\{b\}$ as

$$[P]\,\{v\} = \{b\} \tag{4.43}$$

From which

$$\{v\} = [P]^T \{b\} \tag{4.44}$$

and finally obtain the solution by back substitution

$$[S]\,\{v\} = \{v\} \tag{4.45}$$

A rotation matrices $[P_{j,i}]^T$ is to be evaluated such that it must reduce to zero the elements in positions (j, i) where $j > i$ of the matrix. A typical matrix is

$$\begin{array}{cl} & \begin{array}{cccccc} & & i\text{th column} & & j\text{th column} & \end{array} \\ [P_{j,i}]^T = \left[\begin{array}{cccccc} 1 & \ldots\ldots & \ldots\ldots & \ldots\ldots & \ldots\ldots & \\ \ldots\ldots & \ldots\ldots & \ldots\ldots & \ldots\ldots & \ldots\ldots & \ldots\ldots \\ \ldots\ldots & \ldots\ldots & \cos\theta & \ldots\ldots & \sin\theta & \ldots \\ \ldots\ldots & \ldots\ldots & \ldots\ldots & \ldots\ldots & \ldots\ldots & \ldots\ldots \\ \ldots\ldots & \ldots\ldots & -\sin\theta & \ldots\ldots & \cos\theta & \ldots \\ \ldots\ldots & \ldots\ldots & \ldots\ldots & \ldots\ldots & \ldots\ldots & \ldots\ldots \\ \ldots\ldots & \ldots\ldots & \ldots\ldots & \ldots\ldots & \ldots\ldots & 1 \end{array}\right] & \begin{array}{l} \\ \\ i\text{th row} \\ \\ j\text{th row} \\ \\ \\ \end{array} \end{array} \tag{4.46}$$

where θ is so chosen that the element (j, i) is to reduce to zero. The order in which the elements of the matrix are reduced to zero are given below.

$$\begin{array}{ll} i = 1 & j = 2, 3, \ldots n \\ i = 2 & j = 3, 4, \ldots n \\ \ldots & \ldots\ldots \\ i = n - 1 & j = n \end{array}$$

Let us consider the construction of the matrix $[P_{2,l}]^T$

By taking the matrix product $[\tilde{A}] = [P_{2,1}]^T [A]$, the element (2, 1) in the original matrix is zero i.e.

$$[\bar{A}] = \begin{bmatrix} \cos\theta & \sin\theta & & \\ -\sin\theta & \cos\theta & & \\ & & 1 & \\ & & & 1 \end{bmatrix} \begin{bmatrix} a_{11} & a_{12} & a_{13} & \cdots \\ a_{21} & a_{22} & a_{23} & \cdots \\ a_{31} & a_{32} & a_{33} & \cdots \\ \cdot & \cdot & \cdot & \\ \cdot & \cdot & \cdot & \\ \cdot & \cdot & \cdot & \cdots \end{bmatrix}$$

$$= \begin{bmatrix} \tilde{a}_{11} & \tilde{a}_{12} & \tilde{a}_{13} & \cdots \\ 0 & \tilde{a}_{22} & \tilde{a}_{23} & \cdots \\ \tilde{a}_{31} & \tilde{a}_{32} & \tilde{a}_{33} & \cdots \\ \cdots & \cdots & \cdots & \cdots \\ \cdots & \cdots & \cdots & \cdots \end{bmatrix} \tag{4.47}$$

Now the angle θ can be obtained from the equation

$$-a_{11}\sin\theta + a_{21}\cos\theta = 0 \tag{4.48}$$

Hence, $$\cos\theta = \frac{a_{11}}{(a_{11}^2 + a_{21}^2)^{1/2}};\ \sin\theta = \frac{a_{21}}{(a_{11}^2 + a_{21}^2)^{1/2}} \tag{4.49}$$

If $a_{11}^2 + a_{21}^2 = 0$ it means that there is no transformation

i.e. $\cos\theta = 1, \sin\theta = 0$

Similarly the other rotation matrices and the required products are to be evaluated. The procedure can be explained with help of the following example.

Example 4.14

Use the Givens factorisation to solve the system of equations

$$x_1 + x_2 + x_3 - x_4 = 2$$

$$4x_1 + 4x_2 + x_3 + x_4 = 11$$

$$x_1 - x_2 - x_3 + 2x_4 = 0$$

$$2x_1 + x_2 + 2x_3 - 2x_4 = 2$$

Solution

In the matrix form

$$\begin{bmatrix} 1 & 1 & 1 & -1 \\ 4 & 4 & 1 & 1 \\ 1 & -1 & -1 & 2 \\ 2 & 1 & 2 & -2 \end{bmatrix} \begin{Bmatrix} x_1 \\ x_2 \\ x_3 \\ x_4 \end{Bmatrix} = \begin{Bmatrix} 2 \\ 11 \\ 0 \\ 2 \end{Bmatrix}$$

By the Givens method, for $i = 1, j = 2$

$$\cos\theta = \frac{a_{11}}{\sqrt{a_{11}^2 + a_{21}^2}} = \frac{1}{\sqrt{1^2+4^2}} = \frac{1}{\sqrt{17}} = 0.242536$$

$$\sin\theta = \frac{a_{21}}{\sqrt{a_{11}^2 + a_{21}^2}} = \frac{4}{\sqrt{1^2+4^2}} = \frac{4}{\sqrt{17}} = 0.970413$$

$$[P_{2,1}]^T = \begin{bmatrix} \cos\theta & \sin\theta & 0 & 0 \\ -\sin\theta & \cos\theta & 0 & 0 \\ 0 & 0 & 1 & 0 \\ 0 & 0 & 0 & 1 \end{bmatrix} = \begin{bmatrix} 0.242536 & 0.970143 & 0 & 0 \\ -0.970143 & 0.242536 & 0 & 0 \\ 0 & 0 & 1 & 0 \\ 0 & 0 & 0 & 1 \end{bmatrix}$$

$$[P_{2,1}]^T \cdot [A] = \begin{bmatrix} 0.242536 & 0.970143 & 0 & 0 \\ -0.970143 & 0.242536 & 0 & 0 \\ 0 & 0 & 1 & 0 \\ 0 & 0 & 0 & 1 \end{bmatrix} \begin{bmatrix} 1 & 1 & 1 & -1 \\ 4 & 4 & 1 & 1 \\ 1 & -1 & -1 & 2 \\ 2 & 1 & 2 & -2 \end{bmatrix}$$

$$= \begin{bmatrix} 4.123108 & 4.123108 & 1.212679 & 0.727607 \\ 0 & 0 & -0.727607 & 1.212679 \\ 1 & -1 & -1 & 2 \\ 2 & 1 & 2 & -2 \end{bmatrix}$$

$$[P_{2,1}]^T [b] = \begin{bmatrix} 0.242536 & 0.970143 & 0 & 0 \\ -0.970143 & 0.242536 & 0 & 0 \\ 0 & 0 & 1 & 0 \\ 0 & 0 & 0 & 1 \end{bmatrix} \begin{Bmatrix} 2 \\ 11 \\ 0 \\ 2 \end{Bmatrix} = \begin{Bmatrix} 11.156645 \\ 0.72761 \\ 0 \\ 2 \end{Bmatrix}$$

For $i = 1, j = 3$

$$\cos\theta = \frac{a_{11}^1}{\sqrt{a_{11}^{12} + a_{31}^{12}}} = \frac{4.123108}{\sqrt{4.123108^2 + 1^2}} = 0.971825$$

$$\sin\theta = \frac{a_{31}}{\sqrt{a_{11}^{12} + a_{31}^{12}}} = \frac{1}{\sqrt{4.123108^2 + 1^2}} = 0.235702$$

$$[P_{3,1}]^T = \begin{bmatrix} 0.971825 & 0 & 0.235702 & 0 \\ 0 & 1 & 0 & 0 \\ -0.235702 & 0 & 0.971825 & 0 \\ 0 & 0 & 0 & 1 \end{bmatrix}$$

$$[P_{3,1}]^T [P_{2,1}]^T [A] = \begin{bmatrix} 0.971825 & 0 & 0.235702 & 0 \\ 0 & 1 & 0 & 0 \\ -0.235702 & 0 & 0.971825 & 0 \\ 0 & 0 & 0 & 1 \end{bmatrix} \times$$

$$\begin{bmatrix} 4.123108 & 4.123108 & 1.212679 & 0.72760 \\ 0 & 0 & -0.727607 & 1.212671 \\ 1 & -1 & -1 & 2 \\ 2 & 1 & 2 & -2 \end{bmatrix}$$

$$= \begin{bmatrix} 4.123108 & 3.771237 & 0.942810 & 1.78511 \\ 0 & 0 & -0.727607 & 1.212679 \\ 0 & -1.943650 & -1.257561 & 1.772152 \\ 2 & 1 & 2 & -2 \end{bmatrix}$$

$$[P_{3,1}]^T [P_{2,1}] [b] = \begin{bmatrix} 0.971825 & 0 & 0.235702 & 0 \\ 0 & 1 & 0 & 0 \\ -0.235702 & 0 & 0.971825 & 0 \\ 0 & 0 & 0 & 1 \end{bmatrix} \begin{Bmatrix} 11.156645 \\ 0.72761 \\ 0 \\ 2 \end{Bmatrix} = \begin{Bmatrix} 10.842307 \\ 0.72761 \\ -2.629644 \\ 2.0 \end{Bmatrix}$$

For $i = 1, j = 4$

$$\cos\theta = \frac{a_{11}}{\sqrt{a_{11}^2 + a_{41}^2}} = \frac{4.123108}{\sqrt{4.123108^2 + 2^2}} = 0.904534$$

$$\sin\theta = \frac{a_{41}}{\sqrt{a_{11}^2 + a_{41}^2}} = \frac{2}{\sqrt{4.123108^2 + 2^2}} = 0.426401$$

$$[P_{4,1}]^T [P_{3,1}]^T [P_{2,1}]^T [A] = \begin{bmatrix} 0.904534 & 0 & 0 & 0.426401 \\ 0 & 1 & 0 & 0 \\ 0 & 0 & 1 & 0 \\ -0.426401 & 0 & 0 & 0.904534 \end{bmatrix}$$

$$\begin{bmatrix} 4.123108 & 3.771237 & 0.942810 & 1.78511 \\ 0 & 0 & -0.727607 & 1.212679 \\ 0 & -1.94365 & -1.257561 & 1.772152 \\ 2 & 1 & 2 & -2 \end{bmatrix}$$

$$= \begin{bmatrix} 4.69045 & 3.837613 & 1.705606 & 0.213201 \\ 0 & 0 & -0.727607 & 1.212679 \\ 0 & -1.943650 & -1.257656 & 1.772152 \\ 0 & -0.703525 & 1.407053 & -2.311586 \end{bmatrix}$$

$$[P_{4,1}]^T [P_{3,1}]^T [P_{2,1}]^T [b] = \begin{bmatrix} 0.904534 & 0 & 0 & 0.426401 \\ 0 & 1 & 0 & 0 \\ 0 & 0 & 1 & 0 \\ -0.424601 & 0 & 0 & 0.904534 \end{bmatrix} \begin{Bmatrix} 10.842307 \\ 0.72761 \\ -9.629644 \\ 2.0 \end{Bmatrix} = \begin{Bmatrix} 10.660037 \\ 0.72761 \\ -2.629644 \\ -2.814103 \end{Bmatrix}$$

For $i = 2, j = 3$

$$\cos\theta = \frac{a_{22}}{\sqrt{a_{22}^2 + a_{32}^2}} = \frac{0}{\sqrt{0 + (-1.943650)^2}} = 0$$

$$\sin\theta = \frac{a_{32}}{\sqrt{a_{22}^2 + a_{32}^2}} = \frac{1.94365}{\sqrt{0 + (-1.94365)^2}} = 1$$

$$[P_{3,2}]^T = \begin{bmatrix} 1 & 0 & 0 & 0 \\ 0 & 0 & -1 & 0 \\ 0 & 1 & 0 & 0 \\ 0 & 0 & 0 & 1 \end{bmatrix}$$

$$[P_{3,2}]^T [P_{4,1}]^T [P_{3,1}]^T [P_{2,1}]^T [A] = \begin{bmatrix} 1 & 0 & 0 & 0 \\ 0 & 0 & -1 & 0 \\ 0 & 1 & 0 & 0 \\ 0 & 0 & 0 & 1 \end{bmatrix}$$

$$\begin{bmatrix} 4.69045 & 3.837613 & 1.705606 & 0.213201 \\ 0 & 0 & -0.727607 & 1.212679 \\ 0 & -1.943650 & -1.257656 & 1.772152 \\ 0 & -0.703525 & 1.407053 & -2.311586 \end{bmatrix}$$

$$= \begin{bmatrix} 4.690415 & 3.837613 & 1.705606 & 0.213201 \\ 0 & 1.943650 & 1.257656 & -1.772152 \\ 0 & 0 & -0.727607 & 1.212679 \\ 0 & -0.703525 & 1.407053 & -2.311586 \end{bmatrix}$$

$$[P_{3,2}]^T \ldots [P_{2,1}]^T \{b\} = \begin{bmatrix} 1 & 0 & 0 & 0 \\ 0 & 0 & -1 & 0 \\ 0 & 1 & 0 & 0 \\ 0 & 0 & 0 & 1 \end{bmatrix} \begin{Bmatrix} 10.660037 \\ 0.72761 \\ -2.629644 \\ -2.814103 \end{Bmatrix} = \begin{bmatrix} 10.660037 \\ -2.629644 \\ 0.727610 \\ -2.814103 \end{bmatrix}$$

For $i = 2, j = 4$

$$\cos\theta = \frac{a_{22}}{\sqrt{a_{22}^2 + a_{42}^2}} = \frac{1.943650}{\sqrt{(1.943650)^2 + (-0.703525)^2}} = 0.940298$$

$$\sin\theta = \frac{a_{42}}{\sqrt{a_{22}^2 + a_{42}^2}} = \frac{-0.703525}{\sqrt{(1.943650)^2 + (-0.703525)^2}} = -0.340351$$

$$[P_{4,2}]^T = \begin{bmatrix} 1 & 0 & 0 & 0 \\ 0 & 0.940298 & 0 & -0.340351 \\ 0 & 0 & 1 & 0 \\ 0 & 0.340351 & 0 & 0.940298 \end{bmatrix}$$

$$[P_{4,2}]^T \ldots [P_{2,1}]^T \{A\} = \begin{bmatrix} 1 & 0 & 0 & 0 \\ 0 & 0.940298 & 0 & -0.340351 \\ 0 & 0 & 1 & 0 \\ 0 & 0.340351 & 0 & 0.940298 \end{bmatrix}$$

$$\begin{bmatrix} 4.690415 & 3.837613 & 1.705606 & 0.213201 \\ 0 & 1.943650 & 1.257656 & -1.772152 \\ 0 & 0 & -0.727607 & 1.212679 \\ 0 & -0.703525 & 1.407053 & -2.311586 \end{bmatrix}$$

$$= \begin{bmatrix} 4.690415 & 3.837613 & 1.705606 & 0.213201 \\ 0 & 2.067055 & 0.703681 & -0.879600 \\ 0 & 0 & -0.727607 & 1.212679 \\ 0 & 0 & 1.751094 & 2.776733 \end{bmatrix}$$

$$[P_{4,2}]^{T'} \ldots [P_{2,1}]^T \{b\} = \begin{bmatrix} 1 & 0 & 0 & 0 \\ 0 & 0.940298 & 0 & -0.340351 \\ 0 & 0 & 1 & 0 \\ 0 & 0.340351 & 0 & 0.940298 \end{bmatrix} \begin{Bmatrix} 10.660037 \\ -2.629644 \\ 0.727610 \\ -2.814103 \end{Bmatrix}$$

$$= \begin{bmatrix} 10.660037 \\ 3.430432 \\ 0.727610 \\ -1.751094 \end{bmatrix}$$

For $i = 3, j = 4$;

$$\cos\theta = -0.3837, \sin\theta = 0.923454$$

$$[P_{4,3}]^T [P_{4,2}]^T \ldots [P_{2,1}]^T \{A\} = \begin{bmatrix} 1 & 0 & 0 & 0 \\ 0 & 1 & 0 & 0 \\ 0 & 0 & -0.38710 & 0.93454 \\ 0 & 0 & -0.923454 & -0.38710 \end{bmatrix}$$

$$\begin{bmatrix} 4.690415 & 3.837613 & 1.705606 & 0.213201 \\ 0 & 2.067055 & 0.703681 & -0.879600 \\ 0 & 0 & -0.727607 & 1.212679 \\ 0 & 0 & 1.751094 & 2.776733 \end{bmatrix}$$

$$= \begin{bmatrix} 4.690415 & 3.837613 & 1.705606 & 0.213201 \\ 0 & 2.067055 & 0.703681 & -0.879600 \\ 0 & 0 & 1.896245 & 2.098868 \\ 0 & 0 & 0 & 2.185314 \end{bmatrix}$$

$$[P_{4,3}]^T [P_{4,2}]^T \ldots [b] = \begin{bmatrix} 1 & 0 & 0 & 0 \\ 0 & 1 & 0 & 0 \\ 0 & 0 & -0.38710 & 0.923454 \\ 0 & 0 & -0.923454 & -0.38710 \end{bmatrix} \begin{Bmatrix} 10.660037 \\ 3.430432 \\ 0.727610 \\ -1.751094 \end{Bmatrix}$$

$$= \begin{Bmatrix} 10.660037 \\ 3.430432 \\ -1.896246 \\ -0.000002 \end{Bmatrix}$$

By the process of back substitution we get

$$x_1 = 1, x_2 = 2, x_3 = -1, x_4 = 0$$

4.11 THE HOUSEHOLDER FACTORISATION

This method transforms the matrix into an upper triangular form by making use of reflection matrices; we have

$$[P_H]^T [A] = [S_H] \tag{4.50}$$

where

$$[P_H]^T = [P_{n-1}]^T \ldots [P_2]^T [P_1]^T \tag{4.51}$$

and $[S_H]$ is an upper triangular matrix. The matrices $[P_i]^T$, $i = 1 \ldots n-1$ are reflection matrices computed in such a way that $[P_i]^T$ reduce the subdiagonal elements in column i of the coefficient matrix.

Then we have

$$[P_i]^T = \begin{bmatrix} [I_{i-1}] & 0 \\ 0 & [P_i] \end{bmatrix} \tag{4.52}$$

where $[I_i - _1]$ is the identity matrix of size $i-1$

and $$[\tilde{P}] = 1 - \theta\{w\}\{w\}^T;$$

where $$\theta = \frac{2}{\{W_i\}^T\{W_i\}}$$

Here $[\tilde{P}_i]$ is a symmetric matrix and $\{w_i\}$ is a vector of size $n - i + 1$. The vector $\{w_i\}$ will be chosen as explained later.

Because $[P_i]$ is symmetric, $[P_i]^T = [P_i]$

Now solution of the equation $[A]\{x\} = \{b\}$ can be obtained by the following equation

$$[A] = [P_H][S_H]$$

$$[P_H]\{v\} = \{b\}$$

where $$\{v\} = [S_H]\{x\}.$$

The vector $\{v\}$ is obtained as $\{v\} = [P_H]^T\{b\}$

To explain the transformation, as a first step let us compute the $[P_1]$ i.e.,

$$[\tilde{A}] = [P_1][A] \tag{4.53}$$

and $$[A] = [a_1\,; A_1] \tag{4.54}$$

where a_1 is the first column of $[A]$. Then we have

$$[P_1] = I - \theta\{w_1\}\{w_1\}^T$$

Here we have the first element of the vector $[P_1][a_1]$ to be non zero since the subdiagonal elements of the column 1 of matrix $[\tilde{A}]$ is required to be zero.

Now choose the vector $\{w_1\}$ such that it must fulfil the condition

$$(I - \theta\{w_1\}\{w_1\}^T)[a_1] = \pm \| a_1 \|_2\, e_1 \tag{4.55}$$

where e_1 is a nondimensional unit vector from eq. (4.55).

$$[a_1] - \theta\{w_1\} = \pm \| a_1 \|_2\, e_1 \tag{4.56}$$

where θ is a constant and equal to $e\{w_1\}^T\{w_1\}$.

Let us set $\theta = 1.0$ then we obtain

$$\{w_1\} = [a_1] + \text{sign}\,(a_{11})\, \| a_1 \|_2\, e_1 \tag{4.57}$$

From equation (4.53) we can get

$$\{v_1\}^T = \{w_1\}^T [A] \tag{4.58}$$

hence,
$$\left[\tilde{A}\right] = [A] - \theta\,(\{w_1\}\,\{v_1\}^T)$$

The factorisation is explained in the example.

Example 4.15

Solve the set of equations given in example 4.12 using Householders factorisation method.

The set of equation is

$$\begin{bmatrix} 1 & 1 & 1 & -1 \\ 4 & 4 & 1 & 1 \\ 1 & -1 & -1 & 2 \\ 2 & 1 & 2 & -2 \end{bmatrix} \begin{Bmatrix} x_1 \\ x_2 \\ x_3 \\ x_4 \end{Bmatrix} = \begin{Bmatrix} 2 \\ 11 \\ 0 \\ 2 \end{Bmatrix}$$

Solution

Here the coefficient matrix is unsymmetric from equation 4.57

$$W_1 = \begin{Bmatrix} 1 \\ 4 \\ 1 \\ 2 \end{Bmatrix} + \sqrt{1^2+4^2+1^2+2^2} + \begin{Bmatrix} 1 \\ 0 \\ 0 \\ 0 \end{Bmatrix} = \begin{Bmatrix} 5.690416 \\ 4 \\ 1 \\ 2 \end{Bmatrix}$$

$$[P_1]^T = I_4 - \theta\{w_1\}\,\{w_1\}^T$$

where
$$\theta = \frac{2}{\{W_1\}^T\{W_1\}} = \frac{2}{\{5.690416 \quad 4 \quad 1 \quad 2\}\begin{Bmatrix} 5.690416 \\ 4 \\ 1 \\ 2 \end{Bmatrix}} = 0.037467$$

$$[P_1]^T = \begin{bmatrix} 1 & 0 & 0 & 0 \\ 0 & 1 & 0 & 0 \\ 0 & 0 & 1 & 0 \\ 0 & 0 & 0 & 1 \end{bmatrix} - 0.037467 \begin{Bmatrix} 5.690416 \\ 4 \\ 2 \\ 1 \end{Bmatrix} \{5.690416 \quad 4 \quad 2 \quad 1\}$$

$$\begin{bmatrix} 1 & 0 & 0 & 0 \\ 0 & 1 & 0 & 0 \\ 0 & 0 & 1 & 0 \\ 0 & 0 & 0 & 1 \end{bmatrix} - \begin{bmatrix} 1.213213 & 0.852811 & 0.213203 & 0.426406 \\ 0.852811 & 0.599472 & 0.149868 & 0.299736 \\ 0.213203 & 0.149868 & 0.037467 & 0.074934 \\ 0.426406 & 0.299736 & 0.07494 & 0.149868 \end{bmatrix}$$

$$[P_1]^T[A] = -\begin{bmatrix} 0.213213 & 0.852811 & 0.213203 & 0.426406 \\ 0.852811 & -0.400528 & 0.149868 & 0.299736 \\ 0.213203 & 0.149868 & -0.962533 & 0.074934 \\ 0.426406 & 0.299736 & 0.07494 & -0.850132 \end{bmatrix} \begin{bmatrix} 1 & 1 & 1 & -1 \\ 4 & 4 & 1 & 1 \\ 1 & -1 & -1 & 2 \\ 2 & 1 & 2 & -2 \end{bmatrix}$$

$$= \begin{bmatrix} -4.69047 & -3.83766 & -1.705633 & -0.213192 \\ 0 & 0.599434 & -0.901886 & 1.553074 \\ 0 & -1.850142 & -1.475472 & 2.138269 \\ 0 & -0.700278 & 1.049062 & -1.723474 \end{bmatrix}$$

$$[P_1]^T \{b\} = \begin{Bmatrix} -10.660159 \\ 2.100716 \\ -2.224822 \\ -2.449644 \end{Bmatrix}$$

$$w_2 = \begin{Bmatrix} 0.599434 \\ -1.850142 \\ -0.700278 \\ 2.666494 \\ -1.850142 \\ -0.700278 \end{Bmatrix} + \sqrt{0.599434^2 + (-1.850145)^2 + (-0.700278)^2} \begin{Bmatrix} 1 \\ 0 \\ 0 \\ 0 \end{Bmatrix}$$

For the second step

$$\theta = \frac{2}{\{2.666494 -1.850142 -0.700278\} \begin{Bmatrix} 2.666494 \\ -1.850142 \\ -0.700278 \end{Bmatrix}} = 0.181429$$

$$[P_2]^T = [I_3] - \theta\{W_2\}\{W_2\}^T$$

$$\begin{bmatrix} 1 & 0 & 0 \\ 0 & 1 & 0 \\ 0 & 0 & 1 \end{bmatrix} - 0.181429 \begin{Bmatrix} 2.666494 \\ -1.850142 \\ -0.700278 \end{Bmatrix} \{2.666494 -1.850142 -0.700278\}$$

$$= \begin{bmatrix} -0.289995 & 0.895061 & 0.33878 \\ 0.895061 & 0.378964 & -0.235062 \\ 0.33878 & -0.230562 & 0.911029 \end{bmatrix}$$

$$[P_2]^T [P_1]^T [A] = \begin{bmatrix} -4.690472 & -3.83766 & -1.705633 & 0.213192 \\ 0 & -0.2067063 & -0.703691 & 0.879619 \\ 0 & 0 & -1.612997 & 2.605546 \\ 0 & 0 & 0.997009 & -1.546610 \end{bmatrix}$$

$$[P_2]^T [P_1]^T b = \begin{Bmatrix} -10.660159 \\ -3.430439 \\ 1.612960 \\ -0.997045 \end{Bmatrix}$$

For the next operation

$$W_3 = \begin{Bmatrix} -1.6129997 \\ 0.997009 \end{Bmatrix} + \sqrt{-1.612997^2 + 0.997009^2} \begin{Bmatrix} 1 \\ 0 \end{Bmatrix} = \begin{Bmatrix} 0.283259 \\ 0.997009 \end{Bmatrix}$$

$$\theta = \frac{2}{\{0.283259 \quad 0.997009\}\begin{Bmatrix}0.283259\\0.997009\end{Bmatrix}} = 1.861742$$

$$[P_3]^T = \begin{bmatrix}1 & 0\\0 & 1\end{bmatrix} - 1.861742\begin{Bmatrix}0.2832259\\0.997009\end{Bmatrix}\{0.283259 \quad 0.997009\}$$

$$= \begin{bmatrix}0.856022 & -0.525778\\-0.525778 & -0.850622\end{bmatrix}$$

$$[P_3]^T[P_2]^T[P_1]^T[A] = \begin{bmatrix}-4.690472 & -3.83766 & -1.705633 & -0.213192\\0 & -2.067063 & -0.703691 & 0.879619\\0 & 0 & -1.896256 & 3.029508\\0 & 0 & 0 & -0.054359\end{bmatrix}$$

$$[P_3]^T[P_2]^T[P_1]^T b = \begin{Bmatrix}-10.660159\\-3.430439\\1.896244\\0\end{Bmatrix}$$

$$x_1 = 1, x_2 = 2, x_3 = -1, x_4 = 0.$$

The Givens and Householder factorisations are time consuming when compared to Gaussian elimination scheme. The coefficient matrix losses its symmetry and banded nature. The advantage of these methods is that they are numerically stable and are more effectively used in eigenvalue problems.

PROBLEMS

4.1 Using the method of partitioning find the inverse of the matrices:

(*a*) $\begin{bmatrix}-2 & 1 & 0\\1 & -2 & 1\\0 & 1 & 2\end{bmatrix}$ (*b*) $\begin{bmatrix}4 & 2 & 1\\3 & 7 & 1\\2 & 5 & 5\end{bmatrix}$

4.2 Find the inverse of the square matrix by (*a*) the method of partitioning, (*b*) Gauss Jordan method.

$$[A] = \begin{bmatrix}5 & -4 & 1 & 0\\-4 & 6 & -4 & 1\\1 & -4 & 6 & -4\\0 & 1 & -4 & 5\end{bmatrix}$$

4.3 Solve the set of linear equations given below by matrix inversion using the method of partitioning:

$$x_1 + 2x_2 + 3x_3 + 5x_4 = 21$$
$$-2x_1 + 5x_2 + 7x_3 - 9x_4 = 18$$
$$5x_1 + 7x_2 + 2x_3 - 5x_4 = 25$$
$$-x_1 + 3x_2 - 7x_3 + 7x_4 = 30$$

4.4 Use Gauss Jordan method to find the inverse of the following matrix.

$$[A] = \begin{bmatrix}2 & 1 & -3\\4 & -2 & 3\\-2 & 2 & -1\end{bmatrix}$$

4.5 Use Gaussian elimination scheme to solve the set of equations.

$$2x_1 + x_2 - 3x_3 = 11$$
$$4x_1 - 2x_2 + 3x_3 = 8$$
$$-2x_1 + 2x_2 - x_3 = -6$$

4.6 Solve the system of linear equations by Gaussian elimination method.

$$6x_1 + 3x_2 + 6x_3 = 30$$
$$2x_1 + 3x_2 + 3x_3 = 17$$
$$x_1 + 2x_2 + 2x_3 = 11$$

4.7 Use the method of Gaussian elimination to solve the following system of linear equations:

$$x_1 + 2x_2 + 3x_3 + 4x_4 = 8$$
$$2x_1 - 2x_2 - x_3 - x_4 = -3$$
$$x_1 - 3x_2 + 4x_3 - 4x_4 = 8$$
$$2x_1 + 2x_2 - 3x_3 + 4x_4 = -2.$$

4.8 Using Gaussian elimination method, solve the system of linear equations:

$$2x_1 + x_2 + x_3 - x_4 = 10$$
$$x_1 + 5x_2 - 5x_3 + 6x_4 = 25$$
$$-7x_1 + 3x_2 - 7x_3 - 5x_4 = 5$$
$$x_1 - 5x_2 + 2x_3 + 7x_4 = 11.$$

4.9 Find the inverse of the square matrix using Gauss Jordan method. $\begin{bmatrix} 1 & 1 & 1 \\ 1 & 2 & 2 \\ 1 & 0 & 3 \end{bmatrix}$

4.10 Determine the values of x, y, and z for the following set of linear algebraic, equations by Gauss-Jordan method:

$$2x + y - 3z = 11$$
$$4x - 2y + 3z = 8$$
$$-2x + 2y - z = -6.$$

4.11 Using Cholesky's method of solution, solve the following linear equations.

$$x_1 + x_2 + x_3 = 7$$
$$3x_1 + 3x_2 + 4x_3 = 23$$
$$2x_1 + x_2 + x_3 = 10$$

4.12 Solve the system of equations by Cholesky's factorisation method.

$$12x_1 - 6x_2 - 6x_3 - 1.5x_4 = 1$$
$$-6x_1 + 4x_2 + 3x_3 + 0.5x_4 = 2$$
$$-6x_1 + 3x_2 + 6x_3 + 1.5x_4 = 3$$
$$-1.5x_1 + 0.5x_2 + 1.5x_3 + x_4 = 4$$

4.13 Find the solution to the system of equations using Potters' method.

$$x_1 + x_2 + x_3 = 1$$
$$4x_1 + 3x_2 - x_3 = 6$$
$$3x_1 + 5x_2 + 3x_3 = 4$$

4.14 Solve the set of equations given in Problem 4.4 by Potters' method.

4.15 Solve the system of equations given in Problem 4.8 by Potters' method.

4.16 Use the Jacobi method to solve the set of equations correct to three decimal places.

$$2x - y + 5z = 15$$
$$2x + y + z = 7$$
$$x + 3y + z = 10$$

4.17 Use Gauss-Siedel method to solve the system of equations given in Problem 4.10.

4.18 Use the Gauss-Seidel method to solve the set of equations given in Problem 4.11 correct to three decimal places.

4.19 Find the solution to the equations using Gauss Seidel method.

$$\begin{bmatrix} 4 & 2 & 0 & 0 \\ 2 & 8 & 2 & 0 \\ 0 & 2 & 8 & 2 \\ 0 & 0 & 2 & 4 \end{bmatrix} \begin{Bmatrix} x_1 \\ x_2 \\ x_3 \\ x_4 \end{Bmatrix} = \begin{Bmatrix} 4 \\ 0 \\ 0 \\ 0 \end{Bmatrix}$$

4.20 Solve the system of equations given by $[A]\{x\} = \{b\}$ using Gauss Seidel method. The matrices $[A]$ and $\{b\}$ are given below.

$$[A] = \begin{bmatrix} 4 & 2 & 0 & 0 \\ 2 & 8 & 2 & 0 \\ 0 & 2 & 8 & 2 \\ 0 & 0 & 2 & 4 \end{bmatrix} \quad \{b\} = \begin{Bmatrix} 4 \\ 0 \\ 0 \\ 14 \end{Bmatrix}$$

4.21 Use the Given's Factorisation method to solve the system of equations.

$$\begin{bmatrix} 4 & -1 & 0 & 0 \\ -1 & 4 & -1 & 0 \\ 0 & -1 & 4 & -1 \\ 0 & 0 & -1 & 4 \end{bmatrix} \begin{Bmatrix} x_1 \\ x_2 \\ x_3 \\ x_4 \end{Bmatrix} = \begin{Bmatrix} 1 \\ 0 \\ 0 \\ 0 \end{Bmatrix}$$

4.22 Use the Givens factorisation to solve the system of equations given below.

$$\begin{bmatrix} 4 & 2 & 1 & 1 \\ 2 & 10 & 2 & 1 \\ 1 & 2 & 4 & 2 \\ 1 & 2 & 4 & 8 \end{bmatrix} \begin{Bmatrix} x_1 \\ x_2 \\ x_3 \\ x_4 \end{Bmatrix} = \begin{Bmatrix} 10 \\ 20 \\ 30 \\ 40 \end{Bmatrix}$$

4.23 Use the Householder factorisation to solve the set of equations of Problem 4.14.

4.24 Find the solution to the system of equations using the Householder's Scheme.

$$\begin{bmatrix} 1 & 2 & -1 \\ 2 & -1 & 1 \\ 1 & 2 & 2 \end{bmatrix} \begin{Bmatrix} x_1 \\ x_2 \\ x_3 \end{Bmatrix} = 0$$

4.25 Solve the system of equations given in Problem 4.21 by Householder's factorization method.

4.26 Solve the system of equations given in Problem 4.22 by Householder's factorization method.

REFERENCES

1. Ben Noble, (1969), *Applied Linear Algebra,* Prentice-Hall, Englewood Cliffs. New Jersey.
2. C.M. Bommer and D.A. Symonds, *Matrix Methods of Linear Structural Analysis,* Crosby Lockwood and Sons, London, S.W.7.
3. David I. Steinberg, (1974), *Computational Matrix Algebra,* McGraw-Hill, Kogukusha, Tokyo.
4. Harold I. Laurren, (1966), *Matrix Analysis of Structures,* McGraw-Hill Book Company, New York.
5. Joel N. Franklin, (1968), *Matrix Theory,* Prentice Hall, Inc., Englewood Cliffs, New Jersey.
6. M.G. Salvadori and M.L. Baron, (1961), *Numerical Methods in Engineering,* Prentice Hall, Inc., Englewood Cliffs, New Jersey.
7. Richard Bronson, (1969), *Matrix Methods: An Introduction,* Academic, New York.
8. V. Ramamurti, (1987), Computer Aided Design in Mechanical Engineering, Tata McGraw-Hill, New Delhi.
9. W.W. Bell, (1975), *Matrices for Scientists and Engineers,* Von Nostrand Reinhold Company, New York.
10. Y. Masi and T. Pham, (1985), Microcomputer Aided Stress Analysis. *Proceedings of the International Conference on Computers in Engineering* V. 2. P. 189-195.

CHAPTER 5

TRANSIENT ANALYSIS

5.1 INTRODUCTION

The equations of dynamic equilibrium for a mechanical system in motion can be written as

$$[M]\{\ddot{X}\} + [C]\{\dot{X}\} + [K]\{X\} = \{F(t)\} \tag{5.1}$$

where $[M]$, $[C]$ and $[K]$ are the mass, damping, and stiffness matrices; $\{F(t)\}$ is the external load vector; and $\{X\}$, $\{\dot{X}\}$ and $\{\ddot{X}\}$ are the displacement, velocity, and acceleration vectors, respectively. Eq. (5.1) can also be written from considerations of statics at time t as

$$\{F_I(t)\} + \{F_D(t)\} + \{F_S(t)\} = \{F(t)\} \tag{5.2}$$

where $\{F_I(t)\}$ are the inertia forces, $\{F_I(t)\} = [M]\{\ddot{X}\}$

$\{F_D(t)\}$ are the damping forces, $\{F_D(t)\} = [C]\{\dot{X}\}$

and $\{F_S(t)\}$ are the elastic forces, $\{F_S(t)\} = [K]\{X\}$

In static analysis, the equations of motion (5.1) are considered with the itertia and damping effects neglected and the equations are independent of time, whereas in dynamic analysis, the effect of acceleration-dependent itertia forces, the velocity-dependent damping forces, and the displacement-dependent elastic forces are considered. Eq. (5.1), in general, represents a system of linear second order differential equations and the solution can be determined by standard procedures for differential equations with constant coefficients. However, the solution procedures could become very expensive if the size of the matrices in Eq. (5.1) are very large.

In this chapter, we will consider two methods of solution: *direct integration* and *mode superposition*. Although, these two methods of solution may appear to be distinctly different, they are closely related and the selection of one method over the other merely depends on their numerical effectiveness. In direct integration method, the equations (5.1) are integrated using a numerical step-by-step procedure, the term direct meaning that prior to the numerical integration, no transformation of the equations into a different form is carried out. However, if the integration must be carried out for many time steps, it may be more effective to first transform the equations (5.1) into a form in which the step-by-step solution is faster. The response analysis by mode superposition first requires the solution of the eigenvalues and eigenvectors of the problems, the solution of the decoupled equilibrium equations, and finally, the superposition of the responses in each eigenvector. The solutions obtained using either procedure are identical within the numerical errors of the time integration schemes used.

5.2 SINGLE DEGREE OF FREEDOM SYSTEM

The general equation of a viscously damped single degree of freedom dynamical system which may be linear or nonlinear, can be expressed in the following general form:

$$M\ddot{X} + C\dot{X} + KX + F(t) \tag{5.3}$$

where M, C and K are the mass, damping and stiffness of the system; $F(t)$ is the applied force; and X, $\dot{X}$, and $\ddot{X}$ are the displacement, velocity and acceleration of the system.

5.2.1 Finite Difference Method

If the equilibrium relation (5.1) is regarded as an ordinary differential equation with constant coefficients, it follows that any convenient *finite difference* expressions to approximate the velocities and accelerations in terms of displacements can be used. The central idea in the finite difference method is to use approximations to derivatives. Hence, the general differential equation such as (5.1) and the associated boundary conditions are replaced by the corresponding finite difference equations. The continuous variable t is replaced by the discrete variable t_i and the differential equation is solved progressively in time increments $h = \Delta t$ starting from known initial conditions. The solution obtained is approximate but by suitably selecting the time increment the accuracy of the solution can be improved.

In this method, we replace the solution domain with a finite number of points, known as mesh or grid points, and obtain the solution at these points. The mesh or grid points are generally equally spaced along the independent coordinate as shown in Fig. (5.1). Central difference method is based on the Taylor's series expansion of X_{i+1} and X_{i-1} about the grid point i.

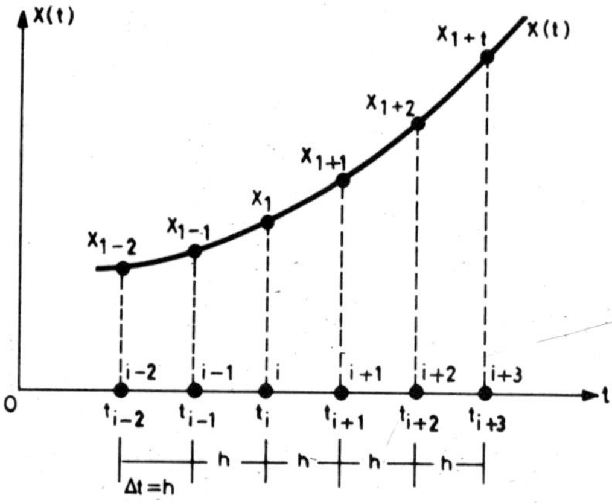

Fig. 5.1 Response X of the system obtained using the central difference method

$$X_{i+1} = X_i + h\dot{X}_i + \frac{h^2}{2}\ddot{X}_i + \frac{h^3}{6}\dddot{X}_i + \ldots\ldots \tag{5.4}$$

$$X_{i-1} = X_i - h\dot{X}_i + \frac{h^2}{2}\ddot{X}_i - \frac{h^3}{6}\dddot{X}_i + \ldots\ldots \tag{5.5}$$

where $X_i = X\ (t = t_i)$ and the time interval $h = t_{i+1} - t = \Delta t$. By taking the first two terms only and substracting Eq. (5.5) from (5.4), we obtain

$$\dot{X}_i = \frac{1}{2h}(X_{i+1} - X_{i-1}) \tag{5.6}$$

Adding Eqs. (5.5) and (5.4), we get

$$\ddot{X}_i \frac{1}{h^2}(X_{i-1} - 2X_i + X_{i+1}) \tag{5.7}$$

Although there exist a number of finite difference schemes, here we consider only two methods selected for their simplicity. They are the central difference method and the Runge-Kutta method.

5.2.2 Central Difference Method

Let the duration over which the numerical solution of Eq. (5.3) is required be divided into n equal parts of interval $h = \Delta t$ each. The initial conditions are assumed to be given by $X(t = 0) = X_0$ and $\dot{X}(t = 0) = \dot{X}_0$.

The accuracy of the solution always depends on the size of the time step. The critical time step is given by $\Delta t_{cri} = \tau_n/\pi$, Where τ_n the natural period of the system. If Δt is selected to be larger than Δt_{cri}, the method becomes unstable, that is the truncation of higher order terms or rounding-off in the computer causes errors to grow and makes the dynamic response calculations meaningless. Numerical methods which requires the use of time step Δt smaller than the critical time step Δt_{cri} are said to be conditionally stable. A safe rule to use is to choose $h \le \tau_n/10$. Substituting Eqs. (5.7) and (5.6) for $\ddot{X}_i$ and $\dot{X}_i$ respectively in Eq. (5.3) at mesh or grid point i gives

$$M\left\{\frac{X_{i+1} - 2X_i + X_{i-1}}{(\Delta t)^2}\right\} + C\left\{\frac{X_{i+1} - X_{i-1}}{2\,\Delta t}\right\} + K\,X_i = F_i \tag{5.8}$$

Where $X = X(t_i)$ and $F_i = F(t_i)$. Solving Eq. (5.8) for X_{i+1} gives

$$X_{i+1} = \left\{\frac{1}{\frac{M}{(\Delta t)^2} + \frac{C}{2\,\Delta t}}\right\}\left[\left\{\frac{2M}{(\Delta t)^2} - K\right\}\{X_i\} + \left\{\frac{C}{2\,\Delta t} - \frac{M}{(\Delta t)^2}\right\}X_{i-1} + F_i\right] \tag{5.9}$$

which is known as the *recurrence formula.*

Thus the displacement of the mass (X_{i+1}) can be calculated using Eq. (5.9) if we know the previous displacements X_i, X_{i-1} and the present external force F_i. Repeated application of Eq. (5.9) gives us the response time history of the system. Since the solution of X_{i+1} Eq. (5.9) is based on the previous displacement X_i Eq. (5.8), the integration procedure is known as an *explicit integration method.* Note that in order to compute X_i, both X_0 and X_{i-1} are required but the initial conditions provide only the values of X_0 and $\dot{X}_0$. Therefore the central difference method is not self-starting. However, the value of X_{i-1} can be obtained from Eqs. (5.6) and (5.7) as follows. First calculate the value of $\ddot{X}_0$ by substituting the given values of X_0 and $\dot{X}_0$ in Eq. (5.3) as

$$\ddot{X}_0 = \frac{1}{M}[F(t=0) - C\dot{X}_0 - KX_0] \tag{5.10}$$

The value of X_{-1} is then obtained by the application of Eqs. (5.6) and (5.7) at $i = 0$.

$$X = X - \Delta t\dot{X} + \frac{(\Delta t)^2}{2}X_0 \tag{5.11}$$

Example 5.1

Find the response of a viscously damped single degree of freedom system subjected to a force

$$F(t) = F_0\left(1 - \text{Sin}\frac{\pi}{t_0}\right)$$

with the following data: $F_0 = 2\,N, t_0 = \pi, M = 2$ Kg, $C = 0.3$, and $K = 1$ N/m. Assume the values of the displacement and velocity of the mass at $t = 0$ to be zero.

Solution

The differential equation of motion is

$$M\ddot{X} + C\dot{X} + KX = F(t) = F_0\left(1 - \text{Sin}\frac{\pi t}{t_0}\right) \tag{a}$$

Since the initial conditions are $X_0 = \dot{X}_0 = 0$, we have from Eq. (5.10)

$$\ddot{X}_0 = \frac{1}{M}[F(t=0) - C\dot{X}_0 - KX_0) = \frac{1}{2}[2 - 0 - 0] = 1$$

Hence Eq. (5.11) gives

$$\ddot{X}_{-1} = X_0 - (\Delta t)X_0 + \frac{(\Delta t)^2}{2}\ddot{X}_0 = \frac{(\Delta t)^2}{2}$$

Therefore Eq. (a) can be written as a recurrence relation:

$$X_{i+1} = \frac{1}{\left[\frac{M}{(\Delta t)^2} + \frac{C}{2(\Delta t)}\right]}\left[\left\{\frac{2M}{(\Delta t)^2} - K\right\}X_1 + \left\{\frac{C}{2\,\Delta t} - \frac{M}{(\Delta t)^2}\right\}X_{i-1} + F_i\right] \cdot \tag{b}$$

$$i = 0, 1, 2, \ldots..$$

with $X_0 = 0, x_{-1} = \frac{(\Delta t)^2}{2}, X_i = X(t_i) = X(i\Delta t)$, and

$$F_i = F(t_i) = F_0\left(1 - \text{Sin}\frac{i\pi\Delta t}{t_0}\right)$$

The undamped natural frequency and the natural period of the system are given by

$$\omega_n = \left(\frac{K}{M}\right)^{\frac{1}{2}} = 1$$

and
$$\tau_n = \frac{2\pi}{\omega_n} = 2\pi$$

Generally speaking, the time step Δt must be $< \frac{\tau_n}{\pi} = 2.0$. Let us find the solution of Eq. (a) by using the time steps $\Delta t = \tau_n/20$. The values of the response X_i obtained according to Eq. (b) are shown in Table 5.1 for ten time steps.

5.2.3 Runge-Kutta Method

In the Runge-Kutta method, an approximation to $X_{t+\Delta t}$ is obtained from X_t in such a way that the power series expansion of the approximation coincides, up to terms of a certain order $(\Delta t)^N$ in the time interval Δt, with the actual Taylor series expansion of $(t + \Delta t)$ in powers of Δt. The method is based on the assumption that the higher derivatives and partial derivatives exist at points required.

Table 5.1 Response X of the system obtained using the central difference method

Time (t_i)	Response (X_i)
0	0
π / 10	0.0493
2 π / 10	0.1606
3 π / 10	0.2988
4 π / 10	0.4347
5 π / 10	0.5481
6 π / 10	0.6298
7 π / 10	0.6821
8 π / 10	0.7175
9 π / 10	0.7564
π	0.8238

The Runge-Kutta method is self starting and has the advantage that no initial values are needed beyond the prescribed values. A brief discussion of its basis is presented here. In the Runge-Kutta method the second-order differential equation is first reduced to two first-order equations. Consider the differential equation for the single degree of freedom system (Eq. 5.3). Eq. (5.3) can be rewritten as

$$\ddot{X} = \frac{1}{M}[F(t) - C\dot{X} - KX] = f(X, \dot{X}, t) \tag{5.12}$$

By letting $X_1 = X$ and $X_2 = \dot{X}$, Eq. (5.12) can be reduced to the following two first-order equations;

$$\dot{X}_1 = X_2 \tag{5.13}$$

$$\dot{X}_2 = f(X_1, X_2, t)$$

By defining

$$X(t) = \begin{Bmatrix} X_1(t) \\ X_2(t) \end{Bmatrix}$$

$$F(t) = \begin{Bmatrix} X_2 \\ f(X_1, X_2, t) \end{Bmatrix}$$

the following recurrence formula is obtained to find the values of $X(t)$ at mesh or grid points t_i according to the fourth order Runge-Kutta method. We omit the details of the derivation of the method.

$$X_{i+1} = X_i + \frac{1}{6}[K_1 + 2K_2 + 2K_3 + K_4]$$

Where

$$K_1 = hF(X_i, t_i)$$

$$K_2 = hF\left(X_i + \frac{1}{2}K_1, t_i + \frac{1}{2}h\right)$$

$$K_3 = hF\left(X_i + \frac{1}{2}K_2, t_i + \frac{1}{2}h\right) \tag{5.14}$$

$$K_4 = hF\left(X_i + \frac{1}{2}K_3, t_{i+1}\right)$$

Although the Runge-Kutta method does not require the computation of derivatives beyond the first, its higher accuracy is obtained by four evaluations of the first derivatives to obtain agreement with the Taylor series solution through terms of order h^4. Since the fourth-order Runge-Kutta method is an explicit method, the maximum time step is usually governed by stability considerations. The change in time step can be easily implemented between iterations and hence the method can be considered as an inherently stable method. The main drawback of the method is that each forward step requires several computations of the functions thus increasing the computational cost. The Runge-Kutta method is applicable and extendable to a system of differential equations.

Example 5.2

Calculate the displacement response of the system considered in Example 5.1 using the Runge-Kutta method.

Solution

Denoting $X_1 = X$ and $X_2 = \dot{X}$, Eq. (5.12) can be written as

$$\ddot{X} = \frac{1}{M}[F(t) - C\dot{X} - KX] = f(X, \dot{X}, t)$$

or

$$\dot{X}_1 = X_2$$

$$\dot{X}_2 = f(X_1, X_2, t)$$

Also by defining $\{X(t)\} = \begin{Bmatrix} X_1(t) \\ X_2(t) \end{Bmatrix}$ and $\{F(t)\} = \begin{Bmatrix} X_2 \\ f(X, \dot{X}, t) \end{Bmatrix}$ or

$$\{F(t)\} = \begin{Bmatrix} \dot{X}(t) \\ \dfrac{1}{M}\left[F_0 1 - \text{Sin}\dfrac{\pi t}{t_0} - C\dot{X}(t) - KX(t)\right] \end{Bmatrix}$$ with the initial

conditions

$$\{X(0)\} = \begin{Bmatrix} 0 \\ 0 \end{Bmatrix}$$

The values of $\{X_{i+1}\}, i = 0, 1, 2....10$ obtained are shown in Table 5.2.

Table 5.2 Response X of the system obtained using the Runge–Kutta method

Time (t_1)	$X_1 = X$	$X_2 = \dot{X}$
0	0	0
$\pi / 10$	0.0433	0.2564
$2\pi / 10$	0.1489	0.3981
$3\pi / 10$	0.2826	0.4372
$4\pi / 10$	0.4154	0.3977
$5\pi / 10$	0.5276	0.3116
$6\pi / 10$	0.6101	0.2146
$7\pi / 10$	0.6649	0.1413
$8\pi / 10$	0.7044	0.1207
$9\pi / 10$	0.7484	0.1723
π	0.8212	0.3039

5.3 MULTI–DEGREE OF FREEDOM SYSTEM

The general form of the equations of motion for a multi-degree of freedom system are written as

$$[M]\{\ddot{X}\} + [C]\{\dot{X}\} + [K]\{X\} = \{F(t)\} \tag{5.15}$$

Where $[M]$, $[C]$, and $[K]$ are the mass, damping, and stiffness matrices for the system and $\{\ddot{X}\}, \{\dot{X}\}$, and $\{X\}$ refer to the acceleration, velocity, and displacement vectors, respectively. $\{F(t)\}$ is the force vector.

Several numerical direct integration schemes are available to determine the approximate solution of a system of equations of motion. For a linear dynamic system, matrices $[M]$, $[C]$ and $[K]$ are independent of time and therefore remain unchanged during the integration procedure. These matrices vary with time for a nonlinear dynamic system and must be modified during the integration of equations of motion. For the solution of equations of motion for a linear dynamic system, either the normal mode superposition method of dynamic analysis or direct numerical integration methods can be used. However, for the solution of nonlinear equations of motion, direct numerical integration methods are generally recommended.

In a direct integration method, the system of equations of motion are integrated successively by using a step-by-step numerical procedure. No transformation of the equations of motion is needed prior to integration and time derivatives are usually approximated by using difference formulae that involve one or more increments of time. Basically, there are two principal approaches used in the direct integration method: explicit and implicit schemes. In an explicit scheme, the response quantities are expressed in terms of previously determined values of displacement, velocity, and acceleration. In an implicit scheme, the difference equations are combined with the equations of motion, and the displacements are calculated directly by solving the equations.

In this section, only selected numerical integration schemes widely used for linear and nonlirear dynamic analyses are considered. Three explicit and four implicit direct integration schemes are examined. A brief description of these schemes is presented and their application is illustrated. The explicit schemes presented are the central difference method, two cycle iteration with trapezoidal rule, and fourth-order Runge-Kutta. The implicit schemes include the Houbolt, Wilson-Theta, Newmark-Beta, and Park Stiffly stable methods. The accuracy, stability, and efficiency of these schemes are examined by comparing the results for sample problems.

5.4 EXPLICIT SCHEMES

As mentioned earlier, in an explicit formulation, the response quantities are expressed explicitly in terms of previously determined values of displacement, velocity, and acceleration.

5.4.1 Central Difference Method

The procedure indicated for the case of a single degree of freedom system can be directly extended to this case. Consider a displacement time history curve as shown in Fig. 5.2. At the middle of the time interval Δt, the velocity is given by

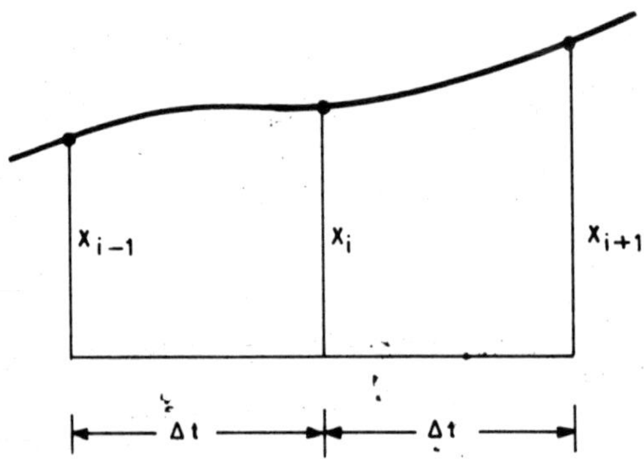

Fig. 5.2 Response X of the system obtain using the central Runge–Kutta method

$$\dot{X}_{i+\frac{1}{2}} = \frac{X_{i+1} - X_i}{\Delta t} \tag{5.16}$$

$$\dot{X}_{i-\frac{1}{2}} = \frac{X_i - X_{i-1}}{\Delta t} \tag{5.17}$$

The acceleration is

$$\ddot{X}_i = \frac{X_{i+\frac{1}{2}} - X_i}{\Delta t} \tag{5.18}$$

Substituting $\dot{X}_{i+\frac{1}{2}}$ and $\dot{X}_{i-\frac{1}{2}}$ from Eqs. (5.16) and (5.17 into Eq. (5.18), we get

$$\ddot{X}_i = \frac{1}{\Delta t^2}(X_{i+1} - 2X_i + X_{i-1}) \tag{5.19}$$

The difference formulas in the central difference method for velocity and acceleration are written in terms of displacement as

$$\{\dot{X}_t\} = \frac{1}{2\Delta t}[\{X_{t+\Delta t}\} - \{X_{t-\Delta t}\}] \tag{5.20}$$

$$\{\ddot{X}_t\} = \frac{t}{\Delta t^2}[\{X_{t+\Delta t}\} - 2\{x_t\} + \{X_{t-\Delta t}\}] \tag{5.21}$$

Substituting $\{\dot{X}_t\}$ and $\{\ddot{X}_t\}$ from Eqs. (5.20) and (5.21), respectively into Eq. (5.15), we get

$$[\overline{M}]\{X_{t+\Delta t}\} = \{\overline{F}_t\} \tag{5.22}$$

where $[\overline{M}]$, the effective mass matrix, and $\{\overline{F}_t\}$, the effective force vector, are given by

$$[\overline{M}] = \frac{1}{\Delta t^2}[M] + \frac{1}{2\Delta t}[C] \tag{5.23}$$

$$\{\overline{F}_t\} = \{F_t\} - \left([K] - \frac{2}{\Delta t^2}[M]\right)\{X_t\} - \left(\frac{1}{\Delta t^2}[M] - \frac{1}{2\Delta t}[C]\right)\{X_{t-\Delta t}\} \tag{5.24}$$

At time $t + \Delta t$, the displacements $\{X_{t+\Delta t}\}$ can be computed by solving Eq. (5.22), and the velocities and accelerations at time t are determined by substituting these values of $\{X_{t+\Delta t}\}$ into Eqs. (5.20) and (5.21). Note that the calculation of $\{X_{t+\Delta t}\}$ involves $\{X_t\}$ and $\{x_{t-\Delta t}\}$. Hence, in order to obtain the solution at time Δt, a special starting procedure is needed.

Table 5.3 summerizes the time integration scheme suitable for implementation in the computer. The local truncation error of this method is of the order of Δt^2. An important consideration in central difference method is that the integration requires a time step Δt which must be smaller than a critical value, Δt_{cr}. This critical value is limited by the highest frequency of the discrete system ω_{max}, where

$$\Delta t \leq \Delta t_{cr} \leq \frac{2}{\omega_{max}} \tag{5.25}$$

If the time step is larger than Δt_{cr}, the integration is unstable, meaning that any errors resulting from the numerical integration or round-off in the computer grow and make the dynamic response calculations questionable.

Table 5.3 Algorithm based on central-difference method

(a) *Initial Computations:*

1. Form stiffness $[K]$, mass $[M]$, and damping $[C]$ matrices.
2. Initialize $\{X_0\}$, $\{\dot{X}_0\}$, and $\{\ddot{X}_0\}$.
3. Select time step Δt and calculate integration constants a_i:

$$a_0 = \frac{1}{\Delta t^2}\,;\; a_1 = \frac{1}{2\Delta t}\,;\; a_2 = 2a_0\,;\; a_3 = \frac{1}{a_2}$$

4. Calculate $\{X_{-\Delta t}\} = \{X_0\} - \Delta t\{\dot{X}_0\} + a_3\{\ddot{X}_0\}$.
5. Form effective mass matrix $[M] = a_0[M] + a_1[C]$.
6. Triangularize $[\overline{M}]$: $[\overline{M}] = [L]\,[D]\,[L]^T$

(b) *For each time step:*

1. Calculate effective force vector at time t:

$$\{\overline{F}_t\} = \{F_t\} - ([K] - a_2[M])\,\{X_t\} - (a_0[M] - a_1[C])\,\{X_{t-\Delta t}\}$$

2. Solve for displacements at time $t + \Delta t$:

$$[\overline{M}]\,\{X_{t+\Delta t}\} = [\overline{F}_t]$$

3. Calculate $\{\dot{X}\}$, and $\{\ddot{X}\}$ at time t:

$$\{\dot{X}_t\} = a_1\,(-\{X_{t-\Delta t}\} - \{X_{t+\Delta t}\})$$

$$\{\ddot{X}_t\} = a_0\,(\{X_{t-\Delta t}\} - 2\,\{X_t\} + \{X_{t+\Delta t}\})$$

Example 5.3

Calculate the response of a simple two degree of freedom system given below by the central difference method.

$$\begin{bmatrix} 2 & 0 \\ 0 & 2 \end{bmatrix} \begin{Bmatrix} \ddot{X}_1 \\ \ddot{X}_2 \end{Bmatrix} + \begin{bmatrix} 4 & 5 \\ 2 & 6 \end{bmatrix} \begin{Bmatrix} X_1 \\ X_2 \end{Bmatrix} = \begin{bmatrix} 5 \\ 2 \end{bmatrix} \tag{a}$$

Assume the initial conditions as $X_1 = X_2 = \dot{X}_1 = \dot{X}_2 = 0$ at $t = 0$

Solution

To find the natural frequencies, we set the determinant of the coefficient matrix $\{X\}$ equal to zero. That is,

$$[[K] - \omega^2[M]]\,\{X\} = 0. \tag{b}$$

$$\begin{bmatrix} 4 - 2\lambda & 5 \\ 2 & 6 - 2\lambda \end{bmatrix} = 0 \tag{c}$$

The expansion of the determinant in Eq. (c) leads to

$$4\lambda^2 - 20\lambda + 14 = 0 \tag{d}$$

By setting $\lambda = \omega^2$, we obtain λ_1 and λ_2 from Eq. (d) as

$$\lambda_1 = \omega_1^2 = 0.84 \text{ and } \lambda_2 = \omega_2^2 = 4.16$$

Then, the periods of oscillation are

$$\tau_1 = 2\pi/\omega_1 = 6.85 \text{ and } \tau_2 = 2\pi/\omega_2 = 3.08$$

Let us choose the time step $\Delta t = (\tau_2/10) = 0.308$ to calculate the response of the system for 10 steps. The first step is to calculate $\{\ddot{X}_0\}$ using the equations (a) at time 0; i.e., we use

$$\begin{bmatrix} 2 & 0 \\ 0 & 2 \end{bmatrix} \{\ddot{X}_0\} + \begin{bmatrix} 4 & 5 \\ 2 & 6 \end{bmatrix} [X_0] = \begin{Bmatrix} 5 \\ 5 \end{Bmatrix}$$

Hence,
$$\{\ddot{X}_0\} = \begin{bmatrix} 5/2 \\ 5/2 \end{bmatrix} = \begin{bmatrix} 2.5 \\ 2.5 \end{bmatrix}$$

Now we follow the calculations in Table 5.3 using $\Delta t = 0.308$

$$a_0 = \frac{1}{(\Delta t)^2} = 10.54$$

$$a_1 = \frac{1}{2(0.308)} = 1.623$$

$$a_2 = 2a_0 = 21.08$$

$$a_3 = \frac{1}{a_2} = 0.0474$$

Hence,

$$\{X_{-\Delta t}\} = \{X_0\} - \Delta t\{\dot{X}_0\} + a_3\{\ddot{X}_0\}$$

$$= \begin{bmatrix} 0 \\ 0 \end{bmatrix} - 0.308 \begin{bmatrix} 0 \\ 0 \end{bmatrix} + 0.0474 \begin{bmatrix} 2.5 \\ 2.5 \end{bmatrix} = \begin{bmatrix} 0.1185 \\ 0.1185 \end{bmatrix}$$

$$[\overline{M}] = a_0[M] + a_1[C] = 10.54 \begin{bmatrix} 2 & 0 \\ 0 & 2 \end{bmatrix} + 1.623 \begin{bmatrix} 0 & 0 \\ 0 & 0 \end{bmatrix} = \begin{bmatrix} 21.08 & 0 \\ 0 & 21.08 \end{bmatrix}$$

The effective force vector at time *t* is

$$\{\overline{F}_t\} = \{F_t\} - ([K] - a_2[M])\{X_t\} - (a_0[M] - a_1[C])\{X_{t-\Delta t}\} = \begin{bmatrix} 5 \\ 5 \end{bmatrix}$$

$$-\left(\begin{bmatrix} 4 & 5 \\ 2 & 6 \end{bmatrix} - 21.08 \begin{bmatrix} 2 & 0 \\ 0 & 2 \end{bmatrix} \begin{Bmatrix} 0 \\ 0 \end{Bmatrix}\right) - \left(10.54 \begin{bmatrix} 2 & 0 \\ 0 & 2 \end{bmatrix} - 1.623 \begin{bmatrix} 0 & 0 \\ 0 & 0 \end{bmatrix}\right) \begin{Bmatrix} 0.1185 \\ 0.1185 \end{Bmatrix} = \begin{Bmatrix} 2.502 \\ 2.502 \end{Bmatrix}$$

Hence we need to solve the following equations for each time step.

$$[\overline{M}]\ \{X_{t+\Delta t}\} = \{\overline{F}_t\} \tag{e}$$

The solution obtained for 10 time steps using Eq. (e) are summarized in Table 5.4.

Table 5.4 Results for Example 5.3 using the central difference method

Time	Δt	$2\Delta t$	$3\Delta t$	$4\Delta t$	$5\Delta t$	$6\Delta t$	$7\Delta t$	$8\Delta t$	$9\Delta t$	$10\Delta t$
X_1	0.1186	0.440	0.887	1.316	1.661	1.865	1.939	1.943	1.954	2.029
X_2	0.1186	0.412	0.722	0.855	0.669	0.137	−0.639	−1.457	−2.083	−2.342

Example 5.4

Determine the displacement response of a simple two degree of freedom system given below by analytical method.

$$\begin{bmatrix} 2 & 0 \\ 0 & 2 \end{bmatrix} \begin{Bmatrix} \ddot{X}_1 \\ \ddot{X}_2 \end{Bmatrix} + \begin{bmatrix} 4 & 5 \\ 2 & 6 \end{bmatrix} \begin{Bmatrix} X_1 \\ X_2 \end{Bmatrix} = \begin{bmatrix} 5 \\ 5 \end{bmatrix} \tag{a}$$

Assume the initial conditions as $X_1 = X_2 = \dot{X}_1 = \dot{X}_2 = 0$ at $t = 0$. Compute the response of the system using time step $\Delta t = 0.308$ sec for 10 equal steps.

Solution:

The response $\{X(t)\}$ of Eq. (a) consists of two parts: first, $\{X_H(t)\}$ is the transient response, i.e., the homogeneous or complementary solution of the equations of motion; and second, $\{X_P(t)\}$ is the steady-state or forced response, i.e., the particular solution of the equations of motion. The particular solution to constant inputs are constants, say Z_1, Z_2. Hence

$$4Z_1 + 5Z_2 = 5$$

$$2Z_1 + 6Z_2 = 5 \tag{b}$$

or $Z_1 = 5/14$ and $Z_2 = 5/7$

The complementary solution to the equations is obtained from

$$2\ddot{X}_1 + 4X_1 + 5X_2 = 0$$

$$2\ddot{X}_2 + 2X_1 + 6X_2 = 0 \tag{c}$$

Let $X_1 = x_1 e^{i\omega t}$ and $X_2 = x_2\, e^{i\omega t}$ and substituting these in Eq. (c), we get

$$(4 - 2\omega^2)x_1 + 5\dot{X}_2 = 0$$

$$2x_1 + (6 - 2\omega^2)x_2 = 0 \tag{d}$$

Solving Eq. (d) for x_1 / x_2 gives

$$\frac{x_1}{x} = \frac{5}{2^2} \underset{2\omega - 4}{=} \frac{2\omega^2 - 6}{2} \tag{e}$$

From Eq. (e), the frequency equation is

$$2(\omega^2)^2 - 10(\omega^2) + 7 = 0$$

from which $\omega_1^2 = \frac{1}{2}(5 - \sqrt{11})$ and $\omega_2^2 = \frac{1}{2}(5 + \sqrt{11})$

At $\omega_1^2 = \frac{1}{2}(5 - \sqrt{11})$, $\quad \left(\dfrac{X_1}{X_2}\right)^{1} = \dfrac{5}{1 - \sqrt{11}} = \lambda_1$

At $\omega_2^2 = \frac{1}{2}(5 + \sqrt{11})$, $\quad \left(\dfrac{X_1}{X_2}\right)^{11} = \dfrac{5}{1 + \sqrt{11}} = \lambda_2$

The two modes of vibration are

$$\begin{Bmatrix} x_1 \\ \overline{x_2} \end{Bmatrix}^I = \begin{Bmatrix} x_1 \\ \overline{x_2} \end{Bmatrix}^I \sin(\omega_1 t - \psi_1)$$

and

$$\begin{Bmatrix} x_1 \\ \overline{x_2} \end{Bmatrix}^{II} = \begin{Bmatrix} x_1 \\ \overline{x_2} \end{Bmatrix}^{II} \sin(\omega_2 t - \psi_2)$$

where $\frac{x_1}{x_2}$ is specified for each mode. The general solution is

$$X_1 = Z_1 + x_1^I \sin(\omega_1 t + \psi_1) + x_1^{II} \sin(\omega_2 t + \psi_2)$$

$$X_2 = Z_2 + x_2^I \sin(\omega_1 t + \psi_1) + x_2^{II} \sin(\omega_2 t + \psi_2) \tag{f}$$

where x_1^1, x_2^1, ψ_1 and ψ_2 are determined from initial conditions. At $t = 0$, $x_1 = x_2 = \dot{x}_1 = \dot{x}_2 = 0$. Substituting Z_1 and Z_2 and the initial conditions in Eqs.(f), we get

$$0 = \frac{5}{14} + x_1^I \sin\psi_1 + x_1^{II} \sin\psi_2$$

$$0 = \frac{5}{7} + x_2^{II} \sin\psi_1 + x_2^{II} \sin\psi_2 \tag{g}$$

$$0 = \omega_1 x_1^I \cos\psi_1 + \omega_2 x_1^{II} \cos\psi_2$$

$$0 = \omega_2 x_2^I \cos\psi_1 + \omega_2 x_2^{II} \cos\psi_2$$

The last of the two equations in (g) give $\cos\psi_1 = 0$ and $\cos\psi_2 = 0$, and $\sin\psi_1 = 1$ and $\sin\psi_2 = 1$. The first of the two equations in (g) gives

$$\lambda_1 x_2^I + \lambda_2 x_2^{II} + \frac{5}{14} = 0 \tag{h}$$

$$x_2^I + x_2^{II} + \frac{5}{7} = 0$$

Solving Eq. (h), we get

$$x_2^I = \frac{5}{154}[2\sqrt{} - 11]$$

$$x_2^{II} = -\frac{5}{154}[2\sqrt{11} - 11]$$

and

$$x_1^I = \frac{25}{154}\left[\frac{(2\sqrt{11} - 11)}{-(1 - \sqrt{11})}\right]$$

$$x_1^{II} = -\frac{25}{154}\left[\frac{(2\sqrt{11} + 11)}{-(1 + \sqrt{11})}\right]$$

Hence, the response of the system is given by

$$X_1 = \frac{5}{14} + \frac{25}{154}\left(\frac{(2\sqrt{11}-11)}{-(1-\sqrt{11})}\right)\cos\omega_1 t - \frac{25}{154}\left(\frac{(2\sqrt{11}+11)}{(1+\sqrt{11})}\right)\cos\omega_2 t \quad \text{(i)}$$

$$X_2 = \frac{5}{7} + \frac{5}{154}(2\sqrt{11}-11)\cos\omega_1 t - \frac{5}{154}(2\sqrt{11}+11)\cos\omega_2 t$$

The solution obtained for 10 *time* steps using Eq. (i) are summarized in Table 5.5

Table 5.5 Results for Example 5.4 from analytical solution

Time	Δt	$2\Delta t$	$3\Delta t$	$4\Delta t$	$5\Delta t$	$6\Delta t$	$7\Delta t$	$8\Delta t$	$9\Delta t$	$10\Delta t$
X_1	–0.4733	–0.1065	.3591	.7628	.9722	.9322	0.6843	0.3482	0.0743	–0.0151
X_2	0.1149	0.4174	.7970	1.1167	1.2645	1.1956	0.9483	0.6287	0.3690	0.2765

Example 5.5

Solve the following system analytically and also using modal super position.

$$2\ddot{x}_1 + 4x_1 + 2x_2 = 5 \quad (1)$$

$$2\ddot{x}_2 + 2x_1 + 4x_2 = 5 \quad (2)$$

Solution

The solution to the coupled second order linear differential equations is of the form

$$x_1 = x_{1(C.F.)} + x_{1(P.I.)} \quad (3)$$

$$x_2 = x_{2(C.F.)} + x_{2(P.I.)} \quad (4)$$

The particular solution to constant inputs are constants

$$x_{1(P.I.)} = Z_1 \quad (5)$$

$$x_{2(P.I.)} = Z_2 \quad (6)$$

Substituting (5), (6) in (1), (2), we get

$$4Z_1 + 2Z_2 = 5 \quad (7)$$

$$2Z_1 + 4Z_2 = 5 \quad (8)$$

Solving (7), (8) we get

$$Z_1 = 5/6 \quad (9)$$

$$Z_2 = 5/6 \quad (10)$$

The complementary part of the solution is obtained from

$$2\ddot{x}_1 + 4x_1 + 2x_2 = 0 \quad (11)$$

$$2\ddot{x}_2 + 2x_1 + 4x_2 = 0 \quad (12)$$

Let the solution be of the form

$$x_1 = X_1 e^{i\omega t} \tag{13}$$

$$x_2 = X_2 e^{i\omega t} \tag{14}$$

Substituting (13), (14) in (11) and (12)

$$(4 - 2\omega^2)X_1 + 2X_2 = 0 \tag{15}$$

$$2X_1 + (4 - 2\omega^2)X_2 = 0 \tag{16}$$

from (15) and (16)

$$\frac{X_1}{X_2} = \frac{2}{2\omega^2 - 4} = \frac{2\omega^2 - 4}{2} \tag{17}$$

from (17), the frequency equation

$$(2\omega^2 - 4)^2 - 4 = 0$$

$$(\omega^2)^2 - 4\omega^2 + 3 = 0 \tag{18}$$

hence

$$\omega_1^2 = 1 \qquad \left(\frac{X_1}{X_2}\right)^I = -1/1 \tag{19}$$

$$\omega_2^2 = 3 \qquad \left(\frac{X_1}{X_2}\right)^{II} = 1/1 \tag{20}$$

The two modes of vibration are

$$\begin{Bmatrix} X_1 \\ X_2 \end{Bmatrix}^I = \begin{Bmatrix} X_1 \\ X_2 \end{Bmatrix}^I \sin(\omega_1 t - \psi_1) \tag{21}$$

$$\begin{Bmatrix} X_1 \\ X_2 \end{Bmatrix}^{II} = \begin{Bmatrix} X_1 \\ X_2 \end{Bmatrix}^{II} \sin(\omega_2 t - \psi_2) \tag{22}$$

Where $\dfrac{X_1}{X_2}$ is specified for each mode

The general solution is

$$x_1 = z_1 + X_1^I \sin(\omega_1 t + \psi_1) + X_1^{II} \sin(\omega_2 t + \psi_2) \tag{23}$$

$$x_2 = z_2 + X_2^I \sin(\omega_1 t + \psi_1) + X_2^{II} \sin(\omega_2 t + \psi_2) \tag{24}$$

where X_I^1, X_2^{II}, ψ_1 and ψ_2 are obtained from initial conditions at $t = 0$, $x_1 = 1$, $x_2 = 2$, $\dot{x}_1 = 0$ and $\dot{x}_2 = 0$

$$1 = \frac{5}{6} + X_1^I \sin\psi_1 + X_1^{II} \sin\psi_2 \tag{25}$$

$$2 = \frac{5}{6} + X_2^I \sin\psi_1 + X_2^{II} \sin\psi_2 \tag{26}$$

$$0 = \omega_1 X_1^I \cos\psi_1 + \omega_2 X_1^{II} \cos\psi_2 \tag{27}$$

$$0 = \omega_1 X_2^I \cos\psi_1 + \omega_2 X_2^{II} \cos\psi_2 \tag{28}$$

from (27) and (28) we get

$$\cos\psi_1 = 0 \text{ and } \cos\psi_2 = 0$$

implying that $\sin\psi_1 = 1$ and $\sin\psi_2 = 1$

From (25) and (26)

$$-X_2^I + X_2^{II} + \frac{5}{6} = 1 \tag{29}$$

$$X_2^I + X_2^{II} + \frac{5}{6} = 2 \tag{30}$$

From (30) and (31)

$$X_2^I = 1/2 \tag{31}$$

$$X_2^{II} = 2/3 \tag{32}$$

Therefore

$$X_1^I = -1/2 \tag{33}$$

$$X_1^{II} = 2/3 \tag{34}$$

The final solution is

$$x_1 = \frac{5}{6} - \frac{1}{2}\cos t + \frac{2}{3}\cos\sqrt{3}\,t \tag{35}$$

$$x_2 = \frac{5}{6} + \frac{1}{2}\cos t + \frac{2}{3}\cos\sqrt{3}\,t \tag{36}$$

The frequencies and ratio of mode shapes are found as before

$$\omega_1^2 = 1 \qquad \left(\frac{X_1}{X_2}\right)^{II} = -\frac{1}{1}$$

$$\omega_2^2 = 3 \qquad \left(\frac{X_1}{X_2}\right)^{II} = \frac{1}{1}$$

Hence the modal matrix is
$$\begin{bmatrix} 1 & 1 \\ -1 & 1 \end{bmatrix} \tag{37}$$

By the model superposition method

$$\begin{bmatrix} 1 & -1 \\ 1 & 1 \end{bmatrix}\begin{bmatrix} 2 & 0 \\ 0 & 2 \end{bmatrix}\begin{bmatrix} 1 & 1 \\ -1 & 1 \end{bmatrix}\begin{Bmatrix} \ddot{q}_1 \\ \ddot{q}_2 \end{Bmatrix} + \begin{bmatrix} 1 & -1 \\ 1 & 1 \end{bmatrix}\begin{bmatrix} 4 & 2 \\ 2 & 4 \end{bmatrix}\begin{bmatrix} 1 & 1 \\ -1 & 1 \end{bmatrix}\begin{Bmatrix} q_1 \\ q_2 \end{Bmatrix}$$

$$= \begin{bmatrix} 1 & -1 \\ 1 & 1 \end{bmatrix}\begin{Bmatrix} 5 \\ 5 \end{Bmatrix} \tag{38}$$

$$\begin{bmatrix} 4 & 0 \\ 0 & 4 \end{bmatrix} \begin{Bmatrix} \ddot{q}_1 \\ \ddot{q}_2 \end{Bmatrix} + \begin{bmatrix} 4 & 0 \\ 0 & 12 \end{bmatrix} \begin{Bmatrix} q_1 \\ q_2 \end{Bmatrix} = \begin{Bmatrix} 0 \\ 10 \end{Bmatrix} \tag{39}$$

The decoupled equations are

$$\ddot{q}_1 + q_1 = 0$$

$$\ddot{q}_2 + 3q_2 = 5/2 \tag{40}$$

The solution to (40) is

$$q_1 = A \cos t + B \sin t$$

$$q_2 = 5/6 + C \cos \sqrt{3}\, t + D \sin \sqrt{3}\, t \tag{41}$$

$$\begin{Bmatrix} x_1 \\ x_2 \end{Bmatrix} = \begin{bmatrix} 1 & 1 \\ -1 & 1 \end{bmatrix} \begin{Bmatrix} q_1 \\ q_2 \end{Bmatrix}$$

$$x_1 = q_1 + q_2 = 5/6 + A \cos t + B \sin t + C \cos \sqrt{3}\, t + D \sin \sqrt{3}\, t$$

$$x_2 = -q_1 + q_2 = 5/6 - A \cos t - B \sin t + C \cos \sqrt{3}\, t + D \sin \sqrt{3}\, t$$

$$\text{at } t = 0, x_1 = 1, x_2 = 2, \dot{x}_1 = 0, \dot{x}_2 = 0$$

From initial conditions we get $A = 2/3$, $C = -1/2$, $B = 0$, $D = 0$ the solution is same as before.

5.4.2 Two-Cycle Iteration with Trapezoidal Rule

The equations of motion at any time t are expressed in the incremental form as

$$[M]\,\{\Delta \ddot{X}_t\} = \{\Delta F_t\} - [K]\,\{\Delta X_t\} - [C]\,\{\Delta \dot{X}_t\} \tag{5.26}$$

The increments in the velocities and displacements are estimated by the use of the following relationships in the first iteration cycle:

For the first time step:

$$\{\Delta \dot{X}_t\} = \Delta t \{\ddot{X}_{t-\Delta t}\} \tag{5.27}$$

For other time steps:

$$\{\Delta \dot{X}_t\} = 2\Delta t \{\ddot{X}_{t-\Delta t}\} - \{\Delta X_{t-\Delta t}\} \tag{5.28}$$

$$\{\dot{X}_t\} = \{\dot{X}_{t-\Delta t}\} + \{\Delta \dot{X}_t\} \tag{5.29}$$

$$\{\Delta X_t\} = \frac{1}{2} \Delta t [\{\dot{X}_{t-\Delta t}\} + \{\dot{X}_t\}] \tag{5.30}$$

By substituting the relations $\{\Delta \dot{X}_t\}$ and $\{\Delta X_t\}$ from Eqs. (5.28), (5.29) and (5.30) into Eq.(5.26) we obtain the increments in the accelerations. These are then employed to obtain the estimate of acceleration at time t as

$$\{\Delta \ddot{X}_t\} = [M]^{-1} (\{\Delta F_t\} - [K]\,\{\Delta X_t\} - [C]\,\{\Delta X_t\}) \tag{5.31}$$

$$\{\ddot{X}_t\} = \{\ddot{X}_{t-\Delta t}\} + \{\Delta \ddot{X}_t\} \tag{5.32}$$

In the second iteration cycle, the increments in the velocities and accelerations are refined as

$$\{\Delta\dot{X}_t\} = \frac{1}{2}\Delta t(\{\ddot{X}_{t-\Delta t}\} + \{\ddot{X}_t\}) \tag{5.33}$$

$$\{\dot{X}_t\} = \{\dot{X}_{t-\Delta t}\} + \{\Delta\dot{X}_t\} \tag{5.34}$$

$$\{\Delta X_t\} = \frac{1}{2}\Delta t(\{\dot{X}_{t-\Delta t}\} + \{\dot{X}_t\}) \tag{5.35}$$

Finally, the relations for $\{\Delta\dot{X}_t\}$ and $\{\Delta X_t\}$ in (5.33) and (5.35) are substituted into (5.31) to compute the new increments in the accelerations. These are then used in Eq. (5.32) to calculate the accelerations at time t. The computational algorithm based on this method is summarized in Table 5.6.

Table 5.6 Algorithm based on two-cycle iteration with trapezoidal rule

1. Form stiffness $[K]$, mass $[M]$, and damping $[C]$ matrices
2. Initialize $\{X_0\}$, $\{\dot{X}_0\}$ and $\{\ddot{X}_0\}$
3. Select time step Δt and calculate for the first time step in the first iteration cycle:

   $$\{\Delta\dot{X}_t\} = \Delta t\{\ddot{X}_{t-\Delta t}\}$$

4. For other time steps:

   $$\{\Delta\dot{X}t\} = 2\Delta t\{\ddot{X}_{t-\Delta t}\} - \{\Delta\dot{X}_{t-\Delta t}\}$$

   $$\{\dot{X}_t\} = \{\dot{X}_{t-\Delta t}\} + \{\Delta\dot{X}_t\}$$

   $$\{\Delta X_t\} = \frac{\Delta t}{2}(\{\dot{X}_{t-\Delta t}\} - \{\dot{X}_t\})$$

5. Compute $\{\Delta\ddot{X}_t\}$ and $\{\dot{X}_t\}$ at time t:

   $$\{\ddot{X}_t\} = \frac{1}{[M]}(\{\Delta F_t\} - [K]\ \{\Delta X_t\} - [C]\ \{\Delta\dot{X}_t\})$$

   $$\{\ddot{X}_t\} = \{\ddot{X}_{t-\Delta t}\} + \{\Delta\ddot{X}_t\}$$

6. Second iteration cycle:

   $$\{\Delta\dot{X}_t\} = \frac{\Delta t}{2}(\{\ddot{X}_{t-\Delta t}\} + \{\ddot{X}_t\})$$

   $$\{\dot{X}_t\} = \{\dot{X}_{t-\Delta t}\} + \{\Delta\dot{X}_t\}$$

   $$\{\Delta X_t\} = \frac{\Delta t}{2}(\{\dot{X}_{t-\Delta t}\} + \{\dot{X}_t\})$$

7. Compute $\{\Delta\ddot{X}_t\}$ in Step 5 using $\{\Delta\dot{X}_t\}$, $\{\dot{X}_t\}$, and $\{\Delta X_t\}$ from Step 6.
8. Finally, compute $\{\ddot{X}_t\}$ from Step 5, using $\{\ddot{X}_t\}$ and $\{\Delta\ddot{X}_t\}$ from Step 7.

5.4.3 Fourth-order Runge-Kutta Method

In the fourth-order Runge-Kutta method, the system of second-order differential equatins (5.15) are converted into state variable form. That is, both the displacements and velocities are treated as unknowns $\{y\}$ defined by

$$\{y\} = \begin{Bmatrix} \{\dot{X}\} \\ \{X\} \end{Bmatrix} \tag{5.36}$$

Using Eq. (5.36), Eq. (5.15) can be rewritten as

$$\{X\} = -[M]^{-1}[K]\{X\} - [M]^{-1}[C]\{\dot{X}\} + [m]^{-1}\{F(t)\} \tag{5.37}$$

Using the identity $\{\dot{y}\} = \{\dot{y}\}$ (5.38)

We obtain from Eqs. (5.36) and (5.37)

$$\{\dot{y}\} = \left\{\frac{\{\dot{X}\}}{\{\ddot{X}\}}\right\} \left[\begin{array}{c|c} \dfrac{[O]}{-[M]^{-1}[K]} & \dfrac{[I]}{-[M]^{-1}[C]} \end{array}\right] \left\{\frac{\{X\}}{\{\dot{X}\}}\right\} + \left\{\frac{\{O\}}{[M]^{-1}\{F(t)\}}\right\} \tag{5.39}$$

or $\{\dot{y}\} = [E]\{Y\} + \{F^{*}(t)\}$ (5.40)

That is $\{\dot{y}\} = \{f(t, y)\}$ (5.41)

In the Runge-Kutta method, an approximation to $\{y_{y+\Delta t}\}$ is obtained from $\{y_t\}$ in such a way that the power series expansion of the approximation coincides, up to the terms of a certain order $(\Delta t)^N$ in the time interval Δt, with an actual Taylor series expansion of $(t + \Delta t)$ in powers of Δt. This method has the advantage that no initial values are required beyond the prescribed ones. The general fourth order algorithms are based on formulae of the form

$$\{y_{t+\Delta t}\} = \{y_t\} + \Delta t\,(aK_1 + bK_2 + cK_3 + dK_4) \tag{5.42}$$

where a, b, c, and d are constants and K_1, K_2, K_3, and K_4 are the appropriate derivative values computed in the interval $t_K < t < t_{K+\Delta t}$. Several fourth-order algorithms have been proposed. The following is due to Runge-Kutta and we omit presenting the details of its derivation.

$$\{y_{t+\Delta t}\} = \{y_t\} + \frac{\Delta t}{6}[K_1 + 2K_2 + 2K_3 + K_4] \tag{5.43}$$

in which

$$\begin{aligned} K_1 &= f(t, y_t) \\ K_2 &= f\left(t + \frac{\Delta t}{2}, y_t + K_1\frac{\Delta t}{2}\right) \\ K_3 &= f\left(t + \frac{\Delta t}{2}, y_t + K_2\frac{\Delta t}{2}\right) \\ K_4 &= f\left(t + \frac{\Delta t}{2}, y_t + K_3\frac{\Delta t}{2}\right) \end{aligned} \tag{5.44}$$

The Runge-Kutta algorithm does not require the calculation of higher derivatives. The method is completely self starting and the step-size can be changed easily between iterations and hence the method can be considered inherently stable. The truncation error e_t for the fourth-order Runge-Kutta scheme is of the form

$$e_t = c(\Delta t)^5 \tag{5.45}$$

where c is a constant which depends on $f(t, y)$ and its higher-order partial derivatives. Runge-Kutta method generates an artificial damping that unduly suppresses the amplitude of the response of a dynamic system.

5.5 IMPLICIT SCHEMES

In an implicit scheme, the difference equations are combined with the equations of motion, and the response to be evaluated is implicitly related to previously determined values. Hence the response quantities are calculated by directly solving the difference equations.

5.5.1 Houbolt Method

The Houbolt method is based on third-order interpolation of displacements X_t, and the multistep implicit formulae for $\dot{X}_t$, and $\ddot{X}_t$ are obtained in terms of X_t by using backward differences.

The difference formulae are summarized in the following with reference to Fig. 5.3. By considering a cubic curve that passes through the four successive ordinates, the following equations can be obtained:

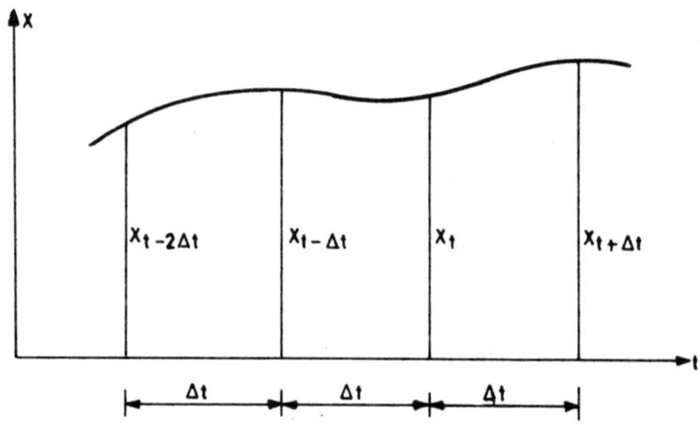

Fig. 5.3 Algorithm based on central difference method

$$X_t = X_{t+\Delta t} - \Delta t\, \dot{X}_{t+\Delta t} + \frac{\Delta t^2}{2} \ddot{X}_{t+\Delta t} - \frac{\Delta t^3}{6} \dddot{X}_{t+\Delta t} \tag{5.46}$$

$$X_{t-\Delta t} = X_{t+\Delta t} - (2\Delta t)\dot{X}_{t+\Delta t} + \left(\frac{2\Delta t}{2}\right)^2 \ddot{X}_{t+\Delta t} - \left(\frac{2\Delta t}{6}\right)^3 \dddot{X}_{t+\Delta t} \tag{5.47}$$

$$X_{t-2\Delta t} = X_{t+\Delta t} - (3\Delta t)\dot{X}_{t+\Delta t} + \left(\frac{3\Delta t}{2}\right)^2 \ddot{x}_{t+\Delta t} - \left(\frac{3\Delta t}{6}\right)^3 \dddot{X}_{t+\Delta t} \tag{5.48}$$

Solving Eqs. (5.46) to (5.48) for $\ddot{X}_{t+\Delta t}$ and $\dot{X}_{t+\Delta t}$, we get

$$\ddot{X}_{t+\Delta t} = \frac{1}{\Delta t^2}(2X_{t+\Delta t} - 5X_t + 4X_{t-\Delta t} - X_{t-2\Delta t}) \tag{5.49}$$

$$\dot{X}_{t+\Delta t} = \frac{1}{6\Delta t^2}(11X_{t+\Delta t} - 18X_t + 9X_{t-\Delta t} - 2X_{t-2\Delta t}) \tag{5.50}$$

The difference formulae in the Houbolt algorithm are therefore given by

$$\{\ddot{X}_{t+\Delta t}\} = \frac{1}{\Delta t^2}[2\{X_{t+\Delta t}\} - 5\{X_t\} + 4\{X_{t-\Delta t}\} - \{X_{t-2\Delta t}\}] \tag{5.51}$$

$$\{\dot{X}_{t+\Delta t}\} = \frac{1}{6\Delta t}[11\{X_{t+\Delta t}\} - 18\{X_t\} + 9\{X_{t-\Delta t}\} - 2\{X_{t-2\Delta t}\}] \tag{5.52}$$

By substituting the expressions for $\{\ddot{X}_{t+\Delta t}\}$ and $\{\dot{X}_{t+\Delta t}\}$ from (5.51) and (5.52), respectively into (5.15), we get

$$[\overline{M}]\{X_{t+\Delta t}\} = \{\overline{F}_{t+\Delta t}\} \tag{5.53}$$

Where $[\overline{M}]$ is the effective mass matrix and $\{\overline{F}_{t+\Delta t}\}$ is the effective force vector.

$$[\overline{M}] = \frac{2}{\Delta t^2}[M] + \frac{11}{6\Delta t}[C] + [K] \tag{5.54}$$

$$\{\overline{F}_{t+\Delta t}\} = \{F_{t+\Delta t}\} + \left(\frac{5}{\Delta t^2}[M] + \frac{3}{\Delta t}[C]\right)\{X_t\}$$

$$-\left(\frac{4}{\Delta t^2}[M] + \frac{3}{2\Delta t}[C]\right)\{X_{t-\Delta t}\} + \left(\frac{1}{\Delta t^2}[M] + \frac{1}{3\Delta t}[C]\right)\{X_{t-2\Delta t}\} \tag{5.55}$$

Note that the equilibrium equation at time $t + \Delta t$ given by, Eq. (5.53) is used in finding the solution for $\{X_{t+\Delta t}\}$. For this reason, this method is called an *implicit integration method.* It can be seen that the velocities and accelerations at time $t + \Delta t$ are obtained by substituting for $\{X_{t+\Delta t}\}$ in (5.52) and (5.51) respectively. Also that a knowledge of $X_t, X_{t-\Delta t}$, and $X_{t-2\Delta t}$ is needed to find solution for $\{X_{t+\Delta t}\}$. Since there is no direct method available to find $\{X_{t-\Delta t}\}$ and $\{X_{t-2\Delta t}\}$, we use the central difference method initially to find solution at time Δt and $2\Delta t$. This makes the method non-self-starting. The method also requires a large computer storage to store displacements for the previous time steps. The step-by-step procedure to,be used in the Houbolt method is summarized in Table 5.7. A basic difference between the Houbolt method in Table 5.7 and the central-difference method in Table 5.3 is the presence of the stiffness matrix K as a factor to the required displacements $X_{t+\Delta t}$ in Houbolt method. The term $KX_{t+\Delta t}$ appears because the equilibrium is considered at time $t + \Delta t$ and not at time t as in the central-difference method. There is no critical time-step limit, and Δt can in general be larger than that given for the central-difference method.

Example 5.6

Calculate the response of the system considered in Example 5.3 using the Houbolt method.

Solution

Taking the time step $\Delta t = 0.308$, and the following Table 5.6, we have

$$a_0 = \frac{2}{(\Delta t)^2} = 21.08$$

$$a_1 = \frac{11}{6\,\Delta t} = 5.952$$

$$a_2 = \frac{5}{(\Delta t)^2} = 52.707$$

$$a_3 = \frac{3}{\Delta t} = 9.74$$

$$a_4 = -2a_0 = -42.166$$

$$a_5 = -a_3/2 = -4.87$$

$$a_6 = \frac{a_0}{2} = 10.5415$$

$$a_7 = a_3/9 = 1.082$$

Table 5.7 Algorithm based on Houbolt Method

(a) *Initial Computations:*

1. Form stiffness $[K]$, mass $[M]$, and damping $[C]$ matrices
2. Initialize $\{X_0\}$, $\{\dot{X}_0\}$. and $\{\ddot{X}_0\}$.
3. Select time step Δt and calculate integration constants:

$$a_0 = \frac{2}{\Delta t^2}; a_1 = \frac{11}{6\Delta t}; a_2 = \frac{5}{\Delta t^2}; a_3 = \frac{3}{\Delta t}; a_4 = -2a_0;$$

$$a_5 = \frac{-a_3}{2}; a_6 = \frac{a_0}{2}; a_7 = \frac{a_3}{9}$$

4. Use special starting procedure, such as central-difference method to calculate $\{X_{\Delta t}\}$ and $\{X_{2\Delta t}\}$.
5. Calculate effective stiffness matrix:

$$[\overline{K}] = [K] + a_0 [M] + a_1 [C].$$

6. Triangularize $[\overline{K}]$: $[\overline{K}] = [L]\,[D]\,[L]^T$

(b) *For each time step:*

1. Calculate effective force vector at time $t + \Delta t$:

$$\{\overline{F}_{t+\Delta t}\} = \{F_{t+\Delta t}\} + [M]\,(a_2\{X_t\} + a_4\,\{X_{t-\Delta t}\} + a_6\{X_{t-2\Delta t}\})$$

$$+ [C]\,(a_3\{X_t\} + a_5\{X_{t-\Delta t}\} + a_7\{X_{t-2\Delta t}\})$$

2. Solve for displacements at time $t + \Delta t$

$$[\overline{K}]\,\{X_{t+\Delta t}\} = \{\overline{F}_{t+\Delta t}\}$$

3. Calculate $\{\dot{X}\}$ and $\{\ddot{X}\}$ at time $t + \Delta t$:

$$\{\dot{X}_{t+\Delta t}\} = a_1\{X_{t+\Delta t}\} - a_3\{X_t\} - a_5\{X_{t-\Delta t}\} - a_7\{X_{t-2\Delta t}\}$$

$$\{\ddot{X}_{t+\Delta t}\} = a_0\{X_{t+\Delta t}\} - a_2\{X_t\} - a_4\{X_{t-\Delta t}\} - a_6\{X_{t-2\Delta t}\}$$

We need $X_{\Delta t}$ and $X_{2\Delta t}$ in order to start the integration, which are taken from the results of central difference method in Example 5.3, as

$$\{X_{\Delta t}\} = \begin{bmatrix} 0.1187 \\ 0.1187 \end{bmatrix}$$

$$\{X_{2\Delta t}\} = \begin{bmatrix} 0.424 \\ 0.429 \end{bmatrix}$$

Next we compute $[\overline{K}]$ given by

$$[\overline{K}] = [K] + a_0\,[M] + a_1\,[C]$$

$$= \begin{bmatrix} 4 & 5 \\ 2 & 6 \end{bmatrix} + 21.08 \begin{bmatrix} 2 & 0 \\ 0 & 2 \end{bmatrix} + 5.952 \begin{bmatrix} 0 & 0 \\ 0 & 0 \end{bmatrix} = \begin{bmatrix} 46.166 & 5 \\ 2.0 & 48.166 \end{bmatrix}$$

$$[\overline{K}]^{-1} = \begin{bmatrix} 0.0218 & -2.226\times 10^{-6} \\ -9.03\times 10^{-4} & 0.0209 \end{bmatrix}$$

For each time step we need $\{\overline{F}_{t+\Delta t}\}$ Which is given by

$$\{\overline{F}_{t+\Delta t}\} = \{F_{t+\Delta t}\} + [M]\,(a_2\{X_t\} + a_4\{X_{t-\Delta t}\} + a_6\{X_{t-2\Delta t}\})$$

$$+ [C]\,(a_3\{X_t\} + a_5\{X_{t-\Delta t}\} + a_7\{X_{t-2\Delta t}\})$$

$$= \begin{bmatrix} 5 \\ 5 \end{bmatrix} + \begin{bmatrix} 2 & 0 \\ 0 & 2 \end{bmatrix} \left(52.707 \begin{bmatrix} 0.424 \\ 0.429 \end{bmatrix} - 42.166 \begin{bmatrix} 0.1187 \\ 0.1187 \end{bmatrix} \right.$$

$$\left. +10.5415 \begin{bmatrix} 0 \\ 0 \end{bmatrix} \right) + \begin{bmatrix} 0 & 0 \\ 0 & 0 \end{bmatrix} \left(9.74 \begin{bmatrix} 0.424 \\ 0.429 \end{bmatrix} - 4.87 \begin{bmatrix} 0.1187 \\ 0.1187 \end{bmatrix} \right.$$

$$\left. + 1.082 \begin{bmatrix} 0 \\ 0 \end{bmatrix} \right)$$

$$= \begin{bmatrix} 39.686 \\ 40.212 \end{bmatrix}$$

We solve $\{X_{t+\Delta t}\}$ for each time step from the following equation

$$[\overline{K}]\,\{X_{t+\Delta t}\} = \{\overline{F}_{t+\Delta t}\}$$

or $$\{X_{t+\Delta t}\} = [\overline{K}]^{-1}\,\{\overline{F}_{t+\Delta t}\}$$

The solution obtained for10 time-steps is summarized in Table 5.8.

Table 5.8 Results for Example 5.6 using the Houbolt Method

Time	Δt	$2\Delta t$	$3\Delta t$	$4\Delta t$	$5\Delta t$	$6\Delta t$	$7\Delta t$	$8\Delta t$	$9\Delta t$	10
X_1	0.1186	0.4406	0.8670	1.30	1.6640	1.9130	2.0450	2.0870	2.0840	2.0
X_2	0.1186	0.4125	0.7809	0.85	0.7308	0.3206	–0.3011	–1.024	–1.683	-2

5.5.2 Wilson Theta Method

The Wilson Theta method assumes that the acceleration of the system varies linearly between two instanats of time. Referring to Fig. 5.4, the acceleration is assumed to be linear from time $t_i = i\Delta t$ to time $t_{i+\theta} = t_i + \theta\Delta t$, where $\theta \geq 1.0$. Because of this reason, the method is known as the Wilson Theta Method.

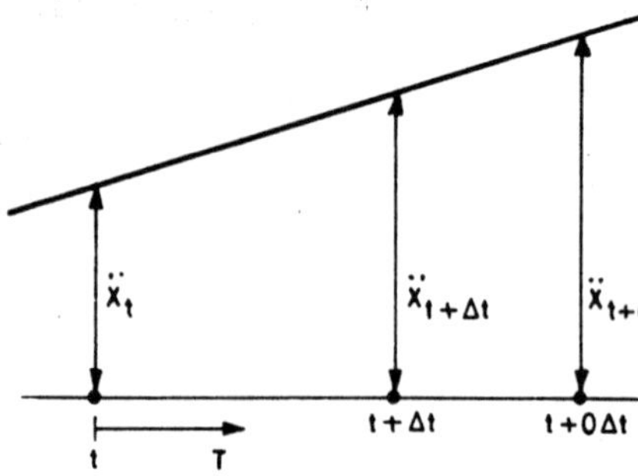

Fig. 5.4 Results for example 3.3 using the central difference method

If τ is time varying between t and $t+\theta\Delta t$, then for time interval t to $t+\theta\Delta t$, it can be assumed that

$$\ddot{X}_{t+\tau} = \ddot{X}_t + \frac{\tau}{\theta\Delta t}(\ddot{X}_{t+\theta\Delta t} - \ddot{X}_t) \tag{5.56}$$

Successive integration for Eq. (5.56) gives the following expressions for $X_{t+\tau}$ and $\dot{X}_{t+\Delta t}$

$$\ddot{X}_{t+\tau} = X_t + \dot{X}_t\tau + \frac{\tau^2}{2\theta\Delta t}(\ddot{X}_{t+\theta\Delta t} - \ddot{X}_t) \tag{5.57}$$

$$\dot{X}_{t+\tau} = X_t + \dot{X}_t\tau + \frac{1}{2}\ddot{X}_t\tau + \frac{\tau^3}{6\theta\Delta t}(\ddot{X}_{t+\theta\Delta t} - \ddot{X}_t) \tag{5.58}$$

Substituting $\tau = \theta\Delta t$ into the above Eqs. (5.57) and (5.58), we obtain the following expressions for $\dot{X}$ and x at time $t+\theta\Delta t$:

$$\dot{X}_{t+\theta\Delta t} = \dot{X}_t + \frac{\theta\Delta t}{2}(\ddot{X}_t + \ddot{X}_{t+\theta\Delta t}) \tag{5.59}$$

$$X_{t+\theta\Delta t} = X_t + \theta\,\Delta t\,\dot{X}_t + \frac{\theta^2\Delta t^2}{6} + (\ddot{X}_{t+\theta\Delta t} - 2\ddot{X}_t) \tag{5.60}$$

Solving Eqs. (5.59) and (5.60) for $\ddot{X}_{t+\theta\Delta t}$ and $\dot{X}_{t+\theta\Delta t}$ in terms of $X_{t+\theta\Delta t}$ we get

$$\ddot{X}_{t+\theta\Delta t} = \frac{6}{\theta^2\Delta t^2}(X_{t+\theta\Delta t} - X_t) - \frac{6}{\theta\Delta t}(\dot{X}_t - 2\ddot{X}_t) \tag{5.61}$$

The difference formulae in the Wilson Theta algorithm are then given by

$$\{\ddot{X}_{t+\theta\Delta t}\} = \frac{6}{\theta^2\Delta t^2}(\{X_{t+\theta\Delta t}\} - \{X_t\}) - \frac{6}{\theta\Delta t}\{\dot{X}_t\} - 2\{\ddot{X}_t\} \tag{5.62}$$

$$\{\dot{X}_{t+\theta\Delta t}\} = \frac{3}{\theta\Delta t}(\{X_{t+\theta\Delta}\} - \{X_t\}) - 2\{\dot{X}_t\} - \frac{\theta\Delta t}{2}\{\ddot{X}_t\} \tag{5.63}$$

We employ Eq. (5.15) at time $t+\Delta t$ to obtain a solution for displacement, velocity, and acceleration at time $t+\Delta t$. Since accelerations vary linearly, a linearly projected force vector is used such that

$$[M]\{\ddot{X}_{t+\theta\Delta t}\} + [C]\{\dot{X}_{t+\theta\Delta t}\} + [K]\{X_{t+\theta\Delta t}\} = \{F_{t+\theta\Delta t}\} \tag{5.64}$$

Where $\{F_{t+\theta\Delta t}\} = \{F_t\} + \theta(\{F_{t+\theta\Delta t}\} - \{F_t\})$

By substituting the expressions for $\{\ddot{X}_{t+\theta\Delta t}\}$ and $\{\dot{X}_{t+\theta\Delta t}\}$ from Eq. (5.62) and (5.63) respectively, into Eq. (5.64), we get

$$[\overline{M}]\{X_{t+\theta\Delta t}\} = \{F_{t+\theta\Delta t}\} \tag{5.65}$$

where the effective mass matrix $[\overline{M}]$ and the effective force vector $\{\overline{F}_{t+\theta\Delta t}\}$ are given by

$$[\overline{M}] = \frac{6}{\theta^2\Delta t^2}[M] + \frac{3}{\theta\Delta t}[C] + [K] \tag{5.66}$$

$$\{\overline{F}_{t+\theta\Delta t}\} = \{F_{t+\theta\Delta t}\} + \left(\frac{6}{\theta^2\Delta t^2}[M] + \frac{3}{\theta\Delta t}[C]\right) + \{X_t\} +$$

$$+\left(\frac{6}{\theta\Delta t}[M] + 2[C]\{\dot{X}_t\}\right) + \left(2[M] + \frac{\theta\Delta t}{2}[C]\{\ddot{X}_t\}\right) \tag{5.67}$$

Table 5.9 Algorithm based on Wilson Theta method

(a) *Initial Computations:*

1. Form stiffness $[K]$, mass $[M]$, and damping $[C]$ matrices
2. Initialize $\{X_0\}$, $\{\dot{X}_0\}$, and $\{\ddot{X}_0\}$.
3. Select time step Δt and calculate integration constants, $\theta = 1.4$ (say):

   $a_0 = \frac{6}{(\theta\Delta t)^2}$; $a_1 = \frac{3}{\theta\Delta t}$; $a_2 = 2a_1$; $a_3 = \frac{\theta\Delta t}{2}$; $a_4 = \frac{a_0}{\theta}$;

   $a_5 = \frac{-a_2}{\theta}$; $a_6 = 1 - \frac{3}{\theta}$; $a_7 = \frac{\Delta t}{2}$; $a_8 = \frac{\Delta t^2}{6}$
4. Form effective stiffness matrix: $[\overline{K}] = [K] + a_0[M] + a_1[C]$
5. Triangularize $[\overline{K}]$: $[\overline{K}] = [L][D][L]^T$

(b) *For each time step:*

1. Calculate effective force vector at time $t + \Delta t$:

   $\{\overline{F}_{t+\theta\Delta t}\} = \{F_t\} + \theta(\{F_{t+\Delta t}\} - \{F_t\}) + [M](a_0\{X_t\} + a_2\{\dot{X}_t\} + 2\{\ddot{X}_t\})$

   $+ [C](a_1\{X_t\} + 2\{\dot{X}_t\} + a_3\{\ddot{X}_t\})$
2. Solve for displacements at time $t + \theta\Delta t$

   $[\overline{K}]\{X_{t+\theta\Delta t}\} = \{\overline{F}_{t+\theta\Delta t}\}$
3. Calculate $\{X\}$, $\{\dot{X}\}$ and $\{\ddot{X}\}$, at time $t + \Delta t$:

   $\{\ddot{X}_{t+\Delta t}\} = a_4(\{X_{t+\theta\Delta t}\} - \{X_t\}) + a_5\{\dot{X}_t\} + a_6\{\ddot{X}_t\}$

   $\{\dot{X}_{t+\Delta t}\} = \{\dot{X}_t\} + a_7(\{\ddot{X}_{t+\Delta t}\} + \{\ddot{X}_t\})$

   $\{X_{t+\Delta t}\} = \{X_t\} + \Delta t\{\dot{X}_t\} + a_8(\{\ddot{X}_{t+\Delta t}\} + 2\{\ddot{X}_t\})$

The solution of Eq.(5.65) gives $\{X_{t+\theta\Delta t}\}$, which is then substituted into the following relationships to obtain the displacements, velocities, and accelerations at time $t + \Delta\tau$.

$$\{\ddot{X}_{t+\Delta t}\} = \frac{6}{\theta^2 \Delta t^2}(\{X_{t+\theta\Delta t}\} - \{X_t\}) - \frac{6}{\theta^2 \Delta t}\{X_t\} + \left(1 - \frac{3}{\theta}\right)\{\ddot{X}_t\} \tag{5.68}$$

$$\{\dot{X}_{t+\Delta t}\} = \{\dot{X}_t\} + \frac{\Delta t}{2}(\ddot{X}_{t+\Delta t}\} - \{\dot{X}_t\} \tag{5.69}$$

$$\{X_{t+\Delta t}\} = \{X_t\} + \Delta t\{\dot{X}_t\} + \frac{\Delta t^2}{6}(\{\ddot{X}_{t+\Delta t}\} - 2\{\ddot{X}_t\}) \tag{5.70}$$

When $\theta = 1.0$, the method reduces to the linear acceleration scheme. The method is unconditionally stable for linear dynamic systems when $\theta \geq 1.37$, and a value of $\theta = 1.4$ is often used for nonlinear dynamic systems. It may also be noted that no special starting procedures are needed, since $X, \dot{X}$, and $\ddot{X}$ are expressed at time $t + \Delta t$ in terms of the same quantities at time t only. The complete algorithm used in the Wilson Theta method is given in Table 5.9.

5.5.3 Newmark Beta Method

The Newmark Beta integration method is also based on the assumption that the acceleration varies linearly between two instants of time. Two parameters α and β this method which can be changed to suit the requirements of a particular problem. The expressions for velocity and displacements are given by

$$\{\dot{X}_{t+\Delta t}\} = \{\dot{X}_t\} + [(1-\alpha)\{\ddot{X}_t\} + \alpha\{\ddot{X}_{t+\Delta t}\}]\Delta t \tag{5.71}$$

$$\{X_{t+\Delta t}\} = \{X_t\} + \{\dot{X}_t \Delta t\} + \left[\left(\frac{1}{2} - \beta\right)\{\ddot{X}_t\} + \beta\{\ddot{X}_{t+\Delta t}\}\right]\Delta t^2 \tag{5.72}$$

The parameters α and β signify the influence of acceleration at the end of the interval Δt on the velocity and displacement, respectively. Therefore, α and β are chosen so as to obtain the desired integration accuracy and stability. When $\alpha = 1/6$, and $\beta = 1/2$, Eqs. (5.71) and (5.72) correspond to the linear acceleration method (which can also be obtained using $\theta = 1$ in the Wilson Theta method). When $\alpha = 1/2$ and $\beta = 0$, the acceleration is constant and equal to $\ddot{X}_t$ during each time interval. If $\alpha = 1/2$ and $\beta = 1/8$, the acceleration is constant from the beginning as $\ddot{X}_t$ and then changes to $\ddot{X}_{t+\Delta t}$ in the middle of the time interval Δt. When $\alpha = 1/2$ and $\beta = 1/4$, this corresponds to the assumption that the acceleration remains constant at an average value of $(\ddot{X}_t + \ddot{X}_{t+\Delta t})/2$. The finite difference formulae for the Newmark Beta scheme are

$$\{\ddot{X}_{t+\Delta t}\} = \frac{1}{\beta\,\Delta t^2}(\{X_{t+\Delta t}\} - \{X_t\}) - \frac{1}{\beta\Delta t}\{\dot{X}_t\} - \left(\frac{1}{2\beta} - 1\right)\{\ddot{X}_t\} \tag{5.73}$$

$$\{\dot{X}_{t+\Delta t}\} = \frac{\alpha}{\beta\Delta t}(\{X_{t+\Delta t}\} - \{X_t\}) - \left(\frac{\alpha}{\beta} - 1\right) - \{\dot{X}_t\} - \Delta t\left(\frac{\alpha}{2\beta} - 1\right)\{\ddot{X}_t\} \tag{5.74}$$

Eq. (5.15) can be employed to obtain a solution for displacements, velocities and accelerations at time $t + \Delta t$. Therefore, by substituting the expressions for $\{\ddot{X}_{t+\Delta t}\}$ and $\{\dot{X}_{t+\Delta t}\}$ from Eqs. (5.73) and (5.74), rspectively, into Eq. (5.15), we get

$$[\overline{M}]\,\{X_{t+\Delta t}\} = \{\overline{F}_{t+\Delta t}\} \tag{5.75}$$

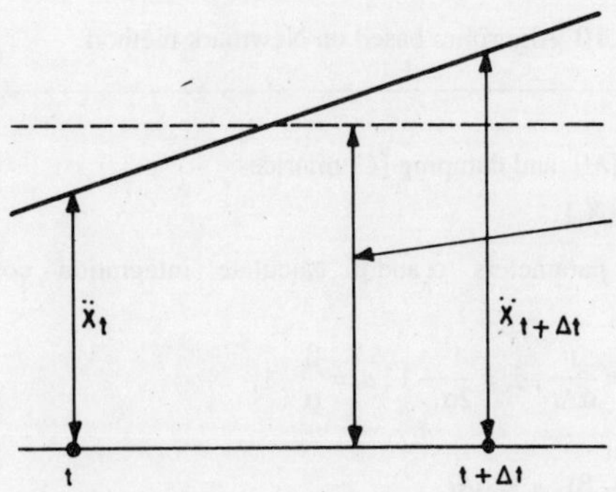

Fig. 5.5 Newmark's constant average-acceleration

where the effective mass matrix $[\overline{M}]$ and the effective force vector $\{\overline{F}_{t+\Delta t}\}$ are given by

$$[\overline{M}] = \frac{1}{\beta\Delta t^2}[M] + \frac{\alpha}{\beta\Delta t}[C] + [K] \quad (5.76)$$

$$\{\overline{F}_{t+\Delta t}\} = \{F_{t+\Delta t}\} + \left[\left(\frac{1}{2\beta} - 1\right)[M] + \Delta t\left(\frac{\alpha}{2\beta} - 1\right)[C]\right]\{\ddot{X}_t\} +$$

$$+\left[\frac{1}{\beta\Delta t}[M] + \left(\frac{\alpha}{\beta} - 1\right)[C]\right]\{\dot{X}_t\} + \left[\frac{1}{\beta\Delta t^2}[M] + \frac{\alpha}{\beta\Delta t}[C]\right]\{X_t\} \quad (5.77)$$

Solution of Eq. (5.75) gives $\{X_{t+\Delta t}\}$, which is then substituted into (5.73) and (5.74) in order to obtain the accelerations and velocities at time $t + \Delta t$. One of the features of Newmark Beta method is that for linear systems the amplitude is conserved and the response is unconditionally stable, provided that $\alpha \geq 1/2$ and $\beta \geq \frac{1}{4}\left(\alpha + \frac{1}{2}\right)^2$.For values of $\alpha = 1/2$ and $\beta = 1/4$ the largest truncation errors occur in frequency of the response as opposed to other β values. It is also important to note that unless $\beta = 1/2$, a spurious damping proportional to $(\beta - 1/2)$ is introduced. If $\beta = 0$, a negative damping results; this involves a self-excited vibration arising solely from the numerical procedure. In a likewise manner, if $\beta > 1/2$, a positive damping is introduced which reduces the magnitude of the response even without the presence of real damping in the system. For a multidegree of freedom system in which a number of modes constitute the total response, the peak amplitude may not be correct.

The complete algorithm using the Newmark Beta integration method is given in Table 5.10.

Example 5.7

Calculate the displacement response of the system considered in Example 5.3 using the Newmark Beta method. Use $\alpha = 0.25$ and $\beta = 0.5$.

Solution

Following the steps of calculations given in Table 5.10 we have

Table 5.10 Algorithm based on Newmark method

(a) *Initial Computations:*

1. Form stiffness $[K]$, mass $[M]$, and damping $[C]$ matrices
2. Initialize $\{X_0\}$, $\{\dot{X}_0\}$, and $\{\ddot{X}_0\}$.
3. Select time step Δt, parameters α and β calculate integration constants, $\beta \geq 0.5$; $\alpha \geq 0.25$; $(0.5+\beta)^2$

$$a_0 = \frac{1}{\alpha(\Delta t)^2};\ a_1 = \frac{\beta}{\alpha \Delta t};\ a_2 = \frac{1}{\alpha \Delta t};\ a_3 = \frac{1}{2\alpha} - 1;\ a_4 = \frac{\beta}{\alpha} - 1;$$

$$a_5 = \frac{\Delta t}{2}\left(\frac{\beta}{\alpha} - 2\right);\ a_6 = \Delta t(1-\beta);\ a_7 = \beta \Delta t.$$

4. Form effective stiffness matrix : $[\overline{K}] = [K] + a_0[M] + a_1[C]$
5. Triangularize $[\overline{K}]$: $[\overline{K}] = [L]\ [D]\ [L]^T$

(b) *For each time step:*

1. Calculate effective force vector at time $t+\Delta t$:

$$\{\overline{F}_{t+\Delta t}\} = \{F_{t+\Delta t}\} + [M]\ (a_0\{X_t\} + a_2\{\dot{X}_t\} + a_3\{\ddot{X}_t\})$$
$$+[C]\ (a_1\{X_t\} + a_4\{\dot{X}_t\} + a_5\{\ddot{X}_t\})$$

2. Solve for displacements at time $t+\Delta t$

$$[\overline{K}]\ \{X_{t+\Delta t}\} = \{\overline{F}_{t+\Delta t}\}$$

3. Calculate $\{\ddot{X}\}$, and $\{\dot{X}\}$, at time $t+\Delta t$:

$$\{\ddot{X}_{t+\Delta t}\} = a_0(\{X_{t+\Delta t}\} - \{X_t\}) - a_2\{\dot{X}_t\} - a_3\{\ddot{X}_t\}$$

$$\{\dot{X}_{t+\Delta t}\} = \{\dot{X}_t\} + a_6\{\ddot{X}_t\} + a_7\{\ddot{X}_{t+\Delta t}\}$$

$$\{X_0\} = \{\dot{X}_0\} = 0 \text{ and } \{\ddot{X}_0\} = \begin{bmatrix} 2.5 \\ 2.5 \end{bmatrix}$$

The integration constants are with time step $\Delta t = 0.308$.

$$a_0 = \frac{1}{\alpha(\Delta t)^2} = \frac{1}{0.25(0.308)^2} = 42.17$$

$$a_1 = \frac{\beta}{\alpha \Delta t} = -\frac{0.5}{0.25(0.308)} = 6.49$$

$$a_2 = \frac{1}{\alpha \Delta t} = -\frac{1}{0.25(0.308)} = 12.99$$

$$a_3 = \left(\frac{1}{2\alpha} - 1\right) = \frac{1}{2(0.25)} - 1 = 1.0$$

$$a_4 = \frac{\beta}{\alpha} - 1 = \frac{0.5}{0.25} - 1 = 1.0$$

$$a_5 = \frac{\Delta t}{2}\left(\frac{\beta}{\alpha} - 2\right) = \frac{0.308}{2}\left(\frac{0.5}{0.25} - 2\right) = 0.0$$

$$a_6 = \Delta t(1-\beta) = 0.308(10.5) = 0.154$$

$$a_7 = \beta\,\Delta t = 0.5(0.308) = 0.154$$

The effective stiffness matrix is

$$[\overline{K}] = [K] + a_0\,[M] + a_1\,[C]$$

$$= \begin{bmatrix} 4 & 5 \\ 2 & 6 \end{bmatrix} + 42.17 \begin{bmatrix} 2 & 0 \\ 0 & 2 \end{bmatrix} + 6.49 \begin{bmatrix} 0 & 0 \\ 0 & 0 \end{bmatrix} = \begin{bmatrix} 88.34 & 5 \\ 2.0 & 90.34 \end{bmatrix}$$

For each time step we need to evaluate

$$\{\overline{F}_{t+\Delta t}\} = \{F_{t+\Delta t}\} + [M]\,(a_0\,\{\dot{X}_t\} + a_2\{X_t\} + a_3\{\ddot{X}_t\}) +$$

$$+ [C]\,(a_1\{X_t\} + a_4\,\{\dot{X}_t\} + a_5\{\ddot{X}_t\})$$

$$= \begin{bmatrix} 5 \\ 5 \end{bmatrix} + \begin{bmatrix} 2 & 0 \\ 0 & 2 \end{bmatrix} \left(42.17 \begin{bmatrix} 0 \\ 0 \end{bmatrix} + 12.99 \begin{bmatrix} 0 \\ 0 \end{bmatrix} + 1 \begin{bmatrix} 2.5 \\ 2.5 \end{bmatrix} \right)$$

$$+ \begin{bmatrix} 0 & 0 \\ 0 & 0 \end{bmatrix} \left(6.49 \begin{bmatrix} 0 \\ 0 \end{bmatrix} + 1 \begin{bmatrix} 0 \\ 0 \end{bmatrix} + \begin{bmatrix} 2.5 \\ 2.5 \end{bmatrix} \right) = \begin{bmatrix} 10 \\ 10 \end{bmatrix}$$

Then, solve for displacements at each time step.

$$[\overline{K}]\,\{X_{t+\Delta t}\} = \{\overline{F}_{t+\Delta t}\}$$

and compute

$$\{\ddot{X}_{t+\Delta t}\} = a_0\,(\{X_{t+\Delta t}\} - \{X_t\}) - a_2\{\dot{X}_t\} - a_3\{\ddot{X}_t\}$$

$$= 42.17\,(\{X_{t+\Delta t}\} - \{X_t\}) - 12.99\,\{\dot{X}_t\} - 1\{\ddot{X}_t\}$$

$$\{\dot{X}_{t+\Delta t}\} = \{\dot{X}_t\} + 0.154\,\{\ddot{X}_t\} + 0.154\,\{\ddot{X}_{t+\Delta t}\}$$

The solution obtained is given in Table 5.11 for 10 time steps.

Table 5.11 Results for Example 5.8 using the Newmark Beta method

Time	Δt	$2\Delta t$	$3\Delta t$	$4\Delta t$	$5\Delta t$	$6\Delta t$	$7\Delta t$	$8\Delta t$	$9\Delta t$	$10\Delta t$
X_1	0.113	0.423	0.849	1.290	1.651	1.882	1.980	1.992	1.9860	2.022
X_2	0.109	0.382	0.677	0.822	0.681	0.212	–0.509	–1.310	–1.979	-2.336

5.5.4 Park Stiffly Stable Method

The Park Stiffly Stable method is an accurate method for low frequency ranges and stable for all higher-frequency components. The velocity in the Park Stiffly stable method is derived by using a linear combination of the following two difference formulae:

$$\dot{X}_{t+\Delta t} = \frac{1}{6\Delta t}[11X_{t+\Delta t} - 18X_t + 9X_{t-\Delta t} - 2X_{t-2\Delta t}] \tag{5.78}$$

$$\dot{X}_{t+\Delta t} = \frac{1}{2\Delta t}(2X_{t+\Delta t} - 4X_t + X_{t-\Delta t}) \tag{5.79}$$

The linear combination of (5.78) and (5.79) gives

$$\dot{X}_{t+\Delta t} = \frac{1}{2}[\frac{1}{2\Delta t}(3X_{t+\Delta t} - 4X_t + X_{t-2\Delta t}) + \frac{1}{6\Delta t}(11X_{t+\Delta t} -$$

$$18X_t + 9X_{t-\Delta t} - 2X_{t-2\Delta t})] \tag{5.80}$$

$$\dot{X}_{t+\Delta t} = \frac{1}{6\Delta t}(10X_{t+\Delta t} - 15\dot{X}_t + 6\dot{X}_{t-\Delta t} - \dot{X}_{t-2\Delta t}) \tag{5.81}$$

Similarly, for the acceleration we obtain

$$\ddot{X}_{t+\Delta t} = \frac{1}{6\Delta t}(10\dot{X}_{t+\Delta t} - 15\dot{X}_t + 6\dot{X}_{t-\Delta t} - \dot{X}_{t-2\Delta t}) \tag{5.82}$$

The difference formulae in the Park Stiffly method are given by

$$\{\ddot{X}_{t+\Delta t}\} = \frac{1}{6\Delta t}[10\{\dot{X}_{t+\Delta t}\} - 15\{\dot{X}_t\} + 6\{\dot{X}_{t-\Delta t}\} - \{\dot{X}_{t-2\Delta t}\}] \tag{5.83}$$

$$\{\dot{X}_{t+\Delta t}\} = \frac{1}{6\Delta t}[10\{X_{t+\Delta t}\} - 15\{X_t\} + 6\{X_{t-\Delta t}\} - \{X_{t-2\Delta t}\}] \tag{5.84}$$

We consider Eq. (5.15) to obtain solution for the displacements, velocities and accelerations at time $t + \Delta t$. By substituting the expressions for $\{\ddot{X}_{t+\Delta t}\}$ and $\{\dot{X}_{t+\Delta t}\}$ from (5.83) and (5.84), respectively, into (5.15), we get

$$[\overline{M}]\,\{X_{t+\Delta t}\} = \{\overline{F}_{t+\Delta t}\} \tag{5.85}$$

where the effective mass matrix $[\overline{M}]$ and the effective force vector $\{\overline{F}_{t+\Delta t}\}$ are given by

$$[\overline{M}] = \frac{100}{36\,\Delta t^2}[M] - \frac{10}{6\Delta t}[C] + [K] \tag{5.86}$$

$$\{\overline{F}_{t+\Delta t}\} = \frac{15}{6\Delta t}[M]\,\{\dot{X}_t\} - \frac{1}{\Delta t}[M]\,\{\dot{X}_{t-\Delta t}\} + \frac{1}{6\Delta t}[M]\,\{\dot{X}_{t-2\Delta t}\} +$$

$$+\left(\frac{150}{36\Delta t^2}[M] + \frac{15}{6\Delta t}[C]\right)\{X_t\} - \left(\frac{10}{6\Delta t^2}[M] + \frac{1}{\Delta t}[C]\right)\{X_{t-\Delta t}\} +$$

$$+\left(\frac{1}{36\Delta t^2}[M] + \frac{1}{6\Delta t}[C]\right)\{X_{t-2\Delta t}\} \tag{5.87}$$

The solution of Eq. (5.85) gives $\{X_{t+\Delta t}\}$, Which is then substituted in Eq. (5.84) to obtain velocities. The values of $\{\ddot{X}_{t+\Delta t}\}$ are then obtained by the use of Eq. (5.83). Note in the Park Stiffly stable method, the calculation of $\{X_{t+\Delta t}\}$ requires the displacements and velocities at t, $t - \Delta t$, and $t - 2\Delta t$. Therefore, in order to obtain the solution at time Δt and $2\Delta t$, a special starting procedure is needed which makes the method non-self-starting. The complete algorithm based on Park Stiffly stable method used in the integration is given in Table 5.12. The method requires a large computer memory in order to store the displacements and velocities for the two previous time steps.

Table 5.12 Algorithm based on Park Stiffly Stable Method

(a) *Initial Computations:*

1. Form stiffness $[K]$, mass $[M]$, and damping $[C]$ matrices
2. Initialize $\{X_0\}$, $\{\dot{X}_0\}$, and $\{\ddot{X}_0\}$.
3. Select time step Δt and calculate integration constants

$$a_0 = \frac{10}{6\Delta t};\ a_1 = \frac{-15}{6\Delta t};\ a_2 = \frac{1}{\Delta t};\ a_3 = \frac{-1}{6\Delta t}$$

4. Form effective stiffness matrix: $[\overline{K}] = a_0^2[M] - a_0[C] + [K]$
5. Triangularize $[\overline{K}]:[\overline{K}] = [L]\ [D]\ [L]^T$

(b) *For each time step:*

1. Calculate effective force vector at time $t + \Delta t$:

$$\{\overline{F}_{t+\Delta t}\} = (-a_1\{X_t\} - a_2\{\dot{X}_{t-\Delta t}\} - a_3\{\dot{X}_{t-2\Delta t}\} - a_0 a_1\{X_t\} - a_0\{X_{t-\Delta t}\}$$

$$+a_3^2\{X_{t-2\Delta t}\})[M] - (a_1\{X_t\} + a_2\{X_{t-\Delta t}\} + a_3\{X_{t-2\Delta t}\})[C]$$

2. Solve for displacements at time $t + \Delta t$

$$[\overline{M}]\ \{X_{t+\Delta t}\} = \{\overline{F}_{t+\Delta t}\}$$

3. Calculate $\{\dot{X}\}$, and $\{\ddot{X}\}$, at time $t + \Delta t$:

$$\{\dot{X}_{t+\Delta t}\} = a_0\{X_{t+\Delta t}\} + a_1\{X_t\} + a_2\{X_{t-\Delta t}\} + a_3\{X_{t-2\Delta t}\}$$

$$\{\ddot{X}_{t+\Delta t}\} = a_0\{\dot{X}_{t+\Delta t}\} + a_1\{\dot{X}_t\} + a_2\{X_{t-\Delta t}\} + a_3\{\dot{X}_{t-2\Delta t}\}$$

5.6 CASE STUDY

5.6.1 Linear Dynamic System

For the displacement response $\{X\}$ of a linear dynamic system, one can use either the normal mode superposition method of dynamic analysis (see sec. 5.7) or direct numerical integration methods. To illustrate the performance of various integration methods and to compare the computational time, efficiency, stability, and accuracy, a linear dynamic system with two degrees of freedom as shown in Fig. 5.6, was used. The equations of motion for this two degrees of freedom linear spring and viscous damper system are

$$\begin{bmatrix} M_1 & 0 \\ 0 & M_2 \end{bmatrix}\begin{bmatrix} \ddot{X}_1 \\ \ddot{X}_2 \end{bmatrix} + \begin{bmatrix} C_1 + C_2 & -C_2 \\ -C_2 & C_2 \end{bmatrix}\begin{bmatrix} \dot{X}_1 \\ \dot{X}_2 \end{bmatrix}$$

$$+\begin{bmatrix} K_1 + K_2 & -K_2 \\ -K_2 & K_2 \end{bmatrix}\begin{bmatrix} X_1 \\ X_2 \end{bmatrix} = \begin{bmatrix} F_1(t) \\ F_2(t) \end{bmatrix} \tag{a}$$

The numerical values of the mass, damping, and stiffness matrices are given as

$$[M] = \begin{bmatrix} 1 & 0 \\ 0 & 10 \end{bmatrix}$$

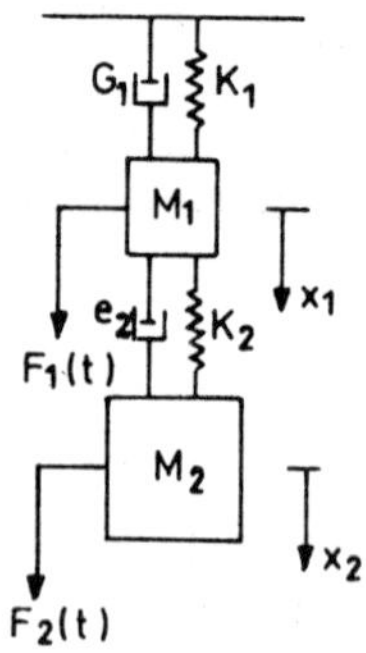

Fig. 5.6 Algorithm based on two cycle integration with trapezoidal rule

$$[K] = \begin{bmatrix} 21 & -1 \\ -1 & 1 \end{bmatrix}$$

$$[C] = \begin{bmatrix} 0.2 & -0.1 \\ -0.1 & 0.1 \end{bmatrix}$$

All the initial conditions are assumed to be zero and the forcing vector is assumed as

$$\begin{Bmatrix} F_1(t) \\ F_2(t) \end{Bmatrix} = \begin{Bmatrix} 0 \\ 4 \end{Bmatrix} \text{ for } t > 0$$

and

$$\begin{Bmatrix} F_1(t) \\ F_2(t) \end{Bmatrix} = \begin{Bmatrix} 0 \\ 0 \end{Bmatrix} \text{ for } t < 0$$

The results obtained by various integration methods are shown in Figs. 5.7 to 5.13. For all the methods, the time step of 0.025 seconds was chosen. A vlaue of $\theta = 1.5$ was used in the Wilson Theta method and the parameters $\alpha = 1/2$ and $\beta = 1/6$ for the Newmark Beta method. All the integration methods gave stable and

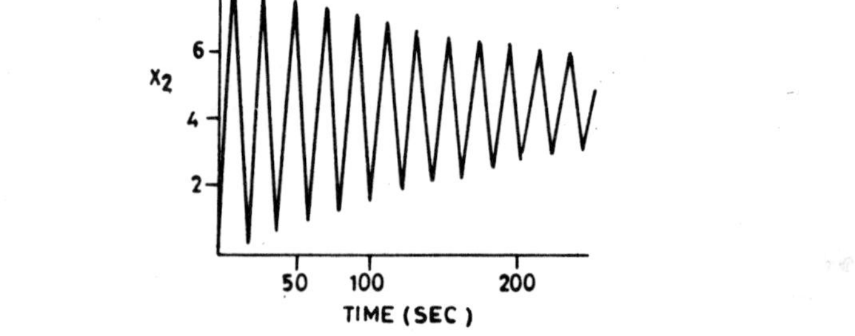

Fig. 5.7(a, b) Algorithm based on Houbolt method

accurate results. The implicit methods were started by using the fourth-order Runge-Kutta method for the initial time steps. The accuracy of these various integration methods is quite evident from the comparison with the analytical solution [15], as shown in Fig. 5.14. The comparison of computational time of various integration methods used in this case study are summarized in Table 5.13.

Table 5.13 Comparison of computational time of various direct integration methods for a linear dynamic system (adapted from Garg and Dukkipati [15])

Integration Method	CPU time (sec)
Explicit Methods:	
1. Central Difference	26.32
2. Two-cycle iteration with trapezoidal rule	25.20
3. Fourth-order Runge-Kutta	27.41
Implicit Methods:	
4. Houbolt	26.04
5. Wilson Theta ($\theta = 1.5$)	27.21
6. Newmark Beta ($\alpha = \frac{1}{2}$ and $\beta = \frac{1}{6}$)	27.95
7. Park Stiffly stable	26.69

*DEC-2050 Computer

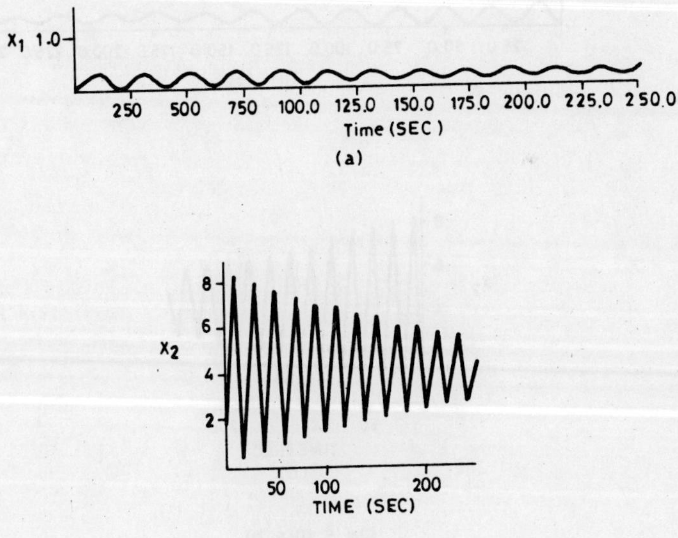

Fig. 5.8(a, b)

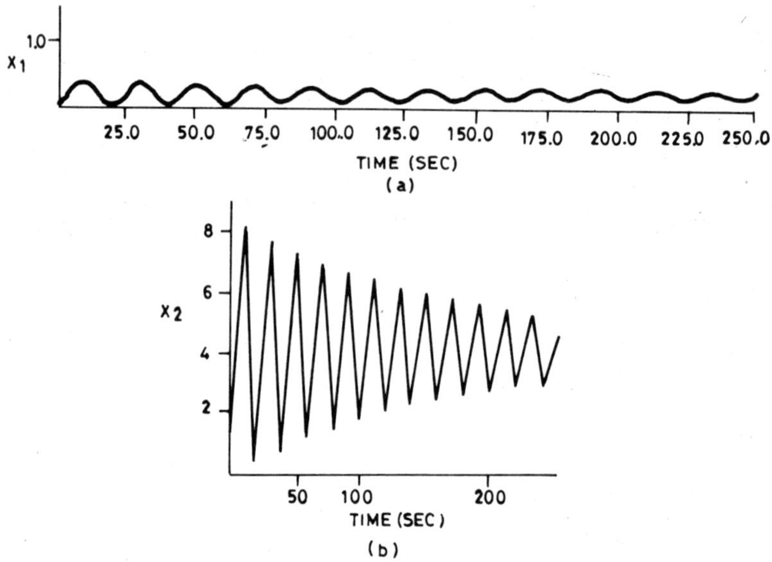

Fig. 5.9(a, b)

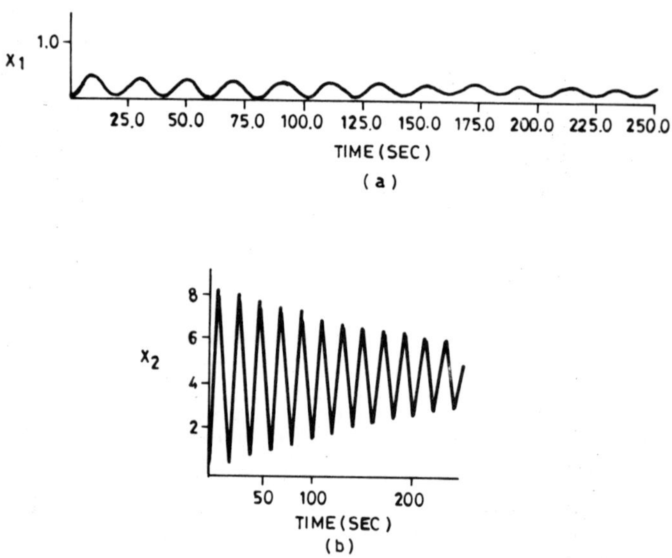

Fig. 5.10(a, b)

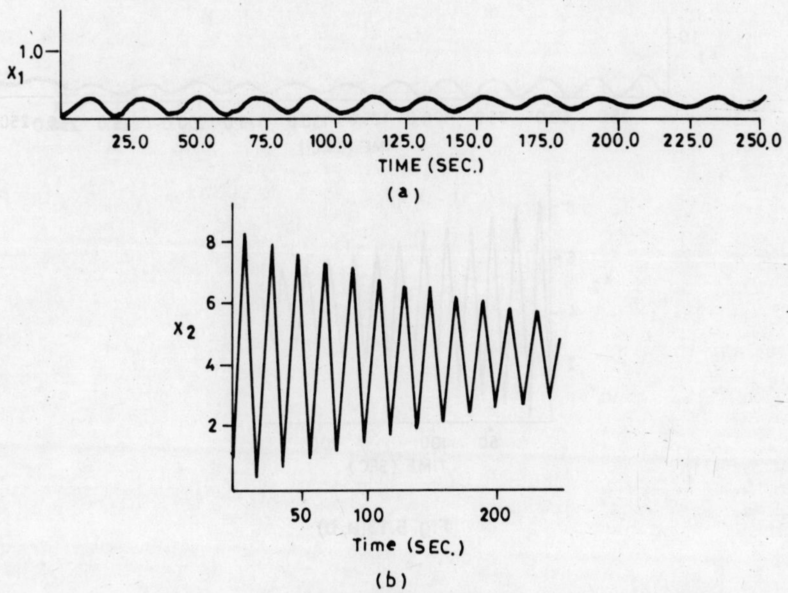

Fig. 5.11(a, b)

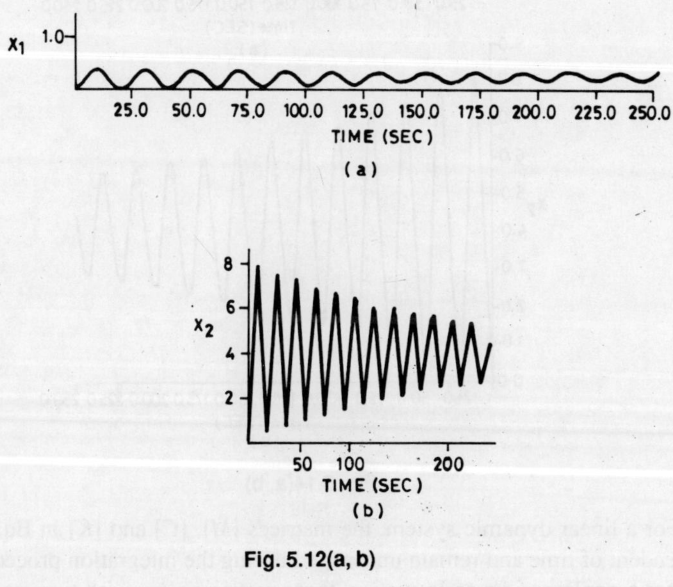

Fig. 5.12(a, b)

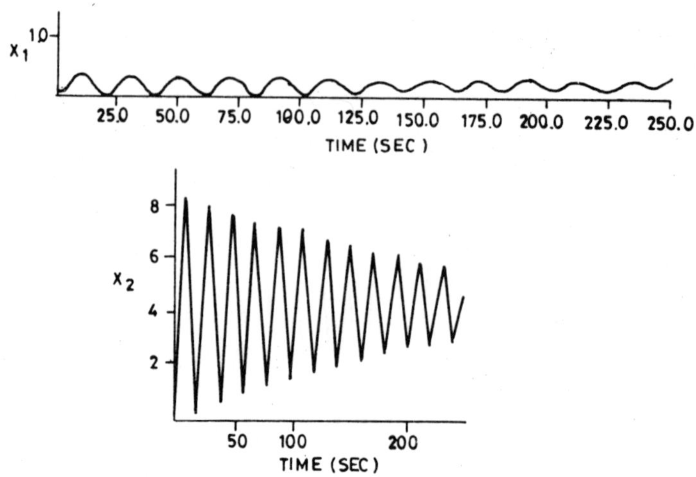

Fig. 5.13(a, b)

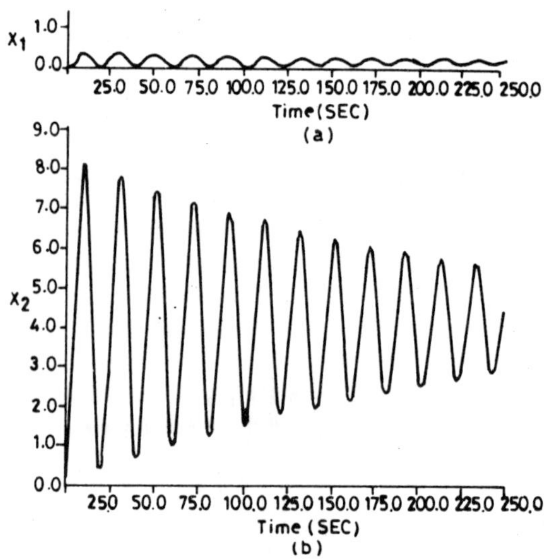

Fig. 5.14(a, b)

For a linear dynamic system, the matrices $[M]$, $[C]$ and $[K]$ in Eq. (5.15) are independent of time and remain unchanged during the integration procedure. However, for a nonlinear dynamic system, these matrices vary with time and therefore should be modified (updated) during integration of the equations of motion. For the displacement response $\{X\}$ of a linear dynamic system represented by a set of equations of motion, one can use either the normal mode superposition method of dynamic analysis or direct numerical integration methods. However, for solution of a dynamic system with a set of nonlinear equations of motion, only the latter procedure is applicable.

5.6.2 Nonlinear Dynamic System

In order to illustrate the performance of various explicit and implicit integration methods, they are applied on a railway wheel-axle set with nonlinear equations of motion. A schematic representation of a railway wheel-axle set is shown in Fig. 5.15. The two non-linear equations of motion for this wheel-axle set, for the lateral and yaw degrees of freedom are:

$$M\ddot{Y} + \frac{2f_{33}}{V}(\dot{y} - V\psi - \frac{2f_{12}}{V}\psi - \frac{2f_{12}}{r_0}\Delta_2(y) + W_A\Delta_L(y)$$

$$+K_y y + C_y \dot{y} = F_y(t) \qquad \text{(a)}$$

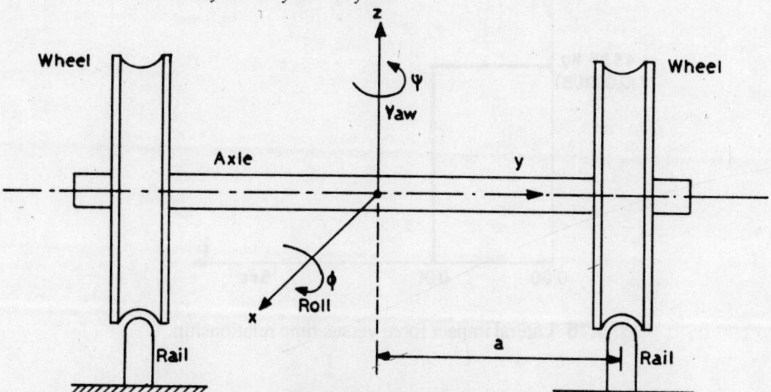

Fig. 5.15 Wheel-axle set

$$I_\omega\ddot{\psi} + \frac{2a^2}{V}f_{11}\dot{\psi} + \frac{2af_{11}}{r_0}\left(\frac{r_L - r_R}{2}\right) + \frac{2f_{22}}{V}\dot{\psi} - \frac{2f_{12}}{V}(\dot{y} - V\psi) -$$

$$-\frac{2f_{22}}{r_0}\Delta_1(y) - a\,\psi\,W_A\,\delta_0 + K_\psi\psi + C_\psi\dot{\psi} = F_\psi(t) \qquad \text{(b)}$$

where M = mass of the wheel-axle set: 5253.804 Nsec^2/m(30 lb sec^2 / in)

I_ω = Yaw moment of inertia of the wheel: 1864.249 Kgm Sec^2 (16,500 lb in sec^2)

a = half of the distance between contact points on two rails: 0.762 m (30 in)

r = radius of the Wheel: 0.508 m (20 in)

f_{33} = longitudinal creep coefficient: 1.633×10^3 Kg(3.6×10^6 1b)

f_{12} = lateral/ spin creep coefficient; 0.209×10^6 Kg(0.46×10^6 1b)

f_{22} = spin creep coefficient: 19.314 Kg m^2(66,000 in^{2}1b)

f_{11} = lateral creep coefficient: 1.769×10^6Kg (3.9×10^6 1b)

W_A = axle load: 29937.096 Kg (66,000 1b)

K_y = lateral stiffness: 87.563×10^4 N/m (5000 lb/in)

C_y = lateral damping: 45.359 Kg sec/rad (100 1b sec/rad)

K_ψ = yaw stiffness: 21.151×10^6 Kg. m/rad (187,200,000 in 1b (rad)

C_ψ = yaw damping: 3525.126 Kg m sec/rad (31,200 1b in sec/rad)
V = axle speed: 382.422 m/sec (15,056 in/sec)
δ_0 = wheel conicity: 0.05
$F_Y(t)$ = lateral input force (given in Fig. 5.16)
$F_\psi(t)$ = Yaw input moment: 0

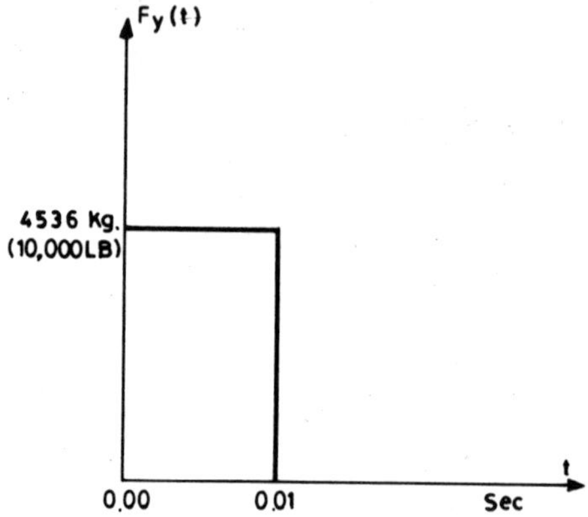

Fig. 5.16 Lateral impact force versus time relationship.

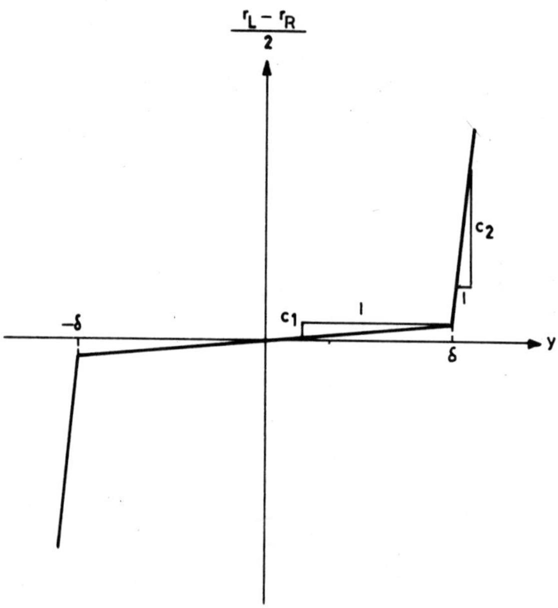

Fig. 5.17 Variation with lateral displacement of the difference in the rolling wheel-axle set shown (c_1 is 0.005, c_2 is 10.2, and δ is 0.35 in.; γ_L and γ_R taneous rolling radii of left and right wheels, respectively.)

The initial conditions at time $t = 0$ are, $y = \dot{y} = \psi = \dot{\psi} = 0$. The variation of the difference in rolling radii $\Delta_1(y), \Delta_2(y)$, and $\Delta_L(y)$ with respect to the lateral displacement, y are given in Figs. (5.17) and (5.18). The given equations of motion (a) and (b) can be arranged in matrix form as

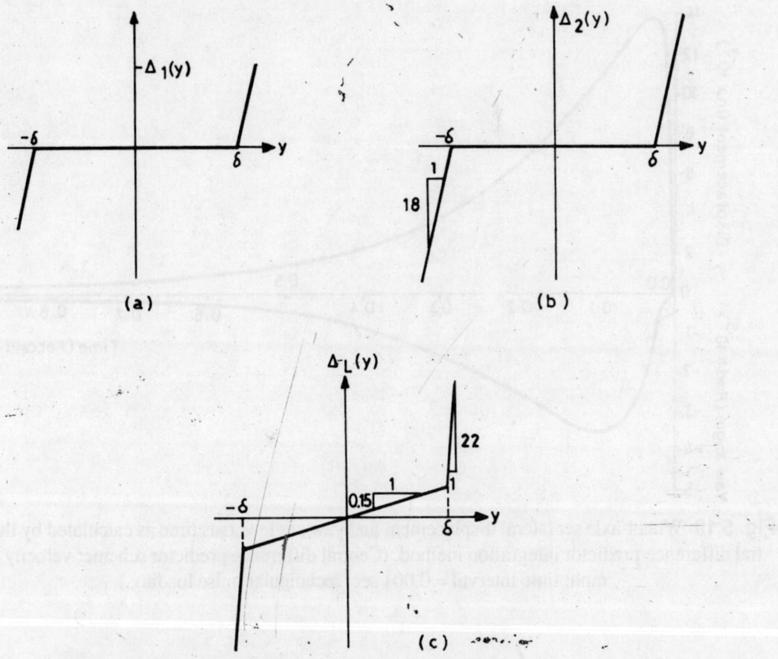

Fig. 5.18 Variation of (a)Δ_1 (y), (b) Δ_2 (y), and (c) ΔL (y) with lateral displacement of the wheel-axle set

$$\begin{bmatrix} M & 0 \\ 0 & I_\omega \end{bmatrix} \begin{Bmatrix} \ddot{Y} \\ \ddot{\psi} \end{Bmatrix} + \begin{bmatrix} \dfrac{2f_{33}}{V} + C_y & -\dfrac{2f_{12}}{V} \\ -\dfrac{2f_{12}}{V} & C_\psi + \dfrac{2a^2 f_{11}}{V} + \dfrac{2f_{22}}{V} \end{bmatrix} \begin{Bmatrix} \dot{y} \\ \dot{\psi} \end{Bmatrix}$$

$$+ \begin{bmatrix} K_y & -2f_{33} \\ 0 & 2f_{12} - a W_A \delta_0 + K_\psi \end{bmatrix} \begin{Bmatrix} y \\ \psi \end{Bmatrix}$$

$$= \begin{Bmatrix} F_y(t) + \dfrac{2f_{12}}{r_0} \Delta_2(y) - W_A \Delta_L(y) \\ F_\psi(t) + \dfrac{2f_{22}}{r_0} \Delta_1(y) - \dfrac{2af_{11}}{r_0} \left(\dfrac{r_L - r_R}{2} \right) \end{Bmatrix} \qquad \text{(c)}$$

with $\alpha = 0.5$ and $\beta = 1/6$ and Park Stiffly stable methods were implemented.

The two equations (c) were solved numerically by using the following direct integration methods: (1) Central difference; (2) Two-cycle iteration with trapezoidal rule; (3) Fourth-order Runge-Kutta; 4) Houbolt; (5) Wilson Theta; (6) Newmark Beta; and (7) Park Stiffly stable method. All the above integration methods were run using time steps of 0.001 sec for a total duration of 1 second, by which time the lateral (y) and yaw (ψ) displacements of the wheel-axle set had reached steady-state values. Time histories for the two parameters y and ψ were then plotted as shown in Figs. 5.19 to 5.25. The results were compared with respect to computing time and stability of solution. Of the three explicit and four implicit integration

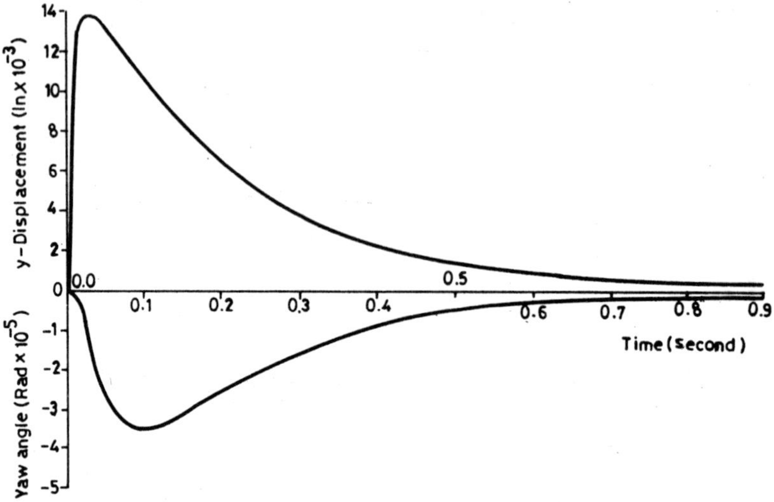

Fig. 5.19 Wheel-axle set lateral displacement and yaw angle versus time as calculated by the central difference predictor integration method. (Central difference predictor scheme: velocity = 60 mph; time interval = 0.001 sec; rectangular pulse loading.)

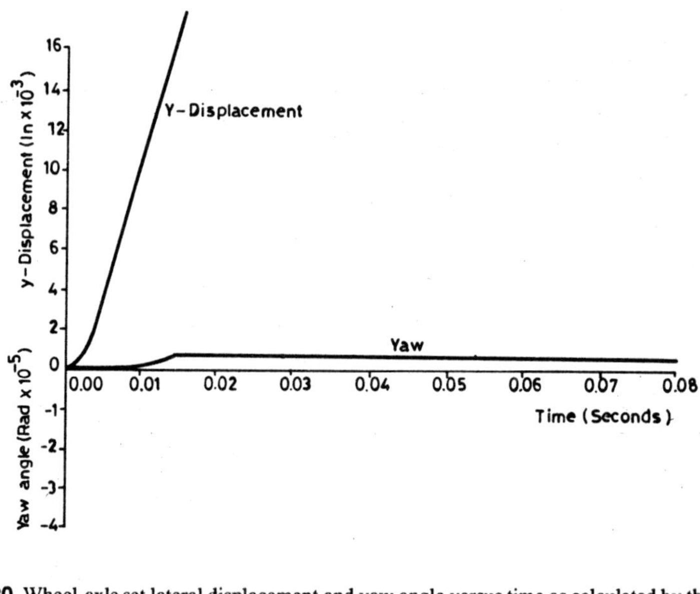

Fig. 5.20 Wheel-axle set lateral displacement and yaw angle versus time as calculated by the two-cycle iteration with trapezoidal rule method. (Two-cycle iteration scheme; velocity = 60 mph; time step = 0.001 sec; rectangular pulse loading.)

methods studied, two of the explicit (central difference and Fourth-order Runge-Kutta) and two of the implicit (Newmark Beta with $\alpha = 0.5$ and $\beta = 1/6$ and Park Stiffly stable) methods were found to be stable. The central difference and Runge-Kutta methods introduce a certain amount of damping. The Runge-Kutta method required the maximum amount of computing time, while all other methods required approximately the same computational time. The results are summarized in Table 5.14.

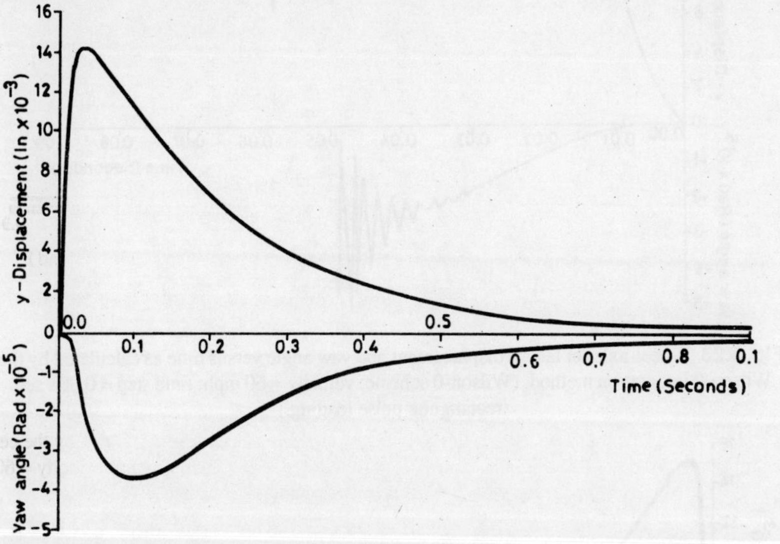

Fig. 5.21 Wheel-axle set lateral displacement and yaw angle versus time as calculated by the Runge-Kutta integration method. (Runge-Kutta scheme: velocity = 60 mph; time step = 0.001 sec; rectangular pulse loading.)

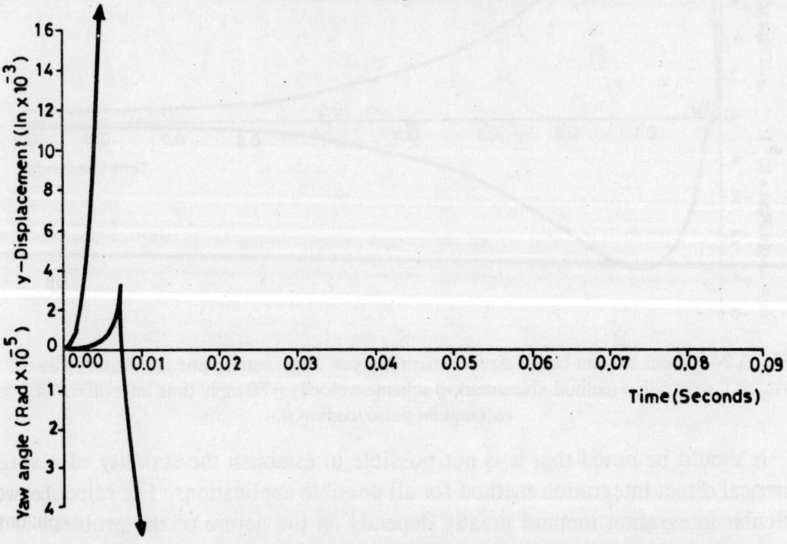

Fig. 5.22 Wheel-axle set lateral displacement and yaw angle versus time as calculated by the Houbolt integration method. (Houbolt scheme: velocity = 60 mph; time step = 0.001 sec; rectangular pulse loading.)

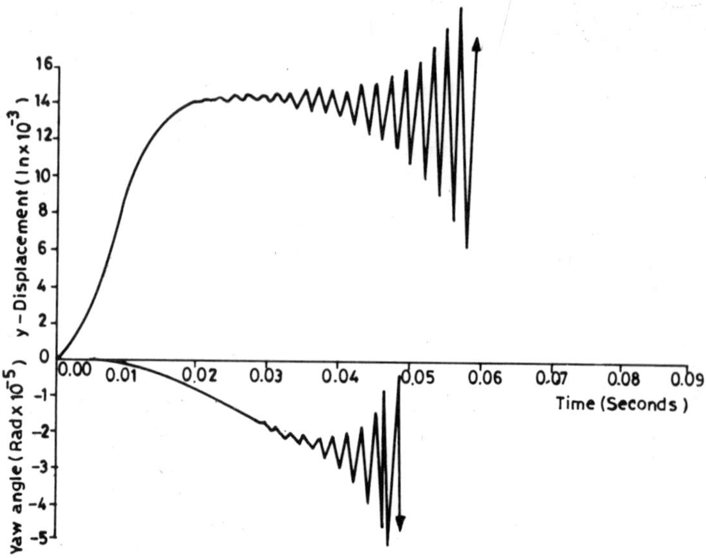

Fig. 5.23 Wheel-axle set lateral displacement and yaw angle versus time as calculated by the Wilson-0 integration method. (Wilson-0 scheme: velocity = 60 mph; time step = 0.001 sec; rectangular pulse loading.)

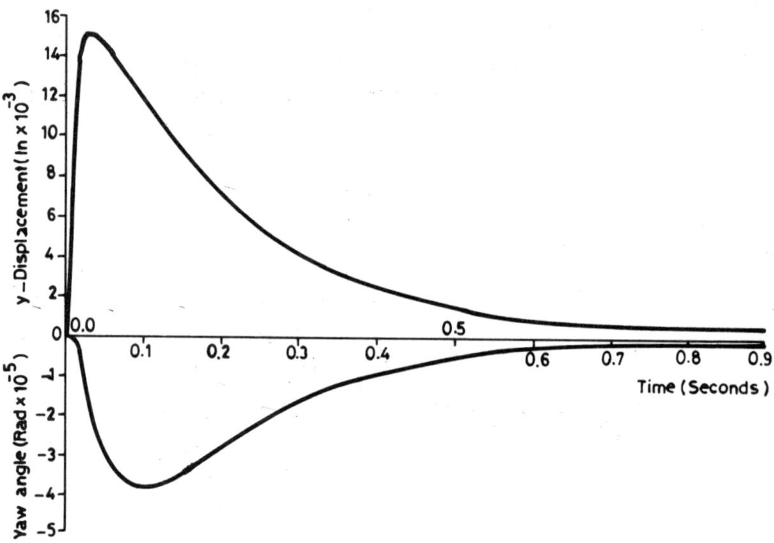

Fig. 5.24 Wheel-axle set lateral displacement and yaw angle versus time as calculated by the Newmark-β integration method. (Newmark-β scheme: velocity = 60 mph; time interval = 0.001 sec; rectangular pulse loading.)

It should be noted that it is not possible to establish the stability of a single numerical direct integration method for all possible applications. The selection of a particular integration method greatly depends on the nature of the problem to be solved and is often dictated by the desired solution accuracy, system nonlinearities, precision of the computing machine, and other associated factors. The selection of the appropriate integration time step is often based on previous experience with similar types of problems.

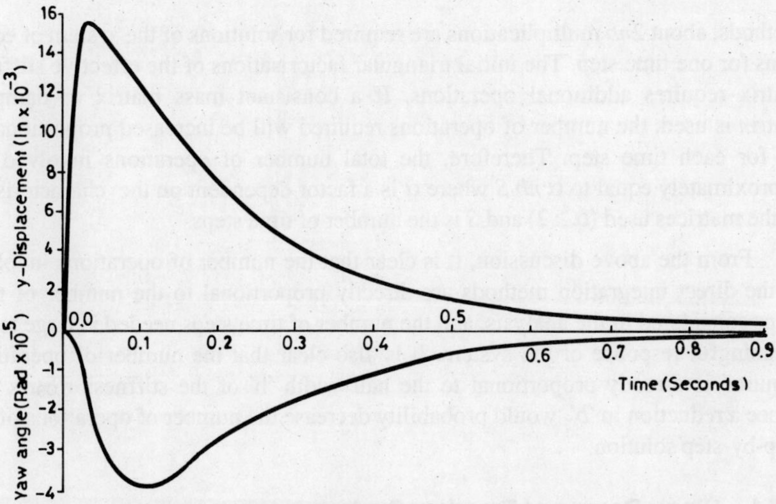

Fig. 5.25 Wheel-axle set lateral displacement and yaw angle versus time as calculated by the Park Stiffly stable integration method. (Park Stiffly stable scheme: velocity = 60 mph; time step = 0.001 sec; rectangular pulse loading.)

Table 5.14 Comparison of various direct integration methods for a nonlinear dynamic system (adapted from Garg and Dukkipati [15])

Integration Method	CPU time* (sec)	Stability	Remarks
Explicit Methods:			
1. Central difference	19.35	stable	introduces damp
2. Two-cycle iteration with trapezoidal rule	25.01	unstable	unstable
3. Fourth-order Runge-Kutta	20.41	stable	introduces damp
Implicit Methods:			
4. Houbolt	19.10	unstable	unstable
5. Wilson Theta ($\theta = 1.4$)	19.24	unstable	unstable
6. Newmark Beta ($\alpha = 0.5$, $\beta = \frac{1}{6}$)	19.85	stable	stable
7. Park Stiffly stable	19.60	stable	stable

* DEC-2050 Computer

5.7 MODE SUPERPOSITION METHOD

All the direct integration methods, presented in the preceding sections (5.4 and 5.5) are very time consuming. If a diagonal mass matrix is assumed for the particular case of an undamped system, the number of multiplications involved in one time step are equal to $2nb$ where n is the size of the matrix and b is the half band width of the stiffness matrix considered. For more multiplications of stiffness matrix with the displacement vector, the number of multiplications involved are $2nb$ in the case of central difference method. In the case of Houboult, Wilson θ and Newmark methods, about $2nb$ multiplications are required for solutions of the system of equations for one time step. The initial triangular factorisations of the effective stiffness matrix requires additional operations. If a consistant mass matrix or damping matrix is used, the number of operations required will be increased proportional to nb for each time step. Therefore, the total number of operations involved are approximately equal to $\alpha\, nb\, S$ where α is a factor dependent on the characteristics of the matrices used ($\alpha \geq 2$) and S is the number of time steps.

From the above discussion, it is clear that the number of operations involved in the direct integration methods are directly proportional to the number of time steps considered in the analysis, and the number of time steps needed is large to get meaningful response of the system. It is also clear that the number of operations required is directly proportional to the half width 'b' of the stiffness matrix and hence a reduction in 'b' would probability decrease the number of operations of the step-by-step solution.

5.7.1 Single Degree of Freedom System

Here we will consider the transient vibration due to an arbitrary excitation $F(t)$ and the solution by means of *superposition*. The method can be implemented readily using computers. Consider the equation of motion for systems with one degree of freedom and an excitation $F(t)$ given by

$$M\ddot{X} + C\dot{X} + KX = F(t) \tag{5.88}$$

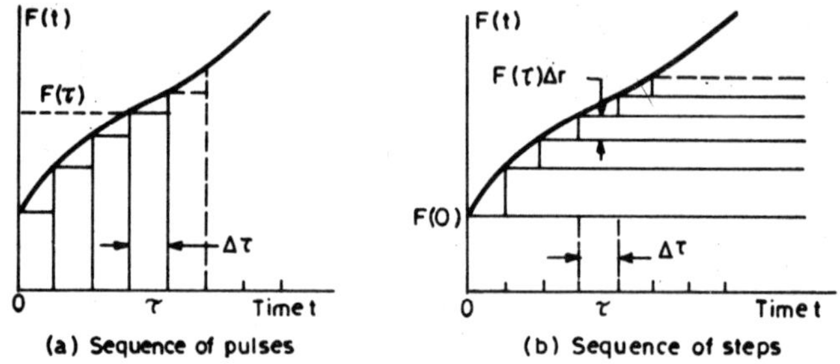

Fig. 5.26 $F(t)$ approximated by pulses and steps.

This equation can be solved to approximate $F(t)$ by a sequence of pulses as shown in Fig. 5.26(a). If the system response to a typical pulse input is known, then the response to $F(t)$ can be determined by means of superposition. That is, the system response to $F(t)$ can be considered as the sum of the responses due to each of the pulses in the sequence. The *strength* of a pulse is defined by the pulse area. The strength of a typical pulse in the sequence at time τ is the area $F(\tau)\Delta\tau$. The system response to a typical pulse is given by the product of the pulse with unit impulse response given by $h(t-\tau)[F(\tau)\Delta\tau]$. By superposition, we can sum the responses due to each of the pulses in the sequence and obtain

$$x(t) = \sum h(t-\tau)\, F(\tau)\Delta\tau \tag{5.89}$$

As $\Delta\tau$ approaches zero, the summation becomes the convolution integral

$$X(t) = \int_0^t F(\tau)h(t-\tau)d\tau = \frac{1}{\omega_d m}\int_0^t F(\tau)e^{-\xi\omega_n(t-\tau)}\sin\omega_d(t-\tau)d\tau \quad (5.90)$$

where ω_d = damped frequency.

Equation (5.90) represents the system response for the input $F(t)$ with zero initial conditions. If the initial conditions are $x(0) = X_0$ and $\dot{X}(0) = \dot{X}_0$, then the complete solution is obtained by the super position of the particular solution due to the excitation and the complementary solution due to the initial conditions. For these initial conditions, the complementary solution is

$$x = e^{-\xi\omega_n t}\left(x_0\cos\omega_d t + \frac{\dot{x}_0 + \xi\omega_n x_0}{\omega_d}\sin\omega_d t\right) \quad (5.91)$$

The particular solution is given by equation (5.3). By superposition, the complete solution is

$$x = e^{-\xi\omega_n t}\left(x_0\cos\omega_d t + \frac{x_0\xi\omega_n x_0}{\omega_d}\sin\omega_d t\right\} + \int_0^t F(\tau)h(t-\tau)d\tau \quad (5.92)$$

The system response due to a unit step input with zero initial conditions is called the *indicial response.* A unit step function $u(t)$ shown in Fig. 5.27(*a*) has the property :

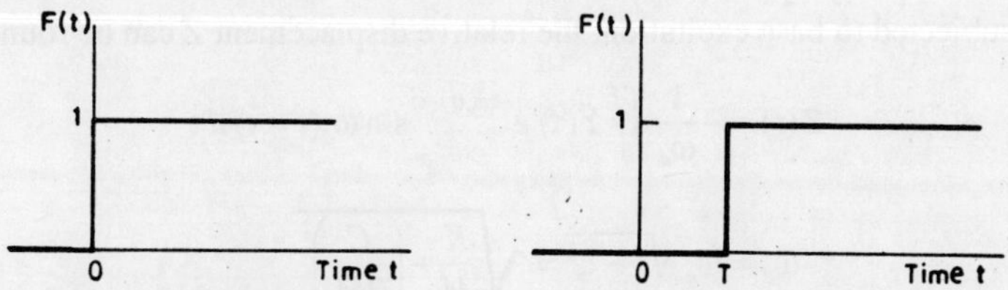

(a) Unit step function u(t) (b) Unit step function u(t−T)

Fig. 5.27 Unit step functions.

$$u(t) = \begin{cases} 1 & \text{for } t > 0 \\ 0 & \text{for } t > \pi \end{cases} \quad (5.93)$$

A unit step translated along the positive time axis by an amount τ to become $u(t-\tau)$ is shown in Fig. 5.27(b)

$$u(t-\tau) = \begin{cases} 1 \text{ for } t > \tau \\ 0 \text{ for } t < \tau \end{cases} \quad (5.94)$$

An arbitrary function $F(t)$ can therefore be approximated by a sequence of steps as illustrated in Fig. 5.26(b). Following the steps enumerated for the impulse response, it can be shown that the indicial response $x_u(t)$ is

$$x_u(t) = \frac{1}{K}\left[1 - \frac{1}{\sqrt{1-\xi^2}}e^{-\xi\omega_n t}\sin(\omega_d + \phi)\right] \quad (5.95)$$

where $\phi = \sin^{-1}\sqrt{1-\xi^2}$. The system response to an arbitrary input $F(t)$ is the superposition of the responses due to each of the individual steps. Thus,

$$X(t) = F(0)X_u(t) + \int_0^t F'(\tau)X_u(t-\tau)d\tau \tag{5.96}$$

where $F'(\tau)$ is the time derivative of $F(t)$ estimated at $t = \tau$. The term $F(0)\,X_u(t)$ is to account for the step at $t = 0$, since the slope does not take into account $F(0)$. Equation (5.96) is referred to as *Duhamel's integral or the superposition integral.*

5.7.2 Base Excitation

Sometimes, the base or support of a single degree of freedom system undergoes motion. Let $Y(t)$ denote the displacement of the base and $X(t)$ the displacement of the mass from its equilibrium position at time t. Then the net elongation of the spring is $X–Y$ and the relative velocity between the two ends of the damper is $\dot{X} - \dot{Y}$. The equation of motion is

$$M\ddot{X} + C(\dot{X} - \dot{Y}) + K(X - Y) = 0 \tag{5.97}$$

Denoting $Z = X - Y$, Eq. (5.97) becomes

$$M\ddot{Z} + C\dot{Z} \cdot + KZ = -M\ddot{Y} \tag{5.98}$$

Equation (5.98) is similar to Eq. (5.88) with the variable Z replacing and the term $-M\ddot{Y}$ replacing the forcing function $F(t)$. Hence, the results for the force excited systems are equally applicable to the base excited system. For an underdamped system subjected to base excitation, the relative displacement Z can be found from:

$$Z(t) = -\frac{1}{\omega_d}\int_0^t \ddot{Y}(\tau)\, e^{-\xi\omega_n(t-\tau)} \sin\omega_d(t-\tau)\, d\tau \tag{5.99}$$

where $$\omega_d = \omega_n\sqrt{1-\xi^2} = \sqrt{\frac{K}{M} - \left(\frac{C}{2M}\right)^2}$$

$$\omega_n = \sqrt{\frac{K}{M}}$$

and $$\xi = \frac{C}{\sqrt{2M\omega_n}}$$

5.8 MODAL ANALYSIS

5.8.1 Change of basis to Modal generalized displacements

Let us transform the equilibrium equations into a more effective form by using the following transformations on the displacement vector $\{X\}$

$$\{X\}\,(t) = [P]\,\{x\}\,(t) \tag{5.100}$$

where $[P]$ is the square matrix and $\{x\}(t)$ is a time-dependent vector of order n. The elements of $\{x\}$ are known as generalized displacements. Substituting Eq. (5.100) in Eq.(5.3) and premultiplying by $[P]^T$ we have

$$[P]^T [M] [P] \{\ddot{x}\} (t) + [P]^T [C] [P] \{\dot{x}\} (t) + [P]^T [K] [P] \{x\} (t) = [P]^T \{F(t)\}$$

This can be written as

$$[\overline{M}] \{\ddot{x}\} (t) + [\overline{C}] \{\dot{x}\} (t) + [\overline{K}] \{x\} (t) = \{\overline{F}\} (t) \tag{5.101}$$

where $[\overline{M}] = [P]^T [M] [P] \,;\, [\overline{C}] = [P]^T [C] [P];$

$$[\overline{K}] = [P]^T [K] [P] \text{ and } \{\overline{F}\} = [P]^T \{F(t)\}$$

This transformation is performed to obtain the generalized displacement basis. The aim of this transformation is to obtain new stiffness, mass and damping matrices with smaller bandwidth than the original system matrices. It should be noted that the transformation matrix $[P]$ should be selected accordingly and it should be a non-singular one. In other words, the rank of $[P]$ must be of the order of n to obtain unique relations between these vectors $\{x\}$ and $\{X\}$.

In order to reduce the bandwidth of the system matrices there can be many different transformation matrices $[P]$. Usually, an effective transformation matrix is obtained by using displacement solutions to the free vibration equilibrium equations neglecting damping,

$$[M] \{\ddot{X}\} + [K] \{X\} = 0 \tag{5.102}$$

The possible solution to Eq. (5.102) is of the form

$$\{x\} = \{\phi\} \text{ Sin}\, \omega (t - t_0) \tag{5.103}$$

where $\{\phi\}$ is a vector of order n, t is the time at any particular instant, t_0 is the initial time and ω is the frequency of vibrations (rad/sec) of the vector $\{\phi\}$. Substituting Eq. (5.103) in Eq. (5.102) we obtain the generalized equation of an eigenvalue problem for which $\{\phi\}$ and ω are the two unknowns to be determined.

$$\omega^2 [M] \{\phi\} + [K] \{\phi\} = 0$$

$$[K] \{\phi\} = \omega^2 [M] \{\phi\} \tag{5.104}$$

The solution of the eigenvalue problem yields the n eigenpairs such as

$$(\omega_1^2, \phi_1), (\omega_2^2, \phi_2), (\omega_3^2, \phi_3)$$

where the eigenvectors are orthonormalized with respect to $[M]$ i.e

$$\{\phi_i\}^T [M] \{\phi_i\} = \begin{Bmatrix} 1 \text{ for } i = j \\ 0 \text{ for } i \neq j \end{Bmatrix} \tag{5.105}$$

and $$0 \le \omega_1^2 \le \omega_2^2 \le \omega_3^2 \le \cdots\cdots \le \omega_n^2$$

The vector $\{\phi_i\}$ is the eigenvector corresponding to the ith mode and ω_i is its natural frequency. Let us define a matrix $[\phi]$ whose columns are the eigenvectors ϕ_i and a diagonal matrix Ω^2 which contains the eigen values ω_i^2. Therefore

$$\{\phi\} = [\phi_1, \phi_2, \cdots \phi_n]$$

$$[\Omega^2] = \begin{bmatrix} \omega_1^2 & & & \\ & \omega_2^2 & & \\ & & \omega_3^2 & \\ & & & \omega_n^2 \end{bmatrix} \tag{5.106}$$

Then the n solutions to Eq. (5.104) can be written as

$$[K]\{\phi\} = [M][\phi][\Omega^2] \tag{5.107}$$

$$[\phi]^T [K][\phi] = [\Omega^2]$$

$$[\phi]^T [M][\phi] = [I]$$

This matrix $[\Phi]$ would be a suitable transformation matrix $[P]$ in Eq. (5.100). Therefore

$$\{X(t)\} = [\Phi]\{x(t)\} \tag{5.108}$$

Now the equations of motion that correspond to the modal generalized displacements are

$$\{\ddot{x}(t)\} + [\Phi]^T [C][\Phi]\{\dot{x}(t)\} + [\Omega^2]\{X(t)\} = [\Phi]^T \{F(t)\} \tag{5.109}$$

The initial conditions for $\{x(t)\}$ can be obtained using Eq. (5.108) and the M-orthonormality of $[\Phi]$. Thus, at time $t = 0$ we have

$$\{X_0\} = [\Phi]^T [M]\{X\}$$

$$\{\dot{X}_0\} = [\Phi]^T [M]\{\dot{X}_0\} \tag{5.110}$$

The above equation shows that if a damping matrix is not included in the analysis, the original equilibrium equations (5.3) are decoupled when the free vibration mode shapes of the system are used in the transformation matrix $[P]$.

5.8.2 Analysis without damping

If the damping effects are neglected in the analysis, equation (5.109) can be written as

$$\{\ddot{x}(t)\} + [\Omega]^2 \{x(t)\} = [\Phi]^T \{f(t)\} \tag{5.111}$$

There are n independent equations of the form

$$\ddot{x}(t) + \omega_i^2 x_i(t) = f_i(t)$$

where
$$f_i(t) = [\Phi_i]^T \{f(t)\} \tag{5.112}$$

in which $i = 1, 2, \ldots\ldots. n$. Equation (5.112) can be recognized as the differential equation of a single degree of freedom system without damping and with unit mass and stiffness ω_i^2. The initial conditions of the system are obtained from Eq. (5.110). We have

$$\dot{x}_i(0) = [m][M]\{\dot{X}_0\} \text{ at } t = 0 \tag{5.113}$$

The solution of the above decoupled equations (3.112) can be obtained by the direct integrations methods. The solution can also be obtained by using the Duhamel integral:

$$x_i(t) = \frac{1}{\omega_i}\int_0^t f_i(\tau)\sin\omega_i(t-\tau)d\tau + \alpha_i \sin\omega_i t + \beta_i \cos\omega_i t \tag{5.114}$$

where α_i and β_i are to be obtained from the initial conditions given in Eq. (3.113).

To obtain the complete response, all the n decoupled equations given in Eq. (3.112) are to be solved, and the total response can be obtained by superposition of all the solutions.

i.e,
$$\{X\}(t) = \sum_{i=1}^{n} [\phi_i]\{x_i(t)\} \tag{5.115}$$

Hence, the response by mode superposition is obtained as the summation of all the solutions of the decoupled equations.

Example 5.8

Consider a simple system for which the governing equilibrium equations are

$$2\ddot{X}_1 + 4X_1 + 2X_2 = 5 \tag{1}$$

$$2\ddot{X}_2 + 2X_1 + 4X_2 = 5 \tag{2}$$

Use mode superposition method to compute the displacement response of the system.

Solution

The solution to these coupled second order linear differential equations is of the form

$$X_1 = X_{1C} + X_{1P} \tag{3}$$

$$X_2 = X_{2C} + X_{2P} \tag{4}$$

The particular solution to constant forcing inputs are constants

$$X_{1P} = Z_1 \tag{5}$$

$$X_{2P} = Z_2 \tag{6}$$

Substituting Eqs. (5) and (6) in Eqs. (1) and (2), we get

$$4Z_1 + 2Z_2 = 5 \tag{7}$$

$$2Z_1 + 4Z_2 = 5 \tag{8}$$

Solving Eqs. (7) and (8), we get

$$Z_1 = \frac{5}{6} \tag{9}$$

and
$$Z_2 = 5/6 \tag{10}$$

The complementary part of the solution is obtained from

$$2\ddot{X}_1 + 4X_1 + 2X_2 = 0 \tag{11}$$

$$2\ddot{X}_2 + 2X_1 + 4X_2 = 0 \tag{12}$$

Assuming

$$X_1 = x_1 \sin \omega t \tag{13}$$

$$X_2 = x_2 \sin \omega t \tag{14}$$

Since there is no damping in the system X_{1C} and X_{2C} oscillate at the same frequency and are either in phase or 180 degrees out of phase. Substituting Eqs. (13) and (14) in Eqs. (11) and (12), we obtain

$$(4 - 2\omega^2)x_1 + 2x_2 = 0 \tag{15}$$

$$2x_1 + (4 - 2\omega^2)x_2 = 0 \tag{16}$$

From Eqs. (15) and (16), we get

$$\frac{x_1}{x_2} = \frac{2}{2\omega^2 - 4} = \frac{2\omega^2 - 4}{2} \tag{17}$$

The frequency equation from Eq. (17) is

$$(2\omega^2 - 4)^2 - 4 = 0$$

or

$$(\omega^2)^2 - 4\,\omega^2 + 3 = 0 \tag{18}$$

Hence

$$\omega_1^2 = 1 \left(\frac{x_1}{x_2}\right)^1 = -\frac{1}{1} \tag{19}$$

$$\omega_2^2 = 3 \left(\frac{x_1}{x_2}\right)^{11} = \frac{1}{1} \tag{20}$$

The two modes of vibration are

$$\begin{Bmatrix} x_1 \\ x_2 \end{Bmatrix}^I = \begin{Bmatrix} x_1 \\ x_2 \end{Bmatrix}^I \sin(\omega_1 t - \psi_1) \tag{21}$$

$$\begin{Bmatrix} x_1 \\ x_2 \end{Bmatrix}^{II} = \begin{Bmatrix} x_1 \\ x_2 \end{Bmatrix}^{II} \sin(\omega_2 t - \psi_2) \tag{22}$$

where $\begin{Bmatrix} \dfrac{x_1}{x_2} \end{Bmatrix}$ is specified for each mode.

The general solution is

$$X_1 = z_1 + x_1^I \sin(\omega_1 t + \psi_1) + x_1^{II} \sin(\omega_2 t + \psi_2) \tag{23}$$

$$X_2 = z_2 + x_2^{II} \sin(\omega_1 t + \psi_1) + x_2^{II} \sin(\omega_2 t + \psi_2) \tag{24}$$

where x_1^I, x_2^{II}, ψ_1 and ψ_2 are obtained from the initial conditions. At $t = 0$: $X_1 = 1$, $X_2 = 2$, $\dot{X}_1 = 0$ and $\dot{X}_2 = 0$. Substituting these into Eqs. (23) and (24), we obtain

$$1 = \frac{5}{6} + x_1^I \sin\psi_1 + x_1^{II} \sin\psi_2 \tag{25}$$

$$2 = \frac{5}{6} + x_2^I \sin\psi_1 + x_2^{II} \sin\psi_2 \tag{26}$$

$$0 = \omega_1 x_1^I \cos\psi_1 + \omega_2 x_2^{II} \cos\psi_2 \tag{27}$$

$$0 = \omega_1 x_2^I \cos\psi_1 + \omega_2 x_2^{II} \cos\psi_2 \tag{28}$$

From Eqs. (27) and (28), we get $\cos\psi_1 = \cos\psi_2 = 0$ implying that $\sin\psi_1 = \sin\psi_2 = 1$. From Eqs. (25) and (26), we obtain

$$-x_2^1 + x_2^{11} + \frac{5}{6} = 1 \tag{29}$$

$$x_2^1 + x_2^{11} + \frac{5}{6} = 1 \tag{30}$$

From Eqs. (29) and (30), we get

$$x_2^I = \frac{1}{2}, x_2^{II} = \frac{2}{3}, x_1^I = -\frac{1}{2} \text{ and } x_1^{II} = \frac{2}{3}$$

Therefore, the complete solution is

$$x_1 = \frac{5}{6} - \frac{1}{2}\cos t + \frac{2}{3}\cos\sqrt{3}\,t \tag{31}$$

$$x_2 = \frac{5}{6} + \frac{1}{2}\cos t + \frac{2}{3}\cos\sqrt{3}\,t \tag{32}$$

The modal matrix is

$$\begin{bmatrix} 1 & 1 \\ -1 & 1 \end{bmatrix} \tag{33}$$

Therefore, by the modal superposition method

$$\begin{bmatrix} 1 & 1 \\ -1 & 1 \end{bmatrix}\begin{bmatrix} 2 & 0 \\ 0 & 2 \end{bmatrix}\begin{bmatrix} 1 & 1 \\ -1 & 1 \end{bmatrix}\begin{Bmatrix} \ddot{x}_1 \\ \ddot{x}_2 \end{Bmatrix} + \begin{bmatrix} 1 & -1 \\ 1 & 1 \end{bmatrix}\begin{bmatrix} 4 & 2 \\ 2 & 3 \end{bmatrix}\begin{bmatrix} 1 & 1 \\ -1 & 1 \end{bmatrix}\begin{Bmatrix} x_1 \\ x_2 \end{Bmatrix}$$

$$= \begin{bmatrix} 1 & 1 \\ -1 & 1 \end{bmatrix}\begin{Bmatrix} 5 \\ 5 \end{Bmatrix} \tag{34}$$

or
$$\begin{bmatrix} 4 & 0 \\ 0 & 4 \end{bmatrix}\begin{Bmatrix} \ddot{x}_1 \\ \ddot{x}_2 \end{Bmatrix} + \begin{bmatrix} 4 & 0 \\ 0 & 12 \end{bmatrix}\begin{Bmatrix} x_1 \\ x_2 \end{Bmatrix} = \begin{Bmatrix} 0 \\ 10 \end{Bmatrix} \tag{35}$$

The decoupled Eqs. (35) are

$$\ddot{x}_1 + x_1 = 0$$

$$\ddot{x}_2 + 3x_2 = 5/2 \tag{36}$$

The solution to Eqs. (36) is

$$x_1 = A\cos\omega t + B\sin\omega t$$

$$x_2 = \frac{5}{6} + C \cos \sqrt{3}\, t + D \sin \sqrt{3}\, t \tag{37}$$

where A, B, C and D are constants to be determined from the initial conditions. Therefore,

$$\begin{Bmatrix} X_1 \\ X_2 \end{Bmatrix} = \begin{bmatrix} 1 & 1 \\ -1 & 1 \end{bmatrix} \begin{Bmatrix} x_1 \\ x_2 \end{Bmatrix} \tag{38}$$

$$X_1 = x_1 + x_2 = \frac{5}{6} + A \cos t + B \sin t + C \cos \sqrt{3}\, t + D \sin \sqrt{3}\, t \tag{39}$$

$$X_2 = -x_1 + x_2 = \frac{5}{6} - A \cos t - B \sin t + C \cos \sqrt{3}\, t + D \sin \sqrt{3}\, t$$

At $t = 0, X_1 = 1, X_2 = 2, \dot{X}_1 = \dot{X}_2 = 0.$

From these initial conditions we get

$$A = \frac{2}{3}, B = 0, C = -\frac{1}{2} \text{ and } D = 0.$$

Therefore, the complete solution is

$$X_1 = \frac{5}{6} - \frac{1}{2} \cos t + \frac{2}{3} \cos \sqrt{3}\, t \tag{40}$$

$$X_2 = \frac{5}{6} + \frac{1}{2} \cos t + \frac{2}{3} \cos \sqrt{3}\, t \tag{41}$$

Note that the Eqs. (40) and (41) are identical to Eqs. (31) and (32). The equation (5.109) reduces to n equations of the form

$$\{\ddot{x}_i(t)\} + 2\omega_i \zeta_i \dot{x}\,(t) + \omega_i^2 x_i\,(t) = f_i(t) \tag{5.118}$$

where ζ_i is the damping ratio $f_i(t)$ and the initial conditions on $x_i(t)$ are defined in Eqs. (5.112) and (5.110) respectively. The response can be obtained by evaluating the Duhamael integral

$$x_i(t) = \frac{1}{\omega_1 \sqrt{1 - \zeta_i^2}\ 0} \int_0^t f_i(\tau)_e - \zeta_i \omega_i (t - \tau) \sin \omega_i \sqrt{1 - \zeta_i^2}\, (t - \tau)\, d\tau$$

$$+ e^{-\zeta_i \omega_i t} \left\{ \alpha_i \sin \left(\omega_i \sqrt{1 - \zeta_i^2} \right) t + \beta_i \cos \omega_i \sqrt{1 - \zeta_i^2} \right\} \tag{5.119}$$

where α_i and β_i are evaluated using the initial conditions in Eq. (5.110).

Important considerations made in arriving at Eq. (5.119) are: the total damping in the system is assumed to be the sum of the individual damping in each mode; the damping in one mode can be evaluated by imposing initial conditions corresponding to that mode only and the decay of the forced damaped vibration can be measured. In the mode superposition analysis, the numerical solution of Eq. (5.3) using the decoupled equations (5.118) the damping matrix [C] is not calculated, only the stiffness and mass matrices [K] and [M] are calculated.

5.8.3 Rayleigh Damping

A systematic method for determining damping matrix [C] of multidegree of freedom system is not available. The material damping present in systems for some of the known materials such as cast iron and mild steel is readily available in literature. The damping ratio reported is based on the fundamental mode.

It is known that the system damping can be evaluated by the free vibration analysis and by the forced vibration method. Damping ratios in each mode can be obtained for a given structure by carrying out experimental modal testing. However, it is not possible to express the elements of the matrix explicitly because the damping is interlinked with stiffness and mass matrices of the system. In any case it is necessary to evaluate the damping matrix [C], which when substituted into (5.117) yields the damping ratios ζ_i , $i = 1.....p$. Rayleigh damping is expressed in the form

$$[C] = \alpha[M] + \beta\,[K] \tag{5.120}$$

where α and β are constants to be determined from two given damping ratios that correspond to two unequal frequencies of vibration. This type of damping is known as *proportional damping* because C is proportional to a linear combination of [M] and [K]. If we post multiply the equation (5.120) by [x] and premultiply the resulting equation by $[X]^T$ we get

$$[X]^T[C]\,[X] = \alpha\,[X]^T\,[M]\,[X] + \beta\,[X]^T[K]\,[X] \tag{5.121}$$

If we write

$$[X]^T[C]\,[X] = 2\begin{bmatrix} \zeta_1\omega_1 & \cdots\cdots\cdots\cdots\cdots 0 \\ 0 \quad \zeta_2\omega_2 & \cdots\cdots\cdots\cdots 0 \\ 0 \quad 0 \quad \zeta_3\omega_3 & \cdots\cdots\cdots 0 \\ \cdots\cdots\cdots\cdots\cdots\cdots & \cdots 0 \\ & \zeta_m\omega_m \end{bmatrix} \tag{5.122}$$

then we have,

$$2\,\zeta_1\,\omega_1 = \alpha + \omega_1^{\,2}\,\beta$$

$$2\,\zeta_2\,\omega_2 = \alpha + \omega_2^{\,2}\,\beta$$

$$\dots \quad \dots \quad \dots \quad \dots$$

$$\dots \quad \dots \quad \dots \quad \dots$$

$$\dots \quad \dots \quad \dots \quad \dots$$

$$2\zeta_m\omega_m = \alpha + \omega^{\,2}_{\;m}\,\beta \tag{5.123}$$

The plot of equations (5.123) of $2\zeta_i\omega_i$ against ω_i^2 would indicate a straight line as shown in Fig. 5.28. The parameters α and β can be determined from Fig. 5.28. In practice, the damping ratio would be as low as 0.03 for the first (fundamental) mode. Damping ratio is of the order of 0.5 for natural frequencies above 10 Hz and hence the rate of decay exp $(-2\pi\zeta\omega_n)$ will be very high. The responses from modes above 10 Hz die down fast.

Example 5.9

For a multidegree of freedom system, the damping ratios for the first two natural frequencies of 1 cycle/second and 4 cycle/second are 0.015 and 0.05. Establish the constants α and β in Rayleigh damping.

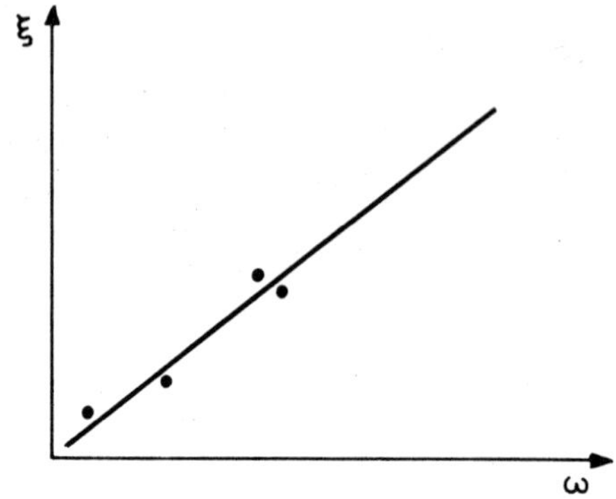

Fig. 5.28 Damping as a function of frequency.

Solution

Given that $\zeta_1 = 0.015$ and $\zeta_2 = 0.05$.

Natural frequencies $f_1 = 1$ cycle / sec or $\omega_1 = 6.2832$ rad/sec.

$f_2 = 4$ cycle/sec or $\omega_2 = 25.1327$ rad/sec.

From Eq.(5.51), we have

$$2\zeta_1\omega_1 = \alpha + \omega_1^2 \beta$$

$$2\zeta_2\omega_2 = \alpha + \omega_2^2 \beta$$

Therefore

$$2(0.015)\,(6.2832) = \alpha + (6.2832)^2 \beta$$

$$2(0.05)\,(25.1327) = \alpha + (25.1327)^2 \beta$$

Solving the above equations for α and β and, we get $\alpha = 0.0335$ and $\beta = 3.9257 \times 10^{-3}$

Hence the damping matrix $[C]$ is given by

$$[C] = \alpha\,[M] + \beta\,[K]$$

$$= 0.0335\,[M] + 3.9257 \times 10^{-3}\,[K]$$

The damping ratio for any other frequency is given by

$$\zeta_i = \frac{\alpha + \beta\,\omega_i^2}{2\,\omega_i} = \frac{(0.0335) + (3.9257 \times 10^{-3})\omega_i^2}{2\,\omega_i}$$

5.9 STABILITY ANALYSIS

For a given initial value problem we have discussed a few direct integration methods in Sec. 3.2 to 3.5 for the dynamic response of a dynamic system. Suppose we have derived the required solutions for the discrete times $0, \Delta t, 2\Delta t, 3\Delta t.....t-\Delta t, t$. For a specific integration method considered it is required to establish a recursive relationship at time $t+\Delta t$ which is

$$\{\hat{X}_{t+\Delta t}\} = [A]\,\{\hat{X}_t\} + \{L\}\,\{f_{t+v}\} \tag{5.124}$$

where $\hat{X}_{t+\Delta t}$ and $\hat{X}_t$ are vectors of solution quantities (displacements, velocities etc.) and f_{t+v} is the load at time $t + v$, Where v may be 0, Δt or $\theta\Delta t$ for the integration method under consideration.

The matrix $[A]$ and vector $[L]$ are known as the *integration approximation* and *load operators,* respectively. When this operation is carried out n times, the response is given by

$$\{\hat{X}_{t+n\Delta t}\} = [A]^n\,\{\hat{X}_t\} + \{A\}^{n-1}\{L\}\,\{f_{t+v}\} + [A]^{n-2}\{L\}\,\{f_{t+\Delta t+v}\}$$

$$+[A]\,\{L\}\,\{f_{t+(n-2)\Delta t+v}\} + \{L\}\,\{f_{t+(n-1)\Delta t+v}\} \tag{5.125}$$

This relationship is used in the study of the stability and accuracy of the integration methods. The derivation of the operators $[A]$ and $[L]$ for a few of the different integration methods is presented in the following sections.

5.9.1 Central Difference Method

In the central difference integration method, acceleration and velocity are approximated at time t. The equilibrium equation considered at time t is

$$\ddot{x}_t + 2\zeta\omega\,\dot{x}_t + \omega^2 x_t = f_t \tag{5.126}$$

$$\ddot{x}_t = \frac{1}{\Delta t^2}\{x_{t-\Delta t} - 2x_t + x_{t+\Delta t}\} \tag{5.127}$$

$$\dot{x}_t = \frac{1}{2\Delta t}\{-x_{t-\Delta t} + x_{t+\Delta t}\} \tag{5.128}$$

Substituting Eqs (5.127) and (5.128) and solving for $x_{t+\Delta t}$ we have

$$x_{t+\Delta t} = \frac{2-\omega^2\Delta t^2}{1+\zeta\omega\Delta t}x_t - \frac{1-\zeta\omega\Delta t}{1+\zeta\omega\Delta t}x_{t-\Delta t} + \frac{\Delta t^2}{1+\zeta\omega\Delta t}f_t \tag{5.129}$$

Writing Eq. (5.129) in the form of (5.124)

$$\begin{Bmatrix} x_{t+\Delta t} \\ x_t \end{Bmatrix} = [A]\begin{Bmatrix} x_t \\ x_{t-\Delta t} \end{Bmatrix} + \{L\}\,\{f_t\} \tag{5.130}$$

where

$$[A] = \begin{bmatrix} \dfrac{2-(\omega\Delta t)^2}{1+\zeta\omega\Delta t} & \dfrac{1-\zeta\omega\Delta t}{1+\zeta\omega\Delta t} \\ 1 & 0 \end{bmatrix} \tag{5.131}$$

$$[L] = \begin{Bmatrix} \dfrac{\Delta t^2}{1+\zeta\omega\Delta t} \\ 0 \end{Bmatrix} \tag{5.132}$$

The largest eigenvalue of the square matrix $[A]$ given by Eq. (5.131) gives an indication of stability. We can see from Eq. (5.131) that whenever $\omega\Delta t/2\pi \le 1/\pi$, the largest eigenvalue is less than 1. Therefore, the central difference method is stable only when $\Delta t/T \le 1/\pi$, where T is the time period of nth mode of vibration.

5.9.2 Houbolt Method

The equilibrium equation in the Houbolt method is considered for acceleration and velocity at time $t+\Delta t$ described by the backward difference formulae. The uncoupled equation at time $t+\Delta t$ is

$$\ddot{x}_{t+\Delta t} + 2\zeta\omega x_{t+\Delta t} + \omega^2 x_{t+\Delta t} = f_{t+\Delta t} \tag{5.133}$$

The backward difference formulae are:

$$\ddot{x}_{t+\Delta t} = \frac{1}{\Delta t^2}\{2x_{t+\Delta t} - 5x_t + 4x_{t-\Delta t} - x_{t-2\Delta t}\} \tag{5.134}$$

$$\dot{x}_{t+\Delta t} = \frac{1}{6\Delta t}\{11x_{t+\Delta t} - 18x_t + 9x_{t-\Delta t} - 2x_{t-2\Delta t}\} \tag{5.135}$$

Substituting Eq. (5.134) and (5.135) in (5.133) we obtain

$$\begin{Bmatrix} x_{t+\Delta t} \\ x_t \\ x_{t-\Delta t} \end{Bmatrix} = [A]\begin{Bmatrix} x_t \\ x_{t-\Delta t} \\ x_{t-2\Delta t} \end{Bmatrix} + [L]\ \{f_{t+\Delta t}\} \tag{5.136}$$

$$[A] = \begin{bmatrix} \dfrac{5\beta}{\omega^2\Delta t^2} + 6K & -\left(\dfrac{4\beta}{\omega^2\Delta t^2} + 3K\right) & \dfrac{\beta}{(\omega\Delta t)^2} + \dfrac{2K}{3} \\ 1 & 0 & 0 \\ 0 & 1 & 0 \end{bmatrix} \tag{5.137}$$

$$\beta = \left(\frac{2}{(\omega\Delta t)^2} + \frac{11\zeta}{3\omega\Delta t} + 1\right)^{-1}$$

$$K = \frac{\zeta\beta}{\omega\Delta t}$$

and

$$L = \begin{Bmatrix} \left(\dfrac{\beta}{\omega^2}\right) \\ 0 \\ 0 \end{Bmatrix} \tag{5.138}$$

5.9.3 Wilson Theta Method

The fundamental assumption in the Wilson θ method is that the acceleration varies linearly over the interval from t to $t+\theta\Delta t$ where $\theta \ge 1$ and is determined to obtain optimum stability and accuracy. The response can be written as

$$\ddot{x}_{t+\tau} = \ddot{x}_t + (\ddot{x}_{t+\Delta t} - \ddot{x}_t)\frac{\tau}{\Delta t} \tag{5.139}$$

$$\dot{x}_{t+\tau} = \dot{x}_t + \ddot{x}_t\tau + (\ddot{x}_{\tau+\Delta t} - \ddot{x}_t)\frac{\tau^2}{2\Delta t} \tag{5.140}$$

$$x_{t+\tau} = x_t + \dot{x}\tau + \frac{1}{2}\ddot{x}_t\tau^2 + (\ddot{x}_{\tau+\Delta t} - \ddot{x}_t)\frac{\tau^3}{6\Delta t} \tag{5.141}$$

for $0 < \tau < \theta\Delta t$. At time $t + \Delta t$ we can get $\tau = \Delta t$

$$\dot{x}_{t+\Delta t} = \dot{x}_t + (\ddot{x}_{t+\Delta t} + \ddot{x}_t)\frac{\Delta t}{2} \tag{5.142}$$

$$x_{t+\Delta t} = x_t + \dot{x}_t\Delta t + (2\ddot{x}_t + \ddot{x}_{t+\Delta t})\frac{\Delta t^2}{6} \tag{5.143}$$

The response of uncoupled equation of equilibrium at time $t + \theta\Delta t$ is given by

$$\ddot{x}_{t+\theta\Delta t} + 2\zeta\omega\dot{x}_{t+\theta\Delta t} + \omega^2 x_{t+\theta\Delta t} = f_{t+\theta\Delta t} \tag{5.144}$$

At time $t = \theta\Delta t$, substituting Eqs. (5.139), (5.140) and (5.141) in Eq. (5.144) we obtain $\ddot{x}_{t+\Delta t}$ and substituting this in Eqs. (5.142) and (5.143) we get the response equations in the following form,

$$\begin{Bmatrix} \ddot{x}_{t+\Delta t} \\ \dot{x}_{t+\Delta t} \\ x_{t+\Delta t} \end{Bmatrix} = [A]\begin{Bmatrix} \ddot{x}_t \\ \dot{x}_t \\ x_t \end{Bmatrix} + \{L\}\ \{f_{t+\theta\Delta t}\} \tag{5.145}$$

where

$$[A] = \begin{bmatrix} 1 - \dfrac{\beta\theta^2}{3} - \dfrac{1}{\theta} - K\theta & \dfrac{1}{\Delta t}(-\beta\theta - 2K) & \dfrac{1}{\Delta t^2}(-\beta) \\ \Delta t\left(1 - \dfrac{1}{2\theta} - \dfrac{\beta\theta^2}{6} - \dfrac{K\theta}{2}\right) & \left(1 - \dfrac{\beta\theta}{2} - K\right) & \dfrac{1}{\Delta t}\left(-\dfrac{\beta}{2}\right) \\ \Delta t^2\left(\dfrac{1}{2} - \dfrac{1}{6\theta} - \dfrac{\beta\theta^2}{18} - \dfrac{K\theta}{6}\right) & \Delta t\left(1 - \dfrac{\beta\theta}{6} - \dfrac{K}{3}\right) & \left(1 - \dfrac{\beta}{2}\right) \end{bmatrix} \tag{5.146}$$

$$\beta = \left(\frac{\theta}{(\omega\Delta t)^2} + \frac{\zeta\theta^2}{\omega\Delta t} + \frac{\theta^3}{6}\right)^{-1}$$

$$K = \frac{\zeta\beta}{\omega\Delta t} \tag{5.147}$$

$$\{L\} = \begin{Bmatrix} \beta/\omega^2\Delta t^2 \\ \beta/2\omega^2\Delta t^2 \\ \beta/6\omega^2 \end{Bmatrix} \tag{5.148}$$

The largest eigenvalue of the square matrix $[A]$ given by Eq. (5.146) gives an indication of stability. Thus, in the Wilson Theta method unconditional stability is obtained when $\theta = 1.37$.

5.9.4 Newmark Beta Method

In the Newmark integration scheme, the velocity and displacement can be expressed at time $t + \Delta t$

$$\dot{x}_{t+\Delta t} = \dot{x}_t + [(1-\delta)\,\ddot{x}_{t+\Delta t}] \tag{5.149}$$

$$x_{t+\Delta t} = x_t + \dot{x}_t \Delta t + [(1/2-\alpha)\,\ddot{x}_t + \alpha\,\ddot{x}_{t+\Delta t}]\,\Delta t^2 \tag{5.150}$$

where δ and α are to be selected such that stability and accuracy are optimum for which $\delta = 1/2$ and $\alpha = 1/4$. Substituting these values of $\ddot{x}_{t+\Delta t}$ and $x_{t+\Delta t}$ from Eqs. (5.149) and (5.150) in the equilibrium equations

$$\ddot{x}_{t+\Delta t} + 2\,\zeta\omega\dot{x}_{t+\Delta t} + \omega^2 x_{t+\Delta t} = f_{t+\Delta t}$$

from which $x_{t+\Delta t}$ can be evaluated.

Now the response at $(t + \Delta t)$ can be written in the following form

$$\begin{Bmatrix} \ddot{x}_{t+\Delta t} \\ \dot{x}_{t+\Delta t} \\ x_{t+\Delta t} \end{Bmatrix} = [A] \begin{Bmatrix} \ddot{x}_t \\ \dot{x}_t \\ x_t \end{Bmatrix} + [L]\,\{f_{t+\Delta t}\} \tag{5.151}$$

where

$$[A] = \begin{bmatrix} -(1/2-\alpha)\beta - 2(1-\delta)\eta & \frac{1}{\Delta t}(-\beta - 2\eta) & \frac{1}{\Delta t^2}(-\beta) \\ \Delta t(1-\delta-(1/2-\alpha)\delta\beta - 2(1-\delta)\delta\eta) & 1-\beta\delta-2\delta\eta & \frac{1}{\Delta t}(-\beta\delta) \\ \Delta t^2(1/2-\alpha-(1/2-\alpha)\alpha\beta - 2(1-\delta)\delta\eta) & \Delta t(1-\alpha\beta-2\alpha\eta) & (1-\alpha\beta) \end{bmatrix} \tag{5.152}$$

$$\beta = \left(\frac{1}{(\omega\Delta t)^2} + \frac{2\zeta\delta}{\omega\Delta t} + \alpha\right)^{-1} ; \eta = \zeta\frac{\beta}{\omega\Delta t}$$

$$\{L\} = \begin{Bmatrix} \frac{\beta}{(\omega\Delta t)^2} \\ \left(\frac{\beta\delta}{\omega^2\Delta t}\right) \\ \frac{\alpha\beta}{\omega^2} \end{Bmatrix} \tag{5.153}$$

The largest eigenvalue of the square matrix $[A]$ given by Eq. (5.152) gives an indication of stability. The Newmark Beta integration method is unconditionally stable if $\delta \geq 0.5$ and $\alpha \geq 0.25(\delta + 0.5)^2$.

5.10 SUMMARY

In this chapter we have briefly reviewed the direct numerical integration methods for the solution of a single or system of differential equations. Many numerical methods are available for the solution of the response of dynamic systems. We have discussed several widely used step-by-step numerical integration methods for linear and nonlinear dynamic response analysis. A brief description of these integration methods is presented and their application is illustrated. The integration schemes considered are three explicit and four implicit methods. The explicit schemes are, the central difference method, two-cycle interaction with trapezoidal rule and the fourth-order Runge-Kutta method, and the implicit schemes are Houbolt method, Wilson Theta method, Newmark Beta method and the Park Stiffly stable method. Application of these direct numerical integration metods is illustrated with a case study of a linear dynamic system.

When these seven integration methods were used to compute the response of a two-degree of freedom nonlinear dynamic system, (the case study of a railway wheel-axle set), it was found that the two-cycle iteration with trapezoidal rule, Houbolt, and Wilson Theta were unstable. The displacement responses from the central difference and the fourth-order Runge-Kutta methods were highly damped. It is not possible to determine the stability, accuracy and efficiency of a single numerical integration method for all possible applications. The use of a particular integration method is mainly dependent on the nature of the problem and is often dictated by the desired solution accuracy and system nonlinearities.

PROBLEMS

5.1 Find the response of a viscously damped single degree of freedom system subjected to a force

$$F(t) = F_0\left(1 - \sin\frac{\pi t}{2t_0}\right)$$

with the following data: $F_0 = 2$, $t_0 = $ c, $M = 2$, $C = 0.3$, and $K = 1$. The values of the displacement and velocity of the mass at $t = 0$ are zero. Use the central difference method.

5.2 Find the solution of the equation $5\ddot{X} + 2.5\dot{X} + 4000X = F(t)$, where $f(t)$ is as shown in Fig. P5.2 for the duration $0 \le t \le 1$. Assume that $X_0 = \dot{X} = 0$ and $\Delta t = 0.05$. Use the central difference method.

5.3 Solve numerically the differential equation 4 X + 2000 X = $F(t)$ with the initial conditions $X_0 = \dot{X}_0 = 0$ and the forcing function $F(t)$ as shown in Fig. P5.3. Use central difference method with $\Delta t = 0.02$ sec.

5.4 Solve numerically the solution to the problem of a spring mass-system excited by a triangular impulse. The differential equation of motion and the initial conditions are given as

$$0.5\ddot{X} + 8\pi^2 X = F(t)$$

with $$X_1 = \dot{X}_1 = 0$$

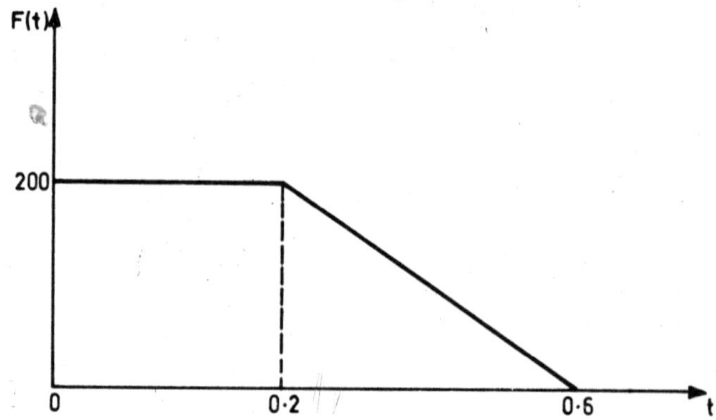

Fig. P5.2

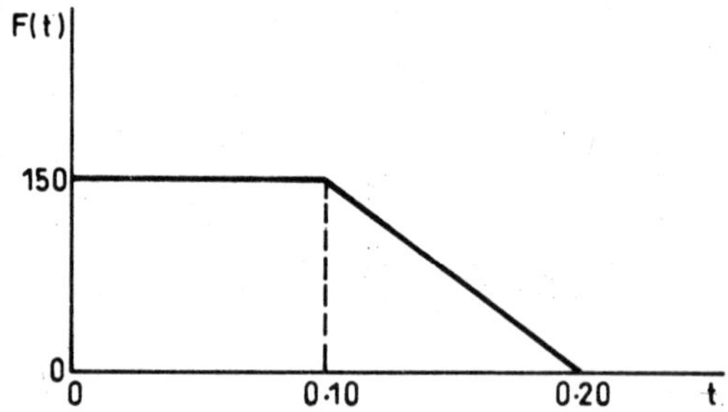

Fig. P5.3

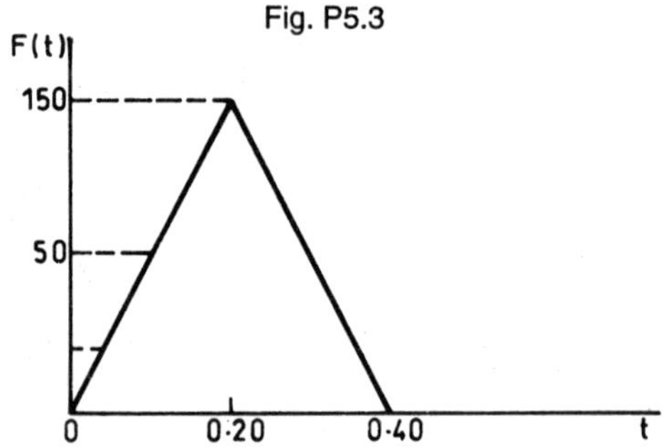

Fig. P5.4

The triangular force is defined in Fig. P5.4. Use central difference method with $\Delta t = 0.05$ sec.

5.5 Solve the following nonlinear vibration problem, using the central difference method.

$$M\ddot{X} + C\dot{X} + KX + K^* X^3 = F \cos \omega t$$

with $M = 1.0$, $C = 0.5$, $K = 1.0$, $K^* = 0.5$, $\Delta t = 0.05$, $t_{max} = 5.0$, and the initial conditions $X_0 = \dot{X}_0 = 0$. Plot the variation of X with t.

5.6 Solve Problem 5.1 using the fourth-order Runge-Kutta method.

5.7 Solve Problem 5.2 using the fourth-order Runge-Kutta method.

5.8 Solve Problem 5.3 by the Runge-Kutta method.

5.9 Solve Problem 5.4 by the Runge-Kutta method.

5.10 Solve Problem 5.5 by the Runge-Kutta method.

5.11 Find the response of the two-degree of freedom system when $F_1(t) = 0$, and $F_2(t) = 10$, using the central difference method. The mass, stiffness, and damping matrices for this system are given as

$$[M] = \begin{bmatrix} 1 & 0 \\ 0 & 10 \end{bmatrix}, [K] = \begin{bmatrix} 11 & -1 \\ -1 & 1 \end{bmatrix}, [C] = \begin{bmatrix} 0.5 & -0.1 \\ -0.1 & 0.1 \end{bmatrix}$$

All the initial conditions are given as zero. Use $\Delta t = 0.05$.

5.12 Solve Problem 5.11 using the two-cycle iteration with trapezoidal rule.

5.13 Solve Problem 5.11 using the fourth-order Runge-Kutta method.

5.14 Solve Problem 5.11 using the Houbolt method.

5.15 Solve Problem 5.11 using the Wilson Theta method.

5.16 Solve Problem 5.11 using the Newmark Beta method.

5.17 Solve Problem 5.11 using the Park Stiffly stable method.

5.18 In the two degree of freedom system shown in Fig. P5.18, the force F_s in the spring connection of the masses M_1 and M_2 is assumed to be related to its displacement X_2 by $F_s = K_2\,(X_s + 0.5\,X^3_s)$, and the equations of motion are given by

$$M_1\ddot{X}_1 + C_1\dot{X}_1 + K_1X_1 - K_2\,[(X_2 - X_1) + 0.5(X_2 - X_1)^3] - C_2[\dot{X}_2 - \dot{X}_1] = F_1$$

$$M_2\ddot{X}_2 + C_2(\dot{X}_2 - \dot{X}_1) + K_2[(X_2 - X_1) + 0.5\,(X_2 - X_1)^3] = F_2$$

The numerical values of the mass, damping, and stiffness are chosen as $M_1 = 1$, $M_2 = 10$, $C_1 = 0$, $C_2 = 0.15$, $K_1 = 19$, and $K_2 = 1$. The initial conditions are selected as zero and the forcing vector is

$$\begin{Bmatrix} F_1(t) \\ F_2(t) \end{Bmatrix} = \begin{Bmatrix} 0 \\ 5 \end{Bmatrix} \text{ for } t > 0$$

and

$$\begin{Bmatrix} F_1(t) \\ F_2(t) \end{Bmatrix} = \begin{Bmatrix} 0 \\ 0 \end{Bmatrix} \text{ for } t < 0$$

in matrix notion, these equations may be written as

$$\begin{bmatrix} M_1 & 0 \\ 0 & M_2 \end{bmatrix} \begin{Bmatrix} \ddot{x}_1 \\ \ddot{x}_2 \end{Bmatrix} + \begin{bmatrix} C_1 + C_2 & -C_2 \\ -C_2 & C_2 \end{bmatrix} \begin{Bmatrix} \dot{x}_1 \\ \dot{x}_2 \end{Bmatrix} +$$

$$\begin{bmatrix} K_1 + K_2 + 0.5K_2(X_2 - X_1)^2 & -K_2 - 0.5K_2(X_2 - X_1)^2 \\ -K_2 - 0.5K_2(X_2 - X_1)^2 & K_2 + 0.5K_2(X_2 - X_1)^2 \end{bmatrix} \begin{Bmatrix} x_1 \\ x_2 \end{Bmatrix} = \begin{Bmatrix} F_1 \\ F_2 \end{Bmatrix}$$

Take $\Delta t = 0.05$ sec. Use the central difference method and compute the response of the resulting nonlinear system.

5.19 Solve problem 5.17 by the two-cycle iteration with trapezoidal rules

5.20 Solve problem 5.17 of the fourth-order Runge-Kutta method.

5.21 Solve problem 5.17 by the Houbolt method.

5.22 Solve problem 5.17 by the Wilson Theta scheme.

5.23 Solve problem 5.17 by the Newmark Beta method.

5.24 Solve problem 5.17 by the Park Stiffly stable method.

5.25 Consider a simple system for which the governing equilibrium equations are

$$\begin{bmatrix} 2 & 0 \\ 0 & 1 \end{bmatrix} \begin{Bmatrix} \ddot{X}_1 \\ \ddot{X}_2 \end{Bmatrix} + \begin{bmatrix} 4 & -1 \\ -1 & 3 \end{bmatrix} \begin{Bmatrix} x_1 \\ x_2 \end{Bmatrix} = \begin{Bmatrix} 0 \\ 10 \end{Bmatrix}$$

(*a*) Calculate the transformation matrix for this system and thus establish the decoupled equations of equilibrium on the basis of mode shape vectors.

(*b*) Compute the exact response by integrating each of the two decoupled equilibrium equations.

5.26 Assume that for a multidegree of freedom system $\omega_1 = 2$ and $\omega_2 = 4$ and that in those two modes we require 2% and 8% critical damping, respectively; that is, we require $\zeta_1 = 0.02$ and $\zeta_2 = 0.08$. Establish the constants α and β for Rayleigh damping in order that a direct step-by-step integration can be carried out.

5.27 The damping ratios for the first two natural frequencies of 1 cycle/sec and 4 cycles/sec are given as 0.015 and 0.05 respectively. Estimate the constants α and β to be used for Rayleigh damping in order that a direct step-by-step integration method can be used.

5.28 The approximate dampings to be specified for a multi-degree of freedom system are given as follows:

$\zeta_1 = 0.003 \qquad \omega_1 = 2.0$

$\zeta_2 = 0.003 \qquad \omega_2 = 3.2$

$\zeta_3 = 0.041 \qquad \omega_3 = 7.0$

$\zeta_4 = 0.095 \qquad \omega_4 = 14.9$

$\zeta_5 = 0.150 \qquad \omega_5 = 20.0$

Find appropriate Rayleigh damping Parameters α and β.

5.29 The approximate dampings to be specified for a multi-degree of freedom system are given as follows:

$\zeta_1 = 0.002$, $\zeta_2 = 0.003$, $\zeta_3 = 0.045$, , $\zeta_4 = 0.090$, and

$\zeta_5 = 0.100$, $\omega_1 = 1.8$, $\omega_2 = 3.3$, $\omega_3 = 6.8$, $\omega_4 = 13.8$, and $\omega_5 = 18.9$.

5.30 The approximate dampings to be specified for a multi-degree of freedom system are given as follows:

$\zeta_1 = 0.001$, $\zeta_2 = 0.002$, $\zeta_3 = 0.030$, $\zeta_4 = 0.060$, and

$\zeta_5 = 0.100$, $\omega_1 = 1.9$, $\omega_2 = 3.6$, $\omega_3 = 7.5$, $\omega_4 = 15.0$, and $\omega_5 = 19.7$.

REFERENCES

1. Ali, R., "Finite difference methods in vibration analysis," *Shock and Vibration Digest,* Vol. 15, March 1983, pp. 3–7.
2. Atkinson, L.V. and Harley, P.J., (1984), Introduction to Numerical Methods with PASCAL, Addison-Wesley, Reading, Mass.
3. Bath, K.J. and Wilson, E.L., (1976), *Numerical Methods in Finite Element Analysis,* Prentice - Hall, Inc., Englewood Cliffs, N.J.
4. Belytschko, T., (1980), Explicit Time Integration of Structure-Mechanical Systems, in J.Dona (Ed.) Advanced Structural Dynamics, PP. 97-122. Applied Science Publishers, London.
5. Belytschko, T. and Mullen, R., Stability of explicit-implicit mesh partitions in time integration, *International Journal for Numerical Methods in Engineering*, Vol. 12, 1978, pp. 1575-1586.
6. Belytschko, T. and Schoeberle, D.F., On the unconditional stability of an implicit algorithm for nonlinear structural dynamics, *Journal of Applied Mechanics*, Vol. 42, 1975, pp. 865-869.
7. Belytschko, T., Holmes, N. and Mullen, R., Explicit integration-stability, solution properties, cost, finite-element analysis of transient nonlinear siructural behavior, *ASME*, AMD Vol. 14, 1975.

8. Brice, C., Luther, H.A. and Wilkes, J.O., (1969), *Applied Numerical Methods*, John Wiley & Sons, Inc., New York.
9. Clough, R.W. and Penzien, J., (1975), *Dynamics of Sturctures*, McGraw-Hill Book Company, New York.
10. Conte, S.D. and DeBoor, c.W., (1972), Elementary Numerical Analysis: An Algorithmic Approach, (2nd Ed.), McGraw-Hill, New York.
11. Cornwell, R.E., Craig, R.R. Jr. and Johnson, C.P., On the application of the modeacceleration method to structural engineering problems, *Earthquake Engineering and Structural Dynamics*, Vol. 11, 1983, pp. 679-688.
12. Denman, E.D., A numerical method for coupled differential equations, *International Journal for Numerical Methods in Engineering*, Vol. 4, 1972, pp. 587-596.
13. Farlow, S.J., A computer program to find analytical solutions of second order linear differential equations, *International Journal for Numerical Methods in Engineering*, Vol. 6, 1973, pp. 603-606.
14. Froberg, C.E., (1969), Introduction to Numerical Analysis, Addison-Wesley Publishing Company, Inc., Reading, Mass.
15. Garg, V.K. and Dukkipati R.V., (1984), Dynamics of Railway Vehicle Systems, Academic Press, Inc., New York,
16. Gerald, C.F. and Wheatley, P.O., (1984), Applied Numerical Analysis, (3rd Ed.), Addison Wesley, Reading, Mass.
17. Gordreu. G.L. and Taylor, R.L., (1973), Evaluation of numerical integration methods in elastodynamics, *Computational Methods in Applied Mechanics and Engineering*, Vol. 2.
18. Hildebrand, F.B., (1956), Introduction to Numerical Analysis, McGraw-Hill Book Company, New York.
19. Hojjat, A., Gere, J,M. and Weaver, W., Algorithms for nonliear structural dynamics, *Journal of the Structural Division*, ASCE, Feb. 1978, pp. 263-297.
20. Houbolt, J.C., A recurrence matrix solution for the dynamic response of elastic aircraft, *Journal of Aeronautical Sciences*, Vol. 17, 1950, pp. 540-550, 594.
21. Hughes, T.J.R., A note on the stability of Newmark's algorithm in nonlinear structural dynamics, *International Journal for Numerical Methods in Engineering*, Vol. 11, 1976 pp. 383–386.
22. Hurty, W.C. and Rubinstein, M.F., (1970), Dynamics of Structures. Prentice-Hall, lnc., Englewood Cliffs, N.J.
23. Jennings, A. and Orr, D.R.L., Application of the simultaneous iteration method to undamped vibration problems, *International Journal for Numerical Methods in Engineering*, Vol. 3, 1971, pp. 13–24.
24. Key, S.W., (1980), Transient response by time integration: Review of implicit and explicit operators, in J. Donea (Ed.), Advanced Structural Dynamics, Applied Science Publishers, London.
25. Krieg, R.D., Unconditional stability in numerical time integration methods, *Journal of Applied Mechanics*, Vo1.40, 1973, pp. 417–421.
26. Lau, P. C. M., Finite difference approximation for ordinary derivatives, *International Journal for Numerical Methods in Engineering*, Vol. 17, 1981, pp. 663–678
27. Leech, J.W., Hsu, P.T., Mack, E.W., Stability of a finite-difference method for solving matrix equations, *AIAA Journal*, Vol. 3, 1965, pp. 2172–2173.
28. Levy, S. and Kroll, W.D., (1951), Errors introduced by finite space and time increments in dynamic response computation, Proceedings, First U.S. National Congress of Applied Mechanics, pp. 1–8.

29. Levy, S. and Wilkinson, J.P.D., (1976), The Component Element Method in Dynamics with Application to Earthquake and Vehicle Engineering, McGraw-Hill, New York.
30. McNamara, J.F., Solution schemes for problems of nonlinear structural dynamics, *Journal of Pressure Vessel Technology*, ASME, May 1974, pp. 96–102.
31. Nakamura, S., (1977), *Computational Methods in Engineering and Science*, John Wiley, New York.
32. Newmark, N.M., A method of computation for structural dynamics, *Journal of Engineering Mechanics Division*, ASCE Vol. 85, 1959, pp. 67–94.
33. Park, K.C., An Improved Stiffly stable method for direct integration of non-linear structural dynamic equations, *Journal of Applied Mechanics*, ASME, June 1975, pp. 464–470.
34. Reali, M., Rangogni, R. and Pennati, V., Compact analytic expressions of two-dimensional finite difference forms, *International Journal for Numerical Methods in Engineering*, Vol. 20, 1984, pp. 121-130.
35. Romanelli, M.J. (1965), Runge-Kutta Method for the solution of ordinary differential equations, in A. Ralston and H.S. Wilf, ed. Mathematical Methods Ior Digital Computers, ed. John Wiley & Sons, Inc., New York.
36. Tillerson, I.R., Stricklin, J.A. and Haisler, W.E., (1973), Numerical Methods for the solution of Nonlinear Problems in Structural Analysis, Winter Annual Meeting of ASME, Detroit, Mich., Nov. 11–15, 1973.15
37. Timoshenko, S.P., Young, D. H., and Weaver, W. Jr., (1974), Vibration Problems in Engineering, (4th Ed.), John Wiley, New York.
38. Wah, T., and Colcote, L.R., (1970), Structural Analysis by Finite Difference Calculus, Van Nostrand Reinhold, New York.
39. Wang, P.C., (1966), *Numerical and Matrix Methods in .Structural Mechanics*, John Wiley & Sons, Inc., New York.
40. Wilson, E.L., Farhoomand, I. and Bathe, K.I., Nonlinear dynamic analysis of complex structures, *International Journal of Earthquake Engineering and Structural Dynamics*, Vol. 1, 1973, pp. 241–252.

CHAPTER 6

DYNAMIC ANALYSIS

6.1 INTRODUCTION

The static and dynamic analysis of structural members and machine components using finite element analysis (F.E.A.) results in a set of equilibrium equations of the form

$$[M]\{\ddot{x}\}+[C]\{\dot{x}\}+[K]\{x\}=\{F\} \tag{6.1}$$

where $[M]$, $[C]$ and $[K]$ are the mass, damping and stiffness matrices, respectively, $[F]$ is the external force vector, and $\ddot{x}$, $\dot{x}$, and x are the acceleration, velocity and displacement vectors respectively. At any instant of time t the equilibrium equations can be written as

$$\{F_I\}+\{F_D\}+\{F_E\}=\{F\} \tag{6.2}$$

where $\{F_I\}$ are the inertia forces, $\{F_D\}$ are the damping forces and $\{F_E\}$ are the elastic forces. All are time dependent and are equal to

$$\{F_I\}=[M]\{\ddot{x}\}$$

$$\{F_D\}=[C]\{\dot{x}\}$$

$$\{F_E\}=[K]\{x\}.$$

Therefore, in dynamic analysis the equilibrium equations at any instant of time can be obtained by taking the effect of acceleration dependent inertia forces and velocity dependent damping forces into consideration in addition to elastic and external forces. In static analysis the inertia and damping forces are not there.

The choice to conduct static analysis or dynamic analysis is generally dependent on the physical nature of the problem. If the motion dependent forces i.e. , inertia and damping forces, are not significant compared to static forces, a static analysis may be sufficient. However, it is rather difficult to obtain solutions neglecting inertia and damping forces in non-linear dynamic analysis.

Equation 6.1 represents a system of linear differential equations of second order. Several solution techniques are available to solve the differential equations with constant coefficients. Most of the solution procedures for the general systems of differential equations are very expensive and time consuming on the computer if the order of the matrices is large, say, more than 100. The coefficient matrices $[M]$, $[C]$ and $[K]$ of mechanical and structural engineering problems have special characteristics which can be effectively utilized in simplifying the analysis. The solution techniques that are considered here are mainly matrix methods. Here we review some of the concepts of eigenvalue problems before discussing the solution techniques.

Some of the concepts involved in eigenvalue problems, properties of matrices, eigenvalues and eigenvectors are discussed in the sections to follow.

6.2 BASIC CONCEPTS OF EIGENVALUE PROBLEMS

The effectiveness of the finite element analysis is mainly based on matrix algebra and the speed and efficient utilization of the storage of the computer. Hence, it is necessary to be familiar with the fundamentals of matrix algebra and linear algebra that are needed for better understanding of the solution techniques. Emphasis is given to those concepts which are important in finite element analysis.

6.2.1 The Trace and other Invariants

The sum of the eigenvalues of an $n \times n$ matrix A is called its trace.

$$T_r[A] = \sum_n \lambda_n$$

$$\det(\lambda I - A) = (\lambda - \lambda_1)(\lambda - \lambda_2)\ldots.(\lambda - \lambda_n)$$

$$= \lambda^n + c_1 \lambda^{n-1} + c_2 \lambda^{n-2} + \ldots + c_n \ldots\ldots\ldots\ldots \quad (6.3)$$

If matrices $[A]$ and $[B]$ are similar, their characteristic polynomials are the same and hence their trace is the same. Hence the trace is invariant in similarity transformation,

$$[B] = [T]^{-1}[A][T] \quad (6.4)$$

where $[T]$ is the matrix used in the similarity transformation.
Setting $\lambda = 0$ in Eq.6.3 we see that $\det(-A) = (-\lambda_1)\ldots.(-\lambda_n)$ and $\det[-A] = (-1)^n \det[A]$. Hence $\det[A] = \lambda_1 \lambda_2 \ldots.\lambda_n$. All the coefficients $c_1 c_2 \ldots c_n$ are invariant. It can also be shown from Eq. 6.3 that the sum of the eigenvalues must be equal to the sum of the diagonal elements.

$$\lambda_1 + \lambda_2 + \lambda_3 + \ldots.\lambda_n = a_{11} + a_{22} + a_{33} + \ldots..a_{nn} \quad (6.5)$$

Therefore

$$T_r[A] = a_{11} + a_{22} + \ldots + a_{nn} \quad (6.6)$$

Example 6.1

Let $[A] = \begin{bmatrix} 5 & 7 \\ -2 & 3 \end{bmatrix}$, then the sum of the eigenvalues of $[A]$ must be equal to 5 + 3 = 8.

6.2.2 The Canonical Diagonal Form

Two matrices $[A]$ and $[B]$ of size $n \times n$ are similar if there exists an $n \times n$ matrix $[T]$ with $\det[T] \neq 0$ for which

$$[T]^{-1}[A][T] = [B] \quad (6.7)$$

Similar matrices are obtained as a result of linear transformation in different coordinate systems.

Further, similar matrices $[A]$ and $[B]$ have the same eigenvalues with the same multiplicities, which can be shown as follows:

$$[T]^{-1}[A][T] = [B]$$

For all complex λ

$$\det[\lambda I - B] = \det[\lambda I - T^{-1}AT]$$

$$= \det[T^{-1}(\lambda I - A)T]$$

$$= \det[T]^{-1}[\det(\lambda I - A)](\det[T])$$

but $(\det[T^{-1}])(\det[T]) = \det([T]^{-1}[T]) = \det[I] = 1$

Therefore, $\det(\lambda I - B) = \det(\lambda I - A)$.

Another important property is that a matrix $[A]$ of size $n \times n$ is similar to a diagonal matrix if and only if $[A]$ has n linearly independent eigenvectors. In particular $[A]$ is similar to a diagonal matrix if $[\Lambda]$ has distinct eigenvalues. A diagonal matrix, $[\Lambda]$, to which $[A]$ is similar is known as a canonical diagonal form related to $[A]$, i.e.,

$$[T]^{-1}[A][T] = \begin{bmatrix} \alpha_1 & & 0 \\ & \alpha_2 & \\ 0 & & \alpha_n \end{bmatrix} = [\Lambda] \tag{6.8}$$

Let us consider $t^1 \ldots t^n$ be the columns of the nonsingular matrix $[T]$, which are linearly independent. Premultiply both sides of (6.6) by $[T]$, then the j th column of $[A][T]$ is $[A]\{t^j\}$. The jth column of $[T][\Lambda]$ is $\alpha_j\{t^j\}$. Therefore (6.6) can be written as

$$[A]\{t_j^j\} = \alpha\{t^j\} \quad \text{for } j = 1, 2, \ldots n \tag{6.9}$$

Thus, the independent vectors t^j are eigenvalues of $[A]$ and α_j are the eigenvalues of $[A]$ with same multiplicities.

Example 6.2

Let
$$[A] = \begin{bmatrix} 0 & -1 \\ 1 & 0 \end{bmatrix}$$

The eigenvalues of $[A]$ are $\alpha_1 = i$ and $\alpha_2 = -i$, where $i = \sqrt{-1}$. The corresponding eigenvectors are

$$\{t\}^1 = \begin{Bmatrix} 1 \\ -i \end{Bmatrix} \text{ and } \{t\}^2 = \begin{Bmatrix} 1 \\ i \end{Bmatrix}$$

$$[T]^{-1}[A][T] = \frac{1}{2i}\begin{bmatrix} i & -1 \\ 1 & i \end{bmatrix}\begin{bmatrix} 0 & -1 \\ 1 & 0 \end{bmatrix}\begin{bmatrix} 1 & 1 \\ -i & i \end{bmatrix}$$

$$= \begin{bmatrix} i & 0 \\ 0 & -i \end{bmatrix} = [\Lambda]$$

6.2.3 Positive Definite Matrix

If all the eigenvalues of a matrix are positive, the matrix is said to be *positive definite* and if the eigenvalues are zero and positive then the matrix is said to be *positive semi-definite*. A matix having positive eigenvalues, positive determinant for itself and for its principal minors is said to be *symmetric positive definite* matrix. Similarly a matrix with zero and positive eigenvalues and zero and positive determinant for itself and for its principal minors is said to be *semi-definite* matrix.

Example 6.3

$$[A] = \begin{bmatrix} 2 & -1 & 0 \\ -1 & 4 & -2 \\ 0 & -2 & 3 \end{bmatrix}$$

Eigenvalues of this matrix are 1, 2.27, 5.73 all are positive. Hence the matrix is positive definite.

6.2.4 Hermitian Matrices

If $[A]$ is a matrix of size $n \times n$ with real or complex components, the adjoint matrix, A^* can be defined as the complex conjugate of the transpose of $[A]$. Thus we have

$$\begin{bmatrix} 1+i & 2-i \\ 3+4i & 5-6i \end{bmatrix}^* = \begin{bmatrix} 1-i & 3-4i \\ 2+i & 5+6i \end{bmatrix}$$

and

$$\begin{bmatrix} -8 & 9 \\ 6 & 7 \end{bmatrix}^* = \begin{bmatrix} -8 & 6 \\ 9 & 7 \end{bmatrix}$$

In both cases above

$$[A]^* = [\overline{A}]^T \tag{6.10}$$

where $[A]^T$ is the transpose of $[A]$. If we define the inner product of two vectors, x and y, to be

$$(\{x\}, \{y\}) = \sum_{k=1}^{n} x_k \, \overline{y}_k \tag{6.11}$$

the adjoint matrix is to satisfy the identity

$$([A]\ \{x\}, \{y\}) = (\{x\}, [A]^* \{y\}) \tag{6.12}$$

Since

$$([A]\ \{x\}, \{y\}) = \sum_{k=1}^{n} \left[\sum_{j=1}^{n} a_{kj}\, x_j \right] \overline{y}_k$$

$$= \sum_{j=1}^{n} \left[\sum_{k=1}^{n} a_{kj}\, \overline{y}_k \right] = [\{x\}, [A]^* \{y\}]$$

Conversely, the identity

$$([A]\ \{x\}, \{y\}) \equiv (\{x\}, [B]\ \{y\}) \quad \text{implies}$$

$$[B] = [\overline{A}]^T = [A]^*$$

This follows from setting $\{x\} = e^j$ and $y = e^k$ which yields

$$a_{kj} = b_{jk}$$

A real symmetric matrix $[A]$ is its own adjoint, ie.,

$$[A] = [A]^T = [A]^*$$

In general, Hermitian matrices are defined as self-adjoint matrices.

$$[H] = [H]^*$$

$$([H]\ \{x\}, \{y\}) = (\{\Lambda\}, [H]\ \{y\}) \quad \text{(for all } x \text{ and } y) \quad (6.11)$$

$$h_{kj} = \overline{h}_{jk} \quad (j,k = 1...n)$$

Another important property is that the eigenvalues of a Hermitian matrix are real and eigenvectors belonging to different eigenvalues are orthogonal.

If $[H] = [H]^*$ and has distinct eigenvalues, then it can be diagonalized by a unitary similarity transformation

$$[U]^{-1}\ [H]\ [U] = [U]^*\ [H]\ [U] = [\Lambda] = \text{diag}(\lambda_1 \ldots .\lambda_n) \quad (6.12)$$

The columns of $[U]$ can be taken as a set of n mutually orthogonal unit eigenvectors corresponding to n different eigenvalues of $[H]$.

The canonical diagonalization (6.12) of Hermitian matrices is always possible, even if the eigenvalues $\lambda_i \ldots \lambda_n$ are not distinct. This can be proved as follows.

If $[H]$ is a Hermitian matrix of size $n \times n$ with eigenvalues $\lambda_1 \ldots \lambda_n$, then $[H]$ has n mutually orthogonal unit eigenvectors $\{U^1\} \ldots . \{U^n\}$, with

$$[H]\ \{u^j\} = \lambda_j\ \{u^j\} \qquad (\text{for } j = 1, 2, \ldots n)$$

and

$$[U]^*\ [H]\ [U] = [\Lambda] \quad (6.13)$$

where $[U]$ is the unitary matrix with columns $\{u^1\}, \ldots \{u^n\}$ and $[\Lambda] = \text{diag}(\lambda_1, \ldots . \lambda_n)$.

6.2.5 Orthogonal Matrices

Here we introduce some important concepts used in the study of eigenvalue problems. Consider two vectors

$$\{x\} = \{x_1, x_2, .., x_n\}^T \text{ and } \{y\} = \{y_1, y_2, \ldots y_n\}^T$$

The inner product of these two vectors can be defined as

$$(\{x\}, \{y\}) = \sum_{j=1}^{n} \overline{x}_j\ y_j = \overline{x}_1\ y_1 + \overline{x}_2\ y_2 + \ldots \overline{x}_n\ y_n \quad (6.14)$$

The inner product of $\{x\}$ and $\{y\}$ is simply the matrix product of the $1 \times n$ row vector $\{x\}$ and $(n \times 1)$ column vector $\{y\}$ resulting in a scalar. The two vectors $\{x\}$ and $\{y\}$ are said to be *orthogonal* if their inner product is zero

or $$(\{x\}, \{y\}) = 0$$

(Note: If $\{x\}$ and $\{y\}$ are three component vectors with real components then $(\{x\}, \{y\}) = 0$ means that $\{x\}$ and $\{y\}$ are mutually perpendicular.

If the inner product of $\{x\}$ with itself is unity then the vector $\{x\}$ is said to be a *Unit* vector.

$$(\{x\},\{x\}) = \sum_{j=1}^{n} |x_j|^2 = 1$$

Let us consider a non zero vector $\{y\}$ is equal to a scalar times a unit vector, $(\{y\}, \{y\}) = c^2 > 0$, where c is a scalar.

Then
$$\{x\} = \frac{1}{c}\{y\}$$

$$(\{x\},\{x\}) = \left(\left\{\frac{1}{c}y\right\},\left\{\frac{1}{c}y\right\}\right) = \frac{1}{c^2}(\{y\},\{y\}) = \frac{c^2}{c^2} = 1$$

Therefore $\{x\}$ is a unit vector. This process of multiplying a vector $\{y\}$ by a scalar to obtain a unit vector $\{x\}$ is known as *normalizing* the vector $\{y\}$. The vector $\{x\}$ is said to be *normalized.*

Observe that if any eigenvector is normalized then the resulting unit vector is also an eigenvector, since $[A]\{x\} = \lambda\{x\}$. Also $[A]\{y\} = \lambda\{y\}$, for $\{y\} = \alpha\{x\}$ (α is any scalar).

Any matrix $[U] = [U_1, U_2, \ldots U_n]$ whose columns are unit vectors that are mutually orthogonal is called a *unitary* matrix with mutually orthogonal columns. That is

$$(\{U_i\},\{U_j\}) = 0 \quad \text{if} \quad i \neq j \quad \begin{array}{l} i = 1,2,\ldots n \\ j = 1,2,\ldots n \end{array} \tag{6.15}$$

Note that each pair of columns is orthogonal. Since each column is a unit vector, we also have

$$(\{U_i\},\{U_i\}) = 1 \quad i = 1,2\ldots n \tag{6.16}$$

Some important properties of unitary matrices are summarized here. If $[U] = [U_1, U_2, \ldots U_n]$ is a unity matrix, then

(a) $[U]^*[U] = [U][U]^* = [I_n]$

(b) $[U]$ is nonsingular

(c) $[U]^{-1} = [U]^*$

If all the elements of a unitary matrix are real, then the matrix is also called *orthogonal* matrix. For example if $[P]$ is an orthogonal matrix, then

$$[P]^T[P] = [I_n] = [P][P]^T$$

$$[P]^{-1} = [P]^T$$

6.2.6 Rotation Matrix

One of the orthogonal matrices very frequently used is the rotation matrix.

$$[P] = \begin{array}{cc}
\begin{array}{cccccc} & i\text{th column} & & j\text{th column} & & \end{array} & \\
\left[\begin{array}{cccccc}
1 & & & & & \\
\cdots & \cdots & \cdots & \cdots & \cdots & \cdots \\
\cdots & \cos\theta & \cdots & -\sin\theta & \cdots & \cdots \\
\cdots & \cdots & \cdots & \cdots & \cdots & \cdots \\
\cdots & \sin\theta & \cdots & \cos\theta & \cdots & \cdots \\
\cdots & \cdots & \cdots & \cdots & \cdots & \cdots \\
 & & & & & 1
\end{array}\right] &
\begin{array}{l}
\\
\\
i\text{th row} \\
\\
j\text{th row} \\
\\
\\
\end{array}
\end{array} \tag{6.17}$$

All other elements are zeros and i and j are arbitrary with $i \neq j$. Consider a matrix of size 2×2, in which case

$$[P] = \begin{bmatrix} \text{Cos}\,\theta & -\text{Sin}\,\theta \\ \text{Sin}\,\theta & \text{Cos}\,\theta \end{bmatrix} \tag{6.18}$$

As shown in Fig. 6.1 we observe that for the base vectors $\{x_1\}$ and $\{x_2\}$ the transformation

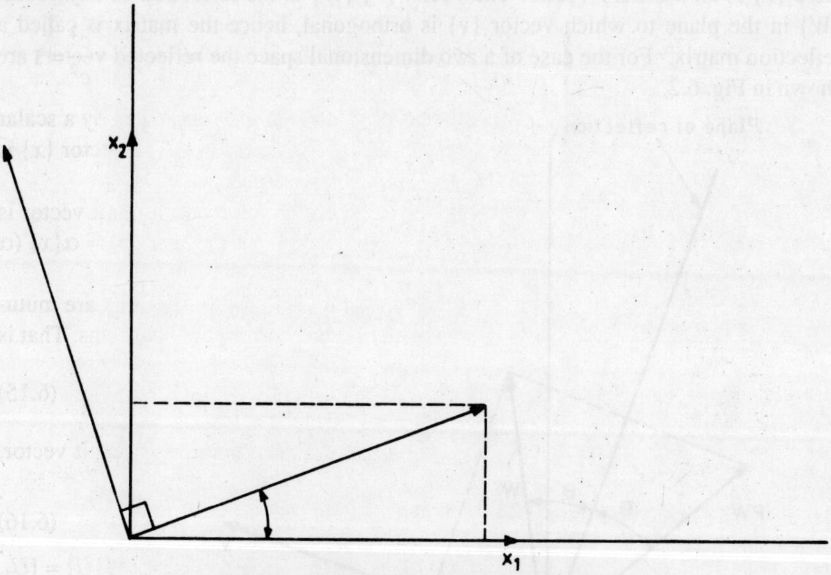

Fig. 6.1 Rotation of vectors $\{x_1\}$ and $\{x_2\}$

$$\{y_1 \quad y_2\} = [P] \quad \{x_1 \quad x_2\}$$

represents rotations by an angle θ. This rotation can be carried out in the n-dimensional space for most general case.

Example 6.4

Rotate the vector $\{x\}$ through an angle 30° where $\{x\} = (2/\sqrt{3}, 0)$. The rotation matrix in this case for $\text{Cos}\ 30° = \dfrac{\sqrt{3}}{2}$ and $\text{Sin}\ 30° = 1/2$

$$[P] = \begin{bmatrix} \dfrac{\sqrt{3}}{2} & -\dfrac{1}{2} \\ \dfrac{1}{2} & \dfrac{\sqrt{3}}{2} \end{bmatrix}$$

The rotated vector $\{y\} = [P]\ \{x\}$

$$[y] = \begin{bmatrix} \dfrac{\sqrt{3}}{2} & -\dfrac{1}{2} \\ \dfrac{1}{2} & \dfrac{\sqrt{3}}{2} \end{bmatrix} \begin{Bmatrix} \dfrac{2}{\sqrt{3}} \\ 0 \end{Bmatrix} = \begin{Bmatrix} 1 \\ \dfrac{1}{\sqrt{3}} \end{Bmatrix}$$

This rotated vector can be represented geometrically.

6.2.7 Reflection Matrix

Another important orthogonal matrix extensively used in the eigenvalue problems is the reflection matrix.

$$[P] = [I] - \alpha \{v\} \{v\}^T \quad \text{where} \quad \alpha = \frac{2}{\{v\}^T \{v\}} \tag{6.19}$$

Here $\{v\}$ is an arbitrary vector. The vector $[P]\{W\}$ is the reflection of any vector $\{W\}$ in the plane to which vector $\{v\}$ is orthogonal, hence the matrix is called a reflection matrix. For the case of a two dimensional space the reflected vectors are shown in Fig. 6.2.

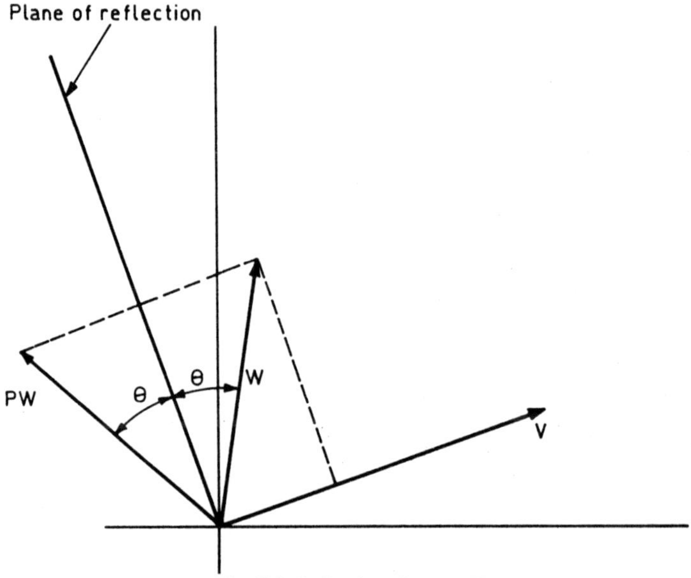

Fig. 6.2 Reflection of vector W

Example 6.5

Establish the reflection matrix to the vector $\{v\} = \begin{Bmatrix} 2 \\ 2 \end{Bmatrix}$ and reflect the vector

$\{W\} = \begin{Bmatrix} 1 \\ 2 \end{Bmatrix}$

we have
$$[P] = [I] - \frac{2}{\{v\}^T \{v\}} \{v\}\{v\}^T$$

$$= \begin{bmatrix} 1 & 0 \\ 0 & 1 \end{bmatrix} - \frac{2}{8} \begin{bmatrix} 4 & 4 \\ 4 & 4 \end{bmatrix} = \begin{bmatrix} 0 & -1 \\ -1 & 0 \end{bmatrix}$$

$[P]\{W\}$ is the reflection of $\{W\}$

$$[P]\{W\} = \begin{bmatrix} 0 & -1 \\ -1 & 0 \end{bmatrix} \begin{Bmatrix} 1 \\ 2 \end{Bmatrix} = \begin{Bmatrix} -2 \\ -1 \end{Bmatrix} = -\begin{Bmatrix} 2 \\ 1 \end{Bmatrix}$$

which is reflection of $\{W\}$.

6.3 BASIC PROPERTIES OF EIGENVALUES AND EIGENVECTORS

Here we present some basic properties of the eigenvalue analysis and indicate some examples relating them to physical problems.

If $[A]$ is any square matrix of order $n \times n$ and if $\{x\}$ is a non-zero vector such that

$$[A]\,\{x\} = \lambda\{x\} \tag{6.20}$$

where λ is some number, then $\{x\}$ is said to be an eigenvector of $[A]$ with the corresponding eigenvalue λ. Premultiplying an eigenvector by the appropriate matrix yields a constant times the eigenvector, where the constant is the eigenvalue.

It is known that the eigenvalues of a square matrix of size $n \times n$ satisfy an nth order polynomial equation. Thus in general there will be n eigenvalues which are not necessarily distinct and real. They are either real or result in complex conjugates if all the matrix elements are real. Another property of eigenvalue problem can be stated as follows. If $[A]$ is a square matrix of size $n \times n$, any eigenvalue λ satisfies the nth degree polynomial equation: $\det(A - \lambda I) = 0$. This equation is also known as the characteristic equations of $[A]$. The proof of this property is that we seek λ and non-zero $\{x\}$ such that

$$[A]\,\{x\} = \lambda\{x\}$$

or

$$[A - \lambda I]\,\{x\} = 0 \tag{6.21}$$

This represents a system of n homogeneous equations in n unknowns $x_1, x_2, \ldots. x_n$. Hence if we require non-zero solutions $\{x\}$ then $[A - \lambda I]$ must be singular or $\det[A - \lambda I] = 0$.

$$\det[A - \lambda I] = \begin{bmatrix} a_{11} - \lambda & a_{12} & \cdots & a_{1n} \\ a_{22} & a_{22} - \lambda & a_{23} & a_{2n} \\ \cdots & \cdots & \cdots & \cdots \\ \cdots & \cdots & \cdots & \cdots \\ a_{n1} & a_{n2} & \cdots & a_{nn} - \lambda \end{bmatrix}$$

or

$$\det[A - \lambda I] = (a_{11} - \lambda)\,(a_{22} - \lambda) \ldots. (a_{nn} - \lambda)$$

The equations $\det[A - \lambda I] = 0$ gives a polynomial equation of nth degree in λ. There will be n eigenvalues and n corresponding eigenvectors. The eigenvalues are $\lambda_1, \lambda_2, \ldots. \lambda_n$ and the corresponding eigenvectors are $\{x^{(1)}\}, \{x^{(2)}\}, \{x^{(3)}\} \ldots \{x^{(n)}\}$. That is

$$[A]\,\{x^{(r)}\} = \lambda_r \{x^r\} \quad \text{where } 1 \le r \le n$$

In general Eq. (6.20) provides a procedure for the calculation of eigenvalues and eigenvectors. The determinant of $[A - \lambda I]$ leads to an explicit polynomial equation. The roots of the polynomial equation give all the eigenvalues $\lambda_1, \lambda_2, \ldots. \lambda_n$. Substituting the eigenvalues λ_r into the eq.6.21 yields n equations, $[A - \lambda_r I]\,\{x^{(r)}\} = 0$ the solution of which gives $\{x^{(r)}\}$.

Example 6.6

Find eigenvalues and the corresponding eigenvectors of the matrix $[A]$

$$[A] = \begin{bmatrix} 2 & 1 & -1 \\ 0 & -2 & -2 \\ 1 & 1 & 0 \end{bmatrix}$$

Solution

$$[A - \lambda I] = \begin{bmatrix} 2-\lambda & 1 & -1 \\ 0 & -2-\lambda & -2 \\ 1 & 1 & -\lambda \end{bmatrix}$$

and $\det [A - \lambda I] = (2-\lambda)\{(2+\lambda)\lambda + 2\} - 1\{0(-\lambda)+2\} - 1\{0(1)+(2+\lambda)\}$

$$= -\lambda^3 + \lambda = 0$$

which is the characteristic equation.
The eigenvalues are 0, 1, and – 1. The corresponding eigenvectors are:

$$x^{(1)} = \frac{1}{\sqrt{3}}\begin{Bmatrix} 1 \\ -1 \\ 1 \end{Bmatrix}, x^{(2)} = \frac{1}{\sqrt{38}}\begin{Bmatrix} 5 \\ -2 \\ 3 \end{Bmatrix}, x^{(3)} = \frac{1}{\sqrt{6}}\begin{Bmatrix} 1 \\ -2 \\ 1 \end{Bmatrix}$$

6.3.1 Further Properties of Eigenvalues and Eigenvectors

In this section we will summarise some important properties of eigenvalues, eigenvectors and their relationships.

(1) If $[A]$ is a square matrix, then the eigenvectors corresponding to distinct eigenvalues are themselves distinct.

(2) The eigenvalues of Hermitian matrix are all real.

Let us suppose that $[A]$ is a Hermitian matrix and has an eigenvalue λ with corresponding eigenvector $\{x\}$ then

$$[A]\{x\} = \lambda\{x\} \tag{6.22}$$

Premultiplying both sides of Eq. 6.22 by $\{\bar{x}\}^T$ yields

$$\{\bar{x}\}^T [A]\{x\} = \lambda\{\bar{x}\}^T\{x\} \tag{6.23}$$

Taking the transpose and complex conjugate of Eq. 6.22 gives

$$[[\bar{A}]\{\bar{x}\}]^T = \bar{\lambda}\{\bar{x}\}^T$$

i.e.,

$$\{\bar{x}\}^T [\bar{A}]^T = \bar{\lambda}\{\bar{x}\}^T$$

so that

$$\{\bar{x}\}^T [\bar{A}] = \bar{\lambda}\{\bar{x}\}^T \tag{6.24}$$

since $[A]$ is Hermitian.
Post multiplying both sides of Eq. (6.24) by $\{x\}$ we get

$$\{\bar{x}\}^T [\bar{A}]\{x\} = \bar{\lambda}\{\bar{x}\}^T\{x\} \tag{6.25}$$

If we compare Eq. 6.22 and 6.25 we have $\lambda = \bar{\lambda}$. Therefore λ is real.

(3) The eigenvectors of a real symmetric matrix can be real.

(4) If $[A]$ is a Hermitian matrix then the eigenvector $\{x^{(r)}\}$ and $\{x^{(s)}\}$ corresponding to two eigenvalues λ_r and λ_s of distinct nature are orthogonal i.e., $\{\bar{x}^{(r)}\}^T \{x^{(s)}\} = 0$.

(5) The eigenvectors corresponding to the eigenvalues of distinct nature of a square matrix $[A]$ of size $n \times n$, are linearly independent in the sense that if $c_1\{x^{(1)}\} + c_2\{x^{(2)}\} + ...c_r\{x^{(r)}\} = 0$ where $\{x^{(1)}\}, \{x^{(2)}\}, ...\{x^{(r)}\}$ are eigenvectors, then

$$c_1 = c_2 = c_3....c_r = 0$$

(6) For the same condition in (5), any vector $\{x\}$ with n components can be written in the form

$$\{x\} = k_1\{x^{(1)}\} + k_2\{x^{(2)}\} + ...k_n\{x^{(n)}\}$$

This property can be extended to Hermitian matrices even if they have coincident eigenvalues.

(7) If $[A]$ is Hermitian matrix of order n, and if it possesses m coincident eigenvalues then there exists m distinct and mutually orthogonal eigenvectors corresponding to these eigenvalues.

(8) If $[A]$ is a triangular matrix then its eigenvalues are the elements of the main diagonal. It can also be shown that the diagonal elements of the above matrix a_{11}, a_{22}, a_{33} ... a_{nn} are its eigenvalues and the eigenvectors corresponding to these eigenvalues a_{ii} are just the vector whose ith component is one and all other components are zeros.

(9) If $[A]$ is a square matrix of size $n \times n$ with eigenvalues λ_1, λ_2, ..., λ_n, the sum and product of all these eigenvalues are given by

(*i*) $\sum_{i=1}^{n} \lambda_i = T_r[A]$

(*ii*) $\prod_{i=1}^{n} \lambda_i = \det [A]$

(10) If $[A]$ and $[B]$ are two similar matrices having the same eigenvalues; if $[B] = [T]^{-1} [A] [T]$ and if $\{x\}$ is an eigenvector of $[A]$ then $[T]^{-1} \{x\}$ is the eigenvector of $[B]$.

This property can be proved by considering $[A]$ whose eigenvalue is λ and corresponding eigenvector is $\{x\}$

$$[B]([T]^{-1}\{x\}) = ([T]^{-1}[A][T])[T]^{-1}\{x\}$$

$$= [T]^{-1}[A][T][T]^{-1}\{x\}$$

$$= [T]^{-1}[A]\{x\} = [T]^{-1}\lambda\{x\}$$

$$= \lambda([T]^{-1}\{x\})$$

Therefore $[T]^{-1} \{x\}$ is the eigenvector of the matrix $[B]$.

(11) If $[A]$ is any square matrix of size $n \times n$ with eigenvalues of distinct nature then there will be a matrix $[T]$ such that $[T]^{-1} [A] [T]$ is a diagonal matrix. The elements of such matrix are the eigenvalues of the matrix $[A]$.

(12) For an arbitrary square matrix, similarity transformations will exist such that $[A]^{-1}$ $[A]$ $[T]$ is triangular and also unitary.

(13) If $[A]$ is a Hermitian matrix then unitary matrix $[T]$ will exist such that $[T]^{-1}$ $[A]$ $[T]$ is diagonal, the diagonal elements of which are the eigenvalues of $[A]$ and the columns of $[T]$ are eigenvectors of $[A]$.

(14) If $[A]$ is a real and symmetric matrix, then there exists an orthogonal matrix such that $[T]^{-1}$ $[A]$ $[T]$ is a diagonal matrix whose elements are the eigenvalues of $[A]$ and the columns of $[T]$ are eigenvectors of $[A]$.

(15) For a square matrix $[A]$ there exists a similarity transformation such that

$$[T]^{-1}[A]\,[T] = \begin{bmatrix} [\Lambda_1] & 0 & 0 & 0 \\ 0 & [\Lambda]_2 & 0 & 0 \\ 0 & 0 & [\Lambda_3] & 0 \\ 0 & 0 & 0 & [\Lambda_m] \end{bmatrix}$$

in the block diagonal form, where the matrices, $\Lambda_1, \Lambda_2, \ldots \Lambda_m$ are such that

$$[\Lambda_j] = \begin{bmatrix} \lambda_j & 1 & 0 & 0\ldots0 \\ 0 & \lambda_j & 1 & 0\ldots0 \\ 0 & 0 & \lambda_j & 1\ldots. \\ \ldots & \ldots & \ldots & \ldots1 \\ 0 & \ldots & \ldots & \ldots\lambda_j \end{bmatrix}$$

where λ_j are the eigenvalues of $[A]$ and a given eigenvalue may appear as the diagonal elements of more than one $[\Lambda_j]$

Example 6.7

Find the eigenvalues and eigenvectors of a matrix

$$[A] = \begin{bmatrix} 3 & 4 \\ 4 & -3 \end{bmatrix}$$

Solution

$$\det[A - \lambda I] = \begin{bmatrix} 3-\lambda & 4 \\ 4 & -3-\lambda \end{bmatrix}$$

$$= -(3-\lambda)(3+\lambda) - 16 = \lambda^2 - 25 = 0$$

is the characteristic equation of the matrix $[A]$. The eigenvalues are

$$\lambda_1 = 5, \lambda_2 = -5.$$

The eigenvector corresponding to $\lambda_1 = +5$ is obtained as follows:

$$\begin{bmatrix} -2 & 4 \\ 4 & -8 \end{bmatrix} \begin{Bmatrix} x_1 \\ x_2 \end{Bmatrix} = \begin{Bmatrix} 0 \\ 0 \end{Bmatrix}$$

That is $$4x_2 = 2x_1$$

or $$x_1 = 2x_2$$

Therefore,

$$\{x\} = \begin{Bmatrix}1\\2\end{Bmatrix}$$

The eigenvector corresponding to $\lambda = -5$ is obtained as follows:

$$\begin{bmatrix}8 & 4\\4 & 2\end{bmatrix}\begin{Bmatrix}x_1\\x_2\end{Bmatrix} = \begin{Bmatrix}0\\0\end{Bmatrix}$$

That is,

$$8x_1 + 4x_2 = 0$$

or

$$x_2 = -2x_1,$$

Therefore,

$$\{x_2\} = \begin{Bmatrix}-1\\2\end{Bmatrix}$$

Let $[P]$ $= [\{x_1\}\ \{x_2\}] = \begin{bmatrix}2 & -1\\1 & 2\end{bmatrix}$

Then $[P]^{-1}$ $= \dfrac{1}{5}\begin{bmatrix}2 & 1\\-1 & 2\end{bmatrix}$

$$[P]^{-1}[A][P] = \frac{1}{5}\begin{bmatrix}2 & 1\\-1 & 2\end{bmatrix}\begin{bmatrix}3 & 4\\4 & -3\end{bmatrix}\begin{bmatrix}2 & -1\\1 & 2\end{bmatrix}$$

$$= \begin{bmatrix}5 & 0\\0 & -5\end{bmatrix} = \begin{bmatrix}\lambda_1 & 0\\0 & \lambda_2\end{bmatrix}$$

Columns of $[P]$ are orthogonal

$$(\{x_1\}, \{x_2\}) = \{2\quad 1\}\begin{Bmatrix}-1\\2\end{Bmatrix} = 0$$

Normalizing these vectors, we obtain

$$\{\{x_1\}, \{x_1\}) = \{2\quad 1\}\begin{Bmatrix}2\\1\end{Bmatrix} = 5$$

$$\{\{x_2\}, \{x_2\}\} = \{-1\quad 2\}\begin{Bmatrix}-1\\2\end{Bmatrix} = 5$$

Thus the normalised vectors are

$$\{y_1\} = \begin{Bmatrix}2/\sqrt{5}\\1/\sqrt{5}\end{Bmatrix}, \{y_2\} = \begin{Bmatrix}-1/\sqrt{5}\\2/\sqrt{5}\end{Bmatrix}$$

Therefore the orthogonal matrix is

$$[B] = \begin{bmatrix}\dfrac{2}{\sqrt{5}} & -\dfrac{1}{\sqrt{5}}\\[2mm] \dfrac{1}{\sqrt{5}} & \dfrac{2}{\sqrt{5}}\end{bmatrix}$$

$$[B]^T[B] = \begin{bmatrix} \frac{2}{\sqrt{5}} & \frac{1}{\sqrt{5}} \\ -\frac{1}{\sqrt{5}} & \frac{2}{\sqrt{5}} \end{bmatrix} \begin{bmatrix} \frac{2}{\sqrt{5}} & -\frac{1}{\sqrt{5}} \\ \frac{1}{\sqrt{5}} & \frac{2}{\sqrt{5}} \end{bmatrix}$$

$$= \begin{bmatrix} 1 & 0 \\ 0 & 1 \end{bmatrix} = [I]$$

It is also shown that $[B]^T = [B]^{-1}$

Example 6.8

If $[A] = \begin{bmatrix} 5 & 0 & 1 \\ 0 & -1 & 0 \\ 1 & 0 & 5 \end{bmatrix}$ is a real symmetric, find the eigenvalues and the corresponding eigenvectors and show that if $[P]$ is orthogonal with eigenvectors of $[A]$ as its columns, then $[P]^T [A] [P] = [\Lambda]$

Solution

$$\det [A - \lambda I] = \begin{bmatrix} 5-\lambda & 0 & 1 \\ 0 & -1-\lambda & 0 \\ 1 & 0 & 5-\lambda \end{bmatrix} = 0$$

That is,

$$(5-\lambda)(-1-\lambda)(5-\lambda) + 1(1+\lambda) = 0$$

$$(\lambda+1)[-\lambda^2 + 10\lambda - 25 + 1] = 0$$

$$(\lambda+1)(\lambda-4)(\lambda-6) = 0$$

Therefore $\lambda = -1, 4, 6$.
Eigenvector corresponding to $\lambda = -1$ can be obtained from

$$[A - \lambda I]\{x_1\} = 0$$

$$\begin{bmatrix} 6 & 0 & 1 \\ 0 & 0 & 0 \\ 1 & 0 & 6 \end{bmatrix} \begin{Bmatrix} x_1 \\ x_2 \\ x_3 \end{Bmatrix} = 0$$

Then $6x_1 + x_3 = 0$ or $x_3 = -6x_1$ and $x_1 = -6x_3$; $x_1 = x_3 = 0$ and x_2 can be arbitrary.

Let us select $\{x_1\} = \begin{Bmatrix} 0 \\ 1 \\ 0 \end{Bmatrix} = \{\bar{x}_1\}$. Since it is a unit vector the eigenvector corresponding to $\lambda_2 = 4$ then we have

$$\begin{bmatrix} 1 & 0 & 1 \\ 0 & -5 & 0 \\ 1 & 0 & 1 \end{bmatrix} \begin{Bmatrix} x_1 \\ x_2 \\ x_3 \end{Bmatrix} = \begin{Bmatrix} 0 \\ 0 \\ 0 \end{Bmatrix}$$

or

$$x_1 = -x_3$$

$$-5x_2 = 0$$

$$x_1 = -x_3$$

If $x_3 = 1$, then $$\{x_2\} = \begin{Bmatrix} -1 \\ 0 \\ 1 \end{Bmatrix}$$

Normalizing $\{x_2\}$ yields $$\{\bar{x}_2\} = \begin{Bmatrix} -1/\sqrt{2} \\ 0 \\ 1/\sqrt{2} \end{Bmatrix}$$

Eigenvector corresponding to eigenvalue $\lambda_3 = 6$

$$\begin{bmatrix} -1 & 0 & 1 \\ 0 & -7 & 0 \\ 1 & 0 & -1 \end{bmatrix} \begin{Bmatrix} x_1 \\ x_2 \\ x_3 \end{Bmatrix} = \begin{Bmatrix} 0 \\ 0 \\ 0 \end{Bmatrix}$$

or

$$x_3 = x_1$$

$$-7x_2 = 0$$

$$x_3 = x_1$$

If we choose $$x_3 = 1, \{x_3\} = \begin{Bmatrix} 1 \\ 0 \\ 1 \end{Bmatrix}$$

Normalizing $$\{\bar{x}_3\} = \begin{Bmatrix} 1/\sqrt{2} \\ 0 \\ 1/\sqrt{2} \end{Bmatrix}$$

Then the othogonal matrix $$[P] = \begin{bmatrix} 0 & -\frac{1}{\sqrt{2}} & \frac{1}{\sqrt{2}} \\ 1 & 0 & 0 \\ 0 & \frac{1}{\sqrt{2}} & \frac{1}{\sqrt{2}} \end{bmatrix}$$

$$[P]^T [A] [P] = \begin{bmatrix} 0 & 1 & 0 \\ -\frac{1}{\sqrt{2}} & 0 & \frac{1}{\sqrt{2}} \\ \frac{1}{\sqrt{2}} & 0 & \frac{1}{\sqrt{2}} \end{bmatrix} \begin{bmatrix} 5 & 0 & 1 \\ 0 & -1 & 0 \\ 1 & 0 & 5 \end{bmatrix} \begin{bmatrix} 0 & -\frac{1}{\sqrt{2}} & \frac{1}{\sqrt{2}} \\ 1 & 0 & 0 \\ 0 & \frac{1}{\sqrt{2}} & \frac{1}{\sqrt{2}} \end{bmatrix}$$

$$= \begin{bmatrix} -1 & 0 & 0 \\ 0 & 4 & 0 \\ 0 & 0 & 6 \end{bmatrix}$$

or
$$= \begin{bmatrix} \lambda_1 & 0 & 0 \\ 0 & \lambda_2 & 0 \\ 0 & 0 & \lambda_3 \end{bmatrix}$$

6.3.2 Eigenvectors of a Real Non Symmetric Matrix

Consider the standard eigenvalue problem

$$[A]\{x\} = \lambda\{x\}$$

where $[A]$ is the real nonsymmetric matrix of order n. Let $[A]^T$ be the transpose of $[A]$, whose eigenvalues are also λ. Rewriting $[A]\{x\} = \lambda\{x\}$ and

$$[A]^T\{y\} = \lambda\{y\} \tag{6.26}$$

for distinct λ, say λ_i and λ_j as

$$[A]\{x_i\} = \lambda_i\{x_i\} \tag{6.27}$$

$$[A]^T\{y_j\} = \lambda_j\{y_j\} \tag{6.28}$$

Taking the transpose of eq. 6.28

$$\{y_j\}^T[A] = \lambda_j\{y_j\}^T$$

Premultiplying Eq. 6.27 by $\{y_j\}^T$ and post multiplying the transposed Eq. 6.28 by $\{x_i\}$ and subtracting, we get

$$\{y_j\}^T[A]\{x_i\} - \{y_j\}^T[A]\{x_i\} = 0$$

$$= (\lambda_i - \lambda_j)\{y_j\}^T\{x_i\}$$

Since $\lambda_i \neq \lambda_j$

$$\{y_j\}^T\{x_i\} = 0 \text{ for } i, j = 1, 2 \ldots\ldots n$$

Hence

$$[Y]^T[X] = [I] \tag{6.29}$$

where

$$[Y]^T = [y_1, y_2 \ldots\ldots y_n]$$

$$[X] = [x_1, x_2 \ldots\ldots x_n]$$

Thus

$$\{y_j\}^T\{x_j\} = 1 \text{ for } j = 1, 2 \ldots\ldots n$$

But from Eq. (6.29), we have

$$[Y]^T = [X]^{-1} \tag{6.30}$$

and
$$[X]^T = [Y]^{-1} \tag{6.31}$$

From the orthogonality property we have

$$[A]\,[X] = [\Lambda]\,[X] \tag{6.32}$$

Premultiplying by $[Y]^T$, we get

$$[Y]^T\,[A]\,\{X\} = [X]^{-1}\,[\Lambda]\,[X] = [\Lambda] \tag{6.33}$$

Example 6.9

Verify the above properties for the following matrix $[A]$ of order two

$$[A] = \begin{bmatrix} 1 & 1+i \\ 1-i & 1 \end{bmatrix}$$

Solution

Matrix $[A]$ is Hermitian. The characteristic equation is given by

$$\det\,[[A] - \lambda[I]] = 0$$

which gives

$$\begin{bmatrix} 1-\lambda & 1+i \\ 1-i & 1-\lambda \end{bmatrix} = 0$$

Expanding we get

$$(1-\lambda)^2 - (1-i)\,(1+i) = 0$$

$$\lambda^2 - 2\lambda - 1 = 0$$

whose roots are the eigenvalues given by

$$\lambda_1 = 1 + \sqrt{2} \text{ and } \lambda_2 = 1 - \sqrt{2}$$

Eigenvector can be obtained from

$$[A]\,\{x_i^{(i)}\} = \lambda_i\{x_i^{(i)}\}$$

For $\lambda_1 = 1 + \sqrt{2}$

$$\begin{bmatrix} 1 & 1+i \\ 1-i & 1 \end{bmatrix} \begin{Bmatrix} x_1 \\ x_2 \end{Bmatrix} = (1+\sqrt{2}) \begin{Bmatrix} x_1 \\ x_2 \end{Bmatrix}$$

which gives

$$x_1 + (1+i)x_2 = (1+\sqrt{2})x_1$$

or

$$(1+i)x_2 = x_1\sqrt{2}$$

Therefore, the first eigenvector can be $\begin{Bmatrix} 1+i \\ \sqrt{2} \end{Bmatrix}$

By normalizing we obtain

$$x^{(1)} = \frac{1}{2}\begin{Bmatrix} 1+i \\ \sqrt{2} \end{Bmatrix}. \text{ Similarly for } \lambda_2 = (1-\sqrt{2}), \quad x^{(2)} = \frac{1}{2}\begin{Bmatrix} 1+i \\ \sqrt{2} \end{Bmatrix}.$$

Now $[Y] = [x^{(1)} \quad x^{(2)}]$

$$= \frac{1}{2}\begin{bmatrix} 1+i & 1+i \\ \sqrt{2} & -\sqrt{2} \end{bmatrix}, \quad [Y]^T = \begin{bmatrix} 1-i & \sqrt{2} \\ 1-i & -\sqrt{2} \end{bmatrix}$$

Now

$$[Y]^T [A] [Y] = \frac{1}{4}\begin{bmatrix} 1-i & \sqrt{2} \\ 1-i & \sqrt{2} \end{bmatrix}\begin{bmatrix} 1 & 1+i \\ 1-i & 1 \end{bmatrix}\begin{bmatrix} 1+i & 1+i \\ \sqrt{2} & -\sqrt{2} \end{bmatrix}$$

$$= \begin{bmatrix} 1+\sqrt{2} & 0 \\ 0 & 1-\sqrt{2} \end{bmatrix}$$

It is observed that for an eigenvalue problem whose mass and stiffness matrices are Hermitian, their eigenvalues are real and the corresponding eigenvectors are complex.

6.4 EIGENVALUE BOUNDS AND INEQUALITIES

The classical method of solving the eigenvalue problem is to solve the characteristic polynomial equation. This method is quite tedious for higher order matrices. Here we describe some other practical methods for the determination of eigenvalues and eigenvectors. These methods require some apporximate idea of the magnitudes of the eigenvalues to be obtained. We also discuss the results concerned with inequalities involved in eigenvalues which will give a bound to the maximum eigenvalue of a given matrix.

6.4.1 Approximate Bounds of Eigenvalues of a Given Matrix

If $[A]$ is a square matrix of order n, whose eigenvalue is λ, then

$$|\lambda| \le \max_{i} \sum_{j=1}^{n} |a_{ij}| \tag{6.34}$$

and

$$|\lambda| \le \max_{j} \sum_{i=1}^{n} |a_{ij}| \tag{6.35}$$

These inequalities state that the magnitude of every eigenvalue is less than the greatest row or column sum of magnitudes of elements.

From Gerschgorin's theorem, if λ is an eigenvalue of the square matrix $[A]$ of size $n \times n$, then it must satisfy

$$|\lambda - a_{ii}| \le \sum_{\substack{j=1 \\ j \ne 1}}^{n} |a_{ij}| \text{ for any } i \tag{6.36}$$

$$\le R_i$$

and

$$|\lambda - a_{ii}| \le \sum_{\substack{j=1 \\ j \ne 1}}^{n} |a_{ji}| \text{ for any } i \tag{6.37}$$

$$\le S_i$$

Each eigenvalue must lie inside at least one of the circles
$|\lambda - a_{ii}| = R_i$ and one of the circles $|\lambda - a_{ii}| = S_i$ in the complex λ plane.

Example 6.10

Obtain the boundaries to the eigenvalues of the given matrix

$$[A] = \begin{bmatrix} 3 & -4 & 2 \\ -4 & 6 & 8 \\ 2 & 8 & -1 \end{bmatrix}$$

Solution

Here the given matrix $[A]$ is real and symmetric so that the eigenvalues are real. The sums of the rows or columns are given by

$$\Sigma \text{Row1} \quad |3|+|-4|+|2| \quad = 9$$

$$\Sigma \text{Row2} \quad |-4|+|6|+|8| \quad = 18$$

$$\Sigma \text{Row3} \quad |2|+|8|+|-1| \quad = 11$$

If λ is an eigenvalue we have that $|\lambda| \le 18$
and

$$|\lambda - a_{ii}| \quad \le \quad \sum_{\substack{j=1 \\ j \ne 1}}^{n} a_{ij}$$

For $i = 1$

$$|\lambda - a_{11}| \quad \le \quad |a_{21}| + |a_{31}|$$

Hence $|\lambda - 3| \le 6$ (1)

For $i = 2$ we have

$$|\lambda - a_{22}| \quad \le \quad |a_{12}| + |a_{32}|$$

Then

$$|\lambda - 6| \quad \le \quad 12 \tag{2}$$

For $i = 3$ we have

$$|\lambda - a_{33}| \quad \le \quad |a_{13}| + |a_{23}|$$

Then

$$|\lambda + 1| \quad \le \quad 10 \tag{3}$$

The regions represented by inequalities (1), (2) and (3) are indicated in Fig. 6.3.

Another method of fixing the bounds to the eigenvalue is that if $[A]$ is a square matrix of order n then any eigenvalue λ must satisfy the inequality.

$$|\lambda|^2 \le \sum_{i,j=1}^{n} |a_{ij}|^2$$

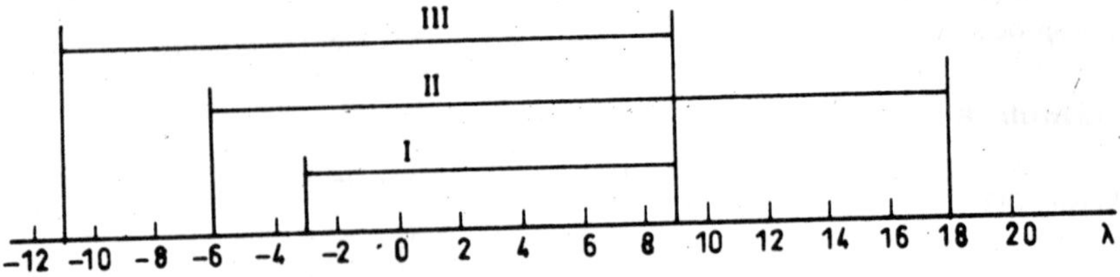

Fig. 6.3 Bounds for eigenvalues in Example 6.10

Example 6.11

For the matrix [*A*] given, obtain the bounds on the eigenvalues.

$$[A] = \begin{bmatrix} 3 & -4 & 2 \\ -4 & 6 & 8 \\ 2 & 8 & -1 \end{bmatrix}$$

Solution

In this case the eigenvalues are real and we have

$$\sum_{i=1}^{n} |\lambda_i|^2 \le \sum_{i,j=1}^{n} |a_{ij}|^2$$

which gives

$$\lambda_1^2 + \lambda_2^2 + \lambda_3^2 \le 9 + 16 + 4 + 16 + 36 + 64 + 4 + 64 + 1 \le 224$$

For the largest eigenvalue λ_m we must have

$$\lambda_m^2 \le 224$$

and so $\lambda_m \le 14.97$ which is much closer than the value obtained previously in example 6.10.

6.4.2 Sturm Sequence

In the preceding sections we have discussed some of the properties of the eigenvalue problems. An important property of the eigenvalues of the problem $[k]\{x\} = \lambda [M]\{x\}$ is that they are the roots of the polynomial equations

$$\det[[k] - \lambda[M]] = f(\lambda) = 0 \tag{6.38}$$

This can be written as

$$[[k] - \lambda_i[M]]\,\{x_i\} = 0.$$

Consider the matrix ($[K] - \mu\,[M]$) where μ is a shift. Cholesky factorisations of $[[K] - \mu\,[M]]$ into $[L]\,[D]\,[L^T]$ can be obtained. The diagonal matrix [*D*] yields the eigenvalues of the problem. It also indicates that the number of negative elements in [*D*] is equal to the number of eigenvalues less than μ. Thus by changing the value of shift, it is easy to locate the eigenvalues. In other words, if $\lambda_1, ..., \lambda_i < \mu < \lambda_{i+1}$, ... λ_n, there are about *i* negative diagonal elements in [*D*]. These considerations also hold good for the case of multiple eigenvalues, and for equal eigenvalues.

The property that the number of negative elements in [D] is equal to the number of eigenvalues smaller than μ can be used directly in obtaining the eigenvalues. The procedure is to assume a value of shift μ and check whether μ is smaller or greater than the required eigenvalue. Repeat the procedure by reducing the shift value till the eigenvalue is obtained.

Example 6.12

For a given system of [k] and [M] compute the natural frequencies using sturm sequence and bisection technique.

$$[k] = \begin{bmatrix} 5 & -4 & 1 & 0 & 0 \\ -4 & 6 & -4 & 1 & 0 \\ 1 & -4 & 6 & -4 & 1 \\ 0 & 1 & -4 & 6 & -4 \\ 0 & 0 & 1 & -4 & 5 \end{bmatrix}; [M] = \begin{bmatrix} 1 & 0 & 0 & 0 & 0 \\ 0 & 2 & 0 & 0 & 0 \\ 0 & 0 & 3 & 0 & 0 \\ 0 & 0 & 0 & 2 & 0 \\ 0 & 0 & 0 & 0 & 1 \end{bmatrix}$$

Solution

Equation of motion for the given problem can be stated as follows

$$[k]\{x\} = \omega^2[M]\{x\}$$

Try with $\mu_1 = 0.01$ and $\mu_2 = 10.0$.
For $\mu_1 = 0.01$

$$[[k] - \mu_1[M]] = \begin{bmatrix} 4.99 & -4 & 1 & 0 & 0 \\ -4 & 5.98 & -4 & 1 & 0 \\ 1 & -4 & 5.97 & -4 & 1 \\ 0 & 1 & -4 & 5.98 & -4 \\ 0 & 0 & 1 & -4 & 4.99 \end{bmatrix}$$

By the method of Gaussian elimination the above matrix can be written as

$$\begin{bmatrix} 4.99 & -4 & 1 & 0 & 0 \\ 0 & -2.7736 & -3.1984 & 1 & 0 \\ 0 & 0 & 2.0813 & -2.8468 & 1 \\ 0 & 0 & 0 & 1.7256 & -2.6322 \\ 0 & 0 & 0 & 0 & 0.4944 \end{bmatrix}$$

All the diagonal elements are positive

when $\mu = 10.0$

$$[[k] - \mu_2[M]] = \begin{bmatrix} -5 & -4 & 1 & 0 & 0 \\ -4 & -14 & -4 & 1 & 0 \\ 1 & -4 & -24 & -4 & 1 \\ 0 & 1 & -4 & -14 & -4 \\ 0 & 0 & 1 & -4 & -5 \end{bmatrix}$$

By Gaussian Elimination this can be written as

$$\begin{bmatrix} -5 & -4 & 1 & 0 & 0 \\ & -10.8 & -4.8 & 1 & 0 \\ & & -22.3778 & -4.2963 & 1 \\ & & & -13.0541 & -4.1986 \\ & & & & -3.6070 \end{bmatrix}$$

All the diagonal elements of the above matrix are negative. Therefore all the eigenvalues are less than $\mu_2 = 10$. When $\mu = 0$, $[\,[k] - \mu\,[M]\,]$ is $[k]$ itself. For upper triangularisation by Gaussian elimination we can write it as

$$\begin{bmatrix} 5 & -4 & 1 & 0 & 0 \\ & 2.8 & 3.2 & 1 & 0 \\ & & 2.1429 & -2.8571 & 1 \\ & & & 1.8336 & 2.6667 \\ & & & & 8.4116 \end{bmatrix}$$

Product of diagonal elements gives det $[k] = 462.7156$. For $\mu_1 = 0.01$, the product of diagonal elements, det $[[k] - \mu_1\,[M]] = 24.5752$. For $\mu_2 = 10.0$, det $[[k] - \mu_2\,[M]\,] = 56898.9465$. $\mu = 0$ and $\mu = 0.01$ are extrapolated for 1st natural frequency

$$\text{Therefore the first natural frequency} = 0.01 + \frac{(0.01)(24.5752)}{(462.7156 - 24.5752)}$$

$$= 0.01056$$

By the method of bisection other natural frequencies are obtained as

$$0.01056 + \frac{(10 - 0.01056)}{3} \text{ and } 0.01056 + \frac{2(10 - 0.01056)}{3}$$

Hence the three natural frequencies are

3.34037, 6.67019 and 10.0

6.5 ITERATION METHODS

In this section we present the determination of the lowest eigenvalues and their corresponding eigenvectors of the eigenvalue problem

$$[k]\,\{x\} = \lambda[M]\,\{x\} \tag{6.39}$$

In general the solution methods of the above eigenvalue problem can be divided into four groups. The first group is vector iteration schemes, which operate on the basic property

$$[k]\,\{x_i\} = \lambda_i[M]\,\{x_i\} \tag{6.40}$$

The second group, using the property

$$[x]^T\,[k]\,[X] = [\Lambda] \tag{6.41}$$

and

$$[x]^T\,[M]\,[X] = [I] \tag{6.42}$$

is known as the transformation methods. The solution techniques for solving the polynomial equation

$$P(\lambda_i) = 0 \tag{6.43}$$

fall under the third group. The solution methods using the Sturm sequence property of the polynomial equations is the fourth group.

$$P(\lambda) = \det[[k] - \lambda[M]] \tag{6.44}$$

To satisfy the Eq.6.39, we assume a vector $\{x_1]$ and its eigenvalue $\lambda_1 = 1$ and substitute in the equation

$$[k]\{x\} = (1)[M]\{x_1\} = \{f_1\} \tag{6.45}$$

That is $[k]\{x_1\} = \{f_1\}$ is true only when $\{x_1\}$ is an eigenvector. Otherwise the resulting equations are similar to the equilibrium equations for static analysis, namely

$$[k]\{x_2\} = \{f_1\} \text{ and } \{x_2\} \neq \{x_1\} \tag{6.46}$$

where $\{x_2\}$ is a displacement vector due to the applied force system $\{f_1\}$. In the iteration process to obtain the eigen pairs, it is quite apparent that $\{x_2\}$ is a better approximation to the vector $\{x_1\}$. By repeating the procedure we obtain progressively better approximations to the eigenvector. This procedure forms the basis for the inverse iteration method.

6.5.1 Inverse Iteration Method

The inverse iteration method scheme is used to determine the eigenvector and the corresponding eigenvalues. In this method we assume $[k]$ is a positive definite stiffness matrix and may be banded. The matrix $[M]$ may be diagonal mass matrix, with or without zero elements or may be banded. In case $[k]$ is positive semi-definite, a shift should be employed before starting the iterations.

The basic equations used in the inverse iteration method are

$$[k]\{\tilde{x}_{r+1}\} = [M]\{x_r\} \tag{6.47}$$

and

$$\{x_{r+1}\} = \frac{\{\tilde{x}_{r+1}\}}{[\{\tilde{x}_{r+1}\}[M]\{\tilde{x}_{r+1}\}]^{\frac{1}{2}}} \text{ for } r = 1, 2, \ldots \tag{6.48}$$

In the first iteration we assume a starting vector $\{x_1\}$ and then evaluate a better vector in subsequent iterations. If the initial vector $\{x_1\}$ satisfies the condition $\{x_1\}^T[M]\{X_1\} \neq 0$ then we have $\{x_{r+1}\} \to \{X\}$ as $r \to \infty$. From Eq. 6.48 we have to obtain a vector $\{x_{r+1}\}$ which satisfies the mass orthonormality

$$\{x_{r+1}\}^T[M]\{x_{r+1}\} = 1 \tag{6.49}$$

If the orthonormality procedure is not included in the iteration method, the vector does not converge to the eigenvector but it will be magnified several times.

Example 6.13

Use the inverse iteration procedure to solve for the fundamental frequency and the corresponding eigenvector of the eigenvalue problem: $[k]\{\phi\} = \lambda[M]\{\phi\}$ where

$$[k] = \begin{bmatrix} 2 & -1 & 0 \\ -1 & 2 & -1 \\ 0 & -1 & 2 \end{bmatrix}, \quad [M] = \begin{bmatrix} 1 & 0 & 0 \\ 0 & 1 & 0 \\ 0 & 0 & 1 \end{bmatrix}$$

Solution

$[k]^{-1}$ is obtained first which is

$$[k]^{-1} = \begin{bmatrix} 0.75 & 0.50 & 0.25 \\ 0.50 & 1.00 & 0.50 \\ 0.25 & 0.50 & 0.75 \end{bmatrix}$$

and

$$[k]^{-1}[M] = \begin{bmatrix} 0.75 & 0.50 & 0.25 \\ 0.50 & 1.00 & 0.50 \\ 0.25 & 0.50 & 0.75 \end{bmatrix}$$

Let us choose the starting vector $\{x_0\}$ as

$$\{x_0\} = \begin{Bmatrix} 1 \\ 1 \\ 1 \end{Bmatrix}$$

Since $\{\phi\} = \lambda[K]^{-1}[M]\{\phi\}$, we have

$\{y_{s+1}\} = \lambda_{s+1}[k]^{-1}[M]\{x_s\}$ where $s = 0, 1, 2...$ and we scale $\{ y_{s+1} \}$ so as to make the largest element of $\{ x_{s+1} \}$ unity.

For $$\{x_0\} = \begin{Bmatrix} 1 \\ 1 \\ 1 \end{Bmatrix}, \{y_1\} = \lambda_1 \begin{Bmatrix} 1.50 \\ 2.00 \\ 1.50 \end{Bmatrix}$$

$$\{x_1\} = \begin{Bmatrix} 0.750 \\ 1.000 \\ 0.750 \end{Bmatrix}, \{y_2\} = \lambda_2 \begin{Bmatrix} 1.250 \\ 1.750 \\ 1.250 \end{Bmatrix}$$

$$\{x_2\} = \begin{Bmatrix} 0.714 \\ 1.000 \\ 0.714 \end{Bmatrix}$$

from which $\lambda_1 = 0.500$ and $\lambda_2 = 0.571$. A better estimate of the eigenvalue can be obtained by computing Rayleigh quotient corresponding to each shape $\{y_{s+1}\}$ as

$$\lambda_{s+1} = \frac{\{y_{s+1}\}^T [k] \{y_{s+1}\}}{\{y_{s+1}\}^T [M] \{y_{s+1}\}} = \frac{\{y_{s+1}\}^T [M] \{x_s\}}{\{y_{s+1}\}^T [M] \{y_{s+1}\}}$$

from which we compute $\{x_{s+1}\}$ as follows

$$\{x_{s+1}\} = \frac{\{y_{s+1}\}}{[\{y_{s+1}\}^T [M] \{y_{s+1}\}]^{1/2}}$$

The iterations using the above procedure are as follows:

$$\{x_0\} = \begin{Bmatrix} 1 \\ 1 \\ 1 \end{Bmatrix}, \{y_1\} = \begin{Bmatrix} 1.50 \\ 2.00 \\ 1.50 \end{Bmatrix}$$

$$\{x_1\} = \begin{Bmatrix} 0.5145 \\ 0.6850 \\ 0.5145 \end{Bmatrix}, \{y_2\} = \begin{Bmatrix} 0.8575 \\ 1.2010 \\ 0.8575 \end{Bmatrix}$$

from which

$$\{x_2\} = \begin{Bmatrix} 0.5024 \\ 0.7037 \\ 0.5024 \end{Bmatrix}$$

Therefore,

$$\lambda_1 = \frac{5.00}{8.5} = 0.588$$

and

$$\lambda \text{ or } \lambda_2 = \frac{1.706}{2.913} = 0.586$$

Hence Rayleigh quotient gives a very good approximation to the exact value of λ_1. After only two iterations, the fundamental frequency and mode shape obtained are:

$$\lambda_1 = 0.586 \text{ and } \phi_1 \cong \begin{Bmatrix} 0.5024 \\ 0.7037 \\ 0.5024 \end{Bmatrix}$$

6.5.2 Forward Iteration Method

In this method we obtain the eigenvector corresponding to the smallest eigenvalue whereas the inverse scheme yields the eigenvector corresponding to the largest eigenvalue. In the inverse iteration scheme we assume the stiffness matrix $[k]$ as positive definite, whereas in this method we assume the mass matrix $[M]$ as positive definite. If it is semi-positive definite some shift is to be used as in the case of inverse iteration method. Initial vector is to be assumed. In forward iteration method, we have

$$[M]\,\{\tilde{x}_{k+1}\} = [k]\,\{x_k\} \text{ for } k = 1, 2, \ldots \tag{6.50}$$

and
$$\{x_{k+1}\} = \frac{\{\tilde{x}_{k+1}\}}{(\{\tilde{x}_{k+1}\}\,[M]\,\{\tilde{x}_{k+1}\})} \tag{6.51}$$

For solving Eqs. 6.50 and 6.51 we decompose the matrix $[M]$.

Alternatively we can solve the eigenvalue problems by forward iteration scheme described as follows

Let
$$[k]\,\{x_1\} = \{y_1\} \tag{6.52}$$

Then
$$[M]\,\{\tilde{x}_{k+1}\} = \{y_k\} \tag{6.53}$$

$$\{\tilde{y}_{k+1}\} = [k]\,\{x_{k+1}\} \tag{6.54}$$

and
$$\{y_{k+1}\} = \frac{\{\tilde{y}_{k+1}\}}{(\{x_{k+1}\}^T\{y_k\})^{1/2}} \tag{6.55}$$

6.5.3 Shift in Vector

The inverse iteration scheme converges to lowest eigenvalue and the rate of convergence is very low or high depending on the magnitude of λ_1 and λ_2 where $\lambda_1 < \lambda_2$. Similarly the convergence rate in the case of forward iteration scheme can be low or high. The shift technique can improve the convergence rate considerably and can be used to predict the lowest eigen pair (λ_1, $\{x_1\}$) in the case of inverse iteration scheme and largest eigen pair (λ_n, $\{x_n\}$) in the case of forward iteration scheme.

If μ is a shift, the eigenvalue problem can be written as

$$[k - \mu M]\{x\} = \eta [M]\{x\} \tag{6.56}$$

where the eigenvalues of the original problem relating to the $[k]\{x\} = \lambda [M]\{x\}$ and the present problem given in Eq. (6.56) are related as follows

$$\eta_i = \lambda_i - \mu \text{ where } i = 1, 2, \ldots n$$

Equation 6.56 can be solved for eigen pairs either by inverse iteration or forward iteration scheme.

6.5.4 Rayleigh Quotient Iteration

The inverse iteration scheme can be improved by implementing the shift and obtaining the fast convergence. The only drawback in this method is the selection of the appropriate shift. The Rayleigh quotient is calculated from

$$p\{\tilde{x}_{k+1}\} = \frac{\{\tilde{x}_{k+1}\}^T \{y_k\}}{\{\tilde{x}_{k+1}\}^T \{\tilde{y}_{k+1}\}} \tag{6.57}$$

where

$$[k]\{\tilde{x}_{k+1}\} = \{y_k\} \text{ for } k = 1, 2 \ldots\ldots \tag{6.58}$$

$$\{\tilde{y}_{k+1}\} = [M]\{\tilde{x}_{k+1}\} \tag{6.59}$$

$$\{y_{k+1}\} = \frac{\{\tilde{y}_{k+1}\}}{(\{\tilde{x}_{k+1}\}^T \{\bar{y}_{k+1}\})^{1/2}} \tag{6.60}$$

The above relationships can be used as the shift for obtaining the eigenvalues. In this procedure the starting iteration vector is $\{x_1\}$ such that

$$\{y_1\} = [M]\{x_1\}$$

The starting shift is usually zero and for other values of $k = 1, 2\ldots$

$$([k] - P\{\tilde{x}_1\}[M])\{\tilde{x}_{k+1}\} = \{y_k\} \tag{6.61}$$

6.5.5 Matrix Deflation and Gram-Schmidt Orthogonalisation

Matrix deflation technique is extensively used in obtaining the solution of standard eigenvalue problems. Any non standard eigenvalue problem is of the form $[k]\{x\} = \lambda [M]\{x\}$ and can be transformed into the standard eigenvalue problem of the form $[A]\{x\} = \lambda \{x\}$.

Considering the deflation of $[A]\{x\} = \lambda \{x\}$, a stable matrix deflation can be carried out by finding an orthogonal matrix $[P]$ whose first column is the calculated eigenvector $\{x_k\}$.

Now $[P]$ is of the form

$$[P] = (\{x_k\}, [P_2] ... [P_n]) \tag{6.62}$$

we have $\{x_k\}^T [P_1] = 0$ for $i = 2, ... n$

Then

$$[P]^T [A] [P] = \begin{bmatrix} \lambda_k & 0 \\ 0 & A_1 \end{bmatrix} \tag{6.63}$$

since $\{x_k\}^T \{x_k\} = 1$.

The eigenvalue of $[A]$ and that of $[P]^T [A] [P]$ are the same. Hence $[A_1]$ must have all eigenvalues of $[A]$ except λ_k. Denoting the eigenvectors of $[P]^T [A] [P]$ by $\{\bar{x}_i\}$, we have

$$\{x_i\} = [P] \{\bar{x}_i\} \tag{6.64}$$

A vector orthonormalisation procedure due to Gram-Schmidt is another approach to extract the eigen pairs. Instead of matrix deflation, it is possible to deflate the iteration vector to get fast convergence to eigen pairs. The basis for this vector deflation is that the iteration vector must not be orthonormal to it. Hence, conversely, iteration vector is orthonormalised to the eigenvectors already calculated. The procedure is used for the case of non standard eigenvalue problem of the form

$$[k] \{x\} = \lambda [M] \{x\}$$

where the calculated eigenvectors are

$$\{x_1\}, \{x_2\}, \{x_3\} ... \{x_n\}$$

If $\{\bar{x}_1\}$ is $[M]$ orthogonalised, then

$$\{\bar{x}_1\} = \{x_1\} - \sum_{i=1}^{m} \alpha_i \{x_i\} \quad \text{for } i = 1, 2, ... m \tag{6.65}$$

where the coefficients α_i are obtained such that $\{x_1\}^T [M] \{\bar{x}_1\} = 0$ for $i = 1, ... m$ and $\{x_i\}^T [M] \{x_j\} = \delta_{ij}$.

Therefore

$$\alpha_i = \{x_i\}^T [M] \{x_i\} \text{ for } i = 1 \tag{6.66}$$

It should be noted that the Gram-Schmidt orthonormalisation procedure can be employed in all the vector iteration methods.

6.5.6 Simultaneous Iteration Method

The vector iteration techniques with use of deflation schemes can be used for extracting the eigenpairs. The first few eigenpairs can be obtained successively. The simultaneous iteration scheme computes the first few eigenpairs simultaneously and hence reduces the computing time considerably. Consider the general eigenvalue problem of the form

$$[k]\{x\} = (1/\lambda)[M]\{x\} \tag{6.67}$$

If $[k]$ is symmetric, it can be decomposed as

$$[k] = [L][L]^T \tag{6.68}$$

Let us denote

$$\{x\} = [L]^{-T}\{y\} \tag{6.69}$$

and substituting Eq. (6.69) and Eq. (6.68) in Eq. (6.67), we get

$$[L][L]^T[L]^{-T}\{y\} = (1/\lambda)[M][L]^{-T}\{y\}$$

$$\lambda\{y\} = [L]^{-1}[M][L]^{-T}\{y\}$$

Denoting $[A] = [L]^{-1}[M][L]^{-T}$ (6.70)

We obtain

$$[A]\{y\} = \lambda\{y\} \tag{6.71}$$

Equation (6.71) is the standard symmetric eigenvalue problem. If $\{y\}$ is replaced by a rectangular matrix of size $n \times m$ where each column of this matrix represents an eigenvector which are mutually independent; by computing such a $n \times m$ matrix, the m eigenvectors are simultaneously computed.

$$\{z\} = [A]\{y\}$$

$$[A]\{y\} = [L]^{-1}[M][L]^{-T}\{y\}$$

If

$$[L]^{-T}\{y\} = \{u\}$$

then we have

$$\{y\} = [L]^T\{u\} \tag{6.72}$$

Since $\{y\}$ and $[L]$ are known, $\{u\}$ can be computed by back substitution,

$$[M]\{u\} = \{v\} \tag{6.73}$$

By forward multiplication, $\{v\}$ can be obtained

$$[L]\{z\} = \{v\} \tag{6.74}$$

Since $\{v\}$ is known $\{z\}$ can be obtained by forward substitutions.

If the initial vector $\{u\}$ is an eigenvector, $\{v\}$ would be the orthogonal vector. For a most general case the vector $\{v\}$ need not be orthogonal and $\{u\}^T\{v\}$ need not be diagonal. If the vector $\{u\}$ converges to eigenvector the above conditions will be satisfied. Let us consider any vector of orthogonal nature

$$\{r\} = \{v\}\{s\} \tag{6.75}$$

$$\{r\}^T\{r\} = [I] \tag{6.76}$$

We can write this as

$$\{s\}^T\{v\}^T\{v\}\{s\} = [I] \tag{6.77}$$

We also know that

$$\{v_0\}^T \{v_0\} = [L_0]\,[L_0]^T = [D] \tag{6.78}$$

Hence

$$\{s\} = [L_0]^{-T}$$

Then

$$\{s\}^{-1} = [L_0]^{-T} \tag{6.79}$$

This can also be written as

$$\{s\}^{-T} = [L_0] \tag{6.80}$$

The coefficients of matrix $\{s\}$ can be obtained directly by Eq.(6.77). Then we have

$$[L_0]^{-1}\,[L_0]\,[L_0]^T\,[L_0]^{-T} = [I]$$

Therefore the new trial vector $\{r\}$ can be used as new trial vector $\{u\}$. The process of iteration is continued until

$$\{u\}^T \{v\} = [\Omega^2] \tag{6.81}$$

converges to diagonal matrix whose elements represent largest eigenvalues, and hence the lowest natural frequencies.

Another approach to this problem is as follows:

$$[k]\,\{u\} = \omega^2[M]\,\{u\}$$

This can be treated as a non standard eigenvalue problem, by assuming a trial vector $\{u'\}$ whose columns are independent. It is easy to compute $[M]\,\{u'\}$ and $\{u'\}$is to be orthonormalized with respect to $[M]$.

If

$$[M]\,\{u'\} = \{x\} \tag{6.82}$$

then

$$[k]\,\{v'\} = \{x\} \tag{6.83}$$

This can be solved by one of the methods discussed in static analysis (Chapter 2). If $\{u\}$ is the eigenvector, it must satisfy the condition

$$\{u\}^T\,[k]\,\{u\} = [\Omega^2] \tag{6.84}$$

Similarly the procedure is repeated for the next iteration if $\{u^2\}$ is the trial vector for the second iteration, it must be orthonormalized with respect to $[M]$. That is

$$\{u^2\}^T\,[M]\,\{u^2\} = [I] \tag{6.85}$$

Modify $\{v'\}$ such that

$$\{v\}\,\{s\} = \{r\} \tag{6.86}$$

If $\{r\}$ replaces $\{u^2\}$ then we have

$$\{s\}^T\,\{v'\}^T\,[M]\,\{v\}\,\{s\} = [I] \tag{6.87}$$

decomposing

$$\{v'\}^T [M] \{v'\} = [L_0] [L_0]^T \tag{6.88}$$

Then

$$\{s\} = [L_0]^{-T} \tag{6.89}$$

The procedure is repeated until it converges completely.

Example 6.14

Compute the two lowest eigenvalues and corresponding eigenvectors of the eigen problem $[k] \{\phi\} = \lambda [M] \{\phi\}$ where

$$[M] = \begin{bmatrix} 1/2 & & \\ & 1 & \\ & & 1/2 \end{bmatrix} \text{ and } [k] = \begin{bmatrix} 2 & -1 & 0 \\ -1 & 4 & -1 \\ 0 & -1 & 2 \end{bmatrix}$$

Solution

The eigenvalues of the above problem are computed first. They are

$$\lambda_1 = 2, \{\phi_1\} = \begin{Bmatrix} \frac{1}{\sqrt{2}} \\ \frac{1}{\sqrt{2}} \\ \frac{1}{\sqrt{2}} \end{Bmatrix}; \lambda_2 = 4, \{\phi_2\} = \begin{Bmatrix} -1 \\ 0 \\ 1 \end{Bmatrix}$$

Let us choose the starting vectors for the simultaneous iteration method with Gram-Schmidt orthogonalisations

$$\{X_1\} = \begin{Bmatrix} 0 & 2 \\ 1 & 1 \\ 2 & 0 \end{Bmatrix}$$

Solve x_2 from $[k] \{x_2\} = [M] \{X_1\}$

$$\{x_2\} = \begin{Bmatrix} 0.25 & 0.75 \\ 0.50 & 0.50 \\ 0.75 & 0.25 \end{Bmatrix}$$

Orthonormalizing $\{x_2\}$ with respect to $[M]$ gives

$$\{X_2\} = \begin{Bmatrix} 0.3333 & 1.1790 \\ 0.6667 & 0.2357 \\ 1.0000 & -0.7071 \end{Bmatrix}$$

$$\{X_2\}^T \{X_2\} = [P_2] = \begin{bmatrix} 1.333 & -1.650 \\ 0 & 2.121 \end{bmatrix}$$

Repeating the procedure, we obtain

$$\{X_3\} = \begin{bmatrix} 0.5222 & 1.108 \\ 0.6963 & 0.123 \\ 0.8700 & -0.861 \end{bmatrix}, [P_3] = \begin{bmatrix} 2.089 & -0.9847 \\ 0 & 3.83 \end{bmatrix}$$

$$\{X_4\} = \begin{bmatrix} 0.6163 & 1.058 \\ 0.7044 & 0.0622 \\ 0.7924 & -0.9339 \end{bmatrix}, [P_4] = \begin{bmatrix} 2.023 & -0.5202 \\ 0 & 3.955 \end{bmatrix}$$

$$\{X_5\} = \begin{bmatrix} 0.6624 & 1.032 \\ 0.7065 & 0.0311 \\ 0.7507 & -0.9678 \end{bmatrix}, [P_5] = \begin{bmatrix} 2.004 & -0.2640 \\ 0 & 3.988 \end{bmatrix}$$

$$\{X_6\} = \begin{bmatrix} 0.6848 & 1.015 \\ 0.7069 & 0.0156 \\ 0.7291 & -0.9842 \end{bmatrix}, [P_6] = \begin{bmatrix} 2.001 & -0.1325 \\ 0 & 3.997 \end{bmatrix}$$

$$\{X_7\} = \begin{bmatrix} 0.6963 & 1.008 \\ 0.7071 & 0.0078 \\ 0.7073 & -0.0079 \end{bmatrix}, [P_7] = \begin{bmatrix} 2.000 & -0.0660 \\ 0 & 3.999 \end{bmatrix}$$

$$\{X_8\} = \begin{bmatrix} 0.7016 & 1.004 \\ 0.7071 & 0.0037 \\ 0.7126 & -0.9960 \end{bmatrix}, [P_8] = \begin{bmatrix} 2.000 & -0.0330 \\ 0 & 4.000 \end{bmatrix}$$

$$\{X_9\} = \begin{bmatrix} 0.7045 & 0.1001 \\ 0.7071 & 0.0021 \\ 0.7099 & -0.9980 \end{bmatrix}, [P_9] = \begin{bmatrix} 2.000 & -0.0166 \\ 0 & 4.000 \end{bmatrix}$$

$$\{X_{10}\} = \begin{bmatrix} 0.7058 & 1.0010 \\ 0.7070 & 0.0010 \\ 0.7084 & -0.9990 \end{bmatrix}, [P_{10}] = \begin{bmatrix} 2.000 & -0.0083 \\ 0 & 4.000 \end{bmatrix}$$

After pth iteration we obtain

$$\{\phi_1\} = \begin{Bmatrix} 0.7058 \\ 0.7070 \\ 0.7084 \end{Bmatrix}, \lambda_1 = 2.00$$

$$\{\phi_2\} = \begin{Bmatrix} 1.0010 \\ 0.0010 \\ -0.9990 \end{Bmatrix}, \lambda_2 = 4.00$$

6.6 TRANSFORMATION METHODS

When the matrix size is small the method commonly employed to solve an eigenvalue problem involves the use of the characteristic equation. However, this method is not used for problems when the matrices are of size more than three. In this section, we indicate the methods which are available for matrices of higher order and suitable for computer implementation.

Generally speaking, there is no single method which can cover all situations. This is due to the fact that what is required may vary from one problem to another. For instance, it may be required to know only the eigenvalues of the largest modulus, or the eigenvalues of the lowest modulus, all eigenvalues but no eigenvectors, and in some other situations all eigenvalues and eigenvectors. In addition, some methods are suited only for certain type of matrices. Therefore it is attempted here to indicate the areas of application of the methods described above.

The transformation method involves the transformation of the original matrix to a new matrix without changing the eigenvalues. The new matrix is in a form that the eigenvalues can be predicted easily. The finite element approach yields the stiffness matrices of banded nature. When solving the eigenvalue problem associated with such matrices, it is necessary to reduce the matrices either to a diagonal or a tridiagonal form. This can be accomplished by a orthogonal transformation using rotation and reflection matrices. Here we present the diagonalization of matrix by the Jacobi's transformation and reduce it into tridiagonal form by Given's and Householder's transformations.

6.6.1 Jacobi's Method

Jacobi's method is valid only for real symmetric matrices. For such matrices the eigenvalues are all real. If $[A]$ is a real symmetric matrix then there exists an orthogonal matrix $[P]$ such that $[P]^T [A] [P] = [\Lambda]$ where $[\Lambda]$ is a diagonal matrix whose diagonal elements are the eigenvalues of $[A]$. Also the columns of $[P]$ are the corresponding eigenvectors of $[A]$. We shall now derive an iterative scheme for finding $[P]$.

Let us consider the two matrices $[A]$ and $[P]$ of order two.

$$[A] = \begin{bmatrix} a_{11} & a_{12} \\ a_{21} & a_{22} \end{bmatrix}, [P] = \begin{bmatrix} p_{11} & p_{12} \\ p_{21} & p_{22} \end{bmatrix}$$

where $p_{11} = \cos\theta = p_{22}$ and $p_{12} = \sin\theta = -p_{21}$, and the value of θ is such that

$$[P]^T [P] = [I]$$

and

$$[P]^T [A] [P] = \begin{bmatrix} \lambda_1 & 0 \\ 0 & \lambda_2 \end{bmatrix} \tag{6.90}$$

in which λ_1 and λ_2 are the eigenvalues of $[A]$ and the (r, q) element and the (q, r) element of $[P]^T [A] [P]$ are zero. Therefore, the value of θ is found from

$$\tan 2\theta = \frac{2a_{rq}}{a_{qq} - a_{rr}}; \; a_{qq} \neq a_{rr}$$

$$\theta = \pi/4 \text{ if } a_{qq} = a_{rr} \tag{6.91}$$

Also $[P]^T [P]$ is symmetric, therefore

$$[P_i]^T [P_j] = \begin{cases} 1 & \text{if } i = j \\ 0 & \text{if } i \neq j \end{cases}$$

Let us consider the following cases:

(i) $i \neq r, q$ *and* $j \neq r, q$:

$$b_{ij} = [e_i]^T [A] [e_j] = [e_i]^T [a_j] = a_{ij}$$

(ii) $i \neq r, q$ *and* $j = r$:

$$b_{ir} = [e_i]^T [A] [P_r] = [e_i]^T \begin{bmatrix} a_{1r}\cos\theta - a_{1q}\sin\theta \\ a_{2r}\cos\theta - a_{2q}\sin\theta \\ \cdots\cdots\cdots \\ \cdots\cdots\cdots \\ a_{nr}\cos\theta - a_{nq}\sin\theta \end{bmatrix}$$

$$= a_{ir}\cos\theta - a_{iq}\sin\theta$$

(iii) $i \neq r, q$ *and* $j = q$:

$$b_{iq} = [e_i]^T [A] [P_q] = [e_i]^T \begin{bmatrix} a_{1r}\sin\theta + a_{1q}\cos\theta \\ a_{2r}\sin\theta + a_{2q}\cos\theta \\ \cdots\cdots\cdots \\ \cdots\cdots\cdots \\ a_{nr}\sin\theta + a_{nq}\cos\theta \end{bmatrix}$$

$$= a_{ir}\sin\theta + a_{iq}\cos\theta$$

(iv) $i = j = r$:

$$b_{rr} = [P_i]^T [A] [P_r] = \begin{bmatrix} 0 .. \overset{(r)}{\cos\theta} .. -\overset{(q)}{\sin\theta} ... 0 \end{bmatrix} \begin{bmatrix} a_{1r}\cos\theta - a_{1q}\sin\theta \\ a_{2r}\cos\theta - a_{2q}\sin\theta \\ \cdots\cdots\cdots \\ \cdots\cdots\cdots \\ a_{nr}\cos\theta - a_{nq}\sin\theta \end{bmatrix}$$

$$= a_{rr}\cos^2\theta - a_{rq}\cos\theta\sin\theta - a_{qr}\sin\theta\cos\theta + a_{qq}\sin^2\theta$$

Since $[A]$ is symmetric matrix $a_{rq} = a_{qr}$

(v) $i = j = q$:

$$b_{qq} = [P_q]^T [A] [P_q] = [e_i]^T = \begin{bmatrix} 0 .. \overset{(r)}{\sin\theta} + \overset{(q)}{\cos\theta} ... 0 \end{bmatrix} \begin{bmatrix} a_{1r}\sin\theta + a_{1q}\cos\theta \\ a_{2r}\sin\theta + a_{2q}\cos\theta \\ \cdots\cdots\cdots \\ \cdots\cdots\cdots \\ a_{nr}\sin\theta + a_{nq}\cos\theta \end{bmatrix}$$

$$= a_{rr}\sin^2\theta + a_{rq}\sin\theta\cos\theta + a_{qr}\cos\theta\sin\theta + a_{qq}\cos^2\theta$$

$$= a_{rr}\sin^2\theta + a_{qq}\cos^2\theta + 2a_{rq}\sin\theta\cos\theta$$

If $i = r$ and $j = q$

$$b_{rq} = [P_r]^T [a] [P_q] = \begin{bmatrix} 0 .. \overset{(r)}{\cos\theta} .. -\overset{(q)}{\sin\theta} ... 0 \end{bmatrix} \begin{bmatrix} a_{1r}\sin\theta + a_{1q}\cos\theta \\ a_{2r}\sin\theta + a_{2q}\cos\theta \\ \cdots\cdots\cdots \\ \cdots\cdots\cdots \\ a_{nr}\sin\theta + a_{nq}\cos\theta \end{bmatrix}$$

$$= a_{rr} \cos\theta \sin\theta + a_{rq} \cos^2\theta - a_{qr} \sin^2\theta - a_{qq} \sin\theta \cos\theta$$

$$= a_{rq}(\cos^2\theta - \sin^2\theta) + (a_{rr} - a_{qq}) \sin\theta \cos\theta$$

$$= a_{rq} \cos 2\theta + \frac{1}{2}(a_{rr} - a_{qq}) \sin 2\theta$$

We observe here that since $[A]$ is symmetric, $[B]$ is also symmetric and

$$[B]^T = ([P]^T [A] [P])^T = [P]^T [A]^T [P] = [P]^T [A] [P] = [B]$$

By choosing proper value of θ we have

$$b_{rq} = b_{qr} = 0$$

$$0 = a_{rq} \cos 2\theta + \frac{1}{2}(a_{rr} - a_{qq}) \sin 2\theta$$

If $a_{rr} - a_{qq} \neq 0$ then

$$\frac{\sin 2\theta}{\cos 2\theta} = \tan 2\theta = \frac{2a_{rq}}{a_{qq} - a_{rr}}$$

If $a_{rr} = a_{qq} = 0$ then

$$a_{rq} \cos 2\theta = 0$$

from which $\theta = \pi/4$

It can also be shown that $[P]^T$ $[A]$ $[P]$ = $[B]$. Here $[A]$ and $[B]$ have the same eigenvalues and at least two off-diagonal elements of $[B]$ are zero, i.e. , $b_{rq} = b_{qr} = 0$ and $[B]$ need not be diagonal.

If it is required to generate a sequence of matrices $[B_1]$, $[B_2]$ ... with the help of the orthogonal matrices $[P_1]$, $[P_2]$ ... each of these matrices will make different pair of elements zero. Consider the following

$$[B_1] = [P_1]^T [A] [P_1]$$

$$[B_2] = [P_2]^T [B_1] [P_2]$$

$$[B_k] = [P_k]^T [B_{k-1}] [P_k]$$

Each $[B_k]$ has the same eigenvalues as $[A]$, if these $[B_1]$, $[B_2]$ ... sequential matrices converge to a diagonal matrix whose elements are the eigenvalues of $[A]$. Unfortunately the sequence which leads to a diagonal matrix is not known, moreover the elements which are forced to zero in one step say $b_{rq} = b_{qr} = 0$, may become non zero elements in the subsequent step.

Example 6.15

Determine the eigenvalues and eigenvectors of the following matrix using the Jacobi's method

$$[A] = \begin{bmatrix} 11 & 2 & 8 \\ 2 & 2 & -10 \\ 9 & -10 & 5 \end{bmatrix}$$

Solution

The elements to be annihilated are the elements of largest modulus at that stage. The first step is to select $r = 2$, $q = 3$ so that $a_{rq} = a_{qr} = -10$ is annihilated from the matrix. Then we have

$$\tan 2\theta_1 = \frac{2a_{23}^{(0)}}{a_{33}^{(0)} - a_{22}^{(0)}} = \frac{2(-10)}{5-2} = \frac{-20}{3}$$

To use this value in the calculations of sin θ, and cos θ, which are required in the [P] matrix, instead of calculating θ use the following equations

$$\tan 2\alpha = \lambda/\mu\,;\ (\mu > 0)$$

then

$$\cos\alpha = \left(\frac{1}{2}\{1 + \mu/[\lambda^2 + \mu^2]^{1/2}\}\right)^{1/2}$$

and

$$\sin\alpha = \frac{\lambda}{(2\{\lambda^2 + \mu^2 + \mu[\lambda^2 + \mu^2]^{1/2}\})^{1/2}}$$

In the present case $\lambda = -20$, $\mu = 3$

By substitution in the above equation, we obtain

$$\cos\theta_1 = 0.76 \text{ and } \sin\theta_1 = -0.65$$

Then

$$[P_1] = \begin{bmatrix} 1 & 0 & 0 \\ 0 & 0.76 & -0.65 \\ 0 & 0.65 & 0.76 \end{bmatrix}$$

$$\{B_1] = [P_1]^T [A] [P]$$

$$= \begin{bmatrix} 1 & 0 & 0 \\ 0 & 0.76 & +0.65 \\ 0 & -0.65 & 0.76 \end{bmatrix} \begin{bmatrix} 11 & 2 & 8 \\ 2 & 2 & -10 \\ 8 & -10 & 5 \end{bmatrix} \begin{bmatrix} 1 & 0 & 0 \\ 0 & 0.76 & -0.65 \\ 0 & 0.65 & 0.76 \end{bmatrix}$$

$$= \begin{bmatrix} 11 & 6.74 & -4.76 \\ 6.74 & -6.61 & 0 \\ -4.76 & 0 & 13.61 \end{bmatrix}$$

The off-diagonal element of largest modulus is -6.74. So we choose $r = 1$, $q = 2$ and calculate $\sin\theta_2$ and $\cos\theta_2$. Thus

$$[P_2] = \begin{bmatrix} 0.95 & -0.32 & 0 \\ 0.32 & 0.95 & 0 \\ 0 & 0 & 1 \end{bmatrix}$$

and $$[B_2] = [P_2]^T [B_1] [P_2]$$

$$= \begin{bmatrix} 0.95 & 0.32 & 0 \\ -0.32 & 0.95 & 0 \\ 0 & 0 & 1 \end{bmatrix} \begin{bmatrix} 11 & 6.74 & -4.76 \\ 6.74 & -6.61 & 0 \\ -4.76 & 0 & 13.61 \end{bmatrix} \begin{bmatrix} 0.95 & -0.32 & 0 \\ 0.32 & 0.95 & 0 \\ 0 & 0 & 1 \end{bmatrix}$$

$$= \begin{bmatrix} 13.28 & 0 & -4.5 \\ 0 & -8.94 & -1.53 \\ -4.5 & -1.53 & 13.61 \end{bmatrix}$$

Note that when a_{12} and a_{21} are annihilated, a_{23} and a_{32} which were annihilated earlier become nonzero, however, with smaller magnitude than before. We repeat the procedure till the matrix converges to a diagonal matrix. The results of the various steps are summarized here.

k	B_k	Sum of the squares of off diagonal elements
0	$\begin{bmatrix} 11 & 2 & 8 \\ 2 & 2 & -10 \\ 8 & -10 & 5 \end{bmatrix}$	336.0
1	$\begin{bmatrix} 11 & 6.74 & -4.76 \\ 6.74 & -6.61 & 0 \\ -4.76 & 0 & 13.61 \end{bmatrix}$	136.00
2	$\begin{bmatrix} 13.28 & 0 & -4.50 \\ 0 & -3.89 & -1.53 \\ -4.50 & -1.53 & 13.61 \end{bmatrix}$	45.25
3	$\begin{bmatrix} 8.94 & -1.06 & 0 \\ -1.06 & -8.94 & 1.10 \\ 0 & 1.10 & 17.95 \end{bmatrix}$	4.66
4	$\begin{bmatrix} 8.94 & -1.06 & 0.04 \\ -1.06 & -8.94 & 0 \\ 0.04 & 0 & 18.0 \end{bmatrix}$	2.24
5	$\begin{bmatrix} 9.00 & 0 & 0.04 \\ 0 & -9.0 & 0.0 \\ 0 & 0.0 & 18.0 \end{bmatrix}$	0.00
6	$\begin{bmatrix} 9.00 & 0.00 & 0 \\ 0.00 & -9.0 & 0.0 \\ 0 & 0.00 & 18.0 \end{bmatrix}$	0.00

Therefore the eigenvalues are 9.00, – 9.00, 18.00 and the corresponding eigenvectors are the columns of the transformation matrix $[P_6]$

$$[P_6] = \begin{bmatrix} 0.67 & -0.33 & 0.67 \\ 0.67 & 0.67 & -0.33 \\ -0.33 & 0.67 & 0.67 \end{bmatrix}$$

6.6.2 Given's Method

In general there is no finite sequence of transformations of the type $[B_k] = [P_k]^T [B_{k-1}] [P_k]$ which results in a diagonal matrix, in the Jacobi method. There is one such finite sequence which leads to a tridiagonal matrix of the form:

$$[A] = \begin{bmatrix} \alpha_1 & \beta_1 & 0 & 0 & \cdots & 0 & 0 \\ \beta_1 & \alpha_2 & \beta_2 & 0 & \cdots & 0 & 0 \\ 0 & \beta_2 & \alpha_3 & \beta_3 & \cdots & 0 & 0 \\ 0 & 0 & \beta_3 & \alpha_4 & \cdots & .. & 0 \\ .. & .. & .. & .. & \cdots & & \\ 0 & 0 & 0 & .. & \alpha_{n-1} & \beta_{n-1} & \\ 0 & 0 & 0 & .. & \beta_{n-1} & \alpha_n & \end{bmatrix} \tag{6.92}$$

In Given's method we consider a real symmetric matrix $[A]$ and make use of the orthogonal matrices $[P_1]$, $[P_2]$ ... of the same type as given in Jacobi's method. We eliminate the elements other than tridiagonal elements such as a_{13}, a_{14} ... a_{1n}; a_{24}, a_{25} ... a_{2n} ; $a_{n-3,n-1}$, $a_{n-3,n}$; $a_{n-2,n}$. In each step we drive out two elements since $[A]$ is a symmetric matrix. This results in a symmetric tridiagonal matrix $[\overline{A}]$ of the form given by eq. 6.92. The minor difference between the matrices $[P_k]$ by Jacobi's method and that of Given's method is in the computations of the angle θ. If $i = r$, $j = q$ then θ is chosen so that the $(r-1, q)$ and $(q, r-1)$ elements are forced to zero in the Given's method whereas (r, q) and (q, r) elements are made zero in Jacobi's method. To annihilate $a^k_{i,q}$ $i \neq r, q$.

$$a^k_{iq} = -a^{k-1}_{ir} \sin\theta_k + a^{k-1}_{iq} \cos\theta_k \text{ for } i \neq p, q$$

where

$$\sin\theta_k = \frac{a^{k-1}_{iq}}{p_k} \text{ and } \cos\theta_k = \frac{a^{k-1}_{ir}}{r_k}$$

$$p_k = \left((a^{k-1}_{ir})^2 + (a^{k-1}_{iq})^2\right)^{1/2}$$

After obtaining the tridiagonal matrix $[\overline{A}]$, the Given's method employs a technique to estimate the boundaries in which the eigenvalues of $[\overline{A}]$ lie. Once the boundaries are known the actual eigenvalues λ_1 ... λ_n and their corresponding eigenvectors are determined.

6.6.3 Householder's Method

In the Given's method it was noted that any real symmetric matrix $[A]$ can be reduced to the tridiagonal from $[\overline{A}]$ in about $\frac{1}{2}(n-1)(n-2)$ transformations of the form

$$[B_k] = [P_k]^T [B_{k-1}] [P_k], \text{ where } k = 0, 1, 2, ...$$

and

$$[B_0] = [A]$$

In the Householder's method the same transformation of any real symmetric matrix into a tridiagonal matrix takes place in $(n - 2)$ operations. However the orthogonal matrix $[P_k]$ are constructed in different manner from those used in Given's or Jacobi's method.

The orthogonal matrix used in Householder's method is of the form

$$[P] = [I_n] - \{w\} \{w\}^T$$

where $\{w\}$ is an n-component vector of unit length such that

$$\{w\}^T \{w\} = 1$$

If the vector $\{w\}$ is properly chosen, only $(n - 2)$ transformations are sufficient to obtain the tridiagonal matrix $[\bar{A}]$. From this step on, Given's method and Householder's method are identical. Householder's method can also be extended to the case of a general square matrix $[A]$.

Wilkinson has shown that Given's and Householder's methods are essentially equivalent, inspite of their different sequence of transformations.

Example 6.16

Use the Householder's method to compute the eigenvalues and the corresponding eigenvectors for the eigenvalue problem.

$$([A] - \lambda[I]) \{x\} = 0$$

where

$$[A] = \begin{bmatrix} 4 & 3 & 2 & 1 \\ 3 & 4 & 1 & 2 \\ 2 & 1 & 4 & 3 \\ 1 & 2 & 3 & 4 \end{bmatrix} = [A_0]$$

Solution

Let us tridiagonalize the given matrix as follows.

$$S_1^{1/2} = 3.742 = -\alpha_{12}^{(1)}$$

$$w_{21}^2 = 0.9010, \ \omega_{21} = 0.9492$$

$$w_{31} = 0.2815, \ \omega_{41} = 0.1408$$

Now

$$w_1^1 = \{0 \quad 0.9492 \quad 0.2815 \quad 0.1408\}$$

$$[P] = \begin{bmatrix} 1 & 0 & 0 & 0 \\ 0 & -0.8020 & -0.5344 & -0.2672 \\ 0 & -0.5344 & 0.8410 & -0.0793 \\ 0 & -0.2672 & -0.07927 & 0.9604 \end{bmatrix}$$

$$[A_1] = [P_1]^T [A_0] [P_1] = \begin{bmatrix} 4 & -3.742 & 0 & 0 \\ -3.742 & 6.572 & -0.5214 & -2.667 \\ 0 & -0.5214 & 2.867 & 1.275 \\ 0 & -2.667 & 1.275 & 2.559 \end{bmatrix}$$

It should be noted that, because of the rounding of errors, the elements $a^{(1)}{}_{13}$, $a^{(1)}{}_{14}$, etc. will not be zero although we have assumed them to be zero.
Then

$$S_2^{1/2} = \{(-0.5214)^2 + (-2.667)^2\}^{1/2} = -2.718 = -a_{23}^{(2)}$$

In order to have $w_{32}^{(2)}$ as large as possible the negative value of $a_{23}^{(2)}$ is taken into consideration

$$w_{32}^2 = 0.5960 \qquad W_{32} = 0.772 \qquad w_{42} = 0.6355$$

Therefore $w_2^1 = \{0 \quad 0 \quad 0.7720 \quad 0.6355\}$

$$[P_2] = \begin{bmatrix} 1 & 0 & 0 & 0 \\ 0 & 1 & 0 & 0 \\ 0 & 0 & -0.1920 & -0.9812 \\ 0 & 0 & -0.9812 & 0.1920 \end{bmatrix}$$

$$[A_2] = [P_2]^T [A_1] [P_2] = \begin{bmatrix} 4 & -3.742 & 0 & 0 \\ -3.742 & 6.572 & 2.718 & 0 \\ 0 & 2.718 & 3.050 & 1.238 \\ 0 & 0 & 1.238 & 2.374 \end{bmatrix}$$

By solving the tridiagonal matrix using sturm sequence we obtain the following eigenvalues

$$\lambda_1 = 10.00 \qquad \lambda_2 = 3.996 \qquad \lambda_3 = 2.0 \qquad \lambda_4 = -0.000329$$

The corresponding eigenvectors are

$$\{Y_1\} = \{0.5001 \quad -0.8018 \quad -0.3229 \quad -0.05242\}^T$$
$$\{Y_2\} = \{0.5003 \quad 0.0004696 \quad 0.6884 \quad 0.5252\}^T$$
$$\{Y_3\} = \{0.4996 \quad 0.2671 \quad 0.2385 \quad -0.7888\}^T$$
$$\{Y_4\} = \{0.5000 \quad 0.5345 \quad -0.6042 \quad 0.3150\}^T$$

6.6.4 QR Method

In the preceding section we have described the Jacob's method which is a reliable method but it requires a large computation time and is valid only for real symmetric matrices. The QR method on the other hand is numerically extremely stable and is applicable to a general matrix. This method also provides a basis for developing a general purpose procedure for determining the eigenvalues and eigenvectors.

The method utilizes the fundamental property that a real matrix can be written as

$$[A] = [Q]\,[U]$$

where $[Q]$ is orthogonal and $[U]$ is upper triangular. This is contrary to the decomposition in the form $[L]$ $[U]$ where $[L]$ is the unit lower matrix and $[U]$ is the upper triangular matrix. The property can be proved as follows.

As in Jacobi's method we introduce here the rotations matrix and denote it by $[R\,(p, q, \theta)]$ to indicate the rows that contain the non-zero, off-diagonal elements. Note that $[R]$ is orthogonal.

$$[R(p,q,\theta)] = \begin{bmatrix} 1 & & & & & & & \\ & 1 & & & & & & \\ & & \cos\theta & & & \sin\theta & & \\ & & & 1 & & & & \\ & & & & 1 & & & \\ & & -\sin\theta & & & \cos\theta & & \\ & & & & & & 1 & \\ & & p & & & q & & 1 \end{bmatrix} \begin{matrix} \\ \\ p \\ \\ \\ q \\ \\ \\ \end{matrix}$$

If any vector $\{x\}$ is multiplied by $[\,R\,(p, q, \theta)\,]$ such that $y = [R]\,\{x\}$ then

$$y_p = r_{pp}\,x_p + r_{pq}x_q$$

$$= \cos\theta\, x_p + \sin\theta\, x_q$$

and

$$Y_q = r_{qp}x_p + r_{qq}x_q$$

$$= -\sin\theta\, x_p + \cos\theta\, x_q$$

i.e., $y_i = x_i$ if $i \neq p$ or q. Therefore it is necessary to select θ such that y_p or y_q is equal to zero. It should also be noted that if $x_p = x_q = 0$ then $y_p = y_q = 0$. If we write

$$[A] = (x^{(1)} x^{(2)} \ldots x^{(n)})$$

then

$$[R(p,q,\theta)]\;[A] = (y^{(1)} y^{(2)} \ldots\, y^{(n)})$$

An element in either pth row or qth row is reduced by a proper choice of θ. Thus all the elements in the first column except the first element can be made zero by suitable values of θ and they remain zero even after multiplying with $[R]$. Similarly for all other columns elements are made zero for the elements below the diagonal elements by proper choice of θ values. Thus we obtain an upper triangular matrix by forming the product

$$[u] = R(n, n-1, \theta_{n,n-1}) R(n, n-2, \theta_{n,n-2}) \ldots R(3,1,\theta_{3,1}) R(2,1,\theta_{2,1})\,[A]$$

$$= \left(\prod_{j=1}^{n-1} \prod_{i=j+1}^{n} R(i, j, \theta_{ij}) \right) [A]$$

Since $[R]$ is an orthogonal matrix, the products of $[R]$ is also orthogonal. Hence we have $[U] = [S]\,[A]$ where $[S]$ is orthogonal and $[U]$ is upper triangular. Since $[S]$ is orthogonal we have $[A] = [S]^{-1}\,[U] = [S]^T\,[U]$. If $[Q] = [S]^T$ then $[A] = [Q]\,[U]$.

We can construct a sequence of matrices $[A_0]$, $[A_1]$ $[A_2]$ ... where

$$[A_0] = [A] = [Q_0]\,[A_0],\ [Q_k]\,[A_k] = [Q_{k-1}]\,[A_{k-1}]$$

for all values of $k \geq 1$. That is, we start with $[A_0] = [A]$ and put it in the form $[Q_0]\,[U_0]$ to obtain $[Q_0]$ and $[U_0]$ and then obtain $[A_1]$ which is equal to the product of $[U_0]\,[Q_0]$ in reverse order. Repeating this procedure we can obtain any number of sequence.

$[A]$	$=$	$[A_0] = [Q_0]\,[U_0]$	determines $[Q_0]$ and $[U_0]$
$[A_1]$	$=$	$[U_0]\,[Q_0]$	determines $[A_1]$
	$=$	$[Q_1]\,[U_1]$	determines $[Q_1]$ and $[U_1]$
$[A_2]$	$=$	$[U_1]\,[Q_1]$	determines $[A_2]$
	$=$	$[Q_2]\,[U_2]$	determines $[Q_2]$ and $[U_2]$
$[A_k]$	$=$	$U_{k-1}]\,[\,Q_{k-1}]$	determines $[A_k]$
	$=$	$[Q_k]\,[U_k]$	determines $[Q_k]$ and $[U_k]$

From the above sequence we can show that the product $Q_0\,Q_1\,Q_2 \ldots Q_k$ converges as $k \to \infty$. Then $[A_k]$ converges to an upper triangular matrix with the eigenvalues of $[A]$ as its diagonal elements. This can be proved as follows. We have

$$[A_k] = [Q_k]\,[U_k] = [U_{k-1}]\,[Q_{k-1}] \tag{6.93}$$

$$[A_{k-1}] = [Q_{k-1}]\,[U_{k-1}] \tag{6.94}$$

From which

$$[U_{k-1}] = [Q_{k-1}]^{-1}\,[A_{k-1}] \tag{6.95}$$

Substituting Eq. (6.95) in Eq. (6.93) we get

$$[A_k] = [Q_{k-1}]^{-1}\,[A_{k-1}]\,[Q_{k-1}]$$

Hence $[A_k]$ is similar to $[A_{k-1}]$. This implies that $[A_k]$ is similar to $[A_0] = [A]$. Therefore it has the same eigenvalues as $[A]$. Also

$$[A_{k-1}] = [Q_{k-2}]^{-1}\,[A_{k-2}]\,[Q_{k-2}]$$

Thus

$$[A_{k+1}] = [Q_k]^{-1}\,[Q_{k-1}]^{-1}\,[Q_0]^{-1}\,[A]\,[Q_0]\,[Q_1] \ldots [Q_k]$$

$$= [P_k]^{-1}\,[A]\,[P_k] \quad \text{where} \quad [P_k] = [Q_0]\,[Q_1] \ldots [Q_k]$$

If $k \to \infty$ $[P_k]$ exists and we denote it by $[P]$.

Then

$$\lim_{k \to \infty} Q_k = \lim_{k \to \infty}([P_{k-1}]^{-1}\,[P_k])$$

$$= \left(\lim_{k \to \infty}[P_{k-1}]^{-1}\right)\left(\lim_{k \to \infty}[P_k]\right)$$

$$= [P]^{-1}\,[P] = [I]$$

Here we have two limiting conditions

1. $$[A_k] = [P_{k-1}]^{-1}[A]\,[P_{k-1}]$$

which means

$$\lim_{k\to\infty}[A_k] = \left(\lim_{k\to\infty}[P_{k-1}]^{-1}\right)[A]\left(\lim_{k\to\infty}[P_{k-1}]\right)$$

$$= [P]^{-1}[A]\,[P]$$

Therefore in the limit $[A_k]$ is similar to $[A]$ and hence has the same eigenvalues as $[A]$.

2. $$[A_k] = [Q_k]\,[U_k]$$

that is

$$\lim_{k\to\infty}[A_k] = \left(\lim_{k\to\infty}[Q_k]\right)\left(\lim_{k\to\infty}[U_k]\right)$$

here we have

$$\lim_{k\to\infty}[Q_k] = [I]$$

which results in

$$\lim_{k\to\infty}[A_k] = \lim_{k\to\infty}[U_k]$$

Since every $[U_k]$ is an upper triangular matrix, the limit of $[A_k]$ is also an upper triangular matrix.

The accuracy of this method mainly depends on the effectiveness of the algorithm used for decompositions of $[A_k]$ into $[Q_k]\,[U_k]$. The limit $k \to \infty$ can exist for large size problems.

6.7 APPROXIMATION METHODS

Computations of dynamic response of any mechanical system require considerable amount of time and computer storage. In static analysis the solutions can be obtained in only one step whereas in dynamic analysis the analysis is required at several discrete points over a period of time. An equation of statics with inertia and damping forces at the end of each discrete time step can be solved for dynamic response using modal superposition analysis. Hence it is required to develop more effective algorithms for the computation of eigenpairs of a given system.

In the case of large eigen systems, the approximate solution methods have been developed to compute the lowest eigen pairs in the problem $[K]\{\phi\} = \lambda [M]\{\phi\}$. For most of the mechanical engineering problems of large size systems it is required to compute the few lowest eigenpairs. Here in this section three approximate methods are presented, all of them can be considered as Ritz analysis. The practical utility, limitations and the assumptions involved in these methods are discussed.

6.7.1 Static Condensation Method

Static condensation technique is one of the effective algorithms which is used in the solution of the equilibrium equations. The technique is used to reduce the degrees of freedom of the element and to perform part of the total finite element system equilibrium equations before arriving at the global matrices $[K]$ and $\{F\}$ of the structure. The displacement degrees of freedom at the internal nodes of an element can be reduced because they do not involve arriving of inter element continuity. The eliminations of such degrees of freedom follows the Gaussian elimination procedure.

The equations used in static condensation technique can be arrived at by assuming that the stiffness matrix, displacement and force vectors of the particular element can be partitioned into the form

$$\begin{bmatrix} K_{aa} & K_{ac} \\ K_{ac} & K_{cc} \end{bmatrix} \begin{Bmatrix} U_a \\ U_c \end{Bmatrix} = \begin{Bmatrix} F_a \\ F_c \end{Bmatrix} \tag{6.96}$$

where U_a and U_c are the displacement vectors to be retained and condensed out, respectively. Similarly the vectors $\{F_a\}$ and $\{F_c\}$ correspond to force vectors. The matrices $[K_{aa}]$, $[K_{ac}]$ and $[K_{cc}]$ correspond to the displacement vectors $\{U_a\}$ and $\{U_c\}$.

From the second equation of (6.96) we get

$$\{U_c\} = [K_{cc}]^{-1}(\{F_{cc}\} - [K_{ca}]\{U_a\}) \tag{6.97}$$

The relation (6.97) is substituted into the first equation of (6.96) to get the condensed equation

$$([K_{aa}] - [K_{ac}][K_{cc}]^{-1}[K_{ca}])\{U_a\} = \{F_a\} - [K_{ac}][K_{cc}]^{-1}\{F_c\} \tag{6.98}$$

It is obvious that the static condensation is nothing but Gauss elimination on the degrees of freedom $\{U_c\}$. Hence static condensation is carried out very effectively by using Gaussian elimination sequentially on each degree of freedom to be condensed out, instead of the present method given in Eqs. (6.96) to (6.98).

The advantage of using static condensation technique on each element is to reduce the order of the system matrices, and by doing so, back up storage is prevented. If all the elements are identical, the stiffness matrix of the first element need to be derived.

Example 6.17

Compute the eigen values and eigen vectors of the problem $[K]\{\phi\} = \lambda[M]\{\phi\}$ using static condensation technique, where

$$[K] = \begin{bmatrix} 4 & -2 & 0 & 0 \\ -2 & 4 & -2 & 0 \\ 0 & -2 & 4 & -2 \\ 0 & 0 & -2 & 2 \end{bmatrix} \text{ and } [M] = \begin{bmatrix} 4 & 0 & 0 & 0 \\ 0 & 2 & 0 & 0 \\ 0 & 0 & 0 & 0 \\ 0 & 0 & 0 & 0 \end{bmatrix}$$

Consider $\{\phi_a\} = (\phi_2, \phi_4)$ and $\{\phi_c\} = (\phi_1, \phi_2)$.

First we rearrange the columns and rows without altering the positions of the diagonal elements to obtain the form

$$\begin{bmatrix} 4 & 0 & -2 & 2 \\ 0 & 2 & 0 & -2 \\ -2 & 0 & 4 & 0 \\ -2 & -2 & 0 & 4 \end{bmatrix} \begin{Bmatrix} \phi_a \\ \phi_c \end{Bmatrix} = \lambda \begin{bmatrix} 2 & & & 0 \\ & 1 & & \\ & & 0 & \\ 0 & & & 0 \end{bmatrix} \begin{Bmatrix} \phi_a \\ \phi_c \end{Bmatrix}$$

After solving for $\{\phi_c\}$ in terms of $\{\phi_a\}$, we can write

$$[K_a] = \begin{bmatrix} 2 & 0 \\ 0 & 1 \end{bmatrix} - \begin{bmatrix} -2 & -2 \\ 0 & -2 \end{bmatrix} \begin{bmatrix} 1/4 & 0 \\ 0 & 1/4 \end{bmatrix} \begin{bmatrix} -2 & 0 \\ -2 & -2 \end{bmatrix} = \begin{bmatrix} 2 & -1 \\ -1 & 1 \end{bmatrix}$$

Therefore

$$\begin{bmatrix} 2 & -1 \\ -1 & 1 \end{bmatrix} \{\phi_a\} = \lambda \begin{bmatrix} 2 & 0 \\ 0 & 1 \end{bmatrix} \{\phi_a\}$$

and we have

$$\det([k_a] - \lambda[M_a]) = 8\lambda^2 - 8\lambda + 1$$

Hence
$$\lambda_1 = \frac{1}{2} - \frac{\sqrt{2}}{4},$$

$$\lambda_2 = \frac{1}{2} + \frac{\sqrt{2}}{4}$$

The corresponding eigenvectors are computed using

$$([K_a] - \lambda_i[M_a])\{\phi_{ai}\} = 0; \{\phi_{ai}^T\} [M_a] \{\phi_{ai}\} = 1$$

Hence
$$\{\phi_{a1}\} = \begin{Bmatrix} \dfrac{\sqrt{2}}{4} \\ \dfrac{1}{2} \end{Bmatrix},$$

$$\{\phi_{a2}\} = \begin{Bmatrix} \dfrac{-\sqrt{2}}{4} \\ \dfrac{1}{2} \end{Bmatrix}$$

Using
$$\{\phi_c\} = -[K_{cc}]^{-1} [K_{ca}] \{\phi_a\}$$

$$\{\phi_{c1}\} = -\begin{bmatrix} \dfrac{1}{4} & 0 \\ 0 & \dfrac{1}{4} \end{bmatrix} \begin{bmatrix} -2 & 0 \\ -2 & -2 \end{bmatrix} \begin{Bmatrix} \dfrac{\sqrt{2}}{4} \\ \dfrac{1}{2} \end{Bmatrix} = \begin{Bmatrix} \dfrac{\sqrt{2}}{8} \\ \dfrac{2+\sqrt{2}}{8} \end{Bmatrix}$$

$$\{\phi_{c2}\} = -\begin{bmatrix} \dfrac{1}{4} & 0 \\ 0 & \dfrac{1}{4} \end{bmatrix} \begin{bmatrix} -2 & 0 \\ -2 & -2 \end{bmatrix} \begin{Bmatrix} \dfrac{-\sqrt{2}}{4} \\ \dfrac{1}{2} \end{Bmatrix} = \begin{Bmatrix} \dfrac{-\sqrt{2}}{8} \\ \dfrac{2-\sqrt{2}}{8} \end{Bmatrix}$$

Solution to the given problem $[K] \{\phi\} = \lambda [M] \{\phi\}$ is

$$\lambda_1 = \frac{1}{2} - \frac{\sqrt{2}}{4} \quad ; \quad \{\phi_1\} = \begin{bmatrix} \sqrt{2}/8 \\ \sqrt{2}/4 \\ \dfrac{2+\sqrt{2}}{8} \\ 1/2 \end{bmatrix}$$

$$\lambda_2 = \frac{1}{2} + \frac{\sqrt{2}}{4} \quad ; \quad \{\phi_2\} = \begin{bmatrix} -\sqrt{2}/8 \\ -\sqrt{2}/4 \\ \dfrac{2-\sqrt{2}}{8} \\ 1/2 \end{bmatrix}$$

$$\lambda_3 = \infty \quad ; \quad \{\phi_3\} = \begin{bmatrix} 2 \\ 0 \\ 0 \\ 0 \end{bmatrix}$$

$$\lambda_4 = \infty \quad ; \quad \{\phi_4\} = \begin{bmatrix} 0 \\ 0 \\ 2 \\ 0 \end{bmatrix}$$

6.7.2 Rayleigh-Ritz Method

An approximate technique often used for determining the lowest natural frequency and corresponding eigenvector of the eigen problem of the form $[K]\{\phi\} = \lambda\,[M]\{\phi\}$ is the Rayleigh-Ritz technique. Ritz basis vectors are assumed in the analysis. The eigen problem that we consider is of the form

$$[K]\,\{\phi\} = \lambda[M]\,\{\phi\} \tag{6.99}$$

where $[K]$ and $[M]$ are both positive definite, in which case all the eigenvalues are positive. The mass matrix $[M]$ is a consistent or lumped mass matrix without zero elements in the main diagonal. Rayleigh minimum principle states that

$$\lambda_1 = \min \rho(\{\phi\}) \tag{6.100}$$

where $\rho\,(\{\phi\})$ is the Rayleigh quotient for all possible vectors, $\{\phi\}$,

$$\rho(\{\phi\}) = \frac{\{\phi\}^T [K]\,\{\phi\}}{\{\phi\}^T [M]\,\{\phi\}} \tag{6.101}$$

This Rayleigh quotient is obtained from the standard eigenvalue problem. Since both $[K]$ and $[M]$ are positive definite matrices, $\rho\,(\{\phi\})$ has finite values for all vectors $\{\phi\}$ and with the limiting values

$$0 < \lambda_1 \le \rho(\{\phi\}) \le \lambda_n < \infty$$

Here we also consider a set of vectors $\{\,\bar{\phi}\,\}$ which are linear combinations of Ritz basis vectors ψ_i, $i = 1, 2....\,q$ which can be given as

$$\{\bar{\phi}\} = \sum_{i=1}^{q} x_i\{\psi_i\} \tag{6.102}$$

where x_i are the Ritz coordinates and $\{\bar{\phi}\}$ cannot be any arbitrary vector and ψ_i for $i = 1, 2, \ldots\, q$ are linearly independent. V_q the Ritz basis vector has dimensions q. The n dimensional space in which $[K]$ and $[M]$ are defined by V_n and our V_q is a part in V_n.

The condition that is used to derive ρ_2 is the procedure used to calculate the approximate higher eigenvalues.

$$\lambda_2 = \min \rho(\{\phi\}) \tag{6.103}$$

where the vector $\{\phi\}$ satisfies the orthogonality condition,

$$\{\phi\}^T [M] \{\phi_1\} = 0 \tag{6.104}$$

The approximate eigen vectors $\{\bar{\phi}_i\}$ obtained in the Rayleigh Analysis satisfy the relation

$$\{\bar{\phi}_i\}^T [M] \{\bar{\phi}_j\} = \delta_{ij} \tag{6.105}$$

where δ_{ij} = Kronecker delta

Hence ρ_2 can be evaluated by

$$\rho_2 = \min \rho(\{\bar{\phi}\}) \tag{6.106}$$

where the vector $\{\bar{\phi}\}$ satisfies the orthogonality condition.

$$\{\bar{\phi}\}^T [M] \{\bar{\phi}_1\} = 0 \tag{6.107}$$

It is to be noticed that the computation of $\{\bar{\phi}_2\}$ and corresponding ρ_2 is based on $\{\bar{\phi}_1\}$ which satisfies the orthogonality condition. Therefore to compute ρ_i and $\{\bar{\phi}_i\}$, it is required to minimize ρ ({ $\bar{\phi}$ }) with the orthogonality condition $\{\bar{\phi}\}$ $[M]$ $\{\bar{\phi}_j\}$ $= 0$ for $j = 1, \ldots i - 1$.

In general, the fact that $(i - 1)$ constraint equations need to be fulfilled in the evaluation of ρ_i also indicates that there is less accuracy in the higher eigenvalue approximations, and high accuracy in the lower eigenvalue approximations for which less constraints are to be imposed.

In practice the dynamic analysis considers the Ritz basis functions computed from the static solutions in which q load patterns are specified in $\{F\}$. Consider

$$[K]\,[\psi] = \{F\} \tag{6.108}$$

where ψ is an $n \times q$ matrix for storing Ritz base vectors.

$$\psi = [\psi_1, \psi_2 \ldots\ldots \psi_q], \quad \text{now evaluate}$$

$$[\bar{K}] = [\psi]^T [K]\,[\psi] \tag{6.109}$$

and

$$[\bar{M}] = [\psi]^T [M]\,[\psi] \tag{6.110}$$

Substituting Eq. (6.108) we have

$$[\bar{K}] = [\psi]^T \{F\} \tag{6.111}$$

Solving the eigen problem $[\bar{K}]\,\{x\} = \rho\,[\bar{M}]\,\{x\}$, the solution of which can be of the form

$$[\bar{K}]\,[X] = [\bar{M}]\,[X]\,[\rho] \tag{6.112}$$

where $[\rho]$ is a diagonal matrix whose elements are the eigenvalue approximations ρ_i and $[x]$ is a matrix of $[\overline{M}]$ orthogonal eigenvectors. They are approximations to the eigenvectors of the problem $[K]\{\phi\} = \lambda [M]\{\phi\}$.

Example 6.18

Compute the eigenvalues of the given system by Rayleigh-Ritz approach and compare the result with that obtained from Rayleigh method.
Given

$$[K] = \begin{bmatrix} 6 & -2 \\ -2 & 4 \end{bmatrix}$$

$$[M] = \begin{bmatrix} 2 & 0 \\ 0 & 1 \end{bmatrix}$$

Solution

Let us assume the displacement vector which represents the fundamental mode.

$$\{u_1\} = \begin{Bmatrix} 1 \\ 2 \end{Bmatrix}$$

$$\omega_1^2 = \frac{\{u_1\}^T [K]\{u_1\}}{\{u_1\}^T [M]\{u_1\}} = \frac{\{1 \quad 2\} \begin{bmatrix} 6 & -2 \\ -2 & 4 \end{bmatrix} \begin{Bmatrix} 1 \\ 2 \end{Bmatrix}}{\{1 \quad 2\} \begin{bmatrix} 2 & 0 \\ 0 & 1 \end{bmatrix} \begin{Bmatrix} 1 \\ 2 \end{Bmatrix}} = \frac{7}{3}$$

1×1 approximation will give us $\omega^2 = 2.33$.

In the Rayleigh-Ritz approach it is required to compute the first two vectors ψ approximately. The stiffness and mass matrices can be computed as follows:
The assumed vectors are of the form

$$\psi = \begin{Bmatrix} 1 & 1 \\ 2 & -1 \end{Bmatrix}$$

where the second vector corresponds to the second mode which is between the two masses.

$$[\overline{K}] = \{\psi\}^T [K]\{\psi\} = \begin{Bmatrix} 1 & 2 \\ 1 & -1 \end{Bmatrix} \begin{bmatrix} 2 & 0 \\ 0 & 1 \end{bmatrix} \begin{Bmatrix} 1 & 1 \\ 2 & -1 \end{Bmatrix} = \begin{bmatrix} 14 & -4 \\ -4 & 14 \end{bmatrix}$$

$$[\overline{M}] = \{\psi\}^T [M]\{\psi\} = \begin{Bmatrix} 1 & 2 \\ 1 & -1 \end{Bmatrix} \begin{bmatrix} 2 & 0 \\ 0 & 1 \end{bmatrix} \begin{Bmatrix} 1 & 1 \\ 2 & -1 \end{Bmatrix} = \begin{bmatrix} 6 & 0 \\ 0 & 3 \end{bmatrix}$$

Hence the eigenvalue problem is

$$[\overline{K}]\{\phi\} = \overline{\omega}^2 [\overline{M}]\{\phi\}$$

The characteristic equations is of the form

$$\begin{bmatrix} 14 - 6\omega^2 & 4 \\ 4 & 14 - 3\omega^2 \end{bmatrix} = 0$$

$$(14 - 6\omega^2)(14 - 3\omega^2) - 16 = 0$$

From which $\omega^2 = 2.05$.

Here the first approximation 1×1 gave $\omega^2 = 2.33$ and 2×2 approximation gave $\omega^2 = 2.05$. It is indicated that the second approximation is less than that of the first. These two values are higher than the actual value. The reader is advised to check this by solving the eigenvalue problem using the polynomial form of frequency equation.

6.7.3 Component Mode Synthesis

In practice there are several systems which are very complex in nature. Branched systems, systems with number of associated components and large structures are common. It is very difficult to analyze such systems with the methods discussed in the previous sections. The component mode synthesis has been developed to analyze such systems. The general procedure of this method is that the structure is divided into a number of components, the analysis of each component being carried out separately. The effects of the associated components on the one being considered is modeled approximately. As an example, let us consider the analysis of a branched piping system. The two branches of the system are divided at the junctions. In the analysis of the side branch we may assume fixing conditions at the junctions and in the analysis of the main branch a concentrated mass spring may be allowed for the side branch. The advantage of this procedure is that the analysis is easy to carry out and the separate groups can work on the analysis and designs of components simultaneously. It is for this reason that the component mode synthesis is very popular in the analysis and design of large structural systems.

The basic formulation of the component mode synthesis is to divide the structure, which may vibrate with a circular frequency ω described by the eigen problem

$$[K]\{\phi\} = \lambda[M]\{\phi\} \tag{6.113}$$

where $\lambda = \omega^2$, into a system of connected substructures and to determine the free vibration behaviour of the entire structure from the free vibration behaviour of the individual structures. This is very advantageous when finite element discretisation of the structure is used which for large structrues often leads to a mathematical model having too many degrees of freedom to be handled easily by digital computers.

For example let us consider two substructures A and B, out of $i = 1, \ldots, N$ substructures, which are joined at the interface r. The equation of motion of the discretized structure as given in Eq. 6.113 leads to the following equations of motion

$$\begin{bmatrix} K_{11} & K_{1r} \\ K_{r1} & K_{rr} \end{bmatrix}^i \begin{Bmatrix} \phi_1 \\ \phi_r \end{Bmatrix}^i - \lambda \begin{bmatrix} M_{11} & M_{1r} \\ M_{r1} & M_{rr} \end{bmatrix}^i \begin{Bmatrix} \phi_1 \\ \phi_r \end{Bmatrix}^i = \begin{Bmatrix} 0 \\ f_r \end{Bmatrix}^i \tag{6.114}$$

$$[K]^i\{\phi\}^i - \lambda[M]^i\{\phi\}^i = f^i$$

where $[K]^i$ and $\{M]^i$ are the stiffness and mass matrices, respectively, of the ith substucture. The vectors ϕ_1^i and ϕ_r^i contain generalized displacements of the substructure index 1 for interior and the index r for interface. Similarly f_r^i contains the generalized forces acting on the interface.

This method differs depending on the assumptions concerning the displacement and forces at the interface. The fixed interface method assumes a rigid clamping at the interface for each substructure, that is $\phi_r^i = 0$, and the free interface method assumes that $f_r^i = 0$. Thus, the individual substructure modes are determined by the eigenvalue problem,

$$[K]^i\{x\}^i = \lambda^i[M]^i\{x\}^i = 0 \tag{6.115}$$

The normal modes $\{x_j\}^i$ are normalized such that

$$\{x_j\}^{iT}\{M\}^i\{x_j\}^i = 1$$

$$\{x_j\}^{iT}\{K\}^i\{x_j\}^i = \lambda_j^i \tag{6.116}$$

and the combined modal matrix $\{u\}^i$.

The dynamic behaviour of the substructures with the forces $\{f_r\}^i$ acting on the interfaces is described by a coordinate transformation relating their physical coordinates $\{\phi\}^i$ to modal coordinates $\{q\}^i$ which is given by

$$\{\phi\}^i = \{u\}^i\{q\}^i = \{u_w\}^i\{q_w\}^i + \{u_{\bar{\phi}}\}^i\{q_{\bar{\phi}}\}^i \tag{6.117}$$

The product $\{u_w\}^i\{q_w\}^i$ is the contribution of modes which are essential and belong to the lowest substructure frequencies while $\{u_{\bar{\phi}}\}\{q_{\bar{\phi}}\}$ indicates the higher ones. By introducing this assumption it is possible to treat the higher order mode shapes. The classical free-interface method by Hov completely neglects the contribution of the higher order modes whereas the basic idea of the method presented here, which was described by Criag and Chang and Schmidt, is to take into consideration the contribution $\{u_{\bar{\phi}}\}^i\{q_{\bar{\phi}}\}^i$ but to replace it by an approximation. This aproximation makes it possible to determine the lowest frequencies of the entire structure with high accuracy, without calculating the matrix $\{u_{ij}\}^i$ which requires large computational effort. The approximation is by substituting Eq. 6.117 ijn Eq. 6.114 and premultiplying it with $\{u\}^{iT}$ which results in, by the use of orthogonality condition of the eigenvectors.

$$\begin{bmatrix}\Lambda_\omega^i & 0\\ 0 & \Lambda_{\bar{\phi}}^i\end{bmatrix}\begin{Bmatrix}q_\omega^i\\ q_{\bar{\phi}}^i\end{Bmatrix} - \lambda\begin{bmatrix}I_\omega^i & 0\\ 0 & I_{\bar{\phi}}^i\end{bmatrix}\begin{Bmatrix}q_\omega^i\\ q_{\bar{\phi}}^i\end{Bmatrix} = \begin{Bmatrix}u_\omega^{iT}\\ u_{\bar{\phi}}^{iT}\end{Bmatrix}f^i \tag{6.118}$$

where the diagonal matrices of the essential and the higher eigenvalues, are

$$[\Lambda_\omega]^i = \{u_\omega\}^{iT}[K]^i\{u_\omega\}^i, \{\Lambda_{\bar{\phi}}\}^i = \{u_{\bar{\phi}}\}^{iT}[k]^i\{u_{\bar{\phi}}\}^i$$

from the lower part of equations (6.118) the vector $\{q_{\bar{\phi}}\}^i$ can be written as

$$\{q_{\bar{\phi}}\}^i = (\Lambda_{\bar{\phi}}^i - \lambda I_{\bar{\phi}})^{-1}\{u_{\bar{\phi}}\}^{iT}\{f\}^i \tag{6.119}$$

It can be assumed that the lowest eigenvalues λ are much less than the smallest value $\lambda_{\bar{\phi}}^{\min}$ of all substructure matrices $\Lambda'_{\bar{\phi}}$.

$$\lambda \ll \lambda_{\bar{\phi}}^{\min} \tag{6.120}$$

The vector $\{q_{\bar{\phi}}\}^i$ from equations (6.119) can be expressed by the approximation

$$\{q_{\bar{\phi}}\}^i \cong (\Lambda_{\bar{\phi}}^i)^{-1}\{u_{\bar{\phi}}\}^{iT}\{f\}^i \tag{6.121}$$

Pre multiplying equation (6.121) by $\{u_{\bar{\phi}}\}^i$ results in

$$\{u_{\bar{\phi}}\}^i \{q_{\bar{\phi}}\}^i \equiv \{u_{\bar{\phi}}\}^i (\Lambda_{\bar{\phi}}^i)^{-1} \{u_{\bar{\phi}}\}^{iT} \{f\}^i = \{G\}^i \{f\}^i \tag{6.122}$$

where $\{G\}^i = \{u_{\bar{\phi}}\}^i (\Lambda_{\bar{\phi}}^i)^{-1} \{u_{\bar{\phi}}\}^{iT}$ can be computed by subtracting the contribution of the essential modes from the flexibility matrix $[K^i]^{-1}$

$$\{G\}^i = \{u_{\bar{\phi}}\}^i (\Lambda_{\bar{\phi}}^i)^{-1} \{u_{\bar{\phi}}\}^{iT} = [K^i]^{-1} - \{u_\omega^i\} (\Lambda_\omega^i)^{-1} \{u_\omega\}^{iT} \tag{6.123}$$

For the rigid body modes of the structures the flexibility matrix $[K^i]^{-1}$ does not exist and an alternative formulation is to be implemented. The displacements $\{\phi\}^i$ according to Eq. 6.117 of each substructure i are replaced by the approximate $\{\bar{\phi}\}^i$ using the relations

$$\{\phi\}^i \equiv \{\bar{\phi}\}^i = \{u_\omega\}^i \{q_\omega\}^i + \{G\}^i \{f\}^i \tag{6.124}$$

The approximate $\{\bar{\phi}\}^i$ for the different substructures i are only relative and fulfill the compatibility condition for the displacements at joint interfaces. For example, for two substructures A and B the relations

$$\{\bar{\phi}_r\}^A = \{\phi_r\}^B \tag{6.125}$$

is valid. On the other hand the equilibrium condition

$$\{f_r\}^A + \{f_r\}^B = 0 \tag{6.126}$$

is true for the interface of the two substructures. From Eq. 6.124 for the displacements it follows that both conditions can only be fulfilled when, in principle, an equation of the form given below exists

$$\{f\}^i = [A]^i \{q_\omega\} \tag{6.127}$$

where the vector $\{q_\omega\} = [q^i{}_\omega]$ (6.128)

consists of all the nodal coordinates of the connected substructure. The matrix $[A]^i$ can be computed by following the procedure given in Ref. 6.15. Then it is possible to compute the force vector$\{f\}^i$ by the Eq. 6.127 which result in the approximate displacement vector.

$$\{\bar{\phi}\}^i = \{u_\omega\}^i \{q_\omega\}^i + [A]^i \{q_\omega\} = ([u_\omega^i] + [A]^i)(q_\omega)$$

$$= [\psi_\omega]^i \{q_\omega\} \tag{6.129}$$

Thus the vector $\{\bar{\phi}\}^i$ is represented by the modal coordinates $\{q_\omega\}$ by approximations which satisfy the compatibility conditions between the substructures. In addition to this matrix $[\psi_\omega{}^i]$ takes into consideration the influence of higher order mode shapes of each substucture on the dynamic behaviour of the entire structure without computing the higher mode shapes of the substructure.

For the purpose of assembling the substructures Ritz method is implemented. The total potential of the entire structure is given by

$$S = U - T \tag{6.130}$$

where

$$U = \frac{1}{2}\{\bar{\phi}^i\}^T [K^i] \{\bar{\phi}^i\}$$

$$T = \frac{1}{2}\lambda\{\bar{\phi}^i\}^T [M^i] \{\bar{\phi}^i\} \tag{6.131}$$

are the potential and kinetic energies respectively, expressed by the displacements.

$$\{\bar{\phi}^i\} = \begin{Bmatrix} \bar{\phi}_1 \\ \cdot \\ \cdot \\ \bar{\phi}^i \\ \cdot \\ \cdot \end{Bmatrix} \tag{6.132}$$

Because of the approximation for the displacements as given in Eq. (6.129) the total potential becomes a function of the modal coordinates $\{q_\omega\}$ which are not known. To obtain its minimum it requires to satisfy

$$\frac{\partial S}{\partial \{q_\omega\}} = 0 \tag{6.133}$$

which results in the reduced eigenvalue problem

$$[\tilde{K}]\{q_\omega\} - \tilde{\lambda}[M]\{q_\omega\} = 0 \tag{6.134}$$

for the total structure. The number of degrees of freedom of this reduced eigenvalue problem is equal to the sum of all essential substructure normal modes and is much less than the order of the original eigenvalue problem of Eq. 6.113. However the eigenvalues $\tilde{\lambda}$ of the reduced system are good approximations for the lowest eigenvalues λ of the total structure.

The computational effort required in this type of component mode synthesis is significantly less, especialy when several identical substructures exist. Therefore, it is very useful in the analysis of bladed disk assemblies and branched systems.

Example 6.19

Solve the branched torsional vibration problem given in Fig. 6.5 using the component mode synthesis method.

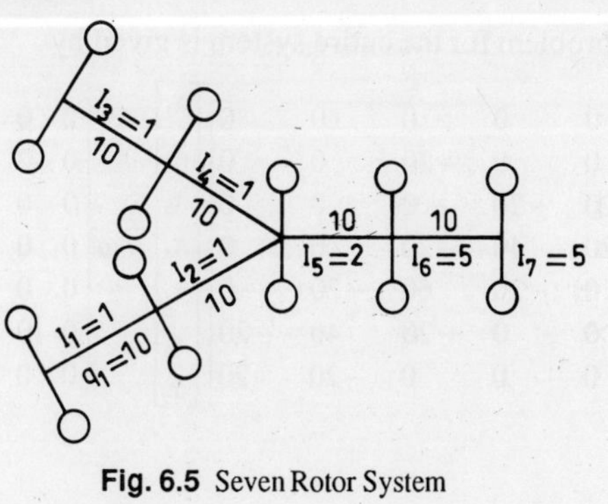

Fig. 6.5 Seven Rotor System

Solution

Let us arrest the Rotor 5 and divide the branched system into three separate systems and solve them independently.

The natural frequencies of the branches given in Fig. 6.6

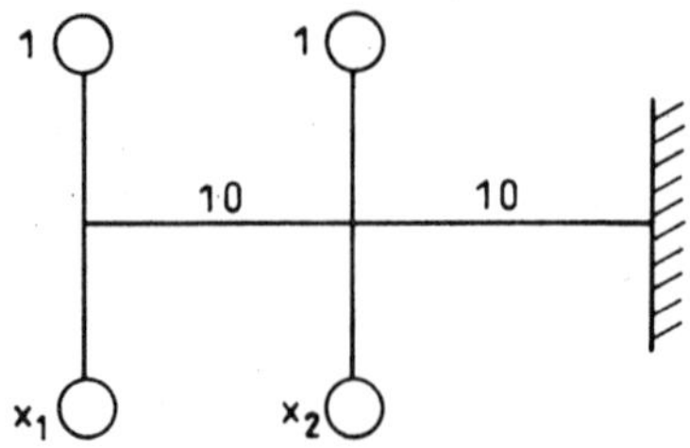

Fig. 6.6 I and II Branches

$$\begin{bmatrix} 20-2\omega^2 & -20 \\ -20 & 40-2\omega^2 \end{bmatrix} = 0$$

Hence $\omega^2 = 3.55$ and 56.4.

The ratio of displacements is given by 1 : 0.645 and 1: – 1.645
The natural frequencies for the branch shown in Fig. 6.7 are given as

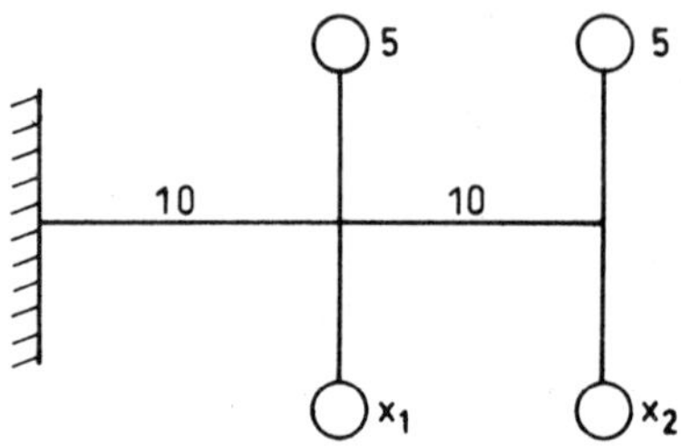

Fig. 6.7 III Branch

$$\begin{bmatrix} (40-10\omega^2) & -20 \\ -20 & 20-10\omega^2 \end{bmatrix} = 0$$

Hence $\omega^2 = 5.23$ and 0.765

The ratio of x_1 adn x_2 is given by

$$1 : 1.645 \text{ and } 1 : -0.645$$

The eigen value problem for the entire system is given by

$$\begin{bmatrix} 20 & -20 & 0 & 0 & 0 & 0 & 0 \\ -20 & 40 & 0 & 0 & -20 & 0 & 0 \\ 0 & 0 & 20 & -20 & 0 & 0 & 0 \\ 0 & 0 & -20 & 40 & -20 & 0 & 0 \\ 0 & -20 & 0 & -20 & 60 & -20 & 0 \\ 0 & 0 & 0 & 0 & -20 & 40 & -20 \\ 0 & 0 & 0 & 0 & 0 & -20 & 20 \end{bmatrix} \begin{bmatrix} x_1 \\ x_2 \\ x_3 \\ x_4 \\ x_5 \\ x_6 \\ x_7 \end{bmatrix} = \omega^2 \begin{bmatrix} 2 & 0 & 0 & 0 & 0 & 0 & 0 \\ 0 & 2 & 0 & 0 & 0 & 0 & 0 \\ 0 & 0 & 2 & 0 & 0 & 0 & 0 \\ 0 & 0 & 0 & 2 & 0 & 0 & 0 \\ 0 & 0 & 0 & 0 & 4 & 0 & 0 \\ 0 & 0 & 0 & 0 & 0 & 10 & 0 \\ 0 & 0 & 0 & 0 & 0 & 0 & 10 \end{bmatrix} \begin{bmatrix} x_1 \\ x_2 \\ x_3 \\ x_4 \\ x_5 \\ x_6 \\ x_7 \end{bmatrix}$$

Rearranging the above equation

$$\begin{bmatrix} 20 & 0 & -20 & 0 & 0 & 0 & 0 \\ 0 & 20 & 0 & -20 & 0 & 0 & 0 \\ -20 & 0 & 40 & 0 & -20 & 0 & 0 \\ 0 & -20 & 0 & 40 & -20 & 0 & 0 \\ 0 & 0 & -20 & -20 & 60 & -20 & 0 \\ 0 & 0 & 0 & 0 & -20 & 40 & -20 \\ 0 & 0 & 0 & 0 & 0 & -20 & 20 \end{bmatrix} \begin{bmatrix} x_1 \\ x_2 \\ x_3 \\ x_4 \\ x_5 \\ x_6 \\ x_7 \end{bmatrix} = \omega^2 \begin{bmatrix} 2 & 0 & 0 & 0 & 0 & 0 & 0 \\ 0 & 2 & 0 & 0 & 0 & 0 & 0 \\ 0 & 0 & 2 & 0 & 0 & 0 & 0 \\ 0 & 0 & 0 & 2 & 0 & 0 & 0 \\ 0 & 0 & 0 & 0 & 4 & 0 & 0 \\ 0 & 0 & 0 & 0 & 0 & 10 & 0 \\ 0 & 0 & 0 & 0 & 0 & 0 & 10 \end{bmatrix} \begin{bmatrix} x_1 \\ x_2 \\ x_3 \\ x_4 \\ x_5 \\ x_6 \\ x_7 \end{bmatrix}$$

Assuming a shift of $\mu = 1.0$ and rewriting $[K]$ as $[K - \mu M]$ we have

$$[K_1] = [K - \mu M] = \begin{bmatrix} 18 & 0 & -20 & 0 & 0 & 0 & 0 \\ 0 & 18 & 0 & -20 & 0 & 0 & 0 \\ -20 & 0 & 38 & 0 & -20 & 0 & 0 \\ 0 & -20 & 0 & 38 & -20 & 0 & 0 \\ 0 & 0 & -20 & -20 & 56 & -20 & 0 \\ 0 & 0 & 0 & 0 & -20 & 30 & -20 \\ 0 & 0 & 0 & 0 & 0 & -20 & 10 \end{bmatrix}$$

$$[K_1]\{\psi\} = \begin{bmatrix} 18 & 0 & -20 & 0 & 0 & 0 & 0 \\ 0 & 18 & 0 & -20 & 0 & 0 & 0 \\ -20 & 0 & 38 & 0 & -20 & 0 & 0 \\ 0 & -20 & 0 & 38 & -20 & 0 & 0 \\ 0 & 0 & -20 & -20 & 56 & -20 & 0 \\ 0 & 0 & 0 & 0 & -20 & 30 & -20 \\ 0 & 0 & 0 & 0 & 0 & -20 & 10 \end{bmatrix} \begin{Bmatrix} 1.0 & 1.0 & 0 \\ 1.0 & 1.0 & 0 \\ 0.645 & -1.645 & 0 \\ 0.645 & -1.645 & 0 \\ 0.0 & 0.0 & 1 \\ -1.0 & 1.0 & 0 \\ -1.645 & -0.645 & 0 \end{Bmatrix}$$

$$= \begin{Bmatrix} 5.1 & 50.9 & 0 \\ 5.1 & 50.9 & 0 \\ 4.51 & -82.51 & -20 \\ 4.51 & -82.51 & -20 \\ -5.8 & 45.8 & 56 \\ 2.9 & 42.9 & -20 \\ 3.55 & -26.45 & 0 \end{Bmatrix}$$

$$\{\psi\}^T [K_1] \{\psi\} =$$

$$\begin{Bmatrix} 1.0 & 1.0 & 0.645 & 0.645 & 0 & -1.0 & -1.645 \\ 1.0 & 1.0 & -1.645 & -1.645 & 0 & 1.0 & -0.645 \\ 0 & 0 & 0 & 0 & 1 & 0 & 0 \end{Bmatrix} \begin{Bmatrix} 5.1 & 50.9 & 0 \\ 5.1 & 50.9 & 0 \\ 4.51 & -82.51 & -20 \\ 4.51 & -82.51 & -20 \\ -5.8 & 45.8 & 56 \\ 2.9 & 42.9 & -20 \\ 3.55 & -26.45 & 0 \end{Bmatrix}$$

$$[\bar{K}] = \begin{bmatrix} 7.26 & -4 & 5.8 \\ -22.0 & 415.18 & 45.8 \\ -45.8 & 45.8 & 56.0 \end{bmatrix}$$

$$[\overline{M}] = \{\psi\}^T [M] \{\psi\} =$$

$$\begin{Bmatrix} 1.0 & 1.0 & 0.645 & 0.645 & 0 & -1.0 & -1.645 \\ 1.0 & 1.0 & -1.645 & -1.645 & 0 & 1.0 & -0.645 \\ 0 & 0 & 0 & 0 & 1 & 0 & 0 \end{Bmatrix} \begin{bmatrix} 2 & 0 & 0 & 0 & 0 & 0 & 0 \\ 0 & 2 & 0 & 0 & 0 & 0 & 0 \\ 0 & 0 & 2 & 0 & 0 & 0 & 0 \\ 0 & 0 & 0 & 2 & 0 & 0 & 0 \\ 0 & 0 & 0 & 0 & 4 & 0 & 0 \\ 0 & 0 & 0 & 0 & 0 & 10 & 0 \\ 0 & 0 & 0 & 0 & 0 & 0 & 10 \end{bmatrix}$$

$$\times \begin{Bmatrix} 1.0 & 1.0 & 0 \\ 1.0 & 1.0 & 0 \\ 0.645 & -1.645 & 0 \\ 0.645 & -1.645 & 0 \\ 0.0 & 0.0 & 1 \\ -1.0 & 1.0 & 0 \\ -1.645 & -0.645 & 0 \end{Bmatrix}$$

$$= \begin{bmatrix} 32.7 & 0 & 0 \\ 0 & 24.82 & 0 \\ 0 & 0 & 4 \end{bmatrix}$$

The fundamental frequency of eigenvalue problem

$$[\overline{K}] \{\phi\} = \omega^2 [\tilde{M}] \{\phi\}$$

Solving the characteristic equation

$$\omega^6 - 31\omega^4 + 218\omega^2 - 80 = 0$$

The fundamental frequency $\overline{\omega}^2$ is 0.38. Since a shift μ of 1.0 was used. Therefore the fundamental frequency ω^2 is given by

$$\omega^2 = 1 + \overline{\omega}^2 = 1 + 0.38 = 1.38$$

6.8 THE DETERMINANT SEARCH METHOD

It is often required to obtain an optimal solution for the extraction of the required eigenpairs for the problem $[k]\ \{x\} = \omega^2\ [M]\ \{x\}$ when the order of $[k]$ and $[M]$ is very large. In this section we present a detailed solution method known as the determinant search technique which is an effective method and has been extensively used in the finite element analysis.

In the finite element analysis, we are generally interested in finding the smallest eigenvalue. The determinant search technique obtains the smallest eigenvalue and corresponding eigenvector by combining and extending the Sturm sequence property of the characteristic polynomials and vector inverse iteration method.

The determinant search technique was developed with a veiw to modify and extend the techniques discussed in the earlier sections to arrive at the optimal solutions method for the smallest eigenvalue and corresponding eigenvector in the problem $[k]\{\phi\} = \lambda[M]\{\phi\}$. No transformation to the standard eigenvalue problem is required. Hence difficulties arising from ill conditioning or loss of band width due to the processes of transformation are avoided.

The determinant search technique is very effective in finite element analysis. It is more effective to employ the determinant search technique as an in-core solution technique. It calculates directly only those eigenvalues and corresponding eigenvectors that are required. In addtion, the advantage of the special characteristics of the matrices $[k]$ and $[M]$ are taken during the solution process. This method is developed for the solution of the p lowest eigenvalues and corresponding eigenvectors, but by using shift strategy. The method can be modified to calculate the largest eigenvalues and corresponding eigenvectors as required in buckling analysis. In essence, the determinant search method is effectively used for in-core solutions of small banded systems.

6.8.1 Preliminary Considerations

The use of the Sturm sequence property is basic technique to obtain an eigenvalue, whereas inverse iteration is a basic technique for extracting an eigenvector. Once an eigenvalue or an eigenvector has been calculated, the other of the pair can be easily evaluated. In the equations

$$[[k] - \lambda_i[M]]\{\phi_i\} = 0$$

if λ_i is known $\{\phi_i\}$ can be computed. If $\{\phi_i\}$ is known, the eigenvalue λ_i can be obtained by Rayleigh quotient.

Initially approximate $\{\phi_i\}$ or λ_i are known. It is required to evaluate one of the eigen pair (λ_i $\{\phi_i\}$) accurately and then to compute the other by the above condition. In a particular case where μ computed by $|\lambda_i - \mu| / |\lambda_j - \mu|$ is very small for all j where $j \neq i$, we can use inverse iteration with shift μ to calculate $\{\phi_i\}$ and accelerate convergence by using Rayleigh quotient. Shift can only be applied once the iteration vector is a close approximation to the eigenvector. In order to evaluate the eigen pairs accurately, it is required to deflate the matrix or the iteration vectors by the eigen pairs already calculated. In the case of nearly equal magnitudes the convergence is very slow. Obviously it is more effective to calculate first and approximate to the unknown eigenvalue using a polynomial iteration scheme and use inverse iteration when a shift close to the required eigenvalue has been obtained.

6.8.2 The Solution Algorithm

Let us consider two approximations μ_{k-1} and μ_k to λ_1 where $\mu_{k-1} < \mu_k \leq \lambda_1$ as indicated in the Fig. 6.8. The purpose of this algorithm is to obtain a shift near λ_1. The next shift μ_{k+1} can be computed by using

$$\mu_{k+1} = \mu_k - \eta \frac{P(\mu_k)}{P(\mu_k) - P(\mu_{k-1})}(\mu_k - \mu_{k-1}) \tag{6.135}$$

where η is a constant. If $\eta = 1$ shows a standard secant iteration in which $\mu_{k+1} \to \lambda_1$ as $k \to \infty$. Since the objective is to obtain a shift near λ_i the algorithm uses $\eta \geq 2$.

For $\eta = 2$ it is obvious that $\mu_{k+1} \le \mu_a$ where μ_a is the smallest stationary point p. Hence the iterations with $\eta = 2$ can only jump over one root which can be detected by a sign change in p. It is obvious that if λ_1 is a multiple root the iteration can still be slow. The algorithm also uses the Sturm sequence property to obtain the boundaries of the eigenvalues and cannot jump far beyond the unknown roots. If the iteration jumps over one or more unknown eigenvalues, vector inverse iteration with Gram-Schmidt orthogonalization is used to calculate accurately the eigenvalue, it may happen that before any jump occurs, two successive iterates in Eq. 6.135 do not differ any more. Therefore the last iteration is then accepted as the place at which it is required to go to inverse iteration with Gram-Schmidt orthogonalization.

The aim of the determinant search algorithm is to calculate effectively the value of $p(\lambda)$ by triangular factorisation of [$[k] - \lambda\,[M]$] into $[L]\,[D]\,[L]^T$. If unacceptable multiplier growth does occur, λ is to be changed in the algorithm and factorisation procedure is to be repeated. The triangular factorisation can be carried out without interchanges. Since the evaluation of $p(\lambda)$ is possible under stable conditions and the specific shift value should not affect the final values of the eigenvalues and eigenvectors. For any other pair (λ_{j+1}, $\{\phi_{j+1}\}$) the deflated polynomial $p(\lambda)$ can be written as

$$p_j(\lambda) = \frac{p(\lambda)}{\prod_{i=1}^{j} [\lambda - \lambda_i^{(l+1)}]} \tag{6.136}$$

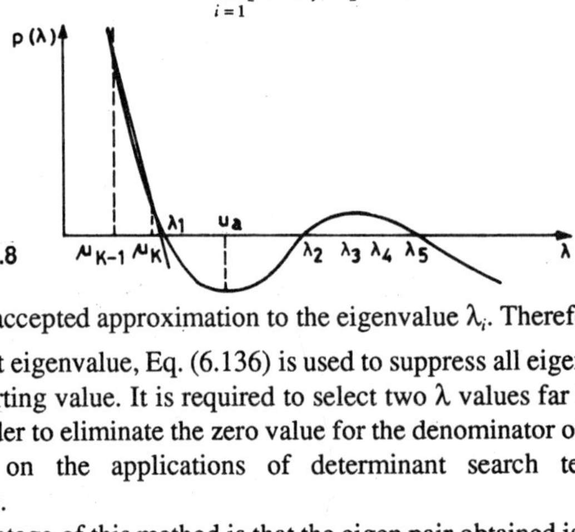

Fig. 6.8

where $\lambda_i^{(l+1)}$ is the accepted approximation to the eigenvalue λ_i. Therefore, to iterate to evaluate the next eigenvalue, Eq. (6.136) is used to suppress all eigenvalues computed from the starting value. It is required to select two λ values far from the calculated roots in order to eliminate the zero value for the denominator of Eq. (6.136). Some highlights on the applications of determinant search technique are summarized below.

1. Main advantage of this method is that the eigen pair obtained is independent of the values obtained previously. The errors involved in the earlier computed eigen pairs will not effect the accuracy of the presently obtained eigen pairs.

2. When a shift is applied to obtain the nearest eigenvalue, Gram-Schmidt orthonormalisation to all previously computed eigen vectors need not be applied. It is only required to orthonormalise the last six computed eigenvectors.

3. In practice $p(\lambda)$ can be much larger than the computer overflow. Scale factors which keep the machine independent implementation must be introduced in computing $p(\lambda)$.

4. It is required to know two lower bounds on λ_1. The first bound can be $\mu_1 = 0.0$ the other bound which is calculated by vector inverse iteration at λ is zero. If $\{x_k\}$ is the iteration vector after $(k-1)$ inverse iterations, then

$$\mu_2 = (1 - 0.01)\frac{\{x_k\}^T [k] \{x_k\}}{\{x_k\}^T [M] \{x_k\}}$$

It is possible that μ_2 can be larger than λ_1. If γ is the number of negative pivots in the triangular factorisation, then μ_2 can be divided by $\gamma + 1$ until γ equals zero.

5. It requires only a few triangular factorisations in computing each eigen pair. Hence the algorithm is efficiently used in an in-core solution process and there may be considerable number of limitations on the size of the system.

6.9 THE SUBSPACE ITERATION SCHEME

It is often required to employ an efficient algorithm for evaluating the required eigen pairs in the problem $[k]\{\phi\} = \lambda [M]\{\phi\}$ if the order of $[k]$ and $[M]$ is large. The solution technique to be employed should take advantage of the specific characteristics of $[k]$ and $[M]$. Of all the methods available, the subspace iteration method is very effective in finite element analysis applications. The technique along with Determinant Search Technique is used extensively in general purpose finite element analysis programs such as SAP, ADINA, ANSYS and NASTRAN.

The subspace iteration method is developed for the solutions of p lowest eigenvalues and corresponding eigenvectors. By using shift technique, the method can be modified to determine the largest eigenvalues and corresponding eigenvectors. This technique is very efficient in the analysis of large banded systems. The subspace iteration method is more generally applicable solution procedure for large size finite element systems.

In the eigenvalue problems when the band width of the matrices $[k]$ and $[M]$ increases, polynomial iterations are much more laborious than vector inverse iteration method. The cost of the polynomial iteration increases if operated out of core, because it involves more storage for reading and writing in a polynomial evaluation than in vector inverse iteration. If inverse iteration is operated simultaneously for all required eigenvectors, the solutions of out-of-core systems will be much more economical. In order to eliminate these problems the subspace iteration method has been designed.

The subspace iteration method operates sequentially in three steps:

1. Chosse the starting iteration vectors q such that $q > p$ where p is the number of eigenvalues and eigenvectors to be calculated.

2. Simultaneously inverse iteration is used on the q vectors. Then extract the best eigenvalue from the initial q vectors by using Ritz analysis.

3. Use the Sturm sequence to verify that the required eigenvalues and corresponding eigenvectors have been calculated after convergence.

The solution procedure is to iterate with a q-dimensional subspace and not to regard as a simultaneous iteration with q individual iteration vectors, hence the procedure is called as subspace iteration method.

6.9.1 Preliminary Considerations

The main aim of the subspace iteration method is to extract the lowest p eigenvalues and corresponding eigenvectors satisfying

$$[k]\{\phi\} = [M]\{\phi\}[\Lambda] \tag{6.137}$$

and

$$\{\phi\}^T [k] \{\phi\} = \Lambda ; \quad \{\phi\}^T [M] \{\phi\} = [I] \tag{6.138}$$

where $[\Lambda]$ = diagonal (λ_i)

$$\{\phi\} = \{\phi_1, \phi_2 \ldots\ldots \phi_p\}$$

and $[I]$ = unit matrix of order p.

It should be noted here that the elements of the diagonal $[\Lambda]$ are the eigenvalues and the vector $\{\phi\}$ stores p eigenvectors corresponding to the p eigenvalues. The relation (6.137) represents a necessary and sufficient condition for the vectors in $\{\phi\}$ to be eigenvectors. However, the orthogonality condition in (6.99) are necessary but not sufficient. For example, if there are q vectors that satisfy the condition (6.138) where $q < \eta$ then these vectors need not be eigenvectors. If the q vectors satisfy the condition (6.137) they are definitely eigenvectors, however, it is required to make sure that they are q specific eigenvectors.

The method can be explained by considering simultaneous vector inverse iteration on q vectors. Simultaneous inverse iteration equation can be written as

$$[k] \{x_{k+1}\} = [M] \{x_k\} \quad \text{where } k = 1, 2 \ldots. \tag{6.139}$$

Numericaly stability can be obtained by generating the orthogonal basis in the subspaces using the Gram-Schmidt process. The iteration equations can be written as

$$[k] \{\overline{X}_{k+1}\} = [M] \{x_k\} \tag{6.140}$$

$$\{X_{k+1}\} = \{\overline{X}_{k+1}\} [R_{k+1}] \tag{6.141}$$

where $[R_{k+1}]$ is an upper triangular matrix which is so chosen that

$$\{X_{k+1}\}^T [M] \{X_{k+1}\} = [I]$$

and we have

$$\{X_{k+1}\} \rightarrow \{\phi\}$$

$$[R_{k+1}] \rightarrow [\Lambda]$$

Equations 6.139, 6.140, and 6.141 generate the same sequence of subspaces.

6.9.2 Subspace Iteration

The subspace iteration algorithm is an orthogonal based scheme which preserves the numerical stability in the iteration and also calculates directly the eigenvectors. This method gives the iteration vectors which are in proper order. The vectors converge to $\{\phi_1\}$, $\{\phi_2\}$, ... and stored in the first, second... columns of $\{X_{k+1}\}$.

Some of the observations on the subspace iteration scheme are that $[k]$ and $[M]$ matrices of the above scheme tend towards the diagonal form as the number of iterations increase. In other words $[k]$ and $[M]$ are diagonal matrices when the columns in the vector $\{X_{k+1}\}$ are multiples of eigenvectors. If the vectors in $\{X_{k+1}\}$ are ordered in such a way that the ith diagonal element in $[\Lambda_{k+1}]$ is larger than the $(i-1)$th element, if $i = 2, \ldots, p$ then the ith column in $\{X_{k+1}\}$ converges linearly to $\{\phi_i\}$ and the convergence rate is $\dfrac{\lambda_i}{\lambda_{p+1}}$. This is an asymptotic convergence rate, and it indicates that the smallest eigenvalues converge faster. Higher convergence rate can be obtained by using q iteration vectors where $q > p$. In practice we found that $q = \min(2p, p + 8)$ is effective. The effectiveness of the algorithm is shown in the few iterations which will give good approximations to the required eigen pairs, the reason may be that the subspace iteration is nothing but Ritz analysis. All characteristics of Ritz analysis pertain also to the subspace iteration, in other words the lowest eigenvalues are approximated best in the iteration and all eigenvalue approximations are proved to be upper bounds on the actual eigenvalues sought.

6.9.3 Starting Iteration Vector

The selection of the starting iteration vectors in $\{x_i\}$ plays a very important role. If starting vectors are used that span the least dominant subspace, the iteration converges in one step, for example, if there are only p non-zero elements in the diagonal mass matrix and the starting vectors are unit vectors with the entries + 1 against the mass degrees of freedom. In this case one subspace iteration is in effect a static condensation analysis since it embodies a Ritz analysis.

In general the starting vectors that span the least dominant subspace could be selected because the mass and stiffness properties have been lumped to a sufficient degree, such lumping may not be possible for accurate stiffness and mass representation of the actual structure. Hence the starting iteration vectors should be constructed to excite those degrees of freedom with which large mass and small stiffness are associated.

Example 6.20

Calculate the first two natural frequencies of the non standard eigenvalue problem by using subspace iteration scheme. The given eigenvalue problem is of the form

$$[k]\{\phi\} = \lambda[M]\{\phi\}$$

where

$$[k] = \begin{bmatrix} 15 & -10 & & \\ -10 & 25 & -15 & \\ & -15 & 35 & -20 \\ & & -20 & 20 \end{bmatrix}$$

and
$$[M] = \begin{bmatrix} 10 & & & \\ & 20 & & \\ & & 30 & \\ & & & 40 \end{bmatrix}$$

Solution

Let us choose the initial vectors as

$$\{x^1\} = \begin{Bmatrix} 1 & 0 \\ 0 & 1 \\ 0 & 0 \\ 0 & 0 \end{Bmatrix}$$

Normalising with respect to [*M*]

$$\{x'\} = \begin{Bmatrix} \frac{1}{\sqrt{10}} & 0 \\ 0 & \frac{1}{\sqrt{20}} \\ 0 & 0 \\ 0 & 0 \end{Bmatrix}, \quad [M]\{x'\} = \begin{Bmatrix} \sqrt{10} & 0 \\ 0 & \sqrt{20} \\ 0 & 0 \\ 0 & 0 \end{Bmatrix}$$

If $[k]\{y^1\} = [M]\{x^1\}$

Then,
$$\{y^1\} = \begin{Bmatrix} \frac{2}{\sqrt{10}} & \frac{4}{\sqrt{20}} \\ \frac{2}{\sqrt{10}} & \frac{6}{\sqrt{20}} \\ \frac{2}{\sqrt{10}} & \frac{6}{\sqrt{20}} \\ \frac{2}{\sqrt{20}} & \frac{6}{\sqrt{20}} \end{Bmatrix}$$

we have
$$[\overline{M}] = \{y^1\}^T [M]\{y^1\} = \begin{bmatrix} 40 & \frac{116}{\sqrt{2}} \\ \frac{116}{\sqrt{2}} & 170 \end{bmatrix}$$

and

$$\{\overline{k}\} = \{y^1\}^T [k]\{y^1\} = \begin{bmatrix} 2 & \frac{4}{\sqrt{2}} \\ \frac{4}{\sqrt{2}} & 6 \end{bmatrix}$$

The eigenvalue problem of the 2×2 subspace is given by

$$[\overline{k}]\{\phi\} = \lambda[\overline{M}]\{\phi\}$$

Now we can write the characteristic equation of the above problem

$$[[\overline{k}] - \mu[\overline{M}]] = \begin{bmatrix} [2-40\lambda] & [(4/\sqrt{2})-(116/\sqrt{2})\lambda] \\ [(4/\sqrt{2})-(116/\sqrt{2})\lambda] & [6-170\lambda] \end{bmatrix} = 0$$

This can be written as

$$(2-40\lambda)(6-170\lambda) - \left(\frac{4}{\sqrt{2}} - \frac{116}{\sqrt{2}}\lambda\right)^2 = 0$$

From which $\lambda = 0.035$ or 1.57, and

$$\{\phi\} = \begin{bmatrix} 0.158 & 0.0246 \\ 0.016 & -0.0724 \end{bmatrix}$$

Now compute the trial vector for the second iteration

$$\{r\} = \{y^1\}\{\phi\} = \begin{Bmatrix} \frac{2}{\sqrt{10}} & \frac{4}{\sqrt{20}} \\ \frac{2}{\sqrt{10}} & \frac{6}{\sqrt{20}} \\ \frac{2}{\sqrt{10}} & \frac{6}{\sqrt{20}} \\ \frac{2}{\sqrt{20}} & \frac{6}{\sqrt{20}} \end{Bmatrix} \begin{bmatrix} 0.158 & 0.0246 \\ 0.016 & -0.0724 \end{bmatrix}$$

$$= \begin{bmatrix} 0.129 & -0.0537 \\ 0.129 & -0.0862 \\ 0.129 & -0.0862 \\ 0.129 & -0.0862 \end{bmatrix}$$

Making use of the above vector as a trial vector for second iteration repeat the same procedure. These iterations are to be carried out until we get the actual value of λ and the corresponding eigenvector.

6.10 THE LANCZOS METHOD

The generalised eigenvalue problem occurs in the finite element idealization of structural dynamics systems. The resulting equations are banded, sparse and of larger order. A good number of algorithms are presently available in literature. The Lanczos methcd is less known in structural analysis. Storage requirement for the Lanczos method is considerably less than the subspace iteration. The Lanczos algorithm has been implemented in many general purpose finite element programs. In order to satisfy the requirements of a large general purpose finite element program, it is often necessary to program an out-of-core version of the algorithm.

6.10.1 The Lanczos Algorithm

The frequency analysis of an undamped system may be expressed in a linearized eigenvalue form as

$$[k]\{X_i\} = \omega_i^2[M]\{X_i\} \tag{6.142}$$

where $[k]$ and $[M]$ are $n \times n$ symmetric positive definite or positive semi-definite stiffness and mass matrices. The parameter ω_i is the ith natural frequency and $\{X_i\}$ is the corresponding eigenvector of the mode. The matrices $[k]$ and $[M]$ are generally sparse and banded.

The stiffness matrix is transformed into Cholesky's factorisation as

$$[k] = [L][L]^T \tag{6.143}$$

where $[L]$ is the lower triangular matrix. If $[k]$ is symmetric and sparse $[L]$ will also be sparse and have the same form as $[k]$. Substituting Eq. 6.143 into Eq. 6.142 gives

$$[L][L]^T\{X\} = \omega_i^2[M]\{X\} \tag{6.144}$$

Eq. 6.144 can be written as

$$[A]\{y\} = \lambda_i\{y\} \tag{6.145}$$

where

$$\{y\} = [L]^T\{X\}$$

and

$$\lambda_i = 1/\omega_i^2$$

$$[A] = [L]^{-1}[M][L]^T$$

The eigenvectors obtained from Eq. (6.145) can be transformed to those required for the solutions of Eq. (6.142). Matrix $[A]$ can be tridiagonalised by using the transformation

$$\lambda[V]^T[V][Q] = [V]^T[A][V][Q] \tag{6.146}$$

where

$$\{V\}[Q] = \{Y\}$$

$$\{V\}^T = \{V\}^{-1} \tag{6.147}$$

and $\{V\}^T[A]\{V\} = [T]$ is a tridiagonal matrix. Eq. (6.146) is then transformed into the eigenvalue problem

$$[T][Q] = \begin{bmatrix} \alpha_1 & \beta_1 & & & & \\ \beta_1 & \alpha_2 & \beta_2 & & & \\ & \beta_2 & \alpha_3 & \beta_3 & & \\ & & & \beta_{n-1} & \alpha_n & \beta_n \end{bmatrix} [Q] = \lambda[Q] \tag{6.148}$$

Using the method of bisections and sturm sequence property Eq. (6.148) can be solved for the required number of eigenvalues. If the number of eigenvalues to be predicted is m where $m < n$, then the new eigenvalue problem is of the form

$$[T_m]\{Z\} = \lambda_i\{Z\} \tag{6.149}$$

where λ_i are the eigenvalues obtained from the truncated tridiagonal matrices. After solving the eigenvalues λ_i by the method by bisection, the eigenvectors are obtained by inverse iteration. It is required to isolate the eigenvectors corresponding to close eigenvalues by orthogonalisations.

The vector $\{V\}$ is generated such that $\{V_i + 1\}$ is orthogonal to $\{V_i\}$ and $\{V_{i-1}\}$. The vector $\{V_{i+1}\}$ is computed by modifying the Eq. (6.147) as

$$[A]\{V\} = \{V\}[T]$$

which can be expanded to give

$$[A]\{V_i\} = \beta_{i-1}\{V_{i-1}\} + \alpha_i\{V_i\} + \beta_i\{V_{i+1}\}$$

The vectors $\{V_i\}$ are selected such that $\{V_i\}^T\{V_i\} = \delta_{ij}$. The parameter δ_{ij} is known as Kronecker delta. The algorithm for obtaining α_i, β_i and $\{V_{i+1}\}$ is given as

$$\{W_i\} = [A]\{V_i\} - \beta_{i-1}\{V_{i-1}\} \quad \text{since } \beta_0 = 0$$

$$\alpha_i = \{V_i\}^T\{W_i\}$$

$$\{C_i\} = \{W_i\} - \alpha_i\{V_i\} \tag{6.150}$$

$$\beta_i = (\{C_i\}^T . \{C_i\})^{1/2}$$

$$\{V_{i+1}\} = (1/\beta_i)\{C_i\}$$

The eigenvectors obtained by the above method are required to be re-othogonalised. For this purpose we consider the operators $\{p_1\}$ $\{p_2\}$ ...... in the form

$$\{p_i\} = [I] - 2\{r_i\}\{r_i\}^T$$

$$\{r_i\}^T\{r_i\} = 1 \tag{6.151}$$

Here the first $(i - 1)$ elements of $\{r_i\}$ are zero. Initial vector $\{V_0\}$ is chosen as the first column of the unit matrix of size m. The re-orthogonalisation procedure is as follows. Consider

$$\{S_{i+1}\} = \{P_i\}\{P_{i-1}\}.....\{P_i\}\{C_i\}$$

for $\quad 1 \le i \le m$ (6.152)

$$\{P_{i+1}\}\{S_{i+1}\} = \{V_i\}\{e_{i+1}\}$$

$$\{V_{i+1}\} = \{P_1\}\{P_2\}......\{P_{i+1}\}\{e_{i+1}\}$$

where e_i = ith column of the unit matrix and $\{V_i\} = \beta_i$. The eigenvectors of $[A]$ are obtained from

$$\{V\} = \{P_1\}\{P_2\}.....\{P_m\}\begin{Bmatrix} Z \\ \hline 0 \end{Bmatrix} \tag{6.153}$$

and the eigenvectors are obtained from

$$\{X\} = [L]^T\{y\} \tag{6.154}$$

EXERCISES

6.1 Consider the eigenvalue problem $[K]\{\phi\} = \lambda[M]\{\phi\}$ where

$$[K] = \begin{bmatrix} 2 & -1 & 0 \\ -1 & 4 & -1 \\ 0 & -1 & 2 \end{bmatrix} \quad \text{and} \quad [M] = \begin{bmatrix} 1/2 & 0 & 0 \\ 0 & 1 & 0 \\ 0 & 0 & 1/2 \end{bmatrix}$$

(a) Using the characteristic polynomial, determine the eigenvalues

(b) Compute the eigenvectors by using the $[M]$ orthogonality condition of the eigenvectors.

6.2 Using the inverse iteration procedure solve for the fundamental mode and frequency of the 3-D .O.F. system for which

$$[K] = \begin{bmatrix} 2 & -1 & 0 \\ -1 & 2 & -1 \\ 0 & -1 & 2 \end{bmatrix} \quad \text{and} \quad [M] = \begin{bmatrix} 1 & 0 & 0 \\ 0 & 1 & 0 \\ 0 & 0 & 1 \end{bmatrix}$$

6.3 Consider the eigen problem

$$\begin{bmatrix} 4 & -2 \\ -2 & 2 \end{bmatrix} \{\phi\} = \lambda \begin{bmatrix} 1 & 0 \\ 0 & 1 \end{bmatrix} \{\phi\}$$

compute the eigen pairs. Then impose a shift $p = -2$ and solve again the eigen pairs.

6.4 Solve the eigenvalue problem $[K]\{\phi\} = \lambda [M]\{\phi\}$

where $$[K] = \begin{bmatrix} 2 & -1 & 0 & 0 \\ -1 & 2 & -1 & 0 \\ 0 & -1 & 2 & -1 \\ 0 & 0 & -1 & 1 \end{bmatrix} \text{ and } [M] = \begin{bmatrix} 0 & & & \\ & 2 & & \\ & & 0 & \\ & & & 1 \end{bmatrix}$$

using Forward iteration scheme.

6.5 Compute the eigen pairs of an unsupported beam whose stiffness matrix is given below, using Inverse iteration scheme.

(Hint : Use shift technique)

6.6 Calculate the eigen pairs of the system given below. Also impose a shift $p = -2$ and solve again for the eigen pairs.

$$\begin{bmatrix} 3 & -3 \\ -3 & 3 \end{bmatrix} \{\phi\} = \lambda \begin{bmatrix} 2 & 1 \\ 1 & 2 \end{bmatrix} \{\phi\}$$

6.7 Consider the problem $[K]\{\phi\} = \lambda [M]\{\phi\}$. Use the Cholesky factorisation of $[M]$ to calculate the matrix $[K^2]$ of a corresponding standard eigenvalue. Also use the spectral decomposition of $[M]$ to calculate the matrix $[K^2]$ of a corresponding standard eigen problem.

6.8 Solve the system of equations given below by using Given's method

$$\begin{bmatrix} 5 & -4 & 1 & 0 \\ -4 & 6 & -4 & 1 \\ 1 & -4 & 6 & -4 \\ 0 & 1 & -4 & 5 \end{bmatrix} \begin{Bmatrix} x_1 \\ x_2 \\ x_3 \\ x_4 \end{Bmatrix} = \begin{Bmatrix} 0 \\ 1 \\ 0 \\ 0 \end{Bmatrix}$$

6.9 Tridiagonolize the given matrix $[A]$ by Householder's method

$$[A] = \begin{bmatrix} 4 & 3 & 2 & 1 \\ 3 & 8 & 6 & 2 \\ 2 & 6 & 8 & 3 \\ 1 & 2 & 3 & 4 \end{bmatrix}$$

and solve for eigenvalues.

6.10 Making use of Gram Schmidt deflation technique compute the first two natural frequencies of the problem $[K]\{x\} = \omega^2 [M][x]$

$$[K] = \begin{bmatrix} 15 & -10 & & \\ -10 & 25 & -15 & \\ & -15 & 35 & -20 \\ & & -20 & 20 \end{bmatrix} \text{ and } [M] = \begin{bmatrix} 10 & 0 & 0 & 0 \\ 0 & 20 & 0 & 0 \\ 0 & 0 & 30 & 0 \\ 0 & 0 & 0 & 40 \end{bmatrix}$$

6.11 Compute the first three natural frequencies of the Example 6.10 by the simultaneous iterations method using the standard eigenvalue problem technique.

6.12 Calculate the first two natural frequencies of the Example 6.10 using the subspace iteration scheme.

6.13 Tridiagonolize the matrix given below using Lanczos' method.

$$[A] = \begin{bmatrix} 4 & 3 & 2 & 1 \\ 3 & 8 & 6 & 2 \\ 2 & 6 & 8 & 3 \\ 1 & 2 & 3 & 4 \end{bmatrix}$$

6.14 Using the Rayleigh quotient iteration on the problem $[A]\{\phi\} = \lambda\{\phi\}$ where $[A] = \begin{bmatrix} 2 & 0 \\ 0 & 6 \end{bmatrix}$

use the initial iteration vector $\{x_1\}$ as (*i*) $\{x_1\} = \begin{Bmatrix} 1 \\ 1 \end{Bmatrix}$ (*ii*) $\{x_2\} = \begin{Bmatrix} 1 \\ 0.1 \end{Bmatrix}$

6.15 Use the threshold Jocobi iteration method to calculate the eigen pairs of the matrix $[K]$

$$\text{where } [K] = \begin{bmatrix} 5 & -4 & 1 & 0 \\ -4 & 6 & -4 & 1 \\ 1 & -4 & 6 & -4 \\ 0 & 1 & -4 & 5 \end{bmatrix}$$

6.16 Triangularise the matrix given below using Lanczos' method.

$$[A] = \begin{bmatrix} 3 & 0 & 2 & 1 \\ 1 & 2 & 5 & 4 \\ 7 & -1 & 2 & 6 \\ 1 & -2 & 3 & 4 \end{bmatrix}$$

6.17 Triangularise the matrix given below using Lanczos' method.

$$[A] = \begin{bmatrix} 1 & 3 & 5 & 7 \\ 2 & -1 & -2 & 4 \\ 3 & 2 & 1 & 1 \\ 4 & 1 & 0 & 6 \end{bmatrix}.$$

REFERENCES

1. Bahram Nour-Omid, B.N. Parlett, and R.L. Taylor, Lanczos verses subspace iteration for solutions of eigenvalue problems, *Int. J. Num. Methods in Engg.*, Vol. 19, 1983.
2. Bathe, B.N. and E.L. Ramaswamy, An accelerated subspace iteration method, *J.Comp. Meth. Appl. Mech. Engg.*, Vol. 23, 1980.
3. Bathe, K.J. and E.L. Wilson, (1978), *Numerical Methods in Finite Element Analysis*, Prentice-Hall of India, New Delhi.
4. Chowdhury, P.C., The truncated Lanczos algorithm for partial solution of the symmetric eigen problem, *Comp. Struct.*, Vol. 8, 1976.
5. Craig, R.R. and M.C.C., Bompton, Coupling of structure for dynamic analysis, *AIAAJ.* Vol. 6, No. 7, 1968.
6. Crandall, R., (1956), *Engineering Analysis*, McGraw-Hill Book Company, New York.
7. Gupta K.K., Solutions of eigenvalue problems by the Sturm sequence method, *Int. J. Num. Methods in Engg.*, Vol. 4, 1972.
8. Jennings, A., A direct iteration method of obtaining latent roots and vectors of a symmetric matrix, *Proc. Cambs. Phi. Soc.*, Vol. 63, 1967.
9. Ojalva I.V. and M. Newman, Vibration modes of large structures by automatic matrix reduction method, *AIAA. J.* Vol. 8, 1970.
10. Parlett, B.N., (1980) *The Symmetric Eigenvalue Problem*, Prentice-Hall, Englewood Cliffs, N.J.
11. Parlett, B.N. and D.S. Scott, The Lanczos algorithm with selective orthogonalisation, *Math. Comp.* 33 (145), 1979.
12. Ramamurti, V., *Computer Aided Design in Mechanical Engineering*, Tata McGraw-Hill Publishing Limited, New Delhi.
13. Weaver, W. and D.M. Yoshida, The eigenvalue problem for banded matrices, *Comp. Structures*, Vol. 1, 1971.
14. Wilkinson, J.H., (1965), *The Algebriac Eigenvalue Problem*, Clarendon press, Oxford.
15. Wilkinson, J.H., The Q.R. Algorithm for Real Symmetric matrices with multiple eigenvalues, *Computer Journal.* Vol. 8, 1965.
16. Craig, R.R., Chang, C.J.: Substrtucuture coupling for dynamic analysis and testing. *NASA Report CR-2781*, 1977.
17. Schmidt, K.J.: Eigenschwingungsanalyse gekoppellter eleasticher Strukturen. Dissertation. Universitat Hannover, 1980. *VDI-Bericht*, Reihe 11 No. 39, 1981, pp. 1-114, *Bericht 37 des Sonderforschungsbereiches 61*, 1981, pp. 1-114.

CHAPTER 7

FINITE ELEMENT ANALYSIS

7.1 INTRODUCTION

Recent technological advances in civil, mechanical, aerospace and other engineering areas have created a need for accurate analysis of very large and complex systems. Geometric complexities, changing material properties and varieties of loading environemnts have resulted in difficulties which exceed the limitations of the mathematical methods. The development of high speed digital computers has created great interest in numerical analysis methods related to the problems of engineering. On the other hand, matrix operations have emerged in formulating many complex engineering analysis problems since they can be adapted to the operation of digial computers. Innovative studies involving the matrix concepts and exploiting the great advantages of digital computers have been made by engineers and scientists. The advanced knowledge of structural analysis using matrix methods resulted in the emergence of the finite element method and subsequent success.

Most of the structures such as frames and trusses are formed by members interconnected at joints. These members are one dimensional elements which, when connected at the joints, generate the whole structure. A general definition of the finite element method would be an analysis method which treats the structure as an assemblage of a finite number of discrete elements (members of the structure) interconnected at finite number of nodal points(joints). When this concept is applied to an elastic continuum, the number of possible elements and nodes among them becomes infinite. Hence it is required to idealize continuum into a structural system with finite and discrete number of elements. This approach and approximation is acceptable for reasonable accuracies. Therefore, any structure or a mechanical system is modeled by a mesh of finite elements and approximations are made on the behaviour of these elements so as to approximate the behaviour of the system.

Before the advent of finite element methods, the finite difference method was in practice for many years for solving structural analysis problems. Solutions of the differential equations are approximated by this method at discrete points and the resulting difference euqations describe the behaviour of the structural system. Therefore, the solution of difference equations gives the solutions to the differential equations. On the other hand, the finite element method divides the structure into discrete elements, generates the equations of equilibrium for each element, and by solving these equations obtains the behaviour of the structure.

Presently, the finite element method is widely used for the analysis of many engineering problems of static, dynamic, thermal stresses and fluid dynamics of machine components and structural systems. The technique is widely used in all branches of engineering and science. Before discussing the details of the method, let us recaptiulate the contirbutions of the pioneers in this area.

Initial concepts of the application of this method were introduced by Hrennikoff, McHenry, and Grinter. They adopted a system of one dimensional elements to solve two dimensional systems. Argyris contributed in the initial stages of the developmet of this method, by presenting a general approach to the computer analysis of structural problems. The use of two dimensional plate element in the analysis of complex structures was introduced by Turner, Clough, Martine and Topp. Clough also presented the use of traingular and rectangular plate elements for the analysis of plane stress elasticity problems. Wilson developed a computer program for solution of plane elasticity problems and subsequently other programs were developed.

The stiffness matrix for an isotropic rectangular plate of uniform thickness was developed by Melosh who also discussed the basis for obtaining the matrices for the direct stiffness method. The application of the finite element method to axially symmetric elastic solids was demonstrated by Colugh and Rasid. They also developed special stiffness matrices for axisymmetric elements. A method for calculating the displacements and stresses in axisymmetric solids of any geometry subjected to thermal and mechanical loads was presented by Wilson. Plane stress analysis with higher order elements was proposed by Tocher and Pian. They also indicated the theoretical development of the conditions to ensure the finite element displacement analysis to converge to the exact values when the element size is reduced; that is analysing with fine mesh. Later, several other concepts were developed such as automatic node labelling scheme by Aky*ü*z and Utku. Subsequently, they extended finite element method into the area of shell analysis. Adini analysed the shell structure by the FEM. The contributions of Utku, Zeinkiewicz, Meek and Ural have fully discussed the FEM and its applications in structural analysis problems, in science and engineering.

Finite element methods were employed to study the dynamic behaviour of turbine blades and other rotating machine components. Durocher and Kane investigated blade deflections with uniformly pre-twisted finite element beam model. They checked the results obtained previously with predictions from three dimensional finite element analysis. An analytical procedure based on the FEM was adopted to determine the deflections and stresses of the blades. Ramamurti and Srinivasa Murthy used a three dimensional 20 noded isoparametric finite element to analyse the rotating blade stresses for various pre-twist angles, skew angles, breadth to length ratios, and breadth to thickness ratios of the blade. These results were supported with experimental results.

Blade loading for the input forces has been investigated with a NASTRAN finite element model. Blade failures due to stresses have also been studied. With the help of elliptical equations and the successive approximate method, stresses at the boundary of blade have been predicted. Simple formulae and nomograms are available for the determination of bending moment components. A computer program has been developed for the three dimensional stress analysis of a blade using FEM.

Several studies are carried out on vibration analysis using finite element methods. Leissa highlighted the advantages and disadvantages of beam theory, plate theory and shell theory with numerical results. In most recent articles FEM has been used to solve blade vibration problems. The dynamic strength of a group of blades has been investigated by considering the blade as a beam model. The effect of root radius, setting angle and tip mass of a rotating beam have been taken itno consideration in the finite element model. Thomas and Sanbunch extended finite element analysis to the behaviour of rotating pre-twisted blades of asymmetric cross section. Vibrational characteristics of the blades were improved using NASTRAN program. Abbas, B.A.H. pointed out the variations due to transverse shear deformations and rotary inertia in his dynamic analysis of thick pre-twisted blades. Bucco, D. and Mazumdar implemented a simple and powerful tool to determine the frequencies of shallow shells. A superparametric shell element is useful to predict the vibrational characteristics of a real blade. Yorgicogh studied a substructure technique for composite rotor blades. The dynamic response of blades with a weighted edge has been analysed for different end conditions and radii of curvature with the help of curved cylindrical finite elements. Using a substructure technique, forced vibration analysis has been carried out for rotating structures subjected to arbitrary forces as a series of rotating forces.

The application and accuracy of the energy method and transmissibility method have been studied by Sheng, C. and Mosimenn. Forced vibrational aspects of rotating blades have been studied using Lagranges equation. The effects of various parameters on dynamics of blades have been carried out using Ritz method, Reissner's variational pricniple, modified lower bound method and Trefftz method.

Leissa and others implemented shallow shell theory and the Ritz method for the analysis of rotating blade vibration. The potential energy method has been extended to analyse blade vibrations. The superiority of the Reissner method was inidcated; speed of rotation, shear deformations, rotary inertia and stagger angle were accounted for.

Vibrational behaviour of turbine blades has been investigated by using a transfer matrix. Experimental and analytical results were also obtained for blades with shrouds by varying the number of blades in a group, the method of connection, geometrical tolerance and centrifugal foce. FEM in combination with transfer matrix method was ued by Chiatti and Sestieri to study the free vibration of turbine blades.

Flexural vibration of the blade was studied by treating it cantilever beam. The discretization technique has been formulated by Downs for blade vibration and compared with other techniques. Wood brought out a new mathematical tool, the boundary integral technique to investigate blade vibration. He also incorporated torsional stiffness, warping stiffness, and shear centre coordinates. The causes of gyroscopic forces and damping have been reported from beam analysis. It was observed that coriolis acceleration due to gyroscopic motion of spinning rotors is creating new regions of instability.

A simple and very efficient method for obtaining the fundamental frequency of blades was presented by Hodges from the composite expansion technique. Leissa and Lee used a numerical integration technique to solve the shallow shell analysis of baldes. They also summarized the effects of rotational inertia, coriolis acceleration, variable curvature and thickness and arbitrary quadrilateral plaenform. Rao, J.S. examined the free and forced vibrations and resonant stresses of rotating blades.

7.2 THEORETICAL BACKGROUND

The concept of the FEM is the idealisation of a continuum by an articulated system for which matrix methods of analysis are directly applicable. In general there are two approaches associated with this method.

(a) The force method is the one which assumes the internal forces as the unknowns of the problem. Using the equilibrium equations, the governing equations are generated and then other equations which are required to obtain the solution are developed. Comaptible conditions are introduced.

(b) The displacement method assumes the displacements of the nodes as the unknowns of the problem. Compatibility conditions are mainly satisfied in this approach. Then the governing equations in terms of nodal displacements are computed for each node using the conditions of equilibrium. The theoretical justification of this method is shown by the use of the principle of minimum potential energy.

The main difference between force and displacement FEM approaches are in the selection of the unknowns and the variations in the associated matrix quantities in the formulation. However, the displacement FEM is simpler from the point of view of its formulation for a majority of engineering problems.

The development of the required matrix quantities for the Finite Element Analysis (FEA) can be automated by the computer programs. The generation of the element stiffness and mass matrices is on the basis of continuum mechanics. The resulting equations are combined and solved by the theory of matrices.

The routine followed to implement the FEM to a particular problem is given below. Each part of this routine will be fully explored and discussed in this chapter.

(1) Idealisation of the physical system. This requires the selection of the type of element and its size to generate the mesh of the problem.
(2) Generation of stiffness and mass matrix quantities for the element in the element local coordinates.
(3) Assembling the element stiffness and mass matrices to develop the global stiffness and mas matrices of the total system.
(4) Determination of the nodal displacements of the system by solving the set of simultaneous linear equations obtained using the equilibrium conditions at the nodal points.
(5) Computations of stress and strains associated with the problem.

Usually the accuracy and effectivenss of the method depends on the type and number of elements used in the mesh generation. Based on the geometry and nature of the structure and loading system, the type element to be implemented in the analysis must be decided. The most widely used elements are beam element, traingular flat element, quadrilateral element, eight noded and twenty noded isoprarametric element, conical segment, tetrahedron, hexahedron, traingular torus, quadrilateral torus, curved shell traingular and curved rectangle. The selection of a particular element or combination of elements will greatly depend on the competence and experience of the analyst. The traingular element is more useful to model any complex system with various types of boundary conditions and the theory is comparatively simple. In FEM the concepts of stiffness, nodal displacements and nodal forces are used. In the analysis of linear elastic structures, the above concepts are analogous to member stiffness matrices, joint displacement and joint forces. Another important aspect of this method is the need for compatibility at the boundaries of adjoining elements. This can be achieved only by assuming proper displacement function for the element.

The displacement approach is applied to many areas of engineering such as the analysis of plates, shells, solids, structure dams, foundations, ship-stability, fluid flow, heat transfer, dynamics, stress concentration, tunnels, fracture mechanics and rock and soil mechanics.

7.2.1 Energy Principle

All the relations in the FEM which are developed for the solution of problems essentially are required to obey the energy principle. It is very much apprarent that the sum of the product of all the displacements and corresponding load components must be equal to the sum of the product of all strains and corresponding stresses. In other words they must represent the true external and internal work related to the system. An idalisation is required since the distributed loads at the boundaries of the element are replaced by equivalent loads applied at the nodes.

The total potential energy of the system must include four components representing four distinct contributions

$$V = U - U_F - U_R - U_S \tag{7.1}$$

where V is the total potential energy of the system, U the internal strain energy, U_F potential energy due to body forces, U_R the potential energy due to nodal forces and U_S the potneital energy due to surface traction.

If the system under consideration for analysis fulfils the internal and external equilibrium, then for any small variation in the displacement, the additional external work introduced must be equal to the resulting internal work. Hence the variation in the total potential energy $d(V)$ must be equal to zero.

$$d(V) = d[U - U_F - U_R - U_S] = 0 \tag{7.2}$$

The total potential energy of the system indicated in the equation (7.2) must have a stationary value and for the equilibrium condition, this value is a minimum. The displacement approach of FEM obeys the principle of minimum potential energy. In other words all displacement expressions must satisfy all displacement boundary conditions and the condition of equilibrium, to make the total potential energy minimum. Another important identity is that the potential energy V of the system is a function of the nodal displacements, and the partial derivative of this quantity with respect to the displacements is zero.

$$\frac{\partial V}{\partial \delta_1} = \frac{\partial V}{\partial \delta_2} = \cdots \frac{\partial V}{\partial \delta_n} = 0 \tag{7.3}$$

The expression (7.3) will provide the basic equilibrium equations. The same energy principle can be applied to develop the element stiffness matrix which will be discussed in the following sections.

7.2.2 Convergence Criteria

The validity and effectiveness of the FEM greatly depends on how best the aproximate solution converges to the exact solution. To ensure convergence to the corect results certain simple requirements must be satisfied.

(1) The displacement within an element must be continuous. Along the boundaries of adjacent elements displacement compatibility must exist. The first part of the above statement can be obtained by the appropriate choice of the continuous polynomials as the general displacement functions. The second part can be prevented by random and independent displacement of adjacent elements at their boundaries.

(2) The displacement fields assumed must have the capability to maintain a state of constant strain. This is requried for an infinitesimal element whose strain approaches a constant value.

(3) The displacement fields assumed must be capable of rigid body motion. This will ensure all the nodes of an element to go through similar displacements.

The analysis of more complex problems require that the above three conditions are satisfied for a careful consideration of the displacement function and the type and size of the finite element.

7.2.3 Adaptability

The finite element analysis is based on the principle of total potential energy using a variation of the Ritz method. The main diference between the Ritz procedures and the finite element method for the solution of stationary value problems lies in the type of functions used in their operations. The Ritz method used smooth displacement functions to describe the behaviour of the entire system whereas the finite element method uses displacement functions for each element of the system. One of the important advantages of this method is its ability to describe a continuous media by discrete, interconnected finite elements of different shapes. Hence, two and three dimensional structural continuum can be idealised into an articulated system which can be analysed using standard structural analysis procedures.

7.2.4 General Formulation of the FEM

Consider a plane stress problem using the constant strain traingular element, such as a thin plate in pure tension in x-y coordinate plane as shown in Fig.7.1. The pltate is divided into number of traingular elements interconnected at the nodal points. For illustration purposes let us consider a coarse mesh gneneration. Since the object under consideration is a plate, the nodes have only two degrees of freedom, namely displacements in the x and y directions.

(a) The unknowns of this method are the displacements of the nodes.

$$\{\delta\}_E = \begin{Bmatrix} \delta_i \\ \delta_j \\ \delta_m \end{Bmatrix} \tag{7.4}$$

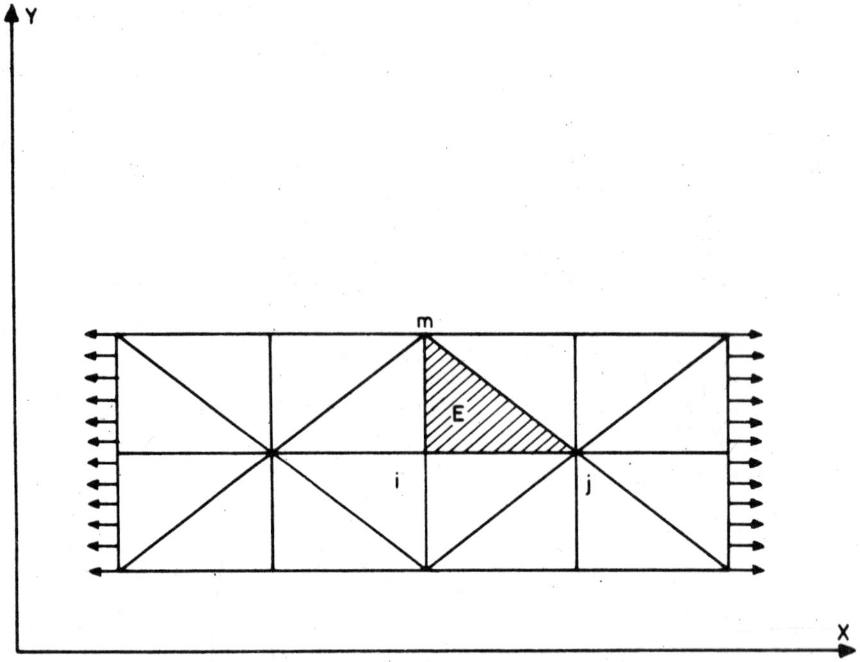

Fig. 7.1

The subscript E denotes the element E, the subscripts i, j and m denote the nodes associated with the element E. Each node has two degrees of freedom, given by

$$\{\delta_i\} = \begin{Bmatrix} u_i \\ v_i \end{Bmatrix} \tag{7.5}$$

where u is the displacement in the x direction and v is the displacement in the y direction. By substituting equation (7.5) in the equation (7.4) node-displacement matrix is generated.

(b) Usually it is essential to assume general displacement exrpessions as functions of nodal dispalcements to describe the behaviour of the elements, as

$$\{\phi\} = \begin{Bmatrix} u(x, y) \\ v(x, y) \end{Bmatrix} \tag{7.6}$$

where $u(x, y)$ and $v(x, y)$ describe the displacement at any point of the element. The nature of the displacement function must be compatible with the type of elements used. The displacement functions in the case of a constant strain traingular element are linear. These functions must also satisfy the displacement compatibility of the adjoining elements at their boundaries. The unknown coefficients of the assumed functions are to be determined by matrix operations.

(c) The process of determination of nodal displacements will result in the computations of the necessary strains in the elements. Each nodal point has three strain components,

$$\{\varepsilon\} = \begin{Bmatrix} \varepsilon_x \\ \varepsilon_y \\ \gamma_{xy} \end{Bmatrix} \tag{7.7}$$

The relations between the displacements and the resulting strains based on the theory of elasticity principles, are given by

$$\{\varepsilon\} = \begin{Bmatrix} \dfrac{\partial u}{\partial x} \\ \dfrac{\partial v}{\partial y} \\ \dfrac{\partial v}{\partial y} + \dfrac{\partial v}{\partial x} \end{Bmatrix} \tag{7.8}$$

It is clear from Eq. (7.8) that a constant strain triangular element should have a linear displacement function associated with it. Strain displacement relation is given by the matrix equation

$$\{\varepsilon\} = [B]\ \{\delta\} \tag{7.9}$$

(d) From the strain values obtained, the computations of stresses in the elements can be carried out using the elastic-strain relations. There are three stress components at any point of an element

$$\{\sigma\} = \begin{Bmatrix} \sigma_x \\ \sigma_y \\ \tau_{xy} \end{Bmatrix} \tag{7.10}$$

By the elasticity transformation matrix, the stress strain relation is written as

$$\{\sigma\} = [D] \quad \{\varepsilon\} \tag{7.11}$$

where $[D]$ is an elasticity matrix containing the material properties given by

$$[D] = \frac{E}{1-\nu^2} \begin{bmatrix} 1 & \nu & 0 \\ \nu & 1 & 0 \\ 0 & 0 & \dfrac{1-\nu}{2} \end{bmatrix} \tag{7.12}$$

(e) The principal stresses are of the form

$$\sigma_{\max} = \frac{\sigma_x + \sigma_y}{2} + \sqrt{\left(\frac{\sigma_x - \sigma_y}{2}\right)^2 + \tau_{xy}^2}$$

$$\sigma_{\min} = \frac{\sigma_x - \sigma_y}{2} - \sqrt{\left(\frac{\sigma_x - \sigma_y}{2}\right)^2 + \tau_{xy}^2} \tag{7.13}$$

The solution of the finite element method depends on the accuracy in determining the unknown nodal displacements. The basic equation used to solve the static analysis problems is

$$\{Q\} = [K]\ \{\delta\} \tag{7.14}$$

where $\{Q\}$ is the equivalent vector which is obtained by lumping the element and edge loads at the nodes, $[K]$ is the global stiffness matrix of the system and $\{\delta\}$ is the unknown nodal displacement vector. The global stiffness matrix is obtained by the assembly of individual element stiffness matrices. Rearranging equation (7.14) will directly result in the displacements

$$\{\delta\} = [K]^{-1}\{Q\} \tag{7.15}$$

The detailed procedure of each step is discussed in the following sections.

7.3 PLANE STRESS AND PLANE STRAIN ANALYSIS

The finite element analysis idealizes a plane stress system by a set of connected elements on which the stiffness matrix method of structural analysis can be applied directly. It is desirable to obtain results in a most general form applicable to any situation. The first successful application of this method was the two dimensional elasticity problems. The general relations will be illustrated with a very simple example of plane stress analysis of a thin plate. It is divided into triangular elements as shown in Fig.7.1. Since they have been widely used because of their ability to define boundaries with relative ease and moreover, exrpessions related to them are simple compared to any other element. The strains in these elements are constant hence they are considered as constant strain triangular elements. Perfect continuity between the elements exists since they are constant strain elements.

A typical finite element is defined by nodes and straight line boundaries. The displacements at any point within the element can be defined by a column vector which are functions of position and represent nodal displacements for a particular element. This will result only in straight line displacements. The loads acting on the structure are replaced by staticially equivalent concentrated loads applied at the nodes of the structure.

In the plane stress and plain strain analysis, the displacement function is uniquely defined by displacement u and v in x and y directions respectively. In the plane stress case the state of stress is defined only by the stress components σ_x, σ_y and τ_{xy} in the x, y and z coordinate system. The analysis of the thin plate is carried out under uniform tensile load as a plane stress problem. In the plane strain case the state of strain is defined by the strain components ε_x, ε_y and v_{xy} in the x, y and z coordinates.

In the case of plane stress analysis, by definition, all other components of stress are zero and therefore give no contribution to internal work. In plane strain analysis, the stress in perpendicular direction to xy plane is not zero, but the strain by definition in that direction is zero and hence there is no contribution to internal work by this stress.

Finally the plane stress and plane strain analysis follow the same logic in their procedure. The only difference will be in the elasticity matrix $[D]$ which gives the stress-strain relation. In this chapter the analysis of two dimensional ealsticity problem using constant strain triangular elements is presented.

7.3.1 Theoretical Development of the Method

The constant strain triangular element shown in Fig.7.2 is considered here, with nodes i,j, m numbered in an anti-clockwise order. The unknowns are the nodal dislacements $\{\delta\}$. Each node will have two degress of freedom; one in x-direction and the other in y-direction, given by

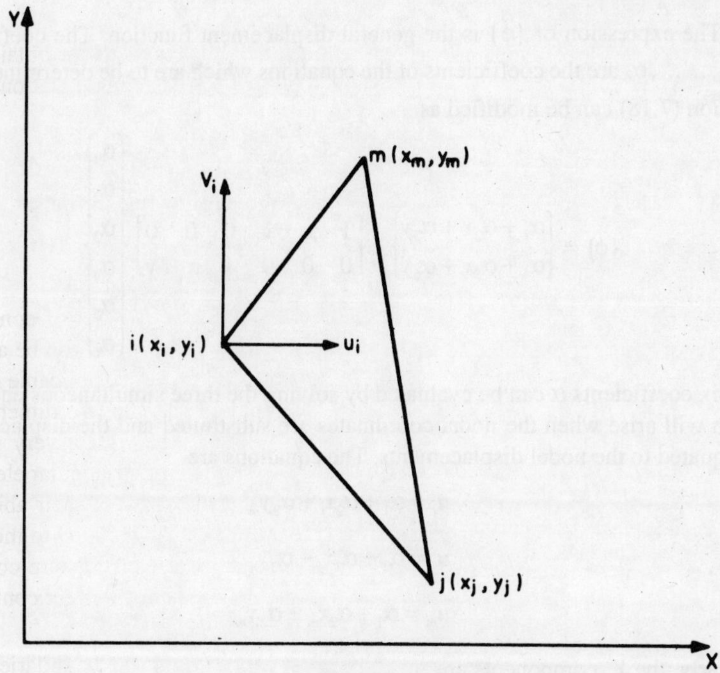

Fig. 7.2

$$\{\delta_i\} = \begin{Bmatrix} u_i \\ v_i \end{Bmatrix} \tag{7.16}$$

Since there are three nodes and each node has two degrees of freedom, the six components of element displacements can be represented as a vector

$$\{\delta\}^e = \begin{Bmatrix} \delta_i \\ \delta_j \\ \delta_m \end{Bmatrix} = \begin{Bmatrix} u_i \\ v_i \\ u_j \\ v_j \\ u_m \\ v_m \end{Bmatrix} \tag{7.17}$$

The X components are represented by u and Y components are represented by v.

This method requires the assumption of a general displacement function for the nodal displacements. The displacements of all the points of the element have to be uniquely defined by these six values. The functions have to be linear functions which are represented by two linear polynomials.

$$\{\phi\} = \begin{Bmatrix} u(x, y) \\ v(x, y) \end{Bmatrix} = \begin{Bmatrix} \alpha_1 + \alpha_2 x + \alpha_3 y \\ \alpha_4 + \alpha_5 x + \alpha_6 y \end{Bmatrix} \tag{7.18}$$

It is obvious that since the partial derivatives of the displacement function and constant strain triangles are used, the two displacement functions have to be linear.

The expression of $\{\phi\}$ is the general displacement function. The coefficients $\alpha_1, \alpha_2, \ldots\ldots, \alpha_6$ are the coefficients of the equations which are to be determined. The equation (7.18) can be modified as

$$\{\phi\} = \begin{Bmatrix} \alpha_1 + \alpha_2 x + \alpha_3 y \\ \alpha_4 + \alpha_5 x + \alpha_6 y \end{Bmatrix} = \begin{bmatrix} 1 & x & y & 0 & 0 & 0 \\ 0 & 0 & 0 & 1 & x & y \end{bmatrix} \begin{Bmatrix} \alpha_1 \\ \alpha_2 \\ \alpha_3 \\ \alpha_4 \\ \alpha_5 \\ \alpha_6 \end{Bmatrix} \tag{7.19}$$

The six coefficients α can be evaluated by solving the three simultaneous equations which will arise when the nodal coordinates are substituted and the displacements are equated to the nodal displacements. The equations are

$$u_i = \alpha_1 + \alpha_2 x_i + \alpha_3 y_m$$

$$u_j = \alpha_1 + \alpha_2 x_j + \alpha_3 y_m$$

$$u_m = \alpha_1 + \alpha_2 x_m + \alpha_3 y_m \tag{7.20}$$

Similarly the Y-components are

$$v_i = \alpha_4 + \alpha_5 x_i + \alpha_6 y_i$$

$$v_j = \alpha_4 + \alpha_5 x_j + \alpha_6 y_i \tag{7.21}$$

$$v_m = \alpha_4 + \alpha_5 x_m + \alpha_6 y_m$$

Using matrix notation, Equation 7.20 is written as

$$\begin{Bmatrix} u_i \\ u_j \\ u_m \end{Bmatrix} = \begin{bmatrix} 1 & x_i & y_i \\ 1 & x_j & y_j \\ 1 & x_m & y_m \end{bmatrix} \begin{Bmatrix} \alpha_1 \\ \alpha_2 \\ \alpha_3 \end{Bmatrix} \tag{7.22}$$

Then we have

$$\begin{Bmatrix} \alpha_1 \\ \alpha_2 \\ \alpha_3 \end{Bmatrix} = \begin{bmatrix} 1 & x_i & y_i \\ 1 & x_j & y_j \\ 1 & x_m & y_m \end{bmatrix}^{-1} \begin{Bmatrix} u_i \\ u_j \\ u_m \end{Bmatrix} \tag{7.23}$$

We obtain finally

$$u = \frac{1}{2A}\{(a_i + b_i x + c_i y)u_i + (a_j + b_j x + c_j y)u_j + (a_m + b_m x + c_m y)u_m\} \tag{7.24}$$

where

$$a_i = x_i y_m - x_m y_j$$

$$b_i = y_j - y_m = y_{im}$$

$$c_i = x_m - x_j = x_{mj} \tag{7.25}$$

By a cyclic operation of subscripts in the order, the other coefficients can be obtained and

$$2\Delta = \det\begin{bmatrix} 1 & x_i & y_i \\ 1 & x_j & y_j \\ 1 & x_m & y_m \end{bmatrix} = 2 \text{ area of the triangle ijm} \tag{7.26}$$

Similarly we also can obtain the vertical displacements

$$v = \frac{1}{2A} \{(a_i + b_i x + c_i y)v_i + (a_j + b_j x + c_j y)v_j + (a_m + b_m x + c_m y)v_m\} \tag{7.27}$$

In order to express the general displacement functions $\{\phi\}$ in a simpler form, we define the following quantities,

$$N_i = (a_i + b_i x + c_i y)$$

$$N_j = (a_j + b_j x + c_j y)$$

$$N_m = (a_m + b_m x + c_m y) \tag{7.28}$$

and from Eqs. (7.24) and (7.27) we obtain

$$u = \frac{1}{2A} (N_i u_i + N_j u_j + N_m u_m)$$

$$v = \frac{1}{2A} (N_i v_i + N_j v_j + N_m v_m) \tag{7.29}$$

Substituting the expressions in Eqs. (7.29) in (7.18) we have

$$\{\phi\} = \begin{Bmatrix} u \\ v \end{Bmatrix} = \frac{1}{2A} \begin{bmatrix} N_i u_i & + & N_j u_j & + & N_m u_m \\ N_i v_i & + & N_j v_j & + & N_m v_m \end{bmatrix} \tag{7.30}$$

which can be written as

$$\{\phi\} = \begin{Bmatrix} u \\ v \end{Bmatrix} = \frac{1}{2A} \begin{bmatrix} N_i & 0 & N_j & 0 & N_m & 0 \\ 0 & N_i & 0 & N_j & 0 & N_m \end{bmatrix} \begin{Bmatrix} u_i \\ v_i \\ u_j \\ v_j \\ u_m \\ v_m \end{Bmatrix} \tag{7.31}$$

In the most general form

$$\{\phi\} = \tfrac{1}{2A} [N_i] \{\delta_i\} \tag{7.32}$$

where the matrix $[N]$ is the position matrix. The nodal displacements vary linearly all along the sides of the triangle, with identical displacements at the nodes. Hence the same displacement will appear along the interface. Therefore the displacement continuity is ensured between adjacent elements.

The strains at any point in the element can be expressed as functions of the general displacement Eq. (7.32). The three components of the strains which can contribute to internal work can be defined as

$$\{\varepsilon\} = \begin{Bmatrix} \varepsilon_x \\ \varepsilon_y \\ \nu_{xy} \end{Bmatrix} = \begin{Bmatrix} \dfrac{\partial u}{\partial x} \\ \dfrac{\partial v}{\partial y} \\ \dfrac{\partial u}{\partial y} + \dfrac{\partial v}{\partial x} \end{Bmatrix} \tag{7.33}$$

Substituting the values of u and v from the Eq. (7.29) we will get

$$\frac{\partial u}{\partial x} = \frac{\partial}{\partial x} \quad (N_i u_i + N_j u_j + N_m u_m) \quad \frac{1}{2A}$$

$$= \left(\frac{\partial N_i}{\partial x} . u_i + \frac{\partial N_j}{\partial x} . u_j + \frac{\partial N_m}{\partial x} . u_m \right) \frac{1}{2A} \tag{7.34}$$

we have

$$\frac{\partial N_i}{\partial x} = \frac{\partial}{\partial x} (a_i + b_i x + c_i y) = b_i \tag{7.35}$$

$$\frac{\partial N_j}{\partial x} = \frac{\partial}{\partial x} (a_j + b_j x + c_j y) = b_j$$

and

$$\frac{\partial N_m}{\partial x} = b_m \tag{7.36}$$

Hence

$$\frac{\partial u}{\partial x} = \frac{1}{2A} \quad (b_i u_i + b_j u_j + b_m u_m) \tag{7.37}$$

In the same way

$$\frac{\partial v}{\partial y} = \frac{1}{2A} \quad (c_i v_i + c_j v_j + c_m v_m) \tag{7.38}$$

can be obtained and the expression $\dfrac{\partial u}{\partial y}$ and $\dfrac{\partial v}{\partial x}$ can be expressed as

$$\frac{\partial u}{\partial y} + \frac{\partial v}{\partial x} = \frac{1}{2A} \quad (c_i u_i + b_i v_i + c_j u_j + b_j v_j + c_m u_m + b_m v_m) \tag{7.39}$$

Hence the expressions for strains can be represented by

$$\{\varepsilon\} = \begin{Bmatrix} \varepsilon_x \\ \varepsilon y \\ \nu_{xy} \end{Bmatrix} = \frac{1}{2A} \begin{bmatrix} b_i & 0 & b_j & 0 & b_m & 0 \\ 0 & c_i & 0 & c_j & 0 & c_m \\ c_i & b_i & c_j & b_j & c_m & b_m \end{bmatrix} \begin{Bmatrix} u_i \\ v_i \\ u_j \\ v_j \\ u_m \\ v_m \end{Bmatrix} \tag{7.40}$$

In the most general form, strain displacement relation is given by

$$\{\varepsilon\} = [B]\,\{\delta\} \tag{7.40A}$$

where $[B]$ is the coefficient matrix. Here the matrix is independent of its position within the element, hence the strains are constant throughout the element.

Besides the strains $\{\varepsilon\}$, there are others which are independent of stress, which may be due to several causes such as shrinkage, crystal growth, temperature changes and will result in an initial strain vector. The initial strains can be represented in matrix form as

$$\{\varepsilon_0\} = \begin{Bmatrix} \varepsilon_{x0} \\ \varepsilon_{y0} \\ \nu_{xy0} \end{Bmatrix} \tag{7.41}$$

This initial strain may depend on the position within the element, and may be defined by the average constant values. This is consistent with the strain conditions in the element.

In an isotropic material element in the plane stress problem when it is subjected to a temperature rise of $\theta°$ with a thermal expansion coefficient α, we have

$$\{\varepsilon_0\} = \begin{Bmatrix} \alpha\theta \\ \alpha\theta \\ 0 \end{Bmatrix} \tag{7.42}$$

since thermal dilation causes no shear strains. In the case of plane strain there is possibility of developing stresses perpendicular to x-y plane even without the main stress components. Therefore the strains will be effected because of elastic constants, which can be represented as

$$\{\varepsilon_0\} = (1+\nu)\begin{Bmatrix} \alpha\theta \\ \alpha\theta \\ 0 \end{Bmatrix} \tag{7.43}$$

where ν is the Poisson's ratio. To obtain the total strains, the initial strains are to be added algebraically to the strains, as

$$\{\varepsilon_{total}\} = \{\varepsilon\} + \{\varepsilon_0\} + \{\varepsilon_T\} \tag{7.44}$$

where ε_T is the strain due to temperature variations.

Materials of special properties such as anisotropic nature will have different thermal expansion coefficient in two mutually perpendicular directions. If x' and y' of Fig.7.3 show the principal directions of the material, the initial strain due to thermal expansions in the plane stress coordinates, are

$$\{\varepsilon'_0\} = \begin{Bmatrix} \varepsilon'_{x0} \\ \varepsilon'_{y0} \\ \nu'_{xy0} \end{Bmatrix} = \begin{Bmatrix} \alpha_1\theta \\ \alpha_2\theta \\ 0 \end{Bmatrix} \tag{7.45}$$

where α_1 and α_2 represents the thermal expansion coefficients in x′ and y′ directions respectively. It is required to transform these strains into the x–y system by a transformation matrix say $[T]$. Consequently

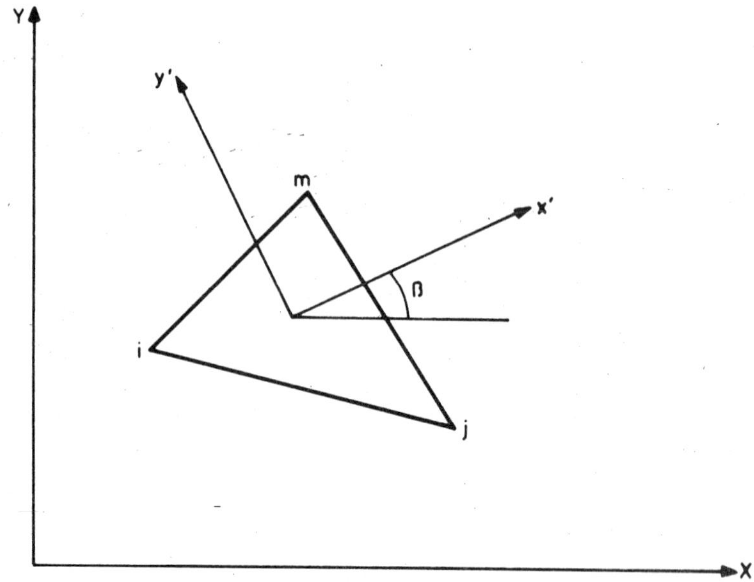

Fig. 7.3

$$\{\varepsilon'_0\} = [T]^T \{\varepsilon_0\} \tag{7.46}$$

The matrix $[T]$ can be obtained as

$$[T] = \begin{bmatrix} \cos^2\theta' & \sin^2\theta' & -2\sin\theta'\cos\theta' \\ \sin^2\theta' & \cos^2\theta' & 2\sin\theta'\cos\theta' \\ \sin\theta'\cos\theta' & -\sin\theta'\cos\theta' & \cos^2\theta' - \sin^2\theta' \end{bmatrix} \tag{7.47}$$

where θ' is the angle defined in Fig.7.3.

The general stress expression is related to strains of the element by a transformation matrix $[D]$ known as the elasticity matrix

$$\{\sigma\} = \begin{Bmatrix} \sigma_x \\ \sigma_y \\ \tau_{xy} \end{Bmatrix} = [D] \begin{bmatrix} \begin{matrix} \varepsilon_x \\ \varepsilon_y \\ v_{xy} \end{matrix} & - & \{\varepsilon_o\} \end{bmatrix} \tag{7.48}$$

In the case of plane stress in an isotropic material the stress strain relations are given by

$$\varepsilon_x = \frac{\sigma_x}{E} - \frac{\nu\sigma_y}{E} + \varepsilon_{x0}$$

$$\varepsilon_y = \frac{\sigma_y}{E} - \frac{\nu\sigma_x}{E} + \varepsilon_{y0} \tag{7.49}$$

$$\mathrm{v}_{xy} = \frac{2(1+\nu)}{E}\tau_{xy} + \mathrm{v}_{xy0}$$

Solving the set of equations given in Eq. 7.49 the elasticity matrix [D] can be obtained as

$$[D] = \frac{E}{1-\nu^2}\begin{bmatrix} 1 & \nu & 0 \\ \nu & 1 & 0 \\ 0 & 0 & \dfrac{(1-\nu)}{2} \end{bmatrix} \tag{7.50}$$

where E is the modulus of elasticity and ν is the poisson's ratio. In the case of plane strain, with isotropic materials there exists a normal component of stress in addition to other components. Including the thermal expansion we have the relations as

$$\varepsilon_x = \frac{\sigma_x}{E} - \frac{\nu\sigma_y}{E} - \frac{\nu\sigma_z}{E} + \alpha\theta$$

$$\varepsilon_y = \frac{\sigma_y}{E} - \frac{\nu\sigma_x}{E} - \frac{\nu\sigma_z}{E} + \alpha\theta \tag{7.51}$$

$$\gamma_{xy} = \frac{2(1+\nu)}{E}\tau_{xy}$$

$$\varepsilon_z = 0 = \frac{\sigma_z}{E} - \frac{\nu\sigma_x}{E} - \frac{\nu\sigma_y}{E} + \alpha\theta$$

by eliminating σ_z and solving for the other three components, we have the elasticity matrix as follows

$$[D] = \frac{E(1-\nu)}{(1+\nu)(1-2\nu)}\begin{bmatrix} 1 & \dfrac{\nu}{(1-\nu)} & 0 \\ \dfrac{\nu}{(1-\nu)} & 1 & 0 \\ 0 & 0 & \dfrac{(1-2\nu)}{2(1-\nu)} \end{bmatrix} \tag{7.52}$$

For an anisotropic material, to define the stress-strain relation in three dimensional case requires twenty-one independent elastic constants. In the case of two dimensional stress-strain relations it requires only six independent constants in the $[D]$ matrix. This is because of the symmetry of properties. The $[D]$ matrix can be written as

$$[D] = \begin{bmatrix} d_{11} & d_{12} & d_{13} \\ 0 & d_{22} & d_{23} \\ S_{ym} & 0 & d_{33} \end{bmatrix} \tag{7.53}$$

for a two dimensional system.

The finite element analysis with displacement approach uses the nodal displacements as unknowns of the problem. The linear equations generated by satisfying the equilibrium conditions at the nodes are to be solved to determine the displacements. The potential energy of the system can be expressed as

$$V = U - U_F - U_R - U_S \tag{7.54}$$

For each element U can be represented as

$$U = \frac{1}{2}\int_{v} \{\varepsilon\}^T \{\sigma\} dv \tag{7.55}$$

If the Eq. (7.48) is substituted in Eq. (7.55), we have

$$U = \frac{1}{2}\int_{v} \{\varepsilon\}^T [D] \{\varepsilon\} dv \tag{7.56}$$

The energy due to body forces (U_F) is

$$U_F = \int_{v} \rho\{\phi\}^T (F) dv \tag{7.57}$$

where $\{F\}$ is the body forces of the system, ρ the mass density of the elastic body and $\{\phi\}$ the displacement function. The external nodal force contributes potential energy which can be expressed as

$$U = \{\delta\}^T \{R\} \tag{7.58}$$

where $\{\delta\}$ is the nodal displacements and $\{R\}$ is the external nodal forces at nodes.

The surface forces yield potential energy U_s which can be expressed as

$$U_s = \int_{\text{area}} \{\phi\}^T \{S\} dA \tag{7.59}$$

where $\{\phi\}$ is the general displacement function and $\{S\}$ is surface traction. Substituting the value of $\{\phi\}$ from the Eq. (7.32) in Eq. (7.59) we have

$$U_s = \int_{\text{area}} \frac{1}{2A} \{\delta\}^T [N]^T \{S\} dA \tag{7.60}$$

Substituting all these energies from Eqs. (7.56) to (7.60) in the Eq. 7.54

$$V = \frac{1}{2}\int_{v} \{\varepsilon\}^T [D] \{\varepsilon\} dv - \int_{v} \rho\{\phi\}^T \{F\} dv - \{\delta\}^T \{R\} - \int_{\text{area}} \frac{1}{2A} \{\delta\}^T [N]^T \{S\} dA \tag{7.61}$$

If the entire structure is divided into n elements for the analysis, then it is required to sum up the energies of all these elements. Hence the total potential energy can be expressed by the Eqs. (7.32) and (7.40A) as

$$V = \sum_{1}^{n} \left[\frac{1}{2}\int_{v} \{\delta\}^T [B]^T [D] [B] \{\delta\} dv - \int_{v} \frac{1}{2A} \rho\{\delta\}^T [N]^T \{F\} dv \right.$$
$$\left. - \{\delta\}^T \{R\} - \int_{\text{area}} \frac{1}{2A} \{\delta\}^T [N]^T \{S\} dA \right] \tag{7.62}$$

The nodal displacements are independent of x and y hence it can be taken out of the integrals of the Eq. 7.62. Thus it can be written as

$$V = \sum_{1}^{n} \left[\frac{1}{2}\{\delta\}^T \int_{v} [B]^T [D] [B] \{\delta\} dv \{\delta\} - \{\delta\}^T \int_{v} \frac{\rho}{2A} [N]^T \{F\} dv \right.$$
$$\left. - \{\delta\}^T \{R\} - \{\delta\}^T \int_{\text{area}} \frac{1}{2A} [N]^T \{S\} dA \right] \tag{7.63}$$

Last three terms of the expression (7.63) represent the total loading system of the structure which can be denoted as $\{Q\}$ and is given by

$$Q = \sum_{1}^{n} \int_{v} \frac{\rho}{2A} [N]^T \{F\} dv + \{R\} + \int_{\text{area}} \frac{1}{2A} [N]^T \{S\} dA \tag{7.64}$$

The expression (7.63) can be simplified by using the identity (7.64) as

$$V = \frac{1}{2} \{\delta\}^T \int_{v} [B]^T [D] [B] dv \{\delta\} - \{\delta\}^T \{Q\} \tag{7.65}$$

The integral $\int_v [B]^T [D] [B] dv$ is defined as the stiffness matrix $[k]$ of an element. That is

$$[k] = \int_{v} [B]^T [D] [B] dv$$

Assembling the stiffness matrices of elements result in the global stiffness matrix of the system, which will usually be denoted as $[K]$

$$[K] = \sum_{1}^{n} [k] \tag{7.67}$$

Substituting Eqs.7.67 in 7.65 we have

$$V = \frac{1}{2} \{\delta\}^T [K] \{\delta\} - \{\delta\}^T \{Q\} \tag{7.68}$$

According to the principle of minimum potential, the Eq. (7.68) yields a condition

$$[K]\{\delta\} = \{Q\} \tag{7.69}$$

which represents a set of equilibrium equations for a static problem. By solving them using any static problem solution techniques given in Chap. 2 of this book the nodal displacements $\{\delta\}$ can be obtained. The strains can be computed by Eq. (7.40A) and the stresses can be computed by Eq. (7.48).

This is the schematic procedure for the logical development of the finite element method using a constant strain triangular element to the plane stress problem.

7.3.2 The Stiffness Matrix

The total stiffness matrix of any system is defined in Eq. (7.67) of the previous section as

$$[K] = \sum_{1}^{n} [k]$$

where $[k]$ is the stiffness matrix of one element and is defined in the general relationship in Eq. (7.66) as

$$[K] = \int_v [B]^T [D] [B] dv$$

Since the matrices $[B]$ and $[D]$ are independent of the coordinates x and y, the above equations can be written as

$$[k] = \int_v \ [B]^T [D] [B] t dx dy \tag{7.70}$$

where t is the thickness of the element and the integration is taken over the area of the triangle. The stiffness matrix given in Eq. (7.70) can be put in the following form

$$[k] = \begin{bmatrix} k_{ii} & k_{ij} & k_{im} \\ k_{ji} & k_{jj} & k_{jm} \\ k_{mi} & k_{mj} & k_{mm} \end{bmatrix} \tag{7.71}$$

where each element is a 2×2 matrix expressed in the general expression,

$$[k_{ij}] = [B_i]^T [D] [B_j] .t. \text{ area} \tag{7.72}$$

Hence the expression (7.70) can be modified as

$$[k] = [B_i B_j B_m]^T [D] [B_i B_j B_m] .t. \text{ area} \tag{7.73}$$

If the matrix operations are carried out, it results in a 3×3 matrix for the element stiffness $[k]$ as indicated

$$[k] = \begin{bmatrix} [B_i]^T [D] [B_i] & [B_i]^T [D] [B_j] & [B_i]^T [D] [B_m] \\ [B_j]^T [D] [B_i] & [B_j]^T [D] [B_j] & [B_j]^T [D] [B_m] \\ [B_m]^T [D] [B_i] & [B_m]^T [D] [B_j] & [B_m] [D] [B_m] \end{bmatrix} .[t. \text{ area}] \tag{7.74}$$

The total stiffness matrix of a system can be obtained by assembling the individual stiffness matrices of the elements properly. This is illustrated in the following example.

Consider a structure which is divided into two elements as shown in Fig.7.4. The stiffness matrix of the first element is obtained from Eq. (7.71) as

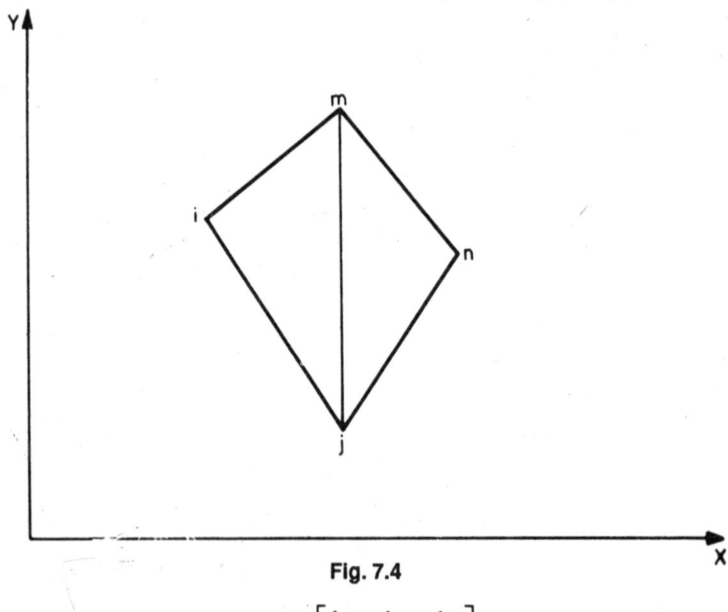

Fig. 7.4

$$[k_1] = \begin{bmatrix} k_{ii} & k_{ij} & k_{im} \\ k_{ji} & k_{jj} & k_{jm} \\ k_{mi} & k_{mj} & k_{mm} \end{bmatrix}$$

and for the second element as

$$[k_2] = \begin{bmatrix} k_{nn} & k_{nm} & k_{nj} \\ k_{mn} & k_{mm} & k_{mj} \\ k_{jn} & k_{jm} & k_{jj} \end{bmatrix}$$

Total stiffness matrix of the two elements can be obtained by assembling properly

$$[k] = \begin{matrix} \\ i \\ j \\ n \\ m \end{matrix} \begin{matrix} \begin{matrix} i & \quad j & \quad n & \quad m \end{matrix} \\ \begin{bmatrix} k_{ii}^1 & k_{ij}^1 & 0 & k_{im}^1 \\ k_{ji}^1 & k_{jj}^1 + k_{jj}^2 & k_{jn}^2 & k_{jm}^1 + k_{jm}^2 \\ 0 & k_{nj}^2 & k_{nn}^2 & k_{nm}^2 \\ k_{mi}^2 & k_{mj}^1 + k_{mj}^2 & k_{mn}^2 & k_{mm}^1 + k_{mm}^2 \end{bmatrix} \end{matrix}$$

Here superscript indicates the element number.

The global stiffness matrix of the structure $[K]$ with two triangular elements is a square, symmetric and postive-definite matrix. In the finite element analysis the solution of the system can be obtained by one of the methods discussed in Chap. 2 under static analysis solution techniques.

In most of the mechanical engineering problems, the stiffness matrix is of banded nature. The bandwidth of the stiffness matrix mainly depends on the geometry of the structure, discretisation and the way the nodes are numbered. If the stiffness matrix is banded, the computer storage requirement is only $n \times b$ where n is the size of the matrix and b is the bandwidth. It can be shown that the time required for the solution of such problems varies approximately as the square of the bandwidth of the matrix. Hence it is essential to reduce the bandwidth of these matrices.

7.3.3 Storage Reduction Techniques

The problem of solving large systems of linear equations with sparse-symmetric, positive-definite coefficient matrices is very important in many areas of engineering. Efficient storage and solution strategies are required in order to minimise the computer storage and solution time. It becomes more important in problems where the system is solved by iterative procedures. This is extremly important in microcomputers where the core limitations are very severe.

The first successful method is very widely used is the Cuthill-McKee (CM) algorithm [12]. Once the adjacent array and a starting node has been found, the starting node must be numbered as node 1. Subsequently, all adjacent nodes should be numbered in increasing order. Thereafter, choose the next node in sequence adjacent to the numbered nodes. Continue the procedure until all the nodes are numbered.

The problem with this method is finding a starting node, the storage and work involved in setting up the adjacent array can be extremely large. The storage for higher order elements can well exceed the size of the stiffness matrix. To find a starting node, Ref. 12 suggests trying all nodes whose degree satisfy.

$$D_{\min} \le D \le D_{\max} + (n/m)^* D_{\max} \text{ with } n = 1 \text{ and } m = 2 \qquad (7.75)$$

and choosing the scheme that gives the minimum bandwidth.

As storage schemes changed from banded to profile, the emphasis changed to profile minimisation. It was found that a simple change to the CM algorithm improved it profile without affecting in bandwidth properties. This modification was done to merely reverse the numbering that resulted from the original algorithm. This scheme was named as Reverse Cuthill-McKee (RCM) algorithm. Reference 8 indicates a comparision of the two methods.

Another more recent method is the Minimum Degree (MD) algorithm. It is an improvement over the graph theory approach. This method uses the nodal degree and the matrix structure in choosing the numbering. By updating the element structure, consistent with its change as a result of each step of the elimination processes of the newly numbered nodes, further use of the structure is considered. The CM method was improved by George and McIntyre. Their approach was to generate a spanning tree for the matrix from an arbitrary node of minimum degree. Then they use the last level of that tree as a starting node. This method is based on an equation solver that utilizes all zero terms of the matrix. The storage for renumbering is not constant but increases as the algorithm progresses.

A method based on searching a spanning tree of the graph of a matrix was very recently proposed by Gibbs *et al.* (GPS). This algorithm starts by finding the pseudo perpheral nodes which are at maximum distance from each other by setting up their spanning trees. The algorithm generates the final minimum spanning tree with the help of spanning tree of the two nodes and graph theory. Finally the nodes are numbered in the structure. The algorithm starts with peripheral node of least degree and orders the nodes level by level, according to increasing degree. Since they use the adjacent structure of the R.C.M. algorithm, the storage is the main drawback. The final spanning tree may not be optimal one because of the starting node. It has been proved that this method is several times faster than the R.C.M. method yet its storage requirement is too large.

The Frontal method was developed by Irons 2 to avoid the problem of large storage demands. This method is mainly based on the assembly of the equations for each element at a time, and reducing the degrees of freedom for which equations are completed. As a result, the entire matrix need not be stored at a time. Hece the storage requirement is greatly reduced but the complexity of the computer implementation may be higher. This method requires a shift from nodal numbering to element numbering. The efficiency of this method depends on the correctness of the element numbering used. The frontal method adds nodes to the front of the element basis and then removes those whose equations are complete. This process consists of removing those nodes in the front with minimum degree. The graph structure is still present but not becomes a combination of an element and nodal level structure. It is apparent that the optimum numbering is controlled by the front and not by the graph structure. Hence the frontal structure indicates the order for nodal numbering.

The Profile-Front Minimisation (PFM) method is developed by satisfying the core storage requirements to accomplish the renumbering to be as small as possible, with the nodal renumbering sequence identical to the frontal technique. The Frontal method is an element based concept, in which the data structure must contain the initial element nodal connectivity. It is also required to find all the elements connected to a given node. Hence there are two sets of arrays in the data structures. The first set is the element connectivity stored in compact form and its pointer array. The second set is the list of elements connected to each node. This is also stored in a compact form with a pointer array. This proves to be the smallest possible for elements with four or more nodes as shown in Fig. 7.5.

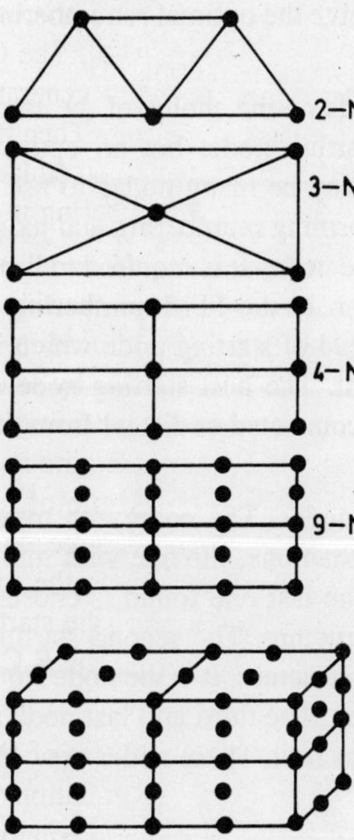

EXAMPLE	ELEMENT TYPE	NUMBER OF ELEMENTS	STORAGE FOR CONNECTIVITY DATA RCM	MD	PEM
	2–NODE	7	19	55	40
	3–NODE	4	21	44	33
	4–NODE	4	49	64	45
	9–NODE	4	289	148	101
	27–NODE	4	2883	420	202

Fig. 7.5

The numbering depends on an element and then on nodal basis. In the first step all the nodes of an element are added to the front. In the second step all the nodes with complete equations are given new numbers and removed from the front. Finally the next element is added to the front and the process is repeated. In the algorithm the procedure is as given below:

(1) Add all the nodes of the elements connected to the starting node to the front.

(2) With the next available number, all the completed nodes are to be numbered. Remove all completed nodes from the front. Quit if there are no nodes left in the front.

(3) Next element is to be chosen to add to the front. (a) Pick the element that completes the most nodes in the front but adds the minimum number of new nodes to the front. (b) In case of a tie choose the element with the least weighted element degree. (c) If there is still a tie, use first element found.

(4) Repeat the steps (2) and (3).

The effectiveness of this method is that, it provides direct connection between the physical structure and the optimum order to perform the Gaussian elimination procedure. The profile equation solver is more effective if the frontal elimination order is implemented to number the nodes which will give the optimal renumbering scheme for the profile solver.

The success of all renumbering algorithms depends on the choice of the starting node. There are several ways of choosing a starting node, but an optimal method is yet to be found. For every problem there may be many nodes to use a starting node, but the best one can be obtained by performing reumbering and judging. In order to avoid the work involved in trying all the nodes it is required to limit the number of starting nodes to a manageable number. In the PFM numbering it can be seen that the starting element is important instead of starting node which is only a pointer for the first element to add to the front. The best starting node is apparent in most of the cases as the one which is least connected or distant from the centre for the structure.

The Global Weight method gives three starting nodes. The node with minimum global degree is the first node. If there is more than one, the one with minimum nodal degree is chosen. If still more than one, the last one found is chosen. The first node is now used as root to form a level structure. The second starting node is chosen from the last level of this primary level structure. It is the node from that level which has minimum nodal and global degrees. The third and last node is found from a level structure formed with second node as root. These nodes are considered for the third node.

This approach generates three most distinct and unconnected nodes present in the structure. These are the nodes used as starting nodes. The optimum starting node out of the three can be obtained by generating the profiles. The best one generates the minimum profile. In the case of a tie the one with minimum bandwidth is considred.

7.4 AXISYMMETRIC STRESS ANALYSIS

7.4.1 Introduction

The problem of stress analysis of axisymmetric solids or bodies of revolution under axisymmetric loading is of practical interest. A spherical solid is an axisymmetric structure which has the z-axis as its axis of symmetry. Let us consider a vertical section of a sphere cut by a plane passing through the origin. The sphere may be loaded uniformly by gravity forces. As it is symmetric by its geometry and by its loads about the z-axis each internal point will have two degrees of freedom for displacements, the two directions being radial and vertical. The radial and vertical coordinates, given by *r* and *z*, respectively, are related to x-y coordinates of the plane stress analysis discussed in the previous section. Obviously the axisymmetric solids can be treated in a similar manner as in two dimensional plane stress problem. A triangular element can be used in the mesh for the structure.

In the plane stress problem the elements are in a plane and their interconnections at nodal points occur in the same planar surface, whereas in the axisymmetric case the elements, lie in the three dimensional space. The elements are of triangular torus, whose cross section at any point will be a plane triangle. The nodal points in the plane stress analysis problem will be points in that plane whereas the nodal points of an axisymmetric traingular element will be circumferential lines. Hence the mathematical formulation to develop the element stiffness matrix will natrually be very complex. An integration procedure must be implemented to satisfy the calculation along the circumferential boundary lines. The stresses will exist only in the x and y directions of a plane stress elasticity problem. The radial displacements will develop circumferential strains which will induce stresses in the same direction. Hence in axisymmetric formulations circumferential stress and strains must be considered.

In the idealisation of the axisymmetric system, triangular form of elements are preferred because they are capable of simulating complex surfaces and are also relatively simple for computation. It is also noted that the finite element procedure is the same for both the cases except for the computation of element stiffness matrix and load matrix. In the finite element approximation of axisymmetric solids, the continuous structure is replaced by a system of axisymmetric element interconected at circumferential joints or nodal circles. Figure 7.6 illustrates a finite element idealisation of a typical axisymmetric solid. Equilibrium equations in terms of unknown nodal circle displacements are developed at each nodal circle. Solution of this set of equations constitutes a solution to the system.

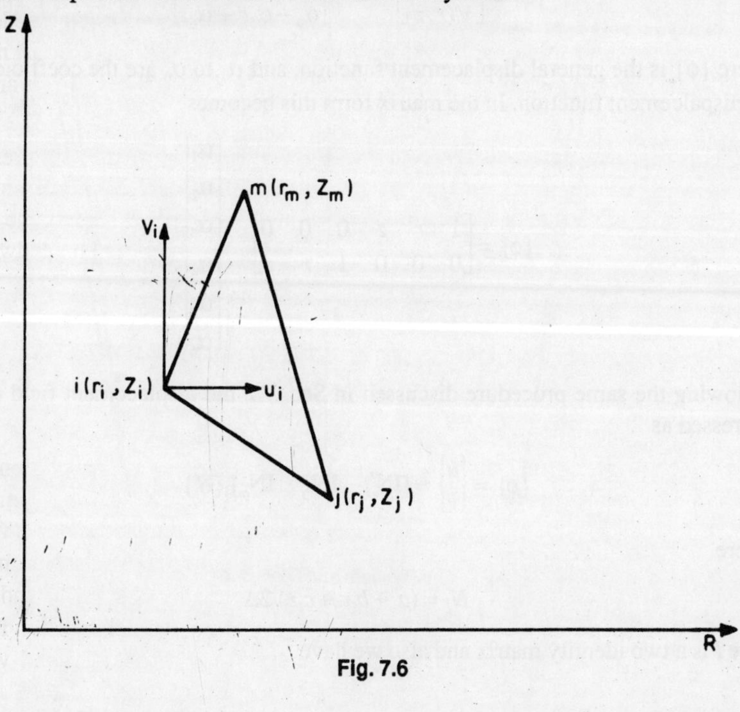

Fig. 7.6

There are many advantages of this method when compared to other numerical approaches. Complex bodies such as bodies of composite materials are easily represented. Since anisotropic materials are automatically included in the formulation, filament structures are easily handled. Displacement or stress boundary conditions may be specified at any nodal circle. Arbitrary thermal, mathematical and accelerational loads are possible. It has been proved that this method converges to the exact solution if the number of elements are increased.

7.4.2 Axisymmetric Analysis Procedure

Consider an axisymmetric triangular element with i, j, m nodes, numbered in the anticlockwise direction, assuming two degrees of freedom per node. The radial displacement is expressed by u and the vertical displacement by v to be compatible with the displacement assumptions of the plane stress analysis. Figure 7.6 shows the nodes and their degrees of freedom. The nodal displacements $\{\delta\}$ are the unknowns of the problem. A triangular axisymmetric element will possess six degrees of freedom, given by

$$\{\delta\} = \begin{Bmatrix} \delta_i \\ \delta_j \\ \delta_m \end{Bmatrix} = \begin{Bmatrix} U_i \\ \theta_i \\ U_j \\ U_m \\ \theta_m \end{Bmatrix} \tag{7.76}$$

The general displacement function to describe the element behaviour is similar to the expression given in Eq. (7.18) which is

$$\{\phi\} = \begin{bmatrix} U(r,z) \\ V(r,z) \end{bmatrix} = \begin{Bmatrix} \alpha_1 + \alpha_2 r + \alpha_3 z \\ \alpha_4 + \alpha_5 r + \alpha_6 z \end{Bmatrix} \tag{7.77}$$

where $\{\phi\}$ is the general displacement function, and α_1 to α_6 are the coefficients of the dispalcement function. In the matrix form this becomes

$$\{\phi\} = \begin{bmatrix} 1 & r & z & 0 & 0 & 0 \\ 0 & 0 & 0 & 1 & r & z \end{bmatrix} \begin{Bmatrix} \alpha_1 \\ \alpha_2 \\ \alpha_3 \\ \alpha_4 \\ \alpha_5 \\ \alpha_6 \end{Bmatrix} \tag{7.78}$$

Following the same procedure discussed in Sec. 7.2 the displacement field can be expressed as

$$\{\phi\} = \begin{Bmatrix} u \\ v \end{Bmatrix} = [\text{I}N'_i \quad \text{I}N'_j \quad \text{I}N_m]\ \{\delta^e\}$$

where

$$N'_i = (a_i + b_i r + c_i z)/2\Delta \tag{7.79}$$

Here I is a two identity matrix and also we have

$$a_i = r_j z_m - r_m z_j$$

$$b_i = z_j - z_m = z_{jm}$$

$$c_i = r_m - r_j = r_{mj} \tag{7.80}$$

The element strains $\{\varepsilon\}$ can be derived from the displacement polynoimals and also as a direct relation of radial displacements. It is to be noted that a fourth strain component, the circumferential strain (ε_θ) is also to be considered in the axi-symmetric analysis. The strains can be defined as follows

$$\{\varepsilon\} = \begin{Bmatrix} \varepsilon_r \\ \varepsilon_z \\ \varepsilon_\theta \\ \nu_{rz} \end{Bmatrix} = \begin{Bmatrix} \dfrac{\partial u}{\partial r} \\ \dfrac{\partial \theta}{\partial z} \\ \dfrac{u}{r} \\ \dfrac{\partial u}{\partial z} + \dfrac{\partial \theta}{\partial r} \end{Bmatrix} \tag{7.81}$$

Using the displacement functions defined in Eqs. (7.79) and (7.80) we have

$$\{\varepsilon\} = [B]\{\delta\}^e = [B_i \quad B_j \quad B_m]\{\delta\}_e \tag{7.82}$$

in which

$$[B_i] = \frac{1}{2\Delta}\begin{bmatrix} 0 & c_i \\ b & 0 \\ \dfrac{a_i}{r} + b_i + \dfrac{c_i z}{r} & 0 \\ c_i & b_i \end{bmatrix} \tag{7.83}$$

It is to be noticed that the matrix $[B]$ of Eq. (7.82) includes the coordinates r and z. Therefore the strains will not be constant as is the case in the plane stress analysis of two dimensional problems when $\varepsilon_\theta = u/r$ is constant, and hence we can treat the strains in the axisymmetric analysis to be constant. This is only possible if u and r are proportional to each other. Once the $\{\delta\}$ is established, we can compute the element strains by Eq. 7.82.

In some practical situations such as stratified anisotropy, which often arises in laminated or fibreglass components of machines and structural members, initial strains may be due to temperature. In general there are about four independent components of strains possible. We have the strain vector as

$$\{\varepsilon_0\} = \begin{Bmatrix} \varepsilon_{z0} \\ \varepsilon_{r0} \\ \varepsilon_{\theta 0} \\ \gamma_{z0} \end{Bmatrix} \tag{7.84}$$

Even though these strains are variable within the element, for easy calculations one can take the initial strains as constant. The initial strains most frequently encountered will be due to the thermal expansion. From isotropic material we shall have

$$\{\varepsilon_o\} = \begin{Bmatrix} \alpha\theta \\ \alpha\theta \\ \alpha\theta \\ 0 \end{Bmatrix} \tag{7.85}$$

where θ is the temperature rise in an element and α is the coefficient of thermal expansion. In the case of a stratified material, the plane of isotropy is normal to the axis of symmetry. The two different expansion coefficients possible are α_z in axial direction and α_r which is normal to it. Now the initial strain vector will become

$$\{\varepsilon_0\} = \begin{Bmatrix} \alpha_z\theta \\ \alpha_r\theta \\ \alpha_r\theta \\ 0 \end{Bmatrix} \tag{7.86}$$

The strain is related to stress by the elastic matrix $[D]$. The strains $\{\varepsilon\}$ and the stresses $\{\sigma\}$ can be represented in the standard form

$$\{\sigma\} = \begin{Bmatrix} \sigma_z \\ \sigma_r \\ \sigma_\theta \\ \tau_{rz} \end{Bmatrix} = [D]\,[\{\varepsilon\} - \{\varepsilon_o\}] \tag{7.87}$$

For an anisotropic stratified material the z-axis representing the normal to the planes of stratification, ignoring the initial strains for convenience, we can write the stress-strain relations as

$$\begin{aligned} \varepsilon_z &= \frac{\sigma_z}{E_2} - \frac{\nu_2\sigma_r}{E_2} - \frac{\nu_2\sigma_\theta}{E_2} \\ \varepsilon_r &= -\frac{\nu_2\sigma_z}{E_2} + \frac{\sigma_r}{E_1} - \frac{\nu_1\sigma_\theta}{E_1} \\ \varepsilon_\theta &= -\frac{\nu_2\sigma_z}{E_2} + \frac{\sigma_\theta}{E_1} - \frac{\nu_1\sigma_r}{E_1} \\ \gamma_{zr} &= \frac{\tau_{zr}}{G_2} \end{aligned} \tag{7.88}$$

Defining $E_1/E_2 = n$ and $G_2/E_2 = M$, and solving for the stresses and substituting Eq. (7.88), we get

$$[D] = \frac{E_2}{(1+\nu_1)(1-\nu_1-2n\nu_1^2)} \begin{Bmatrix} 1-\nu^2 & n\nu_2(1+\nu_1) & n\nu_2(1+\nu_1) & 0 \\ 0 & n(1-n\nu_2^2) & n(\nu_1+n\nu_1^2) & 0 \\ 0 & 0 & n(1-n\nu_2^2) & 0 \\ \textit{symmetric} & 0 & 0 & m(1+\nu_1)(1-\nu_1-2n\nu_2^2) \end{Bmatrix} \tag{7.89}$$

For an isotropic material, as a special case, we can derive the $[D]$ matrix by taking $E_1 = E_2 = E$ or $n = 1$ and $\nu_1 = \nu_2 = \nu$ and using the relation of elastic constants

$$\frac{G_2}{E_2} = \frac{G}{E} = m = \frac{1}{2(1+\nu)}$$

Substituting in Eq. (7.89) we can obtain

$$[D] = \frac{E(1-\nu)}{(1+\nu)(1-2\nu)} \begin{bmatrix} 1 & \dfrac{\nu}{1-\nu} & \dfrac{\nu}{1-\nu} & 0 \\ 0 & 1 & \dfrac{\nu}{(1-\nu)} & 0 \\ \textit{symmetric} & 0 & 1 & 0 \\ 0 & 0 & 0 & \dfrac{1-2\nu}{2(1-\nu)} \end{bmatrix} \tag{7.90}$$

The stiffness matrix $[k]$ of the element ijm under consideration can be easily computed according to the general relation Eq. (7.66). It should also be noted that the volume integral must be taken over the whole ring of the material considered. Then the element stiffness matrix becomes

$$[k]^e = 2\pi \int [B]^T [D] [B] \; r \, d\, r \, d\, z \tag{7.91}$$

with the appropriate matrices of $[B]$ and $[D]$ depending on the material properties. The integration of such an equation is not simple because the $[B]$ matrix depends on the coordinates of the nodes of the element. There are two possibilities to perform this integration, one is by the process of numerical integration and the other is an explicit mutliplication and term-by-term integration. The centroid of the element is given by

$$\bar{r} = \frac{(r_i + r_j + r_m)}{3}$$

and

$$\bar{z} = \frac{(z_i + z_j + z_m)}{3}$$

As a first approximation we have

$$[k] = 2\pi [\bar{B}]^T [D] [\bar{B}] \bar{r} \Delta \tag{7.92}$$

where Δ is the area of the triangle. This approximation is acceptable for obtaining accurate results. There are good number of numerical methods available to carry out the integration more accurately.

7.4.3 External Nodal Forces

The externally applied loads must be expressed in a form compatible with the axi-symmetric nature of the problem. The nodal forces represent the combined effect of all the forces acting throughout the circumference of the circle around the element node. Let Q_{unit} represent the radial component of force per unit length of the circumferential boundary of the element. The external force will be obtained by integrating the Q_{unit} component along the boundary of the element. The total external force Q can be expressed as

$$Q = 2\pi r Q_{unit} \tag{7.93}$$

In the vertical direction or the axial direction, the load is given by

$$Z = 2\pi r Z_{unit} \tag{7.94}$$

which represents the combined effect of axial forces.

Nodal forces due to initial strains can be expressed as

$$\{F\}^e_{\varepsilon_0} = -2\pi \int [B]^T [D] \{\varepsilon_0\} \, r \, d\, r \, d\, z \tag{7.95}$$

Considering ε_0 to be constant and partitioning, we get

$$\{F\}_{\varepsilon_0} = -2\pi \left(\int [B]^T \, r \, d\, r \, d\, z \right) [D] \{\varepsilon_0\} \tag{7.96}$$

The integration can be carried out in the same way as was done to obtain the stiffness matrix. An approximate value of the integral can be expressed as

$$\{\overline{F}_i\} = -2\pi [\overline{B}_i]^T [D] \{\varepsilon_0\} \overline{r} \Delta \tag{7.97}$$

together with a corrective term. Therefore

$$\{F_i\} = \{\overline{F}_i\} + \{F'_i\} \tag{7.98}$$

It is obvious that the corrective term is zero, and hence

$$\{F'\} = 2\pi \left(\int [B'_i] \, r \, dr \, dz \right) [D] \{\varepsilon_0\} = 0$$

Hence we have

$$\{F\}^e_{\varepsilon_0} = -2\pi [\overline{B}]^T [D] \{\varepsilon_0\} \overline{r} \Delta \tag{7.99}$$

7.4.4 Body Forces

Gravitational forces which are acting along the z-axis, centrifugal forces due to rotation of a rotating member which is acting in the radial direction are to be taken into consideration in the analysis of axisymmetric problems. Let us denote the force vector due to distributed body forces as

$$\{P\} = \begin{Bmatrix} R \\ Z \end{Bmatrix} \tag{7.100}$$

per unit volume of the material body in the directions of r and z, respectively. Then we have

$$\{F\}^e_p = -2\pi \int [N]^T \begin{Bmatrix} R \\ Z \end{Bmatrix} r dr \, dz$$

or

$$\{F_i\}^e_p = -2\pi \int \begin{Bmatrix} R \\ Z \end{Bmatrix} N_i \, r dr \, dz \tag{7.101}$$

If the body forces are constant, by approximation, we have

$$\{F_i\}_p = \{F_j\}_p = \{F_m\}_p = -2\pi \begin{Bmatrix} R \\ Z \end{Bmatrix} \bar{r}\frac{\Delta}{3} \tag{7.102}$$

The error involved in this approximation can be reduced by using a fine element mesh. In other words the error reduces with the size of the element.

If the body forces are given by a potential which is defined linearly by its nodal values, the expressions for the forces are given by

$$R = -\frac{\partial \phi}{\partial r}, Z = -\frac{\partial \phi}{\partial z} \tag{7.103}$$

In rotating members the body forces are proprotional to the radius r,

$$R = \omega^2 \rho r \tag{7.104}$$

where ω is the angular velocity and ρ is the density of the material.

It is to be noted that the stresses vary throughout the element, and it is easy to evaluate the average stress at the centroid of the element. Therefore the stress matrix can be written as

$$\{\bar{\sigma}\}_e = [D]\,[\bar{B}]\,\{\delta\}^e - [D]\,\{\varepsilon_o\} \tag{7.105}$$

There is a certain amount of variation in the stress values between elements, and a better approximation can be done by averaging the nodal stresses.

7.4.5 Axisymmetric Analysis Evaluation

Since the finite element analysis of axisymmetric systems follows the same steps as the analysis of two dimensional plane stress problems, its application can be quick and effective. There are several computer programs that have been developed to analyse plane stress, plane strain problems. These programs can also be adapted to the analysis of axisymmetric structural systems. Some important changes that are to be incorporated are:

- The element stiffness matrix generation logic is to be rearranged. Since the elements are circumferential in nature, the operation of integration is to be performed along the circumference of the element ring.
- A new scheme is to be developed to generate the load vectors. Hence direct application of the finite element method to axisymmetric problems has been proved to be faster. There are many structural systems in engineering which are axisymmetric in nature, such as solid or hollow spherical structures, cylindrical pressure vessels, nuclear reactor vessels, thick and thin walled cylindrical systems.

7.5 ISOPARAMETRIC FINITE ELEMENT FORMULATION

7.5.1 Introduction

A very important aspect of FEM is the calculation of the finite element matrices. In the previous sections we have seen the finite element formulation and solution procedures of problems in engineering. It is essential to present the generalized coordinate finite elements to understand the FEM much better. In most practical analyses the use of isoparametric finite elements is more effective. In this section let us concentrate on the formulation of isoparametric finite elements and describe their effective implementation.

In the formulation of generalized coordinate finite element models, we use local element coordinate system x, y and z and assume the element displacements $u(x, y, z)$, $v(x, y, z)$ and $w(x, y, z)$ in the form of polynomials in x, y and z with unknown constant coefficients α_i, β_i and γ_i for $i = 1, 2...$, identified as generalized coordinate systems. It is obvious that the coordinate systems are linear combinations of the element nodal point displacements. It is also essential to take proper care in establishing a unique expression to the generalized coordinates in terms of nodal displacements. The main aim of the isoparametric finite element formulation is to obtain a relation between the element displacements at any point and the element nodal point displacements using shape functions. It is shown that the element matrices corresponding to the required degrees of freedom are obtained directly.

7.5.2 General Formulations

In this formulation it is required to express the element coordinates and displacements in the form of appropriate shape functions using the natural coordinates of the element. The coordinate system depends on whether the problem is one, two or three dimensional.

For a most general case we use the equations of a three dimensional element using the relevant coordinate axes and the appropriate interpolation functions. For this element the shape functions are

$$x = \sum_{i=1}^{q} N_i X_i$$

$$y = \sum_{i=1}^{q} N_i Y_i$$

$$z = \sum_{i=1}^{q} N_i Z_i \qquad (7.106)$$

where x, y, z are the local coordinates at any point of the element and x_i, y_i, z_i where $i = 1...q$ are the coordinates of the 'q' element nodes.

The shape functions N_i are defined in the natural coordinate system of the element with variables of r, s and t each varying in the range from $+1$ to -1. The shape function N_i must have a value of unity at node i and zero at all other nodes. Utilizing this property of the shape functions, a specific nodal point layout can be effected in a systematic manner.

The interpolation functions for a four to eight variable nodes of a two dimensional element are shown in Fig. 7.7. Three dimensional twenty-node element and eight-node elements are shown in Fig. 7.8. An important property of the elements is that these can have any number of nodes between a minimum and maximum. It is obvious that a constant strain triangle can be obtained from the four-noded element shown in Fig.7.7 by providing corner nodes. Similarly a constant strain four-noded element can be obtained from the eight-node brick element as shown in Fig.7.9.

These elements can also have curved boundaries which is a very important advantage over other elements and displacement functions can be very easily formed. It is also to be noticed that the displacement functions and the geometric functions of the isoparametric formulation can be the same. Let u, v, and w be the local element displacements at any point of the element. The displacement at its nodes can be u_i, v_i and w_i where $i = 1 \ldots q$.

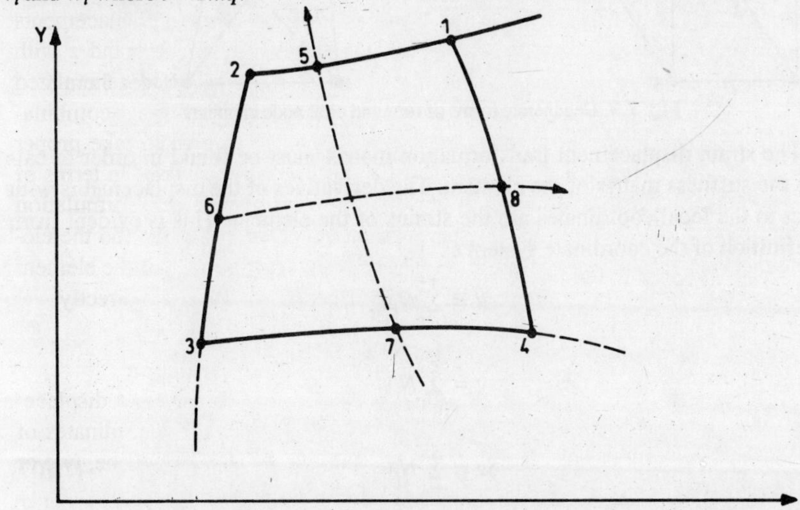

Fig. 7.7 Interpolation functions of four to eight variable-number-node two dimensional element

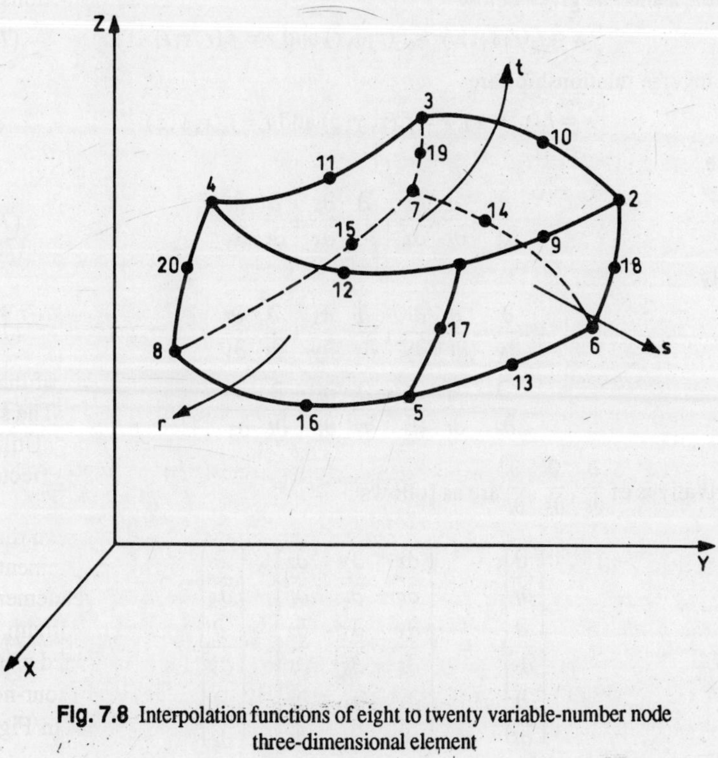

Fig. 7.8 Interpolation functions of eight to twenty variable-number node three-dimensional element

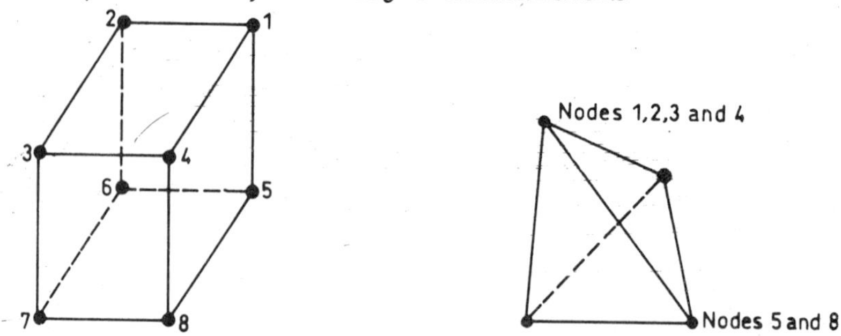

Fig. 7.9 Degenerate forms of four and eitht node elements

The strain displacement transformation matrix must be found in order to calculate the stiffness matrix of the element. The derivatives of the displacements with respect to the local coordinates are the strains of the element. This is evident from the definition of the coordinate system as

$$u = \sum_{i=1}^{q} N_i u_i$$

$$v = \sum_{i=1}^{q} N_i v_i$$

and
$$w = \sum_{i=1}^{q} N_i w_i \tag{7.107}$$

It is also required to relate the derivatives of the coordinate system with the derivatives of r, s and t as given below

$$x = f_1(r,s,t),\ y = f_2(r,s,t) \text{ and } z = f_3(r,s,t) \tag{7.108}$$

and the inverse relationships are

$$r = f_4(x,y,z),\ s = f_5(x,y,z) \text{ and } t = f_6(x,y,z)$$

We have

$$\frac{\partial}{\partial x} = \frac{\partial}{\partial r}\cdot\frac{\partial r}{\partial x} + \frac{\partial}{\partial s}\cdot\frac{\partial s}{\partial x} + \frac{\partial}{\partial t}\cdot\frac{\partial t}{\partial x} \tag{7.109}$$

Similarly

$$\frac{\partial}{\partial y} = \frac{\partial}{\partial r}\cdot\frac{\partial r}{\partial y} + \frac{\partial}{\partial s}\cdot\frac{\partial s}{\partial y} + \frac{\partial}{\partial t}\cdot\frac{\partial t}{\partial y} \tag{7.110}$$

and
$$\frac{\partial}{\partial z} = \frac{\partial}{\partial r}\cdot\frac{\partial r}{\partial z} + \frac{\partial}{\partial s}\cdot\frac{\partial s}{\partial z} + \frac{\partial}{\partial t}\cdot\frac{\partial t}{\partial z} \tag{7.111}$$

The derivatives of $\frac{\partial}{\partial r}, \frac{\partial}{\partial s}, \frac{\partial}{\partial t}$ are as follows

$$\begin{Bmatrix} \frac{\partial}{\partial r} \\ \frac{\partial}{\partial s} \\ \frac{\partial}{\partial t} \end{Bmatrix} = \begin{bmatrix} \frac{\partial x}{\partial r} & \frac{\partial y}{\partial r} & \frac{\partial z}{\partial r} \\ \frac{\partial x}{\partial s} & \frac{\partial y}{\partial s} & \frac{\partial z}{\partial s} \\ \frac{\partial x}{\partial t} & \frac{\partial y}{\partial t} & \frac{\partial z}{\partial t} \end{bmatrix} \begin{Bmatrix} \frac{\partial}{\partial x} \\ \frac{\partial}{\partial y} \\ \frac{\partial}{\partial z} \end{Bmatrix} \tag{7.112}$$

Symbolically, this can be written as

$$\frac{\partial}{\partial r} = [J]\frac{\partial}{\partial x} \quad (7.113)$$

where [J] is the Jacobian operator relating the natural and local coordinate derivatives which can be easily obtained by Eq. 7.106.

Provided that inverse of [J] exists, we can write

$$\frac{\partial}{\partial x} = [J]^{-1}\frac{\partial}{\partial r} \quad (7.114)$$

It is essential to evaluate the derivatives $\frac{\partial u}{\partial x} \cdots \frac{\partial \theta}{\partial x} \cdots \frac{\partial \omega}{\partial x} \cdots$ using the Eqs.7.107 and 7.114 to establish the strain displacement matrix [B] as

$$[\varepsilon] = [B]\,\{u\} \quad (7.115)$$

where $\{u\}$ is the nodal displacement given in Eq. 7.107.

Therefore, the stiffness matrix of the element in the local coordinates is given as

$$[k] = \int_v [B]^T [C]\,[B]\,dv \quad (7.116)$$

It is obvious that the elements of [B] are functions of r, s and t. Hence we have

$$dv = det[J]\,dr\,ds\,dt \quad (7.117)$$

It is very difficult to obtain the $[J]^{-1}$ explicity from Eq. 7.114 and the integration of Eq. 7.117. Hence it is advisable to adopt the numerical solution tehcnique,as givne here. Let us define $[F] = [B]^T [C] [B]$ det [J]. The Eq. 7.116 can be written as

$$[k] = \int_v [F]\,dr\,ds\,dt \quad (7.118)$$

By definition, the elements of [F] are dependent on r, s and t but the functional relation is not clear. However, using numerical integration, the stiffness matrix is now evaluated as

$$[k] = \sum_{i,j,k} \alpha_{ijk} F_{ijk} \quad (7.119)$$

where matrix $[F_{ijk}]$ is the matrix [F] evaluated at points r_i, s_i, t_i and α_{ijk} are dependent on the values of r_i, s_j and t_k. The accuracy of the integration depends on the sampling points r_i, s_j and t_k of the functions.

The element mass matrix and load vectors can be formulated writing the element displacements as follows

$$u(r,s,t) = H\{u\} \quad (7.120)$$

where [H] is the matrix interpolation or shape functions, then we have

$$[M] = \int_v \rho[H]^T [H]\,dv \quad (7.121)$$

$$[R_B] = \int_v [H]^T \{f_B\} dv \tag{7.122}$$

$$[R_s] = \int_s [H_s]^T \{f_s\} ds \tag{7.123}$$

$$[R_I] = \int_v [B]^T \{\tau_I\} dv \tag{7.124}$$

The above matrices are derived by numerical integration as indicated above. It is essential that appropriate functions $[F]$ are used in all computations. The body forces are obtained using $[F] = [H]^T \{f_B\}$ det $[J]$, the surface force vector $\{R_s\}$ is obtained using $[F] = [H_s]^T \{f_s\} \det[J]$, for the initial stress load vector the matrix $[F] = [B]^T \ \{\tau_I\}$ det $[J]$ and finally for the mass matrix the $[F]$ matrix that we use is ρ $[H]^T$ $[H]$ det $[J]$. The element coefficients α_{ijk} remains the same as in the stiffness matrix evaluation. The above formulation is adaptable for one, two and three dimensional elements.

7.5.3 Types of Elements

We assume that the element coordinates are interpolated in a similar manner as the element displacement in the isoparametric finite element derivation. We might find it more convenient in the solution process to introduce the coordinates to a lower degree than the displacements. Characteristically, for the straight sided eight-node quadrilateral in Fig. 7.10, the displacements u and v, are considered parabolically, whereas the coordiantes x and y of the element need only be introduced lineraly as the element edges are straight. Subparametric elements are those elements with a low degree of interpolation on the coordinates than on the displacements. Such elements satisfy the monotonic convergence requirements, since compatibility is satisfied for the same reasons as in the isoparametric formulation. Further, a subparametric element is complete as the associated isoparametric element, which is based exclusively on whether the coordinate interpolations used is complete. This follows from the fact that addition of higher-order displacement interpoltions does not hinder the element from still undergoing rigid body modes and constant strain states.

The coordinates are interpolated to a higher degree than the displacements in another group of elements named superparametric elements. Superparametric elements have been developed for thick and thin shell analysis. The fundamental problems of using isoparametric elements in thick to thin shell analysis are twofold. Firstly excessive shear strain energy is stored in the elements and, secondly, as the element becomes thin, the stiffness coefficients corresponding to the transverse displacement degrees of freedom are considerably larger than those for the longitudinal displacements, which results in numerical ill conditioning. Considering the first problem which is of great consequence when the parabolic elements in Figs.7.7 and 7.8 are used to improve the element behaviour, selective or reduced numerical integration can be employed as disucssed below, and inconsistent displacement modes may be introduced. Next considering the second problem, to prevent or avoid the numerical ill conditioning, relative degrees of freedom can be utilized. However, due to the small relative displacements and also since they do not contribute to the

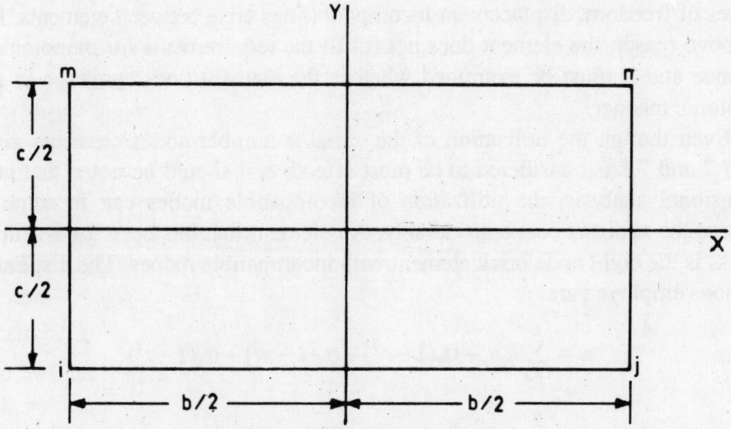

Fig. 7.10

overall response of a thin shell, it may be more effective to employ a superparametric element. The geometry of the element is defined by the original interpolation, but the displacement degrees of freedom are assumed to be rotations and translations at midsurface nodes. Superparametric elements do not necessarily satisfy the convergence criteria and each group of elements must specially be observed for compatibility and completeness.

By the introduction of incompatible modes, we can improve the behaviour of isoparametric elements. Consider the easiest case of addition of incompatible modes to a four node two dimensional element. In this case the coordinate and displacement interpolations used are respectively,

$$x = \sum_{i=1}^{4} h_i, x_i; y = \sum_{i=1}^{4} h_i, \quad y_i \tag{7.125}$$

and

$$u = \sum_{i=1}^{4} h_i u_i + \alpha_1(1-r^2) + \alpha_2(1-s^2) \tag{7.126}$$

$$v = \sum_{i=1}^{r} h_i v_i + \beta_1(1-r^2) + \beta_2(1-s^2)$$

where the $h_1 ... h_4$ are as defined. The $\alpha_1, \alpha_2, \beta_1$ and β_2 are additional degrees of freedom with a higher-order-displacement interpolation than is present in the h_i. If the element which is taken into account as rectangular, the additional degrees of freedom allow the element to represent a constant bending moment and the element will perform much better in stress analysis.

Considering the actual evaluation of the element stiffness matrix, we note that utilizing the interpolation in Eq.7.126 a matrix of order 12 is acquired, and that the degrees of freedom α_1, α_2, β_1 and β_2 are not associated with an element nodal point. To minimize the matrix to order 8, the additional degrees of freedom are eliminated utilizing static condensation technique, which is equivalent to minimizing the element total potential energy with respect to the variables, α_1, α_2, β_1 and β_2.

As the additional degrees of freedom are not in associated with nodal point degrees of freedom, displacement incompatibilities arise between elements. Due to the above reason the element does not fulfill the requirements for monotonic convergence and it must be examined whether the element does converge in a non-monotonic manner.

Even though the utilization of the variable-number-nodes elements given in Figs.7.7 and 7.8 is considered to be most effective, it should be noted that in three dimensional analysis, the utilization of incompatible modes can in some cases decrease the analysis cost considerably. An element that has been used with much success is the eight node brick element with incompatible mdoes. The displacement functions employed are

$$u = \sum_{i=1}^{8} h_i u_i + \alpha_1(1-r^2) + \alpha_2(1-s^2) + \alpha_3(1-t^2)$$

$$v = \sum_{i=1}^{8} h_i v_i + \beta_1(1-r^2) + \beta_2(1-s^2) + \beta_3(1-t^2) \tag{7.127}$$

$$w = \sum_{i=1}^{8} h_i w_i + \gamma_1(1-r^2) + \gamma_2(1-s^2) + \gamma_3(1-t^2)$$

where the $\alpha_1, \alpha_2 \ldots \gamma_3$ are displacement components that are not in association with nodal points and are eliminated using static condensation. The three dimensional brick should be rectangular in all three planes. Observing this rule the element has been employed successfully in a variety of three dimensional and shell analysis. Finally, it should be noted that the concept or the procedure of introducting modes to increase the effectiveness of an element is quite general and can also be employed in the formulation of higher-order elements.

7.6 ELEMENT TYPES FOR FINITE ELEMENT ANALYSIS

7.6.1 Introduction

Conventional engineering structures can be idealized as an assembly of finite number of discrete elements for the purpose of analysis by matrix operations. The finite element method was discussed in the previous chapters using constant strain elements, because of its simplicity for presentation of the basic concepts and logic behind the finite element theory. In this section other improved types of elements and their characteristics are discussed.

A structure of any geometric shape must be discretized into a finite element mesh for analysing the structure. However, based on the behaviour of the structure (static or dynamic) practical constraints may be considered for the choice of the elements. The selected element must be able to represent the appropriate shape of the structural geometry and must fulfill the mathematical requirements of the formualtion in order to obtain acceptable results. The solutions obtained by FEM must converge to the exact solution as the mesh generation becomes finer. It is obvious that if the element size is smaller and smaller, their strain expressions approach constant value. However the designer must be very cautious about the aspect ratio of the element (breadth to length ratio) which should not be less than one third in the case of a triangular element. In case if it is less than that limiting value, there is a problem of numerical instability of the results. So far only very few elements are capable of fulfilling the geometric shapes, practical and mathematical constraints. If the element is of more complicated nature, the mathematical formu-altion with their behaviour becomes more complex.

However, there are certain advantages of using refined and more complex elements which are more suitable to more complicated structures and yield more accurate results even with coarse mesh generation. There are certain complex problems which require sophisticated elements to obtain acceptable and accurate results. Hence it is very essential for the analyst to be familiar with the characteris-tics of all
the elements for which mathematical formulations are to be derived and check their convergency and the acceptability of the results.

In the following section some of the new elements are presented and their convergency, acceptability, accuracy and applicability are discussed.

7.6.2 Quadrilateral Element

Two adjacent triangular elements joining together form a quadrilateral. The stiff-ness matrix of the quadrilateral ijmk would be obtained by summing up the stiff-nesses of the two triangular elements ijm and jmk. If any structure is idealized with quadrilateral elements the sequence of computation may be changed but the nodal displacements equations remain the same. Consequently the nodal displacements and the stresses at these points also remain the same. The advantage in using quad-rilateral elements is in reducing the input data because the number of elements are exactly half of that with triangular elements. There will be considerable improvement in the representation of stress field since the averaging of the two constant triangular stress are taken and implemented at the centroid of quadrilateral. There will be considerable improvement in the accuracy of the analysis even with a coarse mesh. Moreover in averaging two different triangles it is very important to see that two triangles are of the same area.

A polynomial with four coefficeints can be applied to a general quadrilateral such as indicated in Fig.7.7. The displacement continuity which is known as C_0 continuity no longer exists, as there is variation of the function along the line inclined to the x-and y-axis. In order to overcome this difficulty the polynomial must be considered in terms of special coordinates which can take up constant val-ues along the sides of the quadrilateral. The new coordiantes ξ and η are arranged such that the lines with constant ξ and η are straight and take up values of ± 1 at the sides of the quadrilateral and both values increase linearly. Now the displacement u can be written as

$$u = \frac{1}{4}\{(1-\xi)(1-\eta)u_i + (1+\xi)(1-\eta)u_j + (1+\xi)(1+\eta)u_m + (1-\xi)(1+\eta)u_k\} \quad (7.128)$$

The relation between x, y and the new coordinate system is as follows

$$x = \frac{1}{4}\{(1-\xi)(1-\eta)x_i + (1+\xi)(1-\eta)x_j + (1+\xi)(1+\eta)x_m + (1-\xi)(1+\eta)x_k\} \quad (7.129)$$

Similarly

$$y = \frac{1}{4}\{(1-\xi)(1-\eta)y_i + (1+\xi)(1-\eta)y_j + (1+\xi)(1+\eta)y_m + (1-\xi)(1+\eta)y_k\} \quad (7.130)$$

from Eqs.7.129 and 7.130 in 7.128. The displacement can be expressed in terms of x and y. Taking the differentiation with respect to ξ and η we have

$$\frac{\partial}{\partial\xi}=\frac{\partial x}{\partial\xi}\cdot\frac{\partial}{\partial x}+\frac{\partial y}{\partial\xi}\cdot\frac{\partial}{\partial y}$$

$$\frac{\partial}{\partial\eta}=\frac{\partial x}{\partial\eta}\cdot\frac{\partial}{\partial x}+\frac{\partial y}{\partial\eta}\cdot\frac{\partial}{\partial y} \tag{7.131}$$

In matrix form

$$\begin{Bmatrix}\dfrac{\partial}{\partial\xi}\\ \dfrac{\partial}{\partial\eta}\end{Bmatrix} = [J]\begin{Bmatrix}\dfrac{\partial}{\partial x}\\ \dfrac{\partial}{\partial y}\end{Bmatrix} \text{ and } \begin{Bmatrix}\dfrac{\partial}{\partial x}\\ \dfrac{\partial}{\partial y}\end{Bmatrix} = [J]^{-1}\begin{Bmatrix}\dfrac{\partial}{\partial\xi}\\ \dfrac{\partial}{\partial\eta}\end{Bmatrix} \tag{7.132}$$

where $[J]$ is a jacobian matrix which can be obtained by Eq.7.129 and 7.130 which can be written as

$$[J]=\begin{bmatrix}\dfrac{\partial x}{\partial\xi} & \dfrac{\partial y}{\partial\xi}\\ \dfrac{\partial x}{\partial\eta} & \dfrac{\partial y}{\partial\eta}\end{bmatrix}=\frac{1}{4}\begin{bmatrix}-(1-\eta) & (1-\eta) & (1+\eta) & -(1+\eta)\\ -(1-\eta) & -(1+\eta) & (1+\eta) & (1-\eta)\end{bmatrix}\begin{bmatrix}x_i & y_i\\ x_j & y_j\\ x_m & y_m\\ x_k & y_k\end{bmatrix} \tag{7.133}$$

Hence it is very easy to derive the strain matrices in terms of the new coordinates ξ and η.

Similarly, the integration also can be carried out within the limits of -1 to +1 for ξ and η and we have

$$dx\,dy = \text{the det}\, J\, d\xi d\eta \tag{7.134}$$

It is essentially required to apply the numerical integration procedure. Here ξ, η regions are divided into suitable intervals and the $[J]$ matrix can be evaluated at several points. Gauss and other similar approximation techniques can be implemented.

7.6.3 Rectangular Plane Stress Element

A rectangular plane stress element has four nodal points and each node may have two degrees of freedom in the x and y directions. The total number of degrees of freedom of each element is 8. A typical rectangular element is shown in Fig.7.11. The shape function can be assumed as a polynomial with four constants since there are only four nodes. All these constants can be obtained by the coordinates of the nodal points and the assumed displacement functions.

The shape function assumed must be able to express the behaviour of the element and must satisfy the displacement continuity (C_0 continuity) and slope continuity (C_1 continuity). It is also required to be linear along the adjoining boundaries of the rectangular elements. The following functions will satisfy the requirements of the problem since they are linear.

$$u(x,y)=a_1+a_2x+a_3y+a_4xy$$

$$v(x,y)=a_5+a_6x+a_7y+a_8xy \tag{7.135}$$

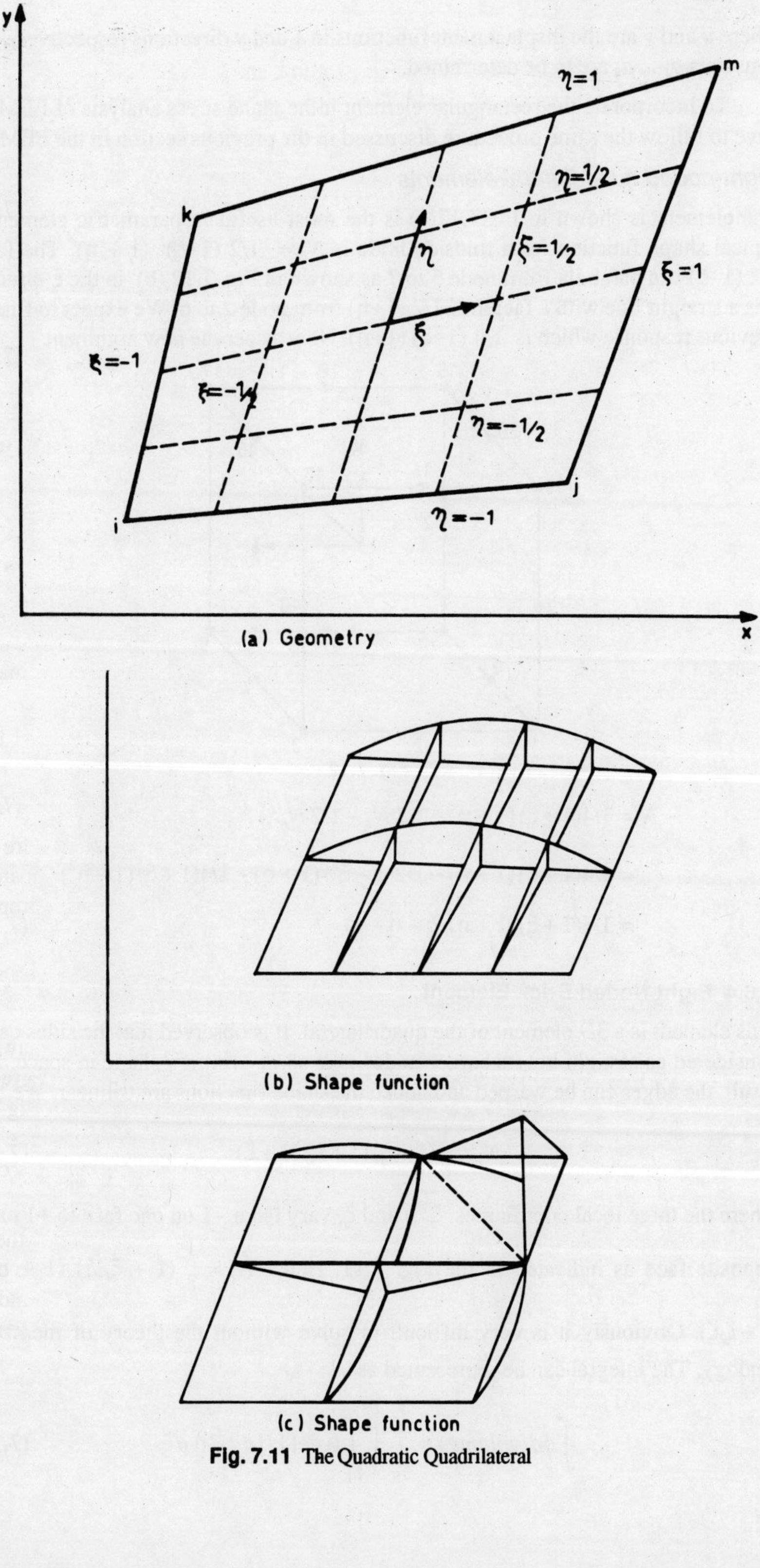

Fig. 7.11 The Quadratic Quadrilateral

where u and v are the displacement functions in x and y directions respectively. The constants a_1 ... a_8 are to be determined.

To incorporate the rectangular element inthe plane stress analysis of FEM, we have to follow the same procedure discussed in the previous section in the FEM.

Eight-noded quadrilateral elements

The element is shown in Fig.7.12(a) is the most useful isoparametric element. A typical shape function for a midside node is $N_6 = 1/2\ (1-\xi)^2\ (1+\eta)$. The factor $1/2\ (1-\xi)$ is a parabola from node 5 to 7 as shown in Fig. 7.12 (b), in the ξ direction it is a straight line with a factor of $1/2\ (1+\eta)$ from node 2 to 6. We expect to find the previous response which is $1/4\ (1+\xi)\ (1+\eta)$. Now as per the new argument

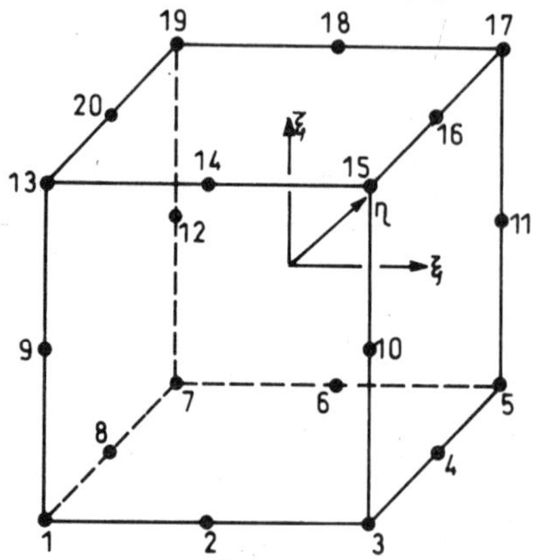

Fig. 7.12

$$N = 1/4(1+\xi)(1+\eta) - 1/2\,N_4 - 1/2\,N_6$$

$$= 1/4(1+\xi)(1+\eta) - 1/2(1-\xi^2)(1+\eta) - 1/4(1+\xi)(1-\eta^2)$$

$$= 1/4(1+\xi)(1+\eta)(\xi+\eta-1) \qquad (7.136)$$

7.6.4 Eight Noded Brick Element

This element is a 3*D* element of the quadrilateral. It is observed that the sides can be considered as straight but its corner nodes take some arbitrary shape in space. As a result, the edges can be warped and hence the shape functions are trilinear. We have

$$N_7 = \frac{1}{8}(1+\xi)(1+\eta)(1+\xi) \qquad (7.137)$$

where the three local coordiantes, ξ, η and ξ, vary from -1 on one face to $+1$ on the opposite face as indicated in the Fig. 7.11. Hence $N_i = \frac{1}{8}\ (1+\xi_i\,\xi)\ (1+\eta_i\,\eta)$ $(1+\zeta_i\zeta)$. Obviously it is very difficult to solve without the theory of membrane analogy. The integral can be represented as

$$\int \phi d(volume) = \int_{-1}^{1}\int_{-1}^{1}\int_{-1}^{1} \phi \det[J]\, d\xi\, d\eta\, d\zeta \qquad (7.138)$$

Twenty noded brick element

This element is more efficient among all the elements developed so far. The edges may be parabolic and the midside nodes should be centrally located as shown in Fig.7.12. The user is advised not to make them too curved. The shape functions resemble those of the eight noded quadrilateral element. As an example

$$N_{18} = 1/4(1-\xi^2)(1+\eta)(1+\zeta)$$

$$N_{17} = 1/8(1+\xi)(1+\eta)(1+\zeta) - 1/2(N_{18} + N_{16} + N_{11}) \quad (7.139)$$

$$N_{17} = 1/8(1+\xi)(1+\eta)(1+\zeta\xi+\eta+\zeta-2) \quad (7.140)$$

Three noded triangle element

This is the simplest isoparametric element, unless we include the two noded tie member. The lienar tetrahedron is so useful for the analysis and we use the linear triangle here as useful tool to introduce the area coordinates.

(1) Let us specify the point p for construction purpose only and we postulate a unit load at the point p on the element. The reactions at the three vertices of the triangle p_i gives L_1, L_2, L_3 the area coordinates as indicated in Fig. 7.13a.

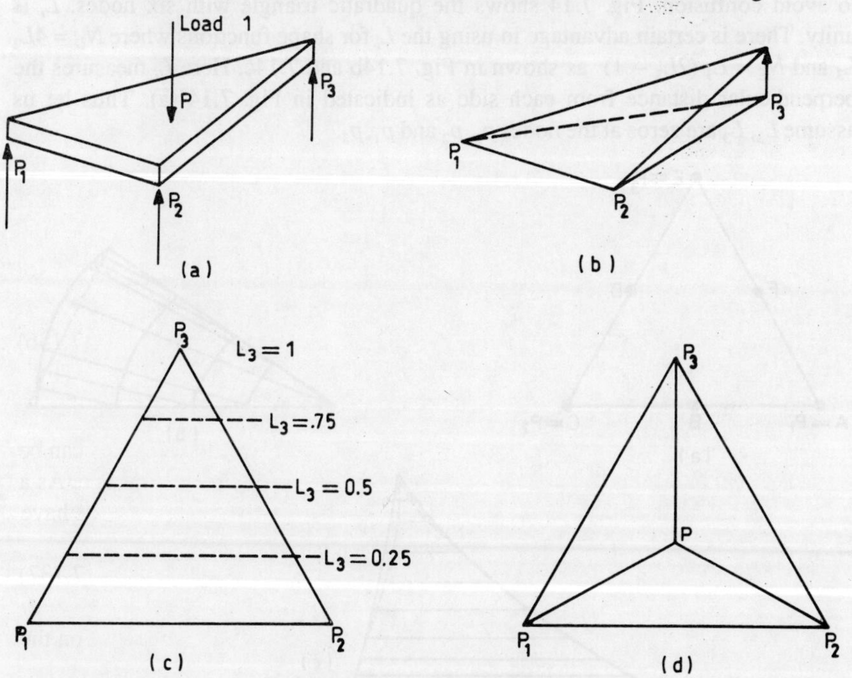

Fig. 7.13 Linear Triangle

(2) They are the shape functions of the linear triangle as shown in Fig. 7.13b.

(3) The line L_3 which is a constant is a line parallel to the base p_1, p_2 as shown in Fig. 7.13c. The L_i are the ratios of the areas of certain triangles as in Fig. 7.13 d. We have

$$L_1 = \frac{\Delta p_2 p_3 p}{\Delta p_1 p_2 p_3}$$

$$L_2 = \frac{\Delta p_3 p_1 p}{\Delta p_1 p_2 p_3}$$

By Cramer's rule

$$L_1 x_1 + L_2 x_2 + L_3 x_3 = x$$

$$L_1 y_1 + L_2 y_2 + L_3 y_3 = y$$

$$L_1 + L_2 + L_3 = 1$$

where p is the load due to the three point masses, L_1, L_2 and L_3 at the vertices.

7.6.5 Six Noded Triangle Element

Using the area coordinates in an element with the eight node quadrilateral element, it is possible to refine the mesh by using the quadrilaterals but it is easier to utilize the triangular elements with six nodes. The element nodes are labelled with letters to avoid confusion. Fig. 7.14 shows the quadratic triangle with six nodes. L_i is unity. There is certain advantage in using the L_i for shape functions where $N_D = 4L_2 L_3$ and $N_E = L_3 (2L_3 - 1)$ as shown in Fig. 7.14b and 7.14c. Here L_i measures the perpendicular distance from each side as indicated in Fig. 7.14 (a). Thus let us assume L_2, L_3 are zeros at the nodes p_1, p_2 and p_1, p_3.

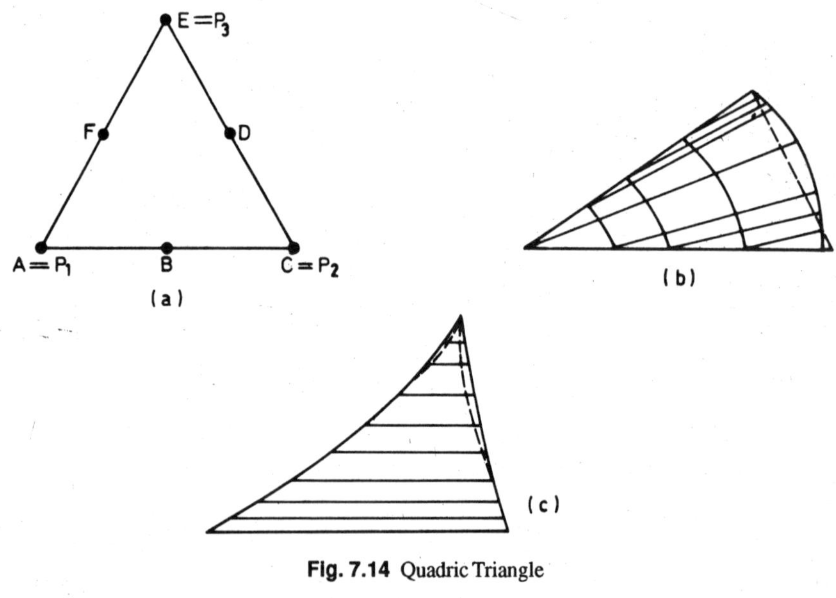

Fig. 7.14 Quadric Triangle

Now $N_D = 4L_2 L_3$ represents the second order near p_i. We can interpret N_E in two different ways. It is possible to take $N_E = 0$ at the five other nodes, by mutliplying the distance from the lower dotted line, $L_3 - 1/2$.

7.7 MESH GENERATION

The users of a finite element program in many cases need to use an existing mesh generation system or write one if necessary. The process of writing a program is time consuming especially for complex structures and the users have to spend many hours in developing the meshes and measuring the coordinates of each nodal point. If the number of nodal points are many it requires much time in obtaining the nodal coordiantes.

In the data generation process use of CAD system has several advantages over other methods. It is possible to see the element connectivity and the position of each element directly on a display when the element generation is in progress. If it is an interactive process, it is also pssible instantaneously to arrive at the best mesh generation to suit a particular problem by manipulating the elements by adding or subtracting. The CAD system can also help as a post processor to represent the data graphically in a faster way.

A CAD system must have the followng capabilities inorder to make use of the system for generation and presentation of data in finite element analysis.

- Mesh generation for two-dimensional-and three-dimensional structures.
- Ability to represent sharp edges and curves and surfaces.
- Capable of controlling the element density and generation of non uniform meshes.
- Capable of identifying a specified region of interest and grading a particular region.
- Quick numbering of nodes and elements of the generated mesh to improve the computational efficiency.
- Possibility to display the idealisation system.
- Capability to view the idealisations of the system in any desired angle.
- Facility to display any portion of the model for verification.
- Facility for on-line iteration for alternative idealisation.
- Capability to derive the required input data for analysis.
- Finally the system should be user oriented, easy to understand and supply the input data, and economical with respect to computer time and manual effort.

A General Finite Element Mesh Generating System (GFEMGS) was developed by Ghassemi at Imperial College for use with a variety of FEM programs. It is to be associated with many of the modules of the GCAD system described in the next section. A user menu is introduced specifically to cope up with functions reqired in the finite element data preparation or the presentation of the results. The system operates in two different modes where one is automatic and the other being manual. The automatic one is used for two dimensional and axisymmetric shapes. Meshes can be generated for a model with quadrilateral elements with different sides. Each quadrilateral element can be divided into triangular elements with three nodes or quadrilateral elements with four nodes. These elements can be transformed into six noded elements or isoparametric elements of triangular or quadrilateral shape of curved edges.

The GFEMGS system also has graphical checking facility to check the coordinates and element connectivity such that if there is any error in the data developed it will be displayed. The user is always guided by the data preparation and course of action will be indicated at each and every stage of the generation. It also has automatic nodal point numbering system which can reduce the bandwidth of the stiffness matrix. The stiffness matrix of manually renumbered nodes can be displayed. If the bandwidth is to be adjusted to the required size, then it may be reumbered by using the automatic mesh generation system.

The user may identify the boundary conditions for a mesh directly from the digitiser. Nodes of the system can be suppressed in any direction or the loads specified. The loads may be applied at the appropriate nodes as soon as the mesh has been generated and the elements which take the external forces have been identified.

Another important feature of this software is its application with finite element program ASKA which is a very popular software in the finite element analysis.

7.8. FEM SOFTWARE

Success of the Finite Element Method is largely due to the availability of high speed electronic digital computers. Analysis of structures with complex geometry and boundary conditions can be solved quite conveniently by finite element method. Several computer programs have been developed which are able to solve a wide variety of problems. There are many FEM software programs which were developed for the analysis of particular type of problems.

7.8.1 Application of the Software

Some of the convenient features of general purpose FEM programmes are given below :

- Input parameters or quantities can be easily prepared and are simple and easily understandable to the users. User need not be familiar with the system hardware and software to solve a specific structural analysis problem.
- FEM software are capable of solving simple or complex problems.
- They are in the form of modules which allows to deal with segments of a program separately. This is an essential requirement in order to incorporate any changes in the program.
- They can be made available in the form of data banks in most of the main frame systems in research and educational institutions.

Some of the disadvantages related to the general purpose programs are

- In most situations the cost of development of general purpose programs are usually very high.
- There may be unnecessary logical steps which increase the length of the program and in general reduce the efficiency of the program.
- If the software is very complex it may not be understandable to the user and as a result it may not be possible to incorporate any changes in the system.

- These general purpose programs require large computer storage. Special purpose programs present altogether different way of utilizing the digital computers. They are more useful and attractive.
- The special purpose programs are much shorter programs when compared to the general purpose programs and they are less expensive also.
- They require limited space for storage since they are pretty small. These programs can be utilized in the pc,pc/XT, pc/AT, etc. one need not have the mainframe computer system.
- Since they are small packages these can be easily extendable without much effort.
- Even complex and moderate size problems can be solved easily.

These special purpose programs are meant for solving small type of analysis and design probelms. The greatest disadvantage of these programs are that they are not capable of solving various types of problems and also they are not user oriented. They cannot solve problems such as preparation of input data, understanding of their abilities and operations.

Some of these software of general purpose and special purpose nature on finite element method of analysis are discussed below .

7.8.2 Software on Finite Element Method

Some of the general purpose software based on the finite elment analysis are discussed here. They are responsible for the success of the method.

ADINA
ANSYS
APPLE SAP
ASKA
ICES-STRUDL (Integrated Civil Engineering System Structural Design Language)
Msc NASTRAN (Nasa Structural Analysis Program)
GENESYS
MARC
SAP7
SAAS-II (Structural Analysis of Axisymmetric Solids)
ELAS program (Elasticity)
STRATA (Stress and thermal analysis program)
Zienkiewicz Program
Wilson's program
BOSOR (Buckling of shells of revolution)
SLADE Program
FEPLS program (finite element analysis of plates)

7.8.3 ADINA

Some of the special features of this program are given below. The analysis of nonlinear reinforced and pre-stressed concrete structures, thermoelastic, plastic and creep analysis of heat treatment fracture mechanic problems, nonlinear dynamic analysis of large fluid structure systems can be successfully carried out.

7.8.4 ANSYS

This is a very useful package with bi-linear elements, heat transfer analysis and fluid flow. This package can be used as a pre-and post-processor.

Perhaps the greatest advantage that ANSYS offers its users is its incredibly wide range of capabilities. ANSYS not only provides all the functions that engineers and scientists expect in an analysis program–such as a variety of analysis types, material representations, and a comprehensive library of elements, it offers much more. Some of the additional features include pre-and post-processing, on line documentation, design optimization, solid modeling and three dimensional graphics. The following analysis capabilities are available in ANSYS.

Static Analysis:

- Linear static analysis assumes that structural equilibrium equations and material properties are linear.
- Nonlinear statics allows for nonlinear behaviour in both geometry and/or material. Large deflections, stress stiffening, plasticity, creep and interface (gap) conditions can be included in the analysis.

Dynamic Analysis:

- Linear transient dynamics efficiently solves for the response of a linear structure.
- Nonlinear transient dynamics incorporates material, geometric, and/or interface nonlinear effects.
- Spectrum analysis envelopes the dynamic response to random vibration or seismic loading.
- Harmonic response determines the steady-state response of a linear structure subjected to harmonically time-varying loads.

Mode Frequency:

- It computes the natural frequencies and associated mode shape of a linear, undamped structure.

Stability Analysis:

- Linear eigenvalue buckling determines the critical loads (bifurcation points) and the associated buckled shapes for a linear structure.
- Large deflection analysis determines the limit load, whether failure occurs by bifurcation or snap through buckling.

Heat Transfer:

- Linear heat transfer assumes non-temperature-dependent material properties.
- Nonlinear heat transfer can have temperature-dependent material properties (including phase change effects) and can include radiation and temperature-dependent convection boundary conditions.
- Transient heat transfer solves the time-dependent temperature distribution within a body. Nonlinear effects may be included.

Magnetostatics:

- It solves for the intensity and flux density of a magnetic field due to current sources and/or permanent magnetic materials.

Coupled Field Analysis:

- Simultaneously solves interacting multiple field effects including two or more of the following: structural displacements and forces, temperature and heat flows, electric voltage and current, magnetic intensity and flux and confined fluid flow pressure and velocity.

Global/Local Modeling:

- Substructuring physically by cutting a piece or multiple pieces of a model and generating corresponding substructures for use in the full analysis at substantial cost savings.
- Submodeling uses the result of a coarsely-modeled structure to obtain an accurate solution of a locally-refined submodel.

Material Representation:

A wide variety of material representations are possible with ANSYS. Material properties may be temperature dependent, isotropic, orthotropic, or anisotropic. Nonlinear material behaviour such as plasticity, creep, swelling and nonlinear elasticity are both available in both static and dynamic analyses. Plasticity material options include:

- The Von Mises yield criterion coupled with kinematic hardening which represents most metal behaviour very well in the plastic range.
- Anisotropic plasticity which allows for different stress and strain behaviour in different directions as well as different behaviour in tension and compression. This option can be used for composites or the metal in which the yield strength is affected by processing (i.e. rolling).
- Drucker-Prager in which the material strength is dependent on the confinement pressure such as for granular materials (i.e. dry soils, rock.).

7.8.5 ASKA (Meijers)

This program was developed by Argyris and his co-workers at the Institut f*ü*r Statik and Dynamic der Luft-und Raumfahrtkonstruktionen, University of Stuttgart.

Applications of this software is mainly for metal forming processes, design of a car body, nuclear reactors and spacecrafts such as rockets and satellite structures, problems relating to soil mechanics. This is adaptable to all types of materials with all types of elements. Analysis capabilities are its applicability to static, dynamic, buckling, post buckling and fracture mechanics problems.

7.8.6 ICES (Integrated Civil Engineering System)

Integrated Civil Engineering System (ICES) was initially conceived in 1964 as a basic software for civil engineering problems. Major part of this was developed in the civil engineering systems laboratory of the Massachusetts Institute of Technology (MIT). Under the general direction of Prof. C.L.Miller who was at that time Head of the department of civil engineering (MIT) the project was initiated and developed to a large extent. The ICES project was a collaborative venture of American government, industry and university groups and developed a large scale software system for civil engineers. This was first implemented on IBM-360 and more recently on the IBM-370.

The ICES systems uses for solving the structural engineering problems of special interest are

- ICSE-COGO–for describing and processing computational and design problems of gemoetries.
- ICES STRUDL–a structural information systems to assist the structural engineer throughout the design process. STRUDL - version II has finite element analysis of one, two-and three dimensional analysis problems. It has more than 40,000 statements in Fortran. It can be used for plane stress and plane strain elasticity problems, plate bending problems, linear plane structural systems and shallow-shell structural systems. Elements used are constant strain triangle with global formulation (CSTG), constant strain triangle with local formulation (CSTL), linear strain triangle (LST), plane stress and strain rectangle (PSR), flat-plate triangle (CPT), flat-plate rectangle (BPR),shallow-shell curved rectangle (SSCR) and flat-plate parallelogram (BPP).

The efficiency of STRUDL depends on the size of the computer hardware and also on the type of the problem. STRUDL can be obtained from Bechtel Engineering Corporation, San Francisco, California.

7.8.7 NASTRAN (Nasa Structural Analysis)

NASTRAN is a general purpose program for the analysis of large complex structures developed by the National Aeronautics and Space Administration, released for general use in the late 1970. Some of the features of NASTRAN which may be of interest are:

- It is mostly a matrix multiplication and numerical data processing program with great power and highly sophisticated capabilities for handling auxiliary storage and interfacing program modules.
- It is a well developed finite element program to solve static and dynamic problems of structures and stability problems of structures. NASTRAN may require more input and more processing time than STRUDL when the cross-section or the loading system varies along the length of the structural member.
- NASTRAN is an analysis program for special or complex problems where the correct method of design may be as an analysis, or may be a member selction by some independent means. It is not useful for the production design of the usual structures.
- For dynamics of elastic structures, NASTRAN has well developed capabilities such as matrix handling and memory management.
- NASTRAN is mainly intended for plotting. It has rather good plotting capabilities, in terms of output selection and compatible plotters. This gives a good view of the physical problem being solved within the limitations of the finite element modeling.

The theory adopted is rather advanced for the usual structural engineering. The engineer with advanced training is definitely well facilitated by the high quality of the documentation of the NASTRAN program made pssible by the resources available. If more refined elements are really needed, this program provides the necessary matrix manipulation and storage management routines. The implementation of new elements, so that they can be handled in a routine manner, is made possible by the documented procedures contained in the software manulas. However, it essentially requires the aid of a system programmer. It is large and promising system to work with and does not depend on any problem orientated language. There are areas in structural engineering where NASTRAN is very useful for example, the static analysis of large free form or shell structures and the dynamic analysis of large structures. Essentially the user must have strong background in advanced structural theory if anybody is to make effective use of the capabilities of NASTRAN for some of these problems.

7.8.8 GENESYS (General Engineering System)

This is a general software system which was originated by the National Computing Center of Great Britain in 1972. Some of its capabilities are discussed below.

- Ability to define a series of commands for subsystems, which may be used by the designer. The use of one or more of these commands will cause the appropriate subroutines to be executed.
- It makes use of both dynamic arrays and dynamic programming. This dynamic array facility permits an efficient use of core and handling of large jobs. The dynamic programming capability permits the user to choose a design path.
- Superior file handling capability.
- A library of problem solving subsystems. The initial subsystems were developed with the support of the British government in order to get the GENESYS project underway. New subsystems are developed by many GENESYS users through internationally operating schemes.

7.8.9 SAAS-II Program

Structural Analysis of Axi-symmetric Solids (SAAS-II) is another finite element analysis program for axisymmetric solids with orthotropic material properties under axisymetric loading conditions. The main features of this program are its capability to generate the mesh required for the analysis procedure and plot the obtained data.

- It deals with problems of axisymmetric solid subjected to axisymmetric loading conditions. The loads that this program undertakes are surface forces or pressures, axial acceleration forces, thermal forces and nodal forces.
- Elements used by the program are triangular, quadrilateral torus elements for the idealisation of the continuous system.
- This program accepts the variations in the material properties and structural complexities in the geometry.

- One of the essentially desired feature of the program is its capability of automatic mesh generation for the problem. This saves considerable amount of time for the user. It also reduces the possibility of committing errors in finding the topology of the system.
- It uses Gaussian elimination procedure to solve the simultaneous linear equations to predict the unknown nodal displacements of the system. The output data can be plotted for evaluation.
- It has a main program and twenty subroutines in FORTRAN-IV language to run the entire FEM as discussed in the previous sections.
- The program has been developed to handle 1000 nodes and 1000 elements, 6 different materials, 12 temperatures and 200 different pressures. The program can run on 216 K memory on IBM–360 or with 142 K on CDC 6600.
- This is a special purpose program for the analysis of axisymmetric solids based on the theory the axisymmetric analysis of finite element method described in Sec. 7.4.

7.8.10 ELAS Program (Elasticity)

This is a general purpose computer program for the equilibrium analysis of linear problems. It was originally written in Fortran-II language. This program ELAS is based on the finite element method with displacement approach. The analysis of one-, two- and three dimensional problems can be handled. It has a large element library and hence has the flexibility of going for any type of element. Mesh generation for any type of problem using beam, triangular, quadrilateral, tetrahedral, conical, hexahedral, torus elements of triangular and quadrilateral shapes can be done. It has special features in logical inter-relations of its subroutines. The program consists of 8000 statements and the object modules including about 1400 binary statements. This can handle 99 varieties of problems of materials, temperature changes, temperature gradients, moment of inertia, cross-sectional areas, thickness, pressures and finally torsional constants.

The general input quantities include the coordinates of the nodes, material properties, loading conditions, the geometry, topology and prescribed displacement at nodal points or assigned loads at these nodes and stresses at the nodes.

The solution technique adopted by this program is Cholesky factorisation scheme for solving the linear simultaneous equations generated by the equilibrium conditions at the nodes. The program is used for several problems such as plane and space trusses, and frames, grid work systems, plane stress and plane strain problems, general solids, plate bending, memberane analysis and bending analysis of general shells, solids and shells of revolution.

7.8.11 STRATA Program (Stress and Thermal Analysis)

This program for the stress and thermal analysis of systems is maily used for the elastic-plastic stress analysis of plane stress and axisymmetric problems. It can be considered as special purpose program. It has been drafted in FORTRAN-IV computer language with about 2000 statements. It is a software compatible to IBM-360–50.

This program uses the quadric expansions for the nodal displacements which cause linear strain variations across the elements. To obtain acceptable results with this approach it requires a fine mesh generation. The plastic stress analysis can be carried out using incremental loading procedure and the Prandtl-Reuss equations to obtain the solution.

STRATA uses a subroutine 'Data check and plots' to check the input data to obtain the correct output.

(a) Element generation and numbering
(b) Nodal numbering
(c) Material boundary conditions
(d) Voids and overlaps of the topology of the system.

7.8.12 Zienkiewicz-Cheung Program

This program was developed by Zienkiewicz and Cheung for the analysis of plane stress and plane strain elasticity problems. It utilizes the constant strain triangular element for the structures. It is a special purpose program which was written in FORTRAN-IV with about 450 statements. Large structures can be partitioned and analysed separately and then assembled for final overall output.

Nodal displacements, coordinates of the centroids of triangular elements, the stress at the centroids of the elements and the value of the anlge of principal axes for each element are available in this program. This program is given in the book on Finite Element Method by Zienkiewicz and Cheung.

7.8.13 BOSOR-3 (Buckling of Shells of Revolution)

This program deals with stress, stability and vibration analysis of complex shells (revolution. The basic assumption of this program is that the material properties a elastic. The thin shell theory is used and the structural system is axisymmetric. Tl idealization process utilizes the shell segments as elements. This program conside the shell segments as elements which are very flexible in nature. It can handle abo 25 shell segments and hence can accommodate at least 97 nodes in a segment, a can have a maximum of 450 nodes.

7.18.14 SLADE Program

A special purpose software for the static analysis of thin shells called SLADE v developed. It uses quadrilateral element doubly curved. For the analysis of sl structures, thin shell theory is assumed. Axisymmetric formulation is used. T program can also handle the composite structures with a maximum of five la and five elastic properties. Another important capability of this program is tha handling shells of variable wall thickness. Automatic mesh generation schemes also incorporated.

7.8.15 FEPLS Program (Finite Element Analysis of Plates)

The program FEPLS is a special purpose digital computer program for f element analysis of plane stress and plane strain problem. Constant strain triangular element is used for the idealization of the structure. The input information to be supplied to the program are the geometry configuration, loading system, boundary conditions and the material properties of the system. For the specified input, the program develops the matrix stiffness and solves for the nodal displacements from which stresses at these nodal points are computed.

7.8.16 SAP (Structural Analysis Program)

SAP IV for the static and dynamic analysis of linear structural systems is the result of several years of research and development. The program has proven to be a very flexible and efficient analysis tool. The program is coded in FORTRAN IV and operates without modifications on the CDC 6400, 6600, 7600 computers. The first version of program SAP was published in September 1970.

Some of the details of the elements used in the programs are as follows:

- Three dimensional truss element
- Three dimensional beam element
- Plane stress and plane strain element
- Two dimensional axisymmetric solid
- Three dimensional solid
- Variable number nodes, thick shell and three dimensional element.
- Thin plate or thin shell element
- Boundary element
- Pipe element (straight and bend)

All the structural elements are used in static or dynamic analysis. The static analysis is carried out by solving the equations of equilibrium followed by the computation of stresses. In a dynamic analysis the choice is between:

- Frequency calculating only
- Frequency calculating followed by response history analysis
- Frequency calculating followed by response spectrum analysis
- Response history analysis by direct integration.

PROBLEMS

7.1 A three-node triangular element is defined in an x, y coordinate system with nodes 1, 2, and 3 located at (x_1, y_1), (x_2, y_2), and (x_3, y_3) respectively, in the global system. Derive the shape functions in terms of the global coordinates.

7.2 Given the form

$$\Phi = N_1\phi_1 + N_2\phi_2 + N_3\phi_3 + N_4\phi_4$$

derive the shape functions N_i for a rectangular element using general x_i, y_i coordinates.

7.3 Derive the local stiffness matrix for plane elasticity for a three-node triangular finite element.

7.4 If a constant uniform pressure P_x is distributed along the side of a triangular finite element between nodes 1 and 2 in the x-coordinate direction, determine the distribution of force to each node.

7.5 If a uniform body force is applied to a plane elasticity problem modeled using triangular elements with

$$\int_V [N]^T f\, dV = \int_A \begin{Bmatrix} N_1 \\ N_2 \\ N_3 \end{Bmatrix} t\, dA$$

Determine the distribution of body force to each mode.

7.6 An open-ended steel cylinder is subjected an internal pressure of 2 Mpa. Determine the deformed shape and the distribution of principal stress.

The cylinder length = 250 mm

Outer diameter = 120 mm

Thickness of cylinder = 20 mm

E = 200 Gpa and Poisson ratio = 0.3.

7.7 Develop a computer program for axisymmetric stress analysis with four-noded quadrilateral elements.

7.8 Derive the interpolation functions for a four-node isoparametric quadrilateral element.

7.9 Derive the Jacobian matrix for a four-node isoparametric finite element.

7.10 Discuss node placement and area coordinates for linear and higher-order triangular isoparametric elements.

7.11 Derive shape functions for the linear, quadratic, and cubic triangular finite elements.

REFERENCES

1. Ashwell, G.D., Gallagher, R.H., (1976), *Finite Elements for Thin Shells and Curved Members*, John Wiley and Sons, New York.
2. Bruce Irons, Sohrab Ahmad, (1986), *Techniques of Finite Elements*, John Wiley and Sons, New York.
3. Elchuri, V., Gallo, A. Michael, and Skalski, S.C., (1981), *Forced Vibration Analysis of Rotating Cyclic Structures in NASTRAN* NASTRAN Manuals, NASA CR 165429.
4. Elchuri, V., Gallo, A. Michael, and Skalski, S.C., (1982), NASTRAN Documentation for Flutter Analysis of Advanced Turbo Propellers, *NASTRAN Manuals*, NASA CR 167927.
5. Elchuri, V., Smith, G.C.C., Gallo, A Michael, and Dale, B.J., (1980), NASTRAN Level 16 Theoretical, user's Programmer's and Demonstration Manuals Updates for Aeroelastic Analysis of Bladed Discs, *NASTRAN Manuals*, NASA CR's 159273-159276.
6. Gallo, A. Michael, Elchuri, V., and Skalski, S.C., (1981), Bladed Shrouded Disc Aeroelastic Analyses: Computer Programme Updates in NASTRAN Level 17.7, *NASTRAN Manuals*, NASA CR 165428.
7. Octay Ural, (1973), *Finite Element Method Basic Concepts and Applications*, Intext Educational Publishers, New York.
8. Smith, G.C.C., and Elchuri, V., (1980), Aetoelastic and Dynamic Finite Element Analyses of a Bladed Shrouded Disc, *Final Technical Report NASA CR* 159728.
9. Whitman Wright, E., (1976), *Structural Design by Computer*, Van Nostrand Reinhold Company Limited, London.
10. Wilson, E.L., (1970), SAP-A General Structrual Analysis Program, *SESM Report 70-20*, Dept. of Civil Engineering, University of California, Berkeley.
11. Zienkiewicz, O.C., Cheung, Y.K., (1967), *The Finite Element Method in Structural and Continuum Mechanics*, McGraw-Hill Publishing Company Limited, London.
12. Zienkiewicz, O.C., Morgan, K., (1983), *Finite Element and Aporoximation*, Jehn Wiley and Sons, New York.

CHAPTER 8

CYCLIC SYMMETRIC STRUCTURES

8.1 INTRODUCTION

Many engineering structures consist of a series of identical sectors connected by identical junctions. Such structures with regularly repeating sectors are referred to as periodic structures. The repeating sectors may form either a closed structure such as pipes, chimneys, pressure vessels and cooling towers or they may extend infinitely such as infinite beams supported periodically, forming linear periodic structures.

Orris and Petyt [8] investigated the vibration behaviour of periodic structures by characteristic propagation constants. The natural frequencies of the finite periodic structures are related to the variation of the pureiy imaginary part of this propagation constant, known as the phase constant. A method was proposed for using the finite element technique to evaluate the phase constant of any arbitrary periodic structure. The method was implemented for two structures. One was an infinite beam periodically supported, and the second a skin rib structure with two models, a beam model and a plate model.

An economical and exact method of analysing the free vibration and the steady state (harmonic) forced vibration of rotationally periodic structure has been described by Thomas [9]. For forced vibrations, his method considered arbitrary harmonic forces acting on the full structure as the sum of a finite number of spatial Fourier harmonics, each of which has the property that all substructures experience identical forces but with a fixed phase difference between the adjacent substructures. The structure was analysed separately for each spatial Fourier harmonic by idealising a single substructure by a finite element model, and applying complex constraints between corresponding displacements of the two substructure boundaries, consistent with phase difference for that harmonic. For each spatial harmonic of forces a corresponding forced vibration equation was solved and the responses of each of the harmonics summed up to give the total response of each substructure.

Free vibration for a given permissible phase relationship between adjacent substructures was a Hermitian eigenvalue problem which was solved to give real eigenvalues (natural frequencies) and complex eigenvectors for a single substructure.

These complex modes may be viewed physically as rotating mode shapes in which the same deflected shape reappears, rotated through one substructure at fixed intervals of time.

Fricker and Potter [2] extended the work of Thomas for the case of transient forced vibration of rotationally periodic structures. A modal method was used to solve the equations of motion which were uncoupled by using the orthogonality properties of the complex eigenvectors. The response in each of the Fourier harmonics was calculated separately and these responses were summed up to give the complete displacement pattern of the structure. A method to obtain seismic response was also proposed. The method proposed by Fricker gave an economical way of solving the transient analysis problem of rotationally periodic structures. Otherwise entire structure would have to be solved which requires more computer storage and time. Considerable amount of time was saved since time required for one substructure was much less than that for the entire structure. The transient analysis of a stator end windings containing 135 substructures under fault conditions was also described.

Static analysis of rotationally periodic structures with Potter's scheme was proposed by Ramamurti and Balasubramanian [6]. Potter's method of solving simultaneous equations having tridiagonal block matrices has been modified for the above problem. The amount of saving in computer storage afforded by implementing the Potter's scheme in this approach was highlighted.

The same authors reported a modified Potter's scheme to solve the simultaneous equations for structural eigenvalue problems to obtain the orthogonalized eignvectors. Simultaneous iteration scheme was used. The modified scheme was applied to the problem of disk flexural vibration and the results were compared with another simultaneous iteration scheme which utilizes the Cholesky's decomposition procedure. It was observed that the convergence of the proposed method was quite fast.

In this chapter static analysis of rotationally periodic structures subjected to axisymmetric and asymmetric loading is presented. Free vibration analysis with and without damping, forced vibration analysis of cyclic symmetric nature of the structures are presented. Modification of the analysis is done considering the effect of centrifugal forces, coriolis forces where they are of first order importance and must be included in the linear analysis. All these analyses with suitable examples are discussed in this chapter.

The finite element method of structural analysis is also considered. A method is presented for obtaining propagation constants by the periodic system of the finite element approach. The imaginary part of the propagation constant is known as the phase constant. The natural frequencies of the finite, periodic structure lie in the frequency bands where the propagation constant is purely imaginary. Hence the phase constant is an important parameter of the periodic structure.

8.2 ADVANTAGES OF CYCLIC SYMMETRY

As mentioned earlier, a periodic structure consists of a finite number of identical substructures. The loads on each substructure may or may not be identical. In either case deflected shape and stress distribution can be obtained by analysing only one substructure by the cyclic symmetric formulation. Hence considerable amount of computer storage and time will be saved.

Very complicated rotationally periodic structures with large number of identical substructures having large number of degrees of freedom and with constraints can be analyzed using the above concept. It is also possible to use node condensation technique to reduce the internal degrees of freedom. The method is also applicable to other eigenvalue problems, such as buckling. Structures with small variations from true rotational periodicity can be analyzed using perturbation technique. The method is also applicable to analyze periodic structures in which the substructures have connections to non adjacent substructures provided the interconnections are of periodic nature. Various types of rotationally periodic structures are discussed in the following sections.

The finite element method of evaluating propagation constants is very simple to apply, and requires no alterations in the existing subroutines. This can easily be extended to obtain propagation constants for structures that are periodic in two or three directions. Finally the method can also be applied to flexural wave propagation.

8.3 STATIC ANALYSIS UNDER SYMMETRIC LOADING

A cylindrical pressure vessel with flange and ribs is a rotationally periodic structure with a number of identical substructures as shown in Fig. 8.1. The structure consists

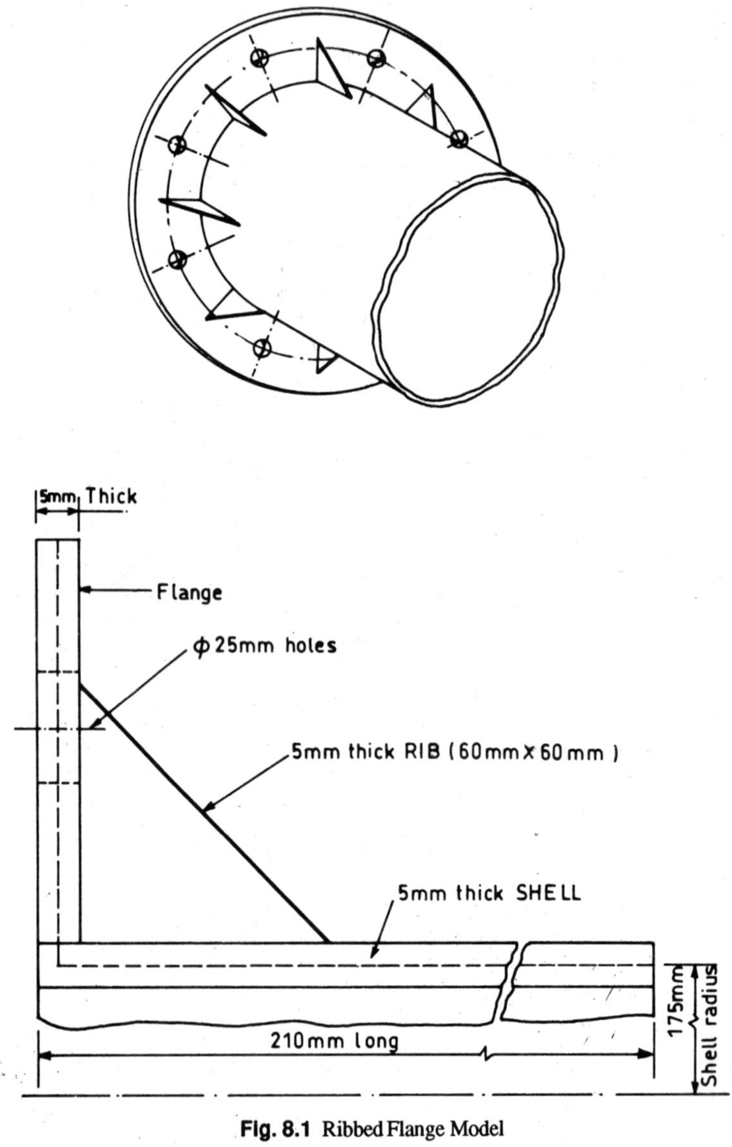

Fig. 8.1 Ribbed Flange Model

of N identical substructures positioned symmetrically about its axis. In the finite element formulation the global stiffness matrix, mass matrix and force vector are required to analyse the structure for static and dynamic analysis. In this method it is enough if one substructure is discretized and the stiffness matrix of this substructure is derived. In addition if the loading is symmetric, the load vector on each substructure is the same. Hence a static analysis under symmetric loading is carried out as follows.

8.3.1 Solution by Potter's method

The equilibrium equation can be written for the entire structure as,

$$\begin{bmatrix} K_{1,1} & K_{1,2} & 0 & \dots & K_{1,N} \\ K_{2,1} & K_{2,2} & K_{2,3} & \dots & 0 \\ 0 & K_{3,2} & K_{3,3} & K_{3,4} & 0 \\ \dots & \dots & K_{N-1,N-2} & K_{N-1,N-1} & K_{N-1,N} \\ K_{N,1} & \dots & \dots & K_{N,N-1} & K_{N,N} \end{bmatrix} \begin{Bmatrix} Z_1 \\ Z_2 \\ \dots \\ Z_{N-1} \\ Z_N \end{Bmatrix} = \begin{Bmatrix} g_1 \\ g_2 \\ \dots \\ g_{N-1} \\ g_N \end{Bmatrix} \tag{8.1}$$

Because of the geometric similarity, the following can be assumed

$$\begin{aligned} K_{1,1} &= K_{2,2} = K_{3,3} = \dots\dots\dots\dots = K_{1,N} \\ K_{1,2} &= K_{2,3} = K_{3,4} = \dots\dots\dots\dots = K_{N,1} \\ K_{2,1} &= K_{3,2} = K_{4,3} = \dots\dots\dots\dots = K_{1,N} \\ g_1 &= g_2 = g_3 = \dots\dots\dots\dots = g_N \\ Z_1 &= Z_2 = Z_3 = \dots\dots\dots\dots = Z_N \end{aligned} \tag{8.2}$$

The stiffness matrix of the entire structure can be obtained by assembling the stiffness matrices of each substructure having n number of station points, which can be written as follows

$$\begin{bmatrix} B_1 A_1 & 0 & & & & C_1 \\ C_2 B_2 & A_2 & & & & \\ \dots & .. & .. & \dots & .. & .. \\ \dots & .. & .. & .. & .. & .. \\ & & & C_{n-1} & B_{n-1} & A_{n-1} \\ A_n & & & & C_n & B_n \end{bmatrix} \tag{8.3}$$

Similarly the displacement load vectors can also be written as

$$[Z_1, Z_2, Z_3 \dots Z_{n-1}, Z_n, Z_1, Z_2, \dots Z_n, \dots Z_1 \dots Z_n]^T \tag{8.4}$$

and

$$[g_1, g_2, g_3 \dots g_{n-1}, g_n, g_1, g_2, \dots g_n, \dots g_1 \dots g_n]^T \tag{8.5}$$

substituting Eqs. 8.4 and 8.5 in Eq. 8.1, equations for each substructure can be obtained as follows:

$$\begin{bmatrix} B_1 & A_1 & 0 & & & & C_1 \\ C_2 & B_2 & A_2 & & & & \\ \cdot & \cdot & \cdot & \cdot & \cdot & \cdot & \cdot \\ \cdot & \cdot & \cdot & \cdot & \cdot & \cdot & \cdot \\ \cdot & \cdot & \cdot & \cdot & \cdot & \cdot & \cdot \\ & & & & C_{n-1} & B_{n-1} & A_{n-1} \\ A_n & & & & & C_n & B_n \end{bmatrix} \begin{Bmatrix} Z_1 \\ Z_2 \\ \cdot \\ \cdot \\ \cdot \\ Z_{n-1} \\ Z_n \end{Bmatrix} = \begin{Bmatrix} g_1 \\ g_2 \\ \cdot \\ \cdot \\ \cdot \\ g_{n-1} \\ g_n \end{Bmatrix} \tag{8.6}$$

Potter's scheme of solving simultaneous equations of tridiagonal block matrices is modified to solve the above equation.

In the first cycle of operation, the above equation is simplified to the following form

$$\begin{bmatrix} I_1 & P_1 & 0 & & & & Q_1 \\ 0 & I_2 & P_2 & & & & Q_2 \\ 0 & 0 & I_3 & P_3 & & & Q_3 \\ \cdot\cdot & \cdot\cdot & \cdot\cdot & \cdots\cdots & \cdot\cdot & & \cdot\cdot \\ & & & 0 & & I_{n-1} & Q_{n-1} \\ A_n & & & & & C_n & B_n \end{bmatrix} \begin{Bmatrix} Z_1 \\ Z_2 \\ \cdot\cdot \\ \cdot\cdot \\ Z_{n-1} \\ Z_n \end{Bmatrix} = \begin{Bmatrix} q_1 \\ q_2 \\ \cdot\cdot \\ \cdot\cdot \\ q_{n-1} \\ g_n \end{Bmatrix} \tag{8.7}$$

where

$$P_1 = B_1^{-1} A_1$$

$$Q_1 = -B_1^{-1} C_1$$

$$q_1 = B_1^{-1} g_1 \tag{8.8}$$

Similarly for other partitions

$$P_i = (B_i - C_i P_{i-1})^{-1} A_i$$

$$Q_i = -(B_i - C_i P_{i-1})^{-1} (C_i Q_{i-1})$$

$$q_i = (B_i - C_i P_{i-1})^{-1} (g_i - C_i q_{i-1})$$

for

$$i = 2, 3, \ldots\ldots\ldots, n-1 \tag{8.9}$$

$$\overline{Q}_{n-1} = P_{n-1} + Q_{n-1} \tag{8.10}$$

The last row in Eq. 8.7 is given by

$$A_n Z_1 + B_n Z_n + C_n Z_{n-1} = g_n \tag{8.11}$$

Substituting for Z_1 from the first row of Eq. 8.7

$$R_1 Z_2 + S_1 Z_n + C_n Z_{n-1} = u_1 \tag{8.12}$$

where

$$R_1 = -A_n P_1, \quad S_1 = B_n - A_n Q_1;$$

$$u_1 = g_n - A_n g_1 \tag{8.13}$$

Substituting for Z_2, Z_3, and so on, the above equation is modified as

$$R_iZ_{i+1} + S_iZ_n + C_nZ_{n-1} = u_i \tag{8.14}$$

where

$$R_i = -R_{i-1}P_i$$

$$S_i = S_{i-1} - R_{i-1}Q_i$$

$$u_i = u_{i-1} - R_{i-1}q_i$$

where $i = 2, 3, ..., n-2$ (8.15)

The $(n-2)^{\text{th}}$ equation is simplified as,

$$(C_n + R_{n-2})Z_{n-1} + S_{n-2}Z_n = u_{n-2} \tag{8.16}$$

This can be simplified as

$$\overline{R}_{n-1}Z_n = u_{n-1} \tag{8.17}$$

where

$$\overline{R}_{n-1} = (R_{n-2} + C_n)(Q_{n-1} + P_{n-1} + S_{n-2})$$

and

$$u_{n-1} = (u_{n-2} - (R_{n-2} + C_n)q_{n-1}) \tag{8.18}$$

Equation 8.17 is solved for Z_n and it is substituted in Eq. 8.7 to find out Z_{n-1}. A series of back substitutions in Eq. 8.7 yield all the other values of Z.

8.3.2 Submatrices Elimination Scheme

Symmetry property of the stiffness matrix is ignored in the modified Potters' scheme. Computational effort can be reduced by incorporating the symmetry property of the stiffness matrix by submatrices eliminations scheme. This is extented to the present analysis.

Due to the property of symmetry Eq. 8.6 can be simplified as

$$\begin{bmatrix} B_1 & A_1 & & & & A_n^t \\ A_1^t & B_2 & A_2 & & & 0 \\ & A_2^t & B_3 & A_3 & & 0 \\ .. & .. & .. & \ldots & .. & .. \\ & & & A_{n-2}^t & B_{n-1} & A_{n-1} \\ A_n & & & & A_{n-1}^t & B_n \end{bmatrix} \begin{Bmatrix} Z_1 \\ Z_2 \\ .. \\ .. \\ Z_{n-1} \\ Z_n \end{Bmatrix} = \begin{Bmatrix} g_1 \\ g_2 \\ .. \\ .. \\ g_{n-1} \\ g_n \end{Bmatrix} \tag{8.19}$$

The above equation is simplified to the form

$$\begin{bmatrix} L_1^t & \overline{P}_1 & .. & .... & .. & .. & \overline{Q}_1 \\ & L_2^t & \overline{P}_2 & .... & .. & .. & \overline{Q}_2 \\ & & L_3^t & \overline{P}_3.. & .. & .. & \overline{Q}_3 \\ .. & .. & .. & .. & .. & .. & .. \\ & & & & L_{n-2}^t & \overline{P}_{n-2} & \overline{Q}_{n-2} \\ & & & & & L_{n-1}^t & \overline{Q}_{n-1} \\ A_n & & & & & A_{n-1}^t & B_n \end{bmatrix} \begin{Bmatrix} Z_1 \\ Z_2 \\ Z_3 \\ .. \\ Z_{n-2} \\ Z_{n-1} \\ Z_n \end{Bmatrix} = \begin{Bmatrix} \overline{q}_1 \\ \overline{q}_2 \\ \overline{q}_3 \\ .. \\ \overline{q}_{n-2} \\ \overline{q}_{n-1} \\ g_n \end{Bmatrix} \tag{8.20}$$

where $L_1, \overline{P}_1$, and $\overline{Q}_1$ can be obtained as follows

$$B_1 = L_1 L_1^t;\quad L_1\overline{P}_1 = A_1;\quad L_1\overline{Q}_1 = A_n^t,\quad L_1\overline{q}_1 = g_1 \tag{8.21}$$

Similarly

$L_i, \overline{P}_i, \overline{Q}_i$ are calculated as follows

$$L_i L_i^t = \left[B_i - \overline{P}_{i-1}^t \cdot \overline{P}_{i-1}\right]$$

$$L_i\overline{P}_i = A_i$$

$$L_i\overline{Q}_i = -\left[\overline{P}_{i-1}^t \cdot \overline{Q}_{i-1}\right]$$

$$L_i\overline{q}_i = \left[g_i - \overline{P}_{i-1}^t \overline{q}_{i-1}\right]$$

$$i = 2, 3, ..., n-1 \tag{8.22}$$

and

$$\overline{\overline{Q}}_{n-1} = [\overline{P}_{n-1} + \overline{Q}_{n-1}] \tag{8.23}$$

From the last row of Eq. 8.20, we have

$$A_n Z_1 + B_n Z_n + A_{n-1}^t \cdot Z_{n-1} = g_n \tag{8.24}$$

Pre multiplication of the first row of Eq. 8.20 by Q'_1 gives rise to

$$\overline{Q}_1' L_1^t Z_1 + \overline{Q}_1' \overline{P}_1 Z_2 + \overline{Q}_1' \overline{Q}_1 Z_N = \overline{Q}_1' \overline{q}_1 \tag{8.25}$$

Here,

$$\overline{Q}_1' L_1^t = (L_1\overline{Q}_1)^t = (A_n^t)^t = A_n \tag{8.26}$$

Substituting Eq. 8.26 in 8.25 and substracting it from Eq. 8.24 gives rise to

$$\left(B_n - \overline{Q}_1'\overline{Q}_1\right) Z_n - \overline{Q}_1'\overline{P}_1 Z_2 + A_{n-1}^t Z_{n-1} = \left(g_n - \overline{Q}_1'\overline{q}_1\right) \tag{8.27}$$

Similarly from the second row of Eq. 8.20, we get

$$\overline{Q}_2' L_2^t Z_2 + \overline{Q}_2' \overline{P}_2 Z_3 + \overline{Q}_2' \overline{Q}_2 Z_n = \overline{Q}_2' \overline{q}_2 \tag{8.28}$$

Applying Eq. 8.22

$$\overline{Q}_2' L_2^t = (L_2\overline{Q}_2)^t = -\left(\overline{P}_1'\overline{Q}_1\right)^t = -\overline{Q}_1'\overline{P}_1 \tag{8.29}$$

Combining Eqs. 8.25 and 8.29 and 8.27 gives rise to

$$\left(B_n - \overline{Q}_1'\overline{Q}_1 - \overline{Q}_2'\overline{Q}_2\right)Z_n - \overline{Q}_2'\overline{P}_2 Z_3 + A_{n-1}^t Z_{n-1} = \left(g_n - \overline{Q}_1'\overline{q}_1 - \overline{Q}_2'\overline{q}_2\right) \tag{8.30}$$

The same procedue is to be repeated for first $(n - 2)$ rows and the resulting equations are as follows.

$$\left(B_n - \overline{Q}_1'\overline{Q}_1 - \overline{Q}_2'\overline{Q}_2 ..... - \overline{Q}_{n-2}'\overline{Q}_{n-2}\right)Z_n - \overline{Q}_{n-2}\overline{P}_{n-2}Z_{n-1} + A_{n-1}^t Z_{n-1}$$

$$= \left(g_n - \overline{Q}_1'\overline{q}_1 - \overline{Q}_2' q_2 ... - \overline{Q}_{n-2}'\overline{q}_{n-2}\right) \tag{8.31}$$

Premultiplying both sides of the $(n - 1)$ th row of Eq. 8.20 by $\overline{\overline{Q}}_{n-1}^t$ gives rise to

$$\overline{\overline{Q}}_{n-1}' L_{n-1}^t Z_{n-1} + \overline{\overline{Q}}_{n-1}' \overline{\overline{Q}}_{n-1} Z_n = \overline{\overline{Q}}_{n-1}' q_{n-1} \tag{8.32}$$

Using Eqs. 8.22 and 8.23

$$\left(\overline{\overline{Q}}_{n-1}\right)^t L_{n-1}^t = \left(L_{n-1}\overline{\overline{Q}} t_{n-1}\right)^t$$

$$= [L_{n-1} \cdot (\overline{P}_{n-1} + \overline{\overline{Q}}_{n-1})]^t$$

$$= [A_{n-1} - P'_{n-1}\overline{Q}_{n-2}]^t$$

$$= A_{n-1}^t - \overline{Q}_{n-1}' P_{n-2} \tag{8.33}$$

Combining Eqs. 8.31, 8.32 and 8.33 we get

$$\overline{B}_n Z_n = \overline{g}_n \tag{8.34}$$

where

$$\overline{B}_n = \left[B_n - \overline{Q}_1'\overline{Q}_1 - \overline{Q}_2'\overline{Q}_2 ..... - \overline{Q}_{n-2}'\overline{Q}_{n-2} - \overline{\overline{Q}}_{n-1}' \cdot \overline{\overline{Q}}_{n-1}\right] \tag{8.35}$$

$$\overline{g}_n = \left[g_n - \overline{Q}_1'\overline{q}_1 - \text{.........} - \overline{Q}_{n-2}' q_{n-2} - \overline{\overline{Q}}_{n-1}' \cdot \overline{q}_{n-1}\right]$$

Hence, Eq.8.20 can be written as

$$\begin{bmatrix} L_1^t & \overline{P}_1 & .. & .. & .. & \overline{Q}_1 \\ & L_2^t & \overline{P}_2 & & & \overline{Q}_2 \\ & & L_3^t & \overline{P}_3 & & \overline{Q}_3 \\ .. & .. & .. & .. & ... & ... \\ & & & L_{n-2}^t & \overline{P}_{n-2} & \overline{Q}_{n-2} \\ & & & & L_{n-1}^t & \overline{\overline{Q}}_{n-1} \\ & & & & & L_n^t \end{bmatrix} \begin{Bmatrix} Z_1 \\ Z_2 \\ Z_3 \\ ... \\ Z_{n-2} \\ Z_{n-1} \\ Z_n \end{Bmatrix} = \begin{Bmatrix} \overline{q}_1 \\ \overline{q}_2 \\ \overline{q}_3 \\ ... \\ \overline{q}_{n-2} \\ \overline{q}_{n-1} \\ \overline{q}_n \end{Bmatrix} \tag{8.36}$$

where L_n^t and $\overline{q}_n$ can be estimated from

$$L_n L_n^t = \overline{B}_n \text{ and } L_n \overline{q}_n = \overline{g}_n \tag{8.37}$$

From the last row of Eq. 8.36, Z_n can be obtained. Using the values of $\overline{P}, \overline{Q}$ and L' for each partition and by the process of back substition of Eq. 8.36 one can obtain the values of $Z_{n-1}, Z_{n-2}, \ldots, Z_2$ and Z_1 sequentially.

8.4 GENERALIZED LOADING (ASYMMETRIC LOADING)

For the finite element analysis of rotationally periodic structures under asymmetric loading, the applied force distribution defined by the forces acting at each degree of freedom (*d. o. f.*) of the finite element idealization must be used. The force acting in the *k*th *d. o. f.* of the *j*th substructure may be expanded in the form of a finite Fourier series. The analysis is carried out for each of the harmonics separately and these are added to define the complete displacement pattern of the structure.

This method provides an economical way of solving the rotationally periodic structure. Without the use of this method, the complete structure must be idealised for the given system of loading. This would require much more computer storage and time.

8.4.1 Fourier Harmonics

A rotationally periodic structure with N identical substructures is shown in Fig. 8.1. Each substructure is idealized as a series of elements. The applied force system is defined by the forces corresponding to the different degrees of freedom. The force acting on the kth degree of the jth substructure may be expanded in the form of a finite Fourier series as

$$a_{jk} = \sum_{p=1}^{N} f_{PK}\, e^{-i(j-1)(2\pi P/N)} \tag{8.38}$$

where f_{PK} are the spatial Fourier harmonic coefficients of forces corresponding to a spatial phase difference of $2\pi\, P/N$ between adjacent substructures and may be complex. Equation 8.38 is applicable to an arbitrary distribution of force system on the structure.

Assume that we know the force distribution acting on the structure. We can use Eq. 8.38 to set up the following matrix equation.

$$\begin{bmatrix} a_{1k} \\ a_{2k} \\ \cdots \\ a_{jk} \\ \cdots \\ a_{Nk} \end{bmatrix} = \begin{bmatrix} 1 & 1 & 1 \\ e^{-i(2\pi/N)} & e^{-i(4\pi/N)} & 1 \\ \cdots\cdots & \cdots\cdots & \cdots \\ e^{-i(j-1)2\pi/N} & & 1 \\ \cdots\cdots & \cdots\cdots & \cdots \\ e^{-i(N-1)2\pi/N} & \cdots\cdots & 1 \end{bmatrix} \begin{bmatrix} f_{1k} \\ f_{2k} \\ \cdots \\ f_{3k} \\ \cdots \\ f_{Nk} \end{bmatrix} \tag{8.39}$$

Hence the Fourier harmonic of the force on the kth degree of freedom will be given by

$$\begin{bmatrix} f_{1k} \\ f_{2k} \\ \cdots \\ f_{jk} \\ \cdots \\ f_{Nk} \end{bmatrix} = \begin{bmatrix} 1 & 1 & 1 \\ e^{-i(2\pi/N)} & e^{-i(4\pi/N)} & 1 \\ \cdots\cdots & \cdots\cdots & \cdots \\ e^{-i(j-1)2\pi/N} & & 1 \\ \cdots\cdots & \cdots\cdots & \cdots \\ e^{-i(N-1)2\pi/N} & \cdots\cdots & 1 \end{bmatrix}^{-1} \begin{bmatrix} a_{1k} \\ a_{2k} \\ \cdots \\ a_{jk} \\ \cdots \\ a_{Nk} \end{bmatrix} \tag{8.40}$$

The *P*th equation of matrix 8.40 is given by

$$f_{pk} = \frac{1}{N} \sum_{j=1}^{N} a_{jk} e^{i(j-1)(2\pi P/N)} \tag{8.41}$$

For a given force acting on kth d.o.f. of each substructure, we can use Eq. 8.41 to obtain the spatial Fourier harmonics of force for that d.o.f. It is important to note that any given d.o.f.o in any substructure is related to a corresponding d.o.f. in another substructure. For example any d.o.f. in the *j*th substructure is obtained by rotating the corresponding d.o.f. in the first substructure through $2\pi\ (J - 1)/N$ radians about the axis of symmetry.

8.4.2 Substructure Stiffness Matrix

The equation of equilibrium of the full structure obtained from the finite element analysis is given by

$$[K]\ \{\delta\} = \{f\} \tag{8.42}$$

where $[K]$ is of size $[Nm, Nm]$, $\{\delta\}$ and $\{f\}$ of size $(Nm, 1)$. N is the number of substructures and m the number of d.o.f. in each substructure. The resulting system of equations is to be solved by expressing the force system in terms of N Fourier components. In other words each term in $\{f\}$ in Eq. 8.42 is a finite series having N terms. Let each one of these terms be given by $\{\delta_p\}$ of size $(mN, 1)$. Since all the substructures are identical and are subjected to forces which differ from those on the next substructure by the same phase multiplier exp $(-\ i\ 2\ \pi\ P/N)$, the effect on the neighbouring substructures must be related in the same way. Thus $\{\delta_p\}$ can be expressed as

$$\begin{bmatrix} \delta'_p \\ \delta'_p \quad e^{-i(2\pi P/N)} \\ \cdots\cdots \\ \cdots\cdots \\ \cdots\cdots \\ \cdots\cdots \\ \cdots\cdots \\ \delta'_p \quad e^{-i(N-1)2\pi/N} \end{bmatrix} \tag{8.43}$$

where $\{\delta'_p\}$ is the deformation of the first substructure. Hence for the first substructure the matrix equation gets simplified to the form

$$[K']\ \{\delta'_p\} = \{f'_p\} \tag{8.44}$$

For any Fourier index p, $[K']$ will be of size (m, m) and $\{\delta'_p\}$ and $\{f'_p\}$ of size $(m, 1)$.

Let us assume that we have solved Eq. 8.44 for each Fourier harmonic P. The resultant displacement vector of the first substructure is then given by

$$\{\delta_1\} = \sum_{p=1}^{N} \{\delta'_p\} \tag{8.45}$$

The deflection of any other substructure j is therefore given by

$$\{\delta_j\} = \sum_{p=1}^{N} \{\delta'_p\} e^{-i(j-1)2\pi P/N} \tag{8.46}$$

The Potters' and submatrices elimination schemes are modified to solve Eq. 8.44.

Example 8.1

Consider a hexagonal structure in which each substructure consists of three nodes assuming only one degree of freedom per node. Determine the constrained stiffness matrix of the structure.

Solution

Consider a single substructure including the joints with other substructures. Let us include 4th node to the first substructure. Applying the complex constraints between node 1 and node 4 we have

$$\begin{Bmatrix} u_1 \\ u_2 \\ u_3 \\ u_4 \end{Bmatrix}_0 = \begin{bmatrix} 1 & 0 & 0 \\ 0 & 1 & 0 \\ 0 & 0 & 1 \\ e^{i\phi} & 0 & 0 \end{bmatrix} \begin{Bmatrix} u_1 \\ u_2 \\ u_3 \end{Bmatrix}_p \tag{1}$$

The constraint stiffness matrix can be obtained by the following equation

$$[k]_p = \begin{bmatrix} 1 & 0 & 0 & e^{-i\phi} \\ 0 & 1 & 0 & 0 \\ 0 & 0 & 1 & 0 \end{bmatrix} \begin{bmatrix} k_{11} & k_{12} & k_{13} & k_{14} \\ k_{21} & k_{22} & k_{23} & k_{24} \\ k_{31} & k_{32} & k_{33} & k_{34} \\ k_{41} & k_{42} & k_{43} & k_{44} \end{bmatrix} \begin{bmatrix} 1 & 0 & 0 \\ 0 & 1 & 0 \\ 0 & 0 & 1 \\ e^{i\phi} & 0 & 0 \end{bmatrix}$$

$$= \begin{bmatrix} k_{11} + k_{41}e^{-i\phi} + k_{14}e^{-i\phi} + k_{44} & k_{12} + k_{42}e^{-i\phi} & k_{13} + k_{43}e^{-i\phi} \\ k_{21} + k_{24}e^{i\phi} & k_{22} & k_{23} \\ k_{31} + k_{34}e^{i\phi} & k_{32} & k_{33} \end{bmatrix}$$

If the structure is more complicated with extra interconnections, then each complex constraint would have been applied independently. Each successive complex constraint is applied to the current constrained matrix until the final constraint gives $[k]_p$.

8.5 FREE VIBRATION ANALYSIS

As mentioned earlier a circumferential periodicity consists of a number of identical substructures coupled together in identical manner to form a closed ring. A substructure may be arbitrarily coupled to other substructures with suitable complex constraints. The advantage of this method is that this reduces the equations of motion for the complete structure to a set of equations of motion for a single substructure. The number of equations reduced in this process is in the same proportion and computational benefits are more.

The free undamped vibrations of circumferentialy rotating periodic structures with the rotation being about the axis of structural symmetry can also be analysed using the present finite element modeling. The relationship between the generalized forces and displacements are established using the elastic stiffness, geometric stiffness, inertia, centrifugal and gyroscopic matrices. All are real and symmetric matrices except for the gyroscopic matrix which is real skew symmetric. The presence of skew-symmetric gyroscopic matrix makes the distinction between the rotating and non-rotating bodies. The free vibration of a rotating elastic body is represented by the following equation of motion

$$[[k]+i\omega[c]-\omega^2[M]]\;\{Z\}\;e^{i\omega t}=0 \tag{8.47}$$

Here $\{Z\}$ is a vector of amplitudes which may be complex, $[k]$ is a real symmetric stiffness matrix including any centrifugal and geometric stiffness, $[M]$ is a mass matrix of real symmetric nature and $[c]$ is a real skew-symmetric gyroscopic matrix. It is assumed that the structure rotates about its axis of structural symmetry with a constant angular velocity Ω.

8.5.1 Free Vibration Analysis without Dampling

Simple case of a rotationally periodic structure divided into N identical substructures each of which contains J degrees of freedom is çonsidered. Consider each substructure to be connected to atleast two neighbouring substructures. The stiffness matrix of the structure can be expressed as a number of $J\times J$ submatrices corresponding to each substructure. Consider the ith substructure whose submatrices are $[k_{ii}^{(i)}]$ which represent the effect on the J degrees of freedom in the substructure and up to $n-1$ substructures $[k_{ji}^{(i)}]$ and $[k_{jj}^{(i)}]$. These traid submatrices represent the interaction between the ith and jth substructure. The equations of motion of the whole structure is given by

$$\begin{bmatrix} \sum\limits_{i=1}^{N} K_{11}^{(i)} & K_{12}^{(1)}+K_{12}^{(2)} & K_{13}^{(1)}+K_{13}^{(3)} & \cdots & K_{1N}^{(1)}+K_{1N}^{(N)} \\ K_{21}^{(2)}+K_{21}^{(1)} & \sum\limits_{i=1}^{N} K_{22}^{(i)} & K_{23}^{(2)}+K_{23}^{(3)} & \cdots & K_{2N}^{(2)}+K_{2N}^{(N)} \\ K_{31}^{(3)}+K_{31}^{(1)} & K_{31}^{(3)}+K_{31}^{(2)} & \cdots & \cdots & \cdots \\ \cdots & \cdots & \cdots & \cdots & \cdots \\ \cdots & \cdots & \cdots & \cdots & \cdots \\ K_{N1}^{(N)}+K_{N1}^{(1)} & K_{N2}^{(N)}+K_{N2}^{(2)} & K_{N3}^{(N)}+K_{N3}^{(3)} & \cdots & \sum\limits_{i=1}^{N} K_{NN}^{(i)} \end{bmatrix}$$

$$-\omega^2\begin{bmatrix} \sum\limits_{i=1}^{N} M_{11}^{(i)} & M_{12}^{(1)}+M_{12}^{(2)} & M_{13}^{(1)}+M_{13}^{(3)} & \cdots & M_{1N}^{(1)}+M_{1N}^{(N)} \\ M_{21}^{(2)}+M_{21}^{(1)} & \sum\limits_{i=1}^{N} M_{22}^{(i)} & M_{23}^{(2)}+M_{23}^{(3)} & \cdots & M_{2N}^{(2)}+M_{2N}^{(N)} \\ M_{31}^{(3)}+M_{31}^{(1)} & M_{32}^{(3)}+M_{32}^{(2)} & \cdots & \cdots & \cdots \\ \cdots & \cdots & \cdots & \cdots & \cdots \\ \cdots & \cdots & \cdots & \cdots & \cdots \\ M_{N1}^{(N)}+M_{N1}^{(1)} & M_{N2}^{(N)}+M_{N2}^{(2)} & M_{N3}^{(N)}+M_{N2}^{(3)} & \cdots & \sum\limits_{i=1}^{N} M_{NN}^{(i)} \end{bmatrix}\begin{bmatrix} Z^{(1)} \\ Z^{(2)} \\ Z^{(3)} \\ \cdots \\ \cdots \\ Z^{(N)} \end{bmatrix}=0 \tag{8.48}$$

Solution to the above free vibration equation is as follows. The two substructures can be combined with complex constraints, all the connections between the substructures are identical. The first row of Eq. 8.48 can be written as

$$\left\{\left[\sum_{i=1}^{N}[K_{11}^{(i)}]\ [K_{12}^{(1)}]+[K_{12}^{(2)}]\ \ldots\ldots\ [K_{1N}^{(1)}]+[K_{1N}^{(N)}]\right]\right.$$

$$\left.-\omega^2\left[\sum_{i=1}^{N}[M_{11}^{(i)}]\ [M_{12}^{(1)}]+[M_{12}^{(2)}]\ \ldots\ldots\ [M_{1N}^{(1)}]+[M_{1N}^{(N)}]\right]\right\}\begin{Bmatrix} Z^{(1)} \\ Z^{(2)} \\ \cdots \\ \cdots \\ Z^{(n)} \end{Bmatrix}=0 \tag{8.49}$$

Here we have all the substructures identical and hence

$$[K_{11}^{(j)}]=[K_{(M+2-j)(N+2-J)}^{(1)}]\quad \text{for } j=2,3,\ldots N$$

and hence

$$\sum_{i=1}^{N}[K_{11}^{(i)}]=\sum_{i=1}^{N}[K_{ii}^{(1)}] \tag{8.50}$$

A similar logic holds good in establishing the mass matrices. Because of the identical coupling terms we have

$$[K_{1j}^{(j)}]=[K_{(N+2-j)1}]\quad \text{for } j=2,3,4\ldots\ldots N \tag{8.51}$$

$Z^{(2)}, Z^{(3)}$ up to $Z^{(N)}$ can be eliminated from Eq. 8.49 by using equation

$$Z^{(j-1)}=e^{i\phi}\{Z^{j}\}\quad \text{or}\quad \{Z^{(j)}\}=e^{i\phi}\{Z^{(j-1)}\} \tag{8.52}$$

and substituting from Eqs. 8.50 and 8.51 into Eq 8.49 yields

$$\left\{\left[\sum_{j=1}^{N}[K_{ij}^{(1)}]+\sum_{j=2}^{N}[K_{ij}^{(1)}]e^{i(j-1)\phi}+\sum_{j=2}^{N}[K_{(N+2-J)}]e^{-i(j-1)\phi}\right]\right.$$

$$\left.-\omega^2\left[\sum_{j=1}^{N}[M_{jj}^{(1)}]+\sum_{j=2}^{N}[M_{1j}^{(1)}]e^{i(j-1)\phi}+\sum_{j=2}^{N}[M_{(N+2-j)}^{(1)}]e^{-i(j-1)\phi}\right]\right\}\{Z^{(1)}\}=0 \tag{8.53}$$

where $\phi=2\pi n/N$

Now let us replace $N+2-j$ by k then we have

$$e^{i(j-1)\phi}=e^{i(N+1-k)\phi}=e^{iN\phi}e^{i(1-k)\phi}=e^{-i(k-1)\phi}$$

since $N\phi$ is a multiple of 2π.

Now we have

$$\sum_{j=2}^{N}[K_{(N+2-j)1}^{(1)}]e^{i(j-1)\phi}=\sum_{k=2}^{N}[K_{(k)1}^{(1)}]e^{-i(k-1)\phi}$$

and replacing the suffix k by j, the Eq. 8.53 can be written as

$$\left\{\left[\sum_{j=1}^{N}[K_{jj}^{(1)}]+\sum_{j=2}^{N}[K_{1j}^{(1)}]e^{i(j-1)\phi}+\sum_{j=2}^{N}[K_{j1}^{(1)}]e^{-i(j-1)\phi}\right]\right.$$

$$\left.-\omega^2\left[\sum_{j=1}^{N}[M_{jj}^{(1)}]+\sum_{j=2}^{N}[M_{1j}^{(1)}\}e^{i(j-1)\phi}+\sum_{j=2}^{N}[M_{(j1)}^{(1)}]e^{-i(j-1)\phi}\right]\right\}\{Z^{(1)}\}=0 \tag{8.54}$$

It is apparent that Eq. 8.54 is an eigenvalue equation consisting of J d.o.f. in one substructure. It is also observed that the substructure is not coupled to any other substructure. Hence its solution results in J eigenvalues and associated eigenvectors $\{Z^{(1)}\}$. By changing the ϕ values we can generate J eigenvectors $\{Z\}$ which represent the complete structure. Here all the $\{Z\}$ eigenvectors are complex and their associated orthogonal pairs of real and imaginary vectors can be easily obtained, which are denoted as $\{u\}$ and $\{\overline{u}\}$ respectively.

The eigenvalue problem of Eq. 8.53 is formed with two complex mass and stiffness matrices. It is obvious that both the matrices are Hermitian which means the real parts of the matrices are symmetric and the imaginary parts are skew symmetric. For such an eigenvalue problem the eigenvalues are real in nature and the eigenvectors are complex, which is the property of an eigenvalue problem whose mass and stiffness matrices are Hermitian. Therefore Eq. 8.53 results in real eigenvalues and complex eigenvectors.

Here Eq. 8.53 represents an eigenvalue problem of one substructure which gives J eigen pairs. There are N such substructures in the total structure. Therefore NJ eigenvalues are obtainable from the Eq. 8.52. This is the same as the total number of degrees of freedom of the entire stucture. All these eigen-vectors of the entire structure can be obtained by N analyses of one substructure. It is observed that the negative values of ϕ correspond to eigenvectors with the same frequencies and mode shapes however, its direction being opposite. Hence it is enough if we solve the Eq. 8.53 for positive values of ϕ.

It is very easy to develop the stiffness and mass matrices of one substructure in Eq. 8.53. The matrices are formed for a single substructure including the coupling terms to all other substructures. The stiffness matrix $[k]$ is of the form

$$[K] = \begin{bmatrix} K_{11}^{(1)} & K_{12}^{(1)} & K_{13}^{(1)} & .. & .. & K_{1N}^{(1)} \\ K_{21}^{(1)} & K_{22}^{(1)} & K_{23}^{(1)} & .. & .. & \phi \\ K_{31}^{(1)} & \Phi & K_{33}^{(1)} & .. & .. & \phi \\ \cdots & \cdots & \cdots & .. & .. & .. \\ K_{N1}^{(1)} & \phi & \phi & .. & .. & K_{NN}^{(1)} \end{bmatrix} \tag{8.55}$$

Obviously this matrix has NJ d.o.f. if none of the rows contain zero terms throughout. This can be reduced to J d.o.f. system by applying complex constraints of the form

$$\{Z^{(j)}\} = e^{i(j-1)\phi}\{Z^{(1)}\} \tag{8.56}$$

The transformed stiffness matrix can be obtained by applying transformation to the matrix such as

$$[K_p] = [P]^T\,[K]\,[P] \tag{8.57}$$

Where

$$[P] = \begin{bmatrix} I_j \\ e^{i\phi} I_j \\ e^{2i\phi} I_j \\ e^{i(N-1)\phi} I_j \end{bmatrix} \tag{8.58}$$

and $[P]^T$ is its conjugate transpose. It many readily be verified that $[K_P]$ evaluated from Eqs. 8.55 and 8.57 is apparently the stiffness matrix of Eq. 8.53. The mass matrix also can be obtained in the same way.

For most of the engineering problems each substructure will only be connected with a small number of other substructures. In the case of many mechanical engineering structures, they will be coupled with only two other substructures, one on either side of the substructures. For such structures the stiffness matrix formed from Eq. 8.55 may only be tridiagonal except for the corner elements which represent the coupling terms. It is also observed that all the tridiagonal elements are only real quantities except the corner elements which are complex terms. This property of the matrices can be utilized in reducing the computer storage and time. This is demonstrated in the following example.

8.5.2 Mode shapes of a periodic structure

As mentioned earlier a rotationally periodic structure consists of N identical substructures. Eigenvalue equations of the structure is indicated in Eq. 8.1. The total number of d.o.f. of the structure is NJ where J is the d.o.f. of each substructure. The eigen-vector of the whole structure can be represented as $\{u\}$ which can be written as

$$\{u\} = \{u^{(1)}u^{(2)}u^{(3)} \ldots.\, u^{(j)} \,..\, u^{(N)}\}^T \tag{8.59}$$

where $\{u^{(j)}\}$ is a vector of length J consisting of displacements of J d.o.f. of the jth substructure. The vector $\{u^{(j)}\}$ are all real.

In the case of axisymmetric structures it is found that most of the modes of vibration are in orthogonal pairs. The possible mode shapes can be categorized into three depending on the shapes of the individual substructures. These are

(a) Axisymmetric modes: All the substructures have the same deflected shape and are also in phase $\{u\} = \{u^1, u^1, \ldots, u^1\}^T$

(b) Antisymmetric modes: Deflected shapes of all the substructures are the same but the adjacent areas are out of phase

$$\{u\} = \{u^1, -u^1, u^1, -u^1, \ldots, -u^1\}^T \tag{8.60}$$

This occurs only in the case of the substructures where N is an even number

(c) All other possible mode shapes.

In most of the situations the mode shapes of class (a) and (b) exhibit degeneracy. Mode shapes of class (a) do not change even if they are rotated through any intergral number of substructures. As mentioned earlier, class (b) mode shapes can exist only when N is even, the rotation of the mode shape through an even number of substructures is unchanged. When it is rotated through an odd number of substructures, it changes its sign i.e. $\{u\}$ will become $-\{u\}$, obviously this change represents the phase shift in the vibration. All other mode shapes are considered as class (c) and they exhibit two-fold degeneracy. An eigenvector $\{u\}$ of mode shape of class (c) has $u^{(j)} \not\equiv u^{(j+1)}$ and $u^j \not\equiv -\, u^{(j+1)}$. In a periodic structure all the substructures are identical, the deflected shape of $\{u\}$ when rotated through one substruture is say $\{u'\}$ with the same eigenvalue. $\{u'\}$ is of the form

$$\{u'\} = \{u^{(N)}u^{(1)}u^{(2)} \ldots..\, u^{(N-1)}\}^T \tag{8.61}$$

and is normalised such that $\{u'\}^T\{u\} = [\Pi]$
$\{u'\}$ can be expressed as a linear combination of two orthogonal eigenvectors $\{u\}$ and $\{\overline{u}\}$.

$$\{u'\} = C\{u\} + S\{\overline{u}\} \tag{8.62}$$

where C and S are constants. Let us consider a vector $\{\overline{u}'\}$ orthogonal to $\{u'\}$ which can be expressed as

$$\{\overline{u}'\} = -S\{u\} + C\{\overline{u}\} \tag{8.63}$$

Expanding Eq. 8.63 to verify its orthogonality

$$\begin{aligned}\{u'\}^T\{\overline{u}\} &= (C\{u\}^T + S\{\overline{u}\}^T)(-S\{\overline{u}\}^T + C\{\overline{u}\}) \\ &= C^2\{u\}^T\{\overline{u}\} - S^2\{\overline{u}\}^T\{u\} - CS\{u\}^T\{u\} + SC\{\overline{u}\}^T\{\overline{u}\} \\ &= 0\end{aligned} \tag{8.64}$$

Therefore the vectors $\{u'\}$ and $\{\overline{u}'\}$ can be expressed as transformation vectors $\{u\}$ and $\{\overline{u}'\}$ by

$$\begin{Bmatrix} u' \\ \overline{u}' \end{Bmatrix} = \begin{bmatrix} C[I_{NJ}] & S[I_{NJ}] \\ -S[I_{NJ}] & C[I_{NJ}] \end{bmatrix} \begin{Bmatrix} u \\ \overline{u} \end{Bmatrix} = [R] \begin{Bmatrix} u \\ \overline{u} \end{Bmatrix} \tag{8.65}$$

Where $[I_{NJ}]$ is the unit diagonal matrix of size NJ. Hence $[R]^j$ is a transformation matrix that rotates the orthogonal vectors $\{u\}$ and $\{\overline{u}\}$ through j substructures. Therefore $[R]^N = [I_{2NJ}]$ as it rotates around N substructures without changing the vectors. We have

$$\{u'\}^T\{u'\} = 1$$

Substituting in Eq. 8.64 we have

$$C^2 + S^2 = 1$$

Therefore,

$$C = \cos\psi \text{ and } S = \sin\psi \tag{8.66}$$

From the Eq. 8.65, the deflated shape of the Nth substructure can be written in terms of deflected shape of the first substructure as

$$\begin{Bmatrix} u^{(N)} \\ \overline{u}^{(N)} \end{Bmatrix} = \begin{bmatrix} C[I_J] & S[I_J] \\ -S[I_J] & C[I_J] \end{bmatrix} \begin{Bmatrix} u^{(1)} \\ \overline{u}^{(1)} \end{Bmatrix} \tag{8.67}$$

Similarly for any other substructure j,

$$\begin{Bmatrix} u^{j-1} \\ \overline{u}^{j-1} \end{Bmatrix} = \begin{bmatrix} C[I_J] & S[I_J] \\ -S[I_J] & C[I_J] \end{bmatrix} \begin{Bmatrix} u^{(j)} \\ \overline{u}^{(j)} \end{Bmatrix} \tag{8.68}$$

Equation 8.65 can be expressed in complex form

$$\{Z'\} = e^{-i\psi}\{Z^j\}$$

where $$\{Z\} = \{u\} + i\{\overline{u}\}$$

and $$\{Z'\} = \{u'\} + i\{\overline{u}'\} \tag{8.69}$$

Eq. 8.68 in the complex vector form

$$\{Z^{j-1}\} = e^{-i\psi}\{Z^j\}$$

$$\{Z^j\} = e^{+i\psi}\{Z^{j-1}\} \tag{8.70}$$

From the Eq. 8.65 in the complex form $e^{iN\psi} = 1$ for which there are N independent values for ψ between $-\pi$ and π. For even number of substructures these are $-\pi$, $-2\pi(N/2-1)/N \ldots -4\pi/N \ldots -2\pi/N, 0, 2\pi/N, 4\pi/N, \ldots 2\pi(N/2-1)/N, \pi$, and for odd number of N they are,

$$-2\pi(N-1)/N \ldots -2\pi/N..0, 2\pi/N, 4\pi/N, \ldots 2\pi(N-1)/2N$$

To obtain all possible modes of vibration of the structure it is necessary to find the modes for N even, to the $N/2+1$ values of ψ given by

$$0, 2\pi/N, 4\pi/N, \ldots 2N(N/2-1)\,N, \pi$$

and for N odd, to the $(N+1)/2$ values of ψ given by

$$0, 2\pi/N, 4\pi/N \ldots 2\pi(N-1)/2N,$$

which means that the negative values of ψ correspond to anticlockwise rotation and the positive values to clockwise. This is because all the anticlockwise eigenvectors are the orthogonal pairs of the clockwise ones. They can be generated if clockwise vectors $\{Z\}$ are known, by generating complex conjugates of $\{Z\}$ for a given value of ψ. Hence it is possible to calculate all the corresponding mode shapes of one substructure from which we get the mode shapes for the whole structure, by computing the mass and stiffness matrices of one substructure without any approximation. Repeating the same for all the possible values of ψ it is possible to obtain all the mode shapes of the complete structure.

8.5.3 Theoretical analysis

For simplicity consider a periodic structure consisting of N identical substructures each having J degrees of freedom. The total number of degrees of freedom of the whole structure will be NJ. The eigenvector of the structure is the vector given in 8.59. All the mode shapes of the rotationally periodic structure fall under $\psi = 0$ and $\psi = \pi$ respectively. Also consider a rotationally periodic structure in which each substructure is connected to two other substructures on either side.

In the finite element analysis, the lumped mass matrix approach reduces the computational effort considerably. It is also proved that the convergence rate is faster when compared to other solution techniques of eigenvalue problems.

A schematic finite element analysis procedure is discussed in this section. The element mass is assumed to be lumped at the nodes of the triangle. The rotary inertia terms are neglected. This in turn gives the diagonal mass matrix for the entire structure. The equation of motion of the structure in terms of the mass and stiffness matrices is as follows

$$\begin{bmatrix} K_{1,1} & K_{1,2} & K_{1,3} & .. & .. & K_{1,N} \\ K_{2,1} & K_{2,2} & K_{2,3} & .. & .. & 0 \\ .. & .. & .. & .. & .. & .. \\ .. & .. & .. & .. & .. & .. \\ K_{N,1} & .. & .. & .. & .. & K_{N,N} \end{bmatrix} \begin{Bmatrix} Z_1 \\ Z_2 \\ Z_3 \\ .. \\ Z_N \end{Bmatrix}$$

$$= [\omega^2]\begin{bmatrix} M_{1,1} & 0 & 0 & .. & .. & 0 \\ 0 & M_{2,3} & 0 & .. & .. & 0 \\ 0 & 0 & M_{3,3} & .. & .. & .. \\ ... & ... & ... & .. & .. & .. \\ 0 & ... & ... & .. & .. & M_{N,N} \end{bmatrix} \begin{Bmatrix} Z_1 \\ Z_2 \\ Z_3 \\ .. \\ Z_N \end{Bmatrix} \tag{8.71}$$

This is a non-standard eigenvalue problem which yields a solution of positive definite and symmetric real matrix.

The deflection of *k*th sector is related to the deflection of the preceding sector by employing wave propagation theory. The equations are as follows:

$$Z_k = Z_{k-1}e^{j\mu} \tag{8.72}$$

and

$$Z_{k-1} = Z_k e^{-j\mu} \tag{8.73}$$

where μ is the wave propagation constant.

A normal mode of vibration is said to be a standing wave if the condition $e^{j\mu N} = 1$ is satisfied. This gives $\mu = 2\pi m/N$

where

$$m = \begin{cases} -(N/2-1), ..., -2, -1, & \\ 0, 1, 2, (N/2-1), N/2 & \text{if } N \text{ is even} \\ -(N-1)/2, ..., -2, -1, & \\ 0, 1, 2, ..., \quad (N-1)/2 & \text{if } N \text{ is odd} \end{cases} \tag{8.74}$$

The negative values associated with waves are the same as the ones associated with the corresponding positive values. Therefore it is enough if positive values are considered. Therefore

$$m = \begin{cases} 0, 1, 2.. \quad .., \quad (N/2-1), N/2 \text{ if } N \text{ is even} \\ 0, 1, 2.. \quad .., \quad (N-3)/2, (N-1)/2 \text{ if } N \text{ is odd} \end{cases} \tag{8.75}$$

For a sector consisting of *n* partitions the stiffness matrix for the entire structure is given in Eq. 8.3.

The eigenvector can be simplified by expressions given in (8.72) and (8.73) as follows:

$$[Z_1, Z_2, ... Z_{n-1}, Z_n, Z_1e^{-i\mu}, Z_2e^{i\mu} \; .... \; Z_ne^{i\mu}, Z_1e^{2i\mu},$$

$$.... \; Z_2e^{2i\mu}, ... \; Z_1e^{-i\mu}, Z_2^{-i\mu} \; ..... \; Z_ne^{-i\mu}] \tag{8.76}$$

Mass Matrix also can be simplified as follows

$$\begin{bmatrix} M_1 & 0 & 0 & .. & .. & 0 \\ 0 & M_2 & 0 & .. & .. & 0 \\ 0 & 0 & M_3 & .. & .. & .. \\ ... & ... & ... & .. & M_{N-1} & .. \\ 0 & ... & ... & .. & 0 & M_N \end{bmatrix} \tag{8.77}$$

The Eq. 8.71 can be written by substituting Eqs. 8.2, 8.76 and 8.77 for first sector which is decoupled from other sectors and is as follows:

$$\begin{bmatrix} B_1 & A_1 & 0 & .. & .. & C_1e^{-i\mu} \\ C_2 & B_2 & A_2 & .. & .. & 0 \\ .. & \cdots & \cdots & .. & .. & .. \\ \cdots & \cdots & \cdots & C_{n-1} & B_{n-1} & A_{n-1} \\ A_N e^{i\mu} & .. & .. & .. & C_n & B_n \end{bmatrix} \begin{Bmatrix} Z_1 \\ Z_2 \\ .. \\ .. \\ Z_n \end{Bmatrix}$$

$$= [\omega^2] \begin{bmatrix} M_1 & 0 & 0 & .. & .. & 0 \\ 0 & M_2 & 0 & .. & .. & 0 \\ .. & .. & .. & .. & .. & .. \\ \cdots & \cdots & \cdots & .. & M_{n-1} & 0 \\ 0 & \cdots & \cdots & .. & .. & M_{N,N} \end{bmatrix} \begin{Bmatrix} Z_1 \\ Z_2 \\ .. \\ .. \\ Z_N \end{Bmatrix} \tag{8.78}$$

To obtain all the eigenvalues of the entire structure the above equation must be solved for $(N/2 + 1)$ values of μ if N is even or $(N + 1)/2$ values of μ if N is odd. The stiffness matrix is complex and the mass matrix is real and diagonal. Hence this is a Hermitian eigenvalue problem. Its eigenvalues are real and eigenvectors are complex. The modes may be a combination of two real orthogonal degenerated modes with a phase difference of $\pi/2$ for all values of μ except for ϕ and π when the eigenvalue problem becomes real. For other sectors the mode shapes can be obtained by Eqs. 8.72 and 8.73.

Simultaneous Iteration Scheme

Simultaneous iteration scheme is a very efficient scheme in computing the first few eigen pairs. Its advantage over other methods is that this scheme computes the eigen pairs simultaneously instead of computing one after the other.

The Hermitian eigenvalue problem obtained in Eq. 8.78 can be represented as

$$[\overline{K}]\,\{\overline{Z}\} = \omega^2[\overline{M}]\,\{\overline{Z}\} \tag{8.79}$$

A schematic procedure for solving the above equation is given below

1. Trial eigenvectors on the right hand side are assumed as $\{\overline{Z}_\phi\}$ and are orthonormalised with respect to mass matrix $[\overline{M}]$.
2. Vector

$$\{\overline{G}\} = [\overline{M}]\,\{\overline{Z}_\phi\} \tag{8.80}$$

is computed.

3. The reduced simultaneous equations of the form

$$[\overline{K}]\,\{\overline{Z}\} = \{\overline{G}\} \tag{8.81}$$

are solved.

4. The new vector $\{\overline{Z}_i\}$ is orthonormalised with respect to $[\overline{M}]$.
5. The interaction matrix is given by

$$[\lambda^2] = \{\overline{Z}_1\}^H\,[\overline{K}]\,\{\overline{Z}_1\} \tag{8.82}$$

6. The orthonormalised new vector $\{\overline{Z}_1\}$ is used in step 2 for next iteration. This is repeated until the convergence of $[\lambda^2]$ is obtained.

Modified Potters' Method

The modified Potters' method is extended to solve the Hermitian simultaneous equations. Equation 8.81 can be expressed as

$$\begin{bmatrix} B_1 & A_1 & 0 & .. & .. & C_1K_1 \\ C_2 & B_2 & A_2 & .. & .. & 0 \\ .. & \cdots & \cdots & .. & .. & .. \\ \cdots & \cdots & \cdots & C_{n-1} & B_{n-1} & A_{n-1} \\ A_nK_2 & .. & .. & .. & C_n & B_n \end{bmatrix} \begin{Bmatrix} Z_1 \\ Z_2 \\ .. \\ .. \\ Z_n \end{Bmatrix} = \begin{Bmatrix} g_1 \\ g_2 \\ .. \\ .. \\ g_n \end{Bmatrix} \tag{8.83}$$

where $K_1 = e^{-j\mu}$ and $K_2 = 1/K_1$

The above equations can be written as

$$\begin{bmatrix} I_1 & P_1 & \Phi & .. & .. & K_1Q_1 \\ 0 & I_2 & P_2 & .. & .. & K_1Q_2 \\ .. & \cdots & \cdots & .. & .. & .. \\ \cdots & \cdots & \cdots & .. & I_{n-1} & \overline{Q}_{n-1} \\ A_NK_2 & .. & .. & .. & C_n & B_n \end{bmatrix} \begin{Bmatrix} Z_1 \\ Z_2 \\ .. \\ Z_{n-1} \\ Z_n \end{Bmatrix} = \begin{Bmatrix} q_1 \\ q_2 \\ .. \\ q_{n-1} \\ q_n \end{Bmatrix} \tag{8.84}$$

where P_1, Q_1 and q_1 are computed from Eq. 8.8. Similarly P, Q and q for other particulars are obtained from Eq. 8.9 and

$$\overline{Q}_{n-1} = P_{n-1} + K_1 Q_{n-1} \tag{8.85}$$

The last row of Eq. 8.84 is

$$K_2A_nZ_1 + B_nZ_n + C_nZ_{n-1} = g_n \tag{8.86}$$

From the last row of Eq. 8.84

$$K_2R_1Z_2 + S_1Z_n + C_nZ_{n-1} = u_1 \tag{8.87}$$

where

$$R_1 = -A_nP_1, S_1 = B_n - A_nQ_1, u_1 = g_n - A_nq_1K_2 \tag{8.88}$$

Expressions for Z_2 and then for Z_3 and so on are substituted in Eq. 8.86 and it reduces to

$$K_2R_iZ_{i+1} + S_iZ_n + C_nZ_{n-1} = u_1 \tag{8.89}$$

where

$$R_i = -R_{i-1}P_i$$

$$S_i = S_{i-1} - R_{i-1}Q_i$$

$$u_i = u_{i-1} - R_{i-1}q_iK_2$$

$$i = 2, 3, 4, ...n-2 \tag{8.90}$$

So far in all the equations except the terms involving load vectors (g_i, q_i, u_i, etc.) all are real. The equation at $(n-2)$ th station is reduced to

$$(C_n + K_2 R_{n-2}) Z_{n-1} + S_{n-2} Z_n = u_{n-2} \tag{8.91}$$

This can be further reduced to

$$\overline{R}_{n-1} Z_n = u_{n-1} \tag{8.92}$$

where

$$\overline{R}_{n-1} = (K_2 R_{n-2} + C_n)(Q_{n-1} K_1 + P_{n-1}) + S_{n-2}$$

and
$$u_{n-1} = [u_{n-2} - (K_2 R_{n-2} + C_2) q_{n-1}] \tag{8.93}$$

The above equation must be solved for Z_n and it is substituted in Eq. 8.84 to find out Z_{n-1}. By back substitutions in Eq. 8.84 one can easily get all the other values of Zs.

For subsequent iterations only the following operations are performed for the new right side vector G'

$$q'_1 = R_1^{-1} g'_1$$

$$q'_i = (B_i - C_i P_{i-1})^{-1} (g'_i - C_i q'_{i-1}) \quad i = 2, 3, 4 \ldots\ldots n-1$$

$$u'_1 = g_n - K_2 A_n q'_1$$

$$u'_i = u_{i-1} - R_{i-1} K_2 q'_i \qquad i = 2, 3, \ldots. n-2$$

$$u'_{n-1} = u'_{n-2} - (R_{n-2} K_2 + C_n) q'_{n-1} \tag{8.94}$$

Then the Eq. 8.92 must be solved for new vector u'_{n-1}. Then by back substitutions all the Zs can be obtained.

The submatrices P and Q are the same for $(n - 1)$ partitions and R and S for $(n - 2)$ partitions and they need not be altered for different values of K. Hence all the equations need not be computed for each value of μ. Only the operations involving g, q and u for $(n - 1)$ partitions and R_{n-1} and u_{n-1} are to be computed. Hence most of the operations for decomposition are to be carried out only once for each value of μ.

Modified Submatrices Elimination Scheme

The stiffness matrix of the structure under consideration is symmetric. This property is not utilized by the Potters' scheme. A better way of solving the Hermitian simultaneous Eqs. 8.81 making use of the symmetric nature of the stiffness matrices is by submatrices elimination scheme. Equation 8.83 can be written as

$$\begin{bmatrix} B_1 & A_1 & 0 & .. & .. & A_1 K_1 \\ A_1^t & B_2 & A_2 & .. & .. & 0 \\ .. & .. & .. & .. & .. & .. \\ .. & .. & .. & A_{n-1}^t & B_{n-1} & A_{n-1} \\ A_n K_2 & .. & .. & .. & A_{n-1}^t & B_n \end{bmatrix} \begin{Bmatrix} Z_1 \\ Z_2 \\ .. \\ Z_{n-1} \\ Z_n \end{Bmatrix} = \begin{Bmatrix} g_1 \\ g_2 \\ .. \\ g_{n-1} \\ g_n \end{Bmatrix} \tag{8.95}$$

$$\begin{bmatrix} L_1^t & P_1 & 0 & .. & .. & Q_1K_1 \\ 0 & L_2^t & P_2 & .. & .. & Q_2K_1 \\ .. & .. & .. & .. & .. & .. \\ .. & .. & .. & L_{n-2}^t & P_{n-2} & Q_{n-1}K_1 \\ .. & .. & .. & .. & L_{n-1}^t & \overline{Q}_{n-1} \\ A_nK_2 & .. & .. & .. & A_{n-1}^t & B_n \end{bmatrix} \begin{Bmatrix} Z_1 \\ Z_2 \\ .. \\ Z_{n-2} \\ Z_{n-1} \\ Z_n \end{Bmatrix} = \begin{Bmatrix} g_1 \\ g_2 \\ .. \\ q_{n-2} \\ q_{n-1} \\ q_n \end{Bmatrix} \quad (8.96)$$

where L_i, P_i and Q_i values are obtained by equating (8.21) and (8.22)

$$\overline{Q}_{n-1} = (P_{n-1} + Q_{n-1}k_1) \quad (8.97)$$

The first row of the Eq. 8.96 is premultiplied by $Q_1^t K_2$ and hence

$$K_2Q_1^tL_1^tZ_1 + K_2Q_1^tP_1Z_2 + Q_1^tQ_1Z_n = K_2Q_1^tq_1 \quad (8.98)$$

Using Eq. 8.26

$$K_2A_nZ_1 + K_2Q_1^tP_1Z_2 + Q_1^tQ_1Z_n = K_2Q_1^tq_1 \quad (8.99)$$

Subtracting the above equation from the last row of Eq. 8.96 gives rise to

$$[B_n - Q_1^tQ_1]Z_n + A_{n-1}^tZ_{n-1} - K_2Q_1^tP_1Z_2 = (g_n - K_2Q_1^t\overline{q}_1) \quad (8.100)$$

Premultiplying the second row of Eq. 8.96 by $K_2\ Q^T$ provides

$$K_2Q_2^tL_2^t\ Z_2 + K_2Q_2^tP_2Z_3 + Q_2^tQ_2Z_n = K_2Q_2^t\overline{q}_2 \quad (8.101)$$

Substituting for $Q_2^t \cdot L_2^t$ from Eq. 8.29 in Eq. 8.101 and combining with 8.100 reduces to

$$[B_n - Q_1^t \cdot Q_1 - Q_2^t \cdot Q_2]Z_n + A_{n-1}^tZ_{n-1} - K_2Q_2^tP_2Z_3$$
$$= (g_n - K_2Q_1^t \cdot \overline{q}_1 - K_2Q_2^t\overline{q}_2) \quad (8.102)$$

The same procedure is repeated upto $(n-2)$th partition and the resulting equation is given by

$$(B_n - Q_1^t \cdot Q_1 - Q_2^t \cdot Q_2 - ... - Q_{n-2}^t\ Q_{n-2})Z_n$$
$$+ A_{n-i}^tZ_{n-1} - K_2\overline{Q}_{n-2}^t \cdot \overline{P}_{n-2} \cdot Z_{n-1}$$
$$= [g_n - K_2 \cdot Q_1^tq_1 - K_2Q_2^tq_2 ... - K_2Q_{n-2}^t \cdot q_{n-2}] \quad (8.103)$$

The $(n-1)$ row of Eq. 8.96 is premultiplied by Q_{n-1}^H and hence

$$\overline{Q}_{n-1}^H \cdot L_{n-1}^t \cdot Z_{n-1} + \overline{Q}_{n-1}^H \cdot \overline{Q}_{n-1} = \overline{Q}_{n-1}^H \cdot \overline{q}_{n-1} \quad (8.104)$$

Using Eqs. 8.22 and 8.97

$$\overline{Q}^H_{n-1} \cdot L^t_{n-1} = (L^H_{n-1} \cdot \overline{Q}_{n-1})^H = [L_{m-1}(P_{n-1} + Q_{n-1}K_1)]^H$$

$$= (L^t_{n-1} \cdot \overline{P}_{n-1} + L^t_{n-1} \cdot Q_{n-1} \cdot K_1)^H$$

$$= [A_{n-1} - K_2 \cdot P^t_{n-2} \cdot Q_{n-2}]^H$$

$$= \left[A^t_{n-1} - K_2 \overline{Q}^t_{n-2} \cdot \overline{P}_{n-2}\right] \tag{8.105}$$

Substituting Eq. 8.105 in Eq. 8.104 reduces to

$$\overline{\overline{B}}_n \cdot Z_n = \overline{\overline{g}}_n \tag{8.106}$$

where

$$\overline{B}_n = \left[B_n - \overline{Q}^t_1 \cdot \overline{Q}_1 - \overline{Q}^t_2 \cdot \overline{Q}_2 - \dots - \overline{Q}^t_{n-2} \cdot \overline{Q}_{n-2}\right] \tag{8.107}$$

$$\overline{\overline{B}}_n = \left[\overline{B}_n - \overline{\overline{Q}}^H_{n-1} \overline{Q}_{n-1}\right] \tag{8.108}$$

$$\overline{\overline{g}}_n = \left[g_n - \overline{Q}^t_1 q_1 - \overline{Q}^t_2 q_2 - \dots - \overline{Q}^t_{n-2} \cdot \overline{q}_{n-2} - \overline{\overline{Q}}^H_{n-1} \cdot \overline{q}_{n-1}\right] \tag{8.109}$$

Hence Eq. 8.96 can be written as

$$\begin{bmatrix} L^t_1 & P_1 & .. & .. & .. & \overline{Q}_1 K_1 \\ 0 & L^t_2 & P_2 & .. & .. & \overline{Q}_2 K_1 \\ .. & .. & .. & .. & .. & .. \\ 0 & & & L^t_{n-2} & \overline{P}_{n-2} & \overline{Q}_{n-2} K_1 \\ 0. & & & & L^t_{n-1} & \overline{\overline{Q}}_{n-1} \\ 0 & & & & & L_n \end{bmatrix} \begin{Bmatrix} Z_1 \\ Z_2 \\ .. \\ Z_{n-2} \\ Z_{n-1} \\ Z_n \end{Bmatrix} = \begin{Bmatrix} \overline{q}_1 \\ \overline{q}_2 \\ .. \\ \overline{q}_{n-2} \\ \overline{q}_{n-1} \\ \overline{q}_n \end{Bmatrix} \tag{8.110}$$

L'_n and $\overline{q}_n$ are obtained from

$$L_n \cdot L^H_n = \overline{\overline{B}}_n \text{ and } L_n \cdot \overline{q}_n = \overline{g}_n \tag{8.111}$$

The back substitution process in the last row of Eq. 8.110 gives Z_n. Having computed the values of $\overline{P}, \overline{Q}$ and L' for each partition, the process of back substitution in each row of Eq. 8.110 gives all the values of $Z_{n-1}, Z_{n-2} \dots Z_2, Z_1$. Here also calculations of $\overline{B}_n, L, \overline{P}$ and $\overline{q}$ are independent of μ value. Hence most of the decomposition operations are in real mode and done only once.

Example 8.2

A regular polygon of N identical particles of mass m are situated at the vertices of a regular Nth order polygon (part of it is shown in Fig. 8.2) and joined together in pairs by identical massless springs along the sides of the polygon having spring constant K and with natural lengths equal to the lengths of the polygon sides. Every particle is connected to the rotating reference frame by a massless spring with spring constant αK acting in the radial directions. Taking the coriolis forces into consideration, compute the natural frequencies.

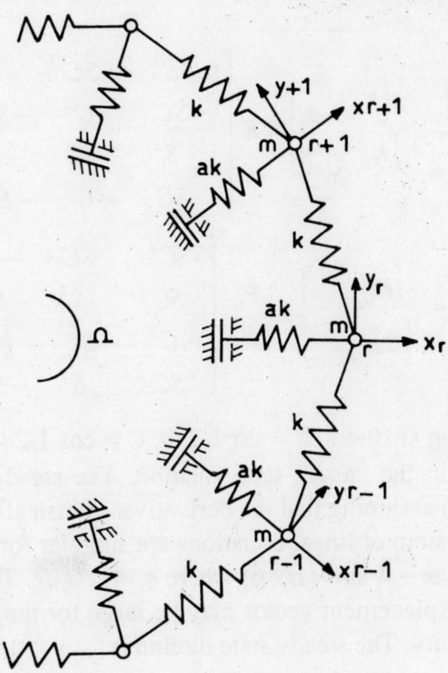

Fig. 8.2 Part of a rotating regular polygon

Solution

The polygon is assumed to rotate about its axis of structural symmetry with angular velocity Ω. A new position of equilibrium is obtained due to rotation.

Let us compute the equations of motion by the principles of energy. When it is vibrating the kinetic energy of the system is

$$T = \frac{1}{2} m \{\dot{Z}\}^T [I] \{\dot{Z}\} + \frac{1}{2} m \Omega^2 \{Z\} [I] \{Z\} + \Omega \{\dot{Z}\}^T [G] \{Z\}$$

$$+ m R \Omega^2 \sum_{r=1}^{N} X_r + m R \Omega \sum_{r=1}^{N} \dot{Y}_r + \frac{1}{2} m R^2 \Omega^2 \quad (1)$$

where $\dot{Z}$ is the velocity vector, $[I]$ is the unit matrix of proper order, R is the radius of the circle connecting the mass particles and $[G]$ is the block matrix on the main diagonal.

It is of the form

$$[G_{rr}^{(r)}] = m \begin{bmatrix} 0 & -1 \\ 1 & 0 \end{bmatrix} \quad (2)$$

The set of equations of motion of the system are

$$[M]\{\ddot{Z}\} + [K_E]\{Z\} + [K_G]\{Z\} - \Omega^2 [M]\{Z\} + 2\Omega [G]\{\dot{Z}\} = m R \Omega^2 \{a\} \quad (3)$$

where the mass matrix is $[M] = m\,[I]$. The vector $\{a\}^T = \{1, 0, 1, 0, \ldots 1, 0\}$ and is of order $2N$. $[K_E]$ is the elastic stiffness matrix, and $[K_G]$ is the geometric stiffness matrix which can be computed from the substructure stiffness matrices respectively.

$$\begin{bmatrix} \left[K_{E_{rr}}^{(r)}\right] & \left[K_{E_{r,r+1}}^{(r)}\right] \\ \left[K_{E_{r+1,r}}^{(r)}\right] & \left[K_{E_{r+1,r+1}}^{(r)}\right] \end{bmatrix} = K \begin{bmatrix} \alpha + S^2 & -SC & S^2 & SC \\ -SC & C^2 & -SC & -C^2 \\ S^2 & -SC & -S^2 & SC \\ SC & -C^2 & -SC & C^2 \end{bmatrix} \quad (4)$$

$$\begin{bmatrix} \left[K_{G_{rr}}^{(r)}\right] & \left[K_{G_{r,r+1}}^{(r)}\right] \\ \left[K_{G_{r+1,r}}^{(r)}\right] & \left[K_{E_{r+1,r+1}}^{(r)}\right] \end{bmatrix} = \frac{F_0}{2RS} \begin{bmatrix} C^2 & SC & -C^2 & SC \\ SC & S^2 & -SC & -S^2 \\ -C^2 & -SC & C^2 & -SC \\ SC & S^2 & -SC & S^2 \end{bmatrix} \quad (5)$$

where K is the spring stiffness, $S = \sin 1/2\ \Phi$, $C = \cos 1/2\ \Phi$, $\Phi = 2\ \Pi/N$, F_0 is the static spring force in the steady state rotation. The steady state motion may be derived from Eq. (3) assuming that the derivatives vanish all the time. The resulting coefficient of the system of linear equations are singular for certain angular velocities Ω such that $f = \alpha + 4 \sin^2 (1/2\ \phi)$ where $\phi = \Omega^2\ m/k$. This leads to divergence which means the displacement vector may be large for the angular velocities near the divergence velocity. The steady state motion is

$$X_r = Rq \quad Y_r = 0, r = 1, 2, 3, \ldots N \quad (6)$$

where

$$q = f/(\alpha + 4S^2 - f) \quad (7)$$

which is nothing but the amplification factor and $f = \Omega^2\ m/K$ is the non dimensional centrifugal factor. For the spring force under steady state conditions, we have

$$F_0 / 2RS = kq \quad (8)$$

At this point we can assume that the steady state motion is attained and the displacement vector $\{Z\}$ is of the steady state motion. Instead of the complete equation of motion of the whole structure which is obtained by complex constraints at the boundaries of the substructures. The reduced equation of motion of the substructure number 1 can be used for the above rotating polygon.

where

$$([S_{11}^{(1)}] + [S_{22}^{(1)}] + [S_{12}^{(1)} e^{i\psi}] + [S_{21}^{(1)} e^{-i\psi}]$$
$$-\Omega^2 [M_{11}^{(1)}] \lambda [C_{11}^{(1)}] + \lambda^2 [M_{11}^{(1)}]) \{Z^{(1)}\} = 0 \quad (9)$$

where

$$[S_{ij}^{(1)}] = \left[K_{E_{ij}}^{(1)}\right] + \left[K_{G_{ij}}^{(1)}\right]$$

$$[C_{11}^{(1)}] = 2\Omega [G_{11}^{(1)}]$$

and $[G^{(1)}{}_{11}]$ is given by Eq. (2). In the Eq. (9) the matrices are either Hermitian or skew-symmetric. This is a special case of the continuous latent root problem where both the matrices Hermitian and Skew-Hermitian are involved. Hence the Eq. (9) is a continous latent root problem.

The stiffness matrix of Eq. (9) is apparently Hermitian hence the eigenvalues are real, the stiffness matrix is

$$[\bar{K}] = \begin{bmatrix} \alpha + 2S^2(1+\cos\psi) + 2C^2(1-\cos\psi)q - f & i(1+q)2SC\sin\psi \\ -i(1+q)2SC\sin\psi & 2C^2(1-\cos\psi) + 2S^2(1+\cos\psi)q - f \end{bmatrix} \quad (10)$$

The numerical values are to be calculated for the given model for which $N = 6$ (masses in the polygon). The number of eigenvalues to be calculated for $\psi = n\phi$, $n = 0, 1, 2, 3$.

Example 8.3

Develop the necessary equations for free, undamped, vibrations of the system shown in the Fig. 8.3.

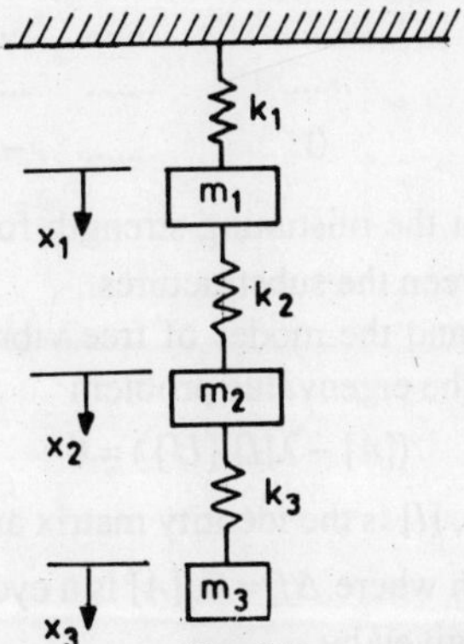

Fig. 8.3

Solution

The structure consists of a cyclic assembly of coupled component systems, where each component system is a single degree of freedom oscillator. Hence the structure is nearly periodic structure. Each substructure is coupled with the adjacent ones through linear springs. In reality the system may be regarded as a simple model of continuously shrouded bladed disks, where each component can be considered as a single blade. The blade model which is considered as a single D.O.F. corresponds to a single structural model approximation of a blade, which may be in bending or in torsion. It is also possible to generalize the system to extract several structural modes per single blade by considering multi-D.O.F. component system. Assuming disk to be rigid the structural coupling between blades is only through shrouds. Springs may be used for coupling between blades through the shroud. The coupling between blades can take different values. The discrepancies among the blades may be assumed as the cause of mistuning of the blades, individual natural frequencies among the blades and stiffness may also result in mistuning of the blades. Hence the governing equations of free, undamped vibration can be shown to be

$$\ddot{q}_i + \omega_{bi}^2 q_i + 2\omega_c^2 q_{i+1} - \omega_c^2 q_{i-1} - \omega_c^2 q_{i+1} = 0 \quad i = 1, 2, \ldots n \quad (1)$$

where $\bar{q}_0 = qN$ and $qN + 1 = \bar{p}_1$

Let us define

$$\omega_{bi}^2 = \omega_b^2\,(1 + \Delta f_i), \qquad i = 1, 2, \ldots\ldots N \quad (2)$$

$$R^2 = \omega_c^2/\omega_b^2 \quad (3)$$

where ω_b is the blade nominal natural frequency and ω_C is the coupling frequency. Equation (1) can be written in the matrix form as

$$\{\ddot{q}\} + \omega_b^2[A]\{q\} = \{0\} \tag{4}$$

where

$$[A] = \begin{bmatrix} 1+2R^2+\Delta f_1 & -R^2 & 0 & & -R^2 \\ -R^2 & 1+2R^2+\Delta f_2 & -R^2 & 0 & \ldots\ldots \\ \ldots\ldots & \ldots\ldots & \ldots\ldots & \ldots\ldots & \ldots\ldots \\ \ldots\ldots & \ldots\ldots & \ldots\ldots & \ldots\ldots & \ldots\ldots \\ \ldots\ldots & \ldots\ldots & \ldots\ldots & \ldots\ldots & \ldots\ldots \\ \ldots\ldots & \ldots\ldots & \ldots\ldots & \ldots\ldots & \ldots\ldots \\ -R^2 & 0 & \ldots\ldots & -R^2 & 1+2R^2+\Delta f_N \end{bmatrix}$$

where Δf_i and $R^2\Delta f_i$ represent the mistuning strength for the ith blade and R^2 is the dimensionless coupling between the substructures.

The natural frequency and the modes of free vibration of the undamped system are obtained by solving the eigenvalue problem

$$([A] - \lambda[I]\{U\}) = 0 \tag{6}$$

where $[A]$ is given by Eq. (5), $[I]$ is the identity matrix and λ is a eigen frequency.

Case 1. For a tuned system where $\Delta f_i = 0$, $[A]$ is a cyclic matrix and its eigenvectors for even values of N are given by

$$(U_k^c\}^T = \{1, \cos\alpha_k \ldots\ldots \cos(N-1)\alpha_k\}, \quad \text{for } k = 1, \ldots N/2+1 \tag{7}$$

$$\{U_k^s\}^T = \{0, \sin\alpha_k \ldots\ldots \sin(N-1)\alpha_k\}, \quad \text{for } k = 1, \ldots N/2 \tag{8}$$

where $\alpha_k = 2\pi(k-1)/N$. Corresponding eigenvalues are

$$\lambda_k = 1 + 2R^2\left[1 - \cos\frac{2\pi(k-1)}{N}\right], \quad k = 1, \ldots\ldots N/2+1 \tag{9}$$

An important observation is that except for $K = 1$ or $N/2 + 1$, double eigenvalues occur, the corresponding eigenvectors being $\{U^c{}_k\}$ and $\{U^s{}_k\}$ and, any linear combination of the two is also an eigenvector. For odd values of N the value $N/2 + 1$ is replaced by $(N + 1)/2$ in all the equations from (7 – 9) and there is only one simple eigenvalue for $K = 1$.

Case 2. Mistuned system with strong internal coupling

An approximate solution can also be obtained by a perturbation approach which can give the effects of mistuning. The unperturbed system is the tuned one and perturbation is the blade mistuning. The unperturbed and perturbed matrices are given by

$$[A_0^c] = \begin{bmatrix} 1+2R^2 & -R^2 & 0 & & 0 \\ -R^2 & 1+2R^2 & -R^2 & 0 & \ldots\ldots \\ \ldots\ldots & \ldots\ldots & \ldots\ldots & \ldots\ldots & \ldots\ldots \\ \ldots\ldots & \ldots\ldots & \ldots\ldots & \ldots\ldots & \ldots\ldots \\ \ldots\ldots & \ldots\ldots & \ldots\ldots & \ldots\ldots & \ldots\ldots \\ \ldots\ldots & \ldots\ldots & \ldots\ldots & \ldots\ldots & \ldots\ldots \\ -R^2 & 0 & \ldots\ldots & -R^2 & 1+2R^2 \end{bmatrix} \tag{10}$$

$$[\delta A^C] = \begin{bmatrix} \Delta f_1 & 0 & \ldots\ldots & \ldots\ldots & 0 \\ 0 & \Delta f_2 & 0 & \ldots\ldots & \ldots\ldots \\ \ldots\ldots & \ldots\ldots & \ldots\ldots & \ldots\ldots & \ldots\ldots \\ \ldots\ldots & \ldots\ldots & \ldots\ldots & \ldots\ldots & \ldots\ldots \\ \ldots\ldots & \ldots\ldots & \ldots\ldots & \ldots\ldots & \ldots\ldots \\ \ldots\ldots & \ldots\ldots & \ldots\ldots & \ldots\ldots & \ldots\ldots \\ 0 & \ldots\ldots & \ldots\ldots & 0 & \Delta f_N \end{bmatrix} \tag{11}$$

The above perturbation scheme is valid for strong coupling. This is also referred to here as classical perturbation method. For the theory of the method the reader is advised to refer to any standard mathematical book on eigenvalue problems.

Case 3. **Mistuned system with weak internal coupling**

For weak internal coupling the unperturbed eigenvalues given by Eq. (9) are close. The order of magnitude of the eigenvector perturbation is determined by $d_{ij}/(\lambda_{oi} - \lambda_{oj})$ and since the distance between eigenvalues is smaller, the eigenvector perturbations become large.

In this case a modified perturbation method (MPM) has to be used. Since the coupling is small, it ought to be considered as a perturbation as well. In order to avoid the repeated eigenvalues for the unperturbed systems, the key idea introduced was to include disorder in the unperturbed system. Then the modified unperturbed system is the mistuned decoupled system, and the perturbation consists of the coupling. Consequently, in the weak coupling case, the MPM is defined by

$$[A_0^m] = \begin{bmatrix} 1+\Delta f_1 & 0 & \ldots\ldots & 0 \\ 0 & 1+\Delta f_2 & 0 & \ldots\ldots \\ \ldots\ldots & \ldots\ldots & \ldots\ldots & \ldots\ldots \\ \ldots\ldots & \ldots\ldots & \ldots\ldots & \ldots\ldots \\ \ldots\ldots & \ldots\ldots & \ldots\ldots & \ldots\ldots \\ \ldots\ldots & \ldots\ldots & \ldots\ldots & \ldots\ldots \\ 0 & & & 1+\Delta f_N \end{bmatrix} \tag{12}$$

$$[\delta A^m] = \begin{bmatrix} 2R^2 & -R^2 & 0 & & -R^2 \\ -R^2 & 2R^2 & -R^2 & 0 & \ldots\ldots \\ \ldots\ldots & \ldots\ldots & \ldots\ldots & \ldots\ldots & \ldots\ldots \\ \ldots\ldots & \ldots\ldots & \ldots\ldots & \ldots\ldots & \ldots\ldots \\ \ldots\ldots & \ldots\ldots & \ldots\ldots & \ldots\ldots & \ldots\ldots \\ \ldots\ldots & \ldots\ldots & \ldots\ldots & \ldots\ldots & \ldots\ldots \\ -R^2 & 0 & & -R^2 & 2R^2 \end{bmatrix} \tag{13}$$

Assuming that the Δf_i 's are distinct, $[A_0^m]$ has simple eigenvalues. Then the eigenvectors will vary continuously from the corresponding unperturbed ones, and it is easy to write to the second order,

$$\{U_i\} = \{U_{oi}\} + \{\delta U_i\} + \{\delta^2 U_i\}, \qquad i = 1,\ldots N \tag{14}$$

$$\lambda_i = \lambda_{oi} + \delta\lambda_i + \delta^2\lambda_i \qquad i = 1,\ldots N \tag{15}$$

Where the modified unperturbed eigen solution is

$$\lambda_{oi} = 1 + \Delta f_i \qquad i = 1, ..., N \tag{16}$$

$$\{U_{oi}\} = \{0, T, 1_{ith}, ..., 0\} i \quad = 1, ..., N \tag{17}$$

The first order perturbation of the eigen solution is found to be

$$\delta\lambda_i = 2R^2 \tag{18}$$

$$\{\delta U_i\}_{i-1} = \frac{-R^2}{\Delta f_i - \Delta f_{i-1}}$$

$$\{\delta U_i\}_i = 0$$

$$\{\delta U_i\}_{i+1} = \frac{-R^2}{\Delta f_i - \Delta f_{i+1}}$$

$$\{\delta U_i\}_j = 0 \tag{19}$$

This procedure demonstrates that in the weak coupling case the mode shapes are perturbations of the modes of the individual decoupled blades, hence each mode is strongly localized about one blade. It is also apparent from Eq. (19) that the localized mode shapes are dependent upon the ratios $\Delta f_i/R^2$, hence the degree of localization depends only on the ratio of mistuning to coupling.

8.5.4 Transient Analysis

The undamped dynamic equation of a rotationally periodic structure, expressed in terms of displacements of a single substructure, for particular harmonic p is given by

$$[M_p]\{\ddot{\delta}_p\} + [K_p]\{\delta_p\} = \{F\} \tag{8.112}$$

Equation 8.112 reduces to a Hermitian eigenvalue problem when $F = 0$. The solution of the above problem gives real values for Ω^2 and values for $\{\delta_p\}$ are complex unless $p = 0$ or $p = N/2$ (for even N). The eigenvectors of the above satisfy the orthogonality conditions of real symmetric matrices such as

$$\{\delta_p\}^T [K_p]\{\delta_p\} = [\Omega^2] \tag{8.113}$$

$$\{\delta_p\}' [M]\{\delta_p\} = [I_m] \tag{8.114}$$

where $\{\delta_p\}$ is a rectangular matrix of size (m, r), where r is the number of eigenvectors and $[\Omega^2]$ is a diagonal matrix of size (r, r) with the diagonal, the first r values of Ω^2. The equation of motion for a given spatial Fourier harmonic can be uncoupled by making use of the conditions of orthogonality into r single D.O.F. equations of motion, each contributing to the response from a single mode shape. The dynamic response at any time t is assumed to be,

$$\{\delta(t)\} = \{\delta_p\}\{q(t)\} \tag{8.115}$$

where $\{\delta(t)\}$ is of size $(m, 1)$, $\{\delta_p\}$ contains the first r eigenvectors of size (m, r) and $q(t)$ the coefficient of size $(r, 1)$ to be determined. Substituting Eq. 8.115 in Eq. 8.112

$$\{\delta_p\}'[M]\{\delta_p\}\{\ddot{q}\}+\{\delta_p\}'[C]\{\delta_p\}\{\dot{q}\}+\{\delta_p\}'[K]\{\delta_p\}\{q\}$$
$$=\{\delta_p\}'\{F\} \tag{8.116}$$

From the orthogonality conditions 8.113 and 8.114 the Eq. 8.116 reduces to

$$[I]\{\ddot{q}\}+2[\xi]\Omega\{\dot{q}\}+[\Omega^2]\{q\}=\{g\} \tag{8.117}$$

where ξ is a diagonal matrix of damping ratios. Equation 8.117 is a set of uncoupled equations, each of which has the form

$$\ddot{q}+2\xi\omega_r\dot{q}+\omega_r^2 q=g \tag{8.118}$$

These uncoupled r equations can be solved by expressing $q(t)$ in the form

$$q(t)=\exp(-\xi\omega_r t)\,[C_1\cos\omega_r t+C_2\sin\omega_r t]+g/\omega_r^2 \tag{8.119}$$

where
$$C_1=q_0-g/\omega_r^2 \tag{8.120}$$

$$C_2=\frac{\dot{q}_0+\omega_r(q_0-g/\omega_r^2)}{(1-\xi^2)\omega_r} \tag{8.121}$$

After solving the Eqs. 8.118 one can obtain the structural response using Eqs. 8.115. This procedure is to be repeated for all the harmonics. However it is enough if we perform for the values of p given by

$$p=0,1,2,\ldots\frac{1}{2}(N-1)\text{ for }N\text{ odd}$$

$$p=0,1,2,\ldots N/2\text{ for }N\text{ even} \tag{8.122}$$

The moving load along the profile of the active tooth is associated with the different nodes as the load progressively moves down. The time interval chosen for computing dynamic displacements has to be smaller than one-tenth of the time period corresponding to the third mode, if the contributions upto the third mode are to be included.

Rayleigh damping is used to simplify the damping term. The material damping present for well known materials has been reported by various investigators. There are two ways of computing the damping present in any system. One by the free vibration analysis and another by the forced vibration method. It is possible to obtain the damping ratios for the first few natural frequencies, by the second method. The elements of the damping matrix are derived using the mass and stiffness matrices.

In practice the damping ratio would increase with natural frequencies, the value being as low as 0.03 for the fundamental mode. It may be mentioned that for value of damping around 0.5 and natural frequencies more than 10 c/s, the rate of decay ($e^{-2\pi\xi\omega}n$) will be very high resulting in response from such frequencies dying down very fast. Having obtained the response for the above harmonics, the total response is obtained by summing up the response of each harmonic as given below.

$$\{q(t)\}=\{q_0(t)\}+2\sum_{p=1}^{(N/2)-1}\{q_p(t)\}+\{q_{N/2}(t)\} \tag{8.123}$$

From the displacements, stresses can be computed for the substructure experiencing the load. The response in the adjacent substructure can be obtained by using the multiplying factor $e^{-i\psi}$ where $\psi = 2\pi j/N$.

Example 8.4

Develop the solution procedure for the flux-shield and armature model using Modal Analysis with Cyclic Symmetry.

Solution

Let us divide the generator into 12 sectors each of 30° slices as shown in the figure, because the structure is composed of N identical segments. Let U_i be the displacement vector of the ith substructure. The Fourier series expansion of the displacement vector is given in the Eq. (1) as

$$\{U\} = \begin{Bmatrix} U_1 \\ U_2 \\ U_3 \\ \cdot\cdot \\ \cdot\cdot \\ U_n \end{Bmatrix} = \begin{bmatrix} 1 & 1 & 0 & \cdots & 1 \\ 1 & \cos\alpha & \sin\alpha & \cdots & -1 \\ 1 & \cos 2\alpha & \sin 2\alpha & \cdots & 1 \\ \cdot\cdot & \cdot\cdot & \cdot\cdot & \cdots & \cdot\cdot \\ \cdot\cdot & \cdot\cdot & \cdot\cdot & \cdots & \cdot\cdot \\ 1 & \cos(N-1)\alpha & \sin(n-1)\alpha & \cdots & 1 \end{bmatrix} \begin{Bmatrix} U_0 \\ U_c^1 \\ U_s^1 \\ \cdot\cdot \\ \cdot\cdot \\ U^{\frac{N}{2}} \end{Bmatrix} \qquad (1)$$

If N is odd, the harmonic mode number $K = N/2$ will not exist and $U^{N/2}$ should be repeated by $U^{(N/2-1)}$ where α is the angle of cyclic symmetry. The subscripts c and s indicate the cosine and sine components respectively. The coefficient vectors are uncoupled vectors with mass matrix and stiffness matrix the same as those of a single substructure. The interfacing modes of the substructure are coupled together with constraint equations.

The natural frequencies of the structure obtained are from different computer runs of different coefficient vector modal solutions. The number of computer runs must be equal to the number of harmonic modes required. (i.e. = $N/2 + 1$). Each run determines one of the corresponding harmonic mode number.

For $K = 0$

(1) Consider one sector for discretisation of the finite element mesh with number of elements and nodes as shown in Fig. 8.4. The system equation of motion can be written as

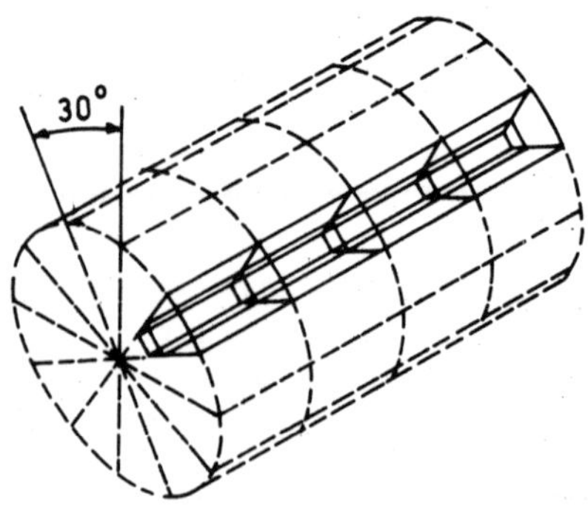

Fig. 8.4

$$[M]\{\ddot{U}^0\} + [K]\{U^0\} = [0] \quad (2)$$

where $[M]$ and $[K]$ are the mass and stiffness matrices of a single segment, respectively.

(2). Introduce constraint equations between two adjacent sectors on both sides. The constraint equations for nodes $j, j+g$ ($j = 1, 2, \ldots, N$) are as follows:

$$\begin{Bmatrix} U_{x_{j+g}} \\ U_{y_{j+g}} \\ U_{z_{j+g}} \end{Bmatrix} = \begin{bmatrix} \cos\alpha & -\sin\alpha & 0 \\ \sin\alpha & \cos\alpha & 0 \\ 0 & 0 & 1 \end{bmatrix} \begin{Bmatrix} U_{x_j} \\ U_{y_j} \\ U_{z_j} \end{Bmatrix} \quad (3)$$

(3) A number of D.O.F. equal to the number of constraint equations are to be considered as non-active D.O.F. The choice of the reduced D.O.F. affects the solutions to a great extent.

(4) The modal analysis provides the natural frequencies of the whole structure and its mode shape $\{U^0\}$. The corresponding mode shape of the whole structure $\{U\}$ can be computed from Eq. (1) which indicates that the deformation vector $\{U_i\}$ of all segments are the same, and equal to $\{U^0\}$ when vibrating at each frequency. The mode shapes corresponding to $K = 0$ could be axial torsional and uniform radial modes.

For $K = 1, 2, \ldots\ldots (N/2 - 1)$

(1) For each value of K it is required to generate the finite element mesh for two identical substructures to represent one for cosine coefficient vector and the other for sine coefficient vector. The nodes of these two substructures are coincident but labeled with different numbers. To discriminate each other the sine coefficient vector components are labeled with numbers h. The system equation of motion for $K = 1$ can be written as

$$\begin{bmatrix} M & 0 \\ 0 & M \end{bmatrix} \begin{Bmatrix} \ddot{U}_C^1 \\ \ddot{U}_S^1 \end{Bmatrix} + \begin{bmatrix} K & 0 \\ 0 & K \end{bmatrix} \begin{Bmatrix} U_C^1 \\ U_S^1 \end{Bmatrix} = \begin{Bmatrix} 0 \\ 0 \end{Bmatrix} \quad (4)$$

(2) Introduce constraint equations between each four corresponding interface modes on both sides and in both cosine and sine vectors. The constraint equations for nodes $j, j+g, j+h, j+g+h$ ($j = 1, 2, \ldots n$) are as given below.

$$\begin{Bmatrix} U_{x_{j+g}} \\ U_{y_{j+g}} \\ U_{z_{j+g}} \\ U_{x_{j+g+h}} \\ U_{y_{j+g+h}} \\ U_{z_{j+g+h}} \end{Bmatrix} = \begin{bmatrix} \phi_1 & -\phi_2 & 0 & \phi_3 & -\phi_4 & 0 \\ \phi_2 & \phi_1 & 0 & \phi_4 & \phi_3 & 0 \\ 0 & 0 & \phi_5 & 0 & 0 & \phi_6 \\ -\phi_3 & \phi_4 & 0 & \phi_1 & -\phi_2 & 0 \\ -\phi_4 & -\phi_3 & 0 & \phi_2 & \phi_1 & 0 \\ 0 & 0 & -\phi_6 & 0 & 0 & \phi_5 \end{bmatrix} \begin{Bmatrix} U_{x_j} \\ U_{y_j} \\ U_{z_j} \\ U_{x_{j+h}} \\ U_{y_{j+h}} \\ U_{z_{j+h}} \end{Bmatrix} \quad (5)$$

where $\quad \phi_1 = \cos\beta\cos\alpha$

$$\phi_2 = \cos\beta\sin\alpha \qquad \phi_5 = \cos\beta$$

$$\phi_3 = \sin\beta\cos\alpha \qquad \phi_6 = \sin\beta$$

$$\phi_4 = \sin\beta\sin\alpha \qquad \beta = K\alpha$$

Same steps are to be followed as in the previous case where $K = 0$.

For $K = N/2$

The equation of motion can be written as

$$[M]\,\{\ddot{U}^{N/2}\} + [K]\,\{U^{N/2}\} = 0$$

The second step is to apply the complex constraints which are the same as $K = 0$

$$\begin{Bmatrix} U_{x_{j+g}} \\ U_{y_{j+g}} \\ U_{z_{j+g}} \end{Bmatrix} = \begin{bmatrix} -\cos\alpha & \sin\alpha & 0 \\ -\sin\alpha & -\cos\alpha & 0 \\ 0 & 0 & 1 \end{bmatrix} \begin{Bmatrix} U_{x_j} \\ U_{y_j} \\ U_{z_j} \end{Bmatrix}$$

The steps 3 and 4 are to be repeated as in the case K = 0.

8.6 FORCED VIBRATION ANALYSIS

8.6.1 Introduction

There are many structures that are cyclically repetitive, either because they are cyclically symmetric about a central axis, or because they may repeat many times. The repetitive nature of the structure can be used so that only single segment need be analysed. To do this appropriate edge boundaries have to be applied to represent the repetitive nature of the structure. This concept has been very successfully applied to the analysis of bladed discs by several authors. Marcus, M.S. and Everstine G.C. carried out frequency analysis of propeller blades on a flexible hub using NASTRAN program. The concept was implemented by Zienkiewicz and Scott to the stress analysis of pump impellors. NASTRAN as a general purpose program with many capabilities has been developed which can analyse cyclic symmetric structures: Modified Potters' scheme which is an out of core technique was developed to solve the equations of cyclic symmetric formulation by Ramamurti and Balasubramanian.

This article elucidates the conditions under which a rotating force distribution is able to excite the resonance vibrations in a rotationally periodic structure which is stationary in space. This force is assumed to rotate about the axis of structural symmetry. A rotationally periodic structure consists of a finite number of identical substructures forming a closed ring. These types of structures are met in many applications such as turbomachinery blades, circular saw blades, gear wheels etc.

The normal modes of vibrations of rotationally periodic structures are known. They consist of harmonically varying displacements in the circumferential direction. The spectrum of natural frequencies is partly degenerated that is some of the natural frequencies appear in pairs, while others are single in nature. The problem of resonances in rotationally periodic structures holds some relationship to the resonance problem of rotationally symmetric structure rotating past a stationary force. It was described that the travelling waves in a rotating circular disc can be excited by a stationary force distribution.

8.6.2 Basic Equations

Forced vibrations of a steadily rotating elastic body are described by the following equations of motion pertaining to a finite element model.

$$[M]\{\ddot{Z}\} + [C]\{\dot{Z}\} + [K]\{Z\} = \{f\} \tag{8.124}$$

where $\{Z\}$ is a numerical vector of generalized displacement and $\{f\}$ is the corresponding generalized force vector. Both contain real elements. $[K]$ is the real symmetric stiffness matrix including centrifugal and geometric stiffness effects. $[C]$ is the real skew-symmetric gyroscopic matrix and $[M]$ is the real symmetric mass matrix.

Here the total structure may consist of N identical substructures each of which is described by J degrees of freedom. Hence the size of the matrices and vectors of Eq. 8.124 are of the order of NJ. The displacement vector $\{Z\}$ may be divided into N sub-vectors of length J. The elements of each sub-vector describes the displacement vector of a sub-structure. Let $\{Z^{(r)}\}$ be the displacement vector of the rth sub-structure. The sub-structure number r varies from 1 to N.

The free vibration analysis of the structure can be described by the Eq. 8.124, if the excitation forces are zero. Here it must be noticed that the free vibrations are described by the backward and forward rotating mode shapes. These can be computed by Eq. 8.124. The latent root problem of Eq. 8.124 yields purely imaginary latent roots and the associated latent vectors consist of complex quantities. Hence a single latent vector cannot be observed in real life, but the solution vectors combined in pairs. Each pair yields a solution which is either a backward or forward rotating mode shape. The complex latent vectors of Eq. 8.124 are denoted by Z_k where $k = 1, 2, \ldots 2NJ$. The complexity is due to the skew-symmetry of the gyroscopic matrix $[C]$. The partitioned latent vectors obey certain complex constraints such as

$$\{Z_k^{(r+1)}\} = e^{i\psi}\{Z_k^{(r)}\} \tag{8.125}$$

where ψ is a phase angle. The ψ value as defined earlier

$$\psi = \pm\, n 2\pi/N$$

where n is a circumferential wave number with the possible values, such as

$$N = 0, 1, 2, \ldots \text{int}(N/2)$$

and int(N/2) denotes the integer value of (N/2) when the complex constraint Eq. 8.125 can be repeatedly used. The displacements of any substructure can be described with reference to a selected substructure, say the first substructure

$$\{Z^{(r+1)}\} = e^{ir\psi}\{Z_k^{(1)}\} \tag{8.126}$$

which can be written as

$$\{Z_k\} = \begin{Bmatrix} Z_k^{(1)} \\ e^{i\psi}Z_k^{(1)} \\ e^{i2\psi}Z_k^{(1)} \\ \ldots\ldots \\ \ldots\ldots \\ e^{i(N-1)\psi}Z_k^{(1)} \end{Bmatrix} \tag{8.127}$$

For simplicity let us denote

$$\{X_k\} = \{Z_k^{(1)}\} \text{ where } k = 1, 2, \tag{8.128}$$

As we know when the total stiffness matrix of the given system is positive semi definite or positive definite there will be $2J$ backward rotating modes and $2J$ forward rotating modes for every wave. It is easy to describe the deformation of the body with the associated complex vectors. Therefore, it is necessary to have at least one pair of modes in each kind. The mode shapes corresponding to the backward rotating mode can be denoted by $\{Z_1\}$ and its complex conjugate by $\{\overline{Z}_1\}$, and the forward rotating mode can be represented by $\{Z_2\}$ and its complex conjugate by $\{\overline{Z}_2\}$. THe choice of the wave number can be arbitrary. The choice of the latent vector is also arbitrary for the chosen wave number. The total description of the mode shape is the summation of all the latent vectors of all the wave numbers. It is enough to study the smallest possible number of components for acceptable results of linearity. The selected vectors in a modal matrix are

$$\{E\} = (Z_1\, Z_2\, \overline{Z}_1\, \overline{Z}_2) \tag{8.129}$$

The associated latent roots are in a diagonal matrix, given by

$$\Lambda = \begin{bmatrix} \lambda & 0 & 0 & 0 \\ 0 & \lambda & 0 & 0 \\ 0 & 0 & \lambda & 0 \\ 0 & 0 & 0 & \lambda \end{bmatrix} \begin{bmatrix} i\omega_{1n} & & & \\ & -i\omega_{2n} & & \\ & & -i\omega_{1n} & \\ & & & -i\omega_{2n} \end{bmatrix} \tag{8.130}$$

where ω_{1n} and ω_{2n} are positive natural frequencies of vibration.

8.6.3 Use of Latent Vectors

In the state space formulation the state space variables are the velocities and displacements given by

$$\{Y\} = \begin{Bmatrix} \dot{Z} \\ Z \end{Bmatrix} \tag{8.131}$$

and the differential equation of motion of Eq. 8.124 can be expressed in the state space formulation as

$$[B]\,\{\dot{y}\} + [L]\,\{y\} = \{F\} \tag{8.132}$$

This is a first order differential equation where,

$$[B] = \begin{bmatrix} 0 & M \\ M & C \end{bmatrix}$$

$$[L] = \begin{bmatrix} -M & 0 \\ 0 & K \end{bmatrix}$$

$$[F] = \begin{Bmatrix} 0 \\ f \end{Bmatrix}$$

Equation 8.132 can be written in terms of the associated latent roots as

$$(\lambda[B]+[L])\{y\}=0 \tag{8.133}$$

Obviously the above Eq. 8.133 has 2(*NJ*) latent roots and associated vectors. Selecting two pairs, as in Eq. 8.129, the latent vector of the Eq. 8.133 can be written as

$$\{y\}=(y_1\ y_2\ \overline{y}_1\ \overline{y}_2) \tag{8.134}$$

and the corresponding roots are the same as in Eq. 8.130. Substituting the Eqs. 8.129 and 8.130 to compute the modal matrix which can be written as

$$\{y\}=\begin{bmatrix}\lambda_1 Z_1 & \lambda_2 Z_2 & \lambda_3 \overline{Z}_1 & \lambda_4 \overline{Z}_2\\ Z_1 & Z_2 & \overline{Z}_1 & \overline{Z}_2\end{bmatrix}=\begin{bmatrix}E\lambda\\ E\end{bmatrix} \tag{8.135}$$

The left vector of Eq. 8.133 is partitioned in the same manner. The modal matrix of the left vector can be written as

$$\{R\}=\begin{bmatrix}\lambda_1 \overline{Z}_1 & \lambda_2 \overline{Z}_2 & \lambda_3 Z_1 & \lambda_4 Z_2\\ \overline{Z}_1 & \overline{Z}_2 & Z_1 & Z_2\end{bmatrix}=\begin{bmatrix}\overline{E}\lambda\\ \overline{E}\end{bmatrix} \tag{8.136}$$

Uncoupled Equation of Motion

The first order differential equation given in Eq. 8.132 can be used for certain types of forcing functions. To solve this equation, the vector can be expressed as a series of latent vectors of the corresponding free vibration. We have

$$\{y\}=[y]\{P\} \tag{8.137}$$

where $[P]$ is a vector of principal coordinates. The coordinates given in Eq. 8.137 can be used in Eq. 8.132. Then the resulting matrix can be premultiplied by the transpose of the modal matrix $[R]$ to obtain the equation of motion in the principal coordinates. These equations are of the form

$$[R]^T\,[B]\,[Y]\,\{P\}+[R]^T\,[L]\,[Y]\,\{P\}=[R]^T\,\{F\} \tag{8.138}$$

The two terms on the right side are of diagonal nature. These equations can be modified as

$$[A_0]=[R]^T\,[B]\,[Y]=[\Lambda]^T\,[E]^H\,[M]\,[E]+[E]^H\,[M]\,\{E\}\,[\Lambda]+[E]^H\,[C]\,\{E\} \tag{8.139}$$

$$[A_1]=[R]^T\,[L]\,[Y]=[E]^H\,[K]\,[E]-[\Lambda]^T\,[E]^H\,[M]\,[E]\,[\Lambda] \tag{8.140}$$

$$Q=[R]^T\,\{F\}=[E]^H\,\{F\} \tag{8.141}$$

where H superscript represents the conjugate transponse of a Hermitian matrix. The mass, gyroscopic and stiffness matrices can be written as

$$[E]^H\,[M]\,[E]=N\begin{bmatrix}M_{11} & M_{12} & & \\ & & 0 & \\ M_{21} & M_{22} & & \\ & & M_{11} & M_{21}\\ & 0 & & \\ & & M_{12} & M_{22}\end{bmatrix} \tag{8.142}$$

$$[E]^H [C] [E] = N \begin{bmatrix} ic_{11} & ic_{12} & & \\ ic_{21} & ic_{22} & & 0 \\ & & -ic_{11} & -ic_{21} \\ 0 & & -ic_{12} & +ic_{22} \end{bmatrix} \quad (8.143)$$

$$[E]^H [K] [E] = N \begin{bmatrix} K_{11} & K_{12} & & \\ K_{21} & K_{22} & & 0 \\ & & K_{11} & K_{21} \\ 0 & & K_{12} & K_{22} \end{bmatrix} \quad (8.144)$$

The matrices are derived from basic principles. Substituting Eqs. 8.142 to 8.143 in Eqs. 8.139 and 8.140 we get

$$A_0 = N \begin{bmatrix} ia_1 & & & \\ & ia_2 & & 0 \\ & & -ia_1 & \\ 0 & & & -ia_2 \end{bmatrix} \quad (8.145)$$

$$A_1 = N \begin{bmatrix} \omega_1 a_1 & & & \\ & -\omega_2 a_2 & & 0 \\ & & \omega_1 a_1 & \\ 0 & & & -\omega_2 a_2 \end{bmatrix} \quad (8.146)$$

where a_1 and a_2 are normalizing constants of the latent vectors which are real quantities. The orthogonality property is utilised in computing $[A_0]$ and $[A_1]$. Now the uncoupled equation of motion of Eq. 8.138 can be written as:

$$[A_0] \{\dot{P}\} + [A_1] \{P\} = \{Q\} \quad (8.147)$$

where $\{Q\}$ is defined in Eq. 8.141.
In the forced vibration analysis these equations can be solved.

(1) Excitation Form

The excitation force vector $\{f\}$ in Eq. 8.124 and Eq. 8.141 must be partitioned in the same way as the displacement vector as shown in the case of latent vector in Eq. 8.127. Obviously each subvector contains the excitation forces acting on one substructure. We have

$$\{f\} = \begin{Bmatrix} f^{(1)} \\ f^{(2)} \\ \cdot \\ \cdot \\ f^{(N)} \end{Bmatrix} \tag{8.148}$$

The generalised force vector $\{Q\}$ in Eq. 8.141 can be represented as Q_k where $k = 1, 2, 3, 4$. These elements can be obtained from the Eqs. 8.141 and 8.148. Making use of Eq. 8.128, the generalised force elements can be expressed as

$$\{Q_1\} = \{Z_1\}^H\{f\} = \{X_1\}^H\{f^{(1)}\} + e^{-i\psi}\{X_1\}^H\{f^{(2)}\} + ... + e^{-i(N-1)\psi}\{X_1\}^H\{f^{(N)}\} \tag{8.149}$$

$$\{Q_2\} = \{Z_2\}^H\{f\} = \{X_2\}^H\sum_{r=1}^{N} e^{-i(r-1)\psi}\{f^{(r)}\} \tag{8.150}$$

$$\{Q_3\} = \{Z_1\}^T\{f\} = \{X_2\}^T\sum_{r=1}^{N} e^{-i(r-1)\psi}\{f^{(r)}\} \tag{8.151}$$

$$\{Q_4\} = \{Z_2\}^T\{f\} = \{X_2\}^T\sum_{r=1}^{N} e^{-i(r-1)\psi}\{f^{(r)}\} \tag{8.152}$$

(2) Point Force

A special case of excitation force is a point force. This can be assummed as a force distribution which exists over a very small stretch in the circumferential direction, and stationary in space acting on the rotating member. The force distribution is so small in the circumferential direction that it can be regarded as a point force. Mathematically this force can be represented as a Dirac delta function. This may have an alternating nature in time with the radian frequency ω_f. Further, it is convenient to introduce the geometric angle V_r at any point in the substructure r, given as

$$V_r = (r-1)2\pi/N = (r-1)\alpha \tag{8.153}$$

where $\alpha = 2\pi/N$. The reference point is taken as the starting point of the substructure No. 1.

(3) Transmission of Force

The force exerted on a body may be written as

$$f(\theta, t) = F(\theta)\,\delta\,(\theta + \Omega t)\cos\omega_f t \tag{8.154}$$

where θ is the angle from the reference point. Ω is the angular rotation of the body. The function $F(\theta)$ takes care of the effects of transformed force to the body which may vary with the angular position of the body, and can be expressed as a Fourier Series given by

$$F(\theta) = \sum_{k=0}^{\infty}(F_k \cos KN\theta + G_k \sin KN\theta) \tag{8.155}$$

(4) Force System on a Substructure

At any instant of time t the force exerted on the rth substructure can be extracted from the general force expression of Eq. 8.154 by integrating the force distribution over θ and by using a wind on the *r*th substructure, which gives

$$f^{(r)}(t) = \int_0^{2\pi} \{f(\theta,t)\Delta r(\theta)d\theta\} = \{F(-\Omega t)\}\Delta r(-rt)\cos\omega_f t \qquad (8.156)$$

where $\Delta_r(\theta)$ is a swatch function which is zero in the interval [0, 2π] except in ((*r* – 1) α, *r*α) where it is unity. It is to be observed that $\Delta\, r(\theta)$ is a periodic with period 2π. In the interval [0, 2π] the functions can be expressed by means of Heaviside's unit step function.

$$\Delta r(\theta) = U[\theta - (r-1)\alpha] - u(\theta - r\alpha] \qquad (8.157)$$

(5) Computing the generalised force

Making use of the expressions 8.156 and 8.157 in Eqs. 8.149 to 8.152, the generalised force in Eq. 8.149 can be expressed as

$$Q_1(t) = \{X_1\}^H \sum_{r=1}^{N} e^{-in(r-1)\alpha}\{F(-\Omega t)\}\ \{\Delta_r(-\Omega t)\}\ \cos\omega_f t \qquad (8.158)$$

Let us denote

$$S = \sum_{r=1}^{N} e^{-in(r-1)\alpha}\{\Delta_r(-\Omega t)\} \qquad (8.159)$$

The summation can be evaluated as follows.
Let us denote $\xi = \Omega\, t$ and making use of the periodic property $\Delta_r\,(\theta)$, the sum can be written as

$$s(\xi) = \sum_{r=1}^{N} e^{-in(r-1)\alpha}\{U[-\xi-(r-1)\alpha+2\pi] - u(-\xi - r\alpha+2\pi)\} = S_1 - S_2 \qquad (8.160)$$

which means the first part becomes

$$s_1(\xi) = \sum_{r=1}^{N} e^{-in(r-1)\alpha} u(-\xi-(r-1)\alpha+2\pi)$$

This results in

$$S_1(\xi) = \sum_{r=1}^{r_1(\xi)} e^{-in(r-1)\alpha} = \frac{e^{-in\alpha r_1(\xi)} - 1}{e^{-in\alpha} - 1} \qquad (8.161)$$

The upper limit of the summation is a step-wise varying function. A similar formula can be obtained for S_2 in Eq. 8.159 with an upper limit $r_2\,(\xi)$ which is $r_2\,(\xi) = r_1\,(\xi)$ – 1. Substituting these values of S_1 and S_2 in Eq. 8.160 we get

$$S(\xi) = e^{in\alpha r_0(\xi)} \qquad (8.162)$$

where $r_0\,(\xi) = -\,r_2\,(\xi)$ has been used. It is noted that $r_0\,(\xi)$ is periodic with period 2π. Hence $S(\xi)$ is also periodic with the same peiod of 2π. Now it can be expanded as a Fourier Series.

$$e^{in\alpha r_0(\Omega t)} = \sum_{m=-\infty}^{\infty} b_m e^{im\Omega t} \qquad (8.163)$$

where

$$b_m = e^{im\alpha/2} Sa(m\alpha/2)\delta_{m,\mu N+n} \qquad (8.164)$$

where the function $sa(\alpha) = \dfrac{\sin\alpha}{\alpha}$, μ is any integer and $\delta_{i,j}$ is the substitution symbol.

For simplifying let us denote

$$c_{\mu,n} = e^{i(\mu N+n)\alpha/2} sa[(\mu N+n)\alpha/2] \tag{8.165}$$

obviously $c_{-\mu,-n} = \overline{c}_{\mu,n}$

Now the generalised force Eq. 8.149 can be written as

$$Q_1(t) = \{X_1\}^H \{F(-\Omega t)\} e^{in\alpha r_0(\Omega t)} \cos\omega_F t \tag{8.166}$$

Making use of Fourier Series expansion $\{F(-\Omega t)\}e^{in\alpha r_0(\Omega t)}$ can be expressed as

$$\begin{aligned}\{F(-\Omega t)\} e^{in\alpha r_0(\Omega t)} &= \frac{1}{2} e^{in\Omega t} \sum_{k=-\infty}^{\infty} \sum_{\mu=-\infty}^{\infty} V_k c_{\mu n} \{F_{k-\mu}\} e^{iKN\Omega t} \\ &= \frac{1}{2} e^{in\Omega t} \sum_{k=-\infty}^{\infty} v_k \{F^1\} e_k^{iKN\Omega t}\end{aligned} \tag{8.167}$$

where $V_0 = 2$, $V_k = 1$, $K \neq 0$ and the modified coefficients of expansion are

$$\{F_k^1\} = \sum_{\mu=-\infty}^{\infty} C_{\mu n} \{F_{k-n}\} \tag{8.168}$$

The coefficients with negative index can be represented as

$$\{F_{-\nu}\} = \{F_\nu\}$$

The terms with the coefficients G_k in Eq. 8.155 can be computed in the same way as the F_k terms are computed.

8.6.4 Forced Response Computation

The equations of motion are solved when the exciting force is a stationary point force treated in the preceding section. Using the Fourier expansions of Eq. 8.155, the equations of motion with the generalised forces supplied from the right hand side can be written in detail. The first force Q_1 (t) is given by expressions (8.166) and (8.167) and other forces are obtained in a similar manner.

$$ia_1\dot{p}_1 + a_1\omega_{1n}p_1 = \frac{1}{2}\{X_1\}^H \sum_{k=-\infty}^{\infty} V_k\{F_k^1\} e^{i(KN+n)\Omega t} \cos\omega_F t \tag{8.169}$$

$$ia_2\dot{p}_2 + a_2\omega_{2n}p_2 = \frac{1}{2}\{X_2\}^H \sum_{k=-\infty}^{\infty} V_k\{F_k^1\} e^{i(KN+n)\Omega t} \cos\omega_F t \tag{8.170}$$

$$ia_1\dot{p}_3 + a_1\omega_{1n}p_3 = \frac{1}{2}\{X_1\}^T \sum_{k=-\infty}^{\infty} V_k\{F_k^{11}\} e^{i(KN+n)\Omega t} \cos\omega_F t \tag{8.171}$$

$$ia_2\dot{p}_4 + a_2\omega_{2n}p_4 = \frac{1}{2}\{X_2\}^T \sum_{k=-\infty}^{\infty} V_k\{F_k^{11}\} e^{i(KN+n)\Omega t} \cos\omega_F t \tag{8.172}$$

where

$$F_k^{11} = \sum_{\mu=-\infty}^{\infty} C_{\mu,-n}\{F_{k-n}\} \tag{8.173}$$

and $\{F^1{}_k\}$ is given in expression (8.168). Making use of this expression, the property $C_{-\mu,-n} = \overline{C}_{\mu n}$ and $\{F_{-m}\} = \{F_m\}$ it is found that

$$\{F_{-k}^{11}\} = \overline{\{F_k^1\}} \tag{8.174}$$

It is observed that Eq. 8.171 is identical Eq. 8.169 if $\overline{p}_3 = p_1$. Similarly from Eqs. 8.172 and 8.170, $\overline{p}_4 = p_2$. From the Eq. 8.147 with the coefficient matrices 8.145 and 8.146 and the general force expressions 8.149 – 8.152 it is found that p_1 and $\overline{p}_3$ both satisfy the identical equations, and so also p_2 and $\overline{p}_4$.
Hence

$$p_3 = \overline{p}_1 \quad ; \quad p_4 = \overline{p}_2 \tag{8.175}$$

It is enough if we solve for the principal co-ordinates p_1 and p_2. The coordinates p_3 and p_4 can be obtained from the Eq. 8.174. Since all the solutions of the equations are simple, they can be obtained readily. With the known principal coordinates it is easy to compute the physical coordinates. This can be accomplished by use of the expression (8.137). For a particular substructure r the displacements in coordinate j can be computed making use of the relation in Eq. 8.175.

$$Z_j^{(r)} = e^{inv_r} k_{j1} p_1 + e^{inv_r} k_{j2} p_2 + e^{-inv_r} \overline{k}_{j1} p_3 + e^{-inv_r} \overline{k}_{j2} p_4$$

$$= 2R_e \left\{ e^{inv_r} (k_{j1} p_1 + k_{j2} p_2) \right\} \tag{8.176}$$

The displacement is a real quantity, a complex quantity is not acceptable. The principal coordinates obtained from the above equation are substituted in Eq. 8.176 to be the desired solution of rotating modes.

$$Z_j^{(r)} = \frac{1}{2a_1} Re \sum_{k=0}^{\infty} \left[\frac{k_{ji}\{k_1\}^H \{F_k^1\} \exp i\{nV_r + [(KN+n)\Omega + \omega_F]t\}}{\omega_{1n} - [(KN+n)\Omega + \omega_F]} \right.$$

$$+ \frac{k_{j1}\{k_1\}^H \{F_{-k}^1\} \exp i\{nV_r + [(KN+n)\Omega - \omega_F]t\}}{\omega_{1n} - [(KN-n)\Omega - \omega_F]}$$

$$+ \frac{k_{j1}\{k_1\}^H \{F_{-k}^1\} \exp i\{nV_r + [(KN-n)\Omega + \omega_F]t\}}{\omega_{1n} - [(KN-n)\Omega + \omega_F]}$$

$$\left. + \frac{k_{j1}\{k_1\}^H \{F_{-k}^1\} \exp i\{nV_r - [(KN-n)\Omega + \omega_F]t\}}{\omega_{1n} + [(KN-n)\Omega + \omega_F]} \right]$$

$$- \frac{1}{2a_2} \mathrm{Re} \sum_{k=0}^{\infty} \left[\frac{k_{j2}\{k_2\}^H \{F_k^1\} \exp i\{nV_r + [(KN-n)\Omega + \omega_F]t\}}{\omega_{2n} + [(KN-n)\Omega + \omega_F]} \right.$$

$$+ \frac{k_{j2}\{k_2\}^H \{F_k^1\} \exp i\{nV_r + [(KN+n)\Omega - \omega_F]t\}}{\omega_{2n} + [(KN+n)\Omega - \omega_F]}$$

$$+ \frac{k_{j2}\{k_2\}^H \{F_{-k}^1\} \exp i\{nV_r - [(KN-n)\Omega + \omega_F]t\}}{\omega_{2n} - [(KN-n)\Omega + \omega_F]}$$

$$+\left.\frac{k_{j2}\{k_2\}^H\{F^1_{-k}\}\exp i\{nV_r-[(KN-n)\Omega+\omega_F]t\}}{\omega_{2n}+[(KN-n)\Omega-\omega_F]}\right] \quad (8.177)$$

The final form of the solution with reference to axisymmetric and periodic structures are discussed separately in the following sections.

Axisymmetric Structures

As mentioned earlier, axisymmetric structures are very common in several mechanical engineering systems. The response of an axisymmetric structure can be obtained from the general response theory discussed in the previous sections. In the case of forced response of axisymmetric structures, it is required to consider only the force vector $\{F_0\}$. For this type of structures there is no limit on the wave number; for circumferentially peiodic structures the minimum number of waves are $N/2$. Hence an axisymmetric body may be regarded as a periodic structure with infinite number of substructures i.e, $N \to \infty$. In such a case the stepwise varying functions r_0 (Ωt) in expression (8.163) slightly deviates from the straight line function, which means that, only one term b_n is taken into consideration. In addition to this, the term when $k = 0$, in solution Eq. 8.177 is taken into consideration. Some important observations about the axisymmetric structural response are given here for general use.

(1) If the force is constant with reference to time i.e. $\omega_F = 0$ there is a possibility of resonance for $n\Omega = \omega_{1n}$ which is nothing but the natural frequency of the backward rotating mode (backward denotes the opposite of the direction of rotation of the structure).

(2) In this case of resonance at $n\Omega = \omega_{1n}$ proves to be a backward rotating mode and hence consistency is achieved.

(3) For harmonic force i.e. $\omega_F > 0$ resonance will occur at the natural frequency of forward rotating mode ω_{2n}. This condition is

$$\omega_F - n\Omega = \omega_{2n}$$

If this condition is satisfied the corresponding mode is forward rotating mode which can be computed from the Eq. 8.177. Hence for the axisymmetric structure the resonance conditions are

$$\omega_{1n} = n\Omega \pm \omega_F \quad (8.178)$$

$$\omega_{2n} = \omega_F - n\Omega \quad (8.179)$$

The above two equations represent straight lines in an (n, ω) diagram. These are shown in the Fig. 8.1 for a particular value of the forcing frequency ω_F and for a given value of angular velocity Ω.

Periodic Structures

In the case of periodic structures the solutions in Eq. 8.177 indicate resonance with backward rotating modes, given by the conditions

$$\omega_{1n} = (k\Omega + n)\Omega \pm \omega_F \quad (8.180)$$

$$\omega_{1n} = -(k\Omega - n)\Omega \pm \omega_F \quad (8.181)$$

Resonance will also occur in the case of forward rotating modes for which the necessary conditions can be computed from Eq. 8.177 as

$$\omega_{2n} = -(kN+n)\Omega + \omega_F \tag{8.182}$$

$$\omega_{2n} = (kN-n)\Omega \pm \omega_F \tag{8.183}$$

Important observations and physical interpretations of these conditions are

(1) For $k = 0$ and $\omega_{1n} = n\,\Omega + \omega_F$, the term

$$\text{Re}\{x_{j1}\{x_1^H\}\,\{F_0^1\}\ \text{exp}i\ [nV_r + (n\Omega + \omega_F)t]\}$$

is a backward rotating mode shape which is also known as the propagation factor. The periodic character of the body is not revealed and the resonance condition is the same as that for the axisymmetric struture of Eq. 8.178.

(2) The resonance $k = 0$ and $\omega_{1n} = n\Omega - \omega_F$ also corresponds to a backward rotating mode shape. Since ω_{1n} is a positive number, the resonance condition is the same as that for the axisymmetric structure as given in Eq. 8.178.

(3) When $k = 0$ and $\omega_{2n} = -n\Omega + \omega_F$, the term

$$\text{Re}\ \{x_{j2}\{x_2\}^H\,\{F_0^1\}\ \text{exp}i\ [nV_r - (\omega_F - n\Omega)t]\}$$

corresponds to a forward rotating mode shape. The resonance condition is the same as the one in Eq. 8.179.

(4) When $k = 1$ and $\omega_{1n} = (N + n)\,\Omega \pm \omega_F$ there is a resonance condition which can appear only in periodic structures. The modes in resonance are rotating backwards.

(5) When $k = 1$ with $\omega_{1n} = \omega_F = (N + n)\,\Omega$ there is a resonance condition with backward rotating mode.

(6) When $k = 1$ and $\omega_{2n} = \omega_F - (N + n)\,\Omega$ there is a resonance condition with forward rotating mode.

(7) When $k = 1$ and $\omega_{2n} = (N - n)\,\Omega \pm\omega_F$ there is a resonance condition with forward rotating modes.

In the same way it is possible to compute several conditions for other values of k. It is apparent that all the seven cases of the resonance conditions may not be satisfied at a time that is for one pair of rotational speeds Ω and the forcing frequency ω_F. It is only possible to arrive at all the resonance conditions by varying the angular velocity or the forcing frequency, or both.

Example 8.5

Derive the expressions for forced response of the structure of example taking viscous damping into consideration.

Solution

A harmonic excitation as external force is taken into consideration. It differs only in phase from substurcture to substurcture. This excitation may be due to the rotation of the system under stationary force in flow field, and has been widely used for bladed disk assemblies.

The equations of motion are given by

$$\{\ddot{q}\} + 2\xi\omega_b\{\dot{q}\} + \omega_b^2[A]\,\{q\} = \frac{1}{m}\{F\} \tag{1}$$

where

$$\{F\}^T = F e^{j\omega t}\{1, e^{j\phi_i}, ...e^{j\phi_i}, ...e^{j\phi_N}\} \quad (2)$$

and

$$\phi_i = \frac{2\pi C(i-1)}{N} \quad (3)$$

The matrix $[A]$ is defined in the exercise.

The forced response of the strongly mistuned system is derived as a perturbation of the response of the tuned system. For the equation of motion 1

$$\{q\} = \{q_0\} + \{\delta q\} \quad (4)$$

$$[A] = [A_0]^c + [\delta A^c] \quad (5)$$

where

$$[A_0^c] = \begin{bmatrix} 1+2R^2 & -R^2 & 0 & & -R^2 \\ -R^2 & 1+2R^2 & -R^2 & 0 & .... \\ .... & .... & .... & .... & .... \\ .... & .... & .... & .... & .... \\ -R^2 & 0 & ... & -R^2 & 1+2R^2 \end{bmatrix} \quad (6)$$

$$[\delta A^c] = \begin{bmatrix} \Delta f_1 & 0 & 0 & ... & ... & 0 \\ 0 & \Delta f_2 & 0 & ... & ... & ... \\ .... & .... & .... & .... & .... & .... \\ .... & .... & .... & .... & .... & .... \\ 0 & ... & ... & ... & 0 & \Delta f_N \end{bmatrix} \quad (7)$$

$\{q_0\}$ is the forced response of the tuned system and $[\delta q]$ refers to the effect of blade mistuning.

Substituting Eqs. (2) and (3) into Eq. (1) and equating the *zero*th and first order terms, we have

$$\{\ddot{q}_0\} + 2\xi\omega_b\{\dot{q}_0\} + \omega_b^2[A_0^c]\{q_0\} = \frac{1}{m}\{F\} \quad (8)$$

$$\{\delta\ddot{q}\} + 2\xi\omega_b\{\delta\dot{q}\} + \omega_b^2[A_0^c]\{\delta q\} = -\omega_b^2[\delta A^c]\{q_0\} \quad (9)$$

By applying modal analysis, the forced response of the tuned system can be obtained from Eq. (8). Also Eq. (9) can be decoupled by using the same modal matrix $[P]$ whose columns are the eigenvectors of the tuned system. $\{U_{oi}\}$ given in the Exercise substituting the equation $\{\delta p\} = [P]\{\delta n\}$ into Eq. (9). $\{\delta n\}$ can be obtained as

$$\{\delta n_i\} = -\frac{T_i}{M_i}\{U_{oi}\}^T[\delta A^c]\{q_0\} \qquad i = 1, 2, ...N \quad (10)$$

$$T_i = \frac{1}{\left[\lambda_{oi} - \frac{\omega^2}{\omega_b^2}\right] + j\left(2\xi\frac{\omega}{\omega_b}\right)} \qquad i = 1, 2, ...N \quad (11)$$

and M_1 is the generalised mass (the square of the norm of { U_{oi} }.

Since [δA^c] is a diagonal matrix, it can be readily shown from Eq. (10) that $\{\delta n\}$ is proportional to the standard deviation of the given mistuning pattern. Therefore the amplitude change $\{\delta \overline{q}\}$ is proportional to the mistuning standard deviation.

EXERCISES

1. Consider a set of eight arbitrary loads acting on eight identical substructures of a structure as given below. Compute the first, second, third and fourth harmonic values of the loads. The loads are 10, 12, 8, 11, 13, 9, 12, 8 N.
2. Consider a maximum in plane force acting at an angle to the tangent at that point of an angular disc. Resolve the force into finite Fourier harmonics. Take the minimum number of subsectors to be eight.
3. A spur gear of 20 teeth of pressure angle 20° is used to transmit 20 Hp at 1400 rpm. Resolve the transmitting force into finite Fourier harmonics.
4. A cyclic symmetric structure with four identical substructures is subjected to a unit load on one side of the structure. Compute the Fourier coefficients.
5. Compute the first four eigen frequencies of the problem given in problem 2 using cyclic symmetric concept.
6. Compute the first four eigen frequencies and mode shapes for the spur gear in problem 3.
7. A square plate has a line load at the central circular hole. Its outer edges are clamped. A uniformly distributed load is assumed to be acting on a very narrow annular space along the inner periphery of the hole. Compute the deflections at different points of the circular hole.

REFERENCES

1. Ezz Ahmed, M., Nathenson, R.D. , Patel, M.R. , (1984), Vibration analysis in large superconducting generator stator using cyclic symmetry, *IEEE Transactions on Power Apparatus and Systems*, Vol. PAS-106, No. 6.
2. Fricker, A.J. and Potter, S., (1981), 'Transient forced vibration of rotationally periodic structures, *Int. Journal of Num. Meths in Engg.* Vol. 17, pp. 957–974.
3. MacNeal, R.H., Harder R.I. , Mason J.B. , (1973), ''NASTRAN Cyclic Symmetry Capability; NASTRAN Users' Experiences'', NASA TM X-2893, National Aeronautics and Space Administration, Washington, D.C.
4. The NASTRAN theorectical manual, (1978) NASA SP. 221(05), Washington, D.C.
5. Ramamurti, V., and Ananda Rao, M. , (1988), Dynamic Analysis of Spur Gear Teeth, *Comp. Structures*, Vol. 29, No. 5, pp. 831–843.
6. Ramamurti, V., and Balasubramanian, P., (1986), 'Static analysis of circumferentially periodic structures with Potters scheme', *Journal Comp. Struct.* Vol. 22, No. 3, pp. 427–431.
7. Ramamurti V. and Balasubramanian, P., (1987), 'Steady state stress analysis of centrifugal fan impellors', *Comp. structures* Vol. 25, No. 1, pp. 129–135.
8. Ruth M. Orris and Petyt, M. , (1974), A finite element study of harmonic wave propagation in periodic structures, *Journal of Sound and vibration*, Vol. 33, pp 223–236.
9. Thomas, D.L., (1979), Dynamics of rotationally periodic structures, *Int. J. Num. Methods in Engg.* Vol. 14, pp.81–102.
10. Wildheim, J., (1981), Excitation of rotating circumferentially periodic structures, *Journal of Sound and Vibration,* Vol. 75, No. 3, pp. 397–416.
11. Wildheim, J., (Dec. 1979) Excitation of rotationally periodic structures, *Trans. ASME*, Vol. 46,
12. Williams, F.W., (1986), An Algorithm for exact eigenvalue calculations for rotationally periodic structures, *Int. Journal for Num. methods in Engg.* , Vol. 23

CHAPTER 9

STRESS ANALYSIS OF STRUCTURAL MEMBERS AND MACHINE COMPONENTS

9.1 INTRODUCTION

Some typical applications of the methods discussed in the previous chapters are presented here. In each case a step-by-step procedure of the particular method is outlined with a view to provide guidelines to the reader. All the case studies presented here are of practical importance. As far as possible true physical situations are taken into consideration. Some case studies are taken from published literature in the area of stress analysis.

9.2 CASES OF STATIC ANALYSIS

With the advent of digital computers, finite element method has become more meaningful and has gained a new dimension in practical application for the numerical solution of engineering problems in the last two decades. In this section some relevant examples to illustrate the application of the method are considered. The general logic used for the formulation of all the static problems are more or less the same and will have the following steps.

(1) The discretisation of the structure by the appropriate element type and size, which is known as the mesh generation for the structure or for the system.
(2) Description of geometric and material properties of the system.
(3) Defining the boundary conditions of the system.
(4) Assumption of the appropriate displacement functions to describe the displacement of the selected elements.
(5) Using the principle of total potential energy, computing the element stiffness matrices.
(6) The assembly of the element stiffness matrices to get the global stiffness matrix of the system.
(7) Computation of the unknown nodal displacements by solving the generated set of linear equations satisfying the conditions of equilibrium at all nodal points of the system.
(8) Obtaining the element strains from the computed nodal displacements.
(9) Computation of the element stresses, using either the known nodal point displacements or strains.

9.2.1 Preliminary Consideration

The stress analysis of frames, truss and beams have only linear elements with two nodal points. The finite element analysis of such problems will be much simpler than those of two-dimensional and three-dimensional problems.

Let us consider the linear members of frames with possible loading conditions. An inclined member of inclination α with reference to x-axis can be considered as a linear element of length L and with two nodes. Each node will have two degrees of freedom as shown in Fig. 9.1.

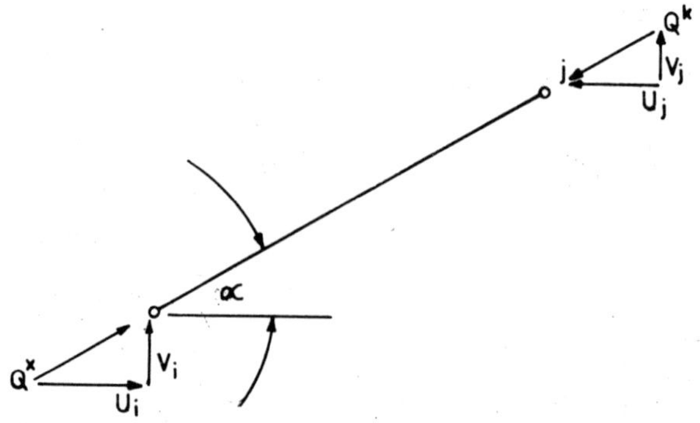

Fig. 9.1

The length L can be expressed in terms of the coordinates of the nodes as

$$L = \sqrt{(x_j - x_i)^2 + (y_j - y_i)^2} \tag{9.1}$$

the angle

$$\alpha = \tan^{-1}\left\{\frac{y_j - y_i}{x_j - x_i}\right\} \tag{9.2}$$

and the nodal coordinates are

$$\{\delta\} = \begin{Bmatrix} \delta_i \\ \delta_j \end{Bmatrix} = \begin{Bmatrix} u_i \\ v_i \\ u_j \\ v_j \end{Bmatrix} \tag{9.3}$$

where u_i and u_j are the x-displacements and v_i and v_j are the y-displacements of the nodes i and j.

Nodal force $\{P\}$ for a linear element can be written as

$$\{P\} = \begin{Bmatrix} P_i \\ P_j \end{Bmatrix} = \begin{Bmatrix} U_i \\ V_i \\ U_j \\ V_j \end{Bmatrix} \tag{9.4}$$

The nodal displacement of Eq. 9.3 will result in the form of member elongations. When these are multiplied by AE/L, forces in the members can be obtained. These components are

$$\{P\} = \begin{Bmatrix} U_i \\ V_i \\ U_j \\ V_j \end{Bmatrix} = \begin{Bmatrix} \cos\alpha \\ \sin\alpha \\ -\cos\alpha \\ -\sin\alpha \end{Bmatrix} \{Q\} \tag{9.5}$$

where $\{Q\}$ is the axial force in the member. Obviously the nodal displacements will induce member deformations. Using the geometric relations which are given in Fig.9.2 axial elnongations are related to the nodal displacements.

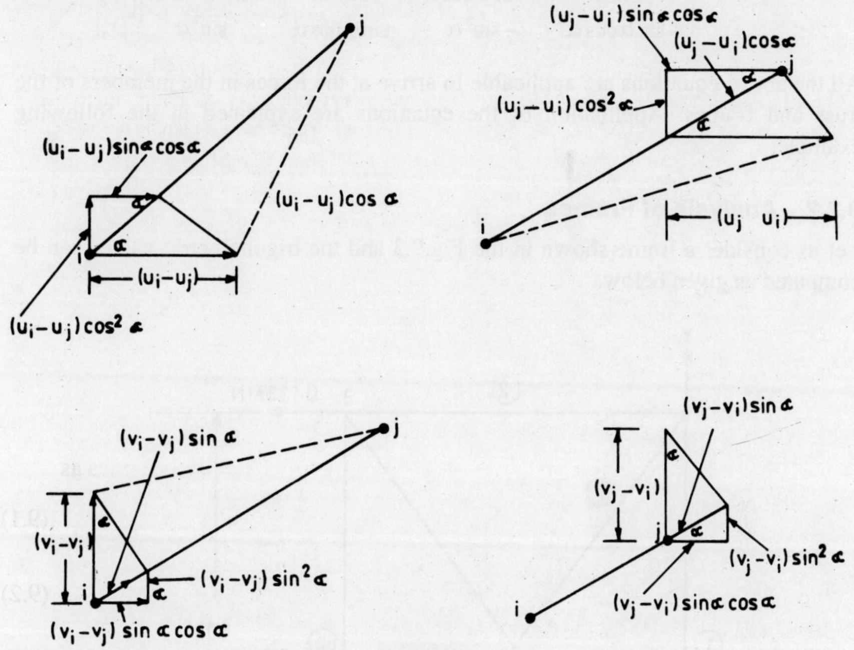

Fig. 9.2

Axial elongation of any member is given by

$$L_{ij} = (u_j - u_i)\cos\alpha + (v_j - v_i)\sin\alpha \tag{9.6}$$

In the matrix form

$$\{L_{ij}\} = \{\cos\alpha \quad \sin\alpha \quad -\cos\alpha \quad -\sin\alpha\}\begin{Bmatrix} u_i \\ v_i \\ u_j \\ v_j \end{Bmatrix} \tag{9.7}$$

x-and y-components of the axial elongation can be obtained by multiplying

$$\begin{Bmatrix} (L_{ij})_{ix} \\ (L_{ij})_{iy} \\ (L_{ij})_{jx} \\ (L_{ij})_{jy} \end{Bmatrix} = \begin{Bmatrix} \cos\alpha \\ \sin\alpha \\ -\cos\alpha \\ -\sin\alpha \end{Bmatrix}\{\cos\alpha \quad \sin\alpha \quad -\cos\alpha \quad -\sin\alpha\}\begin{Bmatrix} u_i \\ v_i \\ u_j \\ v_j \end{Bmatrix} \tag{9.8}$$

$$= \begin{Bmatrix} \cos^2\alpha & \sin\alpha\cos\alpha & -\cos^2\alpha & -\sin\alpha\cos\alpha \\ \sin\alpha\cos\alpha & \sin^2\alpha & -\sin\alpha\cos\alpha & -\sin^2\alpha \\ -\cos^2\alpha & -\sin\alpha\cos\alpha & \cos^2\alpha & \sin\alpha\cos\alpha \\ -\sin\alpha\cos\alpha & -\sin^2\alpha & \sin\alpha\cos\alpha & \sin^2\alpha \end{Bmatrix}\begin{Bmatrix} u_i \\ v_i \\ u_j \\ v_j \end{Bmatrix} \tag{9.9}$$

$$\{P\} = \frac{EA}{L}\begin{Bmatrix} \cos^2\alpha & \sin\alpha\cos\alpha & -\cos^2\alpha & -\sin\alpha\cos\alpha \\ \sin\alpha\cos\alpha & \sin^2\alpha & -\sin\alpha\cos\alpha & -\sin^2\alpha \\ -\cos^2\alpha & -\sin\alpha\cos\alpha & \cos^2\alpha & \sin\alpha\cos\alpha \\ -\sin\alpha\cos\alpha & -\sin^2\alpha & \sin\alpha\cos\alpha & \sin^2\alpha \end{Bmatrix}\begin{Bmatrix} u_i \\ v_i \\ u_j \\ v_j \end{Bmatrix} \quad (9.10)$$

All the above equations are applicable to arrive at the forces in the members of the truss and frames. Application of the equations are explained in the following example.

9.2.2 Analysis of Frames

Let us consider a frame shown in the Fig.9.3 and the trigonometric values can be computed as given below.

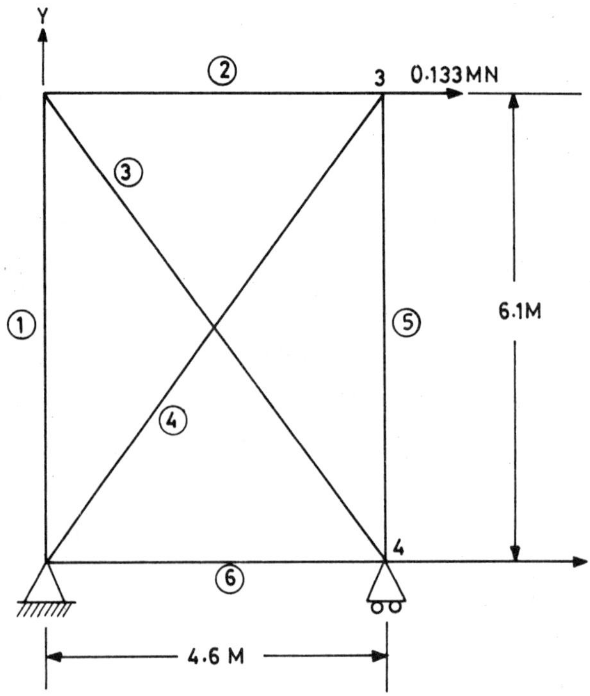

Fig. 9.3

Member	$\cos^2\alpha$	$\sin^2\alpha$	$\cos\alpha\sin\alpha$
1	0	1	0
2	1	0	0
3	0.36	0.64	–0.48
4	0.36	0.64	0.48
5	0	1	0
6	1	0	0

From the equations of equilibrium of each member, the stiffness matrix of each can be computed.

For number 1

$$\frac{EA}{L}\begin{bmatrix} K_{11} K_{12} \\ K_{21} K_{22} \end{bmatrix} \begin{bmatrix} u_1 \\ v_1 \\ u_2 \\ v_2 \end{bmatrix} = \begin{bmatrix} U_1 \\ V_1 \\ U_2 \\ V_2 \end{bmatrix} \tag{9.11}$$

which can be written as

$$\frac{EA}{L}\begin{bmatrix} 0 & 0 & 0 & 0 \\ 0 & 1 & 0 & -1 \\ 0 & 0 & 0 & 0 \\ 0 & -1 & 0 & 1 \end{bmatrix} \begin{bmatrix} u_1 \\ v_1 \\ u_2 \\ v_2 \end{bmatrix} = \begin{bmatrix} U_1 \\ V_1 \\ U_2 \\ V_2 \end{bmatrix} \tag{9.12}$$

since the actual dimension of [K] is 4 × 4.

For member 2, we have

$$\frac{AE}{L}\begin{bmatrix} K_{22} & K_{23} \\ K_{32} & K_{33} \end{bmatrix} \begin{Bmatrix} u_2 \\ v_2 \\ u_3 \\ v_3 \end{Bmatrix} = \begin{Bmatrix} U_2 \\ V_2 \\ U_3 \\ V_3 \end{Bmatrix} \tag{9.13}$$

Numerical values are

$$\frac{EA}{L}\begin{bmatrix} 1 & 0 & -1 & 0 \\ 0 & 0 & 0 & 0 \\ -1 & 0 & 1 & 0 \\ 0 & 0 & 0 & 0 \end{bmatrix} \begin{Bmatrix} u_2 \\ v_2 \\ u_3 \\ v_3 \end{Bmatrix} = \begin{Bmatrix} U_2 \\ V_2 \\ U_3 \\ V_3 \end{Bmatrix} \tag{9.14}$$

Similarly for member 3, we have

$$\frac{AE}{L}\begin{bmatrix} 0.36 & -0.48 & -0.36 & 0.48 \\ -0.48 & 0.64 & 0.48 & -0.64 \\ -0.36 & 0.48 & 0.36 & -0.48 \\ 0.48 & -0.64 & -0.48 & 0.64 \end{bmatrix} \begin{Bmatrix} u_4 \\ v_4 \\ u_2 \\ v_2 \end{Bmatrix} = \begin{Bmatrix} U_4 \\ V_4 \\ U_2 \\ V_2 \end{Bmatrix} \tag{9.15}$$

For member 4

$$\frac{AE}{L}\begin{bmatrix} 0.36 & 0.48 & -0.36 & -0.48 \\ 0.48 & 0.64 & -0.48 & -0.64 \\ -0.36 & -0.48 & 0.36 & 0.48 \\ -0.48 & -0.64 & 0.48 & 0.64 \end{bmatrix} \begin{Bmatrix} u_1 \\ v_1 \\ u_3 \\ v_3 \end{Bmatrix} = \begin{Bmatrix} U_1 \\ V_1 \\ U_3 \\ V_3 \end{Bmatrix} \tag{9.16}$$

For member 5

$$\frac{EA}{L}\begin{bmatrix} 0 & 0 & 0 & 0 \\ 0 & 1 & 0 & -1 \\ 0 & 0 & 0 & 0 \\ 0 & -1 & 0 & 1 \end{bmatrix} \begin{Bmatrix} u_4 \\ v_4 \\ u_3 \\ v_3 \end{Bmatrix} = \begin{Bmatrix} U_4 \\ V_4 \\ U_3 \\ V_3 \end{Bmatrix} \tag{9.17}$$

For member 6

$$\frac{EA}{L}\begin{bmatrix} 1 & 0 & -1 & 0 \\ 0 & 0 & 0 & 0 \\ -1 & 0 & 1 & 0 \\ 0 & 0 & 0 & 0 \end{bmatrix}\begin{Bmatrix} u_1 \\ v_1 \\ u_4 \\ v_4 \end{Bmatrix} = \begin{Bmatrix} U_1 \\ V_1 \\ U_4 \\ V_4 \end{Bmatrix} \tag{9.18}$$

Now the total stiffness matrix of the system can be computed by the overall equations of equilibrium.

$$\frac{AE}{L}\begin{bmatrix} K_{11}^{(1)}+K_{11}^{(4)}+K_{11}^{(6)} & K_{12}^{(1)} & K_{13}^{(4)} & K_{14}^{(6)} \\ K_{21}^{(1)} & K_{22}^{(1)}+K_{22}^{(2)}+K_{22}^{(3)} & K_{23}^{(2)} & K_{24}^{(3)} \\ K_{31}^{(4)} & K_{32}^{(2)} & K_{33}^{(2)}+K_{33}^{(4)}+K_{33}^{(5)} & K_{34}^{(5)} \\ K_{41}^{(6)} & K_{42}^{(3)} & K_{43}^{(5)} & K_{44}^{(3)}+K_{44}^{(5)}+K_{44}^{(6)} \end{bmatrix}\begin{Bmatrix} u_1 \\ v_1 \\ u_2 \\ v_2 \\ u_3 \\ v_3 \\ u_4 \\ v_4 \\ u_5 \\ v_5 \\ u_6 \\ v_6 \end{Bmatrix} = \begin{Bmatrix} U_1 \\ V_1 \\ U_2 \\ V_2 \\ U_3 \\ V_3 \\ U_4 \\ V_4 \\ U_5 \\ V_5 \\ U_6 \\ V_6 \end{Bmatrix} \tag{9.19}$$

With numerical values, we get

$$\frac{AE}{L}\begin{bmatrix} 1.36 & 0.48 & 0 & 0 & -0.36 & -0.48 & -1 & 0 \\ 0.48 & 1.64 & 0 & -1 & -0.48 & -0.64 & 0 & 0 \\ 0 & 0 & 1.36 & -0.48 & -1 & 0 & -0.36 & 0.48 \\ 0 & -1 & -0.48 & 1.64 & 0 & 0 & 0.48 & -0.64 \\ -3.6 & -0.48 & -1 & 0 & 1.36 & 0.48 & 0 & 0 \\ -0.48 & -0.64 & 0 & 0 & 0.48 & 1.64 & 0 & -1 \\ -1 & 0 & -0.36 & 0.48 & 0 & 0 & 1.36 & -0.48 \\ 0 & 0 & 0.48 & -0.64 & 0 & -1 & -0.48 & 1.64 \end{bmatrix}\begin{Bmatrix} u_1 \\ v_1 \\ u_2 \\ v_2 \\ u_3 \\ v_3 \\ u_4 \\ v_4 \end{Bmatrix} = \{P\} \tag{9.20}$$

$$\frac{AE}{L}\begin{bmatrix} 1.36 & -0.48 & -1.0 & 0 & -0.36 \\ -0.48 & 1.64 & 0 & 0 & 0.48 \\ -1.0 & 0 & 1.36 & 0.48 & 0 \\ 0 & 0 & 0.48 & 1.64 & 0 \\ -0.36 & 0.48 & 0 & 0 & 1.36 \end{bmatrix}\begin{Bmatrix} u_2 \\ v_2 \\ u_3 \\ v_3 \\ u_4 \end{Bmatrix} = \begin{Bmatrix} U_2 \\ V_2 \\ U_3 \\ V_3 \\ U_4 \end{Bmatrix} \tag{9.21}$$

Here the total stiffness matrix of the frame is an 8×8 matrix, by introducing the support conditions for which u_1, v_1 and v_4 are all zero. These boundary conditions will reduce the number of equations to 5. Hence, the size of the matrix is only 5×5.

For the given problem the external loads $\{Q\}$ must be equated to the components of forces,

$$\{Q\}_{\text{node}} = \Sigma\,\{P\}_{\text{node}} \tag{9.22}$$

$$= \begin{Bmatrix} 0 \\ 0 \\ 30 \\ 0 \\ 0 \end{Bmatrix} N$$

The unknown nodal displacements can be computed by rearranging Eq. 9.21

$$\{\delta\} = \begin{Bmatrix} u_2 \\ v_2 \\ u_3 \\ v_3 \\ u_4 \end{Bmatrix} = \frac{L}{AE}\begin{bmatrix} 1.36 & -0.48 & -1.0 & 0 & -0.36 \\ -0.48 & 1.64 & 0 & 0 & 0.48 \\ -1.0 & 0 & 1.36 & 0.48 & 0 \\ 0 & 0 & 0.48 & 1.64 & 0 \\ -0.36 & 0.48 & 0 & 0 & 1.36 \end{bmatrix}^{-1}\begin{Bmatrix} 0 \\ 0 \\ 30 \\ 0 \\ 0 \end{Bmatrix} \tag{9.23}$$

$$\{\delta\} = \frac{L}{AE}\begin{Bmatrix} 0.6833337\times 10^2 \\ 0.1640000\times 10^2 \\ 0.8063340\times 10^2 \\ -0.2360002\times 10^2 \\ 0.1230003\times 10^2 \end{Bmatrix} mm \tag{9.24}$$

Now it is easy to obtain the relations to compute the axial forces in each member of the frame.

$$\begin{aligned} P_1 &= \frac{AE}{L}\{(u_2-u_1)\cos\alpha+(v_2-v_1)\sin\alpha\} \\ P_2 &= \frac{AE}{L}\{(u_3-u_2)\cos\alpha+(v_3-v_2)\sin\alpha\} \\ P_3 &= \frac{AE}{L}\{(u_4-u_2)\cos\alpha+(v_4-v_2)\sin\alpha\} \\ P_4 &= \frac{AE}{L}\{(u_3-u_1)\cos\alpha+(v_3-v_1)\sin\alpha\} \\ P_5 &= \frac{AE}{L}\{(u_4-u_3)\cos\alpha+(v_4-v_3)\sin\alpha\} \\ P_6 &= \frac{AE}{L}\{(u_4-u_1)\cos\alpha+(v_4-v_1)\sin\alpha\} \end{aligned} \tag{9.25}$$

The axial forces are given in Eq. 9.26 where the –ve sign represents the compressive force in the member.

$$\begin{Bmatrix} P_1 \\ P_2 \\ P_3 \\ P_4 \\ P_5 \\ P_6 \end{Bmatrix} = \begin{Bmatrix} 16.4 \\ 12.3 \\ -20.5 \\ 29.5 \\ 23.6 \\ 12.3 \end{Bmatrix} \tag{9.26}$$

9.2.3 Analysis of Cylindrical Shells

The analysis described in the previous section is extended to the circular cylindrical pressure vessel with flange and ribs. The finite element descretisation of one repeatable substructure is shown. in Fig.9.4. The entire shell consists of eight ribs and

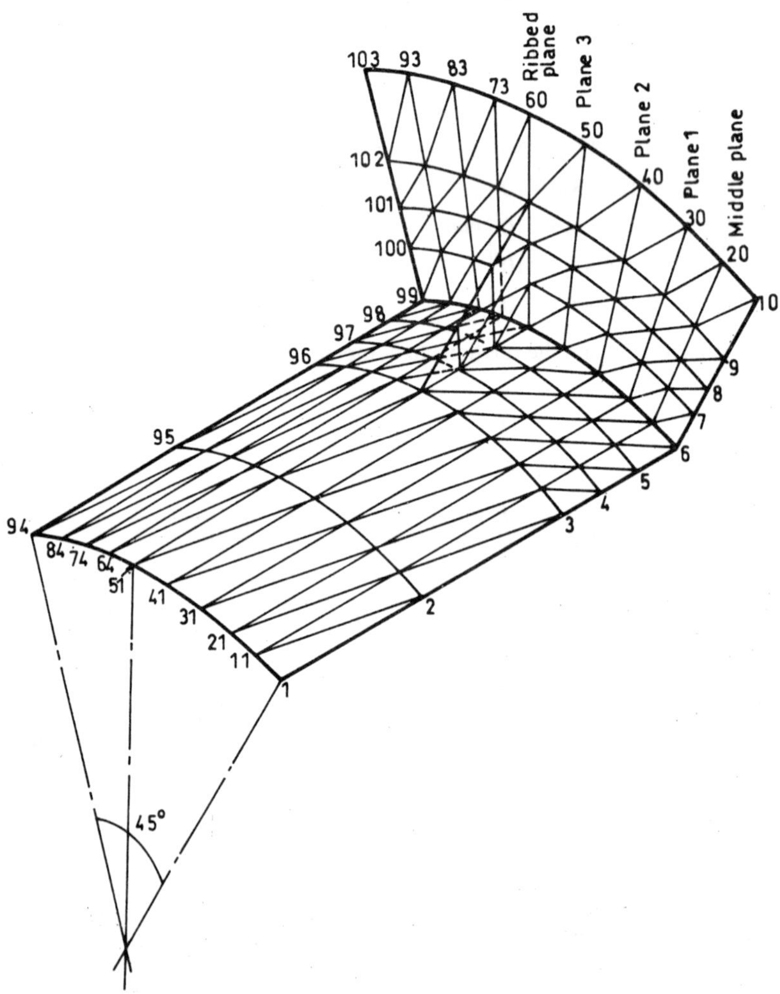

Fig. 9.4 Element discretisation of a sub-structure

hence has eight repeatable substructures. The flanged end is covered with a circular coverplate with the help of eight bolt sets. Hence each repeatable substructure is provided with a rib and a bolt location.

Axisymmetric Loading

When the shell is subjected to internal pressure, the bolts also experience an equal amount of bolt load. Therefore, the repeatable substructure satisifies the conditions for rotational periodicity in geometry and loading.

Let us analyse the axisymmetric structure which consists of eight repeatable substructures. If the substructure is rotated eight times through an angle of 45° about its axis, the equivalent idealistion of the complete shell will be generated. One of the substructures of the shell is idealized as an assembly of flat triangular elements. The number of elements and nodes for each substrcuture is 376 and 103 respectively. The inplane deformation is assumed to be independent of the bending deformation.

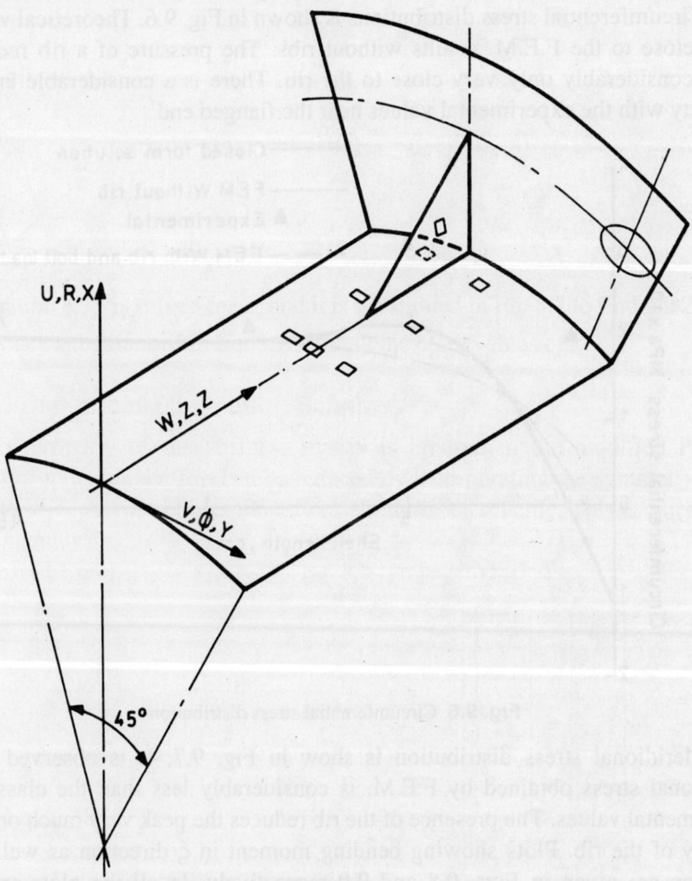

Fig. 9.5 One sub-structure showing strain gauges

The stress distribution is obtained by varying the internal pressure from 0 to 5.75 atmospheres with constant bolt load. The load can be evaluated by distributing the total end thrust equally to all the bolts. The shell is also analysed with internal pressure alone without bolt loads, with ribs and without ribs. To verify the above results, experiments were conducted using strain gauge technique. Details are given in the next section.

The pressure vessel without ribs and bolt loads as a circular cylindrical shell with ends fixed and subjected to internal pressure is analysed theoretically in the literature. The analytical results using cyclic symmetric concept are compared with theoretical results.

Deflections and stresses are computed for uniform internal pressure. The stress distributions and displacement pattern are plotted along the length of the shell. An experimental model is tested for the same internal pressure. Strain measurement at different locations along the length of the pressure vesel is obtained with the help of strain rosettes as indicated in Fig. 9.5. The test is carried out for different pressures varying from 1 to 5.75 atmospheres with constant bolt load.

Circumferential stress distributions is shown in Fig. 9.6. Theoretical values are fairly close to the F.E.M. results without ribs. The pressure of a rib reduces the stress considerably only very close to the rib. There is a considerable amount of disparity with the experimental values near the flanged end.

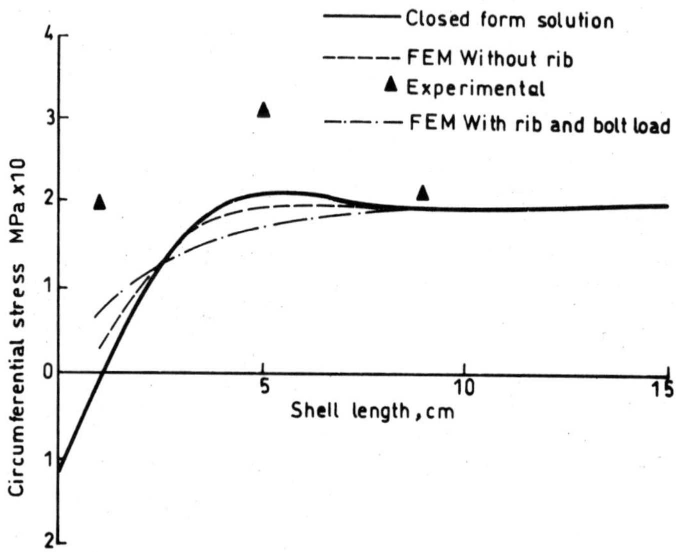

Fig. 9.6 Circumferential stress distribution

Meridional stress distribution is show in Fig. 9.7. It is observed that the meridional stress obtained by F.E.M. is considerably less than the classical and experimental values. The presence of the rib reduces the peak very much only in the vicinity of the rib. Plots showing bending moment in ξ direction as well as in ϕ direction are given in Figs. 9.8 and 9.9 respectively. In all the plots except the bending moment in the ϕ direction, the values are considerably lower than the theoretical values. On the other hand, it is the opposite in the case of bending moment in the ϕ direction.

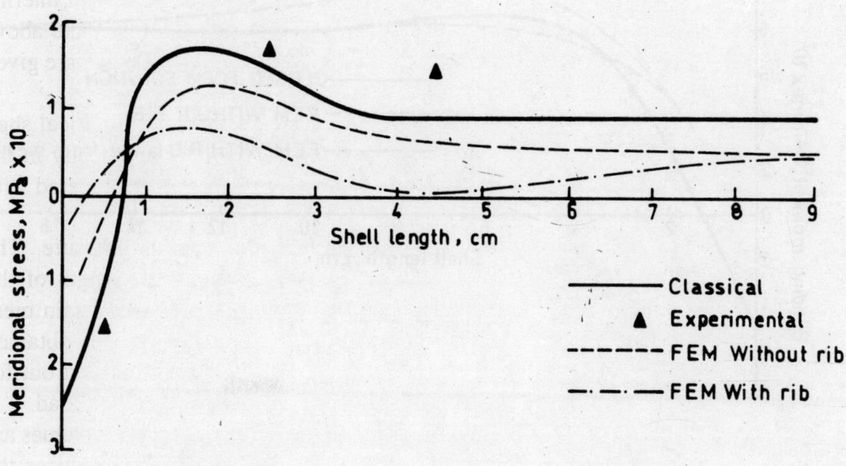

Fig. 9.7 Meridional stress distribution along the shell

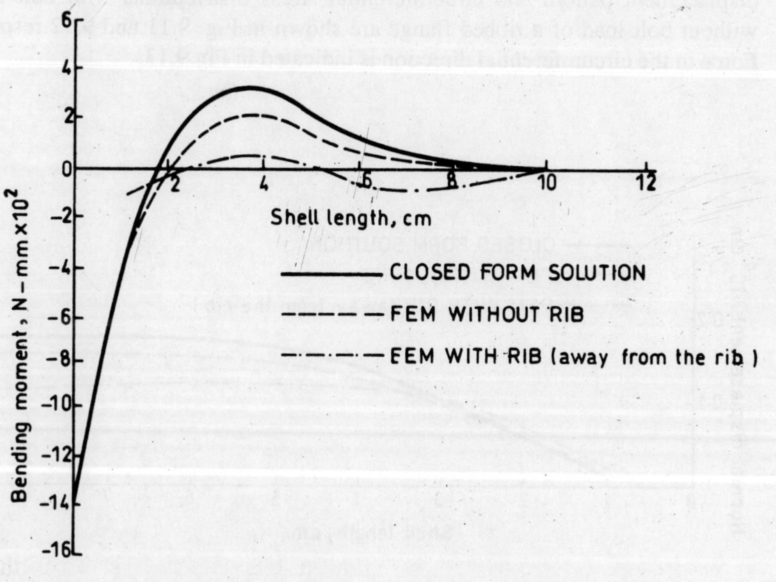

Fig. 9.8 Bending moment along the shell

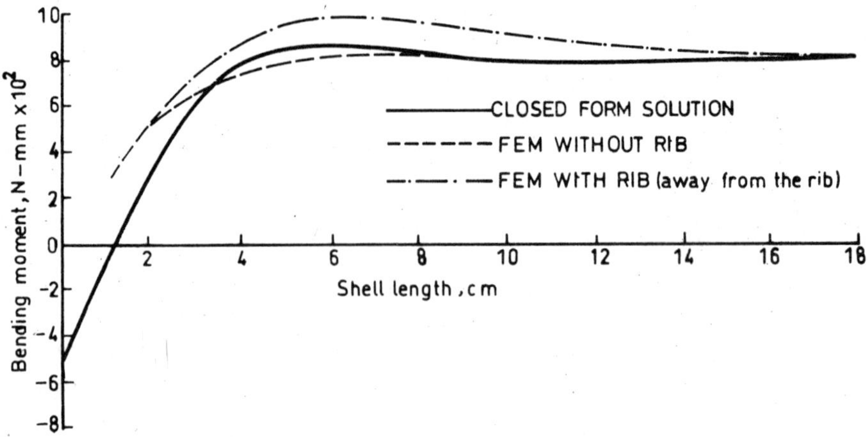

Fig. 9.9 Bending moment in o direction along the shell

A plot showing normal displacement pattern is given in Fig. 9.10. The displacement showing the rib is considerably less. It is also observed that the displacement pattern obtained by F.E.M. without rib is lower than the theoretical. Normal displacement pattern and circumferential stress distributions with bolt load and without bolt load of a ribbed flange are shown in Fig. 9.11 and 9.12 respectively. Force in the circumferential direction is indicated in Fig.9.13.

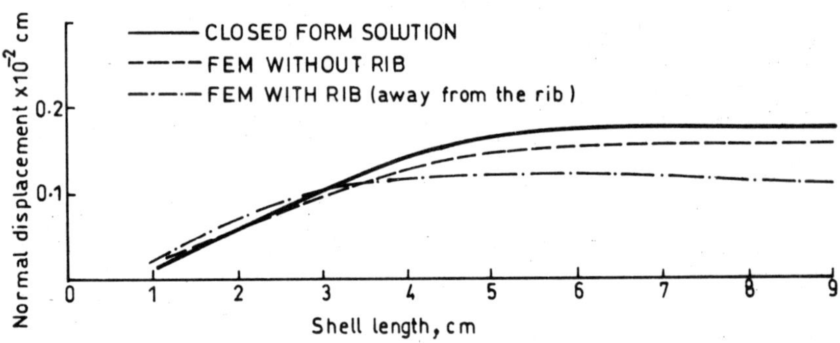

Fig. 9.10 Radial deflection along the shell

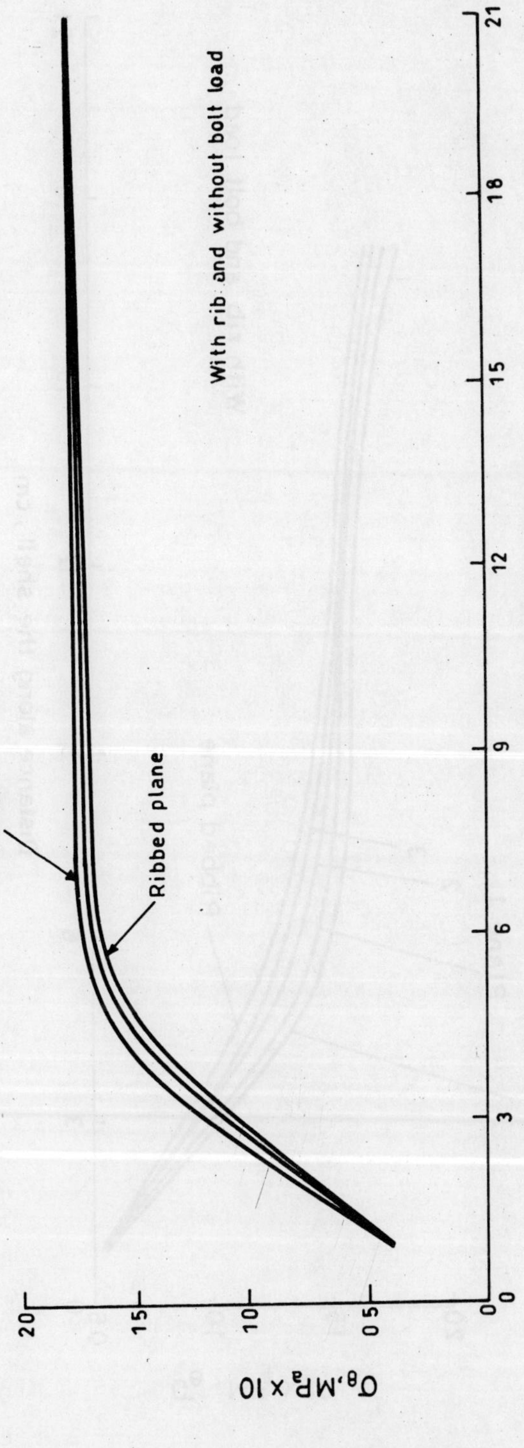

Fig. 9.11 Circumferential stress distribution

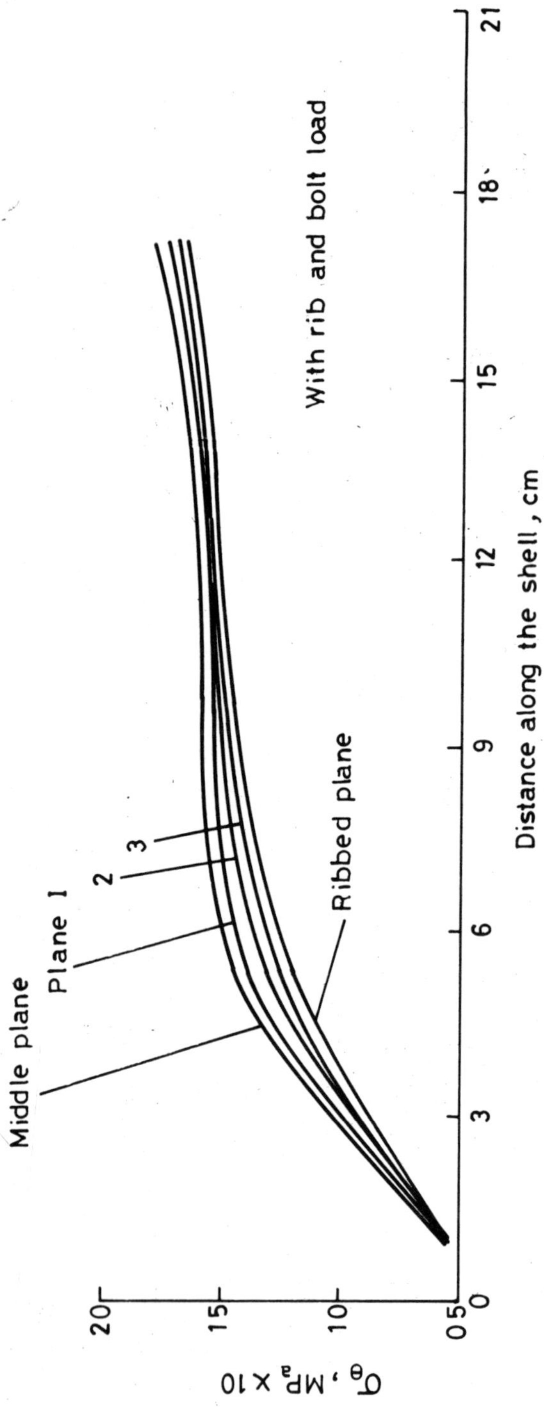

Fig. 9.12 Circumferential stress distribution

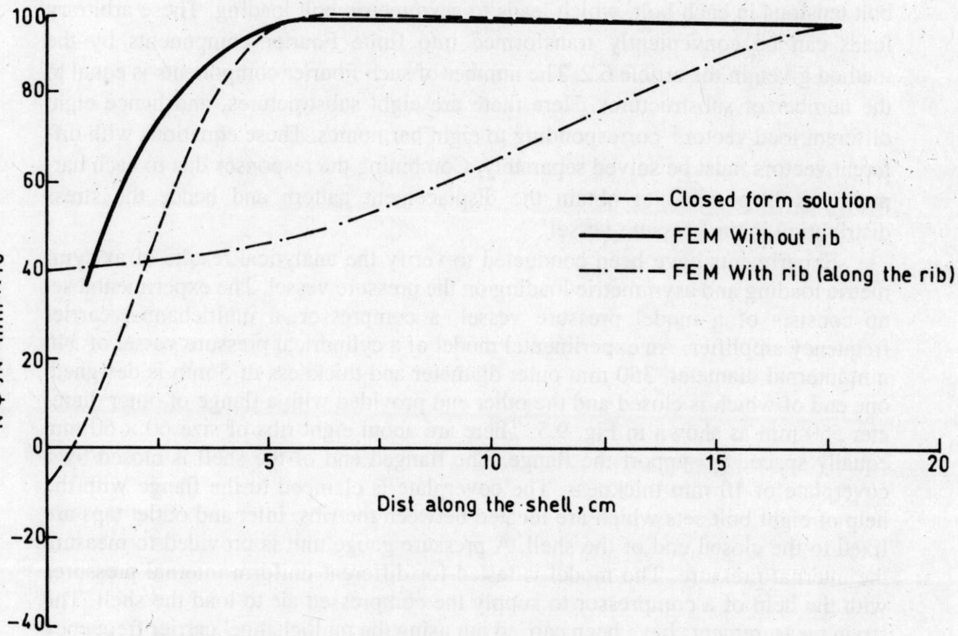

Fig. 9.13 $N\phi v$, distance along the shell

An economical way of stress analysis of rotationally periodic structure subjected to axisymmetric loading has been described. Only one substructure is used to analyse the entire strucutre for varying internal pressure. From the above analysis it can be concluded that the proposed analytical method can be used for any periodic strurcture with required accuracy. Even large size problems can be solved with the help of minicomputers by this approach.

Asymmetric Loading

This method decomposes the loading system into a series of finite Fourier harmonics. The analysis of a substructure is carried out for each of the harmonics separately and these are recombined to define the complete displacement pattern. This method provides an economical way of solving the rotationally periodic structure as opposed to solving the complete structure subjected to the system of loading, which would require much more computer storage and time.

The pressure vessel considered in the previous section is analysed for asymmetric loading of bolts. The effect of bolt holes is neglected. The flexibility of the flange is also neglected for simplicity. A concentrated bolt load is assumed at the bolt location. All such bolt loads are not equal due to uneven tightening. The effect of gasket is not considered in the present analysis.

In reality, it is impossible to tighten all bolts identically, resulting in unequal bolt tensions in each bolt, which leads to asymmetric bolt loading. These arbitrary loads can be conveniently transformed into finite Fourier components by the method given in the article 6.2. The number of such Fourier components is equal to the number of substructures. Here there are eight substructures, and hence eight different load vectors corresponding to eight harmonics. These equations with different vectors must be solved separately. Combining the responses due to each harmonic, it is possible to obtain the displacement pattern and hence the stress distribution in the pressure vessel.

Experiments have been conducted to verify the analytical results of axisymmetric loading and asymmetric loading on the pressure vessel. The experimental set up consists of a model pressure vessel, a compressor, a multichannel carrier frequency amplifier. An experimental model of a cylindrical pressure vessel of 340 mm internal diameter, 350 mm outer diameter and thickness of 5 mm is designed, one end of which is closed and the other end provided with a flange of outer diameter 550 mm as shown in Fig. 9.5. There are about eight ribs of size 60 × 60 mm equally spaced to support the flange. The flanged end of the shell is closed by a coverplate of 10 mm thickness. The coverplate is clamped to the flange with the help of eight bolt sets which are located between the ribs. Inlet and outlet taps are fixed to the closed end of the shell. A pressure gauge unit is provided to measure the internal pressure. The model is tested for different uniform internal pressures with the help of a compressor to supply the compressed air to load the shell. The strain measurements have been carried out using the multichannel carrier frequency amplifer.

The model is tested with known values of bolt on the shell and without internal pressure. The bolt loads are given in Table 9.1.

Table 9.1 Loads at bolt locations

Bolt location	Load ($n \times 10$)	Strain in (micron)
1	1140.02	120.0
2	950.02	100.0
3	760.01	80.0
4	570.01	60.0
5	570.01	60.0
6	760.01	80.0
7	950.02	100.0
8	1140.02	120.0

Comparision between the analytical and experimental strain distributions is presented for longitudinal strain in Fig. 9.14 and for the circumferential strain in Fig. 9.15. The plots correspond to the substructure where the maximum bolt load is acting. Meridional and hoop stress distributions are shown in Figs. 9.16 and 9.17 respectively.

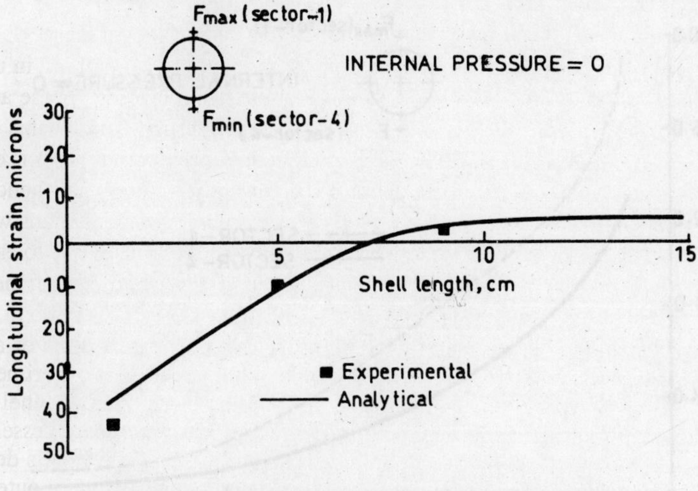

Fig. 9.14 Longitudinal strain distribution along the shell

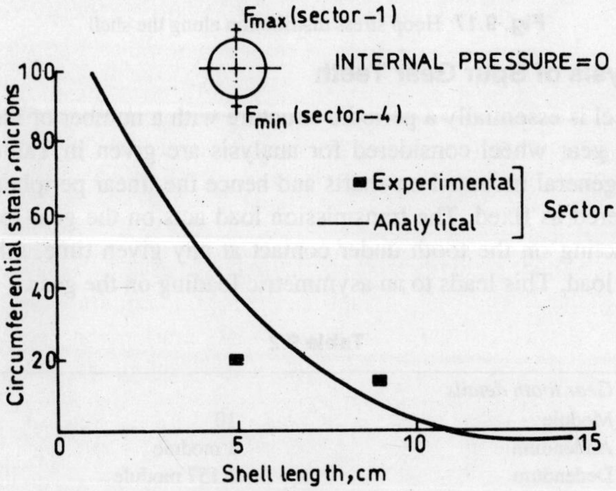

Fig. 9.15 Circumferential strain distribution along the shell

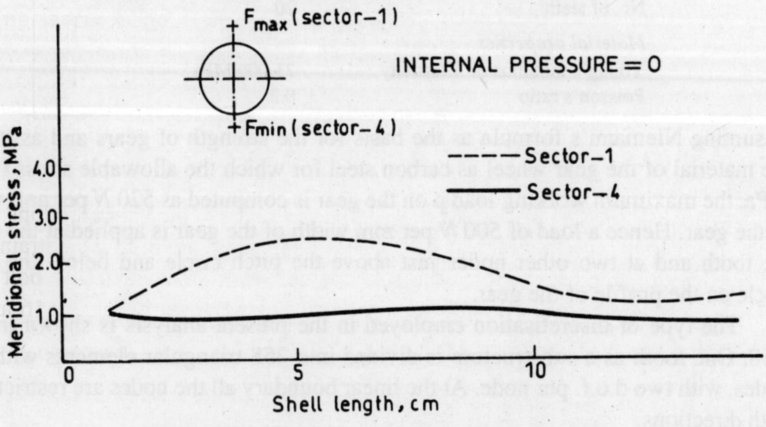

Fig. 9.16 Meridional stress distribution along the shell

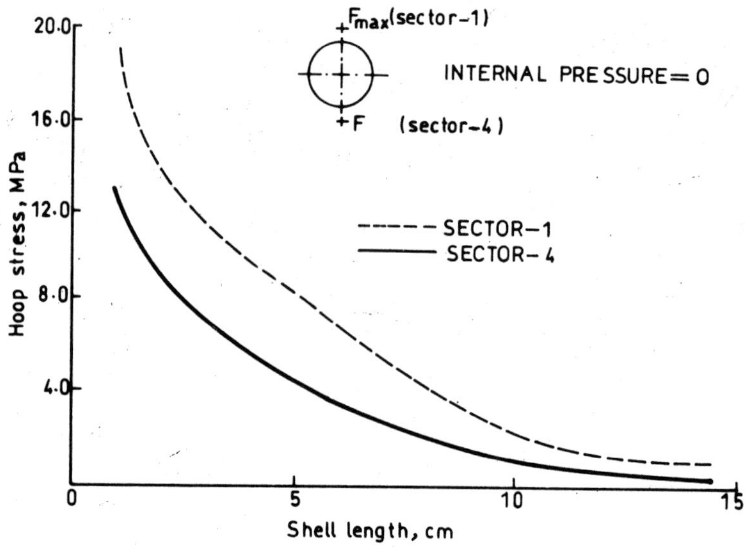

Fig. 9.17 Hoop stress distribution along the shell

9.2.4 Analysis of Spur Gear Teeth

Spur gear wheel is essentially a periodic structure with a number of identical teeth. Details of the gear wheel considered for analysis are given in Table 9.2. These wheels are in general mounted on shafts and hence the linear periphery of the rim can be considered as fixed. The transmission load acts on the gear tooth as a line contact load acting on the tooth under contact at any given time. All other teeth experience no load. This leads to an asymmetric loading on the gear.

Table 9.2

Gear tooth details	
Module	10
Addendum	1 module
Dedendum	1.157 module
Pressure angle	20°
Face width	5 module
No. of teeth	20
Material properties	
Young's modulus of Elasticity	21,000 MPa
Poisson's ratio	0.3

Assuming Niemann's formula as the basis for the strength of gears and assuming the material of the gear wheel as carbon steel for which the allowable stress is 250 MPa, the maximum working load p on the gear is computed as 520 *N* per unit width of the gear. Hence a load of 500 *N* per mm width of the gear is applied at the tip of the tooth and at two other nodes just above the pitch circle and below the pitch circle on the profile of the gear.

The type of discretisation employed in the present analysis is shown in Fig. 9.18. One tooth as a substructure is divided into 358 triangular elements with 206 nodes, with two d.o.f. per node. At the linear boundary all the nodes are restricted in both directions.

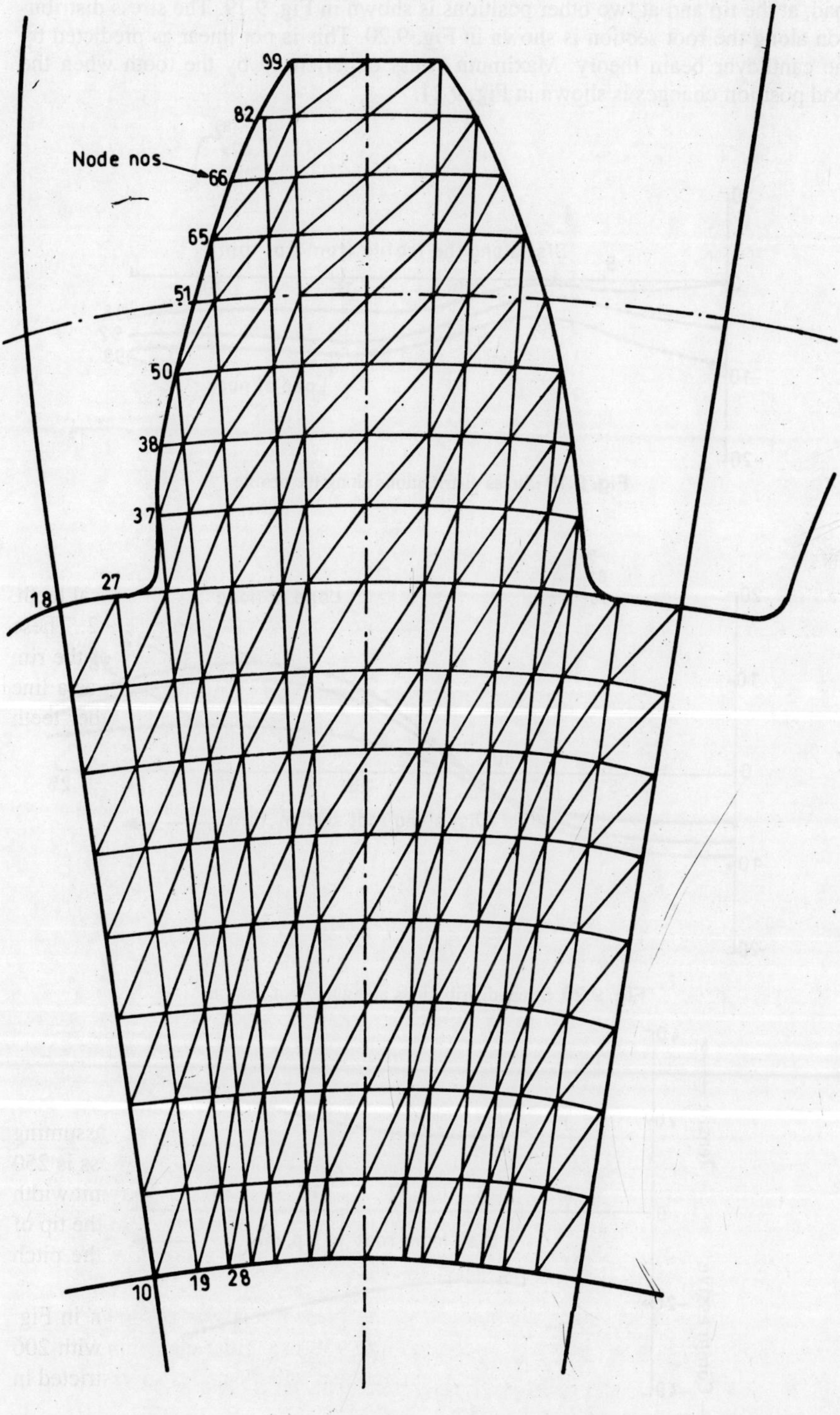

Fig. 9.18 Discretisation of spur gear tooth

The stress distribution along the tooth profile of the tooth experiencing the load, at the tip and at two other positions is shown in Fig. 9.19. The stress distribution along the root section is shown in Fig. 9.20. This is not linear as predicted by the cantilever beam theory. Maximum stress experienced by the tooth when the load position changes is shown in Fig. 9.21.

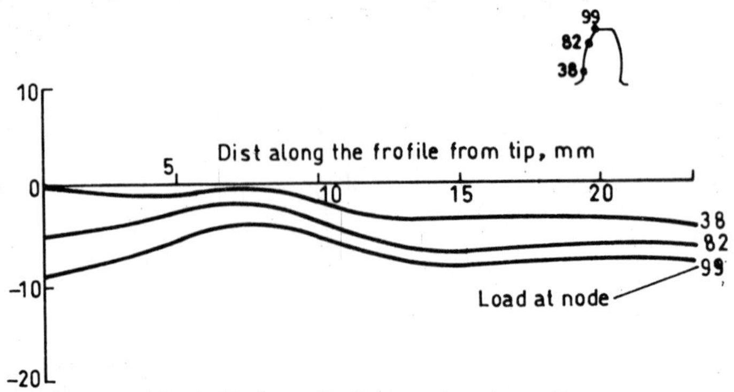

Fig. 9.19 Stress distributions along the profile

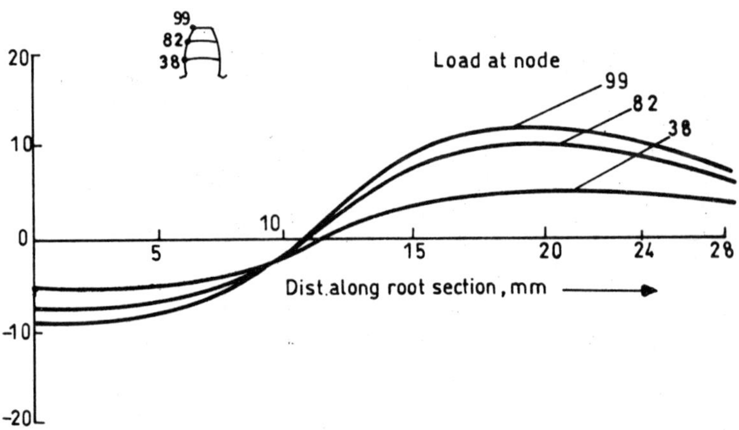

Fig. 9.20 Stress distributions along the root section

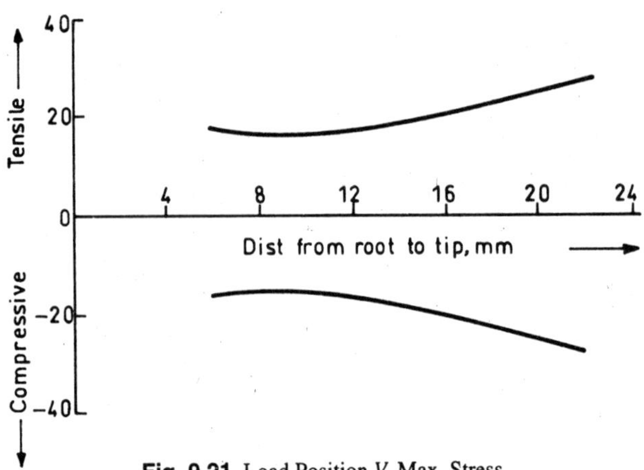

Fig. 9.21 Load Position V_s Max. Stress

The circumferential and radial displacements for the tooth experiencing load at the tip and for the tooth adjacent to it are compared in Fig. 9.22. This shows that the circumferential displacement in the adjacent teeth is negligibly small. It may be observed from Fig. 9.22 that the maximum circumferential displacement obtained is 6.0×10^{-2} mm when the load is at the tip. The value obtained by beam theory assuming the tooth as a contilever subejcted to a concentrated load at the tip of the gear is 6.45×10^{-2} mm. There is a good agreement between these two. The maximum radial stress is about 120 MPa as indicated in Fig. 9.22. The stress may also be obtained by using the expression given below:

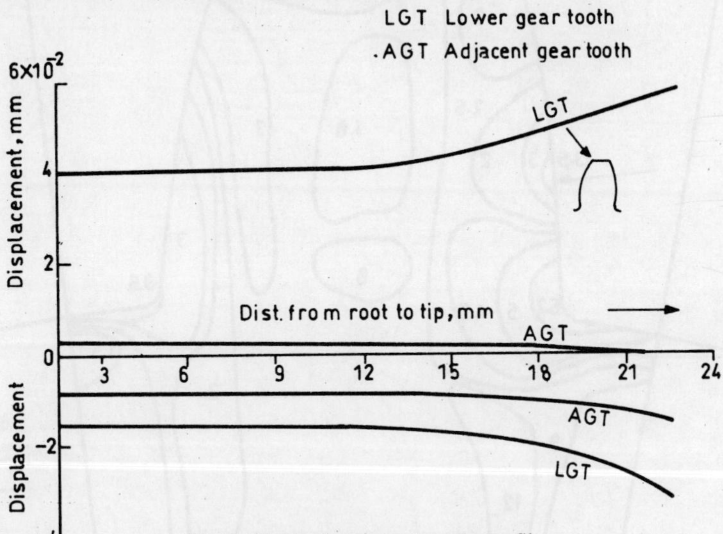

Fig. 9.22 Displacement along the profile

$$\sigma = \sqrt{[(\sigma_b - \sigma_d)^2 + (\mu\tau_{xy})^2]} \tag{9.27}$$

where
$$\sigma_b = \frac{6Pe_f \cos\alpha}{bS_f^2}$$

$$\sigma_d = \frac{P\sin\alpha}{bS_f}$$

$$\tau_{xy} = \frac{P\cos\alpha}{bS_f}$$

e_f is the height of the tooth

S_f is the width of the tooth at the root

P is the normal contact load and

α is the pressure angle.

The value obtained by the above formula is 158.3 MPa. Stress contours are shown in Figs. 9.23, 9.24 and 9.25 for three load positions at the tip, 0.25 module above the pitch point and 0.2 module above the fillet for the loaded gear. It is observed that the stress at the inner radius of the rim is considerably large. Stress contour plots for two adjacent teeth are shown in Figs. 9.26 and 9.27.

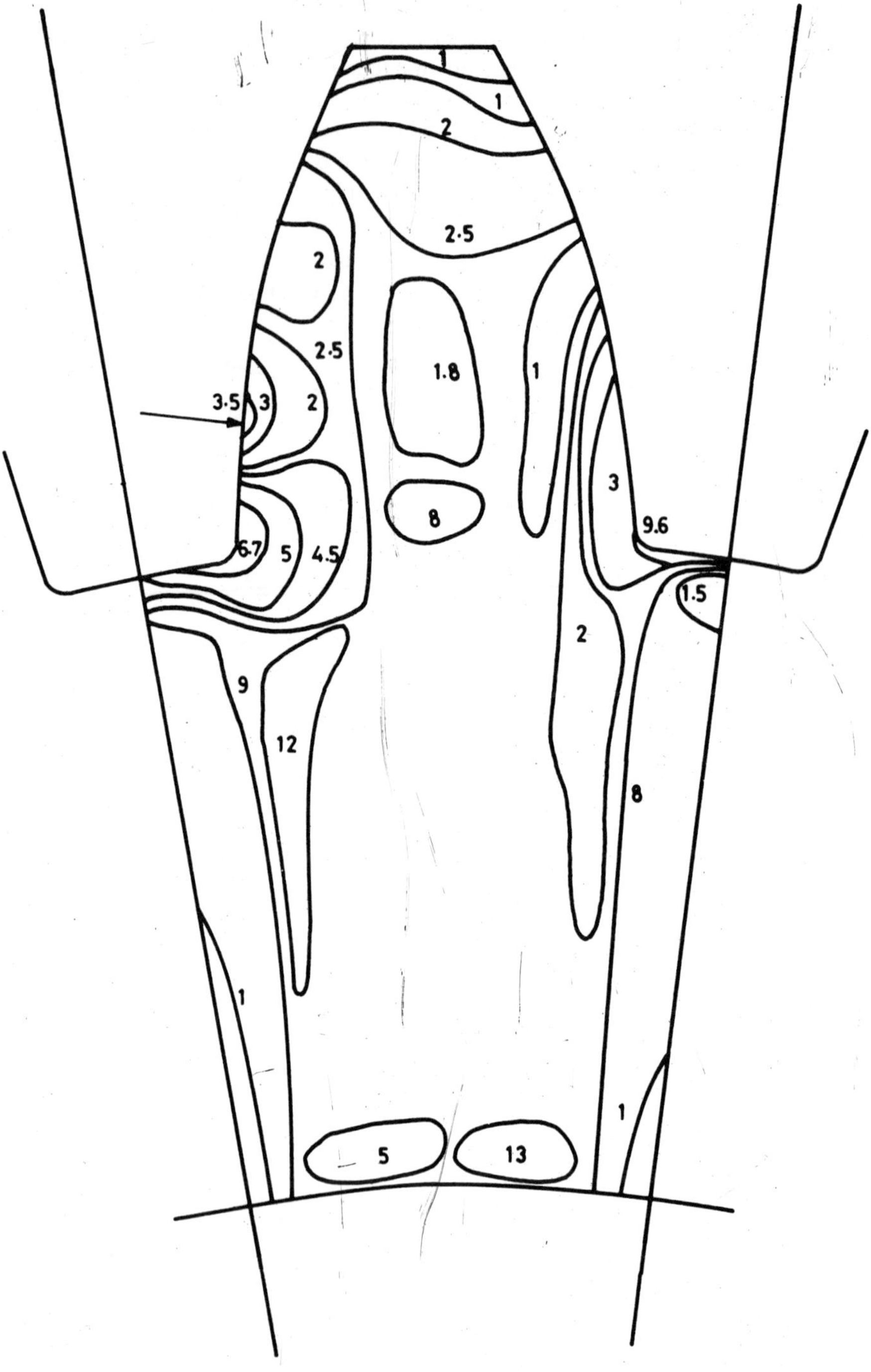

Fig. 9.23 Radial stress contours when the load is at 0.2 module above the Fillet (MPd × 10)

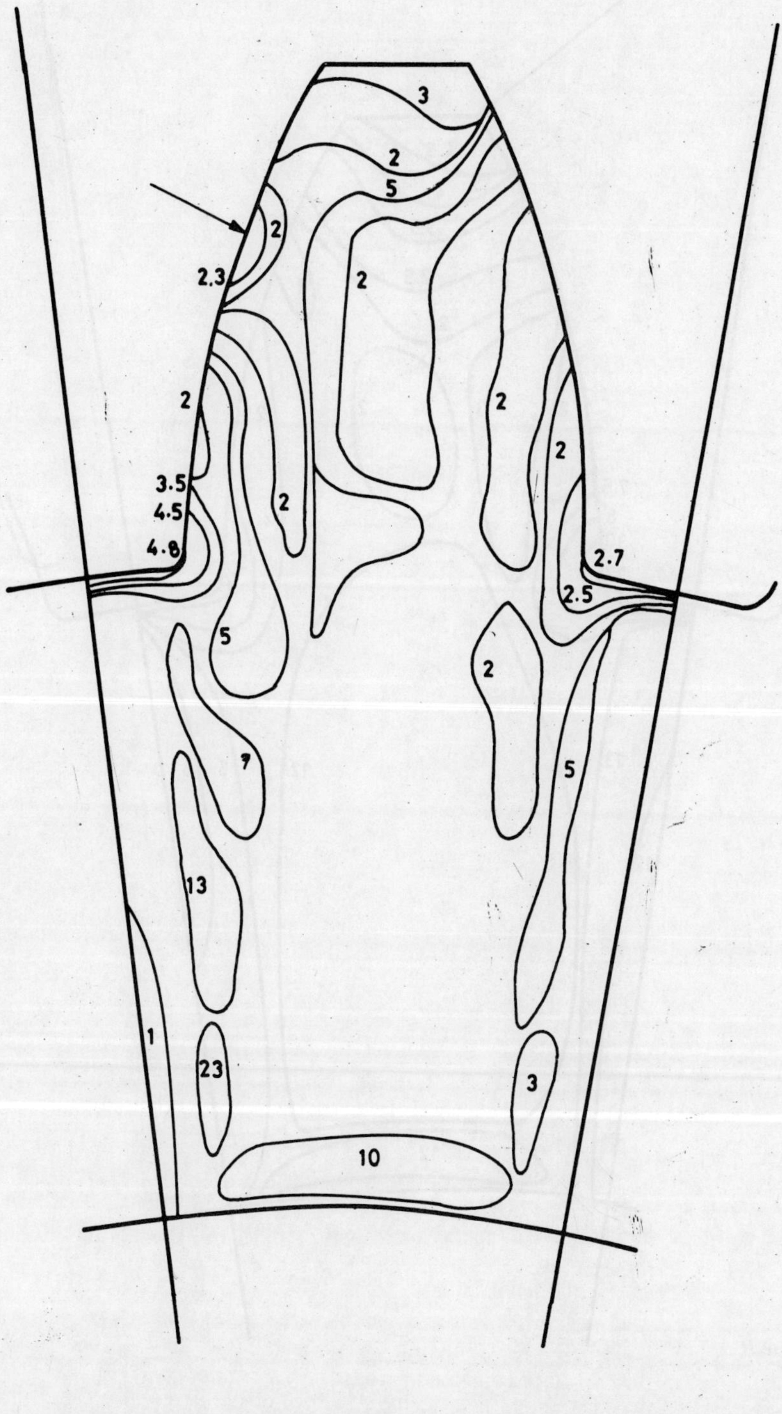

Fig. 9.24 Radial stress contours when the load is at 0.25 Module above the pitch point (MPD × 10)

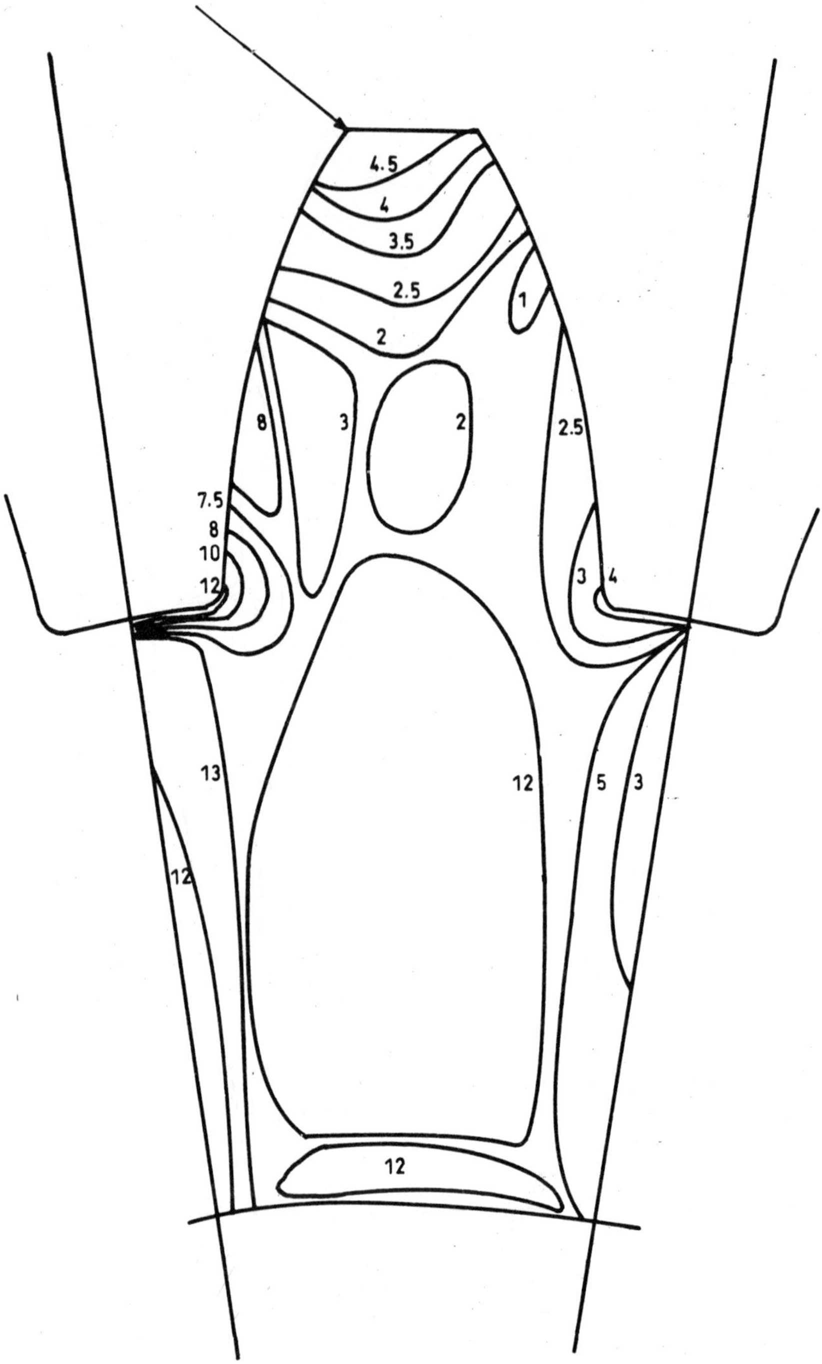

Fig. 9.25 Radial stress contours when the load is at the tip (MPD × 10)

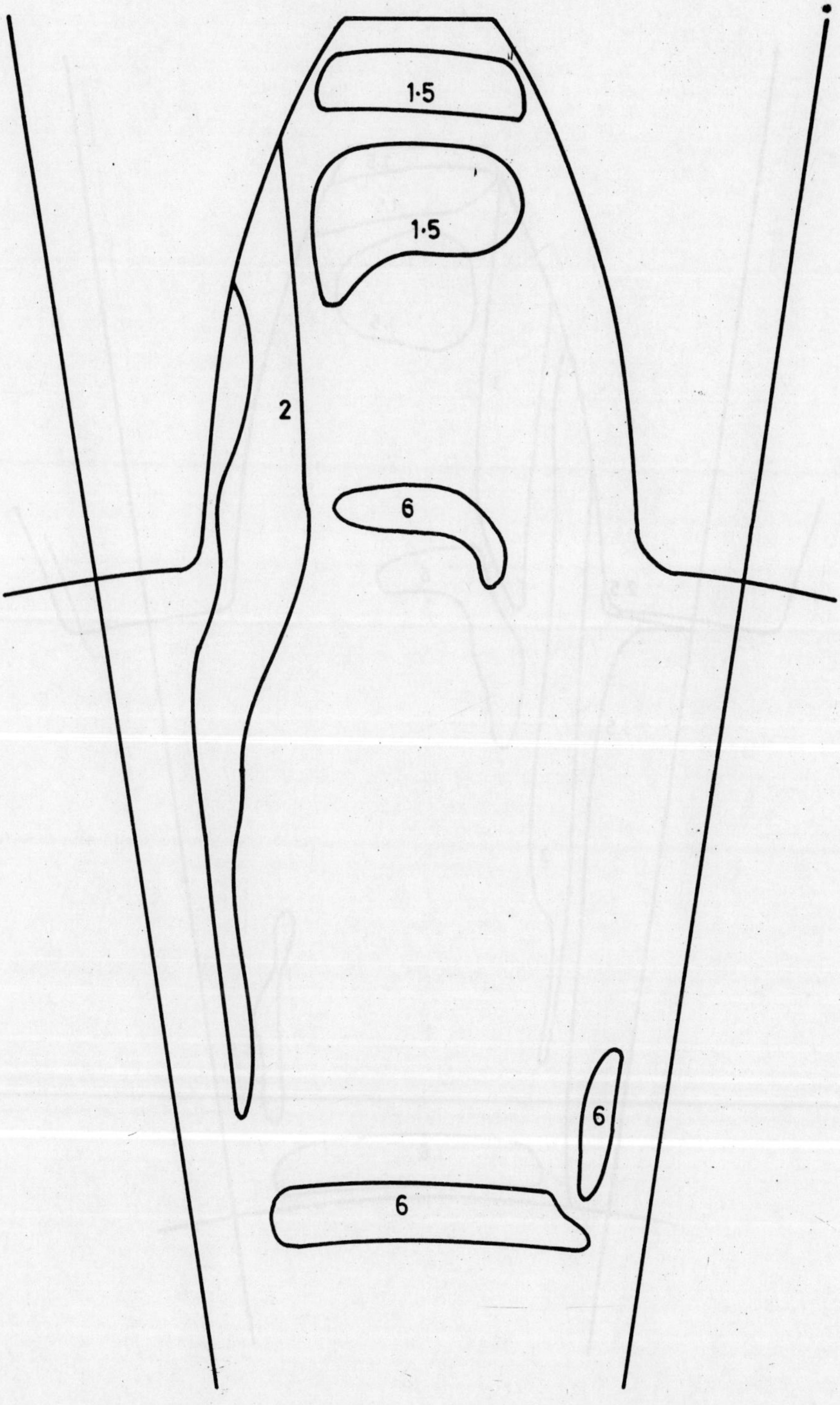

Fig. 9.26 Radial stress contours in the AGT 1 for the 3 load at the tip (MPD × 10)

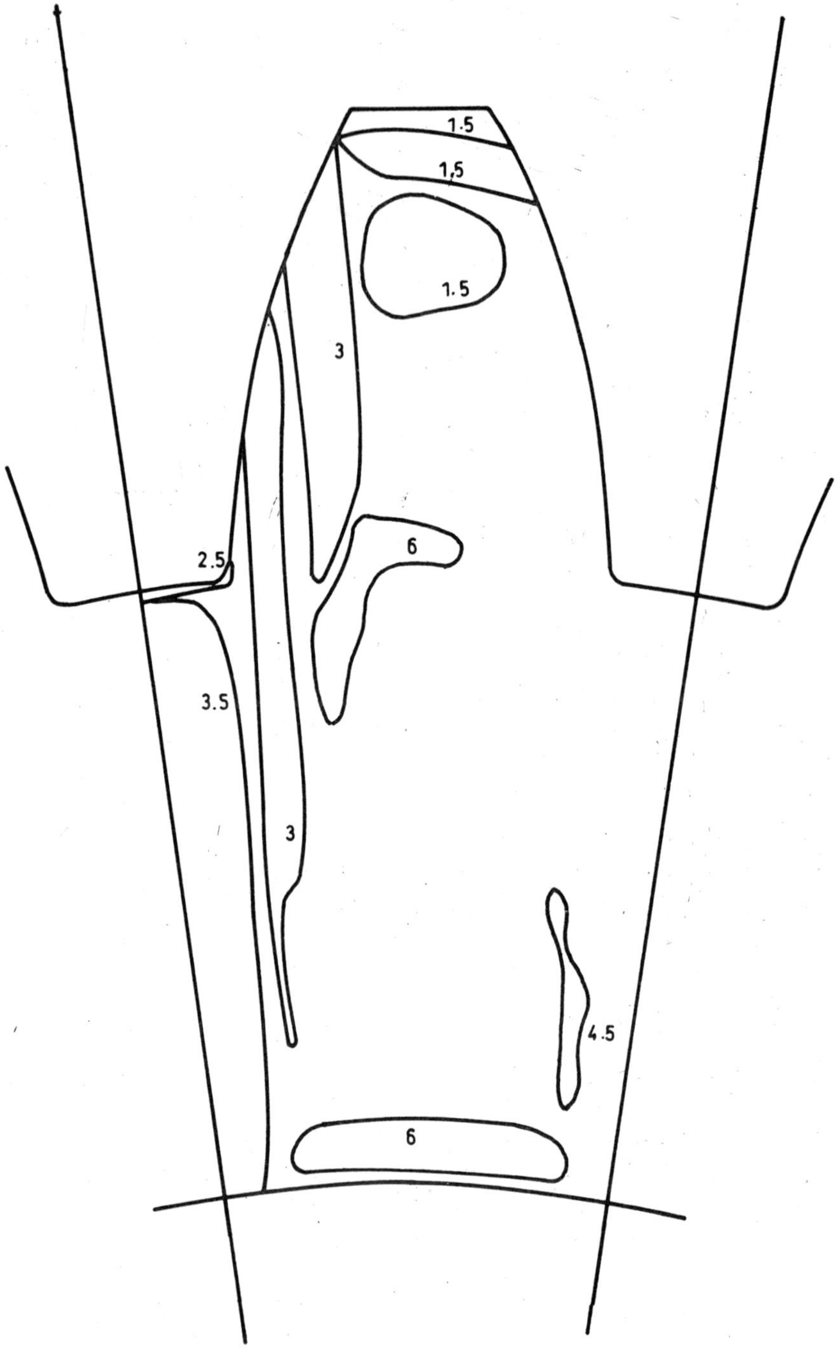

Fig. 9.27 Radial stress contours in the AGT 2 for the load at the tip (MPD × 10)

9.3 COMPUTER AIDED DYNAMIC ANALYSIS: CASE STUDIES

The rotating parts of gas turbines and jet engines are subjected to highly hostile conditions such as centrifugal loads, thermal loads and loading from pressurized gases. The designer is greatly concerned with improvement in performance, life and weight reduction without any loss of reliability. The loads are quite complex and, the life of structural components can be predeicted only with the help of an accurate dynamic analysis. This cannot be achieved without effective and constant development of specific methods and corresponding computer programs to be used by engineers for their calculations. The design of a turbomachine ultimately is a compromise between the requirements of aerodynamics and thermodynamics (for performance) and that of the solid mechanics (for strenght). Hence we are concerned with the dynamic analysis of rotating components and structural members.

9.3.1 Preliminary Consideration

In general there is no single algorithm which is most effective for all the eigenvalue problems. The specific alogrithm will depend on the characteristics of $[K]$ and $[M]$ primarily, such as the order, bandwidth of the matrices and the number of eigen pairs required. For majority of the engineering problems the lowest eigenvalues and corresponding eigenvectors are required. For evaluating this the choice of the appropriate method to match the physical situation lies between the determinant search technique and subspace iteration method. In general for structural analysis problems these two techniques are required. In some of the special-purpose programs Householder-QR-Inverse iteration and the generalized Jacobi, simultaneous method and Lanczos method can also be used effectively.

The most important problem in dynamic analysis is the solution of the lowest eigen pairs. However, in some dynamic analysis specified intermediate range are of interest. If the size of the matrices is not large, Householder-QR-Inverse iterarion technique can give all the eigen paris. If only a very few eigenvalues and eigenvectors are needed simultaneous iteration scheme is very efficient. If large number of eigenvalues are required the Lanczos method is very effective.

It is to be mentioned that the above considerations for the appropriate solution technique are also applicable to standard eigenvalue problems encountered in F.E.M. and solution of the required eigenvalues and eigenvectors of the problem $[K]\{\phi\} = \lambda [M]\{\phi\}$ where $[K]$ is the stiffness matrix and $[M]$ is the mass matrix of the system. In heat transfer problems $[K]$ and $[M]$ would be the conductivity and heat capacity matrices and the eigen solution would be analogous to the solution of the dynamic analysis problem. The problem of buckling analysis is of the form $[K_G]\{\phi\} = \lambda [K]\{\phi\}$ where $[K_G]$ and $[K]$ are the nonlienar and linear strains stiffness matrices, and we require the largest eigenvalue and eigenvector. In this particular case the determinant search and subspace iteration methods can be used. A shift which is larger than the largest eigenvalue must be incorporated before using the above method. The algorithms are also to be modified correspondingly to evaluate the smallest negative eigenvalue which in turn gives the required largest eigenvalue of the problem. In the case of large size buckling analysis problems, determinant search and subspace iteration techniques are to be used.

9.3.2 Dynamic Analysis of Cylindrical Shells

The axisymmetric and asymmetric free vibration analysis of multilayered shells of revolution has been discussed in this section. The free vibrational analysis of any structure requires the structural stiffness and mass matrices. The stiffness matrix formulation was discussed in Chap. 7. The consistent mass matrix is derived following the variational principles. The subspace iteration technique is used in the present analysis to obtain the lowest few eigen pairs. Several examples are studied and compared with the available results.

The fundamental natural frequencies of an isotropic circular cylindrical shell corresponding to axisymmetric mode of vibration for various ratios of length to radius and radius to thickness are obtained. Simply supported conditions are considered at both ends. The frequencies are compared with the results of Leissa [9.9] and those from NASA report on vibration of shells in Table 9.3.

Table 9.3 Nondimensional frequencies of a cylindrical shell

$1/mR$	R/h	NASA Report	Present method
20	20	0.0929296	0.087086
1	500	0.949203	0.93159
4	500	0.464648	0.43887
20	500	0.0929296	0.087086
100	500	0.0185859	0.0168272

The isotropic truncated conical shell is shown in Fig. 9.28 which is simply supported at both ends. The frequencies of axisymmetric modes of vibration of the shell for different semivertex angles, $1/r$ and r/h ratios, are determined and compared with the results of Garnet, H. and Kempner, *J.* [9.10] in Table 9.4

Table 9.4 Nondimensional frequencies of a truncated conical shell

Vertex Angle	h/r	$1/r$	Garnet, *H.* Ref [9.10]	Present method
5°	0.05	0.25	27.785	26.483
5°	0.05	0.375	15.584	15.291
5°	0.05	0.5	12.388	12.362
10°	0.15	0.5	10.379	9.645
15°	0.20	1.0	3.541	3.478
20°	0.10	0.375	5.451	5.310
20°	0.10	0.5	3.580	3.469

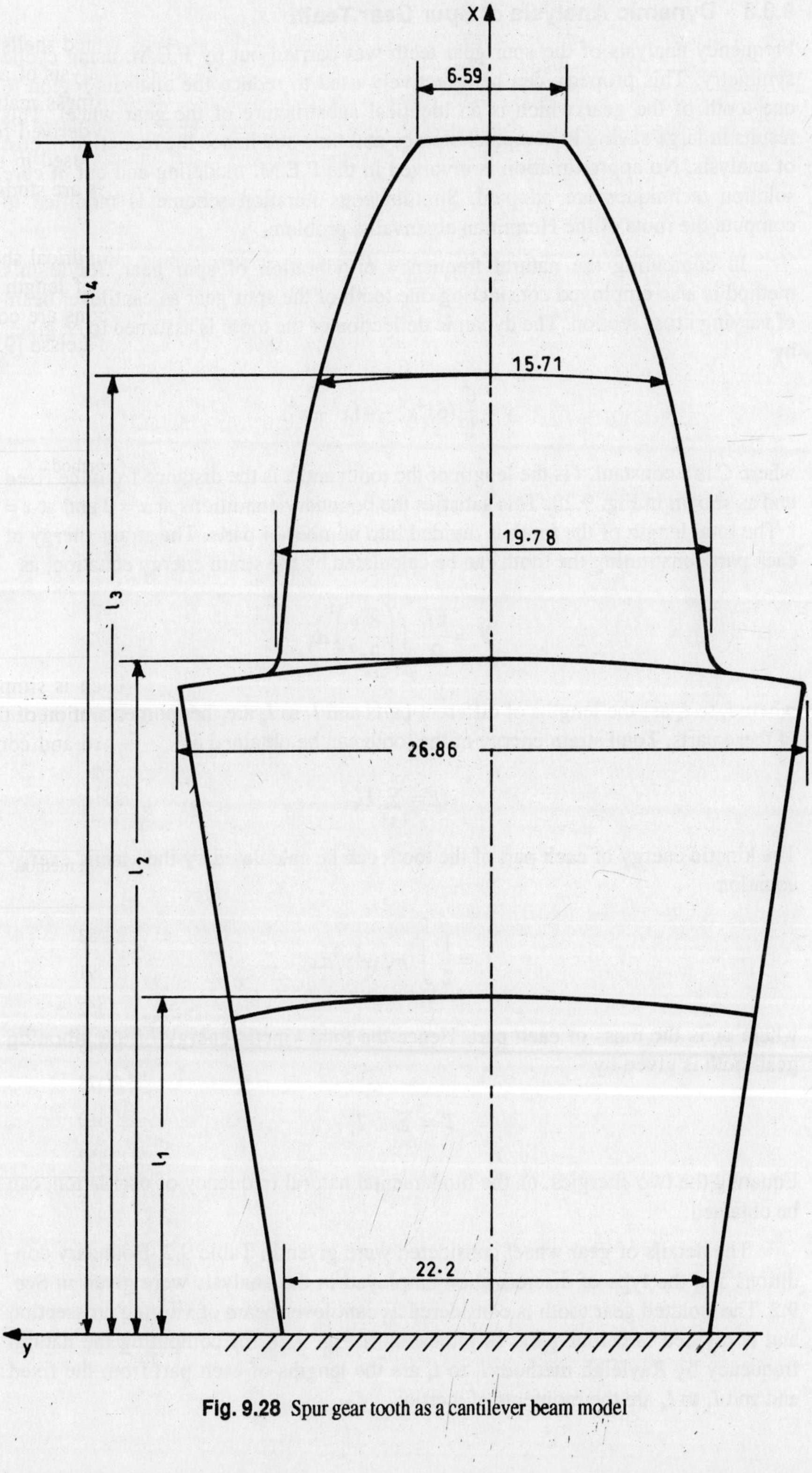

Fig. 9.28 Spur gear tooth as a cantilever beam model

9.3.3 Dynamic Analysis of Spur Gear Teeth

Frequency analysis of the spur gear teeth was carried out by F.E.M. using cyclic symmetry. This property can be effectively used to reduce the analysis region to one tooth of the gear which is an identical substructure of the gear wheel. This results in large saving in computer storage and time and hence the reduction in cost of analysis. No approximation is involved in the F.E.M. modeling and out of core solution techniques are adopted. Simultaneous iteration scheme is modified to compute the roots of the Hermitian eigenvalue problem.

In computing the natural frequency of vibration of spur gear, Rayleigh's method is also employed considering one tooth of the spur gear as cantilever beam of varying cross section. The dynamic deflection of the tooth is assumed to be given by

$$y = \frac{C}{l^3}(6l^2x^2 - 4lx^3 + x^4)$$

where C is a constant, l is the length of the tooth and x is the distance from the fixed end as shown in Fig. 9.28. This satisfies the boundary conditions at $x = 0$ and at $x = l$. The total length of the tooth is divided into number of parts. The strain energy of each part constituting the tooth can be calculated by the strain energy equation, as

$$U_i = \frac{EI_i}{2}\int_{l_{i-1}}^{l_i}\left(\frac{\partial^2 y}{\partial x^2}\right)^2 dx$$

where l_1 to l_n are the lengths of different parts and I_1 to I_n are the moments of inertia of these parts. Total strain energy of the tooth can be obtained as

$$U = \sum_{i=1}^{n} U_i$$

The kinetic energy of each part of the tooth can be calculated by the kinetic energy equation

$$T_i = \frac{1}{2}\int_{l_{i-1}}^{l_i} m_i\, w^2 y_i^2 dx$$

where m_i is the mass of each part. Hence the total kinetic energy of the vibrating gear tooth is given by

$$T = \sum_{i=1}^{n} T_i$$

Equating the two energies, ω, the fundamental natural frequency of oscillation, can be obtained.

The details of gear wheel considered were given in Table 9.2. Boundary conditions and the type of discretization employed in the analysis were given in Sec. 9.2. The isolated gear tooth is considered as cantilever beam of varying crossection and is divided into four parts as indicated in Fig. 9.28 for computing the natural frequency by Rayleigh method. l_1 to l_4 are the lengths of each part from the fixed end and I_1 to I_4 are the moments of inertia.

Transient analysis is carried out for the same gear wheel subjected to a moving line contact load. The analysis is confined to elastic range only. The procedure was outlined in chap. 8.

Natural frequencies obtained by F.E.M. up to 11 harmonics are given in Table 9.5

The fundamental frequency obtained by the present method is 0.746×10^5 rad/s whereas that obtained by Rayleigh's method is 0.86×10^5 rad/s. The frequency obtained by the present method is 15.5% less than the one by Rayleigh's method. Mode shapes for the first three modes are shown in Figs. 9.29 to 9.37 for $P = 0$, 1. and 2.

Table 9.5 Natural frequencies in radians/sec

P	First mode $\times 10^6$ (rad/s)	Second mode $\times 10^6$ (rad/s)	Third mode $\times 10^6$ rad/s
0	0.07463	0.18807	0.19798
1	0.08272	0.17821	0.21225
2	0.09989	0.17057	0.23366
3	0.11439	0.17156	0.25761
4	0.12068	0.18197	0.28314
5	0.12204	0.19693	0.30794
6	0.12214	0.21209	0.32973
7	0.12211	0.22558	0.34710
8	0.12215	0.23626	0.35944
9	0.12222	0.24316	0.36670
10	0.12225	0.24554	0.36908

The transient analysis is carried out using modal superposition methd. A load of 500 N/mm on face width is assumed to travel along the profile. The analysis is confined to elastic range only. The transient response of the tooth experiencing contact load is shown in Fig. 9.38. The effect of the load on the neighbouring teeth is also indicated. The transient stress distribution at the root with respect to time is shown in Fig. 9.39. The stress distribution in the adjacent teeth is also presented. The stress distribution at the root is compared with at the tip in Fig. 9.40 which shows that the stress level is as small as 1/20th of that at the root. The stress distribution at the tip is also compared with that at the adjacent teeth as shown in Fig. 9.41 which indicates that the stress level in the neighbouring teeth is negligibly small. The maximum static stress for the gear analysed as given by Fig. 9.35 is 120 MPa and ; the maximum dynamic stress for the same gear as represented in Fig. 9.39 is 200 MPa. Hence the ratio between maximum dynamic stress and static stress is of the order of 1.67 whereas the ratio is expected to be around 2.0.

The time step chosen for the transient analysis is 1/10th of the time period based on the third natural frequency, which is 0.0000032 sec. Other time steps of 0.000016 sec and 0.0000016 sec. were also tried to check convergence as indicated in Fig. 9.42. The effect of rotational speed on the moving load is shown in Fig. 9.43.

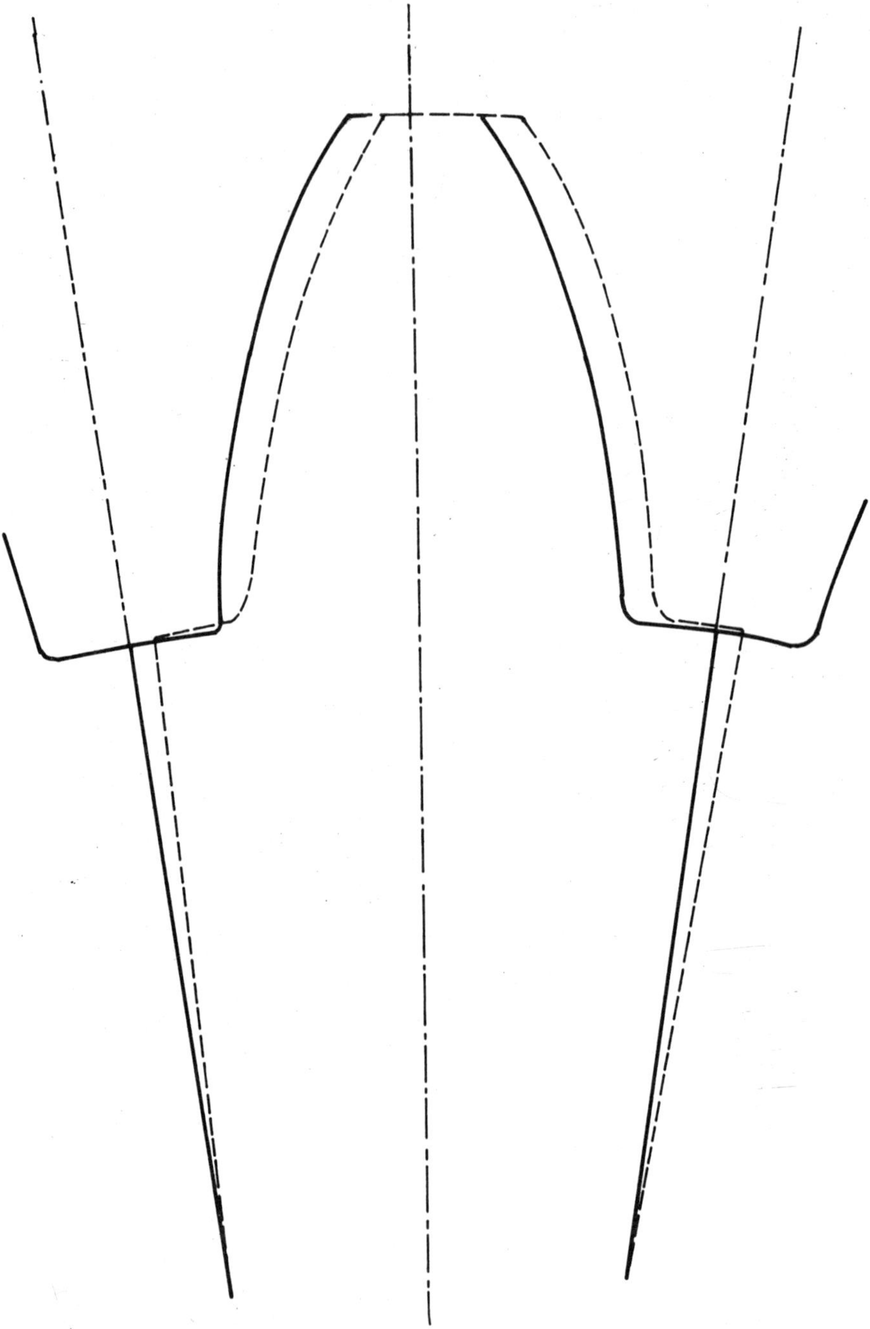

Fig. 9.29 First mode ($P = 0$)

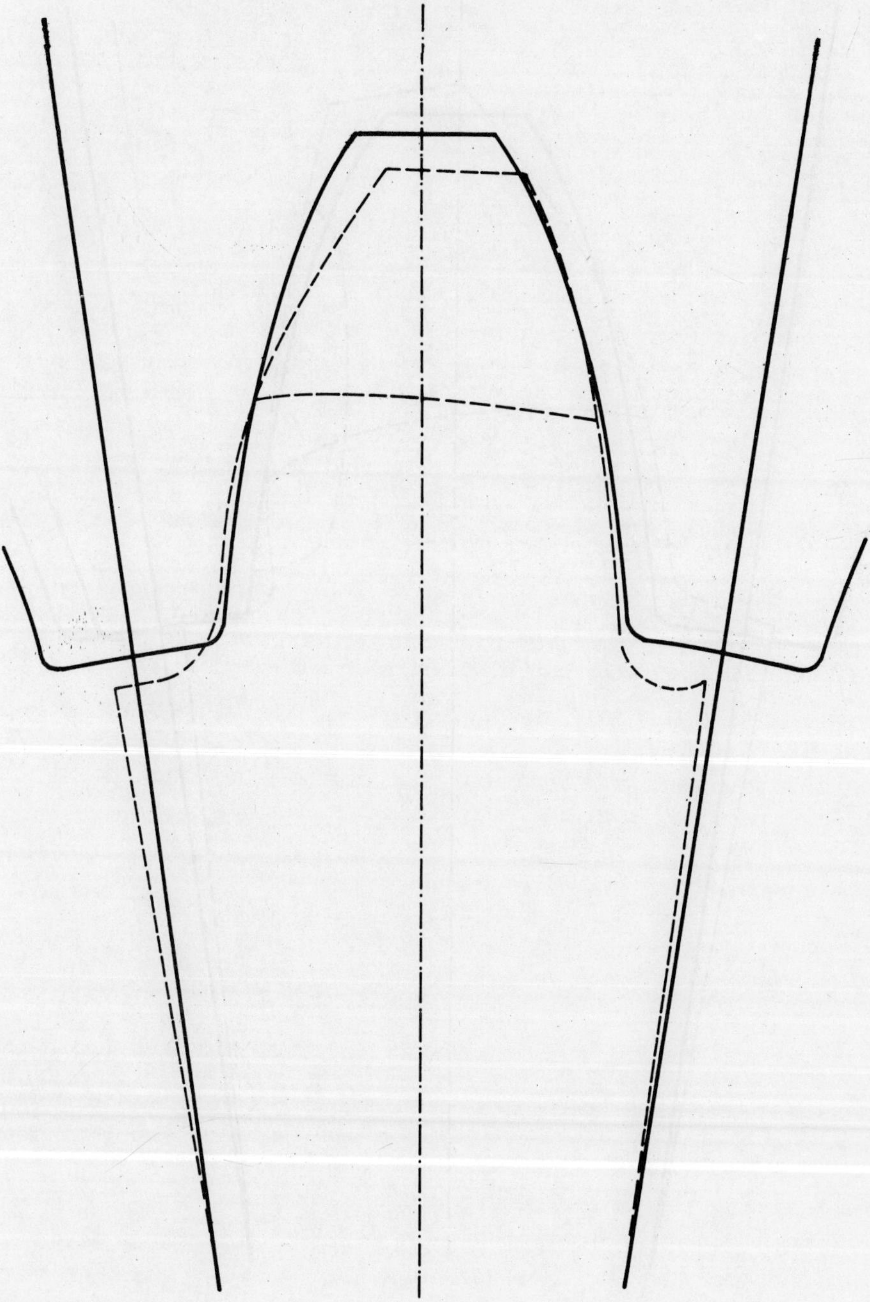

Fig. 9.30 Second mode ($P = 0$)

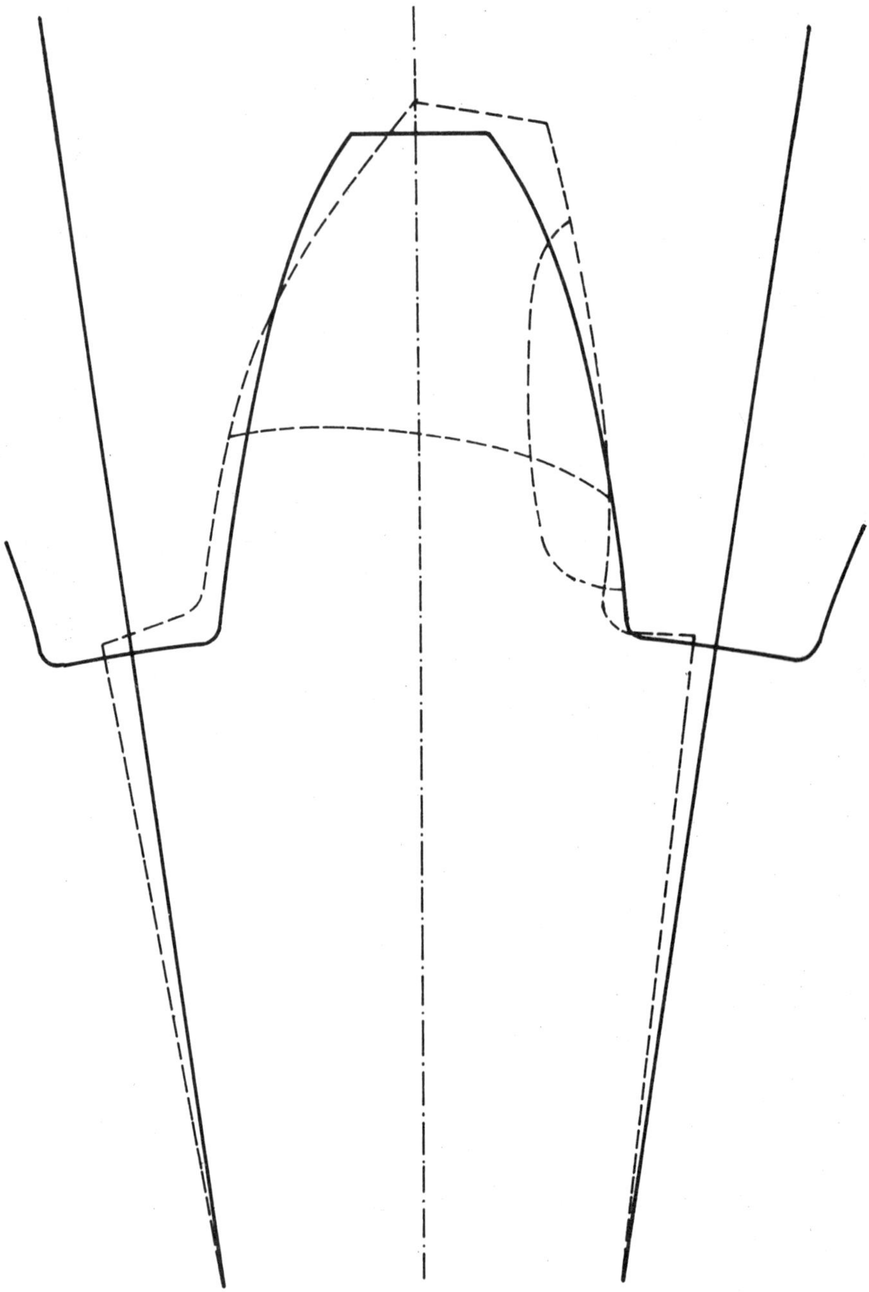

Fig. 9.31 Third mode ($P = 0$)

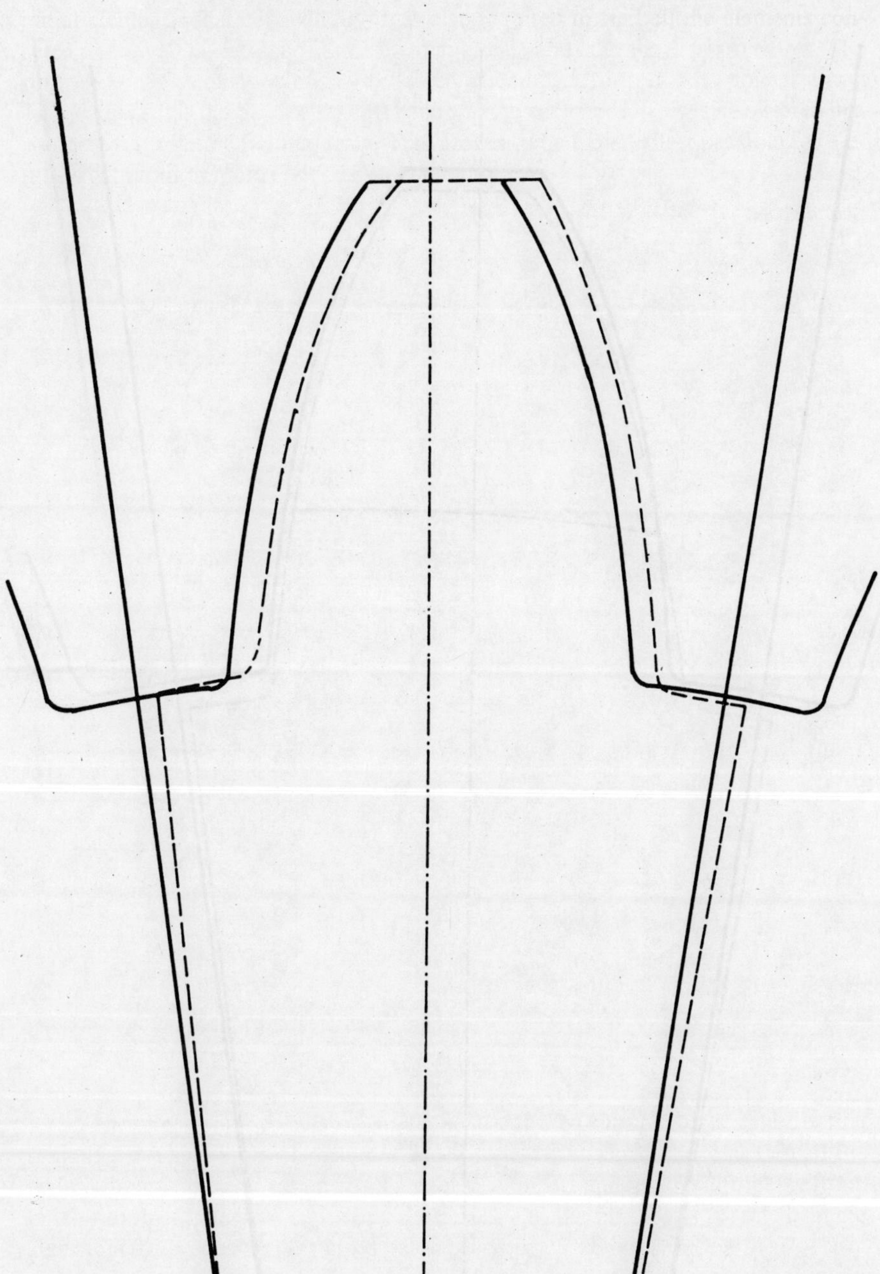

Fig. 9.32 First mode ($P = 1$)

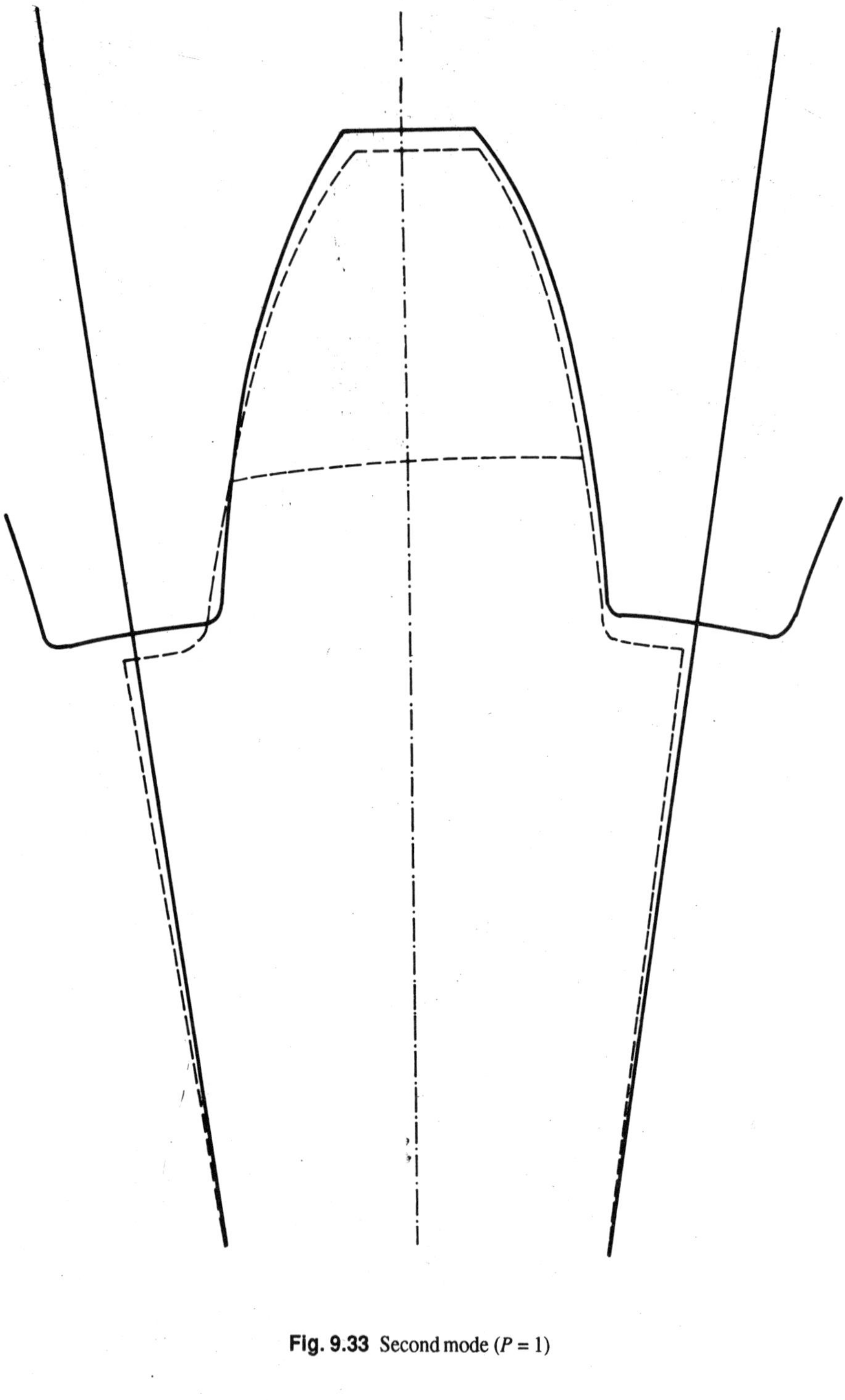

Fig. 9.33 Second mode ($P = 1$)

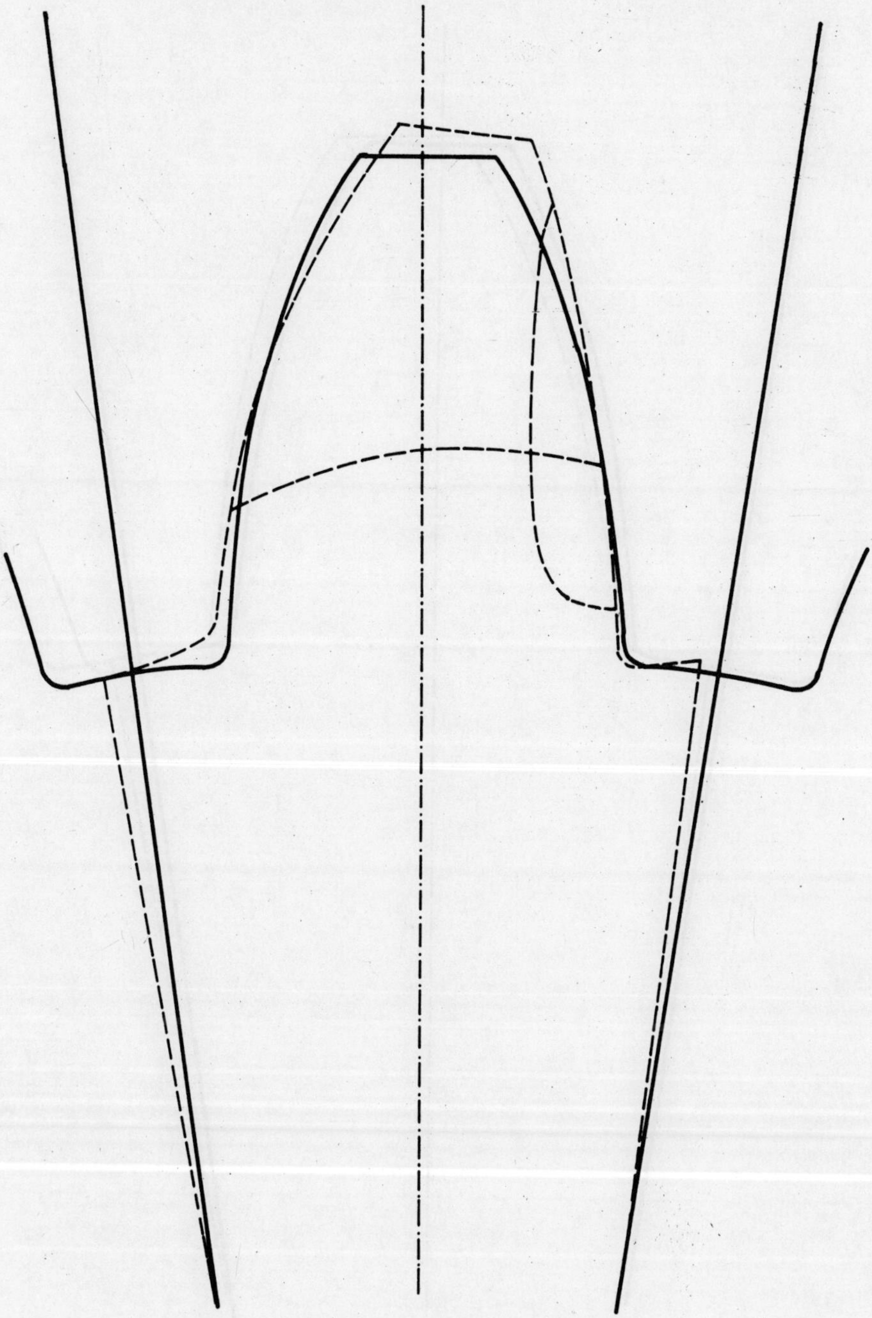

Fig. 9.34 Third mode ($P = 1$)

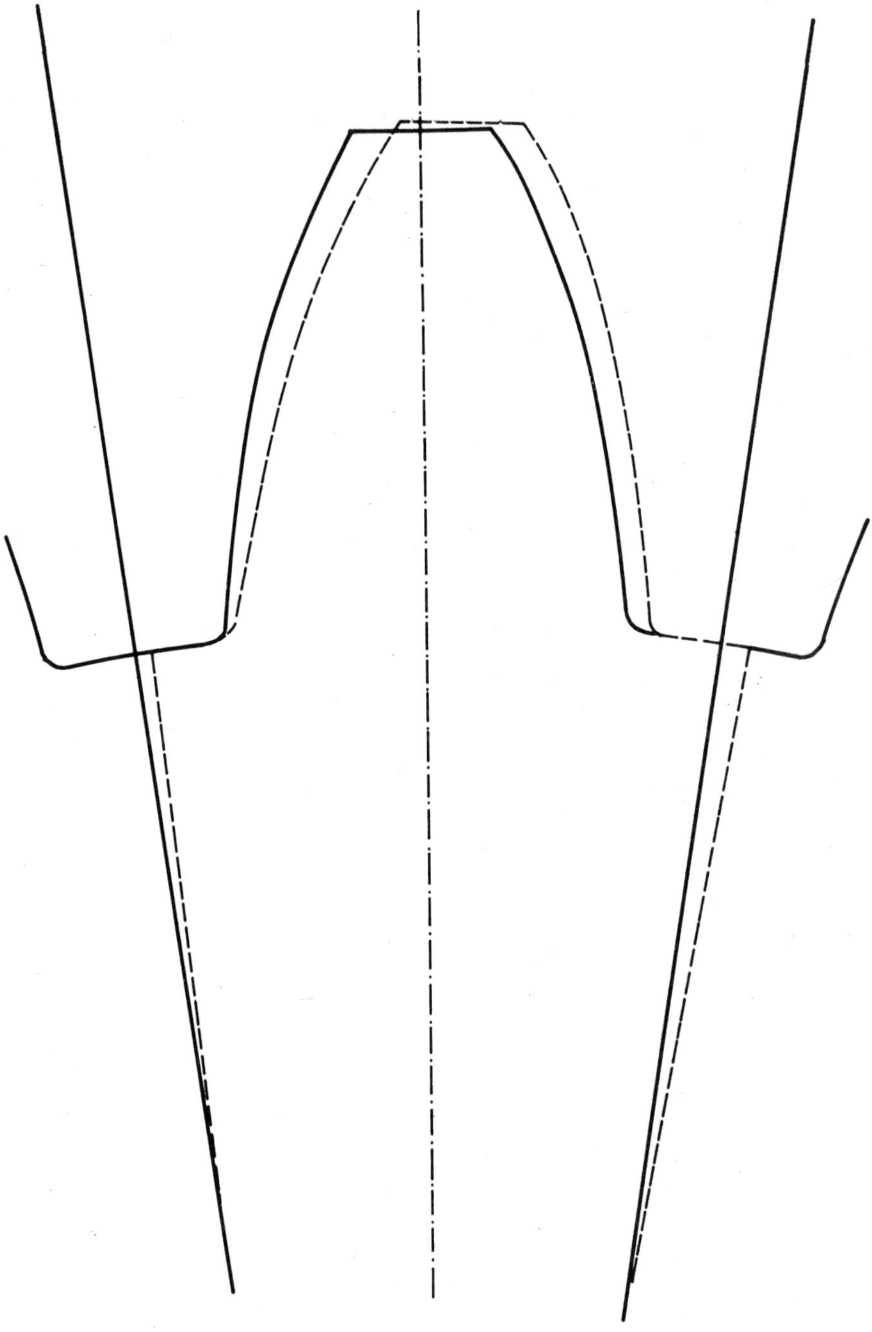

Fig. 9.35 First mode ($P = 2$)

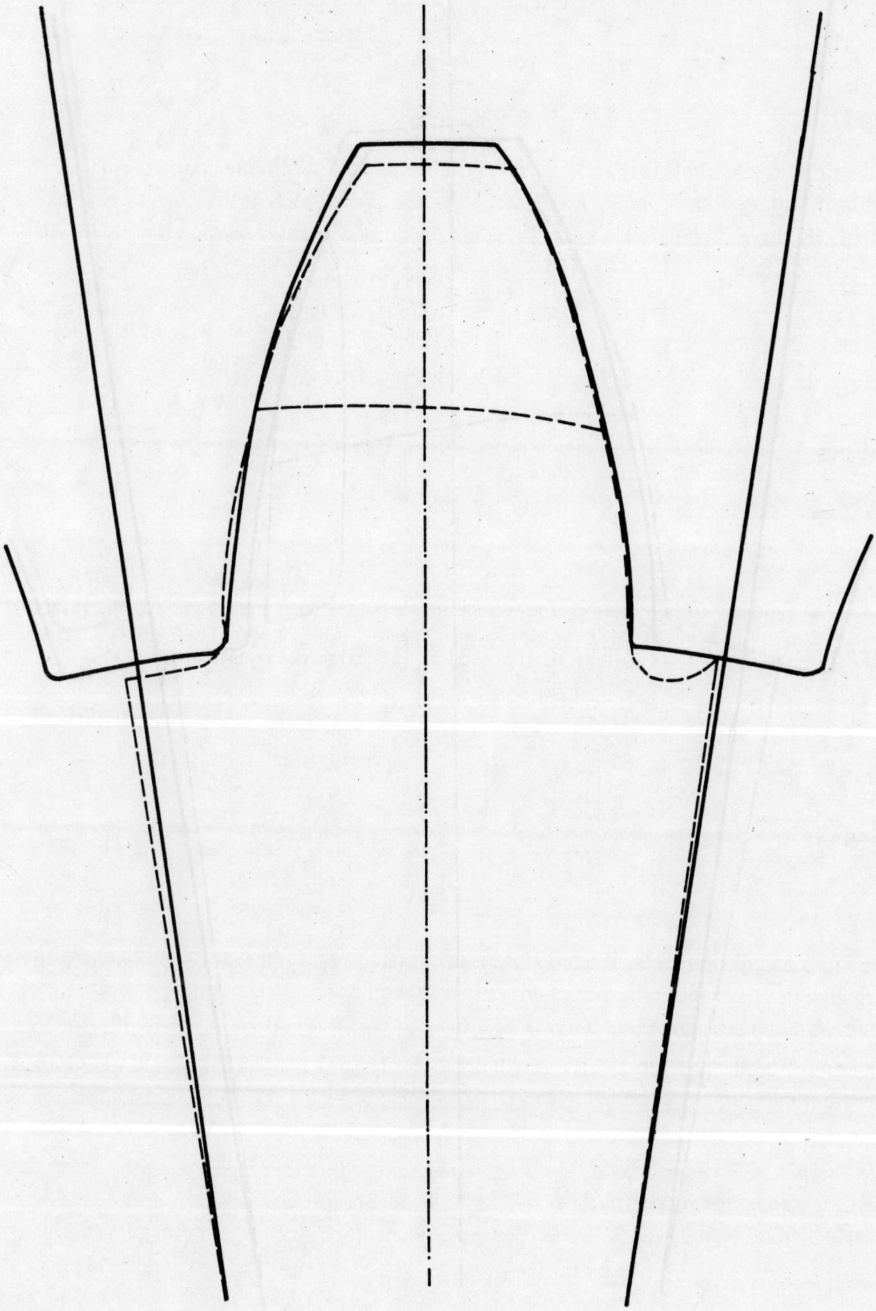

Fig. 9.36 Second mode ($P = 2$)

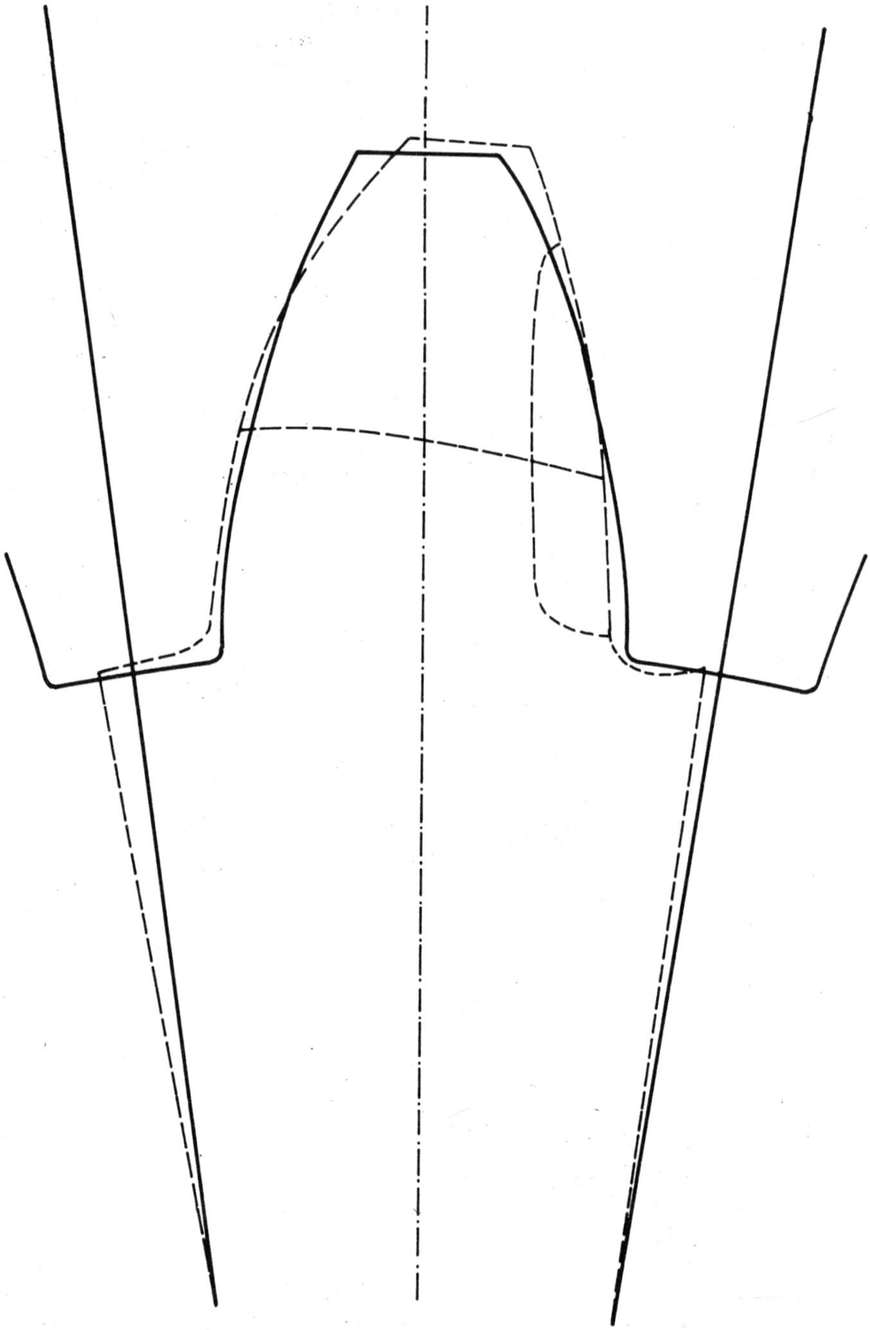

Fig. 9.37 Third mode ($P = 2$)

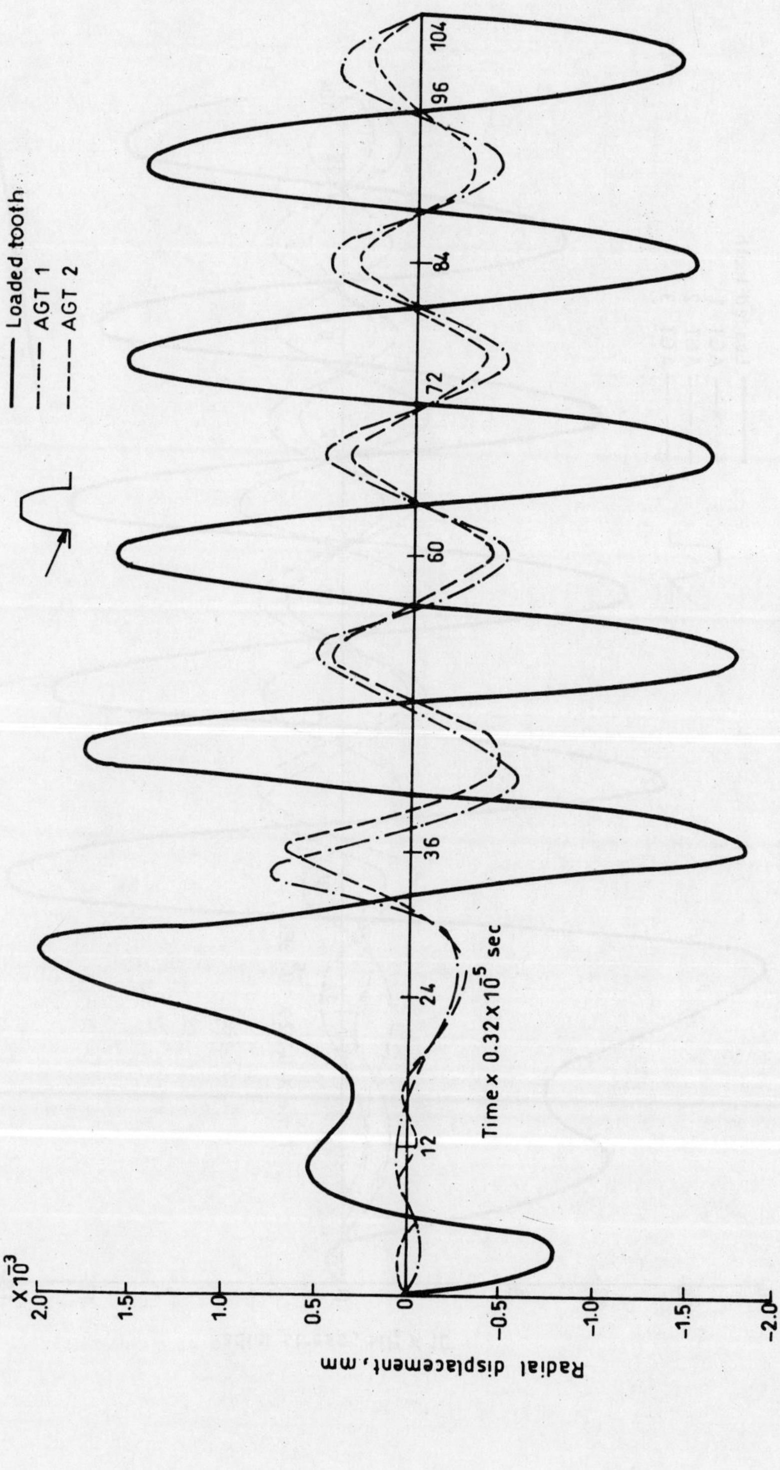

Fig. 9.38 Transient response at the root

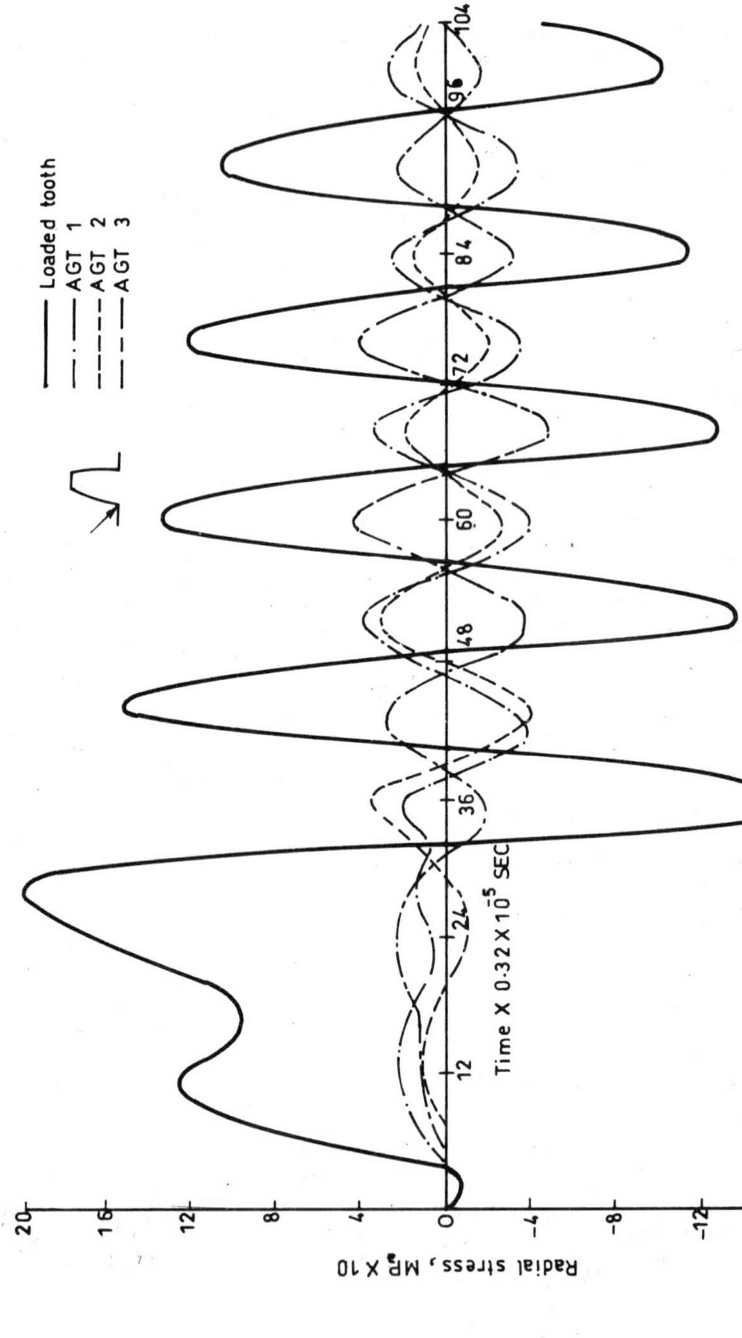

Fig. 9.39 Transient stress response at the root

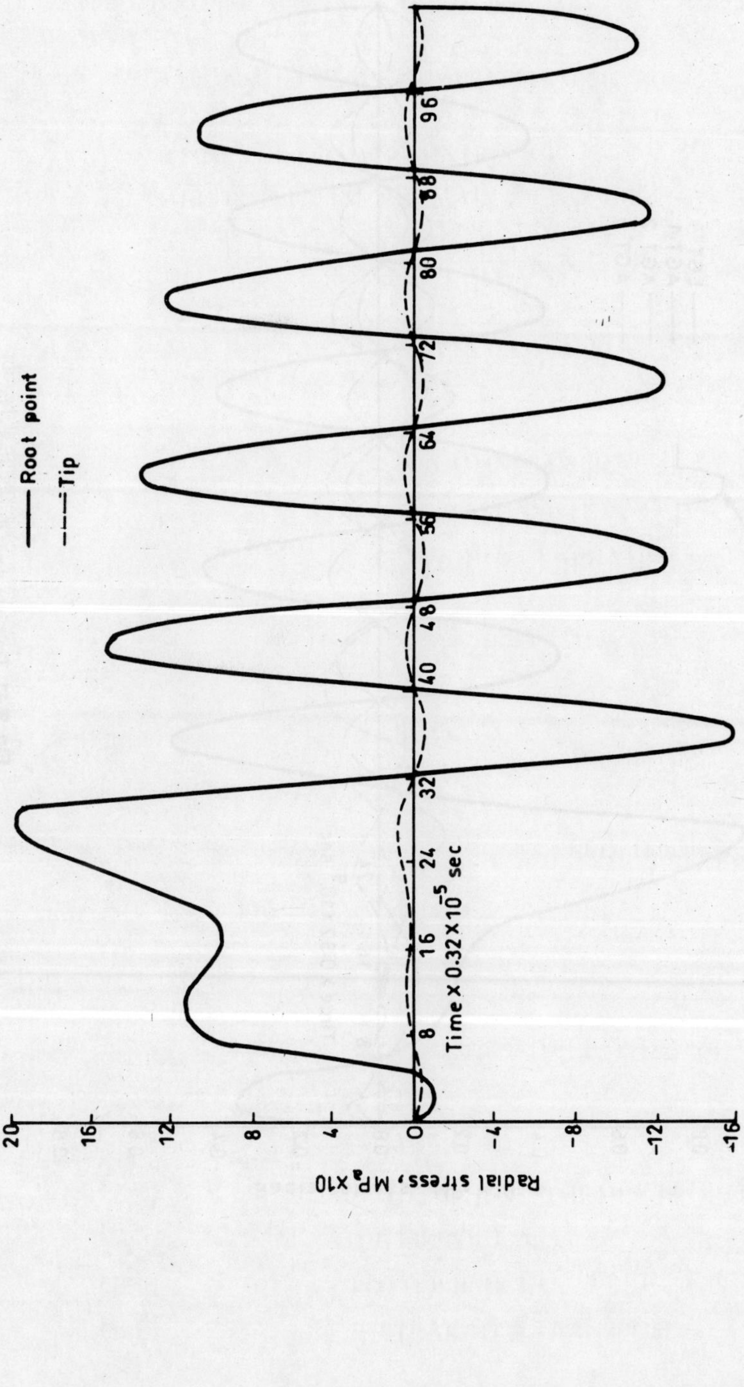

Fig. 9.40 Transient stress distribution

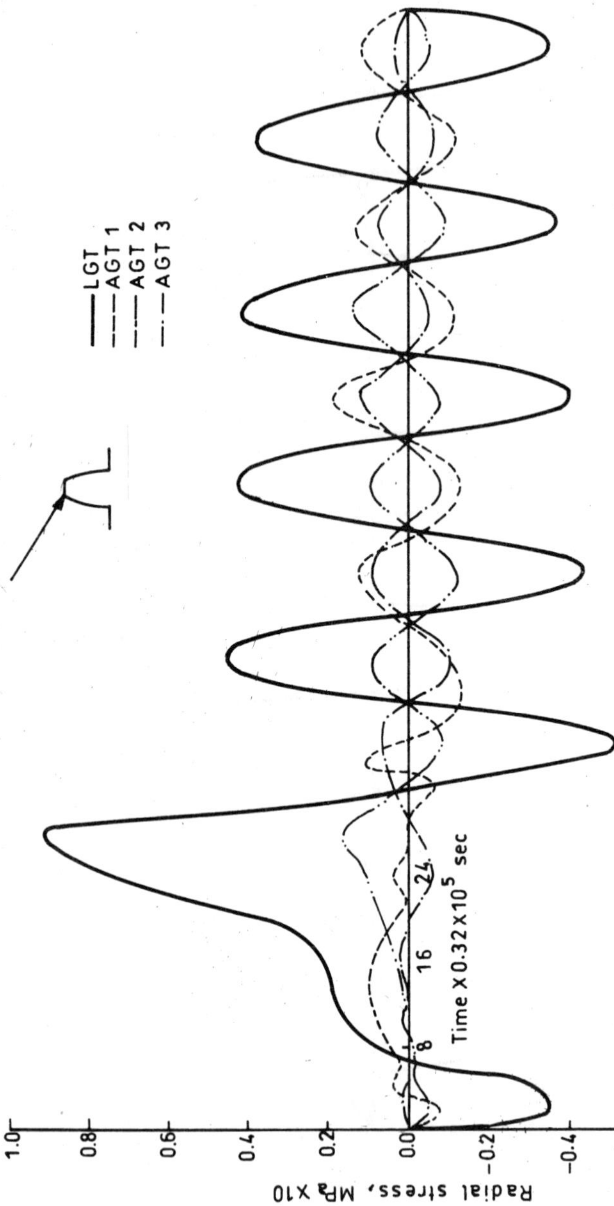

Fig. 9.41 Transient stress distribution at tip

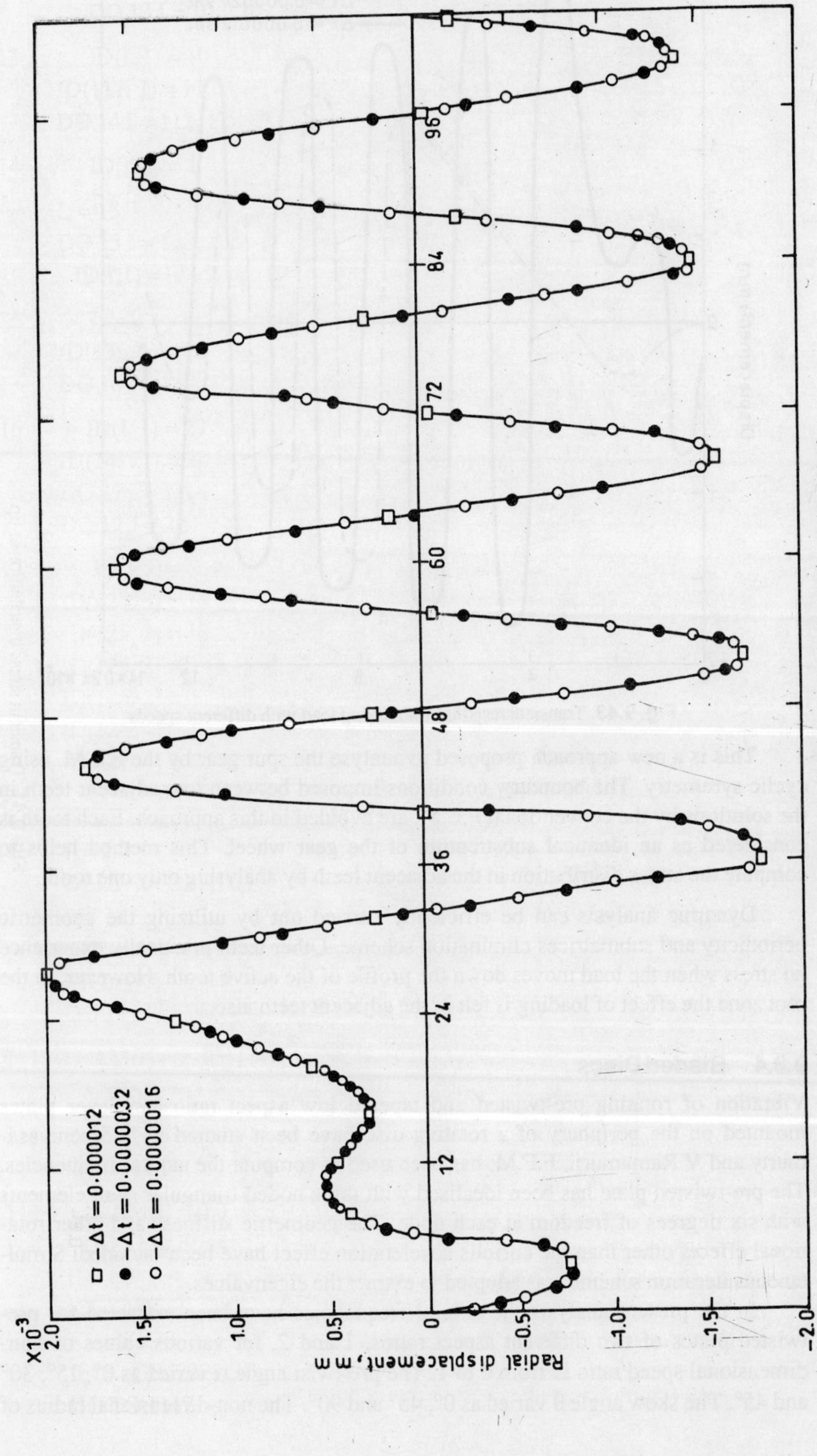

Fig. 9.42 6×4 and 5×5 mesh used in the shell analysis

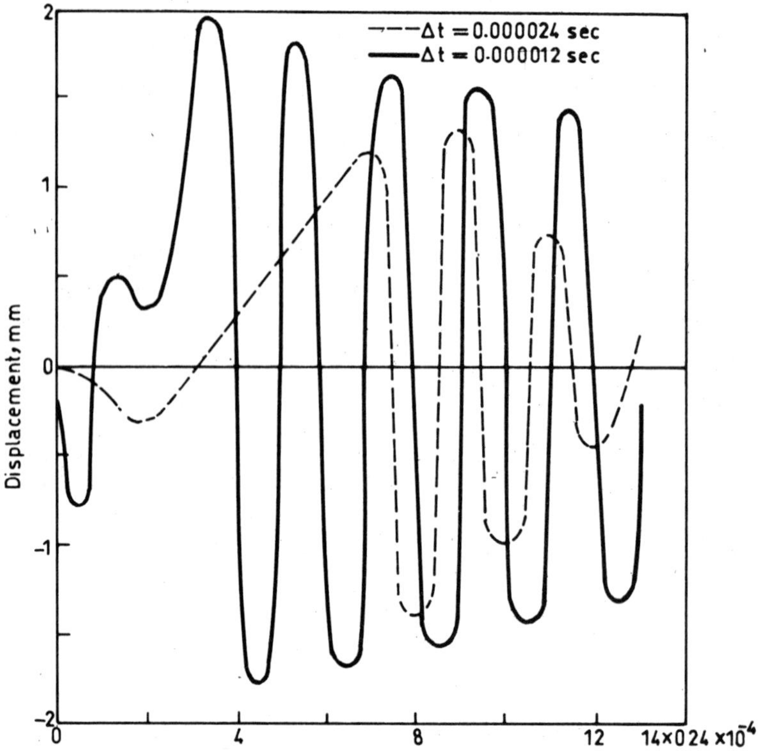

Fig. 9.43 Transient response for moving load with different speeds

This is a new approach proposed to analyse the spur gear by the F.E.M. using cyclic symmetry. The boundary conditions imposed between two adjacent teeth in the solutions by the conventional F.E.M. are avoided in this approach. Each tooth is considered as an identical substrcuture of the gear wheel. This method helps to compute the stress distribution in the adjacent teeth by analysing only one tooth.

Dynamic analysis can be efficiently carried out by utilizing the geometric periodicity and submatrices elimination scheme. Other teeth practically experience no stress when the load moves down the profile of the active tooth. However, in the root zone the effect of loading is felt in the adjacent teeth also.

9.3.4 Bladed Discs

Vibration of rotating pre-twisted and tapered low aspect ratio cantilever plates mounted on the periphery of a rotating disc have been studied by S.Sreenivasamurty and V.Ramamurti. F.E.M. has been used to compute the natural frequencies. The pre-twisted plate has been idealised with three noded triangular shell elements with six degrees of freedom at each node. The geometric stiffness and other rotational effects other than the coriolis acceleration effect have been included. Simultaneous iteration scheme was adopted to extract the eigenvalues.

In the present analysis the natural frequencies have been extracted for pre-twisted plates of two different aspect ratios, 1 and 2, for various values of non-dimensional speed ratio Ω from 0 to 1. The pre-twist angle α varied as 0°, 15°, 30° and 45°. The skew angle θ varied as 0°, 45° and 90°. The non-dimensional radius of the disc r/l varied from 0 to 1. For the same values of Ω, α and θ the frequency analysis of tapered and twisted cantilever plates with taper ratio of 2 (ratio of thickness at the root to the thickness at the tip) have been carried out. The size of the mesh considered were 5×5 and 6×4. The plate is assumed to be homogeneous and isotropic with Poisson's ratio as 0.3.

The results are presented only for a few cases, with an aspect ratio of 2 and for two pre-twist angles $\alpha = 0°, 45°$. Figs. 9.44 to 9.48 represent the first five normalised frequencies, namely first flap-wise bending, first torsional, first edge-wise bending, second flap-wise bending and second torsional modes with the normalized angular speed Ω. It is important to note that each figure is drawn in two parts (a) and (b) to represent the pre-twist angle, 0° and 45°, respectively. In each part the variations for the skew angles 0° and 45°, and 90° are shown. The tapered plates and uniform thickness plates correspond to broken lines and full lines, respectively. For uniform thickness plates the ratio of thickness to length has been chosen as 0.12. For tapered plates the ratio of thickness at the root h_r to the length l is 0.12 and the taper ratio $h_r/h_t = 2$ where h_t is the thickness at the tip. Figs. 9.49 – 9.53 show the variation of the first normalised frequencies. The results calculated for the non-dimensional frequencies are shown in Table 9.6.

Table 9.6 Non-dimensional frequencies when the pre-twisted cantiliver plate is stationary and for any skew angle

		$\alpha = 0°$		$\alpha = 15°$		$\alpha = 30°$		$\alpha = 45°$	
Mode	l/b	ϕ	$\phi\phi$	ϕ	$\phi\phi$	ϕ	$\phi\phi$	ϕ	$\phi\phi$
First	1	3.4695	3.7165	3.4439	3.6914	3.3885	3.6347	3.3027	3.5465
bending	2	3,4286	3.6878	3.3780	3.6298	3.3687	3.622	3.3545	3.6105
First	1	8.5346	7.4019	8.9699	8.1242	10.1943	9.8730	11.6200	11.7925
torsion	2	15.0120	13.2468	14.9827	13.3476	15.2268	13.8340	15.6161	14.5628
Second	1	21.4460	17.3748	22.2910	23.3022	23.5914	24.6833	24.2519	25.8135
bending	2	21.7284	17.8453	21.3737	18.2285	22.0581	19.6379	22.9784	21.0497
Second	1	31.0414	23.2521	30.5328	23.1004	30.6587	23.7347	30.7965	24.5562
torsion	2	49.4121	35.8178	47.9073	35.0076	48.1624	35.6387	48.5370	36.6372

ϕ– Uniform thickness ; $\phi\phi$ – tapered

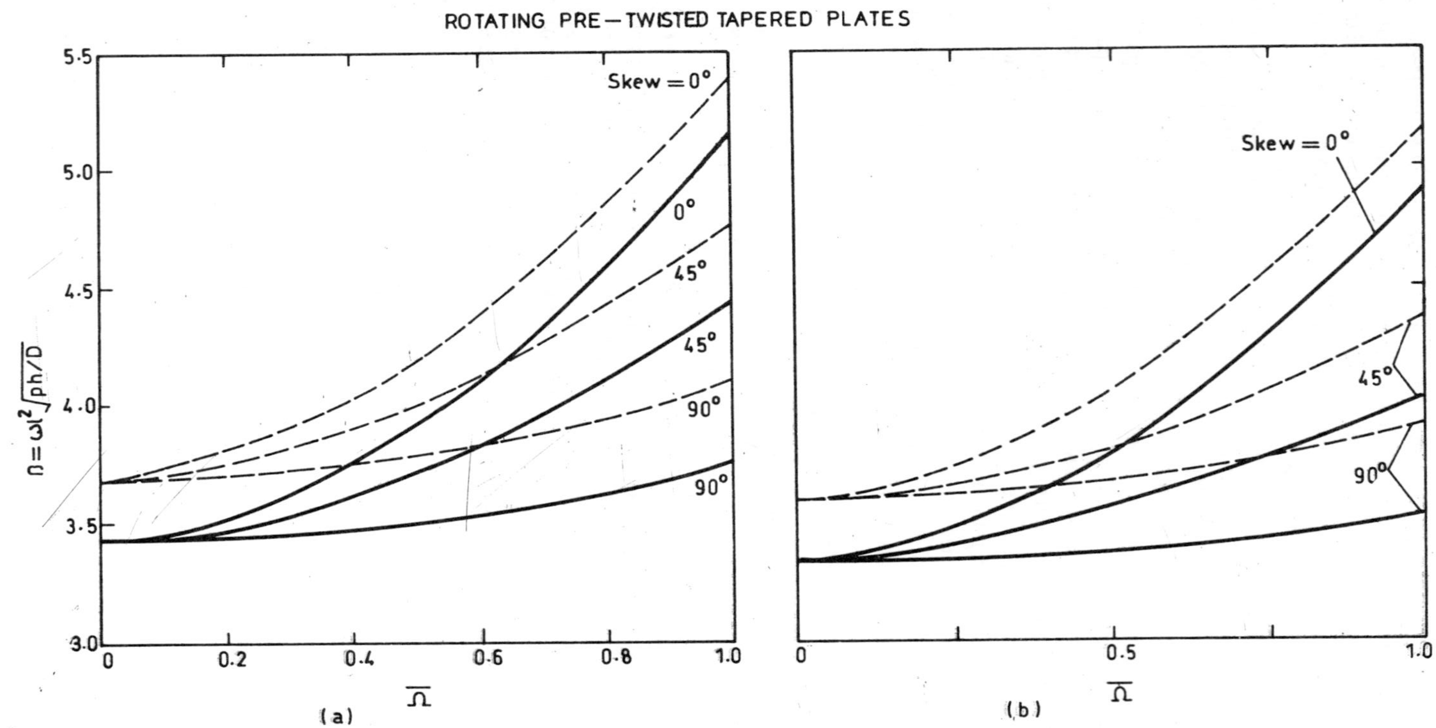

Fig. 9.44 Effect of skew and taper on first flab-wise bending mode frequency (a) $\theta = 0°$ (b) $\theta = 45°$ uniform thickness——, tapered ($h_r/h_t = 2$)., $l/b = 2.$, $h_r/l = 0.12.$, $h = h_r$.

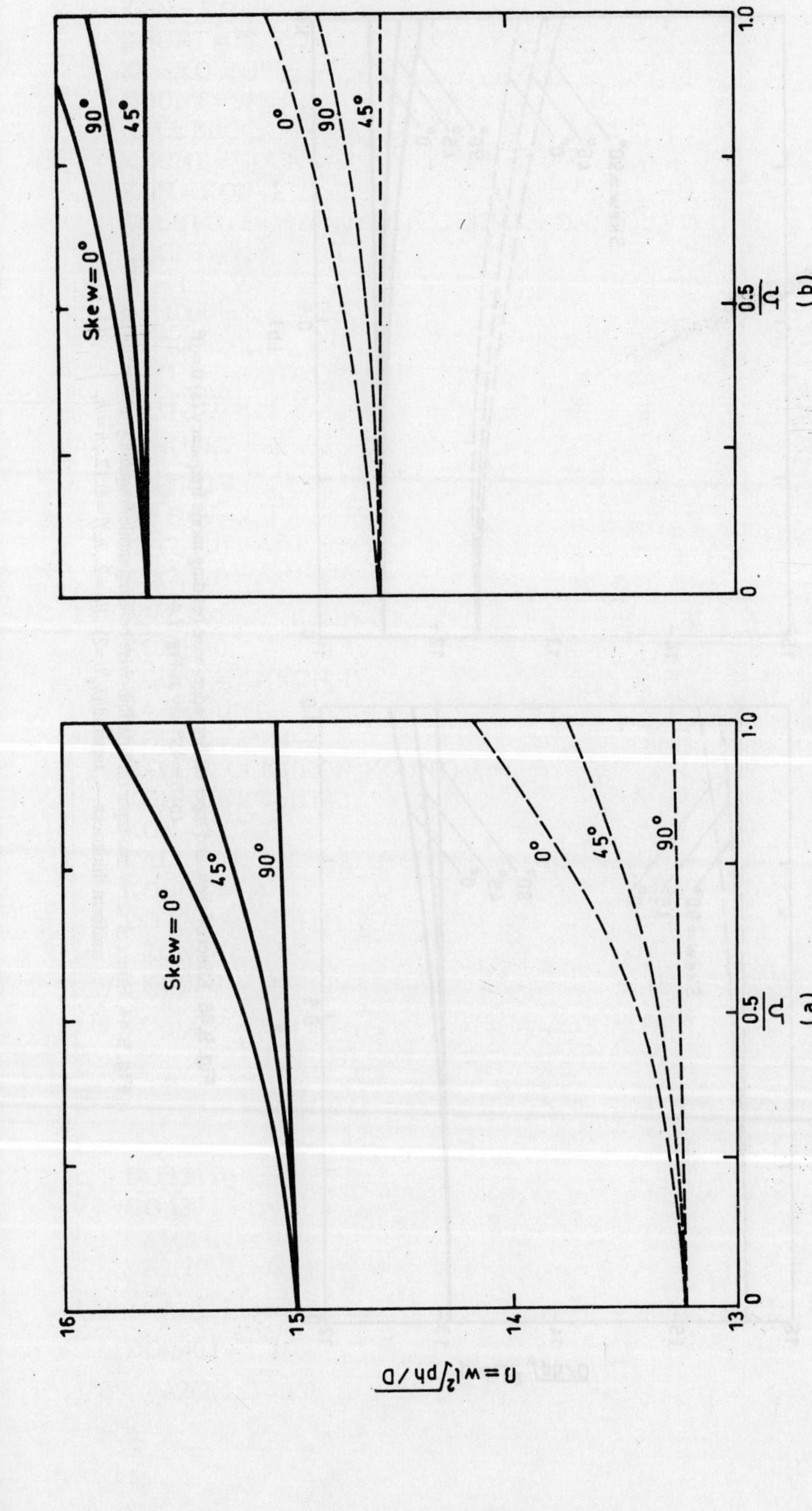

Fig. 9.45 Effect of skew and taper on first torisonal mode frequency (a) θ = 0° (b) θ = 45° key as Fig. 7.44

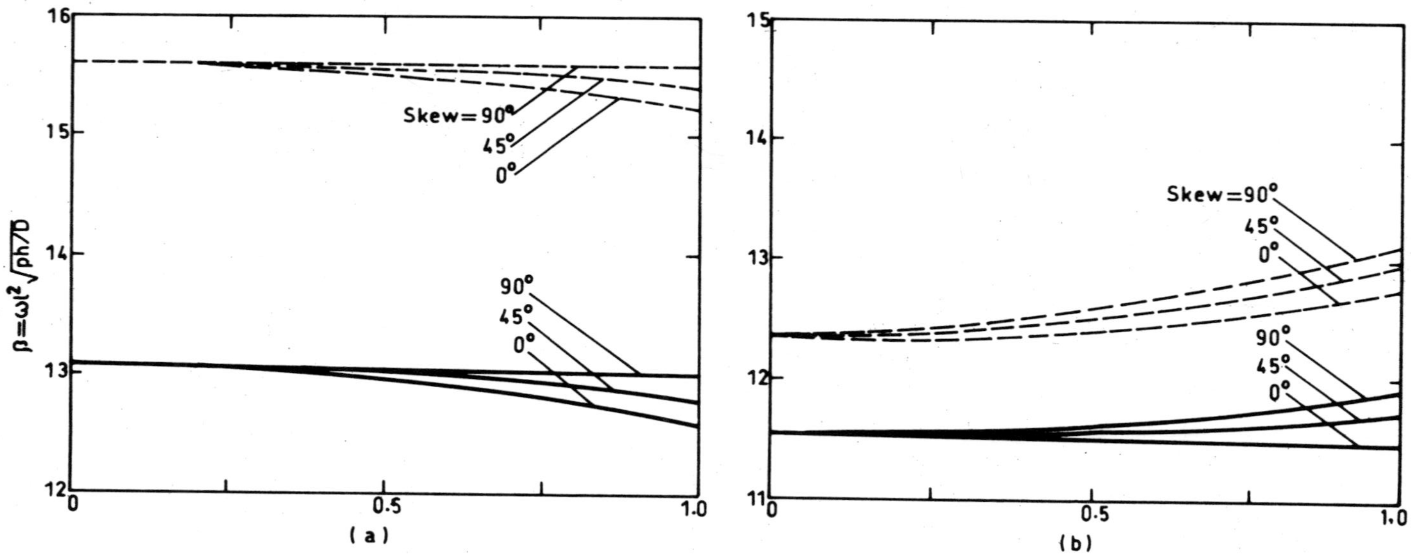

Fig. 9.46 Effect of skew and taper on first edge-wise bending mode frequency (a) $\theta = 0°$ (b) $\theta = 45°$ key as Fig. 7.44

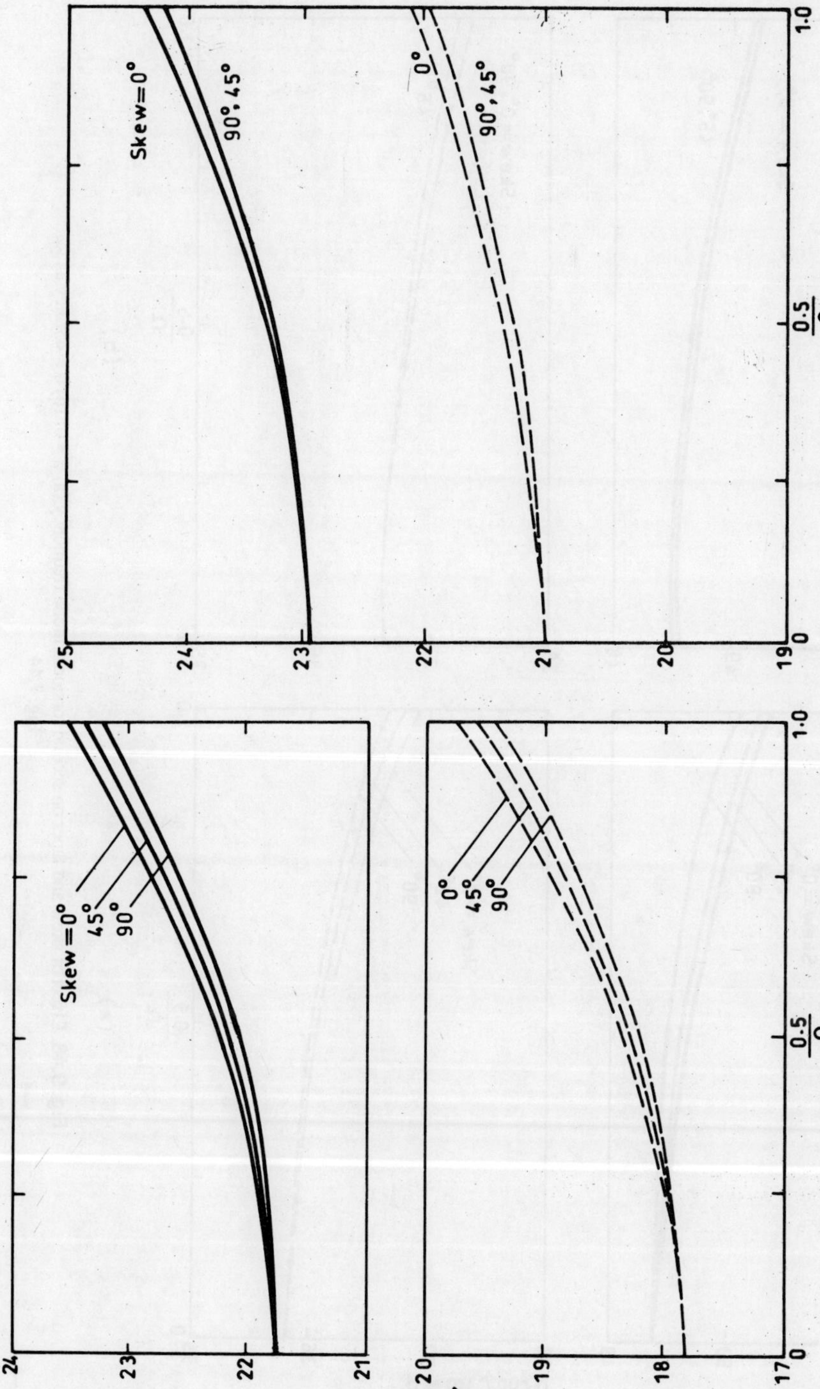

Fig. 9.47 Effect of skew and taper on first flap-wise bending mode frequency (a) θ = 0°(b)θ = 45° uniform thickness—, tapered (h_r/h_t=2)., l/b =2., h_r/l = 0.12., $h = h_r$

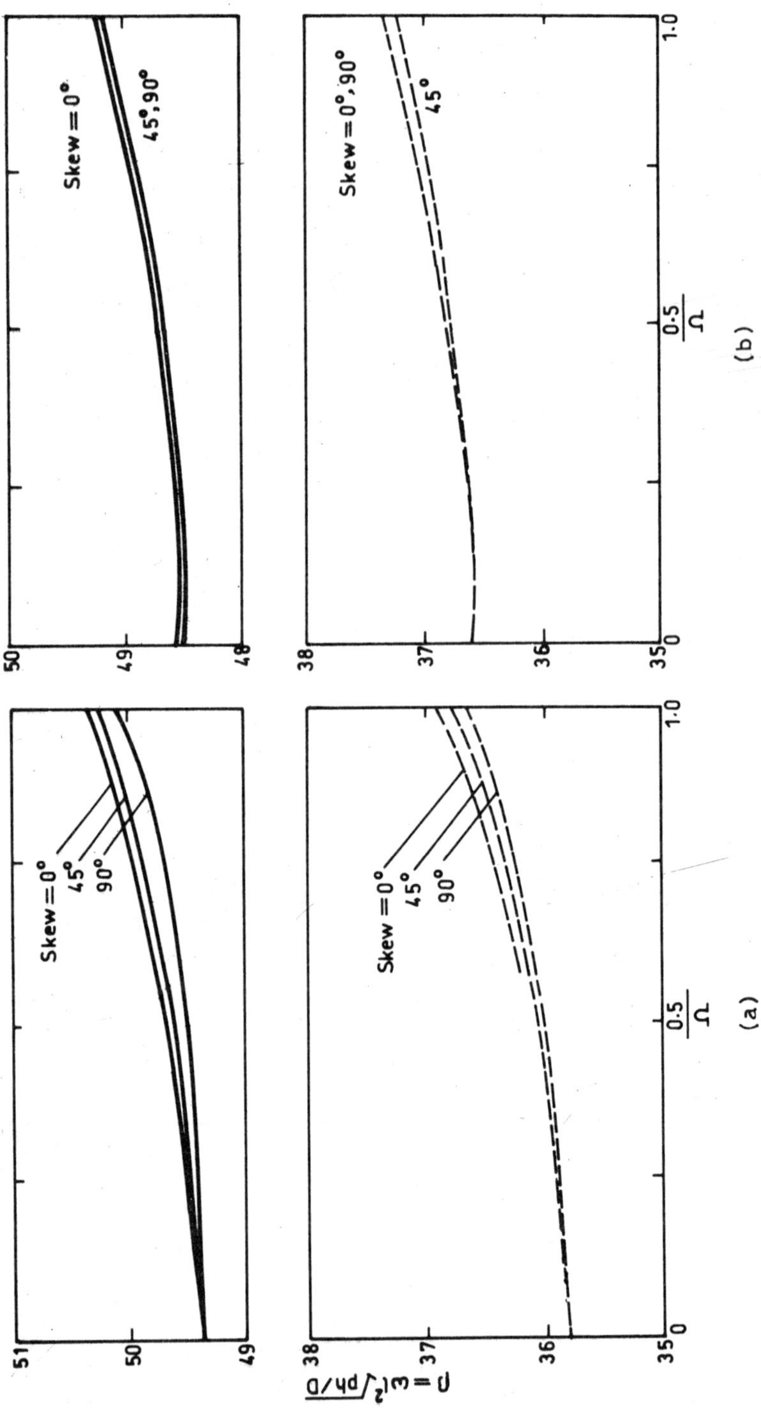

Fig. 9.48 Effect of skew and taper on second torsional mode frequency (a) θ = 0° (b) θ = 45° key as Fig. 7.44

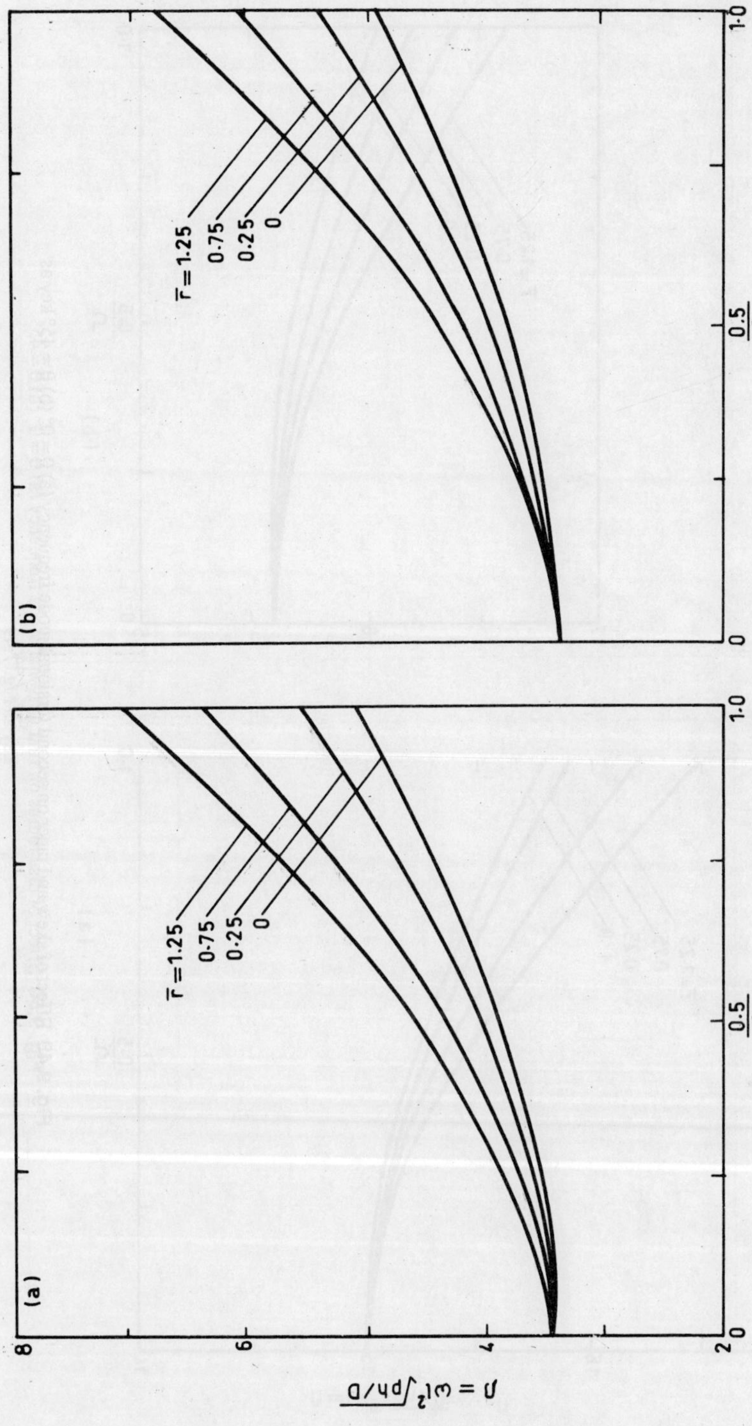

Fig. 9.49 Effect of disc radius on first flap-wise bending mode frequency (a) $\theta = 0°$ (b) $\theta = 45°$
$l/b = 2.$, $h/l = 0.12$

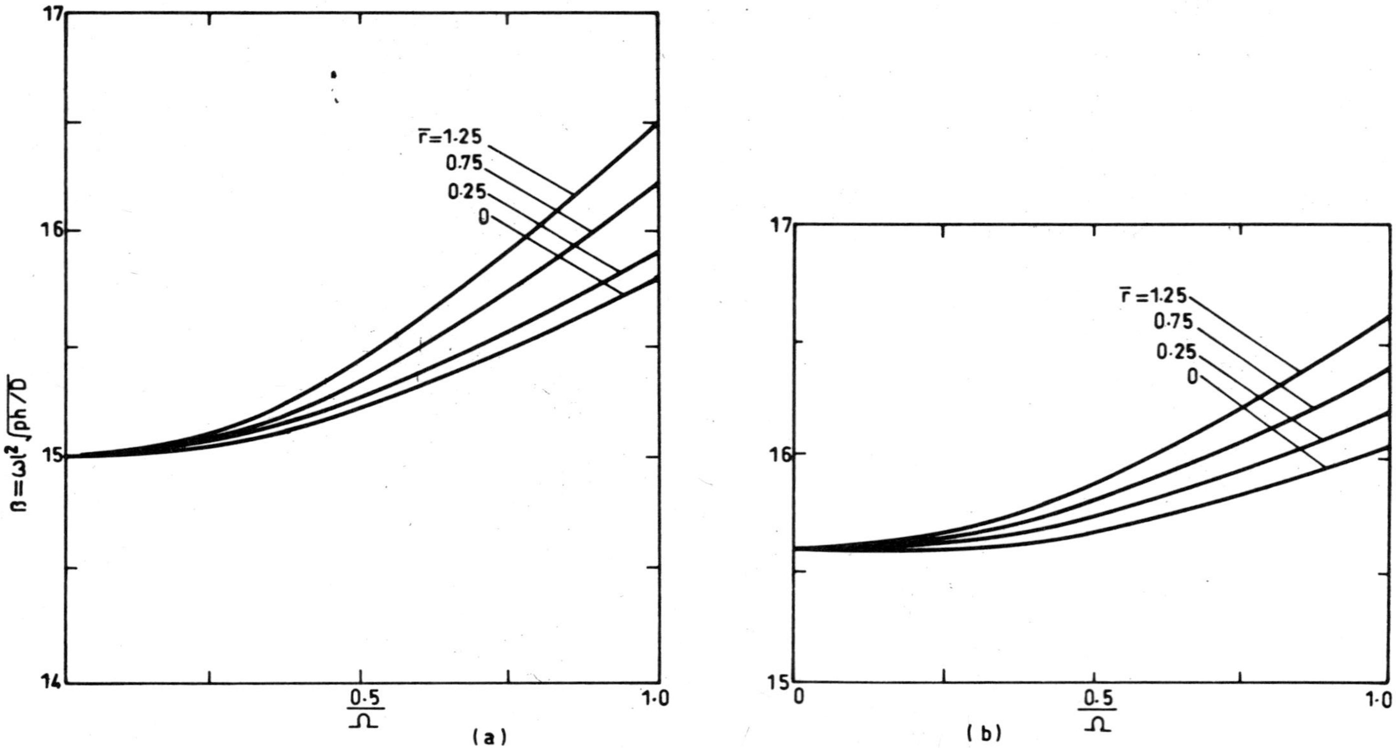

Fig. 9.50 Effect of disc radius on first torisonal mode frequency (a) θ = 0° (b) θ = 45°
key as Fig. 7.49

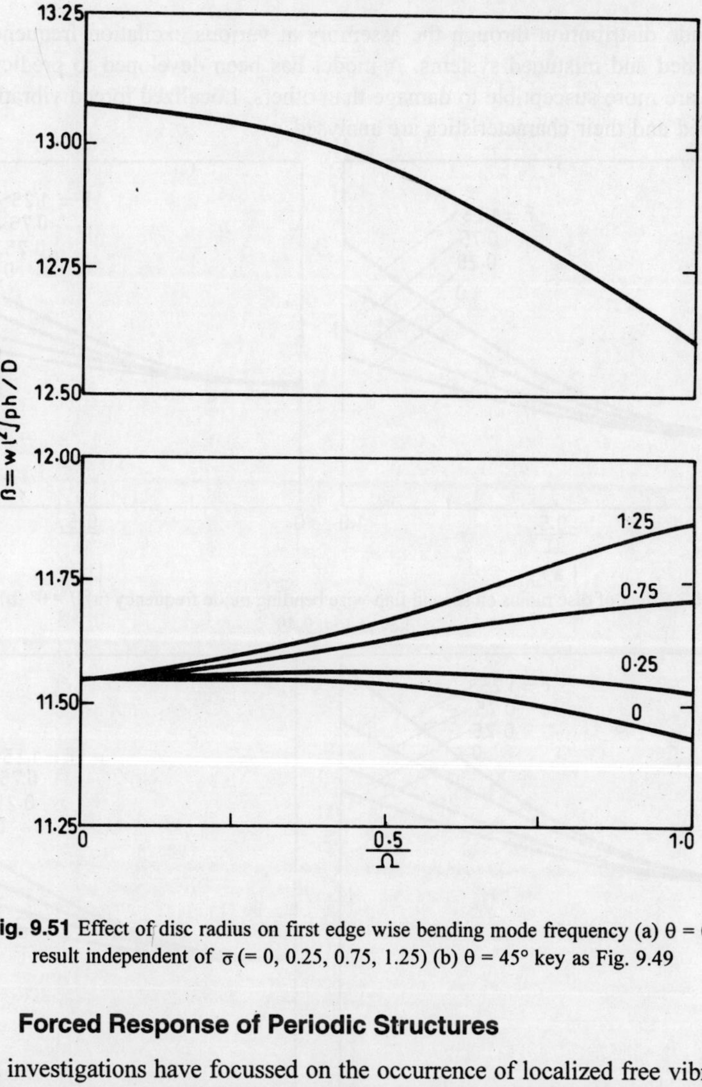

Fig. 9.51 Effect of disc radius on first edge wise bending mode frequency (a) θ = 0° result independent of $\overline{\sigma}$ (= 0, 0.25, 0.75, 1.25) (b) θ = 45° key as Fig. 9.49

9.3.5 Forced Response of Periodic Structures

Recent investigations have focussed on the occurrence of localized free vibrations, and on the confinement of vibrations and waves near a local source of excitation. The objective of this investigation is to determine whether localized forced vibrations occur when all the component systems constituting the nearly periodic structure are excited harmonically.

The effects of mistuning on the response to forced excitation of nearly periodic structures with cyclic symmetric approach are presented. Extensive study has been done on the effects of mistuning on the forced response of bladed disc assemblies. Conflicting conclusions have been arrived as discussed by Wei and Pierre. However, the aim of this study is to show that the sensitivity of forced vibrations to small mistuning is governed by the value of the internal coupling, thereby explaining apparently conflicting previous results that were obtained for widely different coupling values. In this study two important issues were discussed. First the effects of irregularities on the forced response of the system to periodic excitation. The effects of various parameters was studied using perturbation techniques. Secondly, the amplitude distribution through the assembly at various excitation frequencies for both tuned and mistuned systems. A model has been developed to predict which blades are more susceptible to damage than others. Localized forced vibrations are observed and their characteristics are analysed.

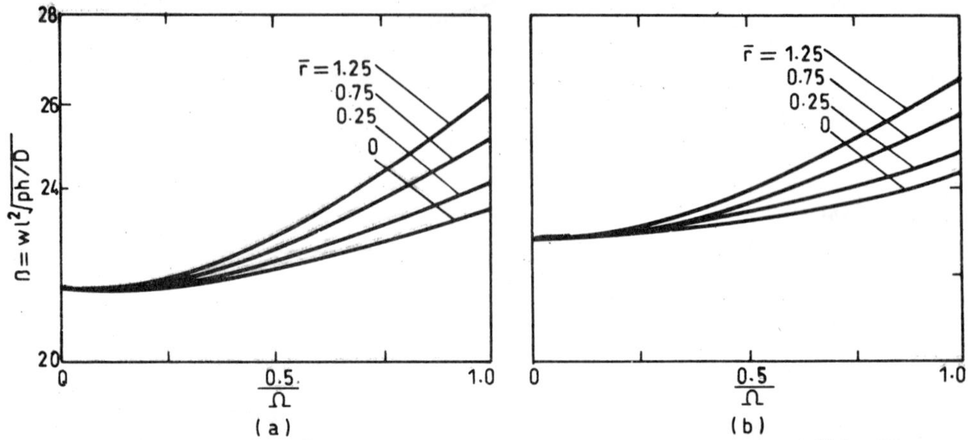

Fig.9.52 Effect of disc radius on second flap-wise bending mode frequency (a) θ = 0° (b) θ = 45° key as Fig. 9.49

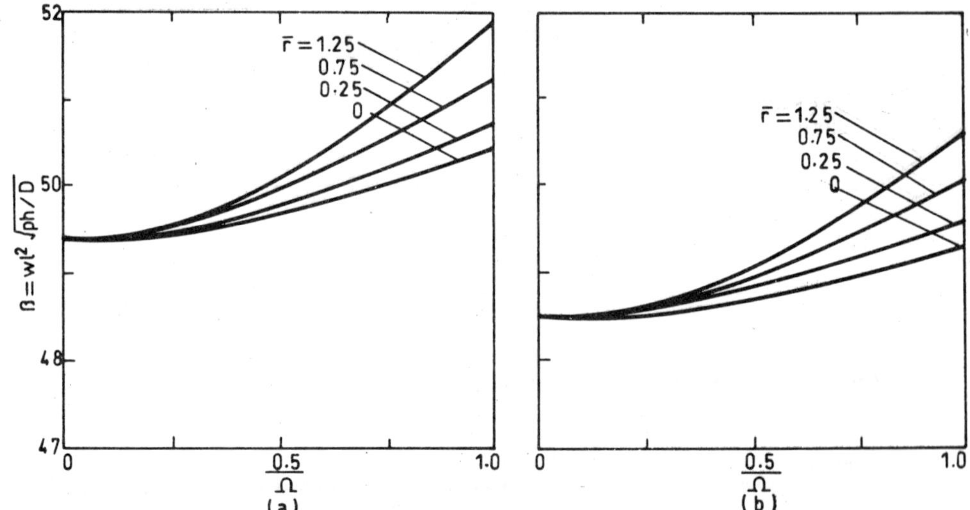

Fig.9.53 Effect of disc radius on second torsional mode frequency (a) θ = 0° (b) θ = 45° key as Fig. 9.49

Formulation and response evaluation was discussed in Chap. 8 under forced vibration analysis. The exact solution for a given tuned system is that all blades experience the same amplitude and stress at a given excitation frequency. It is also observed that the blade amplitude depends on the *C/N* ratio where *C* is the engine order excitation and *N* is the number of blades as shown in Fig.9.54 which displays the largest amplitude versus coupling ratio for different values of *C/N* ratio.

The forced response of mistuned system depends on the interblade coupling, the engine order excitation, the mistuning strength and its distribution and the number of blades. The response of tuned and mistuned systems are compared. Fig. 9.55a-c shows the maximum frequency response for various coupling ratios. Random mistuning of 4% is considered. Largest amplitude changes with coupling is shown in Fig. 9.56. It is also observed that the increase in the largest amplitude is proportional to the square of the coupling (R^2).

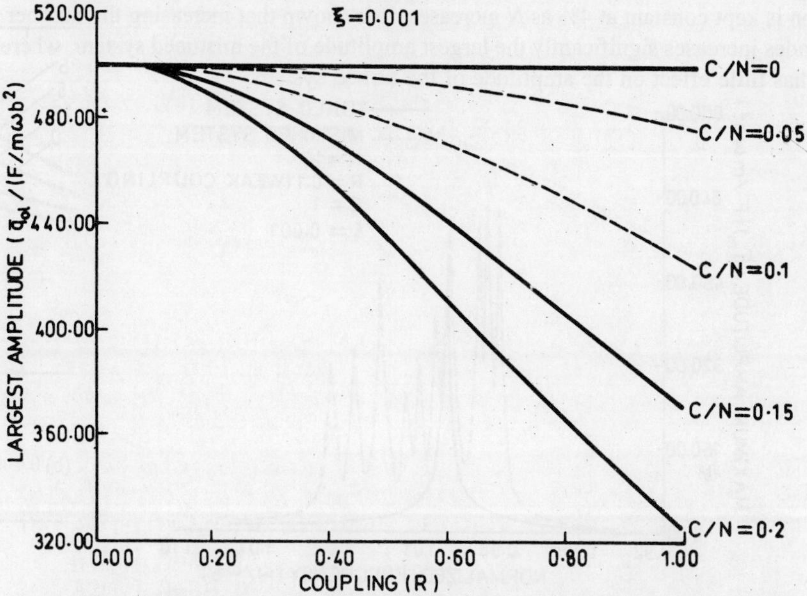

Fig. 9.54 Largest Amplitude of Tuned System throughout the assembly at any excitation frequency versus coupling for different values of C/N. the damping ratio is 0.001.

For a tuned system for which $C \leq N/2$, increasing the engine order excitation shifts the unique peak of the frequency response to a higher frequency, while for $C > N/2$, increasing C decreases the resonance frequency. This is shown in Fig. 9.57a for a strongly coupled mistuned system. The main peaks are shifted to higher excitation frequencies when the engine order excitation is changed from 0.1 to 0.4 For a very weakly coupled mistuned system, it is observed from Fig. 9.57b that the engine order excitation has very little effect on the frequency response of the system. Fig. 9.57c shows that for a slightly larger coupling ratio corresponding to a weakly coupled system, increasing C increases the high frequency peak amplitudes while it decreases the amplitudes of the low frequency peaks.

The effect of mistuning strength on the frequency response is shown in Fig. 9.58 for a weakly coupled system. The frequency response of the weakly coupled system with very small mistuning is very similar to one of the corres-ponding tuned system, except that peak splitting occurs for the mis-tuned system from which it is observed that the important parameter is the ratio of mistuning strength to coupling (σ/R^2). The effect of mistuning strength on the largest amplitude throughout the assembly at any excitation frequency is shown in Fig. 9.59. Figure 9.59a shows the largest amplitude versus standard deviation for several coupling values for the damping ratio $\xi = 0.001$. It is observed in Fig. 9.59 that for small σ (the mistuning strength) the largest amplitude increases linearly with the standard deviation.

The effect of the number of blades on the frequency response of a strongly coupled system ($R = 0.5$) with mistuning strength $\sigma = 4\%$ is shown in Fig. 9.60. It is observed that as the number of blades increases the main two peaks are shifted to lower excitation frequencies and as a result the system is more susceptible to suffer blade damage at low excitation frequencies. Finally the effect of number of blades on the largest amplitudes experienced by mistuned and tuned systems is shown in Fig. 9.61 for the weak coupling case. For the mistuned system the standard deviation is kept constant at 4% as N increases. It is shown that increasing the number of blades increases significantly the largest amplitude of the mistuned system, whereas it has little effect on the amplitude of the turned system.

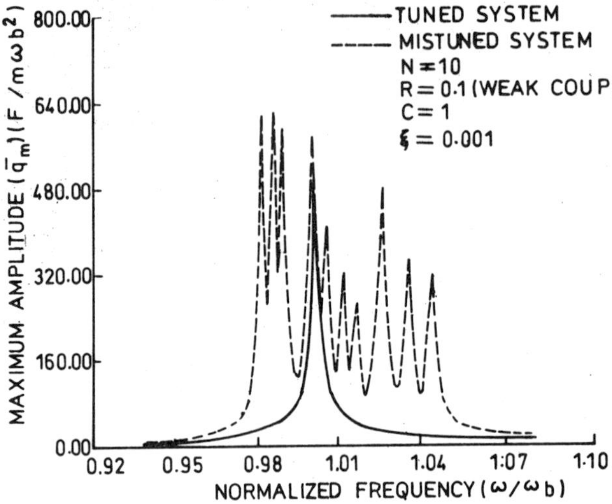

Fig. 9.55a

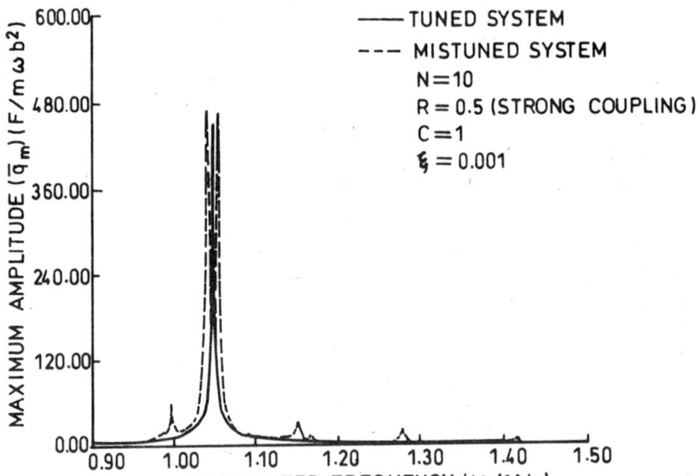

Fig. 9.55b

9.3.6 Transient Vibrations of Turbine Blades

Transient and stationary responses of turbine blades have been investigated by Horst Irretier. He presented his analysis based on the beam theory including the bending-bending and torsional vibrations. The equations of motion are transformed using the technique of modal expansion and solved in the time or frequency domain depending on transient or stationary excitation, respectively.

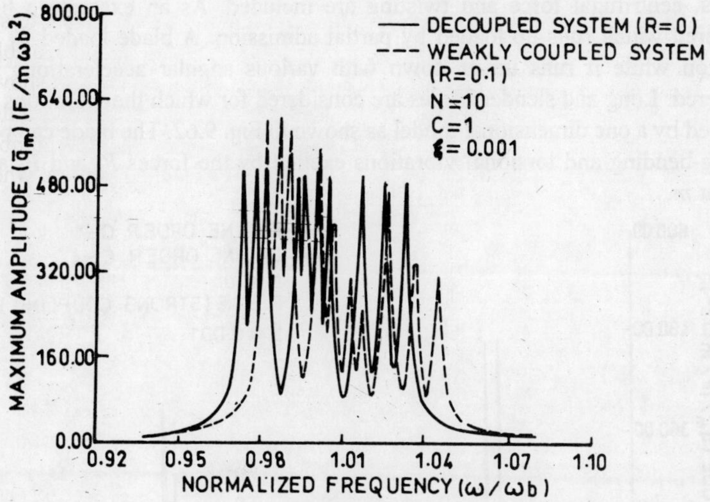

Fig. 9.55c

Fig. 9.55. Maximum Blade Amplitude versus excitation frequency for various coupling ratios. Fig. 9.55(a) shows the frequency responsses of the tuned and mistuned systems for R = 0.1 and Fig. 9.55(b) is for R = 0.5. Fig. 9.55(c) shows the responsses of the decoupled and weakly coupled (R = 0.1) mistuned systems.

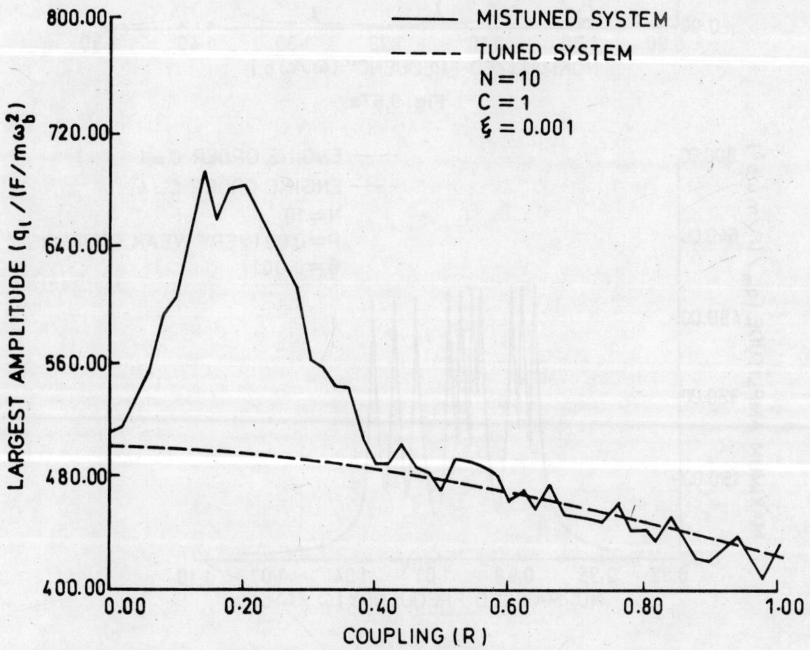

Fig. 9.56 Largest assembly throughout the assembly at any excitation frequency versus coupling for tuned and mistuned systems

In this analysis, a numerical model for transient vibrations of a single cantilever blade for bending-bending and torsional vibrations is presented. In the dynamic analysis, centrifugal force and twisting are included. As an example a blade is considered which runs up loaded by partial admission. A blade loaded by nozzle excitation while it runs up or down with various angular accelerations is also considered. Long and slender blades are considered for which the vibrations can be described by a one dimensional model as shown in Fig. 9.62. The blade can perform bending-bending and torsional vibrations excited by the forces P_2 and P_3 and the moment m.

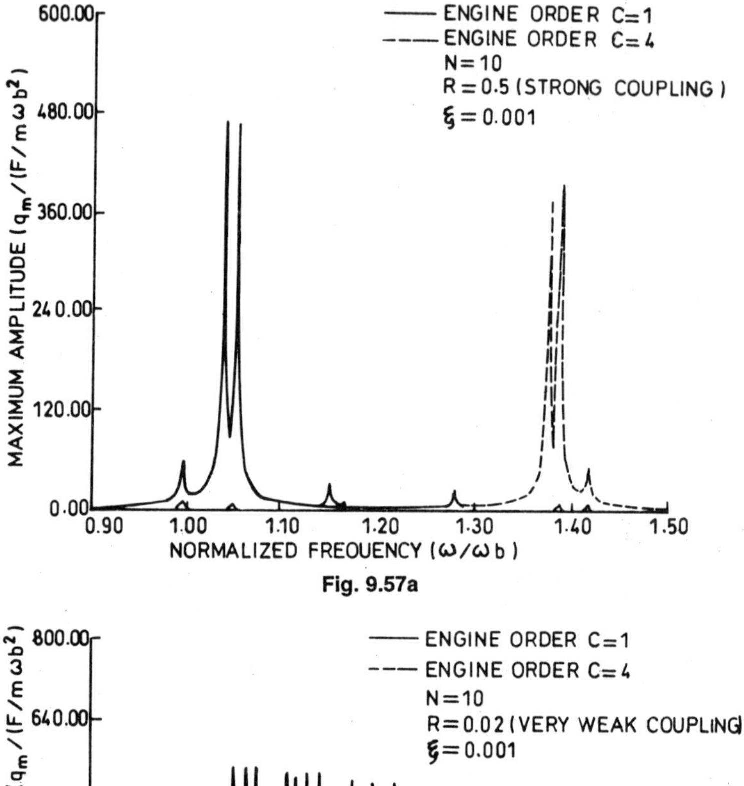

Fig. 9.57a

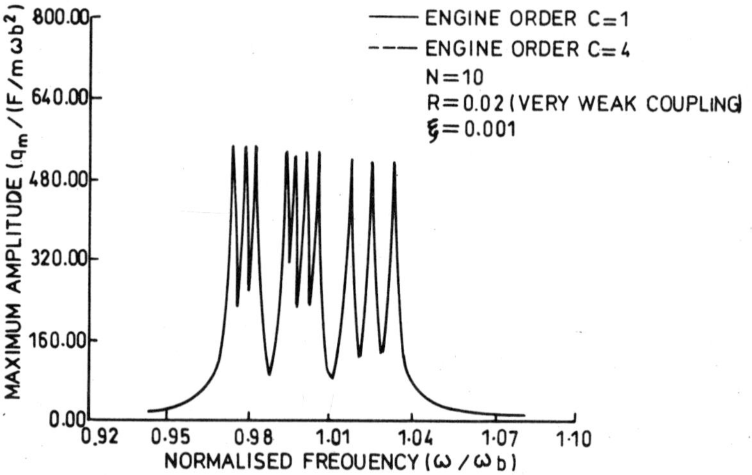

Fig. 9.57b

The modal equations of motion are solved by two methods depending on whether stationary or transient vibrations are considered. The solution in the frequency domain is the most convenient way to solve the equations of motions for different types of excitations.

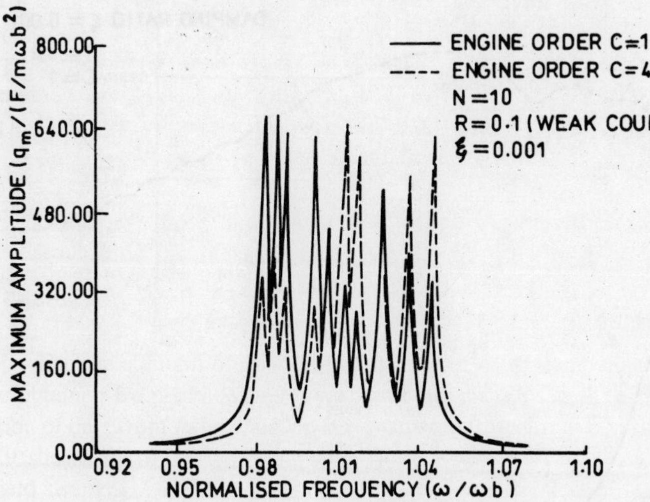

Fig. 9.57c

Fig. 9.57 Maxmimum Blade Amplitude versus excitation frequency for two different engine order excitations (C = 1 and 4). Fig. (a) is for a strongly coupled mistuned system. (R = 0.5) Fig. (b) for a very weakly coupled mistuned system. (R = 0.02) Fig. (c) is for a weakly coupled system (R = 0.1). the mistuning distribution is given in table.

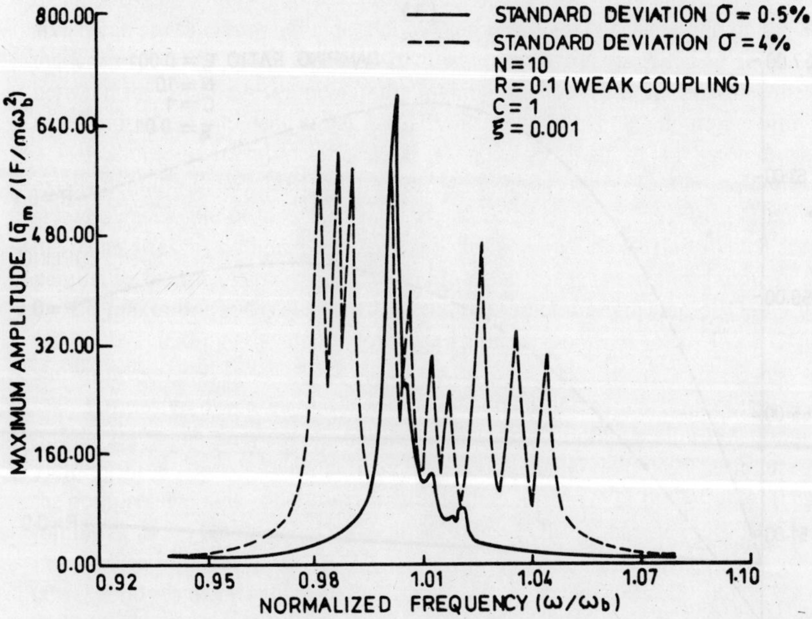

Fig. 9.58 Maximum Blade Amplitude versus excitation frequency for two different mistuning standard deviations. Only the amplitude of the mistuning distribution is varied for the random mistuning pattern given.

To solve the modal equations of motion in the time domain a Runge-Kutta-Fehlberg numerical integration algorithm is used. Thus the complete response of the blade is determined even for the case of non-stationary excitations by time-dependent force spectra.

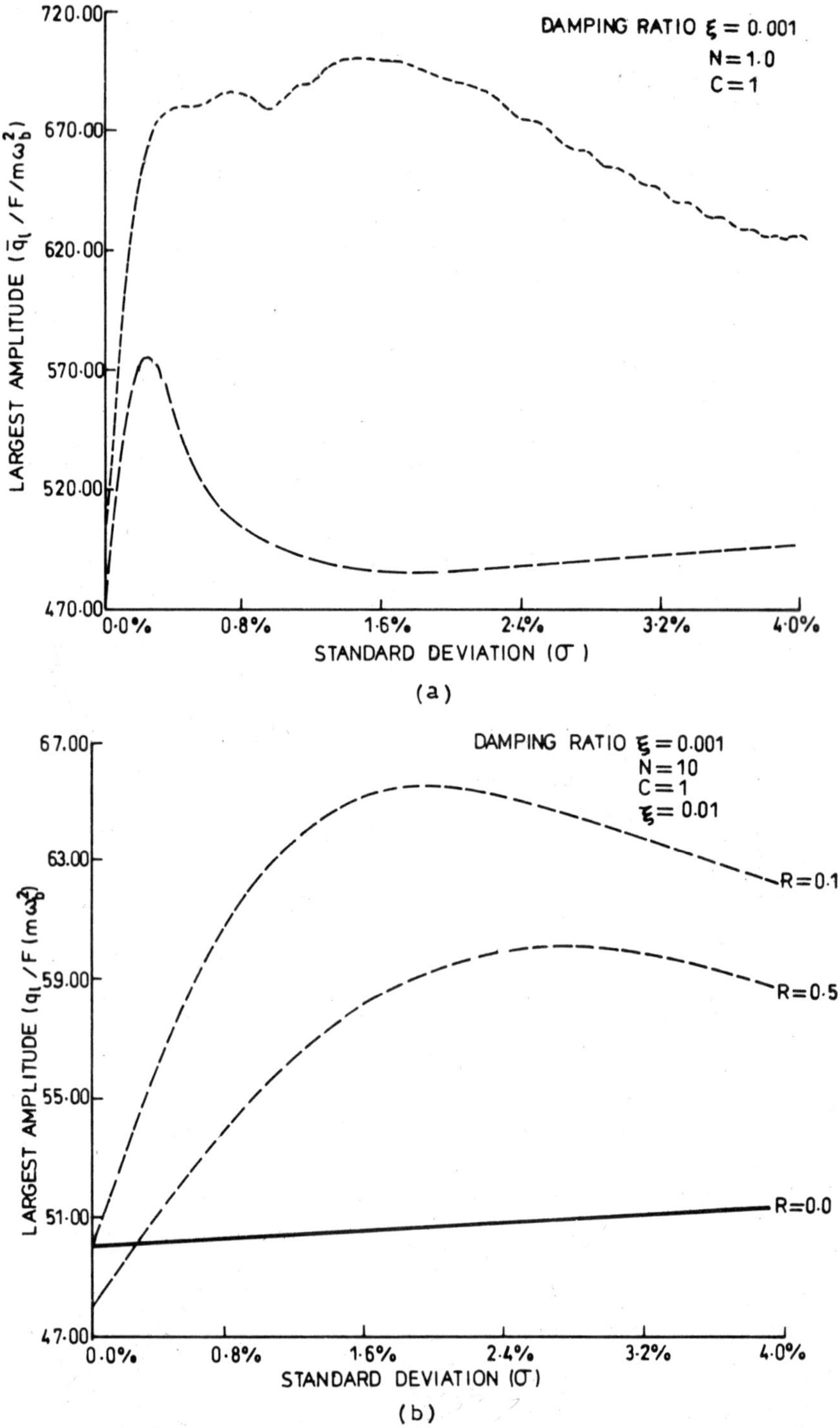

Fig. 9.59 Largest Amplitude throughout the assembly at any excitation frequency versus mistuning standard deviation for various couplings. Only the amplitude of the mistuning distribution is varied for the random mistuning pattern given.

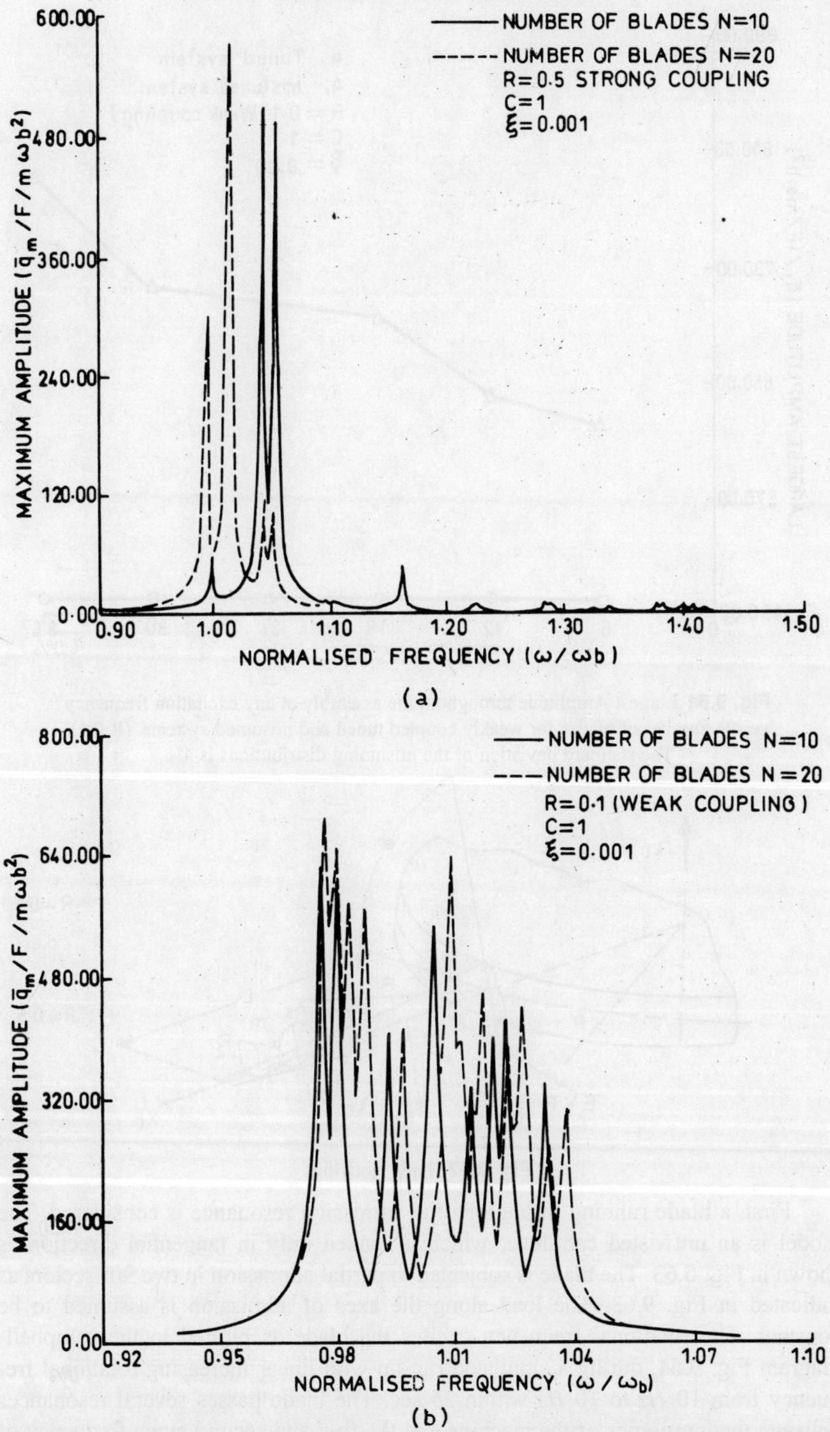

Fig. 9.60 Maximum Blade Amplitude versus excitation frequency for different number of blades (N = 10 and 20) with mistuning strength s = 4%. (Fig (a). is for a strongly coupled mistuned system. Fig (b). is for a weakly coupled mistuned system.

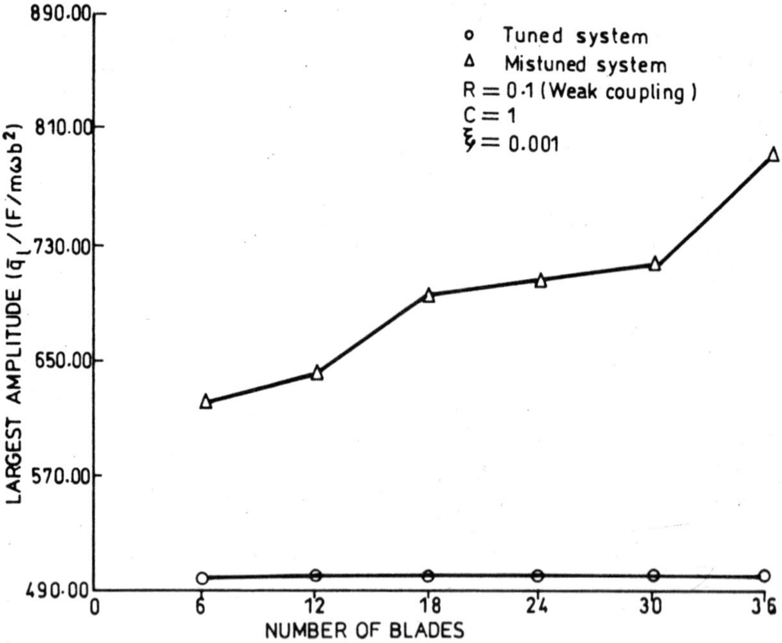

Fig. 9.61 Largest Amplitude throughout the assembly at any excitation frequency versus number of blades for weakly coupled tuned and mistuned systems. (R 0.1). The standard deviation of the mistuning distributions is 4%.

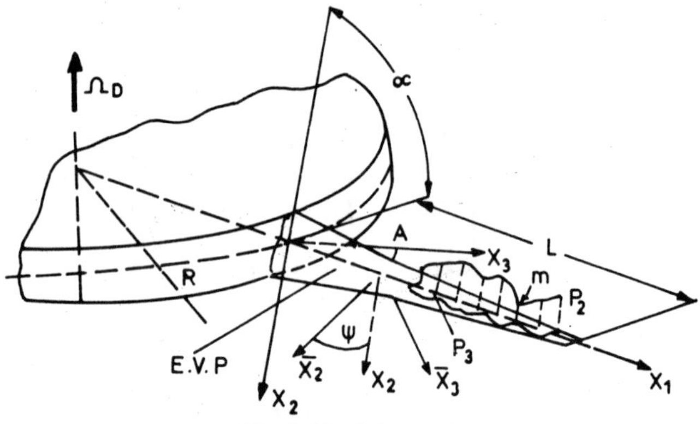

Fig. 9.62 Blade Notations

First, a blade running through partial admission resonance is considered. The model is an untwisted cantilever which is loaded only in tangential direction as shown in Fig. 6.63. The blade is subjected to partial admission in two 90° sectors as indicated in Fig. 9.63. The load along the axes of admission is assumed to be constant. The rotational frequency excites the blade as plotted in the campbell-diagram Fig. 9.64, during a simulated run-up with linear increasing rotational frequency from 10 *Hz* to 10 *Hz* within 25 sec. The blade passes several resonances between the harmonics of the machine and the first and second eigen frequency of the trangential bending vibration. The Campbell plot indicates that the eigen frequencies increase considerably due to rotation. The balde response calculated in the time domain is shown in Fig. 9.65.

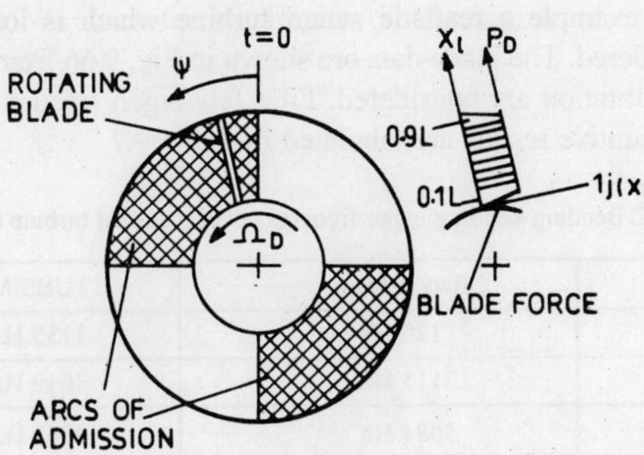

Fig. 9.63 Load distribution for simulation of a runup of a blade subjected to partial admission.

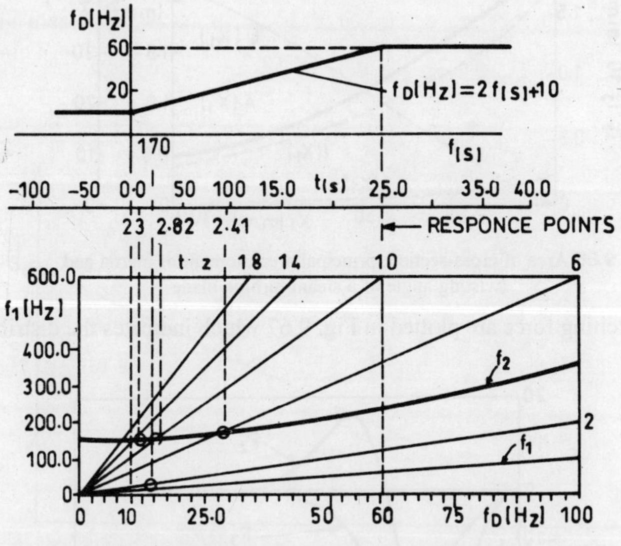

Fig. 9.64 Rotational frequency and Campbell-diagram during run-up.

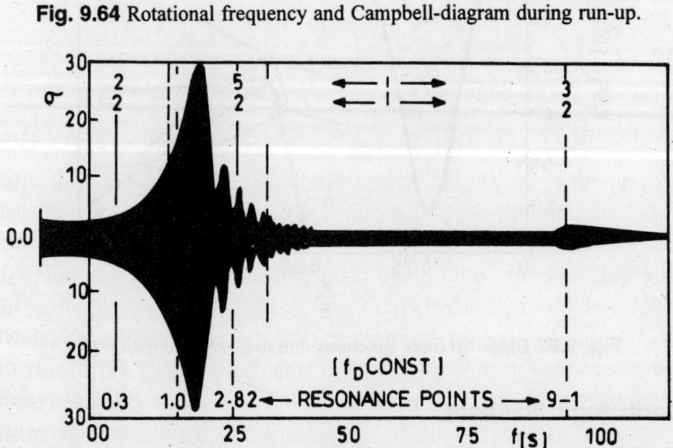

Fig. 9.65 Blade root stress response as function of time during run-up

As a second example a realistic steam turbine which is loaded by nozzle excitation, is considered. The blade data are shown in Fig. 9.66 from which coupled bending-bending vibration are considered. First few eigen frequencies are considered and the comparative results are tabulated in Table 9.7.

Table 9.7 Bending-bending eigen frequencies of a stream turbine blade

Frequency	Rao/Jadvani	TUBSIM
f_1	120 Hz	1155 Hz
f_2	3115 Hz	3049 Hz
f_3	5084 Hz	4861 Hz

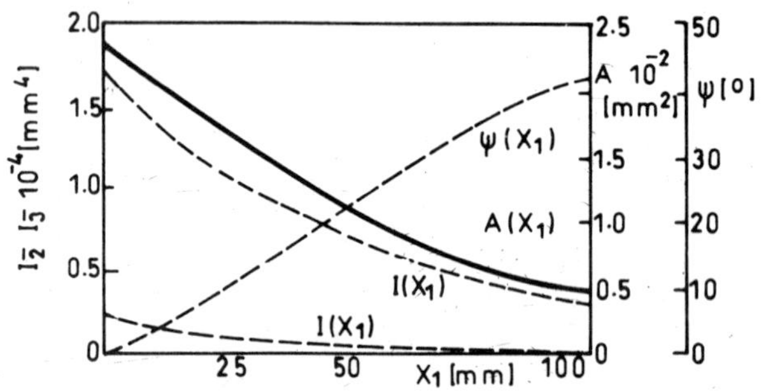

9.66 Area of cross-section, principal area moment of inertia and twisting angle of a steam turbine blade

The data of exciting force are plotted in Fig. 9.67 which indicates the distribution in the nozzle.

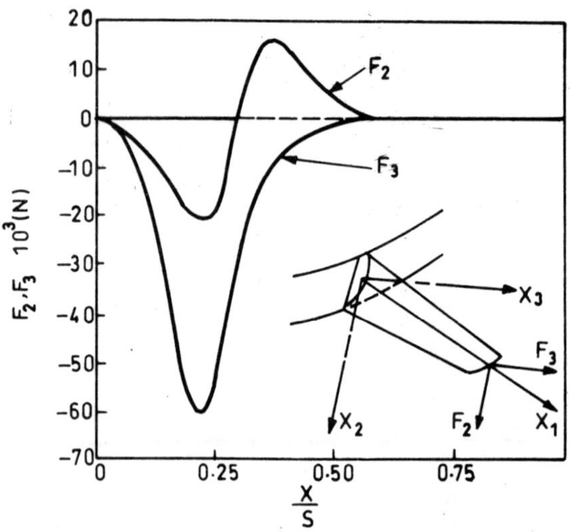

Fig. 9.67 Blade tip force functions due to nozzle excitation (2)

9.3.7 Centrifugal Baskets

A centrifugal basket is a rotationally symmetric vessel rotating at speeds around 1500 rpm and subjected to internal pressure due to induced vortex of the fluid inside the basket and centrifugal force of the basket. The basket is fixed at one end and free at the other, comprises of a circular disc at the bottom and cylindrical shell with hoops on its body. Not much information is available on the stress analysis of such baskets, except for few elementary books. A typical basket analysed here is shown in Fig. 9.68. A rigorous analysis procedure to work out the stresses for a practical basket proposed by V. Ramamurti and B. Prakasam is presented here using Finite Element Method.

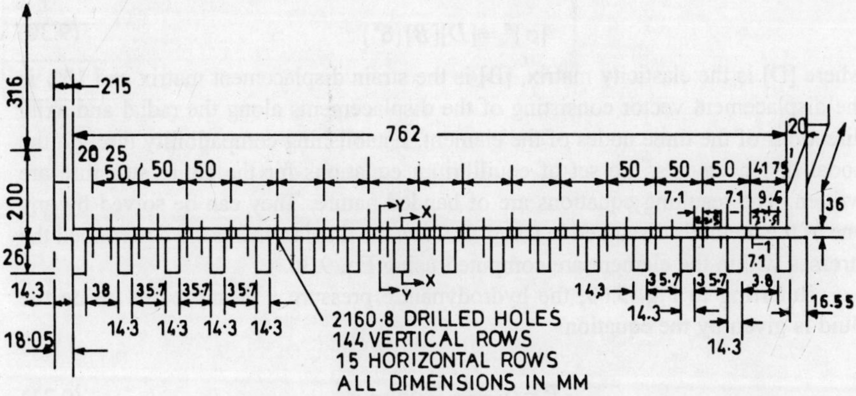

Fig. 9.68 Dimensions of the centrifugal basket

The centrigual basket which is designed to receive the massecuite to be treated, is carried on a vertical shaft, at the upper end of which is the driving motor. The basket is pierced with a number of holes to allow the molasses to escape and is provided with centrifugal hoops to withstand the centrifugal forces. The basket is having a metal gauge linear inside, which helps to retain the sugar while the molasses is passing through. The baskets are of size about 0.75 m to 1.2 m in diameter and of thickness 4 to 6 mm and are made of chrome copper steel and contain 6-16 hoops of nickel steel. The baskets will operate at speeds of 1000 to 1500 rpm. Usually the time taken for each cycle of operation including charging, running, washing and discharging is about 6 min.

It is assumed that the stress is distributed uniformly across its thickness and the resisting force of the basket is equal to the centrifugal force of the massecuite. Using the thin shell theory the maximum circumferential stress is calculated. The radial pressure due to the centrifugal force is given by

$$P = \frac{m\omega^2}{2\pi H} \tag{9.27}$$

where *m* is the mass of the basket and massecuite, and *H* is the height of the basket.

The centrifugal stress developed in it is given by

$$\sigma = \frac{m\omega^2 D}{4\pi H t} \tag{9.28}$$

where *D* is the diameter and *t* is the thickness of the cylindrical basket. The variation in the geometry of the basket is not taken into consideration in the Eq. (9.28). Hence it is required to modify the analysis to consider the geometry and the role of hoops.

Since the problem of centrifugal basket is axisymmetric, the F.E.M. is employed using the triangular ring elements and the linear polynomial as the shape function. The element stiffness matrix and the element stress vector of the triangular element in a body of revolution subjected to axisymmetric loading can be expressed as

$$[K]^e = 2\pi \int \int [B]^T [D][B] r\, dr\, dy \tag{9.29}$$

$$\{\sigma\}^e = [D][B]\{\delta^e\} \tag{9.30}$$

where [D] is the elasticity matrix, [B] is the strain displacement matrix and $\{\delta^e\}$ is the displacement vector consisting of the displacements along the radial and axial directions of the three nodes of the element. Establishing compatibility through the nodal displacements, the set of equilibrium equations for the entire structure are written. The resulting equations are of banded nature. They can be solved by any one of the methods discussed in Chap. 2. Once the displacements are determined the stresses within the element are computed using Eq. 9.30.

Referring to Fig. 9.69, the hydrodynamic pressure p at any point inside the fluid is given by the equation

$$P = \rho \frac{\omega^2 x^2}{2} - \rho g y + c \tag{9.31}$$

where x and y are the coordinates and c is a constant. At the origin $x = y = 0$, $p = 0$ and hence $c = 0$. At the top and at the bottom of the free surface we have

$$y_1 = \frac{\omega^2}{2g} x_1^2 \; ; \; y_2 = \frac{\omega^2}{2g} x_2^2 \tag{9.32}$$

and hence

$$(y_1 - y_2) = \frac{\omega^2}{2g}(x_1 + x_2)(x_1 - x_2) \tag{9.33}$$

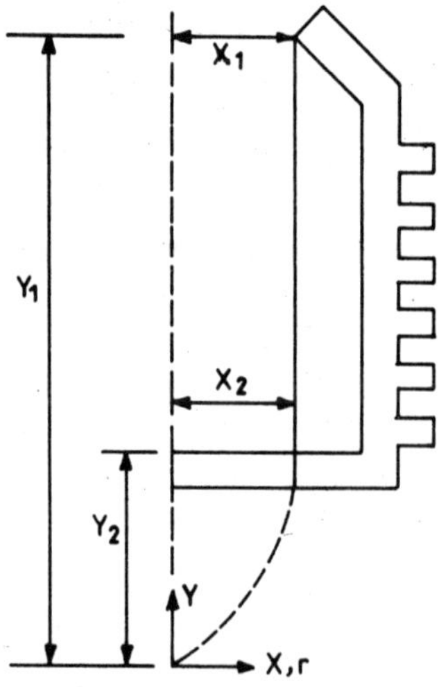

Fig. 9.69 Vertex formation in the basket at high speeds

It could be seen that $(y_1 - y_2)$ from Eq. 9.33 and $(x_1 + x_2)$ is of the same order for a standard basket. For the present model $y_1 - y_2 = 782$ mm whereas $x_1 + x_2 = 2\times314 = 628$ for a basket speed of 1500 rpm and above this speed the $\omega^2/2g$ value is very large and $(x_1 - x_2)$ has to be very small. Hence the free surface of the liquid could be assumed as vertical and we will assume x_1 to be the radius of the free surface. Now the radially outward fluid pressure at any point on the lateral surface of the basket with coordinates r and y can be given as

$$P = \sigma \frac{\omega^2 r^2}{2} - \rho \frac{\omega^2 x_1^2}{2} \tag{9.34}$$

The centrifugal force

The radially outward pressure due to the centrifugal force of the basket can be expressed as

$$P = \frac{\rho_m h}{g} \quad \omega_r^2 \tag{9.35}$$

where ρ_m is the specific weight and h is the radially outward thickness of the basket. The nodal force due to the fluid pressure at a typical node of an element would be the normal pressure p multiplied by half the axial height of the element.

The analysis is carried out for three types of baskets, (1) a standard basket as given in Fig. (2) a model basket as indicated in Fig. 9.70 on which experiments are also conducted and (3) other standard baskets given in handbook of Cane Sugar Engineering.

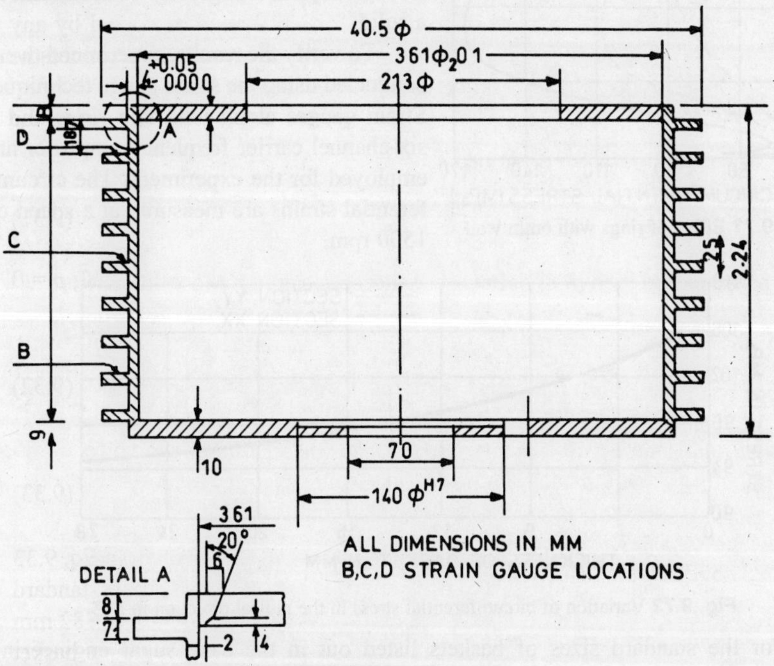

Fig. 9.70 Model Basket

The study is carried out for the behaviour of the basket when running empty, in this case only centrifugal force is present, running with water, with massecuite considered as ideal liquid and ideal soled. Both the stresses and deformations have been investigated.

The hydrodynamic forces are imposed at all the nodes at the inner face of the basket. The equivalent static forces at the nodes of each element due to the centrigual force of the element are computed. For this problem the number of elements and nodes are 1374 and 932 respectively. The basket is fixed at the bottom and is free at the top. The resulting 1858 simultaneous equations are solved. Maximum band-width is only 16. Convergency study is carried out.

All the plots given below refer to the standard basket shown in Fig. 9.68 for the speed of 1500 rpm. Figure 9.71 shows the circumferential stress on the inner face of

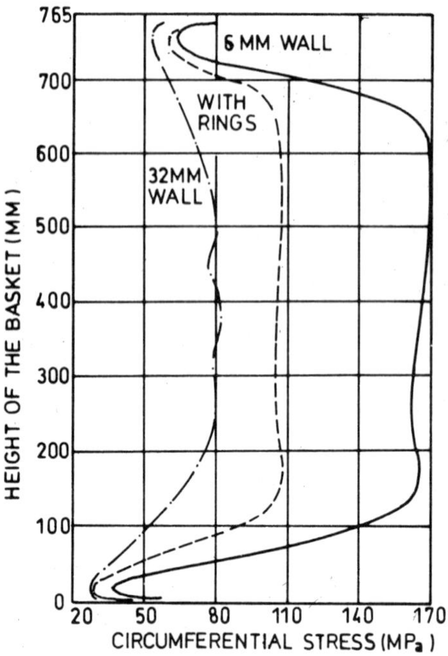

Fig. 9.71 Effect of rings with 6mm wall

the standard basket when filled with water. The variation of circumferential stress of a typical zone of a standard basket are shown in Figs. 9.72 and 9.73. It indicates that the variation along the axis is very small whereas the variation in the radial direction is considerable. The deformation pattern is shown in Fig. 9.74. The axial and radial stresses with massecuite for the same basket are shown in Fig. 9.75. Figure 9.76 shows the circumferential stress for the standard basket with the hoops when running empty, with water, with massecuite as an ideal liquid, (sp. gravity of 1.47) and as a solid.

To verify the results, experiments were conducted using the strain gauge technique. Strain gauges along with slip rings and a six-channel carrier frequency amplifier are employed for the experiment. The circumferential strains are measured at a speed of 1500 rpm.

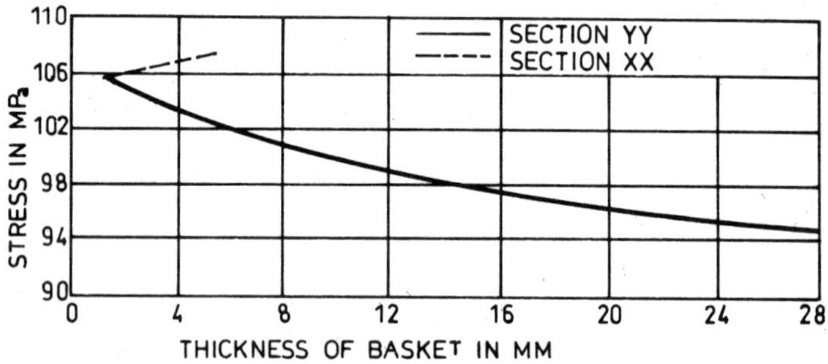

Fig. 9.72 Variation of circumferential stress in the radical direction in MP_a

For the standard sizes of baskets listed out in the cane sugar engineering bandbook, assuming 16 rings in the cylindrical portion, the maximum circumferential stress is analytically computed and presented in Table 9.8.

Table 9.8 Stress in Standard Basket

S. No.	Nominal size (mm)	Actual size (mm)	Basket Thickness (mm)	Ring Axial	Dimensions (mm) Radial	Circumferential Stress (MPa)
1	760 × 460	760 × 460	6	12	7	57
2	915 × 460	916 × 460	6	24	10	98
3	1015 × 510	1016 × 517	6	27	15	102
4	1015 × 610	1016 × 612	6	27	12	122
5	1015 × 760	1016 × 765	6	27	15	105
6	1065 × 610	1066 × 615	6	27	15	134
7	1065 × 760	1066 × 760	6	28	15	122

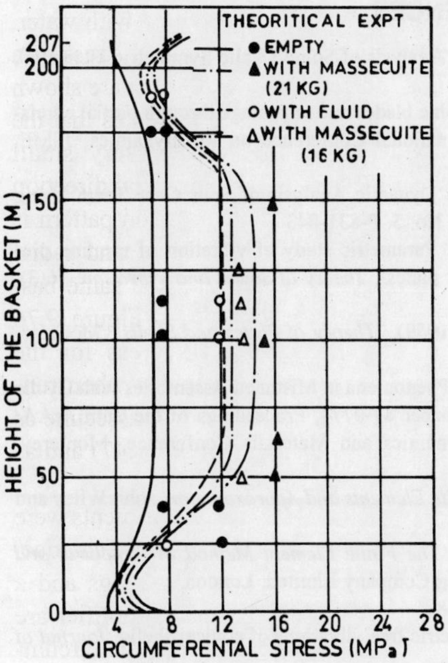

Fig. 9.73 Comparison of results in model basket (inner face)

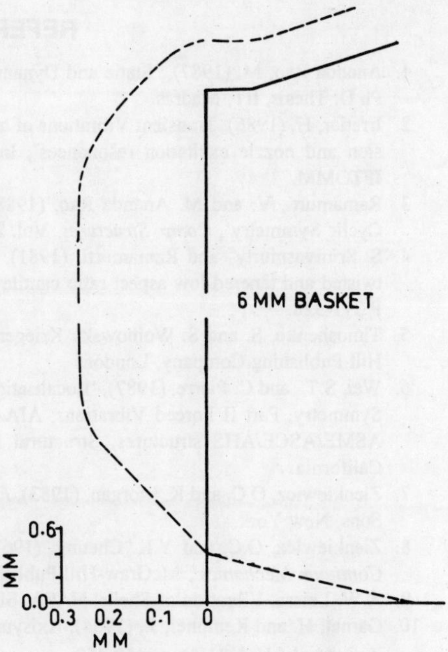

Fig. 9.74 Deflection pattern of the inner face (radical and axial displacement)

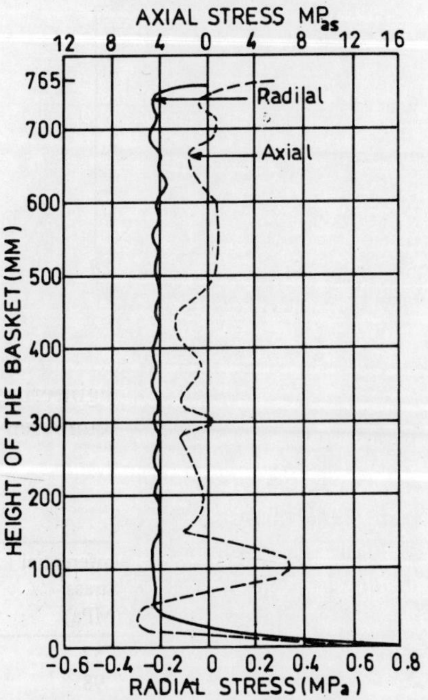

Fig. 9.75 Stress distribution on the inner face (6mm basket with massecuite)

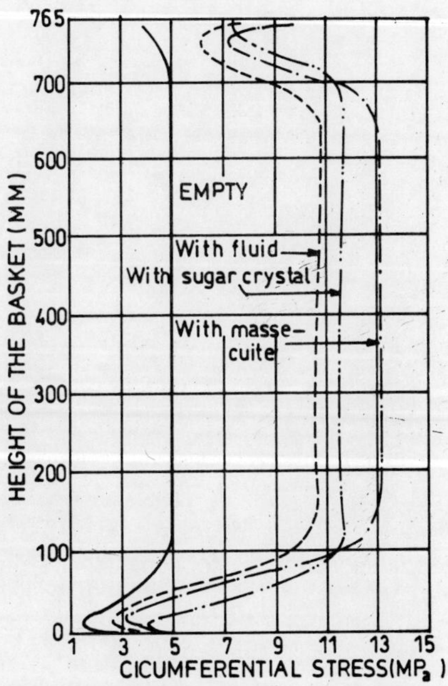

Fig. 9.76 Stress distribution on the inner face (6mm basket)

REFERENCES

1. Ananda Rao, M. (1987), 'Static and Dynamic Analysis of Some Cyclic Symmetric elements', Ph.D. Thesis, IIT, Madras.
2. Irretier, H. (1986), Transient Vibrations of turbine blades due to passage through partial admission and nozzle excitation resonances', International Conference on Rotadynamics, JSME, IFTOMM.
3. Ramamurti, V. and M. Ananda Rao, (1988), 'Dynamic Analysis of Spur Gear Teeth Using Cyclic Symmetry', *Comp. Structures,* Vol. 29, No. 5. P-831-843
4. S. Srinivasmurty and Ramamurti, (1981), 'A Parametric study of vibration of rotating pre-twisted and tapered low aspect ratio cantilever plates', *Theory of Sound and Vibration,* 76(3). P 311-328.
5. Timoshenko, S. and S. Woinowsky Krieger, (1959), *'Theory of Plates and Shells'*, McGraw-Hill Publishing Company, London.
6. Wei, S.T., and C. Pierre, (1987), 'Localisation Phenomena in Mistuned Assemblies with Cyclic Symmetry, Part II Forced Vibrations, AIAA paper 87-0774, Proceedings of the 28th AIAA/ASME/ASCE/AHS structures, Structural Dynamics and Materials Conference, Monterey, California.
7. Zienkiewicz, O.C. and K. Morgan, (1983), *Finite Elements and Approximation,* John Wiley and Sons, New York.
8. Zienkiewicz, O.C. and Y.K. Cheung, (1967), *The Finite Element Method in Structural and Continum Mechanics',* McGraw-Hill Publishing Company Limited, London.
9. A.W. Leissa, Vibration of Shells, NASA, SP-288.
10. Garnet, H. and Kempner, J., (1964), Axisymmetric free vibrations of conical shells, *Journal of App. Mech.,* Vol. 31(3), p. 458-460.

```
C
C ----------------------------------------------------------------------
C
```

SEISMIC ANALYSIS OF A PRESSURE VESSEL DYNAMIC ANALYSIS

```
C                          OUR METHOD
 ***************************************************
C                          METHODOLOGY
C *******************************************************
C **  1.    GENERATE STIFFNESS MATRIX                        **
C **                                                         **
C **  2.    GENERATE MASS MATRIX                             **
C **                                                         **
C **  3.    USE MODIFIED SIMULTANEOUS ITERATION SCHEME       **
  **        FOR UNSYMMETRIC                                  **
            MATRICES TO GET FIRST 8 EIGEN PAIRS
C **
C **  4.    USE MODAL SUPERPOSITION METHOD TO                **
C **        DETERMINE THE RESPONSE                           **
C **  5     POTTERS SCHEME WITH VARIABLE BLOCK SIZE          **
C **        (MAS. 12*12) IS USED.                            **
C *******************************************************
      IMPLICIT REAL*8(A-H, O-Z)
      DIMENSION A(4, 4), A1(2, 4, 4), A2(2, 4, 4), A3(2, 4, 4), A4(12, 12)
      DIMENSION A5(12, 12), A6(12, 12), AM(1128)
      DIMENSION B(4, 4), BC1(4, 4), BC2(4, 4), BETA(4, 4)
      DIMENSION C(4, 4), E(4, 4), ETA(4, 4), FE(4, 4), FORCE(12), G(4, 4),
      GE(4, 4)
      DIMENSION GEM(4, 4), GEP(4, 4), H(4, 4), HM(4, 4), HP(4, 4), ID(141, 4)
      DIMENSION PRUN(12, 12), PSI(12, 12), PSIC(4, 4)
C
C     VARIABLES USED AT THE JUNCTION ONLY ARE
C
       DIMENSION Q4(4, 4), SI(4, 4), EM3(4, 4)
       DIMENSION R3(4, 4), TT1(4, 4), EN3(4, 4)
       DIMENSION S2(4, 4), X2 (4, 4), TT2(4, 4)
       DIMENSION X1(4, 4), Y2(4, 4), Y1(4,4)
     * GE1(4, 4), GE2(4, 4), GE3(4,4 ), H1(4, 4)
     * ,H2(4, 4), H3(4, 4), PSI1(4, 4), PSI2(4, 4)
C ----------------------------------------------------------------------
```

```
      COMMON / COM1 / A1, A2, A3
      COMMON / COM3 / AM
      COMMON / COM2 / ID
      REWIND 4
C     DEFINE FILE 01 (85, 1200, L, KOUNT)
C     DEFINE FILE 02 (285, 1200, L, KON)
C     DEFINE FILE 03(150, 1200, L, IKON)
C-----------------------------------------------------------------
C     NAME          EXPLANATION
C-----------------------------------------------------------------
C     A1 TO A3      NODAL A, B, C OF SIZE(4, 4) TAKEN TWO AT A
                    TIME
C     A4 TO A6      PLOTTER BLOCKS OF MAX. SIZE (12, 12)
                    EQUIVALENT TO
                    A, B, C IN THAT ORDER.
C     AM            MASS MATRIX
C     BC1, BC2      BOUNDARY CONDITION MATRICES
C     ID            FIRST COLUMN GIVES KOUNT.SECOND TO
                    FOURTH
                    GIVE THE SIZES OF POTTER BLOCKS
C     T'S           THICKNESSES
C     D'S           DIAMETRES
C     AC            REFERENCE LENGTH IN MM
C     DELTA1, 2     NON-DIMENSIONAL INTERVAL
C     EW            POISSON'S RATIO
C     DEN           MASS DENSITY OF STEEL
C     YM            YOUNG'S MODULUS OF STEEL
C
C-----------------------------------------------------------------
C                        CERTAIN POINTS
C 1.  TWO NODES CONSTITUTE ONE PARTITION. SO, FOR 280 NODES
C     KON = 1, 141 IS USED (INCLUDING JUNCTION NODE) AS THE
C     PARTITION NO. SINCE IN THE MAIN CYLINDRICAL PORTION,
C     POTTER BLOCKS DO NOT VARY, KOUNT, IS REALISED. FOR
C     KON=10, 110 KOUNT IS SAME. A4, A5, A6 HAVE A MAX. SIZE OF
C     12*12 AND RUNNING SIZES IT1*JT1, IT1*IT1, IT1*JT3 RESPEC-
      TIVELY. IT1, JT1, JT3 ARE GIVEN IN SECOND TO FOURTH COL-
      UMNS OF ID MATRIX IN THAT ORDER.
C 2.  AS & WHEN POTTER BLOCKS ARE FORMED P'S(STRAIGHT)
C     ARE CALCULATED AND WRITTEN ON SCRATCH FILE. AFTER
```

```
C       ALL PARTITIONS ARE OVER P'S(TRANSPOSE) ARE CALCU-
C       LATED. THOUGH APPEALING IT IS NOT A GOOD IDEA -- COM-
C       PUTATIONALLY SPEAKING (CONSIDERING POTTER3 ALSO).
C 3.    TRANSPOSING THE STIFFNESS MATRIX IS JUST INTERCHANGE
C       OF PA AND PC. SPECIAL CARE IS TAKEN AT THE BOUNDARY
C       NODES.
C 4.    FOR STATIC ANALYSIS BY THIS PROGRAM, DO THIS:-
C
C          A> DEFINE THE LOADING MATRIX X.
C          B> CALL POTER3 IN THE MAIN PROGRAM WITH NEIG=1;
C             K1=2
C          C> DELETE CALL POTTER2, CALL UNSYM FROM THE MAIN
C             PROGRAM.
C          D> INSERT THE STRESS-CALCULATION ROUTINE FROM Y1
C             PROGRAM.
C--------------------------------------------------------------
C                   DETAILS OF SUBROUTINES USED
C          NAME                        EXPLANATION
C     Block1, Block2    GROUPING OF NODES-GENERATION OF POTTER
C                       BLOCKS
C     ELF1              GENERATING F MATRIX(THEORY) CALLED BE
C                       IN THE PROGRAM
CC    GARY              GENERATING G
C     HOJO              GENERATES H, GE (PRONOUNCE IT)
C     BACHUS            GENERATES NODAL A, B, C
C     CALLS1            ALL CALL STATEMENTS NEEDED FOR A, B, C
C     CALLS2            USED AT ANY DISCONTINUITY NODE
C     TRANS             TRANSFORMATION MATRIX-DISCONTINUITY
      JUNCTION          GENERATES ALL THE MATRICES AT THE
                        JUNCTION NODE
C     POTER1(2)         GENERATES P'S FOR THE STRAIGHT (TRANS-
                        POSE)
                        PROBLEM
C     POTER3            SOLVES EQNS
C     UNSYM             S.I. METHOD FOR UNSYMMETRIC PROBLEM
C                        SCRATCH FILE DETAILS
C          FILE1                 POTTER BLOCKS
C          FILE2                 P (STRAIGHT & TRANSPOSE)
```

```
C         FILE3                   Q (STRAIGHT & TRANSPOSE)
C         FILE4                   INFORMATION REQD. FOR RESPONSE
C-----------------------------------------------------------------
C*** INPUT QUANTITIES
      T1 = 400.
      T2 = 200.
      T3 = 50.
      T4 = 350.
      D1 = 10.
      D2 = 3210.
      D3 = 3010.
      D4 = 1160.
      AC = 1000.
      DELTA1 = 0.1
      EW = 0.3
      P1 = 4. *DATAN(1.ODO)
      OMZT = 0.0
      EN = 1.ODO
      RSP1 = D2/2.
      RSP2 = D4/2.
      MS1 = 249
      MS2 = 268
      TEST = T2
      DEN = 7833.0
      YM = 2.058E11
C-----------------------------------------------------------------
C                         INITIALISATION
C-----------------------------------------------------------------
      MS = 12
      IT1 = 8
      JT1 = 8
      JT3 = 8
      DO 11 I = 1, MS
      DO 11 J = 1, MS
      A4(I, J) = 0.0
      A5(I, J) = 0.0
11      A6(I, J) = 0.0
C-----------------------------------------------------------------
C                   GENERATION OF (ID) MATRIX
C-----------------------------------------------------------------
      DO 12 I = 1, 9
12      ID(I, 1) = I
```

```
      DO 13 I = 10, 110
13       ID(I, 1) = 10
      ID(111, 1) = 11
      DO 14 I = 112, 122
14       ID(I, 1) = 12
      L = 13
      DO 15 I = 123, 135
        ID(I,1) = L
15       L = L + 1
      ID(136, 1) = 26
      DO 16 I = 137, 140
16       ID(I, 1) = 27
      ID(141, 1) = 28
      DO 17 I = 1, 141
      DO 17 J = 2, 4
17       ID(I, J) = 8
      ID(124, 3) = 12
      ID(125, 2) = 12
      ID(125, 3) = 4
      ID(126, 2) = 4
      ID(126, 4) = 12
      ID(127, 4) = 4
C-----------------------------MASS MATRIX GENERATION---------------------------
      F = 2.0
      DELTA = DELTA1
      DO 1111 K = 1.16
        K2 = 4*K
        K1 = K2-3
      DO 1113 I = K1, K2
1113     AM(I) = 2. 0*DELTA*DEN*F/YM
        AM(K2) = 0.0
1111     CONTINUE
      DO 1114 I = 65, 68
1114       AM(I) = 0.0
        DO 1115 K = 18, 248
      F = 1.0
      K2 = 4*K
      K1 = K2-3
      IF (K. GE. 222) GO TO 1118
      GO TO 1117
```

```
1118 ODD = (K–K/2*2)
     IF (ODD.NE.O)GO TO 1117
1117   DO 1116 I = K1, K2
1116    AM(I) = 2.O*DELTA*DEN*F/YM
     AM(K2) = 0.0
1115   CONTINUE
     DO 1119 I = 885, 888
1119    AM(I) = 0.0
     DO 1131 I= 981, 984
1131    AM(I) = 0.0
     DO 1120 I = 993, 1004
1120    AM(I) = 0.0
     F = 1.0
     ALFAM = DARCOS(RSP2/RSP1)
     DELTA2 = ALFAM/ (MS2-MS1)*RSP1/AC
     DELTA = DELTA2
     DO 1121 K = 250, 267
       K2 = 4*K+8
       K1 = K2–3
     DO 1122 I = K1, K2
1122    AM(I) = 2. *DELTA*DEN*F/YM
       AM(K2) = 0.0
1121    CONTINUE
     DO 1123 I = 1077, 1080
1123     AM(I) = 0.0
     F = T4/T2
     DELTA = DELTA1
     DO 1124 K = 269, 280
       K2 = 4*K + 8
       K1 = K2–3
     DO 1125 I = K1, K2
1125    AM(I) = 2.*DEN*DELTA*F/YM
       AM(K2) = 0.0
1124   CONTINUE
C             MASS MATRIX GENERATED
C -----------------------------------------------------------------
 C             GENERATION OF STIFFNESS MATRIX STARTS
C -----------------------------------------------------------------
C**           AT FIRST NODE --FREE END CONDITIONS   **
    DO 20 I = 1, 4
    DO 20 J = 1, 4
```

```
        A1(1, I, J) = 0.0
        A2(1, I, J) = 0.0
20      A3(1, I, J) = 0.0
      OMZ = 0.0
      OMEGAT = 0.0
      F = T1/T2
      AMDA = T1/AC
      R = D1/2.0
      RHO = R/AC
      GAMA = 1. 0/RHO
      CALL HOJO(RHO, GAMA, OMEGAT, OMZ, EN, H, GE, EW, AMDA, F)
      DO 21 I = 1, 4
      DO 21 J =1, 4
        BC1(I, J) = 0.0
21      BC2(I, J) = 0.0
      BC1(1, 1) = 1.0
      BC1(2, 2) = 1.0
      BC1(3, 3) = 1.0
      BC2(4, 4) = 1.0
      CALL ULT(BC1, H, 4, 4, 4, 4, A, DELTA1)
      CALL ULT(BC1, GE, 4, 4, 4, 4, B, 1.000)
      DO 22 I = 1, 4
      DO 22 J = 1, 4
        A1(1, I, J) = A(I, J)
22        A2(1, I, J) = –A (I, J) + B(I, J) + BC2(I, J)
      K1 = 2
      DO 60 K = 2, 16
        RHO = RHO + DELTA1
        GAMA = 1.0/RHO
       CALL CALLS1 (RHO, GAMA, F, EW, EN, OMZ, OMZT, OMEGAT,
*     AMDA, DELTA1, A, B, C)
      DO 40 I = 1, 4
      DO 40 J = 1, 4
        A1(K1, I, J) = A (I, J)
        A2(K1, I, J)B (I, J)
40    A3 (K1, I, J) = C (I, J)
      IF (K1. NE.2) GOTO 50
      KÓN = K/2
      KOUNT = ID (KON, 1)
      K4 = KOUNT
      KOUNT = 3*K4–2
      CALL BLOCK1 (KON, KOUNT)
      KOUNT = KOUNT–3
      IF (KON.GT.1) KON = KON–1
```

```
      CALL POTER1 (IT1, JT1, IT1, JT3, MS, KON, KOUNT)
      KOUNT = K4
      K1 = 1
      GO TO 60
50     K1 = K1+1
60     CONTINUE
C -----------------------------------------------------------------
      K1 = 1
C*          AT NODE 17 **
C
      K = 17
      RHO = RHO + DELTA1
      GAMA = 1.O/RHO
      CALL HOJO (RHO, GAMA, OMEGAT, OMZ, EN, HM, GEM, EW,
*     AMDA, F)
      OMEGAT = GAMA
      GAMA = 0.0
      AMDA = T2/AC
      F = 1.0
      PHI = PI/2.
      CALL HOJO (RHO GAMA OMEGAT, OMZ, EN, HP, GEP, EW, AMDA,
*     F)
      DO 70 I = 1, 4
      D0 70 J = 1, 4
70          LA1 (K1, I,J) = HP (I, J) / DELTA 1
      CALL TRANS(PHI, PSI)
      CALL CALLS2 (GEM, HM, GEP, HP, DELTA1, PSI, B, C)
      DO 80 I = 1, 4
      DO 80 J = 1, 4
        A2(K1, I, J) = B(I, J)
80      A3(K1, I, J) = C(I, J)
C
C*        AT NODE 18    ***
**    K1 = K1 + 1
      K = 18
      CALL CALLS1(RHO, GAMA, F, EW, EN, OMZ, OMZT, OMEGAT,
*     AMDA, DELTA1, A, B, C)
      MSS = 4
      CALL ULT(C, PSI, MSS, 4, 4, 4, PSIC, 1.ODO)
      DO 90 I = 1, 4
      DO 90 J = 1, 4
          A1(K1, I, J) = A (I, J)
          A2(K1, I, J) = B(I, J)
90          A3(K1, I, J) = PSIC(I, J)
```

```
      KON = K/2
      KOUNT = ID (KON, 1)
      K4 = KOUNT
      KOUNT = 3*K4-2
      CALL BLOCK1 (KON, KOUNT)
      KOUNT = KOUNT-3
      KON = KON-1
      CALL POTER1 (IT1, JT1, IT1, JT3, MS, KON, KOUNT)
      KOUNT = K4
      K1 = 1
      DO 100 I = 1, 4
      DO 100 J =1, 4
      A1 (1, I, J) = A(I, J)
      A2 (1, I, J) = B(I, J)
100   A3(K1, I, J) = C(I, J)
      DO 110 I = 1, 4
      DO 110 J = 1, 4
      A1 (2, I, J) = A1(1, I, J)
      A2 (2, I, J) = A2(1, I, J)
110   A3(2, I, J) = A3(1, I, J)
      KON = 10
      KOUNT = ID (KON, 1)
      K4 = KOUNT
      KOUNT = 3*K4-2
      CALL BLOCK1(KON, KOUNT)
      KOUNT = KOUNT-3
      KON = KON-1
      CALL POTER1(IT1, JT1, IT1, JT3, MS, KON, KOUNT)
      KOUNT = K4
      DO 120 IKON = 11, 110
        KON = IKON-1
        KOUNT = 3*ID (IKON, 1)-2
120     CALL POTER1 (IT1, JT1, IT1, JT3, MS, KON, KOUNT)
C ---------------------------------------------------------------
C***         AT NODE 222     ***
C
      DO 130 I = 1, 4
      DO 130 J = 1, 4
        A1(2, I, J) = 0.0
        A2(2, I, J) = 0.0
130     A3(2, I, J) = 0.0
      DO 140 I = 1, 4
140     A2(2, I, I) = 1.0
```

```
      KON = 111
      KOUNT = ID(KON, 1)
      K4 = KOUNT
      KOUNT = 3*K4-2
      CALL BLOCK2(KON, KOUNT)
      KOUNT = KOUNT-3
      KON = KON-1
      CALL POTER1 (IT1, JT1, IT1, JT3, MS, KON, KOUNT)
      KOUNT = K4
C
C-----------------------------------------------------------------
C**      AT NODE 224   ****
C
      K = 224
      R = D3/2.0
      RHO = R/AC
      OMZ = 0.0
      OMEGAT = 1.0/RHO
      GAMA = 0.0
      F = T3/TEST
      AMDA = T3/AC
      CALL CALL S1 (RHO, GAMA, F, EW, EN, OMZ, OMZT, OMEGAT,
*     AMDA, DELTA1, A, B, C)
      DO 150 I = 1, 4
      DO 150 J = 1, 4
       A1(2, I, J) = A(I, J)
       A2(2, I, J) = B(I, J)
150    A3(2, I, J) = C(I, J)
      KON = K/2
      KOUNT = ID(KON, 1)
      K4 = KOUNT
      KOUNT = 3*K4-2
      CALL BLOCK2(KON,KOUNT)
      DO 160 IKON = 112, 122
        KON = IKON-1
        KOUNT = 3*ID(IKON, 1)-2
160     CALL POTER1(IT1, JT1, IT1, JT3, MS, KON, KOUNT)
C
C-----------------------------------------------------------------
C**   AT NODE 246   **
C
      K=246
      CALL HOJO (RHO, GAMA, OMEGAT, OMZ, EN, HM, GEM, EW,
      AMDA, F)
      PHI = PI/2.0
      GAMA = -1.0/RHO
      OMEGAT = 0.0
```

```
      AMDA = T3/AC
      F = T3/T2
      CALL HOJO (RHO, GAMA, OMEGAT, OMZ, EN, HP, GEP, EW, AMDA,
      F)
      CALL TRANS(PHI, PSI)
      CALL CALLS2(GEM, HM, GEP, HP, DELTA1, PSI, B, C)
      DO 170 I = 1, 4
      DO 170 J = 1, 4
        A1(2, I, J) = HP(I, J)/DELTA1
        A2(2, I, J) = B(I, J)
170     A3(2, I, J) = C(I, J)
      KON = K/2
      KOUNT = ID(KON, 1)
      K4 = KOUNT
      KOUNT = 3*K4–2
      CALL BLOCK2 (KON, KOUNT)
      KOUNT = KOUNT–3
      KON = KON–1
      CALL POTER1 (IT1, JT1, IT1, JT3.MS, KON, KOUNT)
      KOUNT = K4
C
C ----------------------------------------------------------------
C**   AT NODE 248      **
C
      K = 248
      RHO = RSP1/AC+DELTA1
      GAMA = –1.0/RHO
      OMEGAT = 0.0
      AMDA = T3/AC
      F = T3/T2
      CALL CALLS1 (RHO, GAMA, F, EW, EN, OMZ, OMZT, OMEGAT,
      AMDA, DELTA1, A, B, C)
      MSS = 4
      CALL ULT (C, PSI, MSS, 4, 4, PSIC, 1.ODO)
      DO 180 I = 1, 4
      DO 180 J = 1, 4
        A1(2, I, J) = A(I, J)
        A2(2, I, J) = B(I, J)
180     A3(2, I, J) = PSIC(I, J)
      KON = K/2
      KOUNT = ID(KON, 1)
      K4 = KOUNT
      KOUNT = 3*K4–2
      CALL BLOCK2 (KON, KOUNT)
      KOUNT = KOUNT–3
      KON = KON–1
```

```
      JT1 = MS
      CALL POTER1 (IT1, JT1, IT1, JT3, MS, KON, KOUNT)
      KOUNT = K4
C
C ------------------------------------------------------------------
C ***  AT NODE 249    **
C
      DO 190 I = 1, 4
      DO 190 J = 1, 4
        BETA(I, J) = 0.0
190   ETA(I, J) = 0.0
      BETA(1, 1) = 1.0
      BETA(2, 2) = 1.0
      BETA(3, 3) = 1.0
      ETA(4, 4) = 1.0
C--------------------------------FIRST BRANCH--------------------------------
      R = D2/2.0
      RHO = R/AC
      GAMA = 0.0
      OMEGAT = 1.0/RHO
      OMZ = 0.0
      AMDA = T2/AC
      F = 1.0
      CALL HOJO (RHO, GAMA, OMEGAT, OMZ, EN, H1, GE1, EW, AMDA,
*     F)
C -----------------------------SECOND BRANCH--------------------------------
      GAMA = -OMEGAT
      OMEGAT = 0.0
      AMDA = T3/AC
      F = T3/TEST
      CALL HOJO (RHO, GAMA, OMEGAT, OMZ, EN, H2, GE2, EW, AMDA,
*     F)
C ---------------------------THIRD BRANCH----------------------------------
      OMEGAT = -GAMA
      GAMA = 0.0
      OMZ = OMEGAT
      AMDA = T2/AC
      F = 1.0
      CALL HOJO (RHO, GAMA, OMEGAT, OMZ, EN, H3, GE3, EW, AMDA,
*     F)
C ------------------------------------------------------------------
```

```
      PHI1 = 0.O
      PHI2 = -PI/2.0
      DELTA2 = DARCOS (RSP2/RSP1)/(MS2-MS1)*RSP1/AC
      CALL TRANS (PHI1, PSI1)
      CALL TRANS (PHI2, PSI2)
      CALL A1B1C1(H1, GE1, H2, GE2, H3, GE3, Q4, R3, S2, TT2, S1, TT1,
*     EM3, EN3, X2, X1, Y2, Y1, BETA, ETA, DELTA1, DELTA2, PSI1, PSI2)
      KOUNT = ID(125, 1)
      DO 189 I = 1, 12
      DO 189 J = 1, 12
        A4 (I, J) = O.O
        A5 (I, J) = 0.0
189     A6 (I, J) = 0.0
      DO 191 I = 1, 4
        I1 = I + 4
        I2 = I1 + 4
      DO 191 J = 1, 4
        J1 = J + 4
        J2 = J1 + 4
C-----------------------------------------------------------------
        A4 (I, J) = -Q4(I, J)
        A4 (I1, J) = -Q4(I, J)
        A4 (I2, J) = -EM3(I, J)
C-----------------------------------------------------------------
        A5(I, J) = S1(I, J)
        A5(I, J1) = 0.0
        A5(I, J2) = -R3(I, J)
        A5(I1, J) = 0.0
        A5(I1, J1) = S2(I, J)
        A5(I1, J2) = -R3(I, J)
        A5(I2, J) = X1(I, J)
        A5(I2, J1) = X2(I, J)
        A5(I2, J2) = -EN3(I, J)
C-----------------------------------------------------------------
        A6 (I, J) = TT1(I, J)
        A6 (I, J1) = 0.0
        A6 (I1, J) = 0.0
        A6 (I1, J1) = TT2 (I, J)
        A6 (I2, J) = Y1(I, J)
        A6 (I2, J1) = Y2(I, J)
191     CONTINUE
C-----------------------------------------------------------------
       KON = 125
       IT1 = ID(KON, 2)
       JT1 = ID(KON, 3)
       JT3 = ID (KON, 4)
```

```
      K2 = KOUNT
      KOUNT = 3*K2–2
      WRITE (01'KOUNT) ((A4 (I, J), J=1, JT1), I=1, IT1)
      WRITE (01'KOUNT) ((A5 (I, J), J = 1, IT1), I = 1, IT1)
      WRITE (01'KOUNT) ((A6 (I, J), J = 1, JT3), I = 1, IT1)
      KOUNT = K2
      KON = 124
      KOUNT = 3*K2–2
      CALL POTER1 (IT1, JT1, IT1, JT3, MS, KON, KOUNT)
      KOUNT = K2
      K1 = 1
      F = 1.0
      AMDA = T2/AC
      OMZ = AC/RSP1
      ALFAM = DARCOS (RSP2/RSP1)
      DELTA2 = ALFAM/ (MS2–MS1)*RSP1/AC
      DO 240 K = 250, 267

C ---------------------------------------------------------------
C   ALFA IS THE ANGLE BETWEEN THE TANGENT TO THE SURFACE
C     AT THE NODE UNDER CONSIDERATION AND THE VERTICAL,
C        WHICH IS THE TANGENT AT NODE 249. ALFAM IS THAT
C                    ALFA AT NODE 268
C ---------------------------------------------------------------
        ALFA = ALFAM/ (MS2–MS1) * (K–MS1)
        RHO = RSP1/AC*DCOS (ALFA)
        GAMA = –DSIN (ALPHA)/RHO
        OMEGAT = DCOS(ALPHA)/RHO
        CALL CALLS1 (RHO, GAMA, F, EW, EN, OMZ, OMZT, OMEGAT,
     *  AMDA, DELTA2, A, B, C)
        IF (K.EQ.250) GOTO 220
      DO 215 I = 1, 4
      DO 215 J = 1, 4
        A1(K1, I, J) = A(I, J)
        A2(K1, I, J) = B(I, J)
215       A3(K1, I, J) = C(I, J)
      IF (K1.NE.2) GOTO 210
      KON = K/2+1
      KOUNT = ID (KON, 1)
      IF (KON. NE.127) GO TO 213
      DO 216 I = 1, 12
      DO 216 J = 1, 12
        A4(I, J) = 0.0
        A5(I, J) = 0.0
```

```
216       A6(I, J)=0.0
      DO 211 I=1, 4
      I1=I+4
      DO 211 J=1, 4
      J1=J+4
      A4(I1, J)=-A1(2, I, J)
      A5(I, J)=-A2(1, I, J)
      A5(I, J1)=-A1(1, I, J)
      A5(I1, J1)=-A2(2, I, J)
      A5(I1, J)=-A3(2, I, J)
211       A6 (I, J)=-A3(1, I, J)
      IT1=ID (KON, 2)
      JT1=ID (KON, 3)
      JT3=ID (KON, 4)
      K2=KOUNT
      KOUNT=3*K2-2
      WRITE (01'KOUNT) ((A4(I, J), J=1, JT1), I=1, IT1)
      WRITE (01'KOUNT) ((A5(I, J), J=1, IT1), I=1, IT1)
      WRITE (01'KOUNT) ((A6(I, J), J=1, JT3), I=1, IT1)
      KOUNT=3*K2-2
      KON=KON-1
      CALL POTER1 (LT1, JT1, IT1, JT3, MS, KON, KOUNT)
      KOUNT=K2
      K1=1
      GO TO 240
213       CONTINUE
      K4=KOUNT
      KOUNT=3*K4-2
      CALL BLOCK1 (KON, KOUNT)
      KOUNT=KOUNT-3
      KON=KON-1
      JT3=8
      CALL POTER1 (IT1, JT1, IT1, JT3, MS, KON, KOUNT)
      KOUNT=K4
      K1=1
      GO TO 240
210       K1=K1+1
      GO TO 240
220       KOUNT=ID (126, 1)
   DO 222 I=1, 12
   DO 222 J=1, 12
    A4 (I, J)=0.0
    A5 (I, J)=0.0
222    A6(I, J)=0.0
```

```
      DO 221 I=1, 4
      DO 221 J=1, 4
       J1=J+4
       J2=J1+4
       A4 (I, J)=-A (I, J)
       A5 (I, J)=-B (I, J)
221      A6 (I, J)=-C(I, J)
      KON=K/2+1
      IT1=ID (KON, 2)
      JT1=ID (KON, 3)
      JT3=ID (KON, 4)
      K2=KOUNT
      KOUNT=3*K2-2
      WRITE (01'KOUNT) ((A4(I, J), J=1, JT1), I=1, IT1)
      WRITE (01'KOUNT) ((A5(I, J), J=1, IT1), I=1, IT1)
      WRITE (01'KOUNT) ((A6(I, J), J=1, JT3), I=1, IT1)
      KOUNT=3*K2-2
      KON=KON-1
      CALL POTER1 (IT1, JT1, IT1, JT3, MS, KON, KOUNT)
      KOUNT=K2
240      CONTINUE
C
***      AT MODE 268        **
C
      K=268
      K1=2
      RHO=RSP2/AC
      GAMA=-DSIN (ALFAM)/RHO
      OMEGAT=DCOS(ALFAM)/RHO
      CALL HOJO (RHO, GAMA, OMEGAT, OMZ, EN, HM, GEM,
*     EW, AMDA, F)
      GAMA=0.0
      OMEGAT=1.0/RHO
      OMZ=0.0
      AMDA=T4/AC
      F=T4/TEST
      CALL HOJO (RHO, GAMA, OMEGAT, OMZ, EN, HP, GEP, EW,
*     AMDA, F)
      PHI=-ALFAM
      CALL TRANS (PHI, PSI)
      DO 250 I=1, 4
      DO 250 J=1, 4
250      A1(K1, I, J)=HP (I, J)/DELTA1
      CALL CALLS2 (GEM, HM, GEP, HP, DELTA1, PSI, B, C)
      DO 260 I=1, 4
      DO 260 J=1, 4
         A2 (K1, I, J)=B (I, J)
```

```
260     A3 (K1, I, J)= C(I, J)
        KON=K/2+1
        KOUNT=ID (KON, 1)
        K4=KOUNT
        KOUNT=3*K4-2
        CALL BLOCK1 (KON, KOUNT)
        KOUNT=KOUNT-3
        KON=KON-1
        CALL POTER1 (IT1, JT1, IT1, JT3, MS, KON, KOUNT)
        KOUNT=K4
C
***       AT NODE 269       **
C
        K=269
        CALL CALLS1 (RHO, GAMA, F, EW, EN, OMZ, OMZT, OMEGAT,
*       AMDA, DELTA1, A, B, C)
        MSS=4
        CALL ULT (C, PSI, MSS, 4, 4, 4, PSIC, 1.000)
        DO 273  I=1, 4
        DO 273  J=1, 4
          A1(1, I, J)=A(I, J)
          A1(2, I, J)=A(I, J)
          A2(1, I, J)=B(I, J)
          A2(2, I, J)=B(I, J)
          A3(1, I, J)=PSIC(I, J)
273       A3(2, I, J)=C(I, J)
        KON=136
        KOUNT=ID (KON, 1)
        K4=KOUNT
        KOUNT=3*K4-2
        CALL BLOCK1 (KON, KOUNT)
        KOUNT=KOUNT-3
        KON-1
        CALL POTER1 (IT1, JT1, IT1, JT3, MS, KON, KOUNT)
        KOUNT=K4
        DO 274  I=1, 4
        DO 274  J=1, 4
          A1 (1, I, J)=A1(2, I, J)
          A2 (1, I, J)=A2 (2, I, J)
274       A3 (1, I, J)=A3(2, I, J)
        DO 275  I=1, 4
        DO 275  J=1, 4
          A1 (2, I, J)=A1(1, I, J)
          A2 (2, I, J)=A2 (1, I, J)
```

```
275     A3 (2, I, J)=A3(1, I, J)
      KON=137
      KOUNT=ID (137, 1)
      K4=KOUNT
      KOUNT=3*K4-2
      CALL BLOCK1 (KON, KOUNT)
      DO 280 IKON=137, 140
        KON=IKON-1
        KOUNT=3*ID (IKON, 1)-2
280     CALL POTER1 (IT1, JT1, IT1, JT3, MS, KON, KOUNT)
      KON=141
      K=280
      KOUNT=ID(KON, 1)
      DO 290 I=1, 4
      DO 290 J=1, 4
        A1(2, I, J)=0.0
        A2(2, I, J)=0.0
290     A3 (2, I, J)=0.0
      CALL HOJO (RHO, GAMA, OMEGAT, OMZ, EN, H, GE, EW, AMDA, F)
      CALL ULT (BC1, H, 4, 4, 4, 4, C, DELTA1)
      CALL ULT (BC1, GE, 4, 4, 4, 4, B, 1.000)
      DO 300 I=1, 4
      DO 300 J=1, 4
        A2 (2, I, J)=C(I, J)+B(I, J)+BC2(I, J)
300     A3(2, I, J)=-C(I, J)
      DO 301 I=1, 12
      DO 301 J=1, 12
        A4(I, J)=0.0
        A5(I, J)=0.0
301     A6(I, J)=0.0
      DO 310 I=1, 4
        I1=I+4
      DO 310 J=1, 4
        J1=J+4
        A6 (I, J1)=-A3(1, I, J)
        A5 (I, J)=-A2(1, I, J)
        A5 (I, J1)=-A1(1, I, J)
        A5 (I1, J)=-A3(2, I, J)
310     A5(I1, J1)= -A2(2, I, J)
      K1=KOUNT
      KOUNT=3*K1-2
      WRITE (01'KOUNT) ((A4(I, J), J=1, 8), I=1, 8)
```

```
      WRITE (01'KOUNT) ((A5(I, J), J=1, 8), I=1, 8)
      WRITE (01'KOUNT) ((A6(I, J), J=1,8 ), I=1, 8)
      KOUNT=K1
C
      CALL POTER2
C
      N=1128
      NEIG=5
      NIT=10
C
      CALL UNSYM(N, NEIG, NIT)
C --------------------------------
      STOP
      END
C --------------------------------
      SUBROUTINE POTER3 (K1, X, Y, N, NEIG)
C
C     SOLVES (A)* (Y)=(X)
C
C                WHERE   (A) = (K)     IF K1=2
C                        (A) = (K)T    IF K1=1

      IMPLICIT REAL*8(A-H, O-Z)
      DIMENSION Y1 (12, 12)
      DIMENSION ID(141, 4), A4(12, 12), A5(12, 12), A6(12, 12), PA(12, 12),
    *  PC(12, 12), PRUN (12, 12), QRUN(12, 12), Z(12, 12), X(N, NEIG),
    *  Y (N, NEIG), FORCE(12, 12), X1(12, 12), X2(12, 12), PB(12, 12)
      COMMON/COM2/ID
      COMMON/COM3/AM(1128)
      PRINT 1003
1003      FORMAT (/10X, 'POTER3 CALLED'/)
       PRINT 1004, K1
1004   FORMAT (/10X, 'K1 (POTER3)=', I10)
      AMU=0. 1E+05
      MS=12
      DO 1 I=1, 12
      DO 1 J=1, 12
        PB(I, J)=0.0
        PC(I, J)=0.0
        A5(I, J)=0.0
        A6(I, J)=0.0
        A4(I, J)=0.0
        FORCE (I, J)=0.0
```

```
1         QRUN(I, J)=0.0
        KIT1=1
        DO 100 IKON=1, 141
          KOUNT=ID (IKON, 1)
        IT1=ID (IKON, 2)
        JT1=ID (IKON, 3)
        JT3=ID(IKON, 4)
        KIT2=KIT1+IT1-1
C -----------------------------------------------------------------
         L=1
        DO 10 I=KIT1, KIT2
        DO 20 J=1, NEIG
20       FORCE (L, J)=X(I, J)
10       L=L+1
         KIT1=KIT2+1
C -----------------------------------------------------------------
        IF (K1.EQ.1) GO TO 1010
        IF (IKON.EQ.1) GO TO 91
        KON=IKON-1
        READ(02'KON) ((PRUN (I, J), J=1, IT1), I=1, JT3)
91        K2=KOUNT
        KOUNT=3*K2-1
        READ (01'KOUNT) ((A5 (1, J), J=1, IT1), I=1, IT1)
        KOUNT=3*K2
        READ (01'KOUNT) ((A6 (1, J), J=1, JT3), I=1,IT1)
        KOUNT=K2
        DO 30 I=1, 12
        DO 30 J=1, 12
          PB (I, J)=A5(I, J)
30          PC(I, J)=A6(I, J)
        GO TO 90
C -----------------------------------------------------------------
1010        KON1=IKON-1
        IF (IKON.EQ.1) GO TO 1013
        KON=IKON+140-1
        READ (02'KON) ((PRUN(I, J), J=1, IT1), I=1, JT3)
1013        KOUNT=3*KOUNT-1
        READ (01'KON) ((A5 (I, J), J=1, IT1), I=1, IT1)
        IF (IKON.EQ. 1) GO TO 1012
        KOUNT=ID(KON1, 1)
        KOUNT=3*KOUNT-2
        READ (01'KOUNT) ((A4 (I, J), J=1, IT1), I=1, JT3)
```

```
1012      DO 1011 I=1, 12
      DO 1011 J=1, 12
      PB (I, J)=A5 (J, I)
1011      PC(I, J)=A4(J, I)
C ------------------------------------------------------------------
90        IF (IKON. EQ. 1) GO TO 50
      CALL ULT (PC, PRUN, MS, IT1, JT3, IT1, X1, -1,0D0)
      CALL ADD (PB, X1, MS, IT1, IT1, X1, 1.0D0)
       CALL JAI(X1, MS, IT1)
      CALL ULT (PC, QRUN, MS, IT1, JT3, NEIG, X2, -1.0D0)
      CALL ADD (FORCE, X2, MS, IT1, NEIG, X2, 1.0D0)
      CALL ULT(X1, X2, MS, IT1, IT1, NEIG, QRUN, 1.0D0)
      GO TO 60
50        CALL JAI (PB, MS, IT1)
      CALL ULT (PB, FORCE, MS, IT1, IT1, NEIG, QRUN, 1.0D0)
60        WRITE (O3'IKON) ((QRUN (I,J), J=1,NEIG),I=1,IT1)
100       CONTINUE
C         RUNNING BACK
      KIT1=KIT2-IT1+1
      L=1
       DO 120 I=KIT1, KIT2
      DO 110 J=1, NEIG
          Z(L, J)=QRUN(L, J)
110       Y(I, J)=QRUN(L, J)
120         L = L + 1
      DO 230 K = 1, 140
            KON = 141 - K
            IT1 = ID (KON, 2)
            JT1 = ID (KON, 3)
            IF (K1. EQ. 1) KON = KON + 140
            READ (02 'KON) ((PRUN (I, J), J = 1, JT1), I = 1, IT1)
            IF (K1. EQ. 1) KON = KON - 140
            CALL ULT (PRUN, Z, MS, IT1, JT1, NEIG, Y1, - 1.000)
            IKON = 141 - K
            READ (03' IKON) ( (QRUN (I, J), J = 1, NEIG), I = 1, IT1)
            CALL ADD (Y1, QRUN, MS, IT1, NEIG, Z, 1.OOO)
            KIT2 = KIT1 - 1
            KIT1 = KIT2 - IT1 + 1
            L = 1
      DO 170 I = KIT1, KIT2
      DO 180 J = 1, NEIG
180         Y(I, J) = Z(L, J)
```

```
170          L = L + 1
230        CONTINUE
         RETURN
         END
C -------------------------------------------------------------------
      SUBROUTINE UNSYM (N, NEIG, NIT)
C **    METHOD :-
C **    EIGENVALUE PROBLEM FOR UNSYMMETRIC
C **    MATRICES OF THE TYPE A * X = LAMBDA * B * X
C **    DESCRIPTION OF PARAMETERS
C **          N         ORDER OF THE MATRIX A
C **          IC        NO. OF EIGENVALUES REQUIRED
C **          NIT        NO. OF ITERATIONS
C **          A         INPUT STIFFNESS MATRIX
C **          B         INPUT MASS MATRIX
C **      X1, X2, RIGHT AND LEFT EIGENVECTORS
C **      YX1, YXT1, XT1, XT2 ARE WORKING VECTORS
C **      SUBROUTINES REQUIRED :-
C **        SOLVE
C **        DMAT
C **        DLLT
           IMPLICIT REAL * 8 (A-H, O-Z)
           DIMENSION AM (1128)
       *   ,XT1 (1128, 5), XT2 (1128, 5)
       *   ,YX1 (1128, 5), D (5, 5),
       *   DU (5, 5), DLT (5, 5), BE (5, 5)
           DIMENSION ID (141, 4)
           DIMENSION A5 (12, 12)
           DIMENSION D1 (5, 5)
           DIMENSION X2 (1128, 5), X1 (1128, 5)
           DIMENSION RR (12, 5), ZZ (1128, 5)
           DIMENSION AA (12, 36)
           DIMENSION A4 (12, 12), A6 (12, 12)
           COMMON/COM5/X1
           COMMON/COM6/X2, ZZ
           COMMON/COM2/ID
           COMMON/COM3/AM
C **
C **    INITIAL TRIAL VECTORS
C **
      PRINT 1117
1117    FORMAT (/10X, 'UNSYM CALLED' /)
      DO 120 I = 1, N
      DO 120 J = 1, NEIG
```

```
120       YX1(I, J) = 0.0
      YX1 (79, 1) = 1.0
      YX1 (699, 2) = 1.0
      YX1 (119, 3) = 1.0
      YX1 (799, 3) = - 1.0
      YX1 (99, 4) = 1.0
      YX1 (439, 4) = - 1.0
      YX1 (839, 4) = 1.0
      YX1 (79, 5) = 1.0
      YX1 (239, 5) = - 1.0
      YX1 (399, 5) = 1.0
      YX1 (599, 5) = - 1.0
      YX1 (719, 5) = 1.0

C **
C **  ITERATION STARTS
C **  II = 1
      K1 = 1
      DO 2001 I = 1, N
      DO 2001 J = 1, NEIG
        XT1 (I, J) = YX1 (I, J)
2001      XT2 (I, J) = YX1 (I, J)
      GO TO 2002
C ------------------------------------------------------------
194       DO 195 I = 1, N
      DO 195 J = 1, NEIG
195       YX1 (I, J) = AM (I) * YX1 (I, J)
C ------------------------------------------------------------
160       IF (II. NE. 1. AND. K1. EQ. 1) GO TO 170
      K1 = 1
      CALL POTER3 (K1, YX1, XT2, N, NEIG)
      II = II + 1
      GO TO 250
170       K1 = 2
      CALL POTER3 (K1, YX1, XT1, N, NEIG)
------------------------ORTHONORMALISATION ---------------
2002      DO 110 I = 1, NEIG
      DO 110 J = 1, NEIG
110     D1 (I, J) = 0.0
      CALL DMAT (XT2, XT1, N, NEIG, D)
      PRINT 171, II
171       FORMAT (/10X, 'NO. OF ITERATION = ', I10/)
      CALL DLLT (D, NEIG)
      IF (II. EQ. NIT) GO TO 250
```

```
          D0 111 I = 1, NEIG
      DO 111 J = 1, NEIG
111       D1 (I, J) = D (I, J)
      CALL SOLVE (D1, XT2, X2, NEIG, N)
          DO 115 I = 1, NEIG
      DO 115 J = 1, NEIG
115       YX1 (I, J) = X2 (I, J)
      GO TO 194
250       DO 112 I = 1, NEIG
      DO 112 J = 1, NEIG
112       D1 (I, J) = D (I, J)
      CALL SOLVE (D1, XT1, X1, NEIG, N)
      IF (II. NE. NIT) GO TO 2053
      GO TO 251
2053      CONTINUE
        DO 116 I = 1, N
      DO 116 J = 1, NEIG
116       YX1 (I, J) = X1 (I, J)
C ------------------INTERACTION MATRIX------------------
      DO 1002 I = 1, 2
      DO 1002 J = 1, 36
1002   AA (I, J) = 0.0
      N1 = 1
      NBCOL = 1
      DO 1001 I = 1, N
      DO 1001 J = 1, NEIG
1001   ZZ (I, J) = 0.0
      KON = 1
      KOUNT = ID (KON, 1)
      IT1 = ID (KON, 2)
      JT1 = ID (KON, 3)
      JT3 = ID (KON, 4)
      K9 = KOUNT
      KOUNT = 3 * K9 – 2
      READ (01 'KOUNT) ((A4 (I, J), J = 1, JT1), I = 1, IT1)
      KOUNT = 3 * K9 – 1
      READ (01 'KOUNT) ((A5 (I, J), J = 1, IT1), I = 1, IT1)
      KOUNT = K9
      DO 1010 I = 1, IT1
      DO 1010 J = 1, IT1
1010   AA (I, J) = A5 (I, J)
      K5 = IT1 + 1
      K6 = K5 + JT1 – 1
      DO 1011 I = 1, IT1
```

```
        L = 1
      DO 1011 J = K5, K6
        AA(I,J) = A4 (I, L)
1011      L = L + 1
1012      CONTINUE
      N2 = N1 + IT1 + JT1 – 1
      CALL MULT1(AA, N1, N2, RR, IT1)
      DO 1013 L = 1, IT1
      DO 1014 I = 1, NEIG
1014    ZZ (NBCOL, I) = RR (L, I)
1013    NBCOL = NBCOL + 1
      DO 1100 KON = 2, 140
      DO 1015 I = 1, 12
      DO 1015 J = 1, 36
1015    AA (I, J) = 0.0
      KOUNT = ID (KON, 1)
      IT1 = ID (KON, 2)
      JT1 = ID (KON, 3)
      JT3 = ID (KON, 4)
      K9 = KOUNT
      KOUNT = 3 * K9 – 2
      READ (01 'KOUNT) ((A4 (I, J), J = 1, JT1), I = 1, IT1)
      KOUNT = 3 * K9 – 1
      READ (01 'KOUNT) ((A5 (I, J), J = 1, IT1), I = 1, IT1)
      KOUNT 3 * K9
      READ (01 'KOUNT) ( (A6 (I, J), J = 1, JT3), I = 1, IT1)
      DO 1003 I = 1, IT1
      DO 1003 J = 1, JT3
1003    AA (I, J) = A6 (I, J)
      K5 = JT3 + 1
      K6 = K5 + IT1 – 1
      DO 1004 I = 1, IT1
        L = 1
      DO 1005 J = K5, K6
        AA (I, J) = A5 (I, J)
1005    L = L + 1
1004      CONTINUE
      K5 = K6 + 1
      K6 = K5 + JT1 – 1
      DO 1006 I = 1, IT1
        L = 1
      DO 1007 J = K5, K6
        AA (I, J) = A4 (I, L)
1007  L = L + 1
1006  CONTINUE
```

```
      N1 = NBCOL – JT3
      N2 = N1 + IT1 + JT1 + JT3 – 1
      CALL MULT1 (AA, N1, N2, RR, IT1)
      DO 1009 L = 1, IT1
      DO 1008 I = 1, 5
1008    ZZ (NBCOL, I) = RR (L, I)
1009    NBCOL = NBCOL + 1
1100    CONTINUE
      KON = 141
      N1 = 1113
      N2 = 1128
      DO 4115 I = 1, 12
      DO 4115 J = 1, 36
4115    AA (I, J) = 0.0
      KOUNT = ID (KON, 1)
      IT1 = ID (KON, 2)
      JT1 = ID (KON, 3)
      JT3 = ID (KON, 4)
      K9 = KOUNT
      KOUNT = 3 * K9 – 1
      READ (01 'KOUNT) ((A5 (I, J), J = 1, IT1), I = 1, IT1)
      KOUNT = 3 * K9
      READ (01 'KOUNT) ((A6 (I, J), J = 1, JT3), I = 1, IT1)
      KOUNT = K9
      DO 4110 I = 1, IT1
      DO 4110 J = 1, JT3
4110    AA (I, J) = A6 (I, J)
      K5 = JT3 + 1
      K6 = K5 + IT1 – 1
      DO 4111 I = 1, IT1
        L = 1
      DO 4112 J = K5, K6
        AA (I, J) = A5 (I, L)
4112    L = L + 1
4111    CONTINUE
      CALL MULT1 (AA, N1, N2, RR, IT1)
      DO 4114 L = 1, IT1
      DO 4113 I = 1, NEIG
4113     ZZ (NBCOL, I) = RR (L, I)
4114     NBCOL = NBCOL + 1
      CALL MULT2 (BE)
      WRITE (6, 1000)
      WRITE (6, 2000) ((BE (I, J), J = 1, NEIG), I = 1, NEIG)
      GO TO 194
C -----------------------------------------------------------
```

```
C **  ITERATION ARE OVER
251      WRITE (6, 3000)
      DO 400 I = 1, NEIG
         X = DSQRT (BE (I, I))
400      WRITE (6, 4000) I, X
1000     FORMAT (/, 10X, 'INTERACTION MATRIX', /)
2000     FORMAT (5D15. 5/)
3000     FORMAT (/, 10X, 'NATURAL FREQ. IN RAD/SEC. ', /)
4000     FORMAT (/, 10X, 'FREQ (', I3, ') = ', D20. 10/)
      PRINT 4001
4001     FORMAT (/, 10X, 'EIGENVECTORS ARE ', /)
      PRINT 4002
4002     FORMAT (/, 10X, ' X1  IS ', /)
      PRINT 4003, ((X1 (I, J), J = 1, NEIG), I = 1, N)
4003    FORMAT (/10X, 10E12. 3)
      PRINT 4004
4004     FORMAT (///)
   *    WRITE (04) ((X1 (I, J), J = 1, NEIG), I = 1, N), ((X2 (I, J), J = 1, NE (G), I
        = 1, N),
        ((BE (I, J), J = 1, NEIG), I = 1, NEIG), (AM (I), I = 1, N)
        RETURN
        END
C ------------------------------------------------------------------------
      SUBROUTINE MULT1 (AA, N1, N2, RR, IT1)
      IMPLICIT REAL * 8 (A–H, O–Z)
      DIMENSION AA (12, 36), RR (12, 5), X1 (1128, 5)
      COMMON/COM5/X1
      DO 1 I = 1, IT1
      DO 2 J = 1, 5
        RR (I, J) = 0.0
        L = 1
      DO 3, K = N1, N2
        RR (I, J) = RR (I, J) + AA (I, L) * X1 (K, J)
3          L = L + 1
2          CONTINUE
1          CONTINUE
      RETURN
      END
C ------------------------------------------------------------------------
      SUBROUTINE MULT2 (BE)
      IMPLICIT REAL*8  (A–H, O–Z)
      DIMENSION BE (5, 5), X2 (1128, 5), ZZ(1128, 5)
      COMMON/COM6/X2, ZZ
      DO 1 I = 1, 5
      DO 1 J =1, 5
        BE(I, J) = 0.0
      DO 1 K = 1, 1128
```

```
1       BE(I, J) = BE(I, J) + X2(K, I)*ZZ(K, J)
      RETURN
      END
C ----------------------------------------------------------------
      SUBROUTINE SOLVE (D, V, U, IC, N)
C**     FIND U FORM U*D = V
**      D-UPPER TRIANGULAR MATRIX (IC*IC)
**      V-KNOWN VECTOR (N*IC)
**      U-ORTHO-NORMALIZED VECTOR (N*IC)
      IMPLICIT REAL*8(A-H, O-Z)
      DIMENSION D(IC, IC), V(N, IC), U(N, IC)
      DO 10 I = 1, N
      DO 10 J = 1, IC
      JI = J-1
      IF (J. EQ. 1) U(I, J) = V(I, J)/D(J, J)
      IF(J. EQ. 1)) GO TO 10
      X = 0.0
      DO 20 K = 1, J1
20      X = U(I, K)*D(K, J) + X
      X = V(I, J)-X
      U(I, J) = X/D(J, J)
10      CONTINUE
      RETURN
      END
C ----------------------------------------------------------------
      SUBROUTINE DMAT (A, B, N, IC, D)
      IMPLICIT REAL*8(A-H, O-Z)
      DIMENSION A(1128,5 ), B(1128, 5), AM(128), D(IC, IC)
      COMMON/COM3/AM
      DO 260 I = 1, IC
      DO 260 J = 1, IC
        D(I, J) = 0.0
      DO 270 K = 1, N
C ----------------------------------------------------------------
270     D(I, J) = D(I, J) + A(K, I)*AM(K)*B(K, J)
260     CONTINUE
      PRINT 271
271     FORMAT (/10X,' D MATRIX IS '/)
       PRINT 272, ((D(I, J), J = 1, 5), I = 1, 5)
272     FORMAT (/10X, 5E15.5)
      RETURM
      END
C ----------------------------------------------------------------
      SUBROUTINE DLLT(B, N)
C **
**    DECOMPOSE D MATRIX AS L1*L2(T)
C **
```

```
       IMPLICIT REAL*8(A–H, O–Z)
       DIMENSION B(N, N)
       DO 10 I = I, N
       IN = I-1
         DO 10 J = I, N
          SUM1 = B(J, I)
          SUM = B(I, J)
        IF(I–1) 6, 6, 4
C       CONTINUE
4       DO 5 K = 1, IN
        SUM1 = SUM1–B(J, K)*B(K, I)
5       SUM = SUM–B (I, K) *B(K, J)
6          IF(J–I) 7, 8, 7
7          B(I, J) = SUM*TEMP
           B(J, I) = SUM1*TEMP
        GO TO 10
8       B(I, I) = DABS(SUM)
        B(I, I) = DSQRT (B(I, I))
        TEMP = 1.0/B(I, I)
10         CONTINUE
        RETURN
        END
C ----------------------------------------------------------------
        SUBROUTINE POTER1(IT1, JT1, JT2, JT3, MS, /KON/, /KOUNT/)
        IMPLICIT REAL*8(A–H, O–Z)
        DIMENSION A4(12, 12), A5(12, 12), A6(12, 12)
        DIMENSION PRUN (12, 12), X(12, 12)
        COMMON/COM3/AM(1128)
        AMU = 0. 1E + 05
        DO 111    = 1, 12
        DO 111 J = 1, 12
111        PRUN(I, J) = 0.0
        READ (O1' KOUNT) ((A4(I, J), J = 1, JT1), I = 1, IT1)
        READ (O1' KOUNT) ((A5(I, J), J = 1, IT1), I = 1, IT1)
        READ (O1' KOUNT) ((A6(I, J), J = 1, JT3), I = 1, IT1)
        IF (KOUNT. EQ.4) GO TO 2
        READ (O2'KON) ((PRUN(I, J), J = 1, IT1), I = 1, JT3)
7          CALL ULT (A6, PRUN, MS, IT1, JT3, IT1, X, –1.0D0)
        CALL ADD(A5, X, MS, IT1, IT1, X, 1.0D0)
        CALL JAI(X, MS, IT1)
        CALL ULT(X, A4, MS, IT1, IT1, JT1, PRUN, 1.ODO)
        GO TO 3
2          CONTINUE
        CALL JAI(A5, MS, IT1)
        CALL ULT(A5, A4, MS, IT1, IT1, JT1,P RUN, 1.0D0)
```

```
3      WRITE(02'KON) ((PRUN(I, J), J = 1, JT1), I = 1, IT1)
       RETURN
       END
C ---------------------------------------------------------------
        SUBROUTINE POTER2
        IMPLICIT REAL*8(A–H, O–Z)
        DIMENSION A4(12, 12), A5, (12, 12), A6(12, 12),
     *  PA(12, 12), PB(12, 12), PC(12, 12), X(12, 12), PTRUN (12, 12)
        DIMENSION ID(141, 4)
        COMMON/COM2/ID
        COMMON/COM3/AM(1128)
        AMU = 0.1E + 05
        PRINT 1117
1117    FORMAT (/10X, 'POTER2 CALLED'/)
       IKON = 1
         IT1 = ID(IKON, 2)
         JT1 = ID(IKON, 3)
         JT3 = ID(IKON, 4)
       MS = 12
       DO 16 I = 1, 12
       DO 16 J = 1, 12
       A4(I, J) = 0.0
       A5(I, J) = 0.0
16       A6(I, J) = 0. 0
       KOUNT = 2
       READ(O1' KOUNT) ((A5(I, J), J = 1, IT1), I = 1, IT1)
       KOUNT = 6
       READ (01' KOUNT) ((A5(I, J), J = 1, IT1), I = 1, IT1)
       DO 1 I = 1, 12
       DO 1 J = 1, 12
         PA(I, J) = A6(J, I)
         PB(I, J) = A5(J, I)
1          PC(I, J) = 0.0
       CALL JAI(PB, MS, IT1)
       CALL ULT(PB, PA, MS, IT1, IT1, JT1, PTRUN, 1.0D0)
       KON = IKON + 140
       WRITE (02'KON) ((PTRUN (I, J), J = 1, JT1), I = 1, IT1)
       DO 5 IKON = 2, 140
         KON1 = IKON–1
         KON2 = IKON + 1
       DO 15 I = 1, 12
       DO 15 J = 1, 12
15       PTRUN(I, J) = 0.0
       KON = KON1 + 140
       KOUNT = ID (IKON, 1)
       IT1 = ID(IKON, 2)
```

```
      JT1 = ID(IKON, 3)
      JT3 = ID(IKON, 4)
      READ (02'KON) ((PTRUN (I, J), J = 1, IT1), I = 1, JT3)
      KOUNT = 3*KOUNT-1
      READ (01' KOUNT) ((A5 (I, J), J = 1, IT1), I = 1, IT1)
      KOUNT = ID(KON1, 1)
      KOUNT = 3*KOUNT-2
      READ (01' KOUNT) ((A4 (I, J), J = 1, IT1), I = 1, JT3)
      KOUNT = 3*ID(KON2, 1)
      READ (01' KOUNT) ((A6(I, J), J = 1, IT1), I = 1, JT1)
      DO 3 I = 1, 12
      DO 3 J = 1, 12
         PA(I, J) = A6(J, I)
         PB (I, J) = A5 (J, I)

3           PC(I, J) = A4(J, I)
      IF(IKON.NE.111) GO TO 2000
      DO 2001 I = 5, 8
      DO 2001 J = 5, 8
2001     PA(I, J) = 0.0
2000  CONTINUE
      CALL ULT(PC, PTRUN, MS, IT1, JT3, IT1, X, -1.0D0)
      CALL ADD (PB, X, MS, IT1, IT1, X, 1.0D0)
      CALL JAI (X, MS, IT1)
      CALL ULT(X, PA, MS, IT1, IT1, JT1, PTRUN, 1.0D0)
      KON = IKON + 140
      WRITE (02'KON) ((PTRUN (I, J), J = 1, JT1), I = 1, IT1)
5        CONTINUE
      RETURN
      END
C -----------------------------------------------------------------
       SUBROUTINE A1B1C1 (H1, GE1, H2, GE2, H3, GE3, A1, B1, C1, D1,
     * A2, B2,
       A3, B3, C3, D3, E3, F3, B3, BETA, ETA, DELTA1, DELTA2, PSI1,
       PSI2)
     * IMPLICIT REAL*8(A-H, O-Z)
     * DIMENSION A1 (4, 4), B1 (4, 4), C1 (4, 4), D1(4, 4), A2(4, 4), B2(4, 4),
     * A3(4, 4), B3(4, 4), C3(4, 4), D3(4, 4), E3(4, 4), F3(4, 4), ETA(4, 4),
     * BETA(4, 4), H1(4, 4), GE1 (4, 4), H2(4, 4), GE2(4, 4), H3(4, 4), GE3(4,
       4), PSI1 (4, 4), PSI2(4, 4), BEPS1 (4, 4), BEPS2(4, 4), BEJ1(4, 4), BEJ2(4,
       4), ETAJ1(4, 4), ETAJ2(4, 4), ETAJ3(4, 4), BETAG3(4, 4)
       MS=4
       CALL ULT (ETA, H3, MS, 4, 4, 4, A1, DELTA2)
       CALL ULT (ETA, H1, MS, 4, 4, 4, B2, -DELTA1)
       CALL ULT (ETA, H2, MS, 4, 4, 4, D1, -DELTA1)
       CALL ULT (BETA, PSI1, MS, 4, 4, 4, BEPS1, 1.0D0)
```

```
      CALL ULT (BEPS1, GE1, MS, 4, 4, 4, BEJ1, 1.0D0)
      CALL ULT (BEPS1, GE1, MS, 4, 4, 4, BEJ1, 1.0D0)
      CALL ULT (BETA, PS12, MS, 4, 4, 4, BEPS2, 1.0D0)
      CALL ULT (BEPS2, H2, MS, 4, 4, 4, E3, -DELTA1)
      CALL ULT (BEPS1, GE2, MS, 4, 4, 4, BEJ2, 1.0D0)
      CALL ULT (ETA, GE1, MS, 4, 4, 4, ETAJ1, 1.0D0)
      CALL ULT (ETA, GE2, MS, 4, 4, 4, ETAJ2, 1.0D0)
      CALL ULT (ETA, GE3, MS, 4, 4, 4, ETAJ3, 1.0D0)
      CALL ULT (BETA, H3, MS, 4, 4, 4, A3, DELTA2)
      CALL ULT (BETA, GE3, MS, 4, 4, 4, BETAG3, 1.0D0)
      DO 1 I = 1, 4
      DO 1 J = 1, 4

        BI(I, J) = BETA(I, J)-A1(I, J) + ETAJ3(I, J)
        C1(I, J) = BEPS2(I, J)-D1(I, J) + ETAJ2(I, J)
        A2(I,J) = BEPS1(I,J)-B2(I, J) + ETAJ1(I, J)
        B3(I, J) = ETA(I, J) + BETAG3(I, J)-A3(I, J)
        C3(I, J) = -E3(I, J) + BEJ2(I, J) + ETA(I, J)
1       D3(I, J) = -F3(I, J) + BEJ1(I, J) + ETA(I, J)
        RETURN
        END
C --------------------------------------------------------------
      SUBROUTINE CALLS1 (RHO, GAMA, F, EW, EN, OMZ, OMZT,
    * OMEGAT, AMDA, DELTA, A, B, C)
      IMPLICIT REAL*8(A-H, O-Z)
      DIMENSION A(4, 4), B(4, 4), C(4, 4)
       DIMENSION E(4,4 ), FE(4, 4), G(4, 4)
      CALL GARY (RHO, GAMA, OMEGAT, OMZ, OMZT, EN, G, EW,
    * AMDA,
      F)
    * CALL ELFI(RHO, GAMA, OMEGAT, OMZ, OMZT, EN, E, FE, EW,
      AMDA, F)
      CALL BACHUS(A, B, C, E, FE, G, DELTA)
      RETURN
      END
C --------------------------------------------------------------
      SUBROUTINE CALLS2(GEM, HM, GEP, HP, DELTA, PSI, B, C)
      IMPLICIT REAL*8(A-H, O,Z)
      DIMENSION GEM (4, 4), HM(4, 4), GEP(4, 4), HP(4, 4), PSI(4, 4)
      DIMENSION B(4, 4), C(4, 4), GH(4, 4), GHPS(4, 4), GEH(4, 4), SIGE(4, 4)
        MS=4
      CALL ADD(GEP, HP, MS, 4, 4, 4, GH, -DELTA)
      CALL ULT(GH, PSI, MS, 4, 4, 4, GHPS, 1.0D0)
      CALL ADD(GEM, HM, MS, 4, 4, GEH, DELTA)
      CALL ULT(PSI, GEH, MS, 4, 4, 4, SIGE, 1.0D0)
      CALL ADD (GHPS, SIGE, MS, 4, 4, 4, B, -1.0D0)
      CALL ULT(PSI, HM, MS, 4, 4, 4, C, DELTA,
```

```
      RETURN
      END
C -----------------------------------------------------------------
      SUBROUTINE BLOCK1(KON, KOUNT)
      IMPLICIT REAL*8(A-H, O-Z)
      DIMENSION A1(2, 4, 4), A2(2, 4, 4), A3(2, 4, 4), A4(12, 12), A5(12, 12),
*     A6(12)
      DIMENSION ID(141, 4)
      COMMON/COM1/A1, A2, A3
      COMMON/COM2/ID
      IT1 = ID(KON, 2)
      JT1 = ID(KON, 3)
      JT3 = ID(KON, 4)
      DO 1 I = 1, 12
      DO 1 J = 1, 12
        A4(I, J) = 0.0
        A5(I, J) = 0.0
1       A6(I, J) = 0.0
      DO 2 I = 1, 4
        I1 = I + 4
      DO 2 J = 1, 4
        J1 = J + 4
        A4(I1, J) = -A1(2, I, J)
        A6(I, J1) = -A3(1, I, J)
        A5(I, J) = -A2(1, I, J)
        A5(I, J1) = -A1(1, I, J)
        A5(I1, J) = -A3(2, I, J)
2       A5(I1, J1) = -A2(2, I, J)
      WRITE (01'KOUNT) ((A4(I, J), J = 1, JT1), I = 1, IT1)
      WRITE (01'KOUNT) ((A5(I, J), J = 1, IT1), I = 1, IT1)
      WRITE (01'KOUNT) ((A6(I, J), J = 1, JT3), I = 1, IT1)
      RETURN
      END
C -----------------------------------------------------------------
      SUBROUTINE BLOCK2(KON, KOUNT)
      IMPLICIT REAL*8(A-H, O-Z)
      DIMENSION A1(2, 4, 4), A2(2, 4, 4), A3(2, 4, 4), A4(12, 12), A5(12, 12),
*     A6(12, 12), ID(141, 4)
      COMMON/COM1/A1, A2, A3
      COMMON/COM2/ID
      IT1 = ID(KON, 2)
      JT1 = ID(KON, 3)
      JT3 = ID(KON, 4)
      DO 1 I = 1, 12
      DO 1 J = 1, 12
        A4(I, J) = 0.0
        A5(I, J) = 0.0
```

```
1         A6(I, J) = 0.0
        DO 2 I = 1, 4
          I1 = I + 4
        DO 2 J = 1, 4
          J1 = J + 4
          A4(I, J) = -A1(1, I, J)
          A5(I, J) = -A2(1, I, J)
          A4(I1, J1) = -A1(2, I, J)
          A5(I1, J1) = -A2(2, I, J)
          IF(KON.EQ.111)GO TO 3
          A6(I1, J) = -A3(1, I, J)
          A6(I1, J1) = -A3(2, I, J)
          GO TO 2
3         A6(I, J1) = -A3(1, I, J)
2         CONTINUE
        WRITE(01'KOUNT)((A4(I, J), J = 1, JT1), I = 1, IT1)
        WRITE(01'KOUNT)((A5(I, J), J = 1, IT1), I = 1, IT1)
        WRITE(01'KOUNT)((A6(I, J), J = 1, JT3), I = 1, IT1)
        RETURN
        END
C ---------------------------------------------------------------
      SUBROUTINE BACHUS(A, BN, C, E, FE, G, DELTA)
C**********CALCULATION OF A, B, C, MATRICES**************
        IMPLICIT REAL*8(A-H, O-Z)
        DIMENSION A(4, 4), B(4, 4), C(4, 4), E(4, 4), FE(4, 4), G(4, 4)
        DO 100 I = 1, 4
          DO 100 J = 1, 4
             A(I, J) = 0.0D0
             B(I, J) = 0.0D0
100     C(I, J)=0.0D0
        D0 110 I = 1, 4
          DO 110 J = 1, 4
             A(I, J) = 2 *E(I, J)/DELTA + FE(I, J)
             B(I, J) = -4.0*E(I, J)/DELTA + 2.0*DELTA*G(I, J)
110     C(I, J) = 2.*E(I, J)/DELTA-FE(I, J)
        RETURN
        END
C******************
        SUBROUTINE TRANS(PHI, PSI)
        IMPLICIT REAL*8(A-H, O-Z)
        DIMENSION PSI(4, 4)
        DO 111 I = 1, 4
            DO 111 J = 1, 4
        PSI(I, J) = 0
```

```
111   PSI(I, I) = 1.0
      PSI(1, 1) = DCOS(PHI)
      PSI(1, 3) = –DSIN(PHI)
      PSI(3, 1) = –PSI(1, 3)
      PSI(3, 3) = PSI(1, 1)
      RETURN
      END
C –––––––––––––––––––––––––––––––––––––––––––––––––––––––––––
      SUBROUTINE ADD(A, B, MS, IT, JT, C, T)
      IMPLICIT REAL*8(A–H, O–Z)
      DIMENSION A(MS, MS), B(MS, MS), C(MS, MS)
      DO 11 I = 1, IT
      DO 11 J = 1, JT
11       C(I, J) = A(I,J) + B(I,J)/T
      RETURN
      END
C**********************************************************
      SUBROUTINE ADDI(A, B, MS, IT, C, T)
      DIMENSION A(MS, 1), B(MS, 1), C(MS, 1)
      DO 11 I = 1, IT
11    C(I, 1) = A(I, 1) + B(I, 1)/T
      RETURN
      END
C****************************************
      SUBROUTINE ULT(A, B, MS, IT, JT, KT, C, T)
      IMPLICIT REAL*8(A–H, O–Z)
      DIMENSION A(MS, MS), B(MS, MS), C(MS, MS)
      DO 10 I = 1, IT
      DO 10 K = 1, KT
      C(I, K) = 0
10    DO 10 J = 1, JT    C(I, K) = C(I, K) + A(I, J)*B(J, K)/T
      RETURN
      END
C**********************************************************
      SUBROUTINE ULT1(A, B, MS, IT, JT, C, T)
      DIMENSION A(MS, MS), B(MS, 1), C(MS, 1)
      DO 11 I = 1, IT
        C(I, 1) = 0.0
        DO 11 K = 1, KT
11         C(I, 1) =C(I, 1) + A(I, J)*B(J, 1)/T
      RETURN
      END
C**********************************************************
```

```
      SUBROUTINE JAI(AE, MS, NZ)
      IMPLICIT REAL*8(A-H, O-Z)
      DIMENSION AE(MS, MS), BX(100), CE(100)
      NN = NZ - 1
      AE(1, 1) = 1. /AE(1, 1)
      DO 1110 M = 1, NN
      K= M + 1
      DO 1160 I = 1, M
      BX(I) = 0.
      DO 1160 J =1, M
1160    BX(I) = BX(I) + AE(I, J)*AE(J, K)
      D=0
      DO 1170 I=1, M
1170    D = D + AE(K, I)*BX(I)
      D = -D + AE(K, K)
1175    AE(K, K) =1./D
      DO 1180 I = 1, M
1180    AE(I, K) = -BX(I)*AE(K, K)
      DO 1190 J = 1, M
      CE(J) = 0
      DO 1190 I = 1, M
1190    CE(J) = CE(J) + AE(K, I)*AE(I, J)
      DO 1100 J = 1, M
1100    AE(K, J) = -CE(J) * AE(K, K)
      DO 1110 I = 1, M
      DO 1110 J = 1, M
1110    AE(I, J) = AE(I, J) - BX(I)*AE(K, J)
1111    CONTINUE
      RETURN
      END
C -----------------------------------------------------------------
      SUBROUTINE GARY(R, GAMA, OMEGAT, OMZ, OMZT, EN, G, EW,
*     AMDA, F)
      IMPLICIT REAL*8(A-H ,O-Z)
      DIMENSION G(4, 4)
      BE = F/(1.-EW*EW)
      DE = F**2*BE/12
      AA9 = AMDA**2*(1. -EW)*GAMA*OMZ
      AA31 = (OMZT + EW*GAMA*OMZ)*DE
      AA3 = BE*(-EW*OMZ*OMEGAT-GAMA**2-(EN/R)**2/2. *(1 -EW) )
*     -2.*DE*AMDA**2*(1. -EW)*(EN/R)**2*OMZ**2
*     -DE*GAMA**2*(1. -EW*EW)*OMZ**2*AMDA**2
```

```
      AA5 = -GAMA*BE*EN*(3.-EW)/(2.*R) -DE*AMDA**2*(1.-EW)
*     *GAMA*EN*(3 + EW)
*       *OMEGAT*OMZ/R**2
      AA7 = BE*(OMZT + GAMA*(OMZ-OMEGAT))-AMDA**2*DE*(1.
*     -EW)*GAMA*EN**2 *(3. + EW)*OMZ/R**2
      AA11 = EN*BE*(3. -EW)*GAMA/(2. *R) + DE*AMDA**2*(1.-
*     EW)*EN*(-4.*OMZT*OMEGAT-2 *(1. + EW)*OMZ*OMEGAT-4.
*     *OMZ**2*GAMA) / (2. *R)
      AA13 = BE*GAMA*(1. -EW)/2.-DE*AMDA**2*(1. -EM)*GAMA*2.
*     *OMEGAT**2
      + DE*AMDA**2*(1. -EW)*GAMMA**4. *OMEGAT*OMZ
      AA14 = -GAMA*AA13 + (1. -EW)*BE*OMZ*OMEGAT/2.
*     -BE*EN**2/R**2 + DE*AMDA**2*(1.-EW)*(-(1..+ EW)*EN**2*
*     OMEGAT**2/R**2 + 2. *OMEGAT**3*OM
      AA17 = -EN*BE/R*(OMEGAT + EW*OMZ) + DE*AMDA**2*EN*(1.
*     -EW)/(2. *R)*(-2. *(1. + EW)*EN**2*OMEGAT/ (R**2)-4. *GA-
*     MA**2*OMZ + 4. *GAMA**2*OMEGAT + 4. *OMEGAT**2*OMZ)
      AA18 = EW*AMDA**2*OMEGAT*EN/R
      AA20 = -BE*GAMA*(EW*OMZ + OMEGAT) + DE*AMDA**2*GA-
*     MA*(1. -EW**2) * (-GAMMA*OMZT - (EN/R)**2*OMZ+ GAM-
*     MA**2*OMZ + 2. *OMZ**2*OMEHAT - 1. *EN**2*AMDA*2*(1.
      -EW)**OMZT/(R**2))
      AA23 = -BE*EN/R*(OMEGAT + EW*OMZ) + DE*AMDA**2*(1.
*     -EW)*EN/R*- (3. + EW)*OMZ*GAMA**2+2. *GAMA**2*(2.
      +EW)*OMEGAT)
      AA26 = -BE*(OMZ**2 + 2. + EW*OMZ*OMEGAT + OMEGAT**2)
*     +DE*AMDA**2* (1. -EW)*(EN/R)**2 ((1. + EW)*(OMZ*OMEGAT -
      (EN/R)**2
      2. + 2. *GAMA**2) + 2. *(GAMA**2 + OMZ*OMEGAT))
      AA29 = -AMDA**2*((1. -EW)*OMZ*OMEGAT + EW*(EN/R)**2)
      AA32 = DE*EW*EN*OMEGAT/R
      AA35 = DE*EW*EN**2/R**2
      AA36 = -1.
      G(1, 1) = AA3
      G(1, 2) = AA5
      G(1, 3) = AA7
      G(1, 4) = AA9
      G(2, 1) = AA11
      G(2, 2) = AA14
      G(2, 3) = AA17
      G(2, 4) = AA18
      G(3, 1) = AA20
      G(3, 2) = AA23
```

```
      G(3, 3) = AA26
      G(3, 4) = AA29
      G(4, 1) = AA31
      G(4, 2) = AA32
      G(4, 3) = AA35
      G(4, 4 )= AA36
      RETURN
      END
C*****************************************************************
      SUBROUTINE ELFI(R, GAMA, OMEGAT, OMZ, OMZT, EN, E, FE,
     *  EW, AMDA, F)
      IMPLICIT REAL*8(A-H, O-Z)
      DIMENSION E(4, 4), FE(4, 4)
      BE = F/(1.-EW*EW)
      DE = F**2*BE/12
      AA1 = BE
      AA8 = AMDA**2*OMZ
      AA27 = AAMA**2
      AA30 = DE*OMZ
      AA33 = -DE
      AA2 = GAMA*BE
      AA4 = BE*EN*(1. + EW) / (2. *R) + 2. *DE*AMDA**2. *(1.
     *  -EW)*EN*OMZ*OMEGAT/R
      AA6 = BE*EW*OMEGAT + BE*OMZ + 2. *DE*AMDA**2*(1.
     *  -W)*EN**2*OMZ/R**2 + DE*AMDA**2* (1.-EW**2)*
     *  GAMA**2*OMZ
      AA10 = AA4
      AA12 = BE*(1. -EW)/2. +2.*DE*(1. -EW)*AMDA**2*OMEGAT**2
      AA13 = BE*GAMA*(1. -EW)/2. -DE*AMDA**2*(1. -EW)*GA-
     *  MA*2. *OMEGAT**2 + DE*AMDA**2* (1. -EW)*GAMA*4*
     *  OMEGAT*OMZ
      AA15 = 2. *EN*DE*(1. -EW)*OMEGAT*AMDA**2/R
      AA16 = (AMDA**2*DE*(1. -EW)*EN/(2. *R)) * (2. *(1. + EW)*GA-
     *  MA*OMEGAT+ 4.* GAMA*(OMZ - OMEGAT))
      AA19 = AA6
      AA21 = AA15
      AA22 = (-AMDA**2*DE*(1. -EW)*EN*GAMA/R)*(3. + EW)*O-
     *  MEGAT + AMDA**2*DE*(1. -EW) *EN*GAMA* 2*OMZ/R
      AA24 = AMDA**2*DE* (1. -EW)*(2.*EN**2/R**2 +
     *  (1. + EW)*GAMA**2)
```

```
      AA25 = -AMDA**2DE*(1. -EW)*((1. + EW)*GAMA**3 + 2. *GA-
*     MA*EN**2/R**2)     +     (-DE*AMDA**2*(1.     -EW))*2.*GA-
*     MA*OMZ*OMEGAT*(1. + EW)
      AA28 = AMDA**2*GAMA*2. -EW)
      AA34 = -DE*EW*GAMA
      DO 23 I = 1, 4
      DO 23 J = 1, 4
*     E(I, J) = 0.000
23      FE(I, J) = 0.0D0
      E(1, 1) = AA1
      E(2, 2) = AA12
      E(2, 3) = AA15
      E(3, 2) = AA21
      E(3, 3) = AA24
      E(3, 4) = AA27
      E(4, 3) = AA33
      FE(1, 1) = AA2
      FE(1, 2) = AA4
      FE(1, 3) = AA6
      FE(1, 4) = AA8
      FE(2, 2) = AA13
      FE(2, 1) = AA10
      FE(2, 3) = AA16
      FE(3, 1) = AA19
      FE(3, 2) = AA22
      FE(3, 3) = AA25
      FE(3, 4) = AA28
      FE(4, 1) = AA30
      FE(4, 3) = AA34
      RETURN
      END
C**************************************************************
      SUBROUTINE HOJO(R, GAMA, OMEGAT, OMZ, EN, H, GE, EW,
*     AMDA, F)
      IMPLICIT REAL*8(A-H, O-Z)
      DIMENSION H(4, 4), GE(4, 4)
      BE = F/(1.-EW*EW)
      DE = F**2*BE/12.
      BA1 = BE
      BA10 = -AMDA**2*DE*(1. -EW)*0MZ*((1. + EW)*GAMA**2 +
*     EN**2/R**2)
      BA15 = AMDA**2
      BA2 = EW*BE*GAMA
      BA3 = EW*EN*BE/R
```

```
      BA4 = BE*EW*OMEGAT + BE*OMZ
      BA5 = (–BE*(1. –EW)*EN)/(2.*R)–2. *DE*(1. –EW)*
*     AMDA**2*EN*OMZ*OMEGAT/R
      BA6 = BE*(1. –EW)/2. + 2. *DE*(1. –EW)*AMDA**2*OMEGAT**2
      BA7 = –GAMA*BA6
      BA8 = 2. *AMDA**2*OMEGAT*EN*DE*(1. –EW)/R
      BA9 = –GAMA*.BA8
      BA11 = 2. *AMDA**2*DE*(1. –EW)*EN*OMEGAT/R
      BA12 = (–AMDA**2*DE*(1. –EW)*GAMA/EN*((2. *R))*2. *
*     (1. + EW.)*OMEGAT + 4*OMF
      BA13 = AMDA**2*DE*(1. –EW)*(2. *EN**2/R**2 + (1. + EW)*
*     GAMA**2)
      BA14 = –AMDA**2*DE*(1. –EW)*EN**2*GAMA*(3. + EW)/R**2
      BA16 = AMDA**2*GAMA*(1. –EW)
      DO 25 I = 1, 14
      DO 25 J = 1, 14
         H(I, J) = 0.D0
25       GE(I, J) = 0.D0
      H(1, 1) = BA1
      H(2, 2) = BA6
      H(2, 3) = BA8
      H(3, 2) = BA11
      H(3, 3) = BA13
      H(3, 4) = BA15
      H(4, 3) = –1
      GE(1, 1) = BA2
      GE(1, 2) = BA3
      GE(1, 3) = BA4
      GE(2, 1) = BA5
      GE(2, 2) = BA7
      GE(2, 3) = BA9
      GE(3, 1) = BA10
      GE(3, 2) = BA12
      GE(3, 3) = BA14
      GE(3, 4) = BA16
      GE(4, 1) = OMZ
      RETURN
      END
```

```
C ------------------------------------------------------------------
 C
                          RESPONSE – M.TECH
 C
C       THIS PROGRAM IS A TYPICAL MODAL SUPERPOSITION ROU-
C       TINE
        WITH 4 EIGEN PAIRS – THOSE FOR N=1
C       NAME          EXPLANATION
C       X1            ORTHONORMALISED         EIGENVECTOR
                      (STRAIGHT)
C       X2            ORTHONORMALISED         EIGENVECTOR
                      (TRANSPOSE)
C       AID           FIRST COLUMN GIVE TIME SECOND COL-
                      UMN GIVE INPUT ACC.IN M/S**2
C       BE            INTERACTION MATRIX
C       U             DISPLACEMENT  (REL.)  RESPONSE  OF
                      STRUCTURE
C       SLOPE & C     THESE ARE M AND C IN Y = M*X+C FIT
                      FOR  THE  ACCELEROGRAM,  BETWEEN
                      TWO CONSECUTIVE PEAKS
C ------------------------------------------------------------------
      IMPLICIT REAL*8(A–H, O–Z)
      DIMENSION X1(1128, 5), X2((1128, 5), AID(115, 2), P(4), PDOT (4),
*     PIN(4), PDOTIN(4), ZET(4), BE(5, 5), U(1128)
      DIMENSION AM(1128), H(4, 4), GE(4, 4), HH(2, 4, 4), GGE(2, 4, 4),
*     FORCE(4), F(1128), Z1(280, 4)E1(4, 1), E2(4, 1), E3(4, 1), NODE(8)
      REWIND 4
      NOMEG = 4
      NEQ = 1128
      NEIG = 5
      NINT = 115
      READ(04)((X1(I, J), J = 1, NEIG), I=1, NEQ), ((X2(I, J), J = 1, NEIG), I = 1,
*     NEQ) ((BE(I, J), J = 1, NEIG), I = 1, NEIG), (AM(I), I = 1, NEQ)
      REWIND 4
      READ 21, (ZET(I), I = 1, NOMEG)
      READ 21, ((AID (I, J), J =1, 2),I = 1, NINT)
21    FORMAT(6F10.0)
      PRINT 8000
8000    FORMAT(/10X,' TRANSIENT RESPONSE IS '/)
C
C     INPUT QUANTITIES – STRUCTURE DETAILS
C
```

```
      D1 = 10.0
      D2 = 3210.0
      D3 = 3610.0
      D4 = 1160.0
      T1 = 400.0
      T2 = 200.0
      T3 = 50.0
      T4 = 350.0
      AC = 1000.0
      TEST = T2
      DELTA1 = 0.1
      EW = 0.3
      EN = 1.0
      OMZ = 0.0
      MS1 = 249
      MS2 = 268
      RSP1 = D2/2.0
      RSP2 = D4/2.0
      PRINT 3566
3566  FORMAT (/10X,' K', 7X, 'STRES1', 6X, 'STRES2', 6X,'STRESS3',
*     6X, 'STRES4', 6X,' TIME')
      DO 351 K = 1, 2
      IF (K. EQ. 2) GOTO 354
353   RHO = 1.605
      OMEGAT = 1. 0/RH0
      GAMA = 0.0
      AMDA = T2/AC
      FF = 1.0
      OMZ = 0.0
      EN = 1.0
      DELTA = DELTA1
      EW  = 0.3
      GO TO 356
354   R = D3/2.0
      RHO = R/AC
      OMEGAT = 1.0/RHO
      GAMA = 0.0
      FF = T3/T2
      AMDA = T3/AC
356   CALL HOJO(RHO, GAMA, OMEGAT, OMZ, EN, H, GE, EW, AMDA,
*     FF)
      DO 357 I = 1, 4
      DO 357 J = 1, 4
      HH(K, I, J) = H(I, J)
357   GGE(K, I, J) =GE(I, J)
```

```
351   CONTINUE
C --------------------------------------------------------------------
      NINT1 = NINT-1
      NN = 5
      DO 100 NOIN = 1, NINT1
      TIME2 = AID(NOIN + 1, 1)
      TIME1 = AID(NOIN, 1)
      DELT = (TIME2-TIME1)/FLOAT (NN)
      F1 = AID(NOIN, 2)
      F2 = AID(NOIN + 1, 2)
      SLOPE = (F2-F1)/(TIME2-TIME1)
      C = (F1*TIME2-F2*TIME1)/(TIME2-TIME1)
      CIF(NOIN.GT.1) GO TO 50
C ---------------CALCULATE MODAL ININTIAL  CONDITIONS
      DO 40 J = 1, NOMEG
         PIN(J) = 0.0
         PDOTIN(J) = 0.0
40         CONTINUE
C --------------------------------------------------------------------
50         CONTINUE
C --------------------------------------------------------------------
      DO 91 II = 1, NN
         T = TIME1 + (FLOAT(II)*DELT)
      ACC = SLOPE*T + C
      DO 92 I = 1, NEQ
92       F(I) = 0.0
      CONST = 2.056E11*ACC
      DO 93 K = 1,16
         K1 = 4*K-3
         K2 = K1 + 1
         F(K1) =-AM(K1)*CONST
93       F(K2) = AM(K2)*CONST
      DO 94 K = 18, 245
        K1 = 4*K - 2
      K2 = K1 + 1
      F(K1) = AM(K1)*CONST
94       F(K2) = -AM (K2)*CONST
      F(886) = 0.0
      F(887) = 0.0
      F(986) = AM(986)*CONST
      F(987) = -AM(987)*CONST
      F(989) = -AM(989)*CONST
      F(990) = AM(990)*CONST
      DO 95 K = 250, 267
```

```
        K1 = 4*K + 6
95        F(K1) = AM(K1)*CONST
      DO 96 K = 269, 280
        K1 = 4*K + 6
        K2 = K1 + 1
        F(K1) = AM(K1)*CONST
96        F(K2) = -AM(K2)*CONST
      DO 97 J = 1.NOMEG
        FORCE(J) = 0.0
      DO 97 I = 1, NEQ
97      FORCE(J) = FORCE(J) + X1(I, J)*F(I)
C--------------CALCULATE MODAL RESPONSE
      DO 70 I = 1, NOMEG
        Z = ZET(I)
      OM = DSQRT(BE(I, I))
      OM2 = BE(I, I)
      OMD = (1. 0-Z*Z)
      OMD = DSQRT(OMD)*OM
      C1 = PIN(I)-FORCE(I)/OMZ
      C2 = (PDOTIN(I) + Z*OM*C1)/OMD
C     -----------------------------------------------------------
C     ---------abc---SINCE THE ERRSET SUBROUTINE IS NOT FOUND IT IS
C     KEPT
C         IN THE COMMENT STATEMENT
        CALL = ERRSET(208, 256, -1, + 1)
          P(I) = DEXP(-Z*OM*DELT)*(C1*DCOS(OMD*DELT) +
    *     C2*DSIN(OMD*DELT))*(FORCE(I)/OM2)
          PDOT(I) = OM*DEXP(-Z*OM*DELT)*((C2-C1*Z)*DCOS
          (OMD*DELT)
    *     -(C1 + Z*C2))*DSIN(OMD*DELT)
   70       CONTINUE
C-----------------------------------------------------------
      DO 80 I = 1, NEQ
        U(I) = 0.0
      DO 80 J = 1, NOMEG
80      U(I) = U(I) + X2(I, J)*P(J)
C-----------------------------------------------------------
      DO 81 K = 1, 249
        K2 = 4*K
        K1 = K2-3
        L = 1
      DO 82 I = K1, K2
        Z1(K, L) = U(I)
```

```
82        L = L+1
81        CONTINUE
      DO 83 K = 250, 280
        K2 = 4*K + 8
        K1 = K2-3
        L = 1
      DO 84 I = K1, K2
        Z1(K, L) = U(I)
84        L = L + 1
83        CONTINUE
      NODE(1) = 120
      NODE(2) = 140
      NODE(3) = 160
      NODE(4) = 180
      NODE(5) = 228
      NODE(6) = 230
      NODE(7) = 232
      NODE(8) = 234
      DELTA = DELTA1
      EN == 1.0D0
      EW = 0.3
      OMZ = 0.0
      GAMA = 0.0
      DO 3556 KK = 1, 8
        K = NODE(KK)
        IF(KK. GT. 4) GO TO 6667
        RHO = D2/2.0/AC
        OMEGAT = 1.0/RHO
        AMDA = T2/AC

        FF = 1.0
        L = 1
        GO TO 4558
6667      RHO = D3/2.O/AC
      OMEGAT = 1.0/RHO
      L = 2
      AMDA = T3/AC
      FF = T3/T2
4558      CONTINUE
      DO 4556 I=1, 4
      DO 4456 J = 1, 4
        H(I, J) = HH(L, I, J)
4556      GE(I, J) = GGE(L, I, J)
      DO 3557 I = 1, 4
        E1(I, 1) = 0.0
      DO 3557 J = 1, 4
```

```
3557 E1(I, 1) = E1 (I, 1) + GE (I, J)*Z1(K, J)
     DO 3558 I =1, 4
     IF(KK.GT.4)GO TO 4559
     E2(I, 1) = (Z1(K + 1, I) - Z1 (K – 1, I)) / (2.0*DELTA)
     GO TO 3558
4559 E2(I, 1) = (Z1(K + 2, I) - Z1 (K – 2, I)) / (2.0*DELTA)
3558  CONTINUE
       E3(I, 1) = 0.0
     DO 3559 J=1,4
3559   E3(I, 1) = E3(I, 1) + H(I, J)*E2(J, 1)
     DO 3563 I = 1, 4
3563 E1 (I, 1) = E3 (I, 1) + E3 (I, 1)
C
     corrected up to here
C
     B = FF/(1.0–EW**2)
     STRES1 = (E1(1,1))/FF + (6. *AMDA*Z1(K,4))/FF**2
     IF(KK.GT.4)GO TO 5556
     STRES2 = B*GAMA*Z1(K,1) + B*EW*(Z1(K + 1,1)–Z1(K–
*    1,1))/(2.0*DELTA) + Z1(K,3)*B*(OMEGAT + EW*OMZ) +
     B*Z1(K,2)/RHO
     GO TO 5558
5556 STRES2 = B*GAMA*Z1(K,1) + B*EW*(Z1(K + 2, 1)–Z1(K–2,
*    1))/(2.0*DELTA)
      + Z1(K, 3)*B*(OMEGAT + EW*OMZ) + B*Z1(K, 2)/RHO
5558 STRES3 = EW*Z1(K,4 ) + (Z1(K, 1)*OMZ–E1(4, 1)*GAMA)/12.0
     STRES4 = (STRES2)/FF + (6.0*AMDA*STRES3)/FF**2
     PRINT 3564, K, STRES1, STRES2, STRES3, STRES4,T
3564   FORMAT(/10X, I5, 5E12.4)
3556  CONTINUE
C ---------------------------------------------------------
     DO 90 I = 1, NOMEG
       PIN(I) = P(I)
       PDOTIN(I) = PDOT(I)
90      CONTINUE
C ---------------------------------------------------------
100     CONTINUE
     STOP
     END
```

```
C -----------------------------------------------------------------
C
C       SESIMIC ANALYSIS OF A PRESURE VESSEL
C
C       STATIC ANALYSIS (BUDIANSKY METHOD))
C
C
C -----------------------------------------------------------------
      IMPLICIT REAL*8(A-H, O-Z)
      DIMENSION A1(2, 4, 4), A2(2, 4,4 ), A3(2, 4, 4)
      DIMENSION A4(8, 8), A5(8, 8), A6(8, 8)
      DIMENSION A7(140, 8), A8(140, 8, 8), A9(140, 8)
      DIMENSION AM(280, 4), A(4, 4)
      DIMENSION A10(8, 8), A11(8, 1), A5A6(8, 8), A6A10(8, 8)
*     , A6A11(8, 1), Q1(4, 4), S1(4, 4), EM3(4, 4)
      DIMENSION B(4, 4), BETA(4, 4), RR(4, 4), TT1(4, 4), EN3(4, 4)
      DIMENSION C(4, 4), S2(4, 4), X2(4, 4), TT2(4, 4)
      DIMENSION X1(4, 4)
*     E(4, 4), ETA(4, 4), Y2(4, 4), FE(4, 4), Y1(4, 4), G(4, 4), GE(4, 4)
*     , GE1(4, 4), GE2(4, 4), GE3(4, 4), GEM(4, 4), GEP(4, 4), H(4, 4), H1(4, 4),
*     H2(4, 4), H3(4, 4), HM(4, 4), HP(4, 4), ES(4, 4), PSI1(4, 4), PSI2(4, 4)
*     , PSIC(4, 4), P(8, 8), Q(8, 1), Z1(280, 4), FORCE(8, 1)
      DIMENSION DD1(4, 8), DD2(4, 8), DD3(4, 8), SC(8, 8), TT(8, 8), D(8, 8)
*     , E1(4, 1), E2(4, 1), E3(4, 1), EE(8, 1), DE(8, 1), Z1Z2(8, 1), Z(8, 1)
      COMMON/COM1/A1, A2, A3, A4, A5, A6, AT, A8, A9
C -----------------------------------------------------------------
C             NAME EXPLANATION
C -----------------------------------------------------------------
C     A1 TO A3NODAL A, B, C OF SIZE(4, 4) TAKEN TWO
C          AT A TIME
C     A4 TO A6POTTER BLOCKS OF SIZE (8, 8) EQUIVALENT
C          A, B, C IN THAT ORDER
C     A7 LOADING MATRIX
C     A8, A9 P, Q OF POTTER STORED IN THESE
C -----------------------------------------------------------------
C**   INPUT QUANTITIES
      T1 = 400.
      T2 = 200.
      T3 = 50.
      T4 = 350.
      D1 = 10.
      D2 = 3210.
```

```
      D3 = 3610.
      D4 = 1160.
      AC = 1000.
      DELTA1 = 0.1
      EW = 0.3
      PI = 4.*DATAN(1.0D0)
      OMZT = 0.0
      EN = 0.0D0
      RSP1 = D2/2.
      RSP2 = D4/2.
      MS1 = 249
      MS2 = 268
      TEST = T2
C**     LOAD DETAILS
      DO 1 KON = 1,140
      DO 1 J = 1, 8
1        A7(KON, J) = 0.0
      DO 2 KON = 2, 139
      A7(KON, 3) = -1.0
2        A7(KON, 7) = -1.0
      A7(1, 7) = -1.0
      A7(140, 3) = -1.0
      A7(111, 7) = 0.0
      A7(9, 3) = 0.0
      A7(124, 7) = 0.0
      A7(123, 7) = 0.0
C--------------------------------------------------------------
      DO 10 KON = 1, 140
      DO 10 J = 1, 8
      A9(KON, J) = 0.0
      DO 10 L = 1, 8
10       A8(KON, J, L) = 0.0
C--------------------------------------------------------------
C**     AT FIRST NODE **
      DO 20 I = 1, 4
      DO 20 J = 1, 4
      A1(1, I, J) = 0.0
      A2(1, I, J) = 0.0
20       A3(1, I, J) = 0.0
      DO 30 I = 1, 4
30       A2(1, I, I) = 0.0
      OMZ = 0.0
      OMEGAT = 0.0
      F = T1/T2
```

```
      AMDA = T1/AC
      R = D1/2.0
      RHO = R/AC
      K1 = 2
      DO 60 K = 2, 16
      RHO = RHO + DELTA1
      GAMA = 1.0/RHO
      CALL CALLS1(RHO, GAMA, F, EW, EN, OMZ, OMZT, OMEGAT,
     *AMDA, DELTA1, A, B, C)
      DO 40 I = 1, 4
      DO 40 J = 1, 4
      A1(K1, I, J) = A(I, J)
      A2(K1, I, J) = B(I, J)
40       A3(K1, I, J) = C(I, J)
      IF(K1.NE.2)GOTO 50
      KON = K/2
      CALL BLOCK1
         PRINT 41
41       FORMAT(/10X,'Q OF POTTER IS PRINTED'/)
      CALL POTER1(KON)
      K1 = 1
      GO TO 60
50       K1 = K1 + 1
60       CONTINUE
C ****************************************************
      K1 = 1
C**      AT NODE 17 **
      K = 17
      RHO = RHO + DELTA1
      PRINT 61, RHO
61       FORMAT(/10X,'RHO(K= 17) =', E12.4)
      GAMA = 1.0/RHO
      CALL HOJO(RHO, GAMA, OMEGAT, OMZ, EN, HM, GEM, EW,
     *   AMDA, F)
      OMEGAT = GAMA
      GAMA = 0.0
      AMDA = T2/AC
      F = 1.0
      PHI = PI/2.
      F = 1.0
      PHI = PI/2.
      CALL HOJO (RHO, GAMA, OMEGAT, OMZ, EN, HP, GEP, EW, AMDA,
     *   F)
      DO 70 I = 1, 4
      DO 70 J = 1, 4
```

```
70      A1(K1, I, J) = HP(I, J)/DELTA1
      CALL TRANS (PHI, PSI)
      CALL CALLS2 (GEM, HM, GEP, HP, DELTA1, PSI, B, C)
      DO 80 I = 1, 4
      DO 80 J = 1, 4
      A2 (K1, I, J) = B(I, J)
80      A3 (K1, I, J) = C(I, J)
C***          AT NODE 18  **
      K1 = K1 + 1
      K = 18
      CALL CALLS1 (RHO, GAMA, F, EW, EN, OMZ, OMZT, OMEGAT,
*     AMDA, DELTA, A, B, C)
      CALL ULT(C, PSI, 4, 4, 4, PSIC, 1.0D0)
      DO 90 I = 1, 4
      DO 90 J = 1, 4
      A1(K1, I, J) = A(I, J)
      A2(K1, I, J) = B(I, J)
90      A3(K1, I, J) = PSIC(I, J)
      KON = K/2
      CALL BLOCK1
      CALL POTER1 (KON)
      K1 = 1
      DO 100 I = 1, 4
      DO 100 J = 1, 4
      A1 (1, I, J) = A(I, J)
      A2(1, I, J) = B(I, J)
100     A3 (1, I, J) = C(I, J)
      DO 110 I = 1, 4
      DO 110 J = 1, 4
      A1(2, I, J) = A1(1, I, J)
      A2(2, I, J) = A2(1, I, J)
110     A3(2, I, J) = A3(1, I, J)
      KON = 10
      CALL BLOCK1
      CALL POTER1 (KON)
      DO 120 KON = 11, 110
120     CALL POTER1(KON)
C -------------------------------------------------------
      DO 130 I = 1, 4
      DO 130 J = 1, 4
      A1(2, I, J) = 0.0
      A2(2, I, J) = 0.0
130     A3 (2, I, J) = 0
      DO 140 I = 1, 4
```

```
140   A2(2, I, J) = 1.0
      KON = 111
      CALL BLOCK2(KON)
      CALL POTER1(KON)
C**     **AT NODE 224    ***
      K = 224
      R = D3/2.0
      RHO = R/AC
      OMEGAT = 1.O/RHO
      GAMA = 0.0
      F = T3/TEST
      AMDA = T3/AC
      CALL CALLS1 (RHO, GAMMA, F, EW, EN, OMZ, OMZT, OMEGAT,
*     AMA, DELTA1, A, B, C)
      DO 150 I = 1, 4
      DO 150 J = 1, 4
      A1 (2, I, J) = A(I, J)
      A2(2, I, J) = B(I, J)
150      A3(2, I, J) = C(I, J)
      KON = K/2
      CALL BLOCK2(KON)
      DO 160 KON = 112, 122
160      CALL POTER1 (KON)
C ----------------------------------------------------------------
C**    AT NODE     246
      K = 246
      CALL HOJO (RHO, GAMA, OMEGAT, OMZ, EN, HM, GEM, EW,
      AMDA, F)
      PHI = PI/2.0
      GAMA = -1.0/RHO
      OMEGAT=0.0
      AMDA = T3/AC
      F = T3/T2
      CALL HOJO (RHO, GAMA, OMEGAT, OMZ, EN, HP, GEP, EW, AMDA,
      F)
      CALL TRANS (PHI, PSI)
      CALL CALLS2 (GEM, HM, GEP, HP, DELTA1, PS1, B, C)
      DO 170 I = 1, 4
      DO 170 J = 1, 4
      A1 (2, I, J) = HP (I, J)/DELTA1
      A2 (2, I, J) = B (I, J)
170      A3(2, I, J) = C(I, J)
      KON = K/2
      CALL BLOCK2(KON)
      CALL POTER1(KON)
C ----------------------------------------------------------------
```

```
C***                    AT NODE 248
      K = 248
      RHO = RSP 1/AC+DELTA1
      GAMA = -1. 0/RHO
      OMEGAT = 0. 0
      AMDA = T3/AC
      F = T3/T2
      CALL CALLS1 (RHO, GAMA, F, EW, EN, OMZ, OMZT, OMEGAT,
      AMDA, DELTA1, A, B, C)
      CALL ULT(C, PSI,4, 4, 4, PSIC, 1. 000)
      DO 180 I = 1, 4
      DO 180 J = 1, 4
      A1(2, I, J) = A(I, J)
      A2(2, I, J) = B(I, J)

180   A3(2, I, J) = PSIC(I, J)
      KON = K/2
      CALL BLOCK2(KON)
      CALL POTER1(KON)
C ------------------------------------------------------------------
C **          AT NODE 249
         DO 190 I = 1,4
         DO 190 J = 1,4
         BETA(I, J) = 0. 0
190         ETA(I, J) = 0. 0
         BETA(1, 1) = 1. 0
         BETA(2, 2) = 1. 0
         BETA(3, 3) = 1. 0
         ETA(4, 4) = 1. 0
C -----------FIRST BRANCH---------------------------
         R = D2/2. 0
         RHO = R/AC
         GAMA = 0. 0
         OMEGAT = 1. 0/RHO
         OMZ = 0. 0
         EN = 0. 0
         AMDA = T2/AC
         F = 1.0
         CALL HOJO(RHO, GAMA, OMEGAT, OMZ, EN, H1, GE1, EW,
         AMDA, F)
C -----------SECOND BRANCH---------------------------
         GAMA = -OMEGAT
         OMEGAT = 0. 0
         AMDA = T3/AC
         F = T3/TEST
```

```
      CALL HOJO(RHO, GAMA, OMEGAT, OMZ, EN, H2, GE2, EW,
     *  AMDA, F)
C ------------THIRD BRANCH--------------------------------
      OMEGAT = -GAMA
      GAMA = 0. 0
      OMZ = OMEGAT
      AMDA = T2/AC
      F = 1. 0
      CALL HOJO(RHO, GAMA, OMEGAT, OMZ, EN, H3, GE3, EW,
     *  AMDA, F)
C ------------------------------------------------------
      PHI1 = 0. 0
      PHI2 = -PI/2. 0
      DELTA2 = ACOS(RSP2/RSP1)/(MS2-MS1) *RSP1/AC
      CALL TRANS(PHI1, PSI1)
      CALL TRANS(PHI2, PSI2)
      CALL A1B1C1 (H1, GE1, H2, GE2, H3, GE3, Q1, RR, S2, TT2, S1,
     *  TT1, EM3, EN3, X2, X1, Y2, Y1, BETA, ETA, DELTA1, DELTA2,
     *  PSI1,
        PSI2)
C --------- AT JUNCTION 249 ------------------------------
      DO 1111 I = 1, 8
      Q(I, 1) = A9(124, I)
      DO 111 J = 1, 8
1111    P(I,J ) = A8 (124, I, J)
      DO 1112 I = 1, 4
        I1 = I + 4
      DO 1112 I = 1, 4
      J1 = J + 4
      SC (I, J) = S1(I, J)
      SC (I, J1) = O.OD0
      SC (I1, J) = 0.0D0
      SC (I1, J1) = S2(I, J)
      TT(I, J) = TT1 (I, J)
      TT (I, J1) = 0.0D0
      TT(I1, J) = 0.0D0
1112    TT(I1, J1) = TT2(I, J)
      CALL ULT (TT, P, B, 8, 8, 8, D, 1.ODO)
      DO 1113 I = 1, 8
      DO 1113 J = 1, 8
1113    D(I, J) = D(I, J) + SC(I, J)
      CALL ULT(TT, Q, 8, 8, 1, EE, 1.ODO)
      CALL JAI (D, 8)
      DO 1114 I = 1, 4
      DO 1114 J = 1, 4
       J1 = J + 4
```

```
      DD1(I, J) = X1(I, J)
      DD1(I, J1) = X2(I, J)
      DD2(I, J) = Y1(I, J)
1114   DD2(I, J1) = Y2(I, J)
      CALL ULT (DD2, P, 4, 8, 8, DD3, 1.0D0)
      CALL ULT (DD2, Q, 4, 8, 1, E3, 1.0D0)
      DO 1115 I = 1, 4
        DO 1115 J = 1, 8
1115  DD1(I, J) = DD1(I, J) - DD3(I, J)
      CALL ULT(DD1, D, 4, 8, 8, DD3, 1.0D0)
      DO 1116 I = 1, 4
       I1 = I + 4
      DO 1116 J = 1, 4
       JI = J + 4
      SC(I, J) = RR(I, J)
      SC(I, J1) = Q1(I, J)
      SC(I1, J) = RR(I, J)
1116   SC(I1, J1) = Q1(I, J)
      CALL ULT(D, SC, 8, 8, 8, TT, 1.0D0)
      CALL ULT(DD3, SC, 4, 8, 8, DD1, 1.0D0)
      CALL ULT (DD3, EE, 4, 8, 1, E1, 1.0D0)
      DO 1117 I = 1, 4
1117    E2(I, 1) = E3(I, 1)–E1(I, 1)
      DO 1118 I = 1, 4
          DO 1118 J = 1, 4
             J1 = J + 4
             DD2(I, J) = EN3(I,J) – DD1(I, J)
1118    DD2 (I, J1) = EM3(I, J)– DD1(I, J1)
      DO 1119 I = 1, 4
          DO 1119 J = 1, 8
1119    A5 (I, J) = DD2(I, J)
C ----------------
      K = 1
      F = 1.0
      AMDA = T2/AC
      OMZ = AC/RSP1
      ALFAM = DARCOS (RSP2/RSP1)
      DELTA2 = ALFAM/(MS2-MS1)*RSP1/AC
      DO 240 K = 250, 267
C ----------------
C     ALFA IS THE ANGLE BETWEEN THE TANGENT TO THE SURFACE
C     AT THE NODE UNDER CONSIDERATION AND THE VERTICAL,
C     WHICH IS THE TANGENT AT NODE 249. ALFAM IS THAT ALFA AT
      NODE 268
C ----------------
      ALFA = ALFAM/(MS2–MS1) * (K–MS1)
      RHO = RSP1/AC * DCOS (ALFA)
```

```
      GAMA = -DSIN (ALFA)/RHO
      OMEGAT = DCOS (ALFA)/RHO
      CALL CALLS1 (RHO, GAMA, F, EW, EN, OMZ, OMZT, OMEGAT,
*     AMDA, DELTA2, A, B, C)
      IF(K.EQ.250) GOTO 220
      DO 221 I = 1, 4
          DO 221 J = 1, 4
              A1(K1, I, J) = A(I, J)
              A2(K1, I, J) = B(I, J)
221       A3(K1, I,J) = C(I, J)
      IF (K1.NE.2) GOTO 210
      KON = K/2
      CALL BLOCK1
      CALL POTER1 (KON)
      K1 = 1
      GOTO 240
210       K1 = K1 + 1
       GOTO 240
C *********     POTTER BLOCKS FOR KON=125   *******
220   DO 223 I = 1, 8
          DO 223 J = 1, 8
              A4(I, J) = 0.0
223       A6(I, J) = 0.0
      DO 230 I = 1, 4
          I1 = I + 4
          DO 230 J = 1, 4
              J1 = J + 4
              A4(I1, J) = A(I, J)
              A5(I1, J) = C(I, J)
230       A5(I1, J1) = B(I, J)
      KON = 125
C ------------FORCE DETERMINATION----------------
      DO 1012 I = 1, 4
          I1 = I + 4
          FORCE(I, 1) = E2 (I, 1)
1012      FORCE (I1, 1) = A7 (125, I1)
      CALL POTER1 (KON)
240   CONTINUE
C***************** AT NODE 268  *****
      K = 268
      K1 = 2
      RHO = RSP2/AC
      GAMA = -DSIN(ALFAM)/RHO
      OMEGAT = DCOS (ALFAM)/RHO
      PRINT 241, K, GAMA, OMEGAT, RHO
```

```
241     FORMAT (/10X, 'K'=, 15,'GAMA=',E12.3, 'OMEGAT=', E12.3,'RHO
*       = ', E12.3/)
        CALL HOJO (RHO, GAMA, OMEGAT, OMZ, EN, HM, GEM, EW,
*       AMDA, F)
        GAMA = 0.0
        OMEGAT = 1.0/RHO
        OMZ = 0.0
        AMDA = T4/TEST
        CALL HOJO(RHO, GAMA, OMEGAT, OMZ, EN, JP, GEP, EW, AMDA,
*       F)
        PHI = -ALFAM
        CALL TRANS(PHI, PSI)
        DO 250 I = 1, 4
            DO 250 J = 1, 4
250     A1(K1, I, J) = HP (I, J)/DELTA1
        CALL CAL + S2 (GEM, HM, GEP, HP, DELTA1, PS1, B, C)
        DO 260 I = 1, 4
            DO 260 J = 1, 4
                A2(K1, I, J) = B(I, J)
260     A3 (K1, I, J) = C(I, J)
        KON=K/2
        CALL BLOCK1
        CALL POTER1 (KON)
C****** AT NODE 269 *********
        K = 269
        CALL CALLS1(RHO, GAMA, F, EW, EN, OMZ, OMZT, OMEGAT,
*       AMDA, DELTA1, A, B, C)
        CALL ULT(C, PSI, MSS, 4, 4, 4, PSIC, 1. 0D0)
        DO 273 I = 1, 4
            DO 273 J = 1, 4
                A1(1, I, J) = A(I, J)
                A1(2, I, J) = A(I, J)
                A2(1, I, J) = B(I, J)
                A2(2, I, J) = B (I, J)
                A3(1, I, J) = PSIC(I, J)
273     A3(2, I,J) = C(I, J)
        CALL BLOCK1
        KON = 135
        CALL POTER1 (KON)
        DO 274 I = 1, 4
            DO 274 J = 1, 4
                A1(1, I, J) = A1(2, I, J)
                A2(1, I, J) = A2(2, I, J)
274     A3(1, I, J) = A3(2, I, J)
        CALL BLOCK1
        DO 280 KON = 136, 139
```

```
280     CALL POTER1(KON)
      KON = 140
      K = 280
      DO 290 I = 1, 4
        DO 290 J = 1, 4
          A1(2, I, J) = 0. 0
          A2(2, I, J) = 0. 0
290     A3(2, I, J) = 0.0
      DO 300 I = 1, 4
300     A2(2, I, J) = 1.0
        DO 301 I = 1, 8
        DO 301 J = 1, 8
          A4(I, J) = 0. 0
          A5(I, J) = 0. 0
301         A6(I, J) = 0. 0
        DO 310 I = 1, 4
          I1 = I + 4
        DO 310 J = 1, 4
          J1 = J + 4
          A6(I, J1) = -A3(1, I, J)
          A5(I, J) = -A2(1, I, J)
          A5(I, J1) = -A1(1, I, J)
          A5(I, J1) = A1 (1, I, J)
310           A5(I1, J1) = A2(2, I, J)
      DO 320 I = 1,8
      A11 (I, 1) = A9 (139 , I)
      DO 320 J = 1, 8
320     A10 (I, J) = A8 (139, I, J)
      DO 323 I = 1, 8
323     FORCE (I, 1) = A7 (140, I)
      CALL ULT (A6 , A10, 8, 8, 8, A6A10, - 1.0D0)
      CALL ULT (A6, A11, 8, 8, 1, A6A11, - 1.0D0)
      CALL ADD (A5, A6A10, 8, 8, A5A6, 1.0D0)
      CALL ADD (FORCE, A6A11, 8, 1, A11, 1.0D0)
      NZ = 8
      CALL JAI (A5A6, NZ)
      CALL ULT (A5A6, A6A11, 8, 8, 1, Z, 1.000)
      DO 330 I = 1, 4
          I1 = I + 4
          Z1 (279, I) = Z (I, 1)
330     Z1 (280, I) = Z (I1, 1)
C -------------RUNNING BACK-------------
      DO 111 K = 1, 139
```

```
                  KK = 140 – K + 1
                  IF (KK. EQ. 125)  GOTO 112
                  CALL POTER2 (A8, A9, KK, Z1)
                  GOTO 111
112                  DO 113 I = 1, 4
                        I1 = I + 4
                        Z (I, 1) =,Z1 (249, I)
113         Z (I1, I) = Z1 (250, I)
      CALL ULT (TT, Z, 8, 8, 1, Q, 1.0D0)
      CALL ULT (D, EE, 8, 8, 1, DE, 1.0D0)
      DO 114 I = 1, 8
114         Z1Z2 (I, 1) = Q (I, 1) = – DE (I, 1)
      DO 115 I = 1, 8
             Q (I, 1) = A9 (124, I)
             DO 115 J = 1, 8
115         P (I, J) = A8 (124, I, J)
      CALL ULT (P, Z1Z2, 8, 8, 1, Z, – 1.0D0)
      DO 116 I = 1, 4
             I1 = I + 4
             Z1 (247, I) = Z (I, 1) + Q (I, 1)
116         Z1 (248, I) = Z (I1, I) + Q (I, 1)
111         CONTINUE
      DO 350 I = 1, 140
            L3 = I + 1
            I1 = 2 * I – 1
            I2 = I1 + 1
            PRINT 340, I1, (Z1 (I1, J), J = 1, 4), I2, (Z1 (I2, J), J = 1, 4)
*
340  FORMAT (5X, '(', I3, ')', 4E12 4, 5X, ' (', I3, ')', 4E12.4)
350         CONTINUE
C
C     STRESS CALCULATIONS
C
      PRINT 3565
3565 FORMAT (/ 10X, 'STRESSES ARE PRINTED BELOW' /)
      PRINT 3566
3566 FORMAT (/10X, 'K', 7X, 'STRES1, '6X, 'STRES2', 6X, 'STRES3',
    * 6X, 'STRES4')
      DO 351 K = 2, 279
```

```
        IF (K.LE.17) GOTO 352
        IF (K. LE. 249) GOTO 353
        IF (K. LE. 268) GOTO 355
        R = D4/2.0
        RHO = R/AC
        GAMA = 0.0D0
        OMEGAT = 1.0 /RHO
        OMZ = 0.0
        F = T4/T2
        AMDA = T4/AC
        DELTA = DELTA1
        GOTO 356
352     RHO = D1/2.0/AC + (K – 1) * DELTA1
        GAMA = 1.0 /RHO
        OMEGAT = 0.0
        OMZ = 0.0
        EN = 0.0
        EW = 0.3
        AMDA = T1/AC
        F = T1/T2
        DELTA = DELTA1
        GOTO 356
353     RHO = 1.605
        OMEGAT = 1.0/RHO
        GAMA = 0.0
        AMDA = T2/AC
        F = 1.0
        IF (K.GT. 221)  GOTO 354
        GOTO 356
354     ODD = (K – K / 2 *2)
        IF (ODD. NE. 0)  GOTO 356
        R = D3/2.0
        RHO = R/AC
        OMEGAT = 1.0/RHO
        F = T3/T2
        AMDA = T3/AC
        GOTO 356
355     OMZ = AC/RSP1
        ALFA = ALFAM/ (MS2 – MS1) * (K – MS1)
        RHO = RSP1 /AC * DCOS (ALFA)
        GAMA = – DSIN (ALFA)/RHO
        OMEGAT = DCOS (ALFA)/RHO
        DELTA = DELTA2
356       CALL HOJO (RHO, GAMA, OMEGAT, OMZ, EN, H, GE, EW,
*      AMDA, F)
```

```
          DO 3557 I = 1, 4
               E1 (I, 1) = 0.0
               DO 3557 J = 1, 4
3557        E1 (I, 1) = E1 (I, 1) + GE (I, J) * Z1 (K, J)
      DO 3558 I = 1, 4
3558  E2 (I, 1) = (Z1 (K + 1, I) – Z1 (K – 1, I) / (2.0 *
         DELTA)
      DO 3559 I = 1, 4
                    E3 (I, 1) = 0.0
                    DO 3559 J = 1, 4
3559  E3 (I, 1) = E3 (I, 1) + H (I, J) * E2 (J, 1)
      DO 3563 I = 1, 4
3563        E1 (I, 1) = E1 (I, 1) + E3 (I, 1)
            BE = F/ (1.0 – EW ** 2)
            STRES1 = DABS (E1 (1, 1)) /F + DABS (6. *AMDA *Z1 (K,
*        4)) /F ** 2
            STRES2 = BE * GAMA * Z1 (K, 1) + BE * EW * (Z1 (K + 1,
*        1) – Z1 (K – 1, 1)) / (2. * DELTA) + Z1 (K, 3) * BE * (OMEGAT + EW
*        * OMZA)
      STRES3 = EW * Z1 (K, 4) + (Z1 (K, 1) * OMZ – E1 (4, 1)) *
*     GAMA/12.0
      STRES4 = DABS (STRES2)/F + DABS (6.0 * AMDA * STRES3 )
*     / F ** 2
      PRINT 3564, K, STRES1, STRES2, STRES3, STRES4
3564  FORMAT (/10X, I5, 4E12. 4)
351   CONTINUE
      STOP
      END
C ----------------------------------------------------------------
      SUBROUTINE POTER1 (KON)
C
C     CALCULATES AND STORES P'S AND Q'S
C
      IMPLICIT REAL * 8 (A-H, O-Z)
      DIMENSION FORCE (8, 1), A (4, 4), A1 (2, 4, 4), A2 (2, 4, 4),
*     A3 (2, 4, 4)
      DIMENSION A4 (8, 8), A5 (8, 8), A6 (8, 8), A7 (140, 8), A8 (140, 8, 8),
*     A9 (140, 8)
      DIMENSION X (8, 8), X1 (8, 8), Y (8, 1), Y1 (8, 1), P (8, 8), Q (8, 1)
      COMMON/COM1/A1, A2, A3, A4, A5, A6, A7, A8, A9
C     IF (KON. EQ. 125) GOTO FJKSLDJFKLSDJF < --- ADDED COMMENT
```

```
      DO 1 I = 1, 8
1     FORCE (I, 1) = A7 (KON, I)
      IF (KON. EQ. 1) GOTO 3
      KON1 = KON – 1
      DO 2 I = 1, 8
            Q (I, 1) = A9 (KON1, I)
            DO 2 J = 1, 8
2     P (I, J) = A8 (KON1, I, J)
      CALL ULT (A6, P, 8, 8, 8, X, – 1.0D0)
      CALL ADD (A5, X, 8, 8, X1, 1.0D0)
      NZ = 8
      CALL JAI (X1, NZ)
      CALL ULT (X1, A4, 8, 8, 8, P, 1.0D0)
      CALL ULT (A6, Q, 8, 8, 8, Y, – 1.0D0)
      CALL ADD (FORCE, Y, 8, 1, Y1, 1.0D0)
      CALL ULT (X1, Y1, 8, 8, 1, Q, 1.0D0)
      GOTO 4
3     NZ = 8
      CALL JAI (A5, NZ)
      CALL ULT (A5, A4, 8, 8, 8, P, 1.0D0)
      CALL ULT (A5, FORCE, 8, 8, 1, Q, 1.0D0)
4     DO 5 I = 1, 8
      A9 (KON, I) = A (I, 1)
      DO 5 J = 1, 8
5     A8 (KON, I, J) = P (I, J)
      PRINT 7, KON, (A9 (KON, I), I = 1, 8)
7     FORMAT (/10X, 'KON=', I5, 8E12.3)
      RETURN
      END
C ------------------------------------
      SUBROUTINE POTER2 (A8, A9, KK, Z1)
C
C     SOLUTION ROUTINE
C
      IMPLICIT REAL * 8 (A-H, O-Z)
      DIMENSION A8 (140, 8, 8), A9 (140, 8), Z(8, 1), Z1 (280, 4), PZ (8, 1), P
      (8, 8), Q (8, 1)
      KK1 = KK – 1
      KK2 = 2 * KK
      KK3 = KK2 – 1
      DO 2 I = 1, 4
            I1 = I + 4
            Q (I, 1) = A9 (KK1, I)
```

```
          Q (I1, 1) = A9 (KK1, I1)
          Z (I, 1) = Z1 (KK3, I)
          Z (I1, 1) = Z1 (KK2, I)
          DO 2 J = 1, 8
              P (I, J) = AB (KK1, I, J)
2         P (I1, J) = A8 (KK1, I1, J)
      KK4 = 2 * KK1
      KK5 = KK4 - 1
      CALL ULT (P, Z, 8, 8, 1, PZ, - 1. 0D0)
      CALL ADD (Q, PZ, 8, 1, Z, 1. 0D0)
      DO 3 I = 1, 4
              I1 = I + 4
              Z1 (KK5, I) = Z (I, 1)
3     Z1 (KK4, I) = Z (I1, 1)
      RETURN
      END
C ---------------------------------
      SUBROUTINE A1B1C1 (H1, GE1, H2, GEG2, H3, GE3, A1, B1, C1, D1,
*     A2, B2, A3, B3, C3, D3, E3, F3, BETA, ETA, DELTA1, DELTA2, PSI1,
*     PSI2)
      IMPLICIT REAL*8(A–H, 0–Z)
      DIMENSION A1 (4, 4), B1 (4, 4), C1 (4, 4), D1 (4, 4), A2 (4, 4), B2 (4, 4),
*     A3 (4, 4), B3 (4, 4), C3 (4, 4), D3 (4, 4), E3 (4, 4), F3 (4, 4), ETA (4, 4),
*     BETA (4, 4), H1 (4, 4), GE1 (4, 4), H2 (4, 4), GE2 (4, 4), H3 (4, 4), GE3 (4,
*     4), PSI1 (4, 4), PSI2 (4, 4), BEPS1 (4, 4), BEPS2 (4, 4), BEJ1 (4, 4), BEJ2 (4,
*     4), ETAJ1 (4, 4), ETAJ2 (4, 4), ETAJ3
*     (4, 4)
      DIMENSION BETAG3 (4, 4)
      CALL ULT (ETA, H3, 4, 4, 4, A1, DELTA2)
      CALL ULT (ETA, H1, 4, 4, 4, B2, - DELTA1)
      CALL ULT (ETA, H2, 4, 4, 4, D1, - DELTA1)
      CALL ULT (BETA, PSI1, 4, 4, 4, BEPS1, 1. ODO)
      CALL ULT (BEPS1, H1, 4, 4, 4, F3, - DELTA1)
      CALL ULT (BEPS1, GE1, 4, 4, 4, BEJ1, 1.0D0)
      CALL ULT (BETA, PSI2, 4, 4, 4, BEPS2, 1.0D0)
      CALL ULT (BETA, PSI2, 4, 4, 4, BEPS2, 1.0D0)
      CALL ULT (BEPS2, H2, 4, 4, 4, E3, - DELTA1)
      CALL ULT (BEPS2, GE2, 4, 4, 4, BEJ2, 1. 0D0)
      CALL ULT (ETA, GE1, 4, 4, 4, ETAJ1, 1. 0D0)
      CALL ULT (ETA, GE2, 4, 4, 4, ETAJ2, 1. 0D0)
      CALL ULT (ETA, GE3, 4, 4, 4, ETAJ3, 1. 0D0)
      CALL ULT (BETA, H3, 4, 4, 4, A3, DELTA2)
      CALL ULT (BETA, GE3, 4, 4, 4, BETAG3, DELTA2)
      DO 1 I = 1, 4
```

```
          DO 1 J = 1, 4
          B1 (I, J) = BETA (I, J) – A1 (I, J) + ETAJ3 (I, J)
          C1 (I, J) = BEPS2 (I, J) – D1 (I, J) + ETAJ2 (I, J)
          A2 (I, J) = BEPS1 (I, J) – B2 (I, J) + ETAJ1 (I, J)
          B3 (I, J) = ETA (I, J) + BETAG3 (I, J) – A3 (I, J)
          C3 (I, J) = – E3 (I, J) + BEJ2 (I, J) + ETA (I, J)
1     D3 (I, J) = – F3 (I, J) + BEJ1 (I, J) + ETA (I, J)
      RETURN
      END
C --------------------------------------------------
      SUBROUTINE CALLS1 (RHO, GAMA, F, EW, EN, OMZ, OMZT,
*     OMEGAT, AMDA, DELTA, A, B, C)
      IMPLICIT REAL * 8 (A-H, O-Z)
      DIMENSION A (4, 4), B (4, 4), C (4, 4)
      DIMENSION E (4, 4), FE (4, 4), G (4, 4)
      CALL GARY (RHO, GAMA, OMEGAT, OMZ, OMZT, EN, G, EW,
*     AMDA, F)
      CALL ELFI (RHO, GAMA, OMEGAT, OMZ, OMZT, EN, E, FE, EW,
*     AMDA, F)
      CALL BACHUS (A, B, C, E, FE, G, DELTA)
      RETURN
      END
C --------------------------------------------------
      SUBROUTINE CALLS2 (GEM, HM, GEP, HP, DELTA, PSI, B, C)
      IMPLICIT REAL * 8 (A-H, O-Z)
      DIMENSION GEM (4, 4), HM (4, 4), GEP (4, 4), HP (4, 4), PSI
*     (4, 4)
      DIMENSION B (4, 4), C (4, 4), GH (4, 4), GHPS (4, 4), GEH
*     (4, 4), SIGE (4, 4)
      CALL ADD (GEP, HP, 4, 4, GH, –DELTA)
      CALL ULT (GH, PSI, 4, 4, 4, GHPS, 1. 0D0)
      CALL ADD (GEM, HM, 4, 4, GEH, DELTA)
      CALL ULT (PSI, GEH, 4, 4, 4, SIGE, 1. 0D0)
      CALL ADD (GHPS, SIGE, 4, 4, 8, – 1 .0D0)
      CALL ULT (PSI, HM, 4, 4, 4, C, DELTA)
      RETURN
      END
C --------------------------------------------------
      SUBROUTINE BLOCK1
      IMPLICIT REAL * 8 (A-H, O-Z)
      DIMENSION A1 (2, 4, 4), A2 (2, 4, 4), A3 (2, 4, 4),
*     A4 (8, 8), A5 (8, 8), A6 (8, 8)
      DIMENSION A7 (140, 8), A8 (140, 8, 8), A9 (140, 8)
      COMMON/COM1/A1, A2, A3, A4, A5, A6, A7, A8, A9
      DO 1 I = 1, 8
```

```
            DO 1 J = 1, 8
                A4 (I, J) = 0.0
                A5 (I, J) = 0.0
1       A6 (I, J) = 0.0
        DO 2 I = 1, 4
            I1 = I + 4
            DO 2 J = 1, 4
                J1 = J + 4
                A4 (I1, J) = A1 (2, I, J)
                A6 (I, J1) = A3 (1, I, J)
                A5 (I, J) = A2 (1, I, J)
                A5 (I, J1) = A1 (1, I, J)
                A5 (I1, J) = A3 (2, I, J)
2       A5 (I1, J1) = A2 (2, I, J)
        RETURN
        END
C ------------------------------------
        SUBROUTINE BLOCK2 (KON)
        IMPLICIT REAL * 8 (A-H, O-Z)
        DIMENSION A1 (2, 4, 4), A2 (2, 4, 4), A3 (2, 4, 4), A4 (8, 8), A5 (8, 8), A6
*       (8, 8)
        DIMENSION A7(140, 8), A8(140, 8, 8), A9(140, 8)
        COMMON/COM1/A1, A2, A3, A4, A5, A6, A7, A8, A9
        DO 1 I = 1, 8
            DO 1 J = 1, 8
                A4 (I, J) = 0.0
                A5 (I, J) = 0.0
1       A6 (I, J) = 0.0
        DO 2 I = 1, 4
            I1 = I + 4
            DO 2 J = 1, 4
                J1 = J + 4
                A4 (I, J) = A1 (1, I, J)
                A5 (I, J) = A1 (1, I, J)
                A4 (I1, J1) = A1 (2, I, J)
                A5 (I1, J1) = A1 (2, I, J)
                IF (KON. EQ. 111) GOTO 3
                A6 (I, J) = A3 (1, I, J)
                A6 (I1, J1) = A3 (2, I, J)
                GOTO 2
3               A6 (I, J1) = A3 (1, I, J)
2       CONTINUE
```

```
      RETURN
      END
C ---------------------------------
      SUBROUTINE BACHUS (A, B, C, E, FE, G, DELTA)
C **********  CALCULATION OF A, B, C, MATRICES ****
      IMPLICIT REAL * 8 (A-H, O-Z)
      DIMENSION A (4, 4), B (4, 4), C (4, 4), E (4, 4), FE (4, 4),
    * G (4, 4)
      DO 100 I = 1, 4
           DO 100 J = 1, 4
                A (I, J) = 0.0D0
                B (I, J) = 0.0D0
100   C (I, J) = 0.0D0
      DO 110 I = 1, 4
           DO 110 J = 1, 4
                A (I, J) = 2. * E (I, J)/DELTA + FE (I, J)
                B (I, J) = - 4.0 * E (I, J)/DELTA + 2. 0 * DELTA *
    *           G (I, J)
110   C (I, J) = 2. * E (I, J)/DELTA - FE (I, J)
      RETURN
      END
C *******************
      SUBROUTINE TRANS (PHI, PSI)
      IMPLICIT REAL * 8 (A-H, O-Z)
      DIMENSION PSI (4, 4)
      DO 111 I = 1, 4
           DO 111 J = 1, 4
111   PSI (I, J) = 0.
      DO 112 I = 1, 4
112   PSI (I, I) = 1. 0
      PSI (1, 1) = DCOS (PHI)
      PSI (1, 3) = - DSIN (PHI)
      PSI (3, 1) = - PSI (1, 3)
      PSI (3, 3) = PSI (1, 1)
      RETURN
      END
```

SUBJECT INDEX

T

U

V

W

Y

AUTHOR INDEX

T

U

W

Y

Z